This commentary by DeRouchie is a detailed and thorough treatment of the book of Zephaniah from someone who genuinely believes the Bible. The stated approach of this series is discourse analysis, but readers coming from a variety of approaches will find in this commentary many helpful insights with which to interact.

—MICHAEL SHEPHERD, Professor of Biblical Studies, Cedarville University

Often the shorter books of the Old Testament get relatively short treatment. Jason DeRouchie's commentary on Zephaniah is impressive in its scope and depth. Highly recommended.

—IAIN DUGUID, Professor of Old Testament, Westminster Theological Seminary

Jason DeRouchie reminds Christians today that there is nothing "minor" about this Minor Prophet. With exegetical rigor and a clear biblical-theological orientation, this commentary situates Zephaniah within the astounding redemptive work of God in Christ. Though an academic commentary, this volume will aid those in the church, especially preachers and teachers, to hear and heed Zephaniah's invitation to be satisfied in God. DeRouchie will keep your eyes on the text while he lifts your heart to Christ in worship. I could not recommend this commentary more highly!

—ANDREW M. KING, Assistant Professor of Biblical Studies,
Midwestern Baptist Theological Seminary

DeRouchie's volume on Zephaniah is a model commentary. It exhibits minute attention to the biblical text, astute engagement with a wide range of scholarly literature, clear exposition of the text, and robust integration of its rich message in biblical theology as well as clear direction for faithful application and proclamation. This thorough treatment of Zephaniah will richly reward its readers, be they students, scholars, or preachers.

—DANIEL TIMMER, Professor of Biblical Studies,
Puritan Reformed Theological Seminary

The culmination of many years of studying and teaching the book of Zephaniah, Jason DeRouchie's commentary is meticulously researched, clearly written, up to date, and belongs on the shelf of every serious student of Scripture. His careful, warmhearted scholarship shows how Zephaniah prophesied of Christ's kingdom and hence relates to us today. As DeRouchie emphasizes, this kingdom is inhabited by a multiethnic community, and those who love the global church will no doubt be encouraged to see this theme brought out from Zephaniah. The intertwining of this exegetical insight with DeRouchie's family story of adoption makes it all the more compelling.

—KEVIN CHEN, Professor of Old Testament Studies, Gateway Seminary

DeRouchie's decade of intensive reflection on Zephaniah offers pastors, scholars, and serious Bible students an extremely rare blend of linguistic rigor (able to refresh one's facility with Hebrew syntax), exegetical depth, biblical-theological connectivity, and evangelical passion. Especially poignant is DeRouchie's attention to Zephaniah's use of Scripture and the prophet's personal interest in the Lord's global, multiethnic kingdom. I hope this volume convinces many pastors to preach through this gem in the Twelve.

—MATTHEW E. SWALE, Assistant Professor of Bible and Church Ministry,
Warner University

This outstanding commentary will take a rightful place among the major commentaries on Zephaniah. The short prophecy of Zephaniah is a neglected book of the Bible, but those who take the time to study it with this commentary in hand will realize what a profound little gem God has given us through his prophet. Noteworthy features of the commentary include its detailed discourse and exegetical analysis of the Hebrew text, as well as its helpful outlines of the book's structure and message. Those tasked with teaching and preaching Zephaniah will especially appreciate the sections labeled Canonical and Theological Significance, where the author provides thought-provoking theological and applicational insights that facilitate a proper response to God's word through his ancient prophet.

—ROBERT CHISHOLM, Chair and Senior Professor of Old Testament Studies,
Dallas Theological Seminary

What's the first stop to study Zephaniah? Easy. Jason DeRouchie's commentary. This commentary builds on DeRouchie's previous studies on Zephaniah and offers reliable and pointed interpretation. Most important is DeRouchie's emphasis on the expectation for a multiethnic work of Yahweh in Zephaniah 3. This commentary can help with the heavy lifting for those who plan to preach Zephaniah.

—GARY EDWARD SCHNITTJER, Distinguished Professor of Old Testament,
Cairn University, and author of *Old Testament Use of Old Testament*

Anyone seeking a deeper understanding of the significance of Zephaniah should read this commentary. DeRouchie skillfully draws out the richness and beauty of Zephaniah's message through careful analysis of the text, at both the sentence and discourse levels. His analysis explains the relevance of the prophecy within the original context while also highlighting its connections to the rest of scripture. Most notably, he shows the reader how Zephaniah points to the beauty of Christ and the fullness of the gospel revealed in the New Testament.

—JOANNA M. HOYT, Associate Professor of Applied Linguistics, Dallas International University

Some commentaries do an excellent job of addressing the original context but do not attend to broader theological concerns. Others are sensitive to issues in the canon as a whole but override the distinctive contextual contribution of the book. In this commentary on Zephaniah, DeRouchie strikes just the right balance. The result is a substantial and rigorous exposition of the Book of Zephaniah, along with a clear explanation of how it relates to the New Testament and the Church today. I highly recommend this work on an important but often overlooked book.

—ERIC J. TULLY, Professor of Old Testament and Semitic Languages and Director of the PhD
Program in Theological Studies, Trinity Evangelical Divinity School

DeRouchie brings to bear his deep knowledge of Zephaniah in this very strong contribution to Zondervan's series of exegetical commentaries. A particular strength is its hermeneutical strategy for re-reading Scripture, showing how deeply embedded the short prophecy is in the OT canon. Its close discourse and rhetorical analysis of the text is heavily influenced by the author's conviction that the book articulates the prophet's Messianic hope. Its conviction that the prophet proclaims hope for the salvation of the nations is especially flavored by the author's belief that the prophet was of mixed Jewish-African descent, and by his own personal connection with Africa. A rich resource for the Christian study of Zephaniah, and biblical prophecy.

—J. GORDON MCCONVILLE, Professor Emeritus of Old Testament, University of Gloucestershire

ZEPHANIAH

Zondervan Exegetical Commentary on the Old Testament

Editorial Board

General Editor

Daniel I. Block

Gunther H. Knoedler Professor Emeritus of Old Testament, Wheaton College

Associate Editors

Hélène Dallaire

Professor of Old Testament and Director of Messianic Judaism Programs, Denver Seminary

Stephen Dempster

Associate Professor of Religious Studies, Crandall University

Jason S. DeRouchie

Research Professor of Old Testament and Biblical Theology, Midwestern Baptist Theological Seminary

Miles V. Van Pelt

Alan Belcher Professor of Old Testament and Biblical Languages, Reformed Theological Seminary

Zondervan Editors

Katya Covrett

Lee Fields

ZEPHANIAH
The Savior's Invitation to Satisfaction

ZONDERVAN
Exegetical Commentary
ON THE
Old Testament
A DISCOURSE ANALYSIS OF THE HEBREW BIBLE

JASON S. DEROUCHIE

Daniel I. Block, General Editor

ZONDERVAN ACADEMIC

Zephaniah
Copyright © 2025 by Jason S. DeRouchie

Published in Grand Rapids, Michigan, by Zondervan. Zondervan is a registered trademark of The Zondervan Corporation, L.L.C., a wholly owned subsidiary of HarperCollins Christian Publishing, Inc.

Requests for information should be addressed to customercare@harpercollins .com.

Zondervan titles may be purchased in bulk for educational, business, fundraising, or sales promotional use. For information, please email SpecialMarkets@ Zondervan.com.

Library of Congress Cataloging-in-Publication Data

Names: DeRouchie, Jason Shane, 1973- author.
Title: Zephaniah : a discourse analysis of the Hebrew Bible / Jason S. DeRouchie ; Daniel I. Block, general editor.
Description: Grand Rapids, Michigan : Zondervan Academic, [2025] | Series: Zondervan exegetical commentary on the Old Testament | Includes bibliographical references and index.
Identifiers: LCCN 2024044675 | ISBN 9780310942443 (hardcover)
Subjects: LCSH: Bible. Zephaniah--Commentaries.
Classification: LCC BS1645.53 .D47 2025 | DDC 224/.96077--dc23/ eng/20250215
LC record available at https://lccn.loc.gov/2024044675

The Hebrew text is from Deuteronomy 31:11–13, which highlights the importance of "hearing" the voice of Scripture:

> When all Israel comes to appear before יהוה your God at the place he will choose, you shall read this *Torah* before them in their hearing. Assemble the people—men, women and children, and the foreigners residing in your towns—so they can *listen* and learn to fear יהוה your God and follow carefully all the words of this *Torah*. Their children, who do not know this *Torah*, must *hear* it and learn to fear יהוה your God as long as you live in the land you are crossing the Jordan to possess. (NIV, modified)

Unless otherwise noted, Scripture quotations are the author's own translations. • Scripture quotations marked ESV are taken from the ESV® Bible (The Holy Bible, English Standard Version®). Copyright © 2001, 2016 by Crossway, a publishing ministry of Good News Publishers. Used by permission. All rights reserved. • Scripture quotations marked HCSB® are taken from the Holman Christian Standard Bible®, Copyright © 1999, 2000, 2002, 2003, 2009, 2017 by Holman Bible Publishers. Used by permission. Holman Christian Standard Bible®, and HCSB®, are federally registered trademarks of Holman Bible Publishers. • Scripture quotations marked NASB20 are taken from the (NASB®) New American Standard Bible®. Copyright © 1960, 1971, 1977, 1995, 2020 by The Lockman Foundation. Used by permission. All rights reserved. www.lockman.org. • Scripture quotations marked NASB95 are taken from the New American Standard Bible®. Copyright © 1960, 1971, 1977, 1995 by The Lockman Foundation. Used by permission. All rights reserved. www .lockman.org. • Scripture quotations marked NET are taken from the NET Bible®. http://netbible.com. Copyright ©1996, 2019 by Biblical Studies Press, L.L.C. Used by permission. All rights reserved. • Scripture quotations noted as NIV are taken from The Holy Bible, New International Version®, NIV®. Copyright ©1973, 1978, 1984, 2011 by Biblica, Inc.® Used by permission of Zondervan. All rights reserved worldwide. www.Zondervan.com. The "NIV" and "New International Version" are trademarks registered in the United States Patent and Trademark Office by Biblica, Inc.® • Scripture quotations marked NLT are taken from the Holy Bible, New Living Translation. Copyright ©1996, 2004, 2015 by Tyndale House Foundation. Used by permission of Tyndale House Publishers, Inc., Carol Stream, Illinois 60188. All rights reserved. • Scripture quotations marked NRSVue are taken from the New Revised Standard Version Bible, Updated Edition. Copyright ©2022, Division of Christian Education of the National Council of the Churches of Christ in the United States of America. Used by permission. All rights reserved. • Scripture quotations marked NRSV are taken from the New Revised Standard Version Bible. Copyright © 1989 National Council of the Churches of Christ in the United States of America. Used by permission. All rights reserved.

Any internet addresses (websites, blogs, etc.) and telephone numbers in this book are offered as a resource. They are not intended in any way to be or imply an endorsement by Zondervan, nor does Zondervan vouch for the content of these sites and numbers for the life of this book.

All rights reserved. No part of this publication may be reproduced, stored in a retrieval system, or transmitted in any form or by any means—electronic, mechanical, photocopy, recording, or any other—except for brief quotations in printed reviews, without the prior permission of the publisher.

Cover design: Tammy Johnson
Interior design: Beth Shagene

Printed in the United States of America

25 26 27 28 29 30 31 32 33 34 35 36 37 /TRM/ 17 16 15 14 13 12 11 10 9 8 7 6 5 4 3 2 1

To Daniel I. Block and Peter J. Gentry
Brothers who love and lead with godliness for the sake of Christ's church

Contents

Series Introduction xi
Author's Preface and Acknowledgments xv
Abbreviations xvii
Select Bibliography xxiii

Translation of Zephaniah 1
Introduction to Zephaniah 5
Commentary on Zephaniah 57

Part I: Zephaniah 1:1 57
  1. Zephaniah 1:1 59

Part II: Zephaniah 1:2–18 69
  2. Zephaniah 1:2–6 73
  3. Zephaniah 1:7–18 99

Part III: Zephaniah 2:1–3:20b 135

Part III.1: Zephaniah 2:1–3:7 143
  4. Zephaniah 2:1–2 145
  5. Zephaniah 2:3–4 153
  6. Zephaniah 2:5–3:7 168

Part III.2: Zephaniah 3:8–20b 225
  7. Zephaniah 3:8–10 227
  8. Zephaniah 3:11–20b 253

Part IV: Zephaniah 3:20c 307

   9. Zephaniah 3:20c 309

Scripture Index 313
Extrabiblical Index 332
Subject Index 333
Author Index 339

Series Introduction

Prospectus

Modern audiences are often taken in by the oratorical skill and creativity of preachers and teachers. However, they tend to forget that the authority of proclamation is directly related to the correspondence of the key points of the sermon to the message the biblical authors were trying to communicate. Since we confess that "all Scripture [including the entirety of the OT] is God-breathed and is useful for teaching, rebuking, correcting and training in righteousness, so that [all God's people] may be thoroughly equipped for every good work" (2 Tim 3:16–17 NIV), it seems essential that those who proclaim its message should pay close attention to the rhetorical agendas of biblical authors. Too often modern readers, including preachers, are either baffled by OT texts, or they simply get out of them that for which they are looking. Many commentaries available to pastors and teachers try to resolve the dilemma either through word-by-word and verse-by-verse analysis or synthetic theological reflections on the text without careful attention to the flow and argument of that text.

The commentators in this series recognize that too little attention has been paid to biblical authors as rhetoricians, to their larger rhetorical and theological agendas, and especially to the means by which they tried to achieve their goals. Like effective communicators in every age, biblical authors were driven by a passion to communicate a message. So we must inquire not only what that message was, but also what strategies they used to impress their message on their hearers' ears. This reference to "hearers" rather than to readers is intentional, since the biblical texts were written to be heard. Not only were the Hebrew and Christian Scriptures composed to be heard in the public gathering of God's people but also before the invention of moveable type, and few would have had access to their own copies of the Scriptures. While the contributors to this series acknowledge with Paul that every Scripture—that is, every passage in the Hebrew Bible—is God-breathed, we also recognize that the inspired authors possessed a vast repertoire of rhetorical and literary strategies. These included not only the special use of words and figures of speech, but also the deliberate selection, arrangement, and shaping of ideas.

The primary goal of this commentary series is to help serious students of

Scripture, as well as those charged with preaching and teaching the Word of God, to hear the messages of Scripture as biblical authors intended them to be heard. While we recognize the timelessness of the biblical message, the validity of our interpretation and the authority with which we teach the Scriptures are related directly to the extent to which we have grasped the message intended by the author in the first place. Accordingly, when dealing with specific texts, the authors of the commentaries in this series are concerned with three principal questions: (1) What are the principal theological points the biblical writers are making? (2) How do biblical writers make those points? (3) What significance does the message of the present text have for understanding the message of the biblical book within which it is embedded and the message of the Scriptures as a whole? The achievement of these goals requires careful attention to the way ideas are expressed in the OT, including the selection and arrangement of materials and the syntactical shaping of the text.

To most readers syntax operates primarily at the sentence level. But recent developments in biblical study, particularly advances in rhetorical and discourse analysis, have alerted us to the fact that syntax operates also at the levels of the paragraph, the literary unit being analyzed, and the composition as a whole. Discourse analysis, also called macrosyntax, studies the text beyond the level of the sentence (sentence syntax), where the paragraph serves as the basic unit of thought. Those contributing to this series recognize that this type of study may be pursued in a variety of ways. Some will prefer a more bottom-up approach, where clause connectors and transitional features play a dominant role in analysis. Others will pursue a more top-down approach, where genre or literary form begins the discussion. However, we all understand that both approaches are required to understand fully the method and the message of the text. For this reason, the ultimate value of discourse analysis is that it allows the text to set the agenda in biblical interpretation.

One of the distinctive goals for this series is to engage the biblical text using some form of discourse analysis to understand not only what the text says, but also how it says it. While attention to words or phrases is still essential, contributors to this commentary series will concentrate on the flow of thought in the biblical writings, both at the macroscopic level of entire compositions and at the microscopic level of individual text units. In so doing we hope to help other readers of Scripture grasp both the message and the rhetorical force of OT texts. When we hear the message of Scripture, we gain access to the mind of God.

Format of the Commentary

The format of this series is designed to achieve the goals summarized above. Accordingly, each volume in the series will begin with an introduction to the book being explored. In addition to answering the usual questions of date, authorship, and provenance of the composition, commentators will highlight what they consider to be the main theological themes of the book and then discuss broadly how the style and structure of the book develop those themes. This discussion will include a coherent outline of the contents of the book, demonstrating the contribution each part makes to the development of the principal themes.

The commentaries on individual text units that follow will repeat this process in greater detail. Although complex literary units will be broken down further, the commentators will address the following issues.

1. **Main Idea of the Passage:** A one- or two-sentence summary of the key ideas the biblical author seeks to communicate.
2. **Literary Context:** A brief discussion of the relationship of the specific text to the book as a whole and to its place within the broader arguments.
3. **Translation and Exegetical Outline:** Commentators will provide their own translations of each text, formatted to highlight the discourse structure of the text and accompanied by a coherent outline that reflects the flow and argument of the text.
4. **Structure and Literary Form:** An introductory survey of the literary structure and rhetorical style adopted by the biblical author, highlighting how these features contribute to the communication of the main idea of the passage.
5. **Explanation of the Text:** A detailed commentary on the passage, paying particular attention to how the biblical authors select and arrange their materials and how they work with words, phrases, and syntax to communicate their messages. This will take up the bulk of most commentaries.
6. **Canonical and Theological Significance:** The commentary on each unit will conclude by building bridges between the world of the biblical author and other biblical authors and with reflections on the contribution made by this unit to the development of broader issues in biblical theology—particularly on how later OT and NT authors have adapted and reused the motifs in question. The discussion will also include brief reflections on the significance of the message of the passage for readers today.

The way this series treats biblical books will be uneven. Commentators on smaller books will have sufficient scope to answer fully each of the issues listed above on each unit of text. However, limitations of space preclude full treatment of every text for the larger books. Instead, commentators will guide readers through #1–4 and 6 for every literary unit, but full Explanation of the Text (#5) will be selective, generally limited to twelve to fifteen literary units deemed most critical for hearing the message of the book.

In addition to these general introductory comments, we should alert readers of this series to several conventions that we follow. First, the divine name in the OT is presented as YHWH. The form of the name—represented by the Tetragrammaton, יהוה—is a particular problem for scholars. The practice of rendering the divine name in Greek as κύριος (=Heb. אֲדֹנָי, "Adonay") is carried over into English translations as "Lᴏʀᴅ," which represents Hebrew יהוה and distinguishes it from "Lord," which represents Hebrew אֲדֹנָי. But this creates interpretive problems, for the connotations and implications of referring to someone by name or by title are quite different. When rendering the word as a name, English translations have traditionally vocalized יהוה as "Jehovah," which seems to combine the consonants of יהוה with the vowels of אֲדֹנָי. However, today non-Jewish scholars often render the name as "Yahweh," recognizing that "Jehovah" is an artificial construct.

Second, frequently the verse numbers in the Hebrew Bible differ from those in our English translations. Since the commentaries in this series are based on the Hebrew text, the Hebrew numbers will be the default numbers. Where the English numbers differ, they will be provided in square brackets (e.g., Joel 4:12[3:12]).

Third, when discussing specific biblical words or phrases, these will be represented in Hebrew font and in translation, except where the transliterated form is used in place of an English term, either because no single English expression captures the Hebrew word's wide range of meaning (e.g., *hesed* for חֶסֶד, rather than "loving-kindness"), or when it functions as a title or technical expression not readily captured in English (e.g., *gō'ēl* for גֹּאֵל, rather than "kinsman-redeemer").

Daniel I. Block, general editor

Author's Preface and Acknowledgments

I cannot believe that I started this book in the summer of 2014, and now 2024 autumn colors are blazing in the trees of northwest Missouri. My heart and this world have grown and changed in this decade, yet Zephaniah's exclamation remains: "Hush before the Sovereign YHWH, for . . . the great day of YHWH is near—near and hastening fast" (Zeph 1:7, 14). I dwell among a nation not longing for God, yet the prophet calls for all who may hear to seek YHWH together to avoid punishment (2:1, 3); he then urges them to wait for YHWH to enjoy salvation (3:8). May the humble hear, fear, and be glad, and may the offspring of those scattered at Babel now come before the great King in worship (3:9–10).

When I started on the ZECOT editorial board around 2007, I thought I would write on Deuteronomy. But life circumstances showed that God had that project for a later time. Early in my academic ministry, I was able to teach a course on the Minor Prophets ten different times in four years. Semester after semester Zephaniah's prophecy overcame my pride, as God called his remnant from Judah and other lands to "seek humility" (2:4), condemned those who had "become haughty" (2:8; cf. 2:10, 15), and promised to leave only "an afflicted and needy people" in his transformed Jerusalem (3:12). With this, I knew Zephaniah served during "the days of Josiah" (1:1), and I wondered whether the Torah scroll that guided the king's reforms (2 Kgs 22:8; 23:2–3) had influenced the prophet's preaching. Thus, I accepted the opportunity to write on this book.

What I did not realize was that Zephaniah was likely a black Jew whose biracial heritage highly influenced his message of divine punishment and renewal. Having adopted three children from Black Africa, in the region of ancient Cush/Ethiopia, I joined the prophet in celebrating his vision of the reversal of Babel's punishment and international reconciliation. I have also stood in awe of how later biblical writers have seen Zephaniah's testimony of God's end-times victory over evil and new creational renewal realized in the coming of Jesus Christ. The NT authors stress how *all* the prophets spoke of Christ's tribulation and triumph and the days of the church (e.g., Acts 3:18, 24; 10:43; 1 Pet 1:10–11). I hope that preachers and teachers will benefit from this interpretation of Zephaniah's prophecy that accounts for its close, continuing, and complete biblical context and that seeks to show the book's lasting relevance for doctrine and ethics.

The research and writing for this book took place during my tenure at two different institutions. I thank the trustees and administrators of both Bethlehem College and Seminary (Minneapolis, MN) and Midwestern Baptist Theological Seminary (Kansas City, MO) for affirming the importance of this project and for each providing me a research sabbatical. I rejoice that both schools are elevating Scripture's authority, prizing God's glory in the face of Christ, and celebrating God's saving work among the nations. May God keep these schools faithful.

Steve Dempster served as my primary editor for this book, and both he and Dan Block offered helpful and substantial suggestions and guidance on the final form. I thank them both. With them, numerous research assistants have helped me through the years, and among those I remember I thank Jonathon Woodyard, Josh Bremerman, Nicholas Majors, and Brian Verrett. I especially thank Brian for his extended multiyear service and significant efforts in helping me lower the book's wordcount. Finally, I thank Lee Fields and the rest of the Zondervan team for their careful preparation of the final manuscript. The ZECOT formatting includes many demanding issues, and I thank them for their perseverance. For all, I pray that God would keep us faithful.

My six kids have grown up with Dad having Zephaniah as a constant companion, and I thank them (and now my two sons-in-law and three grandkids) for cheering me to the finish line. My wife Teresa remains my dearest friend, closest partner, and best human helper, and I rejoice that I can engage in academic and local church ministry with such a companion.

I dedicate this book to Drs. Daniel I. Block and Peter J. Gentry, both of whom have mentored me in various ways through two and a half decades of ministry training and academic ministry. Dan invited me to study under him during my doctoral education at The Southern Baptist Theological Seminary. He helped me learn to ask the biblical authors not only, "What did you say?" but also "Why did you say it like that?" After graduation Dan invited me to join the editorial team that has overseen what is now the Zondervan Exegetical Commentary on the Old Testament, and I am grateful for our near two-decade partnership on this series. During a nine-month sabbatical that Dan took, Peter stepped in to help guide my dissertation that addressed discourse features and structure in Deuteronomy. Over the last two decades he has grown not only to be a dear mentor but a true friend whose hermeneutical and biblical-theological influence is evident in all these pages. I praise the Lord for how he has used these men to make me who I am, and I pray that in different ways the rigor, care, and concern for Christ and his church that this commentary expresses would honor these upon whose shoulders I stand.

Jason S. DeRouchie
Satisfied in a God who saves sinners, Autumn 2024

Abbreviations

1QS	Rule of the Community
1QS III	Composition S column III (Texts from the Judean Desert)
4Q76	XII^a (Texts from the Judean Desert)
4Q77	XII^b (Texts from the Judean Desert)
4Q78	XII^c (Texts from the Judean Desert)
4Q79	XII^d (Texts from the Judean Desert)
4Q80	XIIe (Texts from the Judean Desert)
4Q81	XII^f (Texts from the Judean Desert)
4Q82	XII^g (unopened scroll) (Texts from the Judean Desert)
8ḤevXII gr	Naḥal Ḥever 8Ḥev 1 (Texts from the Judean Desert)
AB	Anchor Bible
ABD	*Anchor Bible Dictionary*. Edited by David Noel Freedman. 6 vols. New York: Doubleday, 1992
ACCSOT	Ancient Christian Commentary on Scripture: Old Testament
AD	*Anno Domini* (in the year of our Lord)
AION	*Annali dell'Istituto Orientale di Napoli*
ANET	*Ancient Near Eastern Texts Relating to the Old Testament*. Edited by James B. Pritchard. 3rd ed. Princeton: Princeton University Press, 1969
Ant.	Josephus, *Jewish Antiquities*
ASTI	Annual of the Swedish Theological Institute
ASV	American Standard Version
ATSAT	Arbeiten zu Text und Sprache im Alten Testament
AUSS	*Andrews University Seminary Studies*
AYBRL	Anchor Yale Bible Reference Library
b.	Babylonian Talmud
B. Bat.	Baba Batra
BA	*Biblical Archaeologist*
BAR	*Biblical Archaeology Review*
BASOR	*Bulletin of the American Schools of Oriental Research*
BBB	Bonner biblische Beiträge

BBE	Bible in Basic English
BBR	*Bulletin for Biblical Research*
BBRSup	Bulletin for Biblical Research, Supplements
BC	Before Christ
BDAG	Danker, Frederick W., Walter Bauer, William F. Arndt, and F. Wilbur Gingrich. *Greek-English Lexicon of the New Testament and Other Early Christian Literature.* 3rd ed. Chicago: University of Chicago Press, 2000 (Danker-Bauer-Arndt-Gingrich)
BECNT	Baker Exegetical Commentary on the New Testament
BET	Biblical Exegesis & Theology
BHQ	*Biblia Hebraica Quinta* . Edited by Adrian Schenker et al. Stuttgart: Deutsche Bibelgesselschaft, 2004–
BHRG	*A Biblical Hebrew Reference Grammar*. Christo H. J. van der Merwe, Jacobus A. Naudé, and Jan H. Kroeze. 2nd ed. London: Bloomsbury, 2017
Bib	*Biblica*
BibInt	Biblical Interpretation Series
BO	Bibliotheca Orientalis
BRT/RBT	*Baptist Review of Theology / Revue Baptiste de Théologie*
BSac	*Bibliotheca Sacra*
BT	*The Bible Translator*
BZ	*Biblische Zeitschrift*
BZAW	Beihefte zur Zeitschrift für die alttestamentliche Wissenschaft
BZNW	Beihefte zur Zeitschrift für die neutestamentliche Wissenschaft
CANE	*Civilizations of the Ancient Near East*. Edited by Jack M. Sasson. 4 vols. New York, 1995. Repr. in 2 vols. Peabody, MA: Hendrickson, 2006
CBC	Cambridge Bible Commentary
CBQ	*Catholic Biblical Quarterly*
CEB	Common English Bible
COS	*The Context of Scripture*. Edited by William W. Hallo and K. Lawson Younger Jr. 4 vols. Leiden: Brill, 1997–2017
CSB	Christian Standard Bible
CTR	*Criswell Theological Review*
CurBS	*Currents in Research: Biblical Studies*
Darby	J. N. Darby Translation
DCH	*Dictionary of Classical Hebrew*. Edited by David J. A. Clines. 9 vols. Sheffield: Sheffield Phoenix, 1993–2014

DDD	*Dictionary of Deities and Demons in the Bible.* Edited by Karel van der Toorn, Bob Becking, and Pieter W. van der Horse. 2nd rev. ed. Grand Rapids: Eerdmans, 1999
DLNT	*Dictionary of the Later New Testament and Its Developments.* Edited by Ralph P. Martin and Peter H. Davids. Downers Grove, IL: InterVarsity Press, 1997
DNTUOT	*Dictionary of the New Testament Use of the Old Testament.* Edited by G. K. Beale, D. A. Carson, Benjamin L. Gladd, and Andrew David Naselli. Grand Rapids: Baker, 2023
DOTP	*Dictionary of the Old Testament: Pentateuch.* Edited by T. Desmond Alexander and David W. Baker. Downers Grove, IL: InterVarsity Press, 2003
DOTPr	*Dictionary of the Old Testament: Prophets.* Edited by Mark J. Boda and J. Gordon McConville. Downers Grove, IL: InterVarsity Press, 2012
DSBS	Daily Study Bible Series
EBC	Expositors Bible Commentary
EBib	*Etudes bibliques*
Enc	*Encounter*
ESV	English Standard Version
ExpTim	*Expository Times*
FOTL	Forms of the Old Testament Literature
GKC	*Gesenius' Hebrew Grammar.* Edited by E. Kautzsch. Translated by A. E. Cowley. 2nd ed. Oxford: Clarendon, 1910
GTJ	*Grace Theological Journal*
HALOT	*The Hebrew and Aramaic Lexicon of the Old Testament.* Ludwig Koehler, Walter Baumgartner, and Johann J. Stamm. Translated and edited under the supervision of Mervyn E. J. Richardson. 4 vols. Leiden: Brill, 1994–1999. Repr. in 2 vols. Leiden: Brill, 2001
HCOT	Historical Commentary on the Old Testament
Hist.	Herodotus, *Historiae*
HS	*Hebrew Studies*
HSS	Harvard Semitic Studies
HThKAT	Herders Theologischer Kommentar zum Alten Testament
HUCA	*Hebrew Union College Annual*
IBHS	*An Introduction to Biblical Hebrew Syntax.* Bruce K. Waltke and Michael O'Connor. Winona Lake, IN: Eisenbrauns, 1990
ICC	International Critical Commentary
ISBE	*International Standard Bible Encyclopedia.* Edited by Geoffrey W. Bromiley. 4 vols. 2nd ed. Grand Rapids: Eerdmans, 1979–1988

JAOS	*Journal of the American Oriental Society*
JARCE	*Journal of the American Research Center in Egypt*
Jastrow	Marcus Jastrow. *A Dictionary of the Targumim, the Talmud Babli and Yerushalmi, and the Midrashic Literature*. 1903. Repr., New York: Judaica, 1996
JBL	*Journal of Biblical Literature*
JESOT	*Journal for the Evangelical Study of the Old Testament*
JETS	*Journal of the Evangelical Theological Society*
JHebS	*Journal of Hebrew Scriptures*
JNES	*Journal of Near Eastern Studies*
JOTT	*Journal of Translation and Textlinguistics*
Joüon	Joüon, Paul, and T. Muraoka. *A Grammar of Biblical Hebrew*. Translated and revised by T. Muraoka. 2nd English ed. Rome: Pontifical Biblical Institute, 2006
JPOS	*Journal of the Palestine Oriental Society*
JRT	*Journal of Religious Thought*
JSNT	*Journal for the Study of the New Testament*
JSNTSup	Journal for the Study of the New Testament Supplement Series
JSOTSup	Journal for the Study of the Old Testament Supplement Series
JSPHL	*Journal for the Study of Paul and His Letters*
JSS	*Journal of Semitic Studies*
KAT	Kommentar zum Alten Testament
KJV	King James Version
KUSATU	*Kleine Untersuchungen zur Sprache des Alten Testaments und seiner Umwelt*
LHBOTS	The Library of Hebrew Bible/Old Testament Studies
LNTS	The Library of New Testament Studies
LSAWS	*Linguistic Studies in Ancient West Semitic*
LXX	Septuagint
MJT	*Midwestern Journal of Theology*
MT	Masoretic Text
NAC	New American Commentary
NASB20	New American Standard Bible 2020
NASB95	New American Standard Bible 1995
NET	New English Translation
NETS	*A New English Translation of the Septuagint*. Edited by Albert Pietersma and Benjamin G. Wright. New York: Oxford University Press, 2007
NIB	*The New Interpreter's Bible*. Edited by Leander E. Keck. 12 vols. Nashville: Abingdon, 1994–2004

NICNT	New International Commentary on the New Testament
NICOT	New International Commentary on the Old Testament
NIDB	*New Interpreter's Dictionary of the Bible*. Edited by Katherine Doob Sakenfeld. 5 vols. Nashville: Abingdon, 2006–2009
NIDOTTE	*New International Dictionary of Old Testament Theology and Exegesis*. Edited by Willem A. VanGemeren. 5 vols. Grand Rapids: Zondervan, 1997
NIV	New International Version
NIVAC	NIV Application Commentary
NJPS	*Tanakh: The Holy Scriptures: The New JPS Translation according to the Traditional Hebrew Text*
NKJV	New King James Version
NLT	New Living Translation
NRSVue	New Revised Standard Version, Updated Edition
NS	New Series
NSBT	New Studies in Biblical Theology
NT	New Testament
ÖBS	Österreichische biblische Studien
OT	Old Testament
OTL	Old Testament Library
PEQ	*Palestine Exploration Quarterly*
PNTC	Pillar New Testament Commentary
RB	*Revue biblique*
ResQ	*Restoration Quarterly*
RV	Revised Version
SBJT	*Southern Baptist Journal of Theology*
SHCANE	Studies in the History and Culture of the Ancient Near East
Sir	Sirach/Ecclesiasticus
SJT	*Scottish Journal of Theology*
SNTSMS	Society for New Testament Studies Monograph Series
StBibLit	Studies in Biblical Literature (Lang)
TCS	Texts from Cuneiform Sources
TD	*Theology Digest*
TDNT	*Theological Dictionary of the New Testament*. Edited by Gerhard Kittel and Gerhard Friedrich. Translate by Geoffrey W. Bromiley. 10 vols. Grand Rapids: Eerdmans, 1964–1976
TDOT	*Theological Dictionary of the Old Testament*. Edited by G. Johannes Botterweck, Helmer Ringgren, Heinz-Josef Fabry, Holger Gzella. 17 vols. Grand Rapids: Eerdmans 1974–2021
Tg. Neb.	Targum of the Prophets

TGC	The Gospel Coalition Bible Commentary
Them	*Themelios*
TJ	*Trinity Journal*
TLOT	*Theological Lexicon of the Old Testament*. Edited by Ernst Jenni, with assistance from Claus Westermann. Translated by Mark E. Biddle. 3 vols. Peabody, MA: Hendrickson, 1997
TOTC	Tyndale Old Testament Commentaries
TVZ	Theologischer Verlag Zurich
TynBul	*Tyndale Bulletin*
UASV	Updated American Standard Version 2022
UF	*Ugarit-Forschungen*
VT	*Vetus Testamentum*
WAW	Writings from the Ancient World
WBC	Word Biblical Commentary
WEB	World English Bible
WTJ	*Westminster Theological Journal*
WUNT	Wissenshaftliche Untersuchungen zum Neuen Testament
WZKM	*Wiener Zeitschrift für die Kunde des Morgenlandes*
YLT	Young's Literal Translation
ZAW	*Zeitschrift für die alttestamentliche Wissenschaft*

Select Works on Zephaniah

Achtemeier, Elizabeth. *Nahum–Malachi*. Interpretation. Atlanta: John Knox, 1986.

Bailey, Waylon. "Zephaniah." Pages 379–505 in *Micah, Nahum, Habakkuk, Zephaniah*. By Kenneth L. Barker and Waylon Bailey. NAC 20. Nashville: Broadman & Holman, 1999.

Baker, David W. *Nahum, Habakkuk and Zephaniah: An Introduction and Commentary*. TOTC 27. Downers Grove, IL: InterVarsity Press, 1988.

Ball, Ivan Jay, Jr. *A Rhetorical Study of Zephaniah*. Berkeley: BIBAL, 1988.

Bennett, Robert A. "The Book of Zephaniah: Introduction, Commentary, and Reflections." Pages 657–704 in vol. 5 of *NIB*. Edited by Leander E. Keck. Nashville: Abingdon, 1996.

Ben Zvi, Ehud. *A Historical-Critical Study of the Book of Zephaniah*. BZAW 198. Berlin: de Gruyter, 1991.

Berlin, Adele. *Zephaniah: A New Translation with Introduction and Commentary*. AB. New Haven: Yale University Press, 1994.

Bridger, Gordon. *The Message of Obadiah, Nahum and Zephaniah: The Kindness and Severity of God*. The Bible Speaks Today. Downers Grove, IL: InterVarsity Press, 2010.

Bruckner, James. *Jonah, Nahum, Habakkuk, Zephaniah*. NIVAC. Grand Rapids: Zondervan, 2004.

Butcher, Jerry Dale. "The Significance of Zephaniah 3:8–13 for Narrative Composition in the Early Chapters of the Book of Acts." PhD diss., Case Western Reserve University, 1972.

Calvin, John. "Habakkuk, Zephaniah, Haggai." *Commentaries on the Twelve Minor Prophets*. Translated by John Owen. Vol. 15 of *Calvin's Commentaries*. Grand Rapids: Baker Books, 2009.

Clendenen, E. Ray. "The Minor Prophets." Pages 340–96 in *Holman Concise Bible Commentary*. Edited by David S. Dockery. Nashville: Broadman & Holman, 1998.

Craigie, Peter C. *Twelve Prophets: Volume 2: Micah, Nahum, Habakkuk, Zephaniah, Haggai, Zechariah, and Malachi*. Daily Study Bible Series. Louisville: Westminster John Knox, 1985.

DeRouchie, Jason S. "Zephaniah." Pages 561–604 in *Daniel–Malachi*. Vol. 7 of *ESV Expository Commentary*. Wheaton, IL: Crossway, 2018.

———. "Zephaniah." *TGC Bible Commentary* (2021). https://www .thegospelcoalition .org /commentary/zephaniah/.

Dietrich, Walter. *Nahum, Habakkuk, Zephaniah*. ICC. Stuttgart: Kohlhammer Verlag, 2015.

Ferreiro, Alberto, ed. *The Twelve Prophets*. ACCSOT 14. Downers Grove, IL: InterVarsity Press, 2003.

Floyd, Michael H. *Minor Prophets, Part 2*. FOTL 22. Grand Rapids: Eerdmans, 2000.

Gelston, Anthony, ed. *The Twelve Minor Prophets*. BHQ 13. Stuttgart: Deutsche Bibelgesellschaft, 2010.

House, Paul R. *The Unity of the Twelve*. JSOTSup 97. Sheffield: Almond Press, 1990.

———. *Zephaniah: A Prophetic Drama*. JSOTSup 69. Sheffield: Almond Press, 1989.

Irsigler, Hubert. *Gottesgericht und Jahwetag: Die Komposition Zef 1,1–2,3, untersucht auf der Grundlage der Literarkritik des Zefanjabuches.* ATSAT 3. St. Ottilien: Eos, 1977.

———. *Zefanja.* HThKAT. Freiburg im Breisgau: Herder, 2002.

Jerome. *Commentaries on the Twelve Prophets.* Edited by Thomas P. Scheck. 2 vols. *Ancient Christian Texts.* Downers Grove, IL: InterVarsity Press, 2016.

Jones, Barry A. "Zephaniah, Book of." *NIDB* 5:975–98.

Kaiser, Walter C. *Micah, Nahum, Habakkuk, Zephaniah, Haggai, Zechariah, Malachi.* Mastering the Old Testament. Dallas: Word, 1992.

Kapelrud, Arvid S. *The Message of the Prophet Zephaniah: Morphology and Ideas.* Oslo: Universitetsforlaget, 1975.

Keil, Carl F. "The Twelve Minor Prophets." Translated by M. G. Easton. *Commentary on the Old Testament.* 2 vols. 1864–1892. Vol. 10 in repr., 10 vols. Peabody, MA: Hendrickson, 2002. (References to Keil and Delitzsch are cited by both the ten-volume edition and the twenty-five-volume edition with the latter in parentheses).

Luther, Martin. "Lectures on Zephaniah." *Lectures on the Minor Prophets I: Hosea–Malachi.* Edited by Hilton C. Oswald. Translated by Richard J. Dinda. Vol. 18 of *Luther's Works.* St. Louis: Concordia, 1975.

Motyer, J. Alec. "Zephaniah." Pages 897–962 in *The Minor Prophets: An Exegetical and Expository Commentary.* Edited by Thomas Edward McComiskey. Grand Rapids: Baker, 1998.

Patterson, Richard D. *Nahum, Habakkuk, Zephaniah: An Exegetical Commentary.* Minor Prophets Exegetical Commentary. Dallas: Biblical Studies, 2003.

Renaud, B. *Michée, Sophonie, Nahum.* Paris: Gabalda, 1987.

Renz, Thomas. *The Books of Nahum, Habakkuk, and Zephaniah.* NICOT. Grand Rapids: Eerdmans, 2021.

Roberts, J. J. M. *Nahum, Habakkuk, and Zephaniah: A Commentary.* OTL. Louisville: Westminster John Knox, 1991.

Robertson, O. Palmer. *The Books of Nahum, Habakkuk, and Zephaniah.* NICOT. Grand Rapids: Eerdmans, 1990.

Rudolph, Wilhelm. *Micha, Nahum, Habakuk, Zephanja.* Vol. 3 of KAT 13. Gütersloh: Mohn, 1975.

Ryou, Daniel Hojoon. *Zephaniah's Oracles against the Nations: A Synchronic and Diachronic Study of Zephaniah 2:1–3:8.* BibInt 13. Leiden: Brill, 1995.

Sabottka, Liudger. *Zephanja.* BO 25. Rome: Biblical Institute Press, 1972.

Seybold, Klaus. *Nahum, Habakuk, Zephanja.* Zurich: TVZ, 1991.

Shepherd, Michael B. *A Commentary on the Book of the Twelve: The Minor Prophets.* Kregel Exegetical Library. Grand Rapids: Kregel, 2018.

Smith, John Merlin Powis. "A Critical and Exegetical Commentary on the Book of Zephaniah." Pages 157–263 in *A Critical and Exegetical Commentary on Micah, Zephaniah, Nahum, Habakkuk, Obadiah and Joel.* By John Merlin Powis Smith, William Hayes Ward, and Julius A. Bewer. ICC. Edinburgh: T&T Clark, 1911.

Smith, Ralph L. *Micah–Malachi.* WBC 32. Dallas: Word, 1984.

Sweeney, Marvin A. *Zephaniah: A Commentary.* Hermeneia. Minneapolis: Fortress, 2003.

Tachick, Christopher S. *"King of Israel" and "Do Not Fear, Daughter of Zion": The Use of Zephaniah 3 in John 12.* Reformed Academic Dissertations 11. Phillipsburg, NJ: P&R, 2018.

Timmer, Daniel C. *The Non-Israelite Nations in the Book of the Twelve: Thematic Coherence and the Diachronic-Synchronic Relationship in the Minor Prophets.* BibInt 135. Leiden: Brill, 2015.

Vlaardingerbroek, Johannes. *Zephaniah*. HCOT. Leuven: Peeters, 1999.

Walker, Larry L. "Zephaniah." Pages 649–95 in *Daniel–Malachi*. 2nd ed. EBC 8. Grand Rapids: Zondervan, 2008.

Watts, John D. W. *The Books of Joel, Obadiah, Jonah, Nahum, Habakkuk, and Zephaniah*. CBC. Cambridge: Cambridge University Press, 1975.

The Author's Studies on Zephaniah

DeRouchie, Jason S. "The Addressees in Zephaniah 2:1, 3: Who Should Seek YHWH Together?" *BBR* 30.2 (2020): 183–207.

———. "Confronting Idolatry in Zephaniah 1:4–6 and the Twenty-First Century." *MJT* 22.2 (2023): 18–41.

———. "The Day of the Lord." *TGC Essays* (2020). https://www.thegospelcoalition.org/essay/the-day-of-the-lord/.

———. "Made for Praise: Zephaniah 3:20." Pages 108–10 in *Devotions on the Hebrew Bible: 54 Reflections to Inspire and Instruct*. Edited by Milton Eng and Lee M. Fields. Grand Rapids: Zondervan, 2015.

———. "Perspectives on Zephaniah's Macrostructure: Critiques and a Proposal" *MJT* (2024): 20–51.

———. "Preaching the Prophets: Zephaniah as a Case Study for Christian Proclamation." *Pro Pastor* 3.1 (2024): 28–37.

———. "Rejoicing Then and Now: Pleasures on the Day of the Lord (Zeph 3:11–20)." *BSac* 181.3 (2024): forthcoming.

———. "Revering God: Punishment on the Day of the Lord (Zeph 1:2–18)." *BSac* 181.1 (2024): forthcoming.

———. "Seeking God and Waiting: Hope on the Day of the Lord (Zeph 2:1–4; 3:8–10)." *BSac* 181.2 (2024): forthcoming.

———. "YHWH's Future Ingathering in Zephaniah 1:2: Interpreting אָסֹף אָסֵף." *HS* 59 (2018): 173–91.

———. "YHWH's Judgment Is New Every Morning: Zephaniah 3:5 and the Light of the World." *TJ* 43 NS (2022): 131–46.

———. "Zephaniah, Book of." *DNTUOT* 886–90.

———. "Zephaniah." Pages 1621–27 in *NIV Biblical Theology Study Bible*. Edited by D. A. Carson. Grand Rapids: Zondervan, 2018.

———. "Zephaniah." Pages 1839–50 in *NIV Zondervan Study Bible*. Edited by D. A. Carson. Grand Rapids: Zondervan, 2015.

———. "Zephaniah." Pages 561–604 in *Daniel–Malachi*. Vol. 7 of *ESV Expository Commentary*. Wheaton, IL: Crossway, 2018.

———. "Zephaniah." Pages 676–79 in *The Baker Illustrated Bible Background Commentary*. Edited by J. Scott Duvall and J. Daniel Hays. Grand Rapids: Baker Books, 2020.

———. "Zephaniah." *TGC Bible Commentary* (2021). https://www.thegospelcoalition.org/commentary/zephaniah/.

———. "Zephaniah's Macrostructure: A Textlinguistic-Rhetorical Analysis." Presentation at the Macro Analysis of Hebrew Poetic and Prophetic Discourse Conference. Dallas International University, 2023. Presentation at the 2024 Annual Meeting of the Evangelical Theological Society. San Diego, CA, 20 November 2024.

Translation of Zephaniah

Zephaniah 1

[1]YHWH's word that came to Zephaniah the son of Cushi, the son of Gedaliah, the son of Amariah, the son of Hezekiah in the days of Josiah the son of Amon, Judah's king.

[2]I will surely gather everything from on the face of the ground—the utterance of YHWH. [3]I will gather human and beast; I will gather the bird of the heavens and the fish of the sea and the stumbling blocks with the wicked. And I will cut off humanity from on the face of the ground—the utterance of YHWH. [4]So, I will stretch out my hand against Judah and against all the inhabitants of Jerusalem. And I will cut off from this place the remnant of the Baal—the name of the illegitimate priests with the priests, [5]and those who bow down on the roofs to the host of the heavens, and those who bow down, who swear to YHWH but swear by their king, [6]and those who turn away from YHWH and who have neither sought YHWH nor inquired of him.

[7]Hush before the Sovereign YHWH, for the day of YHWH is near, for YHWH has prepared a sacrifice; he has consecrated his invited ones. [8]And it will happen in the day of YHWH's sacrifice that I will visit [punishment] on the officials, and on the king's sons, and on all who dress in foreign attire. [9]Furthermore, I will visit [punishment] on all who step over the threshold in that day—those who fill their Sovereign's house with violence and deception. [10]And there will be in that day—the utterance of YHWH—a sound: a cry from the Fish Gate and a wail from the Second Quarter and a great crash from the heights. [11]The inhabitants of the Mortar have wailed, for all the people of Canaan have been silenced; all those laden with silver have been cut off. [12]And it will happen at that time that I will search Jerusalem with the lamps, and I will visit [punishment] on the men who thicken on their wine dregs, who say in their heart, "YHWH will neither do good nor do ill." [13]Then their wealth will be for spoil and their houses for desolation, and they will build houses, but they will not inhabit; and they will plant vineyards, but they will not drink their wine.

[14]The great day of YHWH is near—near and hastening fast. The sound of the day of YHWH is bitter; a Mighty One is shouting there. [15]That day is a day of wrath—a

day of distress and anguish, a day of ruin and devastation, a day of darkness and gloom, a day of cloud and thick darkness, [16]a day of trumpet blast and battle cry against the unassailable cities and against the high battlements. [17]Surely, I will bring distress to humanity, with the result that they will walk as the blind, for against YHWH they have sinned. Indeed, their blood will be poured out like dust and their belly like dung pellets. [18]Also, their silver—even their gold—will not be able to deliver them in the day of the wrath of YHWH. And in the fire of his jealousy all the earth will be consumed, for a complete, even terrifying, end he will deal against all the inhabitants of the earth.

Zephaniah 2

[1]Bind yourselves together, and become a sheaf, O nation not longing—[2]before a birthing of a decree (like chaff, a day has passed), before the fury of YHWH's anger surely comes on you, before the day of YHWH's anger surely comes on you. [3]Seek YHWH, all the humble of the land who have heeded his just decree. Seek righteousness; seek humility! (Perhaps you may be hidden at the day of YHWH's anger.) [4]For Gaza will be abandoned, and Ashkelon for a desolation. As for Ashdod, by the noonday they will drive her out, and Ekron will be uprooted.

[5]Woe, O inhabitants of the shoreline by the sea, nation of Kerethites! YHWH's word is against you, O Canaan, the land of Philistines. Surely, I will destroy you until there is no inhabitant. [6]The result will be that it [i.e., the land]—namely, the shoreline by the sea—will become grazing grounds with cisterns for shepherds and folds for sheep [7]and that it [i.e., the shoreline] will become a shoreline for the remnant of the house of Judah; on them [i.e., the tracts of shoreline] they will pasture. In the houses of Ashkelon at evening they will lie down, for YHWH their God will visit them, and he will restore their circumstance.

[8]I have heard the reproach of Moab and the abuses of Bene-Ammon by which they have disgraced my people and become haughty against their border. [9]Therefore, by my life—the utterance of YHWH of armies, the God of Israel—surely Moab will become like Sodom, and Bene-Ammon like Gomorrah—a possession of weed and salt pit and desolation perpetually. The remnant of my people will plunder them, and the remainder of my nation will inherit them. [10]This shall be to them in exchange for their pride, because they reproached and became haughty against the people of YHWH of armies. [11]YHWH is fearsome against them, for he has made lean all the gods of the earth, so that all the coastlands of the nations will bow down to him, each from his place.

[12]Also you, O Cushites—slain by my sword are they. [13]So, may he stretch out his hand against the north and destroy Assyria. Then may he place Nineveh for a

desolation, dry as the wilderness, [14]with the result that in her midst herds will lie down—every beast of a nation. Even an owl, also a bustard, will lodge at her capitals. A sound will sing at the window. Devastation will be at the threshold, when he has exposed her cedar work. [15]This is the exultant city—the one dwelling in security, the one saying in her heart, "I am, and my limit is still [unreached]." How she has become a desolation, a resting place for the beast. Each one passing over her will hiss; he will shake his fist.

Zephaniah 3

[1]Woe, O rebellious and defiled one—the oppressive city! [2]She has not listened unto a voice; she has not received instruction. In YHWH she has not trusted; unto her God she has not drawn near. [3]Her officials in her midst are roaring lions. Her judges are evening wolves; they have not gnawed to the morning. [4]Her prophets are reckless, men of treacheries. Her priests have profaned what is holy; they have treated torah violently. [5]YHWH is righteous in her midst. He never does wrong. Morning by morning he gives his judgment for the light; it has never been lacking. But a wrong one never knows shame. [6]I have cut off nations; their battlements have been dismayed. I have laid waste their streets with none passing; their cities have become so desolate as to be without a person, so there is no inhabitant. [7]I said, "Surely you will fear me; you will receive instruction," so that her Shelter would not be cut off—all that I have purposed to visit against her. However, they arose early; they corrupted all their deeds.

[8]Therefore, wait for me—the utterance of YHWH—for the day of my rising as witness. For my judgment is to gather nations, to assemble kingdoms, to pour out on them my indignation—all the fury of my anger, for in the fire of my jealousy all the earth will be consumed. [9]For then I will change for peoples a purified lip so that all of them may call on the name YHWH, to serve him with one shoulder. [10]From beyond the rivers of Cush, my supplicants, the daughter of my scattered ones, will carry my offering.

[11]In that day, you [i.e., Jerusalem] will never be ashamed on account of all your deeds by which you revolted against me. For then I will remove from your midst the exultant ones of your boast, and you will no more increase arrogance at the mountain of my holiness. [12]And I will cause to remain in your midst an afflicted and needy people, and they will take refuge in the name of YHWH—[13]the remnant of Israel. They will never do wrong nor speak a lie, and in their mouth will never be found a tongue of deceit, because they will graze and lie down, and there will be none who cause trembling.

[14]Sing aloud, O daughter of Zion! Shout, O Israel! Be merry, and exult with all

heart, O daughter of Jerusalem. YHWH has removed your judgments; he has turned away your enemy. [15]Israel's King, YHWH, is in your midst. Never fear evil again!

[16]In that day, it will be said to Jerusalem, "Do not fear! O Zion, may your hands not grow slack. [17]YHWH your God is in your midst. As a Mighty One, he will save! May he rejoice over you with merriment; may he renew by his love; may he celebrate over you with song! [18]Those tormented from an appointed time I have gathered. They were away from you; a burden was on her, a reproach." [19]Look, I will be dealing with all who afflict you at that time. And I will save the lame one, and the banished one I will assemble. And I will place them for praise and for a name in all the earth, their [place of] shame. [20]At that time, I will bring you—even at the time of my assembling you, for I will give you for a name and for praise among all the peoples of the earth in my restoring your circumstances before your eyes.

YHWH has spoken.

Introduction to Zephaniah

The Savior's Invitation to Satisfaction

Of Zephaniah Luther declared, "Among the minor prophets, he makes the clearest prophecies about the kingdom of Christ."[1] This fact alone should motivate Christian expositors to engage this book. Perhaps more than any other minor prophet, Zephaniah synthesizes in just fifty-three verses a theology of local and global sin, punishment, and restoration. In Zephaniah, YHWH is "King" who comes as mighty Warrior to gather all the world for judgment, consume the unrepentant wicked in his sacrificial fires of wrath, and save his humble remnant of multiethnic worshipers.[2] These together constitute the new Israel of God in the transformed Jerusalem, all on the day of YHWH. Other OT prophets and the NT clarify the central role Christ would play in YHWH's day of wrath and renewal.

Zephaniah's appeals supply what I call the Savior God's invitation to satisfaction. The prophet encourages a righteous remnant to pursue YHWH together with patience, and he probably intended his message to aid King Josiah's reformation movement in Judah. This commentary introduction will cover the following areas:

1. Zephaniah's Title and Authorship
2. Zephaniah's Date and Occasion
3. Zephaniah's Genre, Literary Features, and Audience
4. Zephaniah's Macrostructure
5. Zephaniah's Hermeneutic and Theology
6. Proclaiming Zephaniah Today

---

1. Martin Luther, "Lectures on Zephaniah," in *Lectures on the Minor Prophets I: Hosea–Malachi*, ed. Hilton C. Oswald, trans. Richard J. Dinda, vol. 18 of *Luther's Works* (St. Louis: Concordia, 1975), 319.

2. This commentary's translations are all the author's unless noted otherwise. The translations are highly form-equivalent, retaining correspondence of words, grammar, and history especially to highlight Hebrew macrostructural signals.

Zephaniah's Title and Authorship

The book title "Zephaniah" indicates the prophetic mouthpiece through whom God proclaimed this message of warning and hope. Zephaniah served as a recipient and covenant spokesman of YHWH's oracle sometime during the reign of Judah's king, Josiah (ca. 640–609 BC; Zeph 1:1). This was roughly a century after Assyria overthrew Israel's northern kingdom (ca. 723 BC) and just prior to Babylon destroying Jerusalem in 586 BC (1:4; 3:7). Only this book mentions the prophet Zephaniah.[3] Nevertheless, an early sixth-century seal found at Lachish may refer to him. It reads, "To Jeremiah, the son of Zephaniah, son of a prophe[t] . . ." (*lyrmyhw bn ṣpnyhw bn nby[?]*). While certain identification is impossible, the bulla states that one named Zephaniah fathered a certain Jeremiah and that either Zephaniah or his father was a recognized prophet.[4] The Babylonian Talmud (b. Meg. 15a) states that Zephaniah's father Cushi was a prophet.

The name "Zephaniah" (צְפַנְיָה) means "YHWH has hidden."[5] Scripture applies the root to God's "cherished" or "treasured" saints (Ps 83:4[3]), city (Ezek 7:22), and servants whom he protects from evil (Pss 27:5; 31:21[20]).[6] Parents were likely affirming God's protective grace when they named their son "Zephaniah" during Manasseh's dark reign (see 2 Kgs 20:21–21:18) or, less likely, Amon's (21:19–26).

King Hezekiah was Manasseh's father, the Southern Kingdom's thirteenth king and reformer, and Zephaniah's great, great grandfather (Zeph 1:1, see commentary). Zephaniah's participation in the royal family explains his awareness of and concern for Israel's covenantal and religious heritage (see below), the international climate (e.g., 2:4–15), and the ethics of Jerusalem's political and religious leadership (esp. 1:4, 8–9; 3:3–4). Furthermore, a Godward orientation accompanying this royal, Davidic heritage highlights that a messianic hope still flickered in the darkness.

Because Zephaniah was "son of Cushi" (1:1) and shows a unique interest in the sin and future restoration of the Cushites (i.e., ancient black Africans, 2:12; 3:9–10), the prophet was likely biracial, bearing both Cushite and royal Judean ancestry (see commentary at 1:1). This could explain his apparent interest in global judgment and restoration (1:2–3, 17–18; 3:8–10). Previous Scripture also strongly influenced Zephaniah's message (see below), and the ministries of his contemporary prophets Nahum, Habakkuk, and Jeremiah may have also impacted it.

---

3. Zephaniah the prophet's genealogy and Godward orientation likely differentiate him from the priest "Zephaniah the son of Maaseiah the priest" whom the king of Babylon slaughtered at Riblah in the land of Hamath in the days of Jeremiah (Jer 29:25; 52:24–27).

4. John M. Berridge, "Zephaniah (Person)," *ABD* 6:1075; cf. Klaus Seybold, *Satirische Prophetie: Studien zum Buch Zefanja* (Stuttgart: Katholisches Bibelwerk, 1985), 64–65.

5. צְפַנְיָה comes from the *qal qatal* form of the verb צפן ("he hid, has hidden") and the abbreviated form of the divine name יָה ("Yah[weh]").

6. Marvin A. Sweeney, *Zephaniah: A Commentary*, Hermeneia (Minneapolis: Fortress, 2003), 47.

Zephaniah's Date and Occasion

Zephaniah's Ministry

Zephaniah was likely born during the dark days of King Manasseh.[7] The end of his kingship witnessed a brief resurgence of YHWH worship following his repentance (2 Chr 33:12–16). However, rampant idolatry and covenant disloyalty were the norm during his fifty-five-year reign (ca. 696–642 BC, 2 Kgs 20:21–21:18) and his son Amon's two-year reign (ca. 642–640 BC, 2 Kgs 21:19–26). The "remnant of the Baal" that Zephaniah confronts (Zeph 1:4) is a holdover from the rampant wickedness of these days.

The book's historical signals, rhetorical thrust, and use of Scripture clarify the date and occasion of Zephaniah's ministry. The superscription states that he served during Josiah's thirty-one-year reign (1:1; ca. 640–609 BC), which included his spiritual reformation. Thus, foreign neighbors within Zephaniah (Philistia, Moab, Bene-Ammon, Cush, and Assyria, 2:5–15) nicely fit the political landscape of this time.[8] Also, the spiritual problems Zephaniah confronts resemble the time of Josiah's reforms in 2 Kgs 21–23.[9] Particularly, Josiah and Zephaniah opposed "the remnant of the Baal," which included the "illegitimate priests" (כְּמָרִים) and those worshiping "the host of the heavens" (צְבָא הַשָּׁמַיִם) (2 Kgs 23:5; Zeph 1:4–5).

Zephaniah's message helps clarify his time. Since the prophet anticipates the destruction of Assyria's capital Nineveh (2:13–15) by the Babylonians and Medes in 612 BC, this is his proclamation's latest possible date.[10] The earliest date would then be 640 BC, when King Josiah began reigning at age eight. But it was not until

---

7. No designated age for prophetic office exists. Manhood began at age twenty (the allowable age to fight in war, Num 1:3), and prophets like Samuel and Jeremiah apparently started their roles quite young. Nevertheless, the Israelites recognized the full status of other religious leaders at age thirty (Num 4:3), with an apprenticeship for Levitical guardianship and service (e.g., carrying the ark; performing sacrifices) beginning at age twenty-five (8:24–26) and then later at age twenty (1 Chr 23:24, 27; 2 Chr 31:17; Ezra 3:8). Thus, Zephaniah likely needed to be at least thirty to get a hearing among the people. This makes a birth during Amon's reign unlikely, for he would have been only twelve to fourteen years old in 628 BC when Josiah's reforms formally began and eighteen to twenty in 622 BC when the Torah Scroll was found.

8. For many comparisons, see Duane L. Christensen, "Zephaniah 2:4–15: A Theological Basis for Josiah's Program of Political Expansion," *CBQ* 46 (1984): 669–82; Robert D. Haak, "Zephaniah's Oracles against the Nations" (presented at the Chicago Society of Biblical Research, 1992); Adele Berlin, "Zephaniah's Oracle against the Nations and an Israelite Cultural Myth," in *Fortunate the Eyes That See: Essays in Honor of David Noel Freedman in Celebration of His Seventieth Birthday*, ed. Astrid B. Beck et al. (Grand Rapids: Eerdmans, 1995), 175–84.

9. Cf. Ehud Ben Zvi, *A Historical-Critical Study of the Book of Zephaniah*, BZAW 198 (Berlin: de Gruyter, 1991), 276–77; Johannes Vlaardingerbroek, *Zephaniah*, HCOT (Leuven: Peeters, 1999), 53.

10. For a description of the fall, see "The Babylonian Chronicle," 3.38–52, trans., A. Leo Oppenheim (*ANET*, 304–5); A. Kirk Grayson, *Assyrian and Babylonian Chronicles*, TCS 5 (Winona Lake, IN: Eisenbrauns, 2000), 94–95. Williams's linking the book's oracle to Jehoiakim's reign (609–598 BC) disregards both the superscription's dating in Zeph 1:1 and the portrayal in 2:13–15 of Assyria/Nineveh's fall as still future (Donald L. Williams, "The Date of Zephaniah," *JBL* 82.1 [1963]: 77–88).

Josiah's eighth year (ca. 632 BC) that he "began to seek the God of his father David" (2 Chr 34:3). And in his twelfth year (ca. 628 BC) he started removing all Canaanite pagan shrines and emblems from Jerusalem, Judah, and the region that was the Northern Kingdom (2 Chr 34:3–7). Finally, in his eighteenth year (ca. 622 BC), Hilkiah the high priest recovered the Torah Scroll of Moses (2 Kgs 22:8, 11; 2 Chr 34:14–15), which probably included Deuteronomy's core (cf. Deut 29:21; 30:10; 31:26).[11] This led the king to institute throughout the land a mass religious reform (2 Chr 34:29–35:19) that included eradicating all remaining signs of Baal worship in Jerusalem and its environs (2 Kgs 23:4–25).

Some scholars reason that Zephaniah focuses on Judah's political and religious elite without mentioning the king (Zeph 1:8–9; 3:3–4) because Josiah himself must have still been a minor lacking influence (2 Kgs 22:1).[12] Similarly, Rudolph claims that the religious syncretism evident in Zeph 1:4–6 makes sense only before Josiah's reform.[13] However, Zephaniah's message closely aligns with Josiah's spiritual reforms (cf. e.g., 2 Kgs 23:5–6, 12–13 with Zeph 1:4–6), and the prophet's freedom to warn and command as he does fits best *after* Josiah had begun his reform.[14] Josiah leading the reform and having already "turned to YHWH with all his heart" (2 Kgs 23:25; cf. 23:3, 21) best explains why Zephaniah did not confront him.[15]

Several features suggest that the prophet ministered in the autumn of 622 BC,

---

11. *Torah* is the anglicized form of the transliterated Hebrew noun *tôrâ* (תּוֹרָה), which is routinely, if inadequately, translated "law." Within Deuteronomy, the "Torah Scroll" specifically relates to the Deuteronomic core that Moses wrote as Israel's constitution to guide their life in the promised land. Sweeney notes that, for most modern critical scholars, dating Deuteronomy's core to the late seventh century is "the fundamental linchpin" for reconstructing both Israelite/Judean religious development and much of the biblical literature's compositional history (Marvin A. Sweeney, *King Josiah of Judah: The Lost Messiah of Israel* [Oxford: Oxford University Press, 2001], 5; cf. Julius Wellhausen, *Prolegomena to the History of Israel*, trans. J. Sutherland Black and Allan Menzies [Edinburgh: Black, 1885; repr., Cleveland, OH: World, 1961], 13). The record of Josiah's reforms aligns closely with much of Deuteronomy's content and terminology yet records long before Josiah's day display many of the identical parallels, clarifying that Deuteronomy's core was available long before the days of Josiah. For a developed list of the biblical evidence, see Michael A. Grisanti, "Josiah and the Composition of Deuteronomy," in *Sepher Torath Mosheh: Studies in the Composition and Interpretation of Deuteronomy*, ed. Daniel I. Block and Richard L. Schultz (Peabody, MA: Hendrickson, 2017), 122–29. For a strong argument that this embedded Torah Scroll should be linked directly to Moses, see Daniel I. Block, "Recovering the Voice of Moses: The Genesis of Deuteronomy," *JETS* 44.3 (2001): 385–408.

12. John Merlin Powis Smith, "A Critical and Exegetical Commentary on the Book of Zephaniah," in *A Critical and Exegetical Commentary on Micah, Zephaniah, Nahum, Habakkuk, Obadiah and Joel*, by John Merlin Powis Smith, William Hayes Ward, and Julius A. Brewer, ICC (Edinburgh: T&T Clark, 1911), 196; J. J. M. Roberts, *Nahum, Habakkuk, and Zephaniah: A Commentary*, OTL (Louisville: Westminster John Knox, 1991), 163.

13. Wilhelm Rudolph, *Micha, Nahum, Habakuk, Zephanja*, vol. 3 of *KAT* 13 (Gütersloh: Mohn, 1975), 255.

14. Understood in this way, "Zephaniah's message reflects the ideas of the group that welcomes and advanced the deuteronomic reform in Josiah's day," and "Josiah and Zephaniah would be on the same side" (Ben Zvi, *Book of Zephaniah*, 36 with n76).

15. So, too, C. F. Keil, "The Twelve Minor Prophets," trans. M. G. Easton, 2 vols., in *Commentary on the Old Testament* (1864–1892; repr. in 10 vols., Peabody, MA: Hendrickson, 2002), 10:442 (2:130); Thomas Renz, *The Books of Nahum, Habakkuk, and Zephaniah*, NICOT (Grand Rapids: Eerdmans, 2021), 432. Ben Zvi further notes the absence of any reference to the king in similar prophetic accounts (Isa 1:21–23[–26]; Mic 7:3). This fact "does not rule out the possibility that the text refers to or reflects the days of Josiah's childhood, but rules out the idea that the text necessarily points to these days" (Ben Zvi, *Book of Zephaniah*, 93).

after the king initially cleansed the land in 628 BC and recovered the Torah Scroll in the spring of 622 BC but before fully implementing his reform. First, Zephaniah regularly alludes to Deuteronomy, suggesting he knew of the Deuteronomic core.[16] However, the Torah Scroll began to influence Josiah's reign directly only after Hilkiah the high priest found it in the temple. This likely happened in early 622 BC, for it led King Josiah in his eighteenth year to institute the Passover (2 Kgs 23:21–23), which always occurs in the spring (in March or April), in the first month of the religious calendar—the 14/15 of Abib (cf. Deut 16:2–8). Second, Zephaniah's message features issues that are consonant with Josiah's 622 BC reform (cf. 2 Kgs 23:4–25): confronting religious syncretism, indifference, covenantal disloyalty, and political and social oppression (Zeph 1:4–13; 3:1–4, 7) and calling people to pray, trust, and seek God (e.g., 1:6; 2:3; 3:2, 8). Third, the book never mentions child sacrifice, suggesting Josiah's reform had already curbed this evil from Manasseh and Amon's reigns (2 Kgs 21:6, 21; cf. 24:3–4; Jer 7:31). Fourth, the book's language of "ingathering" suggests that Zephaniah preached during the autumn's Feast of Ingathering (September–October). This post-harvest celebration ran from the religious calendar's fifteenth through twenty-first days of the seventh month, Ethanim / Tishri.[17] Fifth, a holdout of Baal worship including "illegitimate priests" remained in Jerusalem (Zeph 1:4), which means Josiah's full reformation was not yet complete (cf. 2 Kgs 23:5).

Apparently, Zephaniah's message originally served Josiah's reforms in Judah, all with an eye toward the rising Babylonian crisis and Jerusalem's destruction in 586 BC. Nevertheless, the international (e.g., Zeph 2:4–15) and eschatological (e.g., 3:8–20) scope of the prophet's message applies across cultures today.[18]

The Book's Final Form

The book indicates that its body comes from Zephaniah, but it never states that the prophet himself wrote down his oracle, though other prophets did just this (e.g., Deut 31:9; Isa 30:8; Jer 30:2–3). The superscription (Zeph 1:1) introduces the book and identifies the prophet in the third person. But the prophet himself could have introduced the book in this way, just as YHWH refers to himself in third person throughout the book (e.g., 1:4–6; see below). Indeed, the arguments below suggest

---

16. See Zephaniah's Use of Scripture below. So O. Palmer Robertson, *Books of Nahum, Habakkuk, and Zephaniah*, NICOT (Grand Rapids: Eerdmans, 1990), 254–55; Clint Sheehan, "Kingdom through Covenant: The Structure and Theology of Zephaniah," *BRT/RBT* 6.2 (1996): 8–10.

17. For more on this possibility, see the commentary at Zeph 1:2, 5, 7; 3:18 and Roberts, *Nahum, Habakkuk, and Zephaniah*, 169; Sweeney, *Zephaniah*, 62.

18. Within this commentary, the term "eschatology" re-

fers to the dawning of history's end associated with the day of YHWH and the Messiah's death, resurrection, and lasting reign. See G. K. Beale, "The Eschatological Conception of New Testament Theology," in *Eschatology in Bible and Theology: Evangelical Essays at the Dawn of a New Millennium*, ed. Kent E. Brower and Mark W. Elliott (Downers Grove, IL: InterVarsity Press, 1997), 11–52; cf. Dane C. Ortlund and G. K. Beale, "Darkness over the Whole Land: A Biblical Theological Reflection on Mark 15:33," *WTJ* 75 (2013): 221.

10 Introduction to Zephaniah

that Zephaniah himself likely spoke his message and finalized the written form in the version retained in the Bible. This fulfillment of his immediate predictions likely guided others to recognize the whole as YHWH's message and part of the growing covenantal canon that we call Scripture.[19]

Conversely, many critical scholars advance an exilic or postexilic redaction to the whole.[20] This critical approach often considers the literary prophets as less the words of the man associated with a book's title (e.g., Isaiah, Zephaniah, Zechariah) and more the work of tradents, whom Ben Zvi calls "theologians who reflected on their given traditions, reactualized them and eventually shaped or reshaped them."[21] Many critical scholars hold a naturalistic worldview that denies the possibility of true predictive prophecy.[22] They thus use the situational background of the book's various passages to posit different dates of origin for the parts. This commonly results in the view that "original and early redactional materials tend to announce judgment, while exilic and postexilic materials always announce salvation."[23] The parts of the book that scholars most often assign to someone other than Zephaniah are Zeph 1:2–3; 2:7–11; and 3:8–20.[24]

For two reasons, some critical scholars disagree that situational background determines provenance. First, Sweeney rightly notes that those who restrict futur-

---

19. Gowan, *Theology of the Prophetic Books*, 8–9; Gentry, *How to Read and Understand the Biblical Prophets*, 32–37; cf. Robertson, *Books of Nahum, Habakkuk, and Zephaniah*, 335; Ben Zvi, *Book of Zephaniah*, 236; Michael H. Floyd, *Minor Prophets, Part 2*, FOTL 22 (Grand Rapids: Eerdmans, 2000), 177.

20. E.g., J. M. P. Smith, "Book of Zephaniah," 172–74; Louise Pettibone Smith and Ernest R. Lacheman, "The Authorship of the Book of Zephaniah," *JNES* 9.3 (1950): 137–42; Ben Zvi, *Book of Zephaniah*, 349–52; cf. 291–95, 357–58; Roberts, *Nahum, Habakkuk, and Zephaniah*, 163; Adele Berlin, *Zephaniah: A New Translation with Introduction and Commentary*, AB (New Haven: Yale University Press, 1994), 33; Simon J. De Vries, *From Old Revelation to New: A Tradition-Historical and Redaction-Critical Study of Temporal Transitions in Prophetic Prediction* (Grand Rapids: Eerdmans, 1995), 202; Vlaardingerbroek, *Zephaniah*, 9–10; Hubert Irsigler, *Zefanja*, HThKAT (Freiburg im Breisgau: Herder, 2002), 58–65; Tchavdar S. Hadjiev, "Survival, Conversion and Restoration: Reflections on the Redaction History of the Book of Zephaniah," *VT* 61 (2011): 570–81; Judith Gärtner, "Jerusalem—City of God for Israel and for the Nations in Zeph 3:8, 9–10, 11–13," in *Perspectives on the Formation of the Book of the Twelve: Methodological Foundations, Redactional Processes, Historical Insights*, ed. Rainer Albertz, James D. Nogalski, and Jakob Wöhrle, BZAW 433 (Berlin: de Gruyter, 2012), 269–83. Renz claims Zephaniah is canonical Scripture (Renz, *Books of Nahum, Habakkuk, and Zephaniah*, 606n82) but only associates 1:2–3:5 and 3:8

directly with Zephaniah in the 630s or 620s BC; he dates 3:6–7 to later but pre-597 BC and 3:9–20 to after the days of Ezekiel (Renz, *Books of Nahum, Habakkuk, and Zephaniah*, 585, 606; cf. 432–35, 611, 624). For responses to Renz, see Structure and Literary Form for 3:8–10 along with the commentary on 1:1; 3:6, 15b. See also the perceptive arguments against pseudonymity in Joyce G. Baldwin, "Is There Pseudonymity in the Old Testament?," *Them* 4.1 (1978): 6–12; Stuart Lasine, "Fiction, Falsehood, and Reality in Hebrew Scriptures," *HS* 25 (1984): 24–40.

21. Ben Zvi, *Book of Zephaniah*, 9–10; cf. 89; quote from 9.

22. For De Vries, the OT prophetical books' future predictions are "not always a true prediction" but are the "past/present disguised as future" (De Vries, *From Old Revelation to New*, 55–56).

23. De Vries, *From Old Revelation to New*, 206, 243; cf. 56–59, 246, 254–55. Ben Zvi helpfully clarifies his own guiding presuppositions: "The writer could have been aware of past events and old language but could not have been aware of future developments. . . . One of the basic assumptions of the historical-critical method is that there is a basic uniformity through the ages. Since there is no reliable evidence of people directly aware of future developments in present days, one concludes that the same holds true concerning people who lived in the past" (Ben Zvi, *Book of Zephaniah*, 264).

24. Ben Zvi, *Book of Zephaniah*, 32.

istic prophetic speech to the exilic or postexilic period have "a rather wooden view of prophecy that . . . ignores the rhetorical or persuasive dimensions of prophetic speech." He adds, "A portrayal of an idyllic future is frequently essential to enable the prophet to convince his/her audience that his/her message or assessment of the present situation is cogent."[25] While Sweeney's final comments do not affirm the need for the words themselves to be true to bear lasting authority (cf. Deut 18:21–22), he correctly recognizes the motivational force of prediction.

But the prophet's foretelling is not mere "prophetic imagination."[26] Indeed, if we (1) affirm the superscription's claim that "YHWH's word" came to the prophet (Zeph 1:1; cf. 3:20c; 2 Tim 3:16) and (2) agree that Sovereign YHWH both controls all things (Rom 11:36; Eph 1:11) and can ordain the future (Isa 43:9–13; 44:6–8; cf. Acts 4:27–28), then we should readily accept that God enables predictive prophecy (2 Pet 1:20–21; cf. 1 Pet 1:10–11).[27]

Second, Berlin comments that "the book as it stands . . . presents itself rhetorically and structurally as a unified work (with the possible exception of the superscription) and in its canonical form it was apparently intended to be interpreted as such."[28] Thus, as Kapelrud notes, "either this collection of prophetic words was transmitted practically as they were spoken by the prophet, or a redactor of no common ability did an outstanding piece of work in making uniform the *obiter dicta* [i.e., *words* said in passing] of the prophet.[29] Sweeney affirms that "the book as a whole has a coherent structure which derives from the late seventh-century prophet Zephaniah."[30]

While Berlin is correct that Zephaniah's superscription and body do not require the same dating,[31] at least two additional features suggest that Zephaniah or one closely associated with him in his day inscribed the book in its final form. First, the five-member genealogy in 1:1 includes details that would probably have been unknown to an editor much later than Zephaniah himself. Second, the book would likely have referred to Babylon if it arose in the exilic or postexilic periods, but no

---

25. Sweeney, *Zephaniah*, 200.

26. So Walter Brueggemann, *The Prophetic Imagination*, 2nd ed. (Minneapolis: Fortress, 2001); cf. Floyd, *Minor Prophets, Part 2*, 177–78; Renz, *Books of Nahum, Habakkuk, and Zephaniah*, 623–24.

27. The Scriptures' arguments often hinge on the reality of predictive prophecy. For example, the man of God could foretell some three centuries in advance that a Davidic descendant named Josiah would burn the bones of the northern kingdom's illegitimate priests on Bethel's altar (1 Kgs 13:2; cf. 2 Kgs 23:15–16). Similarly, Isaiah of Jerusalem could predict around one hundred fifty years in advance that a shepherd-king named Cyrus would initiate the return to Jerusalem and the city's rebuilding after the exile (Isa 44:28; 45:13; cf. 2 Chr 36:22–23). Robertson writes, "If the genuineness of Yahweh's intention in history rests on the historical fulfillment of the prophet's word,

then of course it matters whether the prophet spoke before or after the event being prophesied" (Robertson, *Books of Nahum, Habakkuk, and Zephaniah*, 335n2). Motyer also stresses that interpreters should not "deny a message of hope to preexilic prophets" since YHWH's name as revealed in Exod 34:6–7 demands that he be both judge and redeemer (J. Alec Motyer, "Zephaniah," in *The Minor Prophets: An Exegetical and Expository Commentary*, ed. Thomas Edward McComiskey [Grand Rapids: Baker, 1998], 957).

28. Berlin, *Zephaniah*, 20.

29. Arvid S. Kapelrud, *Message of the Prophet Zephaniah: Morphology and Ideas* (Oslo: Universitetsforlaget, 1975), 13–14.

30. Sweeney, *Zephaniah*, 391; cf. John D. W. Watts, *Books of Joel, Obadiah, Jonah, Nahum, Habakkuk, and Zephaniah*, CBC (Cambridge: Cambridge University Press, 1975), 163.

31. Berlin, *Zephaniah*, 69.

such references are present.[32] Zephaniah likely inscribed the whole including the superscription and subscription soon after he preached it, with the written form being dated shortly after the autumn of 622 BC and no later than 612 BC.

Zephaniah's Genre, Literary Features, and Audience

Phrases like "YHWH's word" (Zeph 1:1), "the utterance of YHWH" (1:2, 3, 10; 2:9; 3:8), and "YHWH has spoken" (3:20) mark Zephaniah as a prophetic oracle, a divine covenantal pronouncement through a human ambassador that directs human behavior in the present by instructing, indicting, and predicting punishment and hope. The book uses the expected elevated style of prophetic discourse, especially in chapters 2–3, and this minor prophet resembles Isaiah's content and style more than any other.[33] The grouping of five masculine plural imperatives in 2:1, 3 and the additional masculine plural imperative in 3:8 mark the whole book as prophetic exhortation.[34] Everything else either introduces parenetic speech or motivates in some way.

Frequently within the book, the speaker's identity changes without any clear signal or speech frame. For example, the prophet refers to YHWH in the third person in 1:7, but then YHWH speaks in first person in 1:8. Wendland and Clark call this "the most striking formal feature of Zephaniah."[35] Nevertheless, the oracle reads as a cohesive whole with Zephaniah and YHWH's voices working together to proclaim a single "word" (1:1) *as if* from a single voice.

More specifically, Zephaniah's oracle unfolds as a single covenantal address seeking to correct those in Judah and other lands. The prophetic discourse charges the faithful remnant to "seek" YHWH together (2:1, 3) and to "wait" for him (3:8). Warnings of divine punishment against both the world (1:2–3, 14–18; 2:4–15; 3:8) and Judah (1:4–13; 2:2, 3:1–7) and promises of satisfying salvation for a remnant from the same (2:3; 3:9–10, 11–20) motivate these charges. Other literary features also encourage heeding his charges: further commands (3:14), prohibitions (3:16), statements of "woe" (2:5–7; 3:1–5), climax markers (3:8, 10, 12), causal conjunctions (1:7; 2:4; 3:8b–9), inference markers (2:9; 3:8), indicators of immediate significance

---

32. De Vries affirms a late redaction of the work but recognizes, "We cannot learn from this book what did in fact happen next—the Babylonian exile" (De Vries, *From Old Revelation to New*, 202).

33. Motyer writes, "Zephaniah is nearer in literary spirit and talent to Isaiah than is any other prophet" (Motyer, "Zephaniah," 956; cf. 938). For Zephaniah's use of Isaiah, see the commentary at, e.g., Zeph 1:7; 2:3, 4, 9–11, 15; 3:9–10, 11, 13, 16, 17. For a complete list, see the introduction section on Zephaniah's Use of Scripture.

34. Others call the entire discourse prophetic "parenesis," which means the same thing. See Marvin A. Sweeney, *Isaiah 1–39 with an Introduction to Prophetic Literature*, FOTL 16 (Grand Rapids: Eerdmans, 1996), 527.

35. Ernst R. Wendland and David J. Clark, "Zephaniah: Anatomy and Physiology of a Dramatic Prophetic Text," *JOTT* 16 (2003): 4.

(3:19), temporal signals (1:8, 10, 12; 3:9, 11, 16, 19–20), and repetition (e.g., "gather," 1:2; 3:8, 18; "day," 1:7–10, 14–16, 18; 2:2–3; 3:8, 11, 16; "sacrifice/fire," 1:7, 18; 3:8).

Zephaniah uses second person speech ("you/your") to address Judah as "the nation not longing" (2:1), foreign nations like Philistia (2:5) and Cush (2:12), and the unnamed faithful remnant (2:3; 3:8). Its second-person addresses use masculine plural forms for the remnant (e.g., 2:1, 3; 3:8, 14b, 20) and feminine singular forms for the collective city Jerusalem. When addressing Jerusalem, the book speaks to both its corrupt and pre-punishment state (3:7; cf. 3:1) and its purged and transformed state (3:11–12, 14–19).

Zephaniah's most immediate audience was Judeans who would listen. He also directly addresses Israel's neighbors by stressing global punishment and multiethnic salvation (e.g., 3:8–10), which strongly intimates that his message was not restricted to Judah but was universal for all who would pay attention.[36] Indeed, Zephaniah merges God's eschatological multiethnic community (3:9–10) with the new Jerusalem (3:11–20) likely since the transformed members of the new "Israel" (3:13, 14–15; cf. 2:7, 9) and new "Jerusalem/Zion" (3:16) include a faithful remnant of both Judeans and foreigners (3:9–10, 12; cf. 2:3).

Zephaniah's Macrostructure[37]

Zephaniah's book exhibits a high level of rhetorical and structural unity.[38] The present commentary seeks to enhance understanding of Zephaniah's rhetorical purpose and message by closely attending to the book's macrostructure and thought flow. As such, it discusses the book's organization at length.

Critiquing Alternative Proposals to Zephaniah's Macrostructure and Thought Flow[39]

Five approaches to the book's organization predominate: (1) a three-part structure related to speech-forms;[40] (2) a prophetic drama with two-character dialogue;[41]

---

36. See Jason S. DeRouchie, "The Addressees in Zephaniah 2:1, 3: Who Should Seek YHWH Together?," *BBR* 30.2 (2020): 183–207. In addition, Peter notes that prophets like Zephaniah knew that they were serving the eschatological church when proclaiming the great day of salvation (1 Pet 2:12).

37. What this study refers to as "macrostructure," some linguists call "macro-segmentation."

38. Kapelrud, *Message of the Prophet Zephaniah*, 13–14; Berlin, *Zephaniah*, 20; Wendland and Clark, "Zephaniah," 4.

39. For a more developed critique of these various posi-

tions, see Jason S. DeRouchie, "Perspectives on Zephaniah's Macrostructure: Critiques and a Proposal," *MJT* 23.1 (2024): 20–51.

40. See Rudolph, *Micha, Nahum, Habakuk, Zephanja*, 255–56; Ben Zvi, *Book of Zephaniah*, 19; Roberts, *Nahum, Habakkuk, and Zephaniah*, 162–63; Klaus Seybold, *Nahum, Habakuk, Zephanja* (Zurich: TVZ, 1991), 85–86; Motyer, "Zephaniah," 162–63; Vlaardingerbroek, *Zephaniah*, v–vi, 25–27.

41. See Paul R. House, *Zephaniah: A Prophetic Drama*, JSOTSup 69 (Sheffield: Almond Press, 1989), esp. 105–16.

(3) a dramatic prophecy with thematic development;[42] (4) a thematic chiasm;[43] (5) a two-part argument with exhortations preceded by a setting.[44] This introduction will overview the initial four perspectives on Zephaniah's macrostructure with minimal evaluation and then articulate the fifth using a textlinguistic-rhetorical approach. The commentary will then develop the fifth proposal in detail, presuming all the while that exegesis and theology are principally *literary* disciplines that interpret Scripture in the light of its close, continuing, and complete contexts.

Zephaniah as a Three-Part Structure Related to Speech-Forms

Many scholars approaching Zephaniah's structure posit something akin to the tripartite schema that Westermann identified in many prophets: speeches of (1) judgment to the prophet's own nation (Zeph 1:2–2:3); (2) judgment to foreign nations (2:4–15); and (3) salvation to the prophet's own nation (3:1–20).[45] While some features in the oracle's content align with these categories, the tripartite approach fails to account sufficiently for the logical flow and rhetorical development of Zephaniah's argument both with respect to content and linguistic features. It fails to appreciate that declarations of punishment on Judah (1:4–13; 3:1–7) are intermixed with those against all nations (1:2–3, 14–18; 2:5–15), that the celebrated salvation includes a remnant from many peoples (3:8–20), and that the promises of dread and hope motivate higher-level exhortations to seek the Lord together (2:1–4) and to wait for him (3:8). As Sweeney notes, "Close attention to the grammar and syntax . . . generally demonstrates that other organizational principles determine the present form of prophetic books."[46]

Zephaniah as a Prophetic Drama with Two-Character Dialogue

House argues that Zephaniah is "prophetic drama"[47] and that YHWH and Zephaniah's distinct speeches provide "the key to the book's structure."[48] Specifically, the shifts between first- and third-person address signal seven sets of speeches that shift back and forth between YHWH and his prophet.[49] Here "the characters do not speak directly to one another" but instead "supplement and complement each

---

42. See Wendland and Clark, "Zephaniah," 15.

43. See Sheehan, "Kingdom through Covenant," 7–21; cf. David A. Dorsey, *The Literary Structure of the Old Testament: A Commentary on Genesis–Malachi* (Grand Rapids: Baker Academic, 1999), 310–14.

44. Marvin A. Sweeney, "A Form-Critical Reassessment of the Book of Zephaniah," *CBQ* 53 (1991): 388–408; Sweeney, *Zephaniah*; Floyd, *Minor Prophets, Part 2*, 163–250.

45. Claus Westermann, *Basic Forms of Prophetic Speech* (Louisville: Westminster John Knox, 1991), 95; cf. Ehud Ben

Zvi, "Understanding the Message of the Tripartite Prophetic Books," *ResQ* 35.2 (1993): 93–100. For this approach to Zephaniah, see the resources in n38 above.

46. Marvin A. Sweeney, "Zephaniah: A Paradigm for the Study of the Prophetic Books," *CurBS* 7 (1999): 121; cf. Rolf Rendtorff, *The Old Testament: An Introduction*, trans. John Bowden (Philadelphia: Fortress, 1991), 234.

47. House, *Zephaniah*, esp. 105–16.

48. House, *Zephaniah*, 57.

49. House, *Zephaniah*, 56.

other's words."[50] The result is that "the two characters work as interchangeable revealers, and the word of the two is shown as one united word."[51]

Significantly, House imprecisely distinguishes YHWH's voice from Zephaniah's, for as Wendland and Clark recognize, "The occurrence of third-person references to YHWH is not diagnostic of an utterance of the prophet, except when they happen to occur in the subject position."[52] Furthermore, House reveals inconsistency in his own approach,[53] and he never considers numerous linguistic features that guide the book's macrostructure. Alternating voices add dramatic effect to the book but do not organize it; thematic shifts and formal linguistic features do.[54]

Zephaniah as a Dramatic Prophecy with Thematic Development

Similar to House, Wendland and Clark label Zephaniah a "dramatic prophecy"[55] and view the whole as "an antiphonal text" with three major units or "dialogues."[56] However, they offer a more refined approach to distinguishing YHWH's voice from the prophet's—namely, third-person references to YHWH only signal Zephaniah's voice when occurring in the subject position.[57] Their schematic of the characters' "voices" is, therefore, different than House's, and they do not see these voices as the primary guide for structure.

Instead, they trace the shifts in tone within the book's argument, thus showing how the thematic flow moves from warning and punishment to consolation and blessing.[58] Within this flow, they see an intermixing of "commendation" (1:2–18), appeal (2:1–3), and motivation (*negative* 2:4–3:8 / *positive* 3:9–20)[59] that downplays the strong appeal in 3:8 but highlights the way negative and positive motivation dominate 2:4–3:7 and 3:8b–20b, respectively. They rightly see the imperative plus vocative combination in 2:1 signaling a major unit shift,[60] and they consider 2:3 the book's hortatory peak.[61] However, they fail to clarify how the imperatives in 2:3 relate to those in 2:1 or how this grouping of five imperatives relate to those in 3:8, 14.

Zephaniah as a Thematic Chiasm

As Smith notes, a chiasm is "a figure consisting of two panels where the units comprising the first panel correspond inversely to the units comprising the second;

---

50. House, *Zephaniah*, 58.

51. House, *Zephaniah*, 59.

52. Wendland and Clark, "Zephaniah," 6.

53. For example, House's third set of speeches appear in different scenes and acts, and he treats the different voices in set six as performing different roles in the plot's development. House, *Zephaniah*, 64–67, 120–21.

54. Similarly, Kapelrud writes, "The division between divine and prophetic speech is irrelevant in Zephaniah. It does not add anything to a better understanding of the message of the prophet" (Kapelrud, *Message of the Prophet Zephaniah*, 49).

55. Wendland and Clark, "Zephaniah," 15.

56. Wendland and Clark, "Zephaniah," 4–5.

57. Wendland and Clark, "Zephaniah," 6.

58. Wendland and Clark, "Zephaniah," 38–39. For a comparable adaptation that retains Wendland and Clark's own plot points, see Christopher S. Tachick, *"King of Israel" and "Do Not Fear, Daughter of Zion": The Use of Zephaniah 3 in John 12*, Reformed Academic Dissertations 11 (Phillipsburg, NJ: P&R, 2018), 106.

59. Wendland and Clark, "Zephaniah," 38.

60. Wendland and Clark, "Zephaniah," 9.

61. Wendland and Clark, "Zephaniah," 38.

an explicit center may or may not be present."[62] Sheehan maintains that Zephaniah's content is structurally chiastic, which is "the key to unlocking the theology of Zephaniah."[63] All his proposed parallels are antithetical in nature except the most outer frame (A: Word of YHWH [1:1a]/A': Says YHWH [3:20c]) and inner frame (H: Oracles against the Nations [2:4–10]/H': Oracles against the Nations [2:12–15]), the latter of which surrounds the central verse that captures the book's thesis: "YHWH is fearsome against them, for he has made lean all the gods of the earth, so that all the coastlands of the nations will bow down to him, each from his place" (2:11).[64]

Sheehan's proposal is problematic, for it exhibits three common errors that Thompson and deSilva have noted with proposed chiasms in Scripture: (1) creating a chiasm by discounting formal markers, (2) discovering a chiasm by selectively reading key terms, and (3) developing a chiasm by selectively shaping summary statements for major blocks of text.[65] Sheehan's proposal misses how the imperatives in 2:1, 3, and 3:8 provide the book's highest-level exhortations, and he overlooks the subordinate role 2:11 plays within the argument as a whole. While Zephaniah uses repetition and antithesis, these are incorporated into a greater logical argument associated with the genre of prophetic exhortation.[66]

A Synthesis of Zephaniah as a Two-Part Argument with Setting Followed by Exhortations in Two Stages

The present study's textlinguistic-rhetorical approach assumes that exegesis and theology are principally *literary* disciplines that interpret Scripture in the light of its close, continuing, and complete contexts (for more on these three spheres, see Zephaniah's Hermeneutic and Theology below).

The Method

My method for determining macrostructure within Old Testament prophetic books like Zephaniah resembles what Marvin Sweeney and Michael Floyd refer to as the new form criticism[67] in that it focuses on the literary structure, coherence,

---

62. Craig A. Smith, "Criteria for Biblical Chiasms: Objective Means for Distinguishing Chiasm of Design from Accidental and False Chiasm" (PhD diss., University of Bristol, 2009), 94.

63. Sheehan, "Kingdom through Covenant," 7–21.

64. Sheehan, "Kingdom through Covenant," 16.

65. Ian H. Thomson, *Chiasmus in the Pauline Letters*, JSNTSup 111 (Sheffield: Sheffield Academic, 1995), 30–33; David A. deSilva, "X Marks the Spot? A Critique of the Use of Chiasmus in Macro-Structural Analyses of Revelation," *JSNT* 30.3 (2008): 343.

66. Sheehan could have strengthened his proposal had he considered Smith's criteria for distinguishing "chiasm by de-

sign" from accidental or false chiasm: (1) coherence with other structures; (2) significant correspondences, whether verbal, syntactical, form, scene/setting, conceptual, or phonetic; (3) significant symmetry in ways like arrangement of units, macro-balance between panels, micro-balance between panels, symmetrical distribution of verbal elements; (4) discernable function, whether semantic, rhetorical, aesthetic, mnemonic/ organizational; (5) discernable authorial affinity (C. Smith, "Criteria for Biblical Chiasms," 120–319).

67. Sweeney, "Form-Critical Reassessment"; Sweeney, *Zephaniah*; Floyd, *Minor Prophets, Part 2*, 163–250; cf. Sweeney, *Isaiah 1–39*.

and purpose of larger discourse units and seeks to balance a careful reading of text grammar with the whole rhetorical argument.[68] Like Sweeney and similar to Floyd, I argue that Zephaniah is a two-part argument with a setting followed by exhortations. Nevertheless, my exegetical and theological assessments differ at key points from these scholars (at times substantially), and I organize the book differently especially in relation to the structuring function of the imperatival clauses of Zeph 3:8 and 14.

When interpreting prophetic discourse, the present study seeks to trace Zephaniah's argument and thought flow by carefully assessing discourse features like the following:

- the use of the coordinate conjunction *waw* to create chains of discourse that we are to read together (i.e., text blocks)
- the role of asyndeton to signal disjunction due to a fresh beginning, explication, or something else
- the function of other connecting particles (e.g., כִּי "when, because"; לָכֵן "therefore") to convey various semantic/logical relationships, whether coordinate or subordinate, with the latter expressing support by restatement, distinct statement, or contrary statement
- other discourse markers (e.g., וְהָיָה "and it happened that"; הִנֵּה "Look!")
- verb patterns (e.g., *wayyiqtol/weqatal, qatal/yiqtol*, imperative), word order, and the way both generate marked/unmarked and/or topic/focus/dislocated structures within various discourse types (e.g., historical narrative, directive, anticipatory)
- participant tracking through observing explicit subjects and pronoun referent
- repetition of phrases and patterns

The Argument Diagrams and Exegetical Outlines in This Commentary

The argument diagrams that will follow in the Translation and Exegetical Outline portion of this commentary display a text-hierarchy of clauses, using indentation to distinguish levels of prominence within the text's discourse structure. The following elements should help guide the reading of diagrams and the outline that accompanies them.[69]

---

68. Patterson's *stylistic* analysis of the book is helpful but is only a surface-level, semantic assessment that does not consider text linguistic features of the text itself: Richard Patterson, "A Literary Look at Nahum, Habakkuk, and Zephaniah," *GTJ* 11.1 (1990): 17–28; cf. Richard D. Patterson, *Nahum, Habakkuk, Zephaniah: An Exegetical Commentary*, Minor Prophets Exegetical Commentary (Dallas: Biblical Studies, 2003).

69. For a detailed overview of my approach to identifying discourse units, assessing text grammar, and tracing biblical arguments, see chapters 2, 5–6 in Jason S. DeRouchie, *How to Understand and Apply the Old Testament: Twelve Steps from Exegesis to Theology* (Phillipsburg, NJ: P&R, 2017), 98–127, 181–268.

1. Hebrew moves from right to left, so in the Hebrew display the more primary clauses are to the right, and those that support by restatement or distinct statement are indented to the left.
2. The argument diagram displays only Zephaniah's macrostructure, so each line retains an entire clause, which must include a subject with its predicate. This means that infinitival phrases are *not* distinguished on their own line, but when infinitival phrases or participles operate as predicates in a verbless clause, the whole clause receives its own line.
3. There are only two substantive exceptions to the above schema: (a) Relative אֲשֶׁר clauses functioning attributively rather than adverbially are usually not separated because they do not influence the text's macrostructure. (b) Discourse markers that operate at the text- rather than the clause-level (e.g., וְהָיָה in 1:8a and 12a) are given their own line, seeing as they stand outside the clause structure itself.
4. The text-hierarchy indicates that the connector וְ (gloss = "and") at a clause-head links clauses of equal grammatical value within the overall argument. Even where a וְ-clause expresses semantic subordination (e.g., result or purpose), for the sake of macrostructure, the chain remains intact, and no indentation is made. The text, therefore, creates chains of clauses that together form related thought-units.
5. The lack of connection (= asyndeton) usually signals either a fresh beginning or explication. Indentation often marks support by restatement.
6. Zephaniah's message and thought flow drive the exegetical outline point for point. Every shift in the outline correlates with some formal feature within the Hebrew text itself.

An Overview of Zephaniah's Argument

The present discussion will summarize the book's argument. The commentary's Structure and Literary Form sections will analyze in more detail and engage with others.[70]

Building on the discourse features noted above, figure 0.1 shows the book's organization and argument levels. The bottom row identifies the book's two main units: the setting (1:2–18) and the body, which includes stage 1 (2:1–3:7) and stage 2 (3:8–20b) of the Savior's invitation to satisfaction. The next row marks the various units' major sections, and the third row signals those sections' various parts. An exclamation "Hush!" in 1:7 is followed by two parallel reasons to do so. Nevertheless, the main imperatives only come in 2:1–3 ("bundle together!" [2x]; "seek!" [3x]) and in 3:8 ("wait!").

---

70. For a developed synthesis of Zephaniah's major units and thought flow, see also Jason S. DeRouchie, "Zephaniah's Macrostructure: A Textlinguistic-Rhetorical Analysis" (paper presented at the Hebrew Discourse Conference on *Macro* *Analysis of Hebrew Poetic and Prophetic Discourse*, Dallas International University, 18 October 2023 and at the Annual Meeting of the Evangelical Theological Society, San Diego, CA, 20 November 2024).

		Hush!	For the day of YHWH is near	[For] the great day of YHWH is near	Bundle! Seek!	For	Woe!	Woe!	...: Wait!	For For	In that day	(Sing!)	In that day	
1:1	1:2–6	7a	7b–13	14–18	2:1–3	4	5–15	3:1–7	8a	8b–10	11–13	14–15	16–20b	20c
1:1	1:2–6	7–18			2:1–4		2:5–3:7		3:8–10		11–20			20c
	Setting (1:2–18)				Invitation Stage 1 (2:1–3:7)				Invitation Stage 2 (3:8–20b)					20c

Figure 0.1: Structural Overview of Zephaniah

The Superscription of the Savior's Invitation to Satisfaction (1:1)

The superscription formally introduces the book by highlighting its nature and source (the word of God), its messenger (Zephaniah, a black Judean in the Davidic royal line), and its historical backdrop (the days of Josiah's reformation).

The Setting of the Savior's Invitation to Satisfaction: A Call to Revere YHWH in View of His Coming Day (1:2–18)

The book's body opens without connection (i.e., asyndeton), thus marking its fresh beginning. The setting for the oracle's main hortatory appeals that follow comes in 1:2–18. The unit supplies a call to revere God in view of his coming day of fury, and its two sections are this call's context (1:2–6) and content (1:7–18).

The connector וֹ (gloss = "and") links all the main clauses of the context section, and together they promise global punishment against humanity's rebels (1:2–3) and local punishment against Judah's rebels (1:4–6). Each promise has two halves, the first addressing God's encounter ("gather" / "stretch out my hand") and the second declaring that he would "cut off" the enemies. Destruction will come because of rampant wickedness and idolatrous rebellion.

As a herald prepares an audience for an angry king's arrival, Zephaniah next exclaims that his listeners must "Hush before the Sovereign YHWH" (1:7a). This call to revere God is not an imperative but uses the exclamatory particle הַס ("Hush!") that marks the whole section as low-level prophetic exhortation. The audience must revere YHWH because of his impending judgment day's sacrificial content against Judah (1:7b–13) and the entire earth (1:14–18). The phrase "the day of YHWH is near" (1:7b) announces Judah's imminent destruction, likely in 586 BC. Parallel uses of the discourse marker וְהָיָה ("and it will happen that") introduce two sub-parts wherein YHWH will punish both Jerusalem's leaders (1:8–11) and her complacent people (1:12–13). Then, the phrase "the *great* day of YHWH is near" in 1:14 recalls 1:7b's wording and extends the scope to the world. This day's characteristics (1:14–16) and the punishment's effects (1:17–18) will be horrific, as God carries out his sacrifice (1:18; cf. 1:7) and war (1:15–16) because "against YHWH they have sinned" (1:17c).

The Substance of the Savior's Invitation to Satisfaction: Charges to Seek YHWH Together Patiently (2:1–3:20b)

In view of the call to revere God sparked by YHWH's encroaching day (1:2–18), the book's main exhortation section comes in two stages. These stages combine to charge the righteous remnant to pursue YHWH together patiently. Stage 1 calls the believers in Judah and other lands to seek YHWH together to avoid punishment (2:1–3:7). Stage 2 then charges the same group to wait for YHWH to enjoy satisfying salvation (3:8–20b). The second section builds on the first, and both units display a parallel structure:

1. Command(s) (second masculine plural imperative[s]) (2:1, 3 / 3:8a)
2. Initial reason(s) fronted with "for" (כִּי) (2:4 / 3:8b–10)
3. Two unmarked motivations for heeding the command(s) (whether two reasons, both beginning with "Woe!" [הוֹי, 2:5–15; 3:1–7], or two promises, both beginning with "in that day" [בַּיּוֹם הַהוּא, 3:11–13; 3:16–20])

The only break in the structure comes with the discursive intrusion of 3:14–15, which marks the book's rhetorical motivational peak.

Stage 1: The Appeal to Seek YHWH Together to Avoid Punishment (2:1–3:7)

The lack of connection at the head of 2:1 followed by imperatives plus vocative address marks the start of the book's main hortatory unit. The initial appeal comes in two parts and five imperatives. Those listening must "bind [themselves] together" (2:1) before YHWH's day of wrath comes (2:2), and they must "seek" him in righteousness and humility (2:3a–c). Only by these means may they "perhaps . . . be hidden" from God destroying the wicked (2:3d), like those from Philistia (v. 4).

Next, in 2:5–3:7 come two unmarked reasons supporting why the remnant from Judah and other lands must heed the charges to "bind together . . . seek" (2:1, 3) and "wait" (3:8). God promises to bring his fury on the rebels from (a) the foreign nations (2:5–15) and (b) Jerusalem (3:1–7). Each reason opens with the term "Woe!" (הוֹי, 2:5; 3:1), suggesting that they are two sides of the same outpouring of wrath.

The first reason for pursuing God relates to the lamentable state and fate of the rebels from the foreign nations (2:5–15). With the call to repentance and loyalty in focus (2:1–4), these verses build a compass of punishment around Judah, announcing God's wrath against the Philistines to the west (vv. 5–7), the Moabites and Ammonites to the east (vv. 8–11), and the Cushites and Assyrians to the south and north, respectively (vv. 12–15). Implied is that the punishment that spans the populated world will reach Judah (cf. Hab 2:16–17) unless they return to YHWH and become part of the preserved remnant (see Zeph 2:7, 9).

The second reason for seeking YHWH concerns the lamentable state and fate of Jerusalem's rebels (3:1–7). These verses describe the sinful condition and certain punishment of those in Judah's capital city by highlighting their stubborn resistance to learn from God's disciplining hand against them and the foreign nations. YHWH speaks of the city Jerusalem in feminine singular address and notes how he urged her to fear him so that she would not lose him as her Shelter (3:7). Nevertheless, those in the city only increased their corruption.

Stage 2: The Appeal to Wait for YHWH to Enjoy Salvation (3:8–20b)

The oracle now returns to the primary level of exhortation. YHWH calls the remnant not only to seek him together (2:1–3) but also to wait (i.e., patiently trust) for him (3:8). The subordinate conjunction כִּי ("for") then begins two reasons (3:8b, 9–10) supporting this call in 3:8a: YHWH will (1) judge the rebel nations (3:8b) and (2) save a group from these nations, reversing the effects of the tower of Babel (3:9–10; cf. Gen 11:9). Specifically, on the very day YHWH brings judgment as covenant witness (Zeph 3:8), "then" he will bring about a new creation (3:9–10). In this he will transform peoples throughout the world into true worshipers who will call on his name and serve him in unity. Those bringing tribute will include some from Cush, ancient black Africa from which some of Zephaniah's own relatives came (see comments at 1:1).

Two more promises then motivate the remnant to wait on YHWH to destroy his enemies and make a multiethnic people centered in a new Jerusalem (3:11–13, 16–20). They both begin with the phrase "in that day" (בַּיּוֹם הַהוּא) and use feminine singular to address the new Jerusalem.

The first promise is that Jerusalem will never again be ashamed (3:11a). This is because (כִּי) YHWH will remove the proud (3:11b–c) yet preserve the humble (3:12). This multiethnic "remnant of Israel" will rightly value God and those he made in his image as they rest with lasting protection (3:13).

Imperatival charges to rejoice (3:14) supported by two unmarked reasons (3:15) intrude before the second motivating promise comes. These two verses do not add to the exhortations in 2:1, 3 and 3:8 but instead provide a rhetorical peak of motivation for heeding these injunctions. Three discursive calls to rejoice in 3:14 include four imperatives plus vocatives. The first imperative is feminine singular, the second is masculine plural, and the final two are feminine singular and conjoined. The ethnically diverse community that YHWH names "the daughter of my scattered ones" in 3:10 Zephaniah now calls the "daughter of Zion," "Israel," and the "daughter of Jerusalem" (3:14a–b, d). But why should the transformed community rejoice? The unmarked reasons and *qatal* verbs in 3:15 explain: King YHWH has removed the curses (3:15a–b) and is near (3:15c–d). Here the prophet seeks to motivate the remnant to wait for YHWH to act on their behalf by treating the promised deliverance as if it has already happened. The certainty of future salvation should produce present joy even amid pain.

YHWH next adds the second promise beginning with the phrase "in that day" (בַּיּוֹם הַהוּא) to motivate the remnant to obey God's call from 3:8a to endure patiently. He will save his people completely, delivering them, delighting in them, and securing their provision and protection (3:16–20). In 3:16–18 YHWH predicts a future speech, and in 3:19–20b he notes the speech's implications. After predicting that an unnamed prophet will speak on the day of YHWH (3:16a), YHWH supplies the content of the speech. The speech prohibits fear (3:16b–c) and gives two unmarked reasons not to fear: (1) YHWH, the saving Warrior, is near (3:17), and (2) he has gathered his remnant (3:18). YHWH's day of wrath and new creation will develop in an already-but-not-yet way so those God has redeemed will need to remember that he will completely save.

The book's body ends with YHWH promising that he will save Jerusalem (3:19) and that the whole remnant will participate in this salvation (3:20a–b). Whereas 3:19 includes the feminine singular address to Jerusalem, YHWH ends the oracle in 3:20 with more personal terms, returning to the masculine plural address found in the main exhortations of 2:1, 3 and 3:8.

The highest motivation for answering the call to seek YHWH together and to wait for him (2:1–3; 3:8) is the joy set before us—both our joy in God (3:14) and his joy in us (3:17). Hearers should hunger and hope, entreat and trust, look and long. YHWH will completely remove every oppressor, heal the broken, and sing over those he has saved (3:17, 19–20b), and his saving work will ultimately exalt *his* "praise" and *his* "name" in all the earth (3:19d, 20b).

The Subscription of the Savior's Invitation to Satisfaction (3:20c)

The book closes recalling 1:1. All that precedes is what God said to Zephaniah and makes up the Savior's invitation to satisfaction (3:20c).[71]

---

71. For a brief verse-by-verse overview of the whole book, see Jason S. DeRouchie, "Zephaniah," *TGC Bible Commentary* (2021), https://www .thegospelcoalition .org /commentary /zephaniah/. For a more extended commentary, see Jason S. DeRouchie, "Zephaniah," in *Daniel–Malachi*, vol. 7 of *ESV Expository Commentary* (Wheaton, IL: Crossway, 2018), 561–604.

Figure 0.2: Zephaniah's Main Idea and Exegetical Outline
Zephaniah's Main Idea: In view of his coming day of wrath, Savior YHWH invites his faithful remnant to seek him together to avoid punishment and wait for him to enjoy salvation.

I. **The Superscription of the Savior's Invitation to Satisfaction (1:1)**

II. **The Setting of the Savior's Invitation to Satisfaction: A Call to Revere YHWH in View of His Coming Day (1:2–18)**

    A. The Context of the Call to Revere YHWH: Coming Punishment (1:2–6)

    B. The Content of the Call to Revere YHWH (1:7–18)

III. **The Substance of the Savior's Invitation to Satisfaction: Charges to Seek YHWH Together and to Wait (2:1–3:20b)**

    III.1 **Stage 1: The Appeal to Seek YHWH Together to Avoid Punishment (2:1–3:7)**

        A. The Charge to Unite in Submission to YHWH (2:1–2)

        B. The Charge to Seek YHWH in Righteousness and Humility (2:3–4)

            1. The Charge to Seek YHWH (2:3)

            2. An Initial Reason to Seek YHWH: The Devastation of Philistia (2:4)

        C. Further Reasons to Seek YHWH Together (2:5–3:7)

            1. The Lamentable State and Fate of the Rebels from the Foreign Nations (2:5–15)

            2. The Lamentable State and Fate of the Rebels from Jerusalem (3:1–7)

    III.2 **Stage 2: The Appeal to Wait for YHWH to Enjoy Salvation (3:8–20)**

        A. The Charge to Wait for YHWH to Act (3:8–10)

            1. The Charge to Wait for YHWH (3:8a)

            2. Two Reasons to Wait for YHWH (3:8b–10)

        B. Promises to Motivate Waiting for YHWH: The Remnant's Satisfying Salvation (3:11–20b)

            1. The Promise that YHWH Will Not Shame Jerusalem (3:11–13)

            2. A Discursive Charge to Rejoice as if the Great Salvation Has Already Occurred (3:14–15)

            3. The Promise That YHWH Will Save Completely (3:16–20b)

IV. **The Subscription of the Savior's Invitation to Satisfaction (3:20c)**

Zephaniah's Hermeneutic and Theology

This section of the introduction analyzes Zephaniah's hermeneutic and theology. The various Canonical and Theological Significance sections in the rest of the commentary extend these reflections in detailed ways. Five parts shape this unit:

1. Introductory Comments
2. Zephaniah's Place and Role Within the Twelve
3. Zephaniah's Use of Scripture
4. Zephaniah's Vision of the Day of YHWH
5. Zephaniah's Celebration of YHWH's Exaltation

Introductory Comments

With the apostles, I affirm that Zephaniah is Christian Scripture that God intended for our instruction today (Rom 15:4; 1 Cor 10:11; cf. 2 Tim 3:15–17). Zephaniah is "YHWH's word" (Zeph 1:1) for all time, and its close, continuing, and complete contexts within the Christian canon all are extremely significant.[72] The *close* or immediate context relates to a passage's literary placement within the whole book and includes what and how the text communicates. The *continuing* context considers the passage within God's story of salvation, which includes evaluating how antecedent Scripture may have informed any given passage and how every passage contributes to God's unfolding redemptive-historical drama. The *complete* context concerns a text's place and function within the broader canon, which includes how later Scripture in either the Old or New Testament cites or builds upon an OT text.

G. K. Beale has given five principles for considering the divine Son's role within the Testaments' relationship and covenants. These principles derive from the OT's own story of salvation history that guided the NT authors' OT interpretive conclusions:[73]

1. The authors always assume *corporate solidarity*, in which one can represent the many (e.g., Rom 5:18–19).
2. The Messiah *represented the true (remnant) Israel* of the old covenant *and the true (consummate) Israel, the church*, of the new covenant (Isa 49:3, 6 with Luke 2:32 and Acts 26:23).[74]
3. God's wise and sovereign plan *unites salvation history* in such a way that earlier parts correspond to later parts (Luke 16:16; cf. Isa 46:9–10; Eph 1:11).
4. Christ has initiated *the age of eschatological fulfillment* (Mark 1:15; Gal 4:4).[75]
5. Christ stands as the climax and center of history such that his life, death, and resurrection provide *the interpretive lens* for fully understanding the earlier portions of the OT and its promises (Rom 16:25–26; 2 Cor 3:14–16).[76]

Within God's redemptive purposes, Jesus culminates salvation history and provides both the beginning and end of OT interpretation.[77] God removes a veil through Jesus

---

72. For more on these distinctions with examples from Zephaniah, see Jason S. DeRouchie, "Preaching the Prophets: Zephaniah as a Case Study for Christian Proclamation," *Pro Pastor* 3.1 (2024): 28–37.

73. G. K. Beale, "Did Jesus and His Followers Preach the Right Doctrine from the Wrong Texts?," *Them* 14.3 (1989): 392; G. K. Beale, *Handbook on the New Testament Use of the Old Testament: Exegesis and Interpretation* (Grand Rapids: Baker Academic, 2012), 52–53, 95–102.

74. Cf. Acts 13:47; 26:18.

75. Cf. Luke 16:16; Acts 2:17; 1 Cor 10:11; Heb 1:2; 9:26; 1 John 2:18.

76. Cf. 1 Cor 2:13–14.

77. See especially Jason S. DeRouchie, *Delighting in the Old Testament: Through Christ and for Christ* (Wheaton, IL: Crossway, 2024), 15–70; cf. Jason S. DeRouchie, "The Mystery Revealed: A Biblical Case for Christ-Centered Old Testament Interpretation," *Them* 44.2 (2019): 226–48; Jason S. DeRouchie, "Question 21: What Role Does 'Mystery' Play in Biblical Theology?," in *40 Questions about Biblical Theology*, by Jason S.

(2 Cor 3:14), thus allowing us to read Zephaniah in a way that all but the remnant in previous generations had missed (Rom 16:25–26; cf. Mark 4:11–12).

Since Zephaniah was among the prophets, he "sought out and inquired" to learn about the Messiah's "person and time" (1 Pet 1:10–11), he clarified both the Messiah's sufferings and the subsequent new creational glories (Acts 3:18, 24), and he was "carried along by the Holy Spirit" and thus "spoke from God" (2 Pet 1:21). God even disclosed to the prophets that they were writing for the benefit of future generations living in the latter days of the Messiah.[78] That is, when Zephaniah proclaimed the coming great salvation, he knew that he was serving not himself but the messianic community, upon whom "the end of the ages has come" (1 Cor 10:11; 1 Pet 1:10–12). Therefore, the need today is for spiritual people (i.e., true Christians) prayerfully to understand Zephaniah's book in view of the rest of Scripture as the Spirit himself interprets God's meaning to us (1 Cor 2:13–14).[79]

Zephaniah Place and Role Within the Twelve

Placing all the minor prophets together as a unified "Scroll of the Prophets" was one of the features that concluded the OT's formation (see Acts 7:42; cf. 13:40; 15:15). This scroll has twelve parts and came to be regarded simply as "the Twelve" (b. B. Bat. 13b, 14b, ca. AD 200).[80] While historical witnesses display some fluidity regarding the order of the initial six books,[81] the arrangement of the latter six is consistent, with each standing in chronological order (Nahum, Habakkuk, Zephaniah, Haggai, Zechariah, Malachi). However, in the Hebrew Bible, the prophets for whom the initial six books are named are probably not in chronological sequence, so the arrangement of the whole appears intentional, thematic, and theologically significant.[82]

DeRouchie, Oren R. Martin, and Andrew David Naselli, 40 Questions (Grand Rapids: Kregel, 2020), 205–14.

78. See, e.g., Deut 30:8–14; Isa 29:18; 30:8, 20–21; 32:1, 3–4; Jer 30:21–22; 31:1, 31, 33–34; Dan 12:4, 8–10.

79. Cf. 2 Tim 2:7, 15; 2 Pet 3:16–17.

80. Though the Babylonian Talmud was not put into writing until ca. AD 550, this portion is a baraita attributed to the Tannaim (תנו רבנן, "our Rabbans taught"; see b. B. Bat. 13b) and can be dated to ca. AD 200. Sirach (ca. 200 BC) also grouped all the voices together (Sir 49:10), and the Dead Sea scrolls 4Q76–82 (XII[a–g], ca. 150–25 BC) all combine the books on a single scroll (with all following the same order as MT except 4Q76, which places Jonah after Malachi). Furthermore, the earliest Greek witness that includes the prophets (8ḤevXII gr, ca. 50 BC–AD 50) includes them on a single scroll. The NT authors did connect citations with a particular prophet, whether unnamed (Matt 2:5, 15; 21:4) or named (Acts 2:16; Rom 9:25; cf. Tob 2:6), which shows that they viewed the various books

as discrete witnesses, while still treating them as part of a larger whole. Furthermore, the Masoretes marked the middle verse of each of the major prophets with a note in the margin (see Isa 33:21; Jer 28:11; Ezek 26:1), but they did not mark the middle of each of the twelve prophets from Hosea to Malachi. Instead, they noted that Mic 3:12 was the middle of the Twelve's single scroll. For an overview of the historical evidence for the unity of the Twelve, see Michael B. Shepherd, *A Commentary on the Book of the Twelve: The Minor Prophets*, Kregel Exegetical Library (Grand Rapids: Kregel, 2018), 22–23.

81. The standard LXX order has Hosea, Amos, Micah, Joel, Obadiah, Jonah, which represents all prophets except Jonah in chronological order. Nevertheless, the earliest extant Greek scroll (8ḤevXII gr) follows the order of the MT.

82. Stephen G. Dempster, "Twelve," in *What the Old Testament Authors Really Cared About: A Survey of Jesus' Bible*, ed. Jason S. DeRouchie (Grand Rapids: Kregel, 2013), 299. This view stands against, e.g., Ehud Ben Zvi, "Twelve Prophetic

Each of the Twelve retains its own literary style and message and shows evidence of independent shaping without later editorial influence. Nevertheless, a final compiler placed the volumes where he did to produce a greater theological message than any of the independent volumes makes on its own.[83] Dempster observes, "The inclusion of the twelve prophets in one scroll ensured that they sang together, not only in physical unison but also in theological harmony. . . . When we listen to their voices together, we hear far more than if we listen only to the individual parts."[84] He also notes that, when read as a whole, the Book of the Twelve "presents a more panoramic view of the future than is found in the previous prophets."[85]

Zephaniah's Links to Its Adjacent Books

The presence of catchword-thematic linkage (i.e., vocabulary parallels and thematic repetition) between all adjacent books in the Hebrew arrangement of the Twelve is strong evidence that the compiler intended us to read the whole as a literary unit. These canonical "seams" suggest intentionality in the positioning of each volume.[86]

Habakkuk ends with longing for YHWH's deliverance (Hab 3:17–19), and Zephaniah explains that YHWH will secure this salvation. Specifically, Habakkuk (1) urges the earth to "hush" (הַס) before YHWH's judgment (2:20); (2) anticipates "a day of trouble" (יוֹם צָרָה, 3:16; cf. Nah 1:7); (3) commits to "wait" (חכה) for God's answer (2:3), which includes that "one righteous [צַדִּיק] by his faith will live" (2:4);[87] and (4) will "exult" (עלז) in YHWH and "celebrate" (גיל) the God of his "salvation" (יֵשַׁע, 3:18). Developing this hope, Zephaniah (1) urges listeners to "hush!" (הַס) before YHWH's judgment (Zeph 1:7), (2) warns of a coming "day of trouble" (יוֹם צָרָה, Zeph 1:15; cf. 1:7, 14), (3) charges the remnant to seek "righteousness" (צֶדֶק, 2:3) and to "wait" (חכה) for God to act (3:8), and (4) envisions that the daughter of Jerusalem

---

Books or 'The Twelve': A Few Preliminary Considerations," in *Forming Prophetic Literature: Essays on Isaiah and the Twelve in Honor of John D. W. Watts*, ed. James W. Watts and Paul R. House, JSOTSup 235 (Sheffield: Sheffield Academic, 1996), 125–56.

83. Shepherd's compositional analysis on the Twelve has helped identify the divine author's strategy in shaping the Twelve and its unified message. Yet Shepherd's insistence that a later "author" altered the individual books to create this unified message goes against the claims of the books themselves that link all their words to respective prophets. God led someone to arrange the books as they are and by this highlighted the Twelve's amazing coherence, created progressively as the Spirit directed each prophet (1 Pet 1:10–11; 2 Pet 1:21). See Michael B. Shepherd, "Compositional Analysis of the Twelve," *ZAW* 120 (2008): 184–93; Shepherd, *Commentary on the Book of the Twelve*, esp. 23–36.

84. Dempster, "Twelve," 298.

85. Stephen G. Dempster, *Dominion and Dynasty: A Biblical Theology of the Hebrew Bible*, NSBT 15 (Downers Grove, IL: InterVarsity Press, 2003), 182; cf. Paul R. House, *Old Testament Theology* (Downers Grove, IL: InterVarsity Press, 1998), 347.

86. For one scholar's overview of the various catchword-thematic links through the Twelve, see Shepherd, "Compositional Analysis of the Twelve," 184–93; Shepherd, *Commentary on the Book of the Twelve*, 23–34.

87. For the reading of אֱמוּנָה in Hab 2:4 as "faith" rather than "faithfulness," see Michael B. Shepherd, *The Twelve Prophets in the New Testament*, StBibLit 140 (New York: Lang, 2011), 47–54; Michael B. Shepherd, *The Text in the Middle*, StBibLit 162 (New York: Lang, 2014), 30–36; E. Ray Clendenen, "Salvation by Faith or by Faithfulness in the Book of Habakkuk?," *BBR* 24 (2014): 505–13.

must "exult" (עלז) in YHWH's certain deliverance (3:14) and that YHWH will "celebrate" (גיל) over those he "saves" (*hiphil* of ישע, 3:17, 19).

Shepherd asserts that Zephaniah and Haggai bear "the fewest marks" of compositional linkage among the Twelve.[88] Nevertheless, many lexical ties exist between the books. For example, Zephaniah declares how YHWH will gather "human and beast" (אָדָם וּבְהֵמָה) for judicial assessment (1:3), and Haggai notes how God had called a curse down "on the human and on the beast" (עַל־הָאָדָם וְעַל־הַבְּהֵמָה) (Hag 1:11). Zephaniah also promises that those in Jerusalem would plant vineyards but not "drink" (שתה) wine from them (Zeph 1:13), and Haggai claims that those who returned to Jerusalem from exile were "drinking" (שתה) but never being satisfied (Hag 1:6). Furthermore, Zephaniah envisions an eschatological, purified "remnant" (שְׁאֵרִית, Zeph 2:7, 9; 3:13), and Haggai foreshadows this group when he describes the returned "remnant" (שְׁאֵרִית) as those who "listened . . . to YHWH's voice" (Hag 1:12, 14; 2:2).[89]

Perhaps most significantly, Zephaniah's dominant use of the day of YHWH and the repeated phrase "in that day" (בַּיּוֹם הַהוּא, Zeph 1:9–10; 3:11, 16; cf. 1:7, 14) parallels the use of the same phrase in Hag 2:23. On this latter link, Shepherd observes:

> The text of Zephaniah 3:9–20 exerts a great influence on how the following book of Haggai is read. Much the same way that Ezekiel's vision of the temple in Ezekiel 40–48 serves to illustrate the eschatological restoration prophesied in Ezekiel 33–39, so the historical prophecies of Haggai with regard to the rebuilding of the temple now provide pre-figurative images of the future and final restoration envisioned by Zephaniah 3:9–20.[90]

Like Zephaniah (3:8–10), Haggai envisions that YHWH would cause the universe to quake in a way that would overthrow kingdoms and result in the nations gathering like treasure to God's transformed house (Hag 2:6–7, 21–22; cf. Heb 12:26–29). "In that day" a Davidic descendant would rise to rule and restore (Hag 2:23).

Zephaniah as the Climax of the Twelve's Plot

Thematic plot development throughout the Twelve further supports reading it as a literary unity. In its final form within the Hebrew Scriptures, the Scroll/Book of the Twelve prophets dramatically outlines God's "cosmic history" of redemption, which includes (1) Israel's sin to reflect the whole world's rebellion, (2) YHWH's just and impending punishment as an outworking of covenant curse, and (3) the restorative hope of messianic salvation for a multiethnic remnant in

---

88. Shepherd, "Compositional Analysis of the Twelve," 190.
89. Cf. Zeph 3:2; Deut 30:8–14.

90. Shepherd, *Commentary on the Book of the Twelve*, 375–76.

the last days.[91] While all three elements are present in successive order in many of the books, House has effectively argued that the whole is a "unified prophecy" whose *stress* progresses from rebellion (Hosea–Micah) through wrath (Nahum–Zephaniah) to restoration (Haggai–Malachi).[92]

Within this framework, House further notes that Zephaniah's importance "as a plot-shaper in the Twelve can hardly be over-estimated."[93] Specifically, YHWH's fury against Judah and the rest of the world climaxes in Zephaniah, portraying an Edenic new creation for a multiethnic remnant. Zephaniah provides "a bridge between the sin, punishment, and restoration sections of the Twelve. . . . It embodies both the climax and the falling action of the Twelve's story line. Put another way, it completes the bottom of the U-shaped [*sic*] and begins the journey upwards."[94] The prophet does this by supplying one of Scripture's most developed and balanced accounts of YHWH's day. From this point forward in the Twelve, the hope (Haggai, Zechariah) and the need (Malachi) for true restoration from sin through the Messiah's work on YHWH's day dominate.

Zephaniah's Messianic Context within the Twelve

Having established Zephaniah's place within the Twelve, interpreters must read Zephaniah in view of the whole composition. That is, the final compiler intended that the other eleven prophets inform our reading of Zephaniah. This section will sketch the Twelve's informing messianic context.

Hope for the Messiah and His Age in Hosea–Habakkuk

Hosea opens the Twelve anticipating that YHWH will mercifully fulfill the Abrahamic covenant promises of numerous offspring and gather a reunited Judah and Israel under the Davidic King in the latter days after the exile (Hos 2:1–2[1:10–11]; 3:5; cf. Rom 9:26). His restoration will look like both a victorious third-day resurrection over death (Hos 6:1–2; 13:14) and like a second exodus (3:5; 11:10–11; cf. 11:1). The King will represent Israel, embody an Eden-like garden, and be the one in whom the redeemed find healing and habitation (14:5–9[4–8]).

Both Joel and Amos use new creation imagery to depict the coming day of restoration. Joel foresees the outpouring of God's Spirit on all who call on YHWH and are saved (Joel 2:25–26; 3:1–2[2: 28–29], 5[2:32]). God will operate as a stronghold

---

91. See Paul R. House, *The Unity of the Twelve*, JSOTSup 97 (Sheffield: Almond Press, 1990), 111–62; cf. House, *Old Testament Theology*, 346–401.

92. Dempster sees the pattern of sin, punishment, and restoration repeated in many books of the Twelve but not serving as a structuring device for the whole (Dempster, *Dominion and Dynasty*, 182n23). Instead, the 6 + 3 + 3 groupings retell Israel's

history, such that the initial six prophets alternate addressing "the northern and southern kingdoms until the northern kingdom was decimated. . . . Then three prophets spoke to the southern kingdom until it was destroyed. Finally, three post-exilic prophets spoke to a restored Judah" (Dempster, "Twelve," 299).

93. House, *Unity of the Twelve*, 151.

94. House, *Unity of the Twelve*, 151.

for his people in a secure, elevated Jerusalem from which will flow waters of life for a transformed world (3:16–18). Amos anticipates the new Davidic kingdom to include a remnant from the nations (Amos 9:11–12; cf. Acts 15:16–18) and a bountiful new creation (Amos 9:13–15).

Obadiah and Jonah address YHWH's global wrath. Obadiah notes how God's eschatological reign will be centered at Mount Zion and encompass enemy territory (Obad 20–21). No survivor will remain from those who once opposed YHWH, yet some will escape to Mount Zion and thereby gain new identities (vv. 17–18; cf. Amos 9:12; Ps 87). Such is possible because, as Joel declared, "*Everyone* who calls on the name YHWH will be delivered" (Joel 3:5[2:32]; cf. Acts 2:21; Rom 10:13). In Jonah, YHWH proves this point by delivering the foreign sailors and Ninevites who called on his name (Jon 1:14; 3:8). Their salvation as gentiles represented how YHWH would mercifully restore some from every nation (4:2).

Micah predicts that in the latter days, after Jerusalem's desolation, YHWH will exalt a new Jerusalem as the center of his reign; to him nations will gather to hear his Torah and enjoy justice and peace (Mic 4:1–4; cf. Isa 2:2–4). After Jerusalem's destruction, a Shepherd-King will rise from Bethlehem, rule in YHWH's strength, and work peace to the ends of the earth (Mic 5:2–5). His saving deeds will recall the first exodus, and the nations will fear YHWH (7:14–17). God will forgive, restore, and fulfill his Abrahamic covenant promises of blessing (7:18–20).

Nahum and Habakkuk provide further additional detail of YHWH's coming fury on the world. Nahum stresses that YHWH is both a just, overwhelming flood of wrath against his enemies and a merciful refuge for those looking to him (Nah 1:2–8). The prophet foresees a messenger coming with good news of peace, declaring that YHWH is restoring his people's majesty (2:1, 3[1:15; 2:2]; cf. Isa 52:7). Habakkuk, too, affirms that God will destroy his enemies but preserve those who believe (Hab 2:4). YHWH's pattern is to work on behalf of the Davidic king, bringing salvation and destroying opposition (3:13). In God alone does one find salvation and strength (3:18–19).

Hope for the Messiah and His Age in Haggai–Malachi

Haggai and Zechariah both focus on how the coming Messiah will restore God's presence in a new temple. Building on Zephaniah's eschatological context, Haggai envisions the coming of YHWH's day. All creation will shake, the kingdoms of men will fall, and a remnant from the nations will gather as treasures to a restored, glorious temple (Hag 2:6–7, 21–22). In that day, YHWH will raise up the royal Davidic figure whose life Zerubbabel represented (2:23). Indeed, a Priest-King, known also as the new creational "Branch," will bring forgiveness, rule justly, and generate worship as he reigns from YHWH's temple-palace, which he will build with the aid of distant peoples (Zech 3:8–9; 6:12–13, 15; cf. 2:11; 8:23). In accordance with God's purposes,

YHWH's people will reject, slaughter, and pierce his Shepherd-King, and by this God will open a fountain of cleansing from sin and uncleanness (12:10; 13:1; cf. 3:9). In that day, Jerusalem will be a life-giving center, and God will reign over the earth (14:8–9).

Malachi concludes the Twelve noting that a messenger, a new Elijah, will prepare people for YHWH's arrival on his day (Mal 3:1; 3:23–24[4:5–6]). Representing YHWH, a different messenger of the covenant will return to his temple/palace as a refining fire that will destroy evil ones but make the righteous flourish (3:1–2; 3:19–20[4:1–2]).

Conclusion

From a literary-canonical perspective, the Twelve's message and theology, including its messianism, most immediately informs Zephaniah's theology. Hearing Zephaniah's distinctive message requires that we understand the Scripture that could have informed his words *and* that we rightly grasp how later biblical authors and/or editors interpreted Zephaniah and sought to guide our reading. As we will see, while Zephaniah himself never explicitly portrays a messianic figure, the book's close, continuing, and complete contexts strongly suggest that Zephaniah hoped in the Messiah and associated him with YHWH's day of punishment and renewal.

Zephaniah's Use of Scripture[95]

Zephaniah draws on Scripture frequently, especially from Genesis, Deuteronomy, and Isaiah. Figure 0.3 attempts to capture at least most of the citations to these books, whether quotations or allusions.[96]

Zephaniah portrays YHWH's day as a climactic de-creation and re-creation that will both echo and reverse all negative effects of the primeval curses associated with the garden of Eden, the flood, and the tower of Babel. He also characterizes the day of wrath as a new divine conquest by which God will put an end to rebellion and reestablish a new promised land with global scope. In the process YHWH will carry out his Mosaic covenant curses and restoration blessings, fulfill his Abrahamic covenant promises to create a multiethnic remnant of worshipers, and realize his universal kingdom through covenant in a new creation.

---

95. Much of the following section adapts Jason S. DeRouchie, "Zephaniah, Book of," *DNTUOT*, 886–90.

96. Citations are authorially intended references to previous biblical texts. A quotation is a direct citation of an OT passage, evidenced through clear and unique verbal parallelism. An allusion is an indirect citation of an OT passage, such that the author indicates a conscious dependency on an earlier text yet in a way that does not directly reproduce the original wording. For more on the distinctions, see Jeffery M. Leonard, "Identify-

ing Inner-Biblical Allusions: Psalm 78 as a Test Case," *JBL* 127 (2008): 241–65; Russell L. Meek, "Intertextuality, Inner-Biblical Exegesis, and Inner-Biblical Allusion: The Ethics of Methodology," *Bib* 95.2 (2014): 280–91; Christopher A. Beetham, "Quotation, Allusion, Echo," *DNTUOT*, 684–92. Interpreters should note that Zephaniah draws material from chapters 1–33 in Deuteronomy and chapters 1–66 in Isaiah. This fact should inform the discussions of composition and provenance that surround these books.

Introduction to Zephaniah

Figure 0.3: Potential Citations of Genesis, Deuteronomy, and Isaiah in Zephaniah			
Zephaniah	**Genesis**	**Deuteronomy**	**Isaiah**
1:2	6:7; 7:3–4, 23; 8:8		
1:3	1:20–28		
1:4			14:26–27
1:6			50:5; 59:13
1:7		28:49–52	13:3–6
1:8–9			10:3; 29:6
1:9	6:11, 13		
1:12			41:23
1:13		6:10–11; 28:30, 39	42:22; 62:4; 65:21–22
1:14			10:21; 13:6; 42:13
1:15		4:11; 5:22; 28:29, 53, 55, 57	5:30; 8:22; 10:3
1:16		1:28; 3:5; 9:1; 28:52	2:12, 15, 17
1:17	2:7; 3:19	9:4–5; 28:28–29	24:5–6; 59:10
1:18		4:23–24; 32:21–22	10:23; 13:8–9, 13; 28:22; 29:6; 30:30; 66:15–16
2:2			42:14–16
2:3		16:20	51:1
2:4			54:1, 6; 62:2–4
2:5–15	10:6–20		
2:6–7			5:17; 65:10
2:7		30:3	10:3
2:8–9	19:25–26, 28, 37–38		
2:8–10			16:6
2:9		29:23	7:23–25
2:9–11			11:14
2:11		7:21; 10:17, 21	45:23
2:12		32:41; 33:29	66:16
2:15			47:8, 10
3:2		6:4; 28:45, 62; 31:12–13	
3:3		1:16–17; 16:18–19	
3:4		33:10	
3:5		32:4	59:9
3:7	6:11–12	5:29; 6:24; 10:12; 26:15; 32:5; 33:27	1:4

continued on next page

Zephaniah	Genesis	Deuteronomy	Isaiah
3:8		19:15–16	13:4; 24:21–22; 66:15
3:9		6:13	
3:9–10	2:10–14; 10:6, 10; 11:1–9		19:21–22
3:10		4:27; 28:64	11:12; 18:1, 7
3:11		33:26, 29	1:2; 13:3; 29:22–23; 43:27; 45:17; 61:7; 66:24
3:12			14:32; 25:4
3:13		28:26	53:9
3:14			12:5–6; 25:9; 35:6, 10; 54:1; 62:11; 65:18
3:15		33:5	44:6
3:16			13:7; 35:3–4
3:17		10:17; 28:63; 30:9	10:21; 42:13; 43:4; 62:5; 65:17–19
3:18			51:23
3:19			30:26; 35:5–6
3:19–20		26:19; 30:4	11:12; 56:4–8; 55:13
3:20		28:10; 30:3	

Examples of Zephaniah's OT Allusions
Coming Fires of Judgment Parallel the Waters of Judgment at the Flood

Zephaniah's oracle opens with YHWH's promise to gather "everything from on the face of the ground" for global judicial assessment: "human and beast . . . the bird of the heavens and the fish of the sea, and the stumbling blocks with the wicked" (Zeph 1:2–3). The phrase "from on the face of the ground" (מֵעַל פְּנֵי הָאֲדָמָה, 1:2–3) consistently occurs in contexts of divine punishment (e.g., Exod 32:12; Jer 28:16; Amos 9:8), and the use of "ground" recalls the sphere of the original curse (Gen 3:17–19). Zephaniah likely links the coming global judgment with the past flood punishment (6:7; 7:3–4, 23; 8:8).[97] Nevertheless, the scope of YHWH's new judicial assessment will exceed that at the time of the flood since Zephaniah includes "fish" (Zeph 1:3) and the great deluge never explicitly targeted sea creatures. Zephaniah fully respects YHWH's earlier promise that "never again will all flesh be cut off *by the waters of the flood*" (Gen 9:11; cf. 8:21; Isa 55:9–10) since he makes no mention

---

97. See esp. Michael DeRoche, "Zephaniah 1:2–3: The 'Sweeping' of Creation," *VT* 30.1 (1980): 104–9.

of water[98] and since the most natural reading of Zeph 1:2–3 is that YHWH promises to "gather" *all* creatures but only to "cut off" mankind (cf. Zeph 1:18; 3:8).[99]

The Day of YHWH as a New Conquest to Claim a Global Promised Land

By alluding to the original conquest of Canaan, Zephaniah suggests that the day of YHWH would be a greater divine conquest atoning for sin and establishing a global kingdom. First, in Zeph 1:11b, the prophet declares that Jerusalem's inhabitants would wail when YHWH silenced "all the people of Canaan" (ESV = "traders"). These were most likely the Philistine merchants (see 2:5) who negatively influenced Judah with both their worldly goods and perspectives (cf. Isa 2:6–8; Hos 12:8[7]). Their destruction recalls the original conquest when the Canaanites' wickedness along with God's choice of their land demanded their extermination (Deut 7:1–2; 9:4–5; 20:16–17). Similarly, Zephaniah's mention of the war "trumpet blast" (שׁוֹפָר) and of God overpowering "unassailable cities" (הֶעָרִים הַבְּצֻרוֹת) (Zeph 1:15–16) likely alludes to Israel subduing (Deut 6:10–11; Josh 6:5, 20) Canaanite strongholds (Num 13:28; Deut 9:1).

Second, the prophet depicts Jerusalem as spiritually deaf, heedless, faithless, and motionless (Zeph 3:2; cf. 1:6, 12). They had lost sight of YHWH's greatness and had sourced their strength and affluence from the Canaanite traders. These foreigners had reshaped Judah's worship (1:4–5), dress (1:8), and lifestyle (1:6, 9) so much that Zephaniah called these Judeans "the remnant of the Baal" (i.e., the Canaanites' chief god, 1:4b). And having identified with Canaan, they would receive the same punishment (Deut 8:19–20; cf. 20:18). Thus, Zephaniah says for those in Jerusalem, "Then their wealth will be for spoil and their houses for desolation, and they will build houses, but they will not inhabit; and they will plant vineyards, but they will not drink their wine" (Zeph 1:13). This wording recalls Mosaic covenant curses, which foretold that one evidence of divine wrath would be sustained futility in building, planting, and other endeavors (Deut 28:30, 39; cf. Amos 5:11; Mic 6:15). Even more, the language indicates that God was reversing his original covenant blessings and treating Israel as Canaanites. He had pledged that Israel would enjoy "great and good cities that you did not build, and houses full of all good things that you did not fill, and cisterns that you did not dig, and vineyards and olive trees that you did not plant" (Deut 6:10–11; cf. Jer 29:5–7). Now, they would experience substantive loss, as YHWH would reestablish a new promised land for his earthly kingdom and faithful remnant.

---

98. Against DeRoche, "Zephaniah 1:2–3," 105–6; Berlin, *Zephaniah*, 82.

99. See Jason S. DeRouchie, "YHWH's Future Ingathering in Zephaniah 1:2: Interpreting אָסֹף אָסֵף," *HS* 59 (2018): 173–91.

Third, one of the Mosaic covenant's original blessings will become a restoration blessing for "the remnant of the house of Judah" who survives the day's tribulation: "In the houses of Ashkelon at evening [the remnant of the house of Judah] will lie down" (Zeph 2:7; cf. Isa 65:18–22; Ezek 28:26). Thus, Zephaniah recalls the original conquest to stress how YHWH's day will both cleanse the earth and establish God's restored, now global kingdom.

Cush, the Table of Nations, and the Reversal of the Tower of Babel Judgment

Features from the early chapters of Genesis appear to have conceptually and literarily guided Zephaniah's portrayal of devastation and deliverance in 2:1–3:20. In 2:5–3:7, YHWH's wrath surrounds Judah—Philistia to the west, Moab and Bene-Ammon to the east, Cush and Assyria to the south and north, respectively. Berlin helpfully proposes that the prophet chose the particular nations in 2:5–15 based on the Table of Nations in Gen 10, thus highlighting that their pride arose from Babel (Gen 11:1–9).[100] Zephaniah "made the reality of his time fit the pattern in Genesis 10 by choosing the countries from Genesis 10 that were important [Philistia, Assyria], omitting those that were obscure [e.g., Put], and adding crucial ones, lacking in Genesis 10, in terminological equivalents to those in Genesis [Moab, Bene-Ammon]."[101]

By smiting Cush (2:12), God began universally eradicating the human pride that dispersed from the tower of Babel, thus signifying the nations' salvation (Gen 10:32–11:9).[102] On the very day when YHWH gathers the world for judgment (Zeph 3:8), he will "change for peoples a purified lip" and form a community of "supplicants, the daughter of my scattered ones" from "beyond the rivers of Cush" (3:9–10). The imagery of purified speech connotes the reversal of the tower of Babel's judgment in which God confused the "language/speech" and "scattered" the rebels across the globe to counteract communal pride (Gen 11:7, 9). Even some from the most distant lands upon which YHWH has poured his wrath (Zeph 2:11–12) will become "the remnant of Israel" (3:13). It is as if God's worshipers from these distant lands follow the rivers of life back to the garden of Eden for fellowship with the great King (Gen 2:13; cf. Rev 22:1–2). As many prophets anticipate (e.g., Isa 2:2–3; Jer 3:17; Zech 8:23), the new covenant people (i.e., a "daughter" of the dispersed) will include a worldwide, multiethnic community descending from the seventy nations whom YHWH "scattered" at Babel (Gen 11:8–9). Indeed, even some from Cush, Zephaniah's own heritage (Zeph 1:1), would gain new birth certificates declaring that they were born in Zion (Ps 87:4; cf. Isa 18:7; 45:14).

---

100. Berlin, *Zephaniah*, 120–24; Berlin, "Zephaniah's Oracle against the Nations," 175–84.

101. Berlin, *Zephaniah*, 121. However, Berlin fails to appreciate that God, showing no ethnic favoritism, promises to

destroy Judah and Jerusalem (3:1–7) along with her neighbors (2:5–15).

102. Floyd, *Minor Prophets, Part 2*, 210–13.

Zephaniah's Hermeneutical and Theological Strategy

Three factors apparently guided Zephaniah's hermeneutical use of Mosaic covenant blessings and curses and of the accounts of the flood, the Table of Nations, the tower of Babel, and the conquest: (1) typology, (2) redemptive-historical reversal, and (3) event as blueprint.

Typology

Zephaniah appears to portray the coming day of judgment's scope with flood imagery not only as an analogy between the two events but also to highlight mankind's coming destruction as indirectly fulfilling what the flood anticipated. Typology analyzes how biblical "persons, events, and institutions (i.e., antitypes) fulfill Old Testament persons, events, and institutions (i.e., types) by repeating the Old Testament situations at a deeper, climactic level in salvation history."[103] Two reasons suggest that Zephaniah views earlier materials as types and not just analogies: (1) Following the fall, God promised to overthrow the source of all evil and reconstitute creation through a male deliverer (Gen 3:15). The rest of the Pentateuchal narratives, in turn, present every defeat of serpent-like hostility against God as intentionally foreshadowing the coming ultimate deliverance. (2) The same inherent wickedness that prompted the flood-punishment (6:5–7) continued after the deluge (8:21). Thus, the biblical author portrays the flood account as anticipating a greater global destruction that would produce a more lasting new creation.

Zephaniah's use of the conquest and blessing-curse materials displays a similar hermeneutical step. Israel conquered the land God promised Abraham (Gen 15:18; 17:8) in the Mosaic covenant period (e.g., Exod 2:24; Deut 6:10), as realized in the days of Joshua and Solomon (Josh 21:43; 1 Kgs 4:21). Nevertheless, hope existed for the time when the "land" would extend to the "lands" of a multitude of nations (Gen 17:4–6; 26:3–4) and when YHWH's royal deliverer would perform a greater conquest of evil and bring God's blessing to the ends of the earth (3:15; 22:17–18).[104] Zephaniah's use of the conquest narrative signals that God both fulfills his original curses against rebellious Judah (Deut 8:19–20) and punishes his people's enemies with Deuteronomy's curses in the eschatological era (30:7). What the Canaanites were in the original conquest, all the world's evil ones are to YHWH. Thus, God eventually bringing "distress to humanity . . . for against YHWH they have sinned" (Zeph 1:17) heightens hope for a worldwide purified kingdom.

---

103. Andrew David Naselli, "Question 8: How Should Biblical Theology Approach Typology?," in *40 Questions about Biblical Theology*, by Jason S. DeRouchie, Oren R. Martin, and Andrew David Naselli, 40 Questions (Grand Rapids: Kregel, 2020), 81.

104. Cf. Gen 24:60; 49:8–10; Num 24:7–9, 17–19.

Redemptive-Historical Reversal

Zephaniah believes the day of YHWH will definitively reverse the tower of Babel episode and reconstitute a people who are more concerned with his name than with their own (cf. Gen 4:26; 11:4; Zeph 3:9). God portrays the faithful remnant as "the daughter of my scattered ones" (3:10)—that is, the offspring of those whose language YHWH once altered and whom he scattered across the globe away from Babylon (Gen 11:8–9). Noah's grandson Nimrod, a Cushite, built Babel (10:8, 10), and then following YHWH's punishment, the Cushites established their kingdom in what the ancients considered the southernmost region on the planet—near where the Blue and White Nile converge in modern day Sudan. Zephaniah envisioned YHWH's day of wrath as already starting with Cush (Zeph 2:12), and he used a remnant from this region to represent God's future global restoration (3:10). Whereas YHWH once confused the "lip/language" of the earth (Gen 11:8–9), he now would purify the "lip/ speech," not by recreating a common tongue but by uniting a remnant of humanity in worshipful partnership so "that all of them may call on the name YHWH, to serve him with one shoulder"—that is, in complete partnership (Zeph 3:9). Zephaniah's use of redemptive-historical reversal signals that God will inaugurate the new creation that he first anticipated in Gen 3:15 and then announced to Abraham through his promises of blessing all the families of the ground (e.g., 12:3; 28:14).

Event as Blueprint

As Berlin argues, the Table of Nations in Gen 10 possibly supplied a blueprint for the structure of Zeph 2:5–15. With this, Zephaniah's likely biracial link to the Cushites (Zeph 1:1) may have drawn him to Gen 10, which focuses heavily on the Hamitic line (Gen 10:6–20), from which the Philistines, Canaanites (= Sodom and Gomorrah), Cushites, and Assyrians all arose. The Table of Nations (Gen 10:1–32) preceding the account of the tower of Babel (11:1–9) also worked to the prophet's advantage. He first addresses the scope of God's judgment (Zeph 2:5–3:7) and then clarifies how YHWH's blessing would counter the effects of the Babel judgment and restore a lasting age where all survivors of YHWH's day worship his name forever (3:9–20).

Zephaniah Elsewhere in Scripture

Other biblical authors allude to Zephaniah's message of the day of YHWH, and the reader should consult the associated Explanation of the Text and Canonical and Theological Significance sections of the commentary for relevant discussions. The most important Scriptural allusions to Zephaniah relate to:

- *The eschatological ingathering to punish and save:* Zeph 1:2–3 and 3:8 in Jer 3:8; Zech 14:2; and Matt 13:24–30 (cf. 3:12; 25:32, 46)

- *The inauguration of YHWH's day in Christ's death and resurrection and the church's birth:* (1) Zeph 3:8–10 in Acts 1:2–3, 22; 2:1–47; 8:26–40; (2) Zeph 3:14–15 in Zech 9:9 and John 12:13, 15

Zephaniah's Vision of the Day of YHWH

The Day of YHWH as Punishment, Renewal, and Motivation in Zephaniah[105]

Throughout the Prophets, the phrase יוֹם יְהוָה ("the day of YHWH") and its abbreviated parallels ("the/this/that day") refer to the ultimate time when YHWH will punish and restore the whole world and to the periodic penultimate days that clarify and anticipate it. That is, the day of YHWH includes (1) God's final and decisive move to execute justice and to reestablish right order in the world (e.g., Zeph 1:14–18; 3:8–10; cf. 2 Thess 1:9–10; 2 Pet 3:10) and (2) any number of historical foretastes of this end time wherein God restores peace by judging wickedness for either the wider world (e.g., Jer 46:10; Joel 4:9–16[3:9–16]; Obad 15)[106] or Israel/Judah (Ezek 13:5; Amos 5:18; Zech 14:1).[107] Zephaniah anticipates YHWH's day in both respects (e.g., typological: Zeph 1:7; 3:7; ultimate: 1:14; 3:8), and in the process he supplies what von Rad calls some of "the most important material at our disposal concerning the concept of the Day of Yahweh."[108] For Zephaniah, the nearness of YHWH's day (1:7b, 14a) requires an immediate response.

The Day of YHWH as Punishment[109]

The day of YHWH is coming against all the wicked of the world (Zeph 1:2–3, 14–18; 2:5–3:7), including those found in Judah (1:4–6, 7–13; 3:1–7). God's jealousy will blaze forth with fury (1:18; 3:8) against leader (1:8–11; 3:3–4) and commoner (1:12–13; 3:2) alike because "against YHWH they have sinned" (1:17). Chaff is chaff regardless of where it is found, and though in Zephaniah's Judah the faithful remnant was mixed with the rabble majority, on the day of wrath, God "will clear

---

105. Some of this section is adapted from Jason S. DeRouchie, "The Day of the Lord," *TGC Essays* (2020), https://www.thegospelcoalition.org/essay/the-day-of-the-lord/. See also Zephaniah's Day of YHWH within Its Biblical Context in the Canonical and Theological Significance section at the end of Zeph 1:7–18.

106. Cf. Isa 2:10–22; 13:1–22; Ezek 30:1–9.

107. Cf. Isa 3:1–4:1; Joel 1:15; 2:1–11; 3:4[2:31]; Mal 3:23[4:5].

108. Gerhard von Rad, "The Origin of the Concept of the Day of Yahweh," *JSS* 4 (1958): 102. For more on this theme, see the commentary and Douglas K. Stuart, "The Sovereign's Day

of Conquest: A Possible Ancient Near Eastern Parallel to the Israelite Day of Yahweh," *BASOR* 221 (1976): 159–64; Richard H. Hiers, "Day of the Lord," *ABD* 2:82–83; G. K. Beale, "Eschatology," *DLNT*, 330–45; Mark A. LaRocca-Pitts, "The Day of Yahweh as a Rhetorical Strategy among Hebrew Prophets" (PhD diss., Harvard University, 2000); J. D. Barker, "Day of the Lord," *DOTPr* 132–43; Ortlund and Beale, "Darkness over the Whole Land," 221–38.

109. For a further synthesis of this theme, see Jason S. DeRouchie, "Revering God: Punishment on the Day of the Lord (Zeph 1:2–18)," *BSac* 181.1 (2024): forthcoming.

his threshing floor and gather his wheat into the barn, but the chaff he will burn with unquenchable fire" (Matt 3:12; cf. Zeph 2:1–2). He will eradicate all forms of iniquity as he did at the flood (Gen 6:11–13; cf. Zeph 1:2–3) and gather and destroy everyone who multiplies corruption instead of fears him (3:7). The Warrior-King (3:15, 17) will decisively remove arrogance from his city (3:12) and eliminate those who afflicted her (3:19). He will cleanse the earth and reconstitute the mountain of his holiness for his presence (3:11–12; cf. 3:5, 15, 17). When he comes, the day will be unexpected and filled with cataclysm, conquest, and sacrifice.

Cataclysm

With echoes of YHWH's encounter with Adam and Eve following their sin (Gen 3:8) and his appearance before Israel at Mount Sinai (Exod 19:16; Deut 4:11), Zephaniah and the other biblical prophets often associate YHWH's day of wrath with darkness, wind, earthquake, and clouds. "That day is a day of wrath . . . a day of darkness and gloom, a day of cloud and thick darkness" (Zeph 1:15). The foreboding images of tempest and shadow, gloom and quaking display YHWH's fierce and impending presence and highlight the day of destruction's nearness against both individuals (2 Sam 22:12; Job 15:22) and nations (Isa 13:10; 30:30; cf. Ezek 30:3), including Israel/Judah (Isa 5:30; cf. Joel 2:2; Amos 5:18).

Whereas many in Israel envisioned YHWH's day to be one of light, the prophets stressed that for all the unrepentant, it would indeed be night. "Woe to those desiring the day of YHWH. . . . It is darkness, and not light" (Amos 5:18; cf. Ezek 32:7–8; Joel 2:2). Daily YHWH gave "his judgment for the light," foreshadowing the coming day of judgment against sin (Zeph 3:5). But for all who fail to heed his warnings, his coming will bring darkness.

When God enters our space and time, the natural forces react; storms awaken and ground quakes. "From YHWH of armies you will be visited with thunder and earthquake and a great sound, whirlwind and storm and a flame of consuming fire" (Isa 29:6; cf. 30:30; Joel 3:3–4[2:30–31]). With Joel, we must declare, "Great and very fearsome is the day of YHWH, and who can endure it?" (Joel 2:11). Such depictions of YHWH's day should cause hearts to tremble. "Hush before the Sovereign YHWH, for the day of YHWH is near!" (Zeph 1:7).

Conquest

The darkness of YHWH's day may at times refer not to a storm but to the sensory experience of a victim dying from divine war. On the day of YHWH, the lights of life are extinguished for God's enemies, so Zephaniah speaks of "distress and anguish . . . ruin and devastation . . . darkness and gloom . . . cloud and thick darkness." It is "a day of trumpet blast and battle cry against the unassailable cities and against the high battlements" (1:15–16). Such images recall YHWH's conquest of Canaan[110] and portray his day of wrath as a more ultimate conquest, wherein God reestablishes a new people in a transformed land (cf. 1:13 with Deut 6:10–11; 28:30, 39).

Trumpets often served as battle alarms, whether for offense (Num 10:9; Job 39:24) or defense (Jer 42:14; Amos 3:6; Neh 4:20). The trumpet could warn the target (e.g., Jer 6:1; Ezek 33:3; Joel 2:1), or it could arouse the aggressor (Jer 51:27; Zech 9:14). Zephaniah appears to use it in the latter way (Zeph 1:16). He also notes other common sounds associated with war: cries of pain, terror, and tumult (1:10–11). Indeed, "the sound of the day of YHWH is bitter" as "a Mighty One"—YHWH the Sovereign Warrior—"is shouting there" (1:14).

"Israel's King, YHWH" will remove the enemy and stand in the new Jerusalem's midst (3:15); "as a Mighty One, he will save!" (3:17). He is a roaring lion (e.g., Jer 25:30; Joel 4:16[3:16]; Amos 1:2), and he fights against his adversaries to deliver his faithful remnant (cf. Exod 15:3; Ps 24:8; Joel 2:11). At times, the text explicitly mentions that other powers will serve as the agents of God's retribution, operating as the "rod" of his anger (Isa 10:5; cf. Mic 6:9) and his "weapon" of war (Isa 13:5; Jer 51:20). This is the best identification of the "invited ones" in Zeph 1:7 (cf. Isa 13:3). Nevertheless, in Zephaniah, YHWH is chiefly to be feared, "for a complete, even terrifying, end he will deal against all the inhabitants of the earth" (Zeph 1:18).

Sacrifice

After highlighting the nearness of YHWH's day, Zephaniah grounds his declaration in the reality that God had already "prepared a sacrifice" (Zeph 1:7). Atonement reestablishes right order by killing either the sinner or a substitute (Lev 17:11; Num 35:33; Isa 22:12–14; Heb 9:22). By failing to "draw near" to YHWH (Zeph 3:2) principally through his provision of a substitute sacrifice (cf. Lev 9:1–10:3), those in Jerusalem and beyond had prepared themselves as the sacrifice.

Sacrificial fires are nothing less than a divine war against wickedness. Hence, after describing the day with cataclysmic and conquest imagery, God stressed, "I will bring distress to humanity . . . for against YHWH they have sinned" (Zeph 1:17). He then appropriates images of sacrifice to describe what he would do against his enemies: "Their blood will be poured out like dust and their belly like dung pellets. . . . And in the fire of his jealousy all the earth will be consumed" (1:17–18; cf. 2:2; 3:8; Mal 2:3). Zephaniah and other prophets commonly associate fire with the day of YHWH, and it aligns well with images of cataclysm, conquest, and sacrifice.[111] With this,

---

110. Cf. Num 13:28; Deut 1:28; 3:5; 9:1 with Deut 6:10–11; Josh 6:5, 20.

111. E.g., Hos 8:14; Mic 1:7; Zeph 2:2; 3:8; Mal 3:19[4:1];

cf. Isa 29:6; Joel 2:3, 5; 3:3[2:30]; Amos 5:6; Obad 18; Mic 1:4; Nah 1:6; 3:15.

both Jeremiah and Ezekiel compare YHWH's punishing of his enemies with a great sacrifice (Jer 46:10; Ezek 39:17, 20–21).

The Law (i.e., Pentateuch) set forth a clear pattern of substitution (e.g., Exod 12:12–14; Lev 16:15–22, 33–34). Furthermore, the prophets show that this pattern pointed to the sufferings of a righteous Servant, who would "count righteousness . . . for the many, and their iniquities he will bear" (Isa 53:11). Within the Book of the Twelve, the Davidic royal Deliverer (e.g., Hos 3:5; Mic 5:2–5; Zech 6:12–13) triumphs only through great tribulation. Through him God would "remove the iniquity of this land in a single day" (Zech 3:9). He is associated closely with the covenant blood that will set prisoners free (9:11), and his "piercing" (12:10) opens a spring "for the house of David and the inhabitants of Jerusalem for sin and for cleansing" (13:1). His representational death will save God's people and reconstitute right order. "And there will be one day. . . . And it will happen that at evening time will be light. And it will happen in that day that living waters will flow from Jerusalem. . . . And YHWH will be King over all the earth" (14:7–9).

The blended images of war and sacrifice depict how YHWH justly secures atonement and reestablishes a rightly ordered context in which the redeemed celebrate him as supreme and value those made in his image (cf. Isa 22:14; 34:2, 6). Such is the goal of the day of YHWH.

Near Yet Unexpected

Zephaniah portrayed YHWH's day as "near and hastening fast" (Zeph 1:14; cf. Isa 13:6; Ezek 30:3).[112] For the unrepentant living in darkness, the day would come like a thief, catching the victims unaware (Joel 2:9; cf. Jer 48:11–12; Mic 3:11). Zephaniah may suggest this when he claims that YHWH will "search Jerusalem with the lamps"—that is, at night, when unexpected (Zeph 1:12). The need, therefore, was to remain spiritually alert (Joel 1:5) and to respond immediately. Only those who unify and seek him in the present (Zeph 2:1, 3; cf. 3:7) have any hope for shelter when the storms of wrath blow (cf. Isa 33:14–16; Joel 2:14; Amos 5:15).

Old Testament statements regarding the day of YHWH are often unclear as to what applies to the immediate versus the final. Time clarifies, however, and initial, partial fulfillments establish the certainty that complete fulfillment is coming (cf. Jer 28:9; Ezek 33:33). Many in OT Israel likely perceived each historical intrusion of divine wrath as potentially the consummate judgment of the ages (e.g., against Judah, Lam 2:21; or against Babylon, Isa 13:13, 19). However, in time, the faithful recognized them as foreshadowing the ultimate punishment and salvation (see Ezek 38:17; 39:8; cf. Rev 20:7–10).

Zephaniah does more than many to distinguish the immediate and consummate

---

112. See also Joel 2:1; 4:14[3:14]; Obad 15; Zeph 1:7.

destructions, but the two still blend and are mutually interpreting. In distinguishing "the day" (1:7b) from "the *great* day" (1:14a), he at least differentiates Jerusalem's local punishment (1:7b–13; cf. 1:4–6; 2:2; 3:7) from a universal punishment of "all the inhabitants of the earth" (1:18; cf. 1:2–3, 14–18; 3:8). This distinction is also likely temporal, shifting from the coming 586 BC Babylonian takeover of Judah to the complete destruction of evil at the end of the age. Because the overthrow of Cush had likely already occurred (2:12; cf. 3:6), the prophet appears to see the tide shifting and anticipates that the waves of destruction would soon reach Judah's shore. The time to repent was now!

The Day of YHWH as Renewal

On the very day that YHWH rises as judge of the earth, he promises to do two things: (1) gather the nations to execute punishment and (2) redeem a transformed multiethnic community of worshipers who will call upon his name (Zeph 3:8–10).[113] On that very day, he will eradicate both sin and sinners from his presence while also ending curses, overcoming the enemy, and creating a context where his faithful remnant will never fear retribution (3:11–20).[114] With God having pardoned their sins and counted them righteous (Isa 53:11; Jer 31:34; Zech 3:9), he will then save completely and evoke rejoicing and singing (Zeph 3:14–15, 17; cf. Isa 65:19). YHWH's day is nothing less than a reconstituted, eschatological Sabbath (Heb 4:9, 11), wherein God the Creator acts as Warrior to reestablish kingdom rest and order (Zeph 3:14–20), ultimately through his messianic, sin-overcoming Deliverer (Gen 3:15; Zech 13:1; Matt 11:28–30).[115] Here YHWH will be exalted through his messianic Davidic King, who will rule forever with justice and righteousness (e.g., Isa 11:1–10; Jer 23:5; Zech 9:9–10; cf. Zeph 3:15 with John 12:13, 15).[116] Those submitting to his reign will enjoy God's presence and be holy and at peace (Zeph 3:11–20).[117]

Central to YHWH's day is his personal presence among his people (cf. Ezek 37:27; Mal 3:1–2). In Zephaniah, the transformed, ethnically diverse community of worshipers will gather to YHWH's presence (Zeph 3:10), call upon his name (3:9), and find refuge in his name at the mountain of his holiness (3:11–12). Joel further records that God will save those calling on his name at Mount Zion, and upon them he will pour his Spirit (Joel 2:11–13; 3:1–2[2:28–29], 5[2:32]).[118] Twice Zephaniah stresses that YHWH will be in their midst (Zeph 3:15, 17). On that day, God will

---

113. For more on this latter theme, see Jason S. DeRouchie, "Seeking God and Waiting: Hope on the Day of the Lord (Zeph 2:1–4; 3:8–10)," *BSac* 181.2 (2024): forthcoming.

114. For more on this theme, see Jason S. DeRouchie, "Rejoicing Then and Now: Pleasures on the Day of the Lord (Zeph 3:11–20)," *BSac* 181.3 (2024): forthcoming.

115. So, too, Meredith G. Kline, *Kingdom Prologue: Genesis*

Foundations for a Covenantal Worldview (Eugene, OR: Wipf & Stock, 2006), 33–38.

116. See also Isa 9:6–7; Ezek 37:24–25; Mic 5:4–5.

117. E.g., Isa 2:2–4; 4:2–6; Amos 9:11–15; Mic 2:1–4; cf. Joel 3:1–5[2:28–32]; Zech 14:1–21.

118. Cf. Ezek 36:27; 37:14.

fulfill his kingdom promises to David, causing all the earth to flourish under the new David's rule (Isa 11:1–10; Ezek 37:24–28; Amos 9:11–14). Israel's King will be with them (Zeph 3:15), and they will uniquely display and revel in his holiness (3:19–20; Zech 14:7–9, 20).

Significantly, Zephaniah envisioned the day of YHWH to unfold progressively in stages (= already-but-not-yet). After initiating the great ingathering of his remnant (Zeph 3:18; cf. 3:19–20), enemies will still oppose the transformed Jerusalem, requiring its community to hear, "Do not fear! O Zion, may your hands not grow slack" (3:16). Indeed, while God will have gathered those who humbly heeded his warnings of coming punishment (3:18), they will still need to know: "YHWH your God is in your midst. As a Mighty One, he will save!" (3:17). Yet in that day the remnant will be able to rest, as YHWH exalts himself through them before the earth's onlooking peoples who are bound for eternal destruction (3:20; cf. Ezek 36:23).

The Day of YHWH as Motivation for Patiently Pursuing YHWH Together

The prophet was convinced that our hopes and fears for tomorrow can change who we are today. God intends that his promises of blessing and curse motivate radical Godward surrender (2 Pet 1:4). Zephaniah employs dread and hope to awaken his audience to return to the basics of Yahwistic-messianic faith. He wants them to do two things. First, they must seek YHWH together by nurturing righteousness and humility (Zeph 2:1, 3). This was only possible by fleeing idolatry and looking to God in devotion and prayer (1:6), by heeding his warning and joining with other believers (1:7; 2:1, 3), and by turning from resistance and starting to respond through fearing God and heeding his instruction (3:2, 7). Second, the remnant must wait in faith for YHWH to rise as judge and work his new creative powers (3:8–10), even as they rejoice in hope of a sure and better day (3:14–15). The remnant in Judah and other lands must seek YHWH together to avoid punishment, and they must wait for YHWH to enjoy satisfying salvation. This is the Savior's invitation to satisfaction. "Seeking" God together and "waiting" for him today (2:1, 3; 3:8) will result in lasting joy tomorrow, both for those the Savior saves (3:14–15) and for the Warrior-King himself (3:17).

Zephaniah's Day of YHWH and the Glories of Christ and His Church

Peter declared that "*all* the prophets" foretold Christ's sufferings and the subsequent glories, including the glories seen in and through the church today (Acts 3:18, 24; 1 Pet 1:10–11). Zephaniah never explicitly mentions the Messiah, which may be part of his rhetoric to stress how dark his days were. Nevertheless, his twin themes of new exodus and new conquest likely imply a new Moses and a new Joshua, and he would have expected his audience to recognize the messianic contexts he engages in books like Genesis and Isaiah. Furthermore, the overall messianic thrust of the

Book of the Twelve informs Zephaniah's message today (see above), and Zephaniah's link between the day of YHWH as cataclysm, conquest, and sacrifice falls within a salvation-historical and canonical context that climaxes in the Messiah's tribulation and triumph.

To be specific, Zephaniah anticipates Jesus and his mission in at least three ways:

1. Portraying the day of YHWH as cataclysm, conquest, and sacrifice foreshadows the atoning work of Christ at the cross.
2. Zephaniah predicted what we call the church age by portraying YHWH's day as a period of already-but-not-yet new creation during which God has already gathered a multiethnic community of worshipers but has not removed all their opposition.
3. Christ's second coming will realize the final defeat of all evil and the complete reconstitution of right order and ultimate satisfaction that Zephaniah anticipated.

The following discussion places Zephaniah's theology within the larger context of Christ's saving work and the church age and of his return and kingdom consummation.

Christ's Saving Work and the Church Age as Initial Fulfillment of Zephaniah's Day of YHWH

The biblical authors apparently saw Christ's saving work (i.e., his life, death, and resurrection) as inaugurating the day of YHWH as both punishment and renewal. The cross event mingles elements of divine cataclysm, conquest, and sacrifice in a way that calls us to see the birth of the church as initially realizing the age of satisfying salvation for which Zephaniah longed. Numerous factors point in this direction:

1. In fulfillment of Malachi's predictions (Mal 3:1–2; 3:23–24[4:5–6]), John the Baptizer's ministry prepared the way for YHWH's day of anger and his covenant messenger's arrival at his temple (Matt 11:9–15). John anticipated that a fiery display of divine fury would distinguish the righteous from the wicked on the day of YHWH, and he saw Jesus as both the Warrior and Sacrifice through whom God would bring both destruction and deliverance (Matt 3:11–12; John 1:29). Zephaniah, too, anticipated that the sacrificial fires of YHWH's jealousy would inaugurate YHWH's day (Zeph 1:18; 3:8; cf. 1:7), and he foresaw YHWH coming as the royal Mighty One to save (3:15, 17).
2. Zephaniah said King YHWH would be among his people during the day of judgment and salvation (3:8, 11, 15, 17), and Jesus is "God with us" (Matt 1:23) who has received "all authority in heaven and on earth" (28:18). He is both God's tabernacling presence and the temple (John 1:14; 2:19–22), for which the prophets hoped (cf. Hag 2:7–9).

3. In Jesus's triumphal entry, John alludes to Zeph 3:15 by calling Jesus "Israel's King" whose coming victory means the "daughter of Zion" should "fear not" (John 12:13, 15; cf. Zech 9:9). To Jesus the ethnically diverse crowds cry, "Hosanna!" ("Please save!"; John 12:13; cf. Zeph 3:9–10), and Jesus "casts out" "the ruler of this world" (John 12:31; cf. Zeph 3:15, 19). For John, Jesus inaugurated YHWH's end-times reign on YHWH's day for which Zephaniah hoped.[119]

4. Building on imagery already linked to the messianic King in Ps 18:8–16[7–15], each of the synoptic Gospels apply cataclysmic phenomena typically associated with the day of YHWH to Christ's death (Matt 27:45, 51; Mark 15:33; Luke 23:44).[120] These images of darkness and destruction recall Zephaniah's vision of YHWH's day as punishment (Zeph 1:15–16).

5. Luke saw the Spirit's work at Pentecost as fulfilling *both* Joel's and Zephaniah's prophecies about the day of YHWH (Acts 2:16–21; cf. Joel 3:1–4[2:28–31]; Zeph 3:8–10). Luke highlights that numerous cosmological signs including darkness would occur "*before* the day of the Lord comes" (Acts 2:20 with Joel 2:31; cf. Zeph 3:15). Furthermore, like Zephaniah, Luke indicates how those God saves experience transformed speech, call on his name, and enjoy unity (Acts 2:4–6, 21, 42; cf. Zeph 3:9) and how they come from as far as Ethiopia (the Greek term for "Cush"; Acts 8:26–39; cf. Zeph 3:10).

6. Zephaniah saw the day of YHWH as bringing an end to one age and inaugurating a new one (Zeph 3:8–10). Likewise, Jesus's first coming marks the beginning of the end of the first creation and initiates the new creation, which corresponds to the new covenant (2 Cor 5:17; Gal 6:15; Heb 8:13). Christians together are God's end-times, multiethnic bride and are those upon whom "the end of the ages has come" (1 Cor 10:11). We are the peoples from all the nations and kingdoms that Zephaniah envisioned YHWH would gather and transform as worshipers at his new Jerusalem (Zeph 3:8–10; cf. Eph 2:13–22; Heb 12:22–29).

These factors support the notion that Jesus's death marks the intrusion of the day of YHWH as punishment into the middle of history (Zeph 3:8; cf. 1:18) and that his resurrection and the birth of the church at Pentecost signals the dawn of the new creation for which Zephaniah hoped (3:9–10). At the cross, God poured his end-time wrath out on Christ on behalf of the many whom he would count as righteous (Rom 5:18–19; cf. Isa 53:10–11). At the cross, Jesus was judging the world, casting out its evil ruler, and drawing all people to himself (John 12:31–32; cf. Zeph 3:9–10, 15, 19). Jesus became sin and a curse for us (2 Cor 5:21; Gal 3:13). We were once God's enemies bound for destruction, but now, having been justified by Christ's blood, we

---

119. See esp. Tachick, *Use of Zephaniah 3 in John 12.*
120. See J. Bergman Kline, "The Day of the Lord in the Death and Resurrection of Christ," *JETS* 48 (2005): 757–70; Ortlund and Beale, "Darkness over the Whole Land," 221–38.

will "be saved from the wrath of God" that is still to come (Rom 5:9). Believers today are protected from the final day of fury because Christ has already borne the penalty anticipated at the day of YHWH (e.g., Rom 5:1, 9–11; cf. Isa 53:5; 1 Pet 2:24).

The intrusion of YHWH's day brought suffering to Jesus, as he represented all the elect under God's wrath. YHWH's day also launched Christ's church into the period of renewal, as Zephaniah expected. In Jerusalem, Jesus initiated a great second exodus through which he would save many peoples (Luke 9:31; cf. Zeph 3:10, 18). He died "not for the [Jewish] nation only, but also to gather into one the children of God who are scattered abroad" (John 11:51–52; cf. 10:16–18; Isa 49:5–6). Through the great commission and the ever-expanding transcultural church (Matt 28:18–20; Acts 1:8), Jesus is fulfilling the Abrahamic covenant promises of blessing (Gen 12:3; 22:17–18; cf. Acts 3:25–26) and realizing Zephaniah's hopes of a new "Israel" made up of the world's "peoples"—a remnant of descendants of those God once "scattered" at the tower of Babel (Zeph 3:9–10, 13; cf. Gen 11:1–9). Today Jews and Gentiles in Christ together make up the one people of God, the church (Gal 3:8, 29; Eph 2:14–16). As the new covenant community, we have already gathered "to Mount Zion and to the city of the living God, the heavenly Jerusalem" (Heb 12:22; cf. Zeph 3:10–12; Gal 4:26), and we are already realizing many of Zephaniah's hopes by offering sacrifices of praise and good deeds (Rom 12:1; Heb 13:15–16; cf. Zeph 3:10) as we carry out priestly duties in God's service (Rom 15:16; 1 Pet 2:5).

Christ's Return and Kingdom Consummation as Final Fulfillment of Zephaniah's Day of YHWH

Nevertheless, just as Zephaniah himself anticipated (esp. Zeph 3:16–18), the day of YHWH works itself out in stages. We still look ahead to the new heavens and earth, when "the holy city, new Jerusalem," will descend from heaven "as a bride adorned for her husband" (Rev 21:2) and there will no longer be "anything accursed" (22:3). Indeed, in Christ's death the ultimate future day of YHWH intrudes into the middle of history on behalf of the elect. And so, we must also recognize that the consummation of YHWH's day is still to come. "Concerning the coming of our Lord Jesus Christ and our being gathered together to him," Paul said that "the day of the Lord . . . will not come, unless the rebellion is first, and the man of lawlessness, the son of destruction, is revealed" (2 Thess 2:1–3; cf. Mark 13:7).

Like Zephaniah (Zeph 1:7, 14), the apostles stress this day's nearness (Phil 4:5; Rev 1:3; 22:10), but they also highlight that God is faithful and that any sense of delay results from his patient desire to see more saved (2 Pet 3:8–9). For the unrepentant, the day of wrath will still come completely unexpected; it will come like "a thief in the night" (1 Thess 5:2; cf. Joel 2:9; Matt 24:43).[121] But for those spiritually awake and

---

121. See also 1 Thess 5:4; 2 Pet 3:10; Rev 3:3; 16:15.

living in the light, the day will not come as a surprise (1 Thess 5:4; cf. Mark 13:33–37; Rev 3:2–3).[122]

Elsewhere Jesus spoke of the future "day of judgment" wherein God would judge all people according to their deeds (Matt 12:36; cf. 7:23; John 12:48). All those on earth "will see the Son of Man coming on the clouds of heaven with power and great glory" (Matt 24:30; cf. Acts 1:9–11). At this time, "he will send out his angels with a great trumpet call, and they will gather his elect" (Matt 24:31; cf. 1 Thess 4:16; Rev 8:7). Jesus associates Zephaniah's great day of ingathering directly with his second coming (Matt 24:36, 42; cf. Mark 13:32; Luke 17:24) and with the future resurrection (John 6:39–40, 44, 54). At this time, Christ will gather all nations to himself, separate the wicked from the righteous (Matt 25:31–32; cf. Zeph 1:2; 3:8), and punish the former with "unquenchable fire" (Matt 3:12; cf. 2 Thess 1:7–10; 2 Pet 3:7–10). However, he will welcome and feast with the latter (Matt 25:34; 26:29; Mark 14:25).

Paul stressed that "each one's work will become evident, for the Day will disclose it, because by fire it will be revealed, and what sort of work each one's is the fire will test" (1 Cor 3:13; cf. 2 Cor 5:10; 2 Thess 1:8–10). Similarly, Peter emphasized: "The day of the Lord will come like a thief, in which the heavens will pass away with a roar, and the elements will be burned up by melting, and the earth and the works that are in it will not be found" (2 Pet 3:10; cf. 1 Thess 5:2; Rev 3:3). John tagged the culminating battle of the ages "the great day of God the Almighty" (Rev 16:14) and "the great day of their wrath," of which he queried, "Who can stand?" (6:17). In that day, Christ will be called "Faithful and True" and "King of kings and Lord of lords" (19:11, 16). We read: "In righteousness he judges and wages war. . . . And from his mouth comes a sharp sword by which he might strike the nations. And 'he will shepherd them with an iron rod,' and he treads the winepress of the wine of the fury of the wrath of God the Almighty" (19:11, 15; citing Ps 2:9). Like the day of YHWH in Zephaniah (Zeph 1:7), John also envisioned that the results of this final war against evil as a sacrificial feast for the birds (Rev 19:17–18; cf. Ezek 39:17–20).

Conclusion

Zephaniah saw YHWH's day as punishment and renewal, both of which are realized through Jesus's person and work. Concerning punishment, at his first coming he stood as the *object* of God's wrath on behalf of his elect, but at his second coming he will be the *agent* of God's wrath on behalf of the elect. Concerning renewal, Jesus rose on the Lord's day, God's saving light bursting through the darkness and initiating the beginning of the end of one age and the dawn of the new (see 1 Thess 5:5, 8–9). But we still await the day when tears and death will be no more and when God will have reconciled all things to himself.

---

122. See also Matt 24:42–43; Eph 5:14; 1 Thess 5:6.

At one level, Christians are already experiencing the day of YHWH as both punishment and renewal: "Therefore, much more, having now been justified by [Christ's] blood will we be saved through him from the wrath. . . . We were reconciled to God through the death of his Son" (Rom 5:9–10). In Christ's first coming, the day of YHWH intruded, as "the saving grace of God has appeared for all people" (Tit 2:11), initiating the new creation. Nevertheless, we are still "awaiting the blessed hope and the appearing of the glory of our great God and Savior Jesus Christ" (Tit 2:13; cf. Rom 8:18; Heb 9:28).

As Zephaniah hoped (Zeph 3:8–20; cf. Gen 3:15; Zech 3:9), Jesus restores God's end-times Sabbath by overcoming darkness with light (Matt 4:15–17), initiating kingdom rest and order (11:28–12:8), and overpowering the enemy (12:22–32). Nevertheless, he does so in a way that will only reach consummation when he returns (Heb 4:9, 11). Through Jesus, YHWH our God is already in our midst, and "as a Mighty One, he will save" (Zeph 3:17). Therefore, may we continue to "seek YHWH" together and "wait" for him to act (2:1, 3; 3:8), finding present delight in the certainty of our coming complete deliverance (3:14–15, 17, 19–20; cf. Rom 5:1–5). And "may we hold unswervingly the confession of the hope. . . . And may we consider one another for encouragement of love and good works, not forsaking our gathering, as is a custom of some, but exhorting, and so much more as you see the Day nearing" (Heb 10:23–25).

Zephaniah's Celebration of YHWH's Exaltation[123]

A key purpose of the book of Zephaniah is to exalt YHWH God as the judging and saving Warrior-King who deserves the world's reverence. The proper name "YHWH" (יהוה) most commonly designates him in the book (34x), with ten of these coming from God himself. The name firmly fits the book within the Mosaic covenant (cf. Exod 3:14–16; 6:6–8; 34:6–7), as do the frequent allusions to the Law in the various indictments, instructions, curses, and blessings. As Exod 3:14–16 suggests, the name derives from the causative *hiphil* stem of the verb היה ("to be") and thus carries the sense "he causes to be"—a meaning that is then explained in the narrative of Exodus as YHWH sovereignly guides human disability and will, nature, life and death, victory and defeat, and everything else.[124] He thus stands as the only uncaused

---

123. This section is adapted from DeRouchie, *How to Understand and Apply*, 291–93.

124. Surls has helpfully argued that scholars should look to the Exodus narrative as a whole to discern how God himself clarifies the meaning of the Tetragrammaton (יהוה) (Austin Surls, *Making Sense of the Divine Name in the Book of Exodus: From Etymology to Literary Onomastics*, BBRSup 17 [Winona Lake, IN: Eisenbrauns, 2017]). Surls completely rejects any ety-

mologically based core-meaning for the divine name because he rightly claims that biblical names speak more to the character or faith of the name-*giver* rather than the name-*bearer* (pp. 9–10). Nevertheless, he missteps by failing to account for the fact that YHWH names himself in Exod 3:14–15 and by this urges the etymological association between אֶהְיֶה and יהוה. Sonnet balances these elements when he observes that YHWH provided "authorized etymology" for his name in Exodus 3 *and*

one, who creates and controls all things visible and invisible, material and immaterial and does so on behalf of his people and for his glory (see Rom 11:36; Col 1:16; Heb 1:3). Zephaniah confirms and builds upon this point by summarizing the book's contents (Zeph 1:1) and God's purposed activity (2:5) as "YHWH's word." Zephaniah also emphasizes both YHWH's "utterance" (1:2, 3, 10; 2:9; 3:8) and the outworking of his "decree" (2:2), all he has "purposed" (3:7), and his "judgment" (3:8).

Zephaniah joins the name YHWH with the title "their/your God" (2:7; 3:17) to comfort the remnant with the coming restoration. In contrast, the prophet calls him "the Sovereign YHWH" (1:7) when his impending day of fury demands reverence. Accordingly, God castigates Moab and Bene-Ammon as "YHWH of hosts/armies" (2:9–10) for their pride and aggression against his people and then underlines his favor toward his own with the title "the God of Israel" (2:9). Elsewhere Zephaniah designates YHWH as "her [Jerusalem's] God" (3:2), and then Zephaniah calls him "Israel's King" (3:15; cf. YHWH's word of judgment in 2:5) and "a Mighty One" (3:17; cf. 1:14) when stressing the remnant's certain deliverance. He is also Jerusalem's "Shelter," which the city will lose due to rampant corruption (3:7). Beyond these titles, the prophet designates YHWH's character as "righteous" (3:5a) and notes that his homage-demanding presence is both "fearsome" (2:11a) and "in your [Jerusalem's] midst" (3:15c, 17a; cf. 3:5). When God is present and celebrated, there is no need to fear (3:15–17).

All thirty-seven different verbal roots used in relation to YHWH are fientive, focusing on God's actions. What follows synthesizes all roots used two or more times, along with some others. Though the complacent in Jerusalem declared that God would neither "do good" nor "do ill" (1:12), YHWH will "gather" and "assemble" to punish (1:2–3; 3:8) and restore (3:18–20). When he "visits" someone, there is either chastisement (1:8–9, 12; 3:7) or redemption (2:7). When he "stretches out" his hand (1:4; 2:13), he "cuts off" (1:3–4, 11; 3:6–7) and "destroys" (2:5, 13). He "pours out" both indignation (3:8) and blood (1:17) to "consume" all opponents (1:18; 3:8) since "against YHWH they have sinned" (1:17; cf. 2:8–9). YHWH never "does" wrong (3:5) and will "deal" with all the wicked (1:18), including oppressors (3:19). He will "remove" the proud opposition (3:11, 15) but "save" his humble followers (3:17, 19) and "restore" their previous circumstances (2:7; 3:20). He will "place" Nineveh for a desolation (2:13) but his redeemed for praise and renown (3:19). Indeed, he will

---

that the phrase אֶהְיֶה אֲשֶׁר אֶהְיֶה pushes the reader to the rest of the Exodus narrative to fill out the divine name's meaning (Jean-Pierre Sonnet, "*Ehyeh Asher Ehyeh* [Exodus 3:14]: God's 'Narrative Identity' among Suspense, Curiosity, and Surprise," *Poetics Today* 31 [2010]: 342). For an argument that we must not reject all etymological understandings of the divine name, see Elizabeth Robar, "Review of *Making Sense of the Divine Name in Exodus: From Etymology to Literary Onomastics*, by

Austin Surls," *BBR* 28.3 (2018): 464–66. On viewing the Tetragrammaton as a causative *hiphil* of the verb היה ("to be") with the pronunciation "Yahweh" (יַהְוֶה), see Frank Moore Cross, "Yahweh and *ʾĒl*," in *Canaanite Myth and Hebrew Epic: Essays in the History of the Religion of Israel* (Cambridge: Harvard University Press, 1973), 44–75, esp. 65; David Noel Freedman, Helmer Ringgren, and M. O'Connor, "יהוה *YHWH*," *TDOT* 5:512–14.

"give" his elect for acclaim and praise (3:20), as he carries on his daily purpose to "give" his judgment for the light (3:5). In 3:20 the prophet couches all his words as that which YHWH "has said," but God also has two embedded reported-speech acts that declare his past longing for his people's repentance (3:7) and his future commitment to fully save and savor his redeemed (3:16–17).

As the supreme Sovereign, Savior, and Satisfier, YHWH deserves highest allegiance. His just "jealousy" for the honor of his own name kindles his sacrificial fires of punishment against the ungodly (1:18; 3:8; cf. Exod 34:14). Because he has diminished "all the gods of the earth," every knee "will bow down" to him (Zeph 2:11; cf. Isa 45:23; Rom 14:11), some as condemned prisoners of war (Zeph 3:15, 19; cf. Isa 45:14) and others as redeemed worshipers (Zeph 3:9–10; cf. Isa 2:3; Zech 8:22–23). In the end, YHWH will celebrate over his purified, faithful remnant (Zeph 3:17), whom he is transforming as a people of joy (3:14) for *his* "praise" and his "name" throughout the earth (3:19–20; cf. Jer 13:11; 33:9).

God is fulfilling all these things through the first and second appearing of Jesus. The Word who was "in the beginning . . . with God . . . was God" (John 1:1). The very Son who would be named Jesus "was in the form of God" (Phil 2:6), was the very "image of the invisible God" (Col 1:15), and was "the radiance of the glory and the exact imprint of his essence" (Heb 1:3). When Jesus acts and speaks, God is acting and speaking (John 14:9; cf. 5:18). In his description of all YHWH would accomplish on his great day, Zephaniah portrayed Christ's coming and the glories that would follow (Acts 3:18, 24). May we with the apostles celebrate Zephaniah's contribution to the OT portrait of the Messiah and missions (Luke 24:25–27; Acts 26:22–23), and may we include this fifty-three-verse treasure in Christian preaching.

Proclaiming Zephaniah Today

This book of prophecy is an ideal choice for Christian preachers to memorize, recite, and preach from start to finish within the local church (2 Tim 3:15–17; 4:2; 1 Pet 1:10–12). It totals only fifty-three verses, and it perhaps delineates better than any other minor prophet all three of the most common issues that God's covenantal enforcers address: *sin*, *punishment*, and *restoration*.[125] Thus, Zephaniah captures all prophetic theology within three chapters. The book is a God-given means for magnifying the beauties of Christ and his gospel (Luke 24:27; John 5:39; Acts 3:18; 1 Pet 1:10–12).

---

125. For more on these themes in the Book of the Twelve, see House, *Unity of the Twelve*, 63–110.

While some have preached solidly on the whole book in a single sermon,[126] preachers will serve their flocks by preaching the treasures of this book over the course of several sermons. Personally, I have preached the book over fifteen weeks, but also over a shorter period. Six potential sermons include:

1. No Salvation for Those in Sin (1:1–6)
2. Revere the Savior or Die (1:7–18)
3. Seek Shelter in the Only Savior (2:1–4)
4. Reasons to Seek the Savior Together (2:5–3:7)
5. Wait for the Savior to Act (3:8–10)
6. A Satisfying Salvation—True Motivation (3:11–20)

Note that each sermon is tied to the book's overarching theme: "The Savior's Invitation to Satisfaction." With this, every passage unit aligns with the main structural divisions of Zephaniah's flow of thought. In these verses the Savior is calling for a united, patient pursuit of him, and he motivates his exhortation with a stark display of sin and punishment and an even more remarkable portrayal of satisfying salvation. Consider carefully how the prophet's words anticipate the sufferings of Christ and the subsequent glories, and then magnify his majesty and the hope of the gospel.[127]

---

126. See, e.g., John Piper, "The Lord Will Rejoice over You," preached Sept 25, 1982, DesiringGod.org: https://www .desiringgod .org /messages /the -lord -will -rejoice -over -you; Mark Dever, "The Message of Zephaniah: What's There to Be Thankful For?," in *The Message of the Old Testament: Promises Made* (Wheaton, IL: Crossway, 2006), 861–81; Mike Bullmore,

"God's Great Heart of Love toward His Own (Zephaniah)," in *The Scriptures Testify about Me: Jesus and the Gospel in the Old Testament*, ed. D. A. Carson (Wheaton, IL: Crossway, 2013), 127–43.

127. For more interpreting OT prophecy, see DeRouchie, "Preaching the Prophets," 28–37.

Brief Outline of Zephaniah

I. The Superscription of the Savior's Invitation to Satisfaction (1:1)

    A. Origin, Author, and Setting of the Prophecy (1:1)
        1. The Nature and Source (1:1)
        2. The Messenger (1:1)
        3. The Historical Context (1:1)

II. The Setting of the Savior's Invitation to Satisfaction: A Call to Revere YHWH in View of His Coming Day (1:2–18)

    A. The Context of the Call to Revere YHWH: Coming Punishment (1:2–6)
        1. Global Punishment against the Rebels of Humanity (1:2–3)
        2. Local Punishment against the Rebels of Judah and Jerusalem (1:4–6)

    B. The Content of the Call to Revere YHWH (1:7–18)
        1. The Call to Revere YHWH (1:7a)
        2. A Reason to Revere YHWH Related to Jerusalem (1:7b–13)
        3. Another Reason to Revere YHWH Related to the Whole World (1:14–18)

III. The Substance of the Savior's Invitation to Satisfaction: Charges to Seek YHWH Together and to Wait (2:1–3:20b)

III.1 Stage 1: The Appeal to Seek YHWH Together to Avoid Punishment (2:1–3:7)

    A. The Charge to Unite in Submission to YHWH (2:1–2)
        1. The Need to Unite (2:1)
        2. The Time to Unite (2:2)

    B. The Charge to Seek YHWH in Righteousness and Humility (2:3–4)
        1. The Charge to Seek YHWH (2:3)
        2. An Initial Reason to Seek YHWH: The Devastation of Philistia (2:4)

    C. Further Reasons to Seek YHWH Together (2:5–3:7)
        1. The Lamentable State and Fate of the Rebels from the Foreign Nations (2:5–15)
        2. The Lamentable State and Fate of the Rebels from Jerusalem (3:1–7)

III.2 Stage 2: The Appeal to Wait for YHWH to Enjoy Salvation (3:8–20b)

    A. The Charge to Wait for YHWH to Act (3:8–10)
        1. The Charge to Wait for YHWH (3:8a)
        2. Two Reasons to Wait for YHWH (3:8b–10)

    B. Promises to Motivate Waiting for YHWH: The Remnant's Satisfying Salvation (3:11–20b)
        1. The Promise that YHWH Will Not Shame Jerusalem (3:11–13)
        2. A Discursive Charge to Rejoice as if the Great Salvation Has Already Occurred (3:14–15)
        3. The Promise That YHWH Will Save Completely (3:16–20b)

IV. The Subscription of the Savior's Invitation to Satisfaction (3:20c)

    A. YHWH Has Spoken (3:20c)

Outline of Zephaniah

I. The Superscription of the Savior's Invitation to Satisfaction (1:1)
  A. Origin, Author, and Setting of the Prophecy (1:1)
    1. The Nature and Source (1:1)
    2. The Messenger (1:1)
    3. The Historical Context (1:1)

II. The Setting of the Savior's Invitation to Satisfaction: A Call to Revere YHWH in View of His Coming Day (1:2–18)
  A. The Context of the Call to Revere YHWH: Coming Punishment (1:2–6)
    1. Global Punishment against the Rebels of Humanity (1:2–3)
      a. YHWH's Ingathering of Everything for Judicial Assessment (1:2–3b)
        (1) The Declaration of Ingathering (1:2)
        (2) The Details of Ingathering (1:3a–b)
          (a) Human and Beast (1:3a)
          (b) Bird and Fish and Idols (1:3b)
      b. YHWH's Punishment of Rebel Humanity (1:3c)
    2. Local Punishment against the Rebels of Judah and Jerusalem (1:4–6)
      a. YHWH's Extension of His Hand against Judah and Jerusalem (1:4a)
      b. YHWH's Punishment of Remaining Paganism in Judah and Jerusalem (1:4b–6)
        (1) The Declaration and Object of Punishment (1:4b)
        (2) The Composition of the Object of Punishment (1:4c–6)
          (a) The Identities of the Illegitimate Priests with the Priests (1:4c)
          (b) The Star-Worshipers (1:5a)
          (c) The Syncretistic Hypocrites (1:5b)
          (d) The Self-Ruled, Self-Dependent (1:6)
  B. The Content of the Call to Revere YHWH (1:7–18)
    1. The Call to Revere YHWH (1:7a)
    2. A Reason to Revere YHWH Related to Jerusalem (1:7b–13)
      a. The Impending Sacrificial Nature of YHWH's Punishment (1:7b–d)
      b. The Implications of YHWH's Punishment for Jerusalem (1:8–13)
        (1) YHWH's Punishment of the City's Political and Religious Leaders (1:8–11)
          (a) YHWH's Punishment of the Leaders (1:8–9)
          (b) The Resulting Impact on the City: Loss of the Source of Their Self-Exaltation (1:10–11)
        (2) YHWH's Punishment of the City's Complacent People (1:12–13)
          (a) YHWH's Punishment of the Complacent People (1:12)
          (b) The Resulting Impact on the City: Loss of the Objects of Their Misplaced Satisfactions and Securities (1:13)
    3. Another Reason to Revere YHWH Related to the Whole World (1:14–18)
      a. The Characteristics of the Coming Day of Punishment (1:14–16)
        (1) The Imminence of the Day (1:14a)
        (2) The Torturous Sound of the Day (1:14b–c)
        (3) The Terror of the Day (1:15–16)
      b. The Effects of the Coming Punishment (1:17–18)
        (1) Humanity's Distress (1:17)
          (a) The Promise (1:17a)

(b) The Content (1:17b–d)
- Inflicted Disability (1:17b–c)
- Sacrificial Dismemberment (1:17d)
(2) Humanity's Destruction (1:18)
(a) The Impossibility of Deliverance (1:18a)
(b) The Complete Destruction of Every Inhabitant (1:18b–c)

III. The Substance of the Savior's Invitation to Satisfaction: Charges to Seek YHWH Together and to Wait (2:1–3:20b)

III.1 Stage 1: The Appeal to Seek YHWH Together to Avoid Punishment (2:1–3:7)

A. The Charge to Unite in Submission to YHWH (2:1–2)
1. The Need to Unite (2:1)
2. The Time to Unite (2:2)

B. The Charge to Seek YHWH in Righteousness and Humility (2:3–4)
1. The Charge to Seek YHWH (2:3)
a. The Charge Voiced (2:3a)
b. The Charge Explicated (2:3b–c)
c. A Parenthetical Motivation for the Charge (2:3d)
2. An Initial Reason to Seek YHWH: The Devastation of Philistia (2:4)
a. The Desertion of Gaza and Desolation of Ashkelon (2:4a–b)
b. The Expulsion of Ashdod and Uprooting of Ekron (2:4c–d)

C. Further Reasons to Seek YHWH Together (2:5–3:7)
1. The Lamentable State and Fate of the Rebels from the Foreign Nations (2:5–15)
a. A Woe Speech against Philistia to the West (2:5–7)
(1) Its Audience (2:5a)
(2) Its Nature (2:5b–7)
(a) The Promise of the Philistines' Annihilation (2:5b–c)
(b) The Result of the Philistines' Annihilation: A Reclaiming of Homeland for the Remnant of Judah (2:6–7)
b. Further Declarations of International Punishment Surrounding Judah (2:8–15)
(1) Against Moab and Bene-Ammon to the East (2:8–11)
(a) The Reason for Their Punishment (2:8)
(b) The Nature of Their Punishment (2:9–11)
- The Declaration of Punishment (2:9a–b)
- The Explanation of Punishment with Universal Implications (2:9c–11)
  – The Plundering and Dispossession of Moab and Bene-Ammon by YHWH's Remnant (2:9c–d)
  – The Certainty of YHWH's Victory and Receipt of Global Praise (2:10–11)
(2) Against the Cushites to the South and Assyria to the North (2:12–15)
(a) The Context for Assyria's Demise: The Slaying of the Cushites (2:12)
(b) The Declaration of Assyria's Demise (2:13–15)
- A General Plea for Assyria's Demise (2:13a–b)
- A Specific Plea and Promise of Nineveh's Desolation (2:13c–15)
  – The Plea for Her Desolation (2:13c–14a)
  – The Promise of Her Desolation (2:14b–e)
  – The Appraisal of Her Desolation (2:15)

2. The Lamentable State and Fate of the Rebels from Jerusalem (3:1–7)
   a. Jerusalem's Characteristics (3:1)
   b. Jerusalem's Fundamental Failures (3:2–7)
      (1) An Overview of Her Fundamental Failures (3:2)
         (a) Her Initial Resistance (3:2a–b)
         (b) Her Resulting Unresponsiveness (3:2c–d)
      (2) An Elaboration of Her Fundamental Failures (3:3–7)
         (a) Her Crooked Leaders (3:3–5)
            • Their Tendencies (3:3–4)
               – The Political Leaders (3:3)
               – The Religious Leaders (3:4)
            • Their Contrast to YHWH (3:5)
               – His Righteousness and Steadfast Judgment (3:5a–d)
               – The Shamelessness of the Iniquitous (3:5e)
         (b) Her Resistance to Growth (3:6–7)
            • Its Context (3:6a–7d)
               – YHWH's Past Punishments of Other Nations (3:6)
               – YHWH's Pedagogical Intent for Such Punishments (3:7a–d)
            • Its Nature (3:7e–f)

III.2 Stage 2: The Appeal to Wait for YHWH to Enjoy Salvation (3:8–20b)

A. The Charge to Wait for YHWH to Act (3:8–10)
   1. The Charge to Wait for YHWH (3:8a)
   2. Two Reasons to Wait for YHWH (3:8b–10)
      a. YHWH's Intent to Punish All the Wicked of the Earth (3:8b–c)
      b. YHWH's Promise to Create a Community of Worshipers from the Whole Earth (3:9–10)
         (1) The Details of the Promise (3:9)
         (2) The Exposition of the Promise (3:10)

B. Promises to Motivate Waiting for YHWH: The Remnant's Satisfying Salvation (3:11–20b)
   1. The Promise that YHWH Will Not Shame Jerusalem (3:11–13)
      a. The Details of the Promise (3:11a)
      b. The Bases of the Promise (3:11b–13)
         (1) Basis 1: YHWH's Removal of the Proud (3:11b–c)
            (a) The Divine Promise (3:11b)
            (b) The Result (3:11c)
         (2) Basis 2: YHWH's Leaving the Humble (3:12–13)
            (a) The Divine Promise (3:12a)
            (b) The Result (3:12b–13f)
   2. A Discursive Charge to Rejoice as if the Great Salvation Has Already Occurred (3:14–15)
      a. Three Calls to Rejoice (3:14)
      b. Two Reasons to Rejoice (3:15)
         (1) YHWH's Removal of the Curses (3:15a–b)
         (2) YHWH's Nearness (3:15c–d)

3. The Promise That YHWH Will Save Completely (3:16–20b)
  a. The Prediction of a Future Speech Prohibiting Fear (3:16–18)
    (1) The Prediction of the Future Speech (3:16a)
    (2) The Contents of the Future Speech (3:16b–18)
      (a) The Prohibition Not to Fear (3:16b–c)
      (b) Two Reasons Not to Fear (3:17–18)
        • Reason 1: The Saving Warrior's Nearness (3:17)
        • Reason 2: YHWH's Gathering of His Remnant (3:18)
  b. The Promissory Implications of the Future Speech (3:19–20b)
    (1) Jerusalem's Complete Salvation (3:19)
    (2) The Remnant's Complete Participation (3:20a–b)

IV. The Subscription of the Savior's Invitation to Satisfaction (3:20c)

A. YHWH Has Spoken (3:20c)

PART I

Zephaniah 1:1

The Superscription of the Savior's Invitation to Satisfaction

Main Idea of Zephaniah 1:1

The superscription stresses that the book contains God's very word that he delivered to his prophetic emissary Zephaniah during the reign of the Judean king, Josiah.

> **I. The Superscription of the Savior's Invitation to Satisfaction (1:1)**
> II. The Setting of the Savior's Invitation to Satisfaction: A Call to Revere YHWH in View of His Coming Day (1:2–18)
> III. The Substance of the Savior's Invitation to Satisfaction: Charges to Seek YHWH Together and to Wait (2:1–3:20b)
>   III.1 Stage 1: The Appeal to Seek YHWH Together to Avoid Punishment (2:1–3:7)
>   III.2 Stage 2: The Appeal to Wait for YHWH to Enjoy Salvation (3:8–20b)
> IV. The Subscription of the Savior's Invitation to Satisfaction (3:20c)

Literary Context of Zephaniah 1:1

Following the pattern of many Old Testament prophetic writings (e.g., Hos 1:1; Hag 1:1; Zech 1:1), the book of Zephaniah opens with a superscription in 1:1. This heading introduces the content that follows as "YHWH's word," which includes both the setting for the Savior's invitation to satisfaction (1:2–18) and the substance of that invitation (2:1–3:20b).

Zephaniah 1:1

A. Origin, Author, and Setting of the Prophecy (1:1)

Main Idea of the Passage

The superscription stresses that the book contains God's very word that he delivered to his prophetic emissary Zephaniah during the reign of the Judean king, Josiah.

Literary Context

The superscription identifies Zephaniah as God's human mouthpiece who speaks as a heavenly ambassador delivering the "word" (דְּבַר) God gave him. Thus, the book's heading characterizes the prophet's entire message (and perhaps even the superscription itself) as God's "word" to the prophet, which the rest of the book characterizes as a single, coherent oracle. Consequently, everything in the book has a divine origin and authority and derives from a unified will.[1] The book itself bears canonical consciousness.[2]

---

1. Cf. Hans Walter Wolff, *Hosea: A Commentary on the Book of the Prophet Hosea*, trans. Gary Stansell, Hermeneia (Philadelphia: Fortress, 1974), 4. A "vision" (חָזוֹן; e.g., Isa 1:1; Obad 1:1; Nah 1:1), an "oracle/burden" (מַשָּׂה; e.g., Isa 13:1; 15:1; 17:1; 19:1; 21:1, 11, 13; 23:1; 30:6; Nah 1:1; Hab 1:1; Zech 9:1; 12:1; Mal 1:1), or simply "the words of X, who . . ." (e.g., Deut 1:1; Jer 1:1; Amos 1:1) introduce other prophetic messages.

2. For more on canon consciousness, see Ched Spellman, *Toward a Canon-Conscious Reading of the Bible: Exploring the History and Hermeneutics of the Canon*, New Testament Monographs 34 (Sheffield: Sheffield Phoenix, 2014). On the link between divine origin and canon, see Meredith G. Kline, *The Structure of Biblical Authority*, 2nd ed. (Eugene, OR: Wipf & Stock, 1997), 27–75. Wolff believes the singular use of "word" in such contexts provides "an important step toward the formation of the canon," but he does not think the title yet means "Holy Scripture," for "the Word of God is an event that confronts the prophet again and again" (Wolff, *Hosea*, 4). The superscription, however, equates the whole written oracle that follows with the "word" that God delivered to the prophet, so the distinction between the revelatory "word" as event and the revelatory "word" as document is only one of form, not content, origin, or authority.

In three ways the prophet emphasizes that God is the oracle's source: (1) by repeating the oracular formula "the utterance of YHWH" (נְאֻם־יְהוָה; 1:2–3, 10; 2:9; 3:8),[3] (2) by closing the book with the speech formula "YHWH has spoken" (אָמַר יְהוָה; 3:20),[4] and (3) by letting God regularly speak in first-person ("I/me"; e.g., 1:2–4).[5] Zephaniah needed *God's* authority to confront Jerusalem's political and religious elite (1:4, 8–8; 3:3–4). Through his prophet, *God* himself promises an impending day of punishment for both Judah and the world (1:2–18). *God* calls his righteous remnant to seek him together and to wait for him in joyful hope (2:1, 3; 3:8, 14). *God* motivates such a call by warning of the global destruction of the proud (2:4–3:8) and predicting the worldwide restoration of the humble (3:9–20). *God* himself as Savior King promises to satisfy completely his redeemed in his presence and celebrate those (3:14–17) whom he has recreated for his glory (3:19–20). Following the superscription (1:1), God's word through Zephaniah graphically portrays the day of YHWH against Judah and the world (1:2–18) and then builds on this foundation by calling for a united, persistent pursuit of God to avoid punishment and enjoy salvation (2:1–3:20).

> ➡ **I. The Superscription of the Savior's Invitation to Satisfaction (1:1)**
>   **A. Origin, Author, and Setting of the Prophecy (1:1)**
>   **1. The Nature and Source (1:1)**
>   **2. The Messenger (1:1)**
>   **3. The Historical Context (1:1)**

Translation and Exegetical Outline

(See page 61.)

Structure and Literary Form

Zephaniah 1:1 contains no sentence but stands simply as the book's title. It consists of a noun phrase and a relative descriptive clause. The noun phrase ("YHWH's word") clarifies the book's nature and source. The relative descriptive clause indicates the book's messenger ("Zephaniah") and the time he prophesied (during Josiah's reign).

---

3. Sweeney, *Isaiah 1–39*, 546; also called the "signatory formula" in Daniel I. Block, *The Book of Ezekiel: Chapters 1–24*, NICOT (Grand Rapids: Eerdmans, 1997), 33.

4. Sweeney, *Isaiah 1–39*, 547.

5. Even when Zephaniah blurs YHWH's voice by referring to God in third person ("he/him"; e.g., 1:5–7), the divine origin and authority of the prophet's pronouncements remain unchanged. Cf. Vlaardingerbroek, *Zephaniah*, 29.

Zephaniah 1:1 [1]

1:1	דְּבַר־יְהוָ֣ה ׀ אֲשֶׁ֣ר הָיָ֗ה אֶל־צְפַנְיָ֙ה בֶּן־כּוּשִׁ֣י בֶן־גְּדַלְיָ֔ה בֶּן־אֲמַרְיָ֖ה בֶּן־חִזְקִיָּ֑ה בִּימֵ֛י יֹאשִׁיָּ֥הוּ בֶן־אָמ֖וֹן מֶ֥לֶךְ יְהוּדָֽה׃	YHWH's word that came to Zephaniah the son of Cushi, the son of Gedaliah, the son of Amariah, the son of Hezekiah in the days of Josiah the son of Amon, Judah's king.

I. **The Superscription of the Savior's Invitation to Satisfaction (1:1)**

A. Origin, Author, and Setting of the Prophecy (1:1)

    1. The <u>Nature and Source</u> (1:1)

    2. The <u>Messenger</u> (1:1)

    3. The Historical Context (1:1)

---

1. For information on the guidelines used for tracing the argument, see The Method in the introduction, pp. XX.

Formally, verse 1 is a "superscription" that introduces the book.[6] A prophetic word formula (here = ‏דְּבַר־יְהוָה אֲשֶׁר הָיָה אֶל־‎, "YHWH's word that came to") constitutes the heading, of which variations are common throughout the OT's prophetic revelatory contexts.[7] The present pattern occurs elsewhere only in Hos 1:1, Joel 1:1, and Mic 1:1 (also LXX Jer 1:1), which suggests to some that a common preexilic editor may have completed these minor prophetic books.[8] While possible, because the formula varies from book to book and because the fronted placement at the books' beginnings explains the distinctive wording, this view is unnecessary. The prophetic word formula itself characterizes the content of the book as the written expression of a revelatory encounter that YHWH speaks "to" a (usually named) human messenger for another audience.[9] The "coming" (translating ‏היה‎, "to be") of the word means that God's message in some way "became a reality" for Zephaniah.[10] Only in Gen 15:1 is the formula accompanied by a specific mode of delivery (i.e., a "vision"). Elsewhere we learn that, apart from YHWH conversing "mouth to mouth" with Moses (Num 12:6, 8), he spoke to his prophets through visions, dreams, and the Urim (1 Sam 28:6; Jer 31:26), all guided by his Spirit (e.g., Zech 7:12; Neh 9:30; 2 Pet 1:21).[11] The prophets' sustained use of Scripture[12] also indicates that God's Spirit inspired fresh words by "interpreting"[13] not only these oracular revelations but also other written canonical revelation through a process of exegesis, as the prophets "sought out and inquired" about the Messiah's "person and time" (1 Pet 1:10–11). Zephaniah draws on much earlier Scripture,[14] but his book gives no other clues as to the means God used to convey his "word" to the prophet.

Two other significant features include genealogy and the temporal context of the original revelation. Through the repetition of the construct chain "the son of X" (‏[x]־בֶּן‎), the superscription names Zephaniah's father, grandfather, great-grandfather, and great-great-grandfather. While other prophetic books open with similar constructions (Isa 1:1; Jer 1:1; Hos 1:1; Joel 1:1; Jonah 1:1; Zech 1:1), only Zephaniah includes a five-member genealogy. The superscription also uses genealogy to connect

---

6. Sweeney, *Isaiah 1–39*, 539–40.

7. Sweeney, *Isaiah 1–39*, 546; also called the "word-event formula" (Block, *Book of Ezekiel: Chapters 1–24*, 32). What follows is a sampling of instances in the Law, Prophets, and Writings of "YHWH's word" (‏דְּבַר־יְהוָה‎) plus a form of the verb "to be" (‏היה‎) plus the preposition "to" (‏אֶל־‎): *Law:* Gen 15:1, 4; *Prophets:* 1 Sam 15:10; 2 Sam 7:4; 1 Kgs 6:11; 2 Kgs 20:4; Jer 1:2; Ezek 1:3; Isa 38:4; Hos 1:1; Joel 1:1; Jonah 1:1; 3:1; Mic 1:1; Zeph 1:1; Hag 2:10, 20; Zech 1:1; Mal 2:1; *Writings:* Dan 9:2; 2 Chr 11:2.

8. Wolff, *Hosea*, 4; Sweeney, *Zephaniah*, 46.

9. Berlin adds, "The syntax (with a noun, 'the word of the Lord,' at the head of the clause) does not seem to emphasize the process of communication to the prophet as much as to

specify ownership of the oracle to follow" (Berlin, *Zephaniah*, 64). Three texts specify the ultimate addressee as the object of the preposition ‏אֶל‎ and not the prophetic vehicle or messenger of the "word" (1 Kgs 16:7; Zech 4:6; Mal 2:1).

10. Motyer, "Zephaniah," 908.

11. See also 1 Sam 10:6, 10; 1 Kgs 22:24; Mic 3:8; Joel 3:1–2[2:28–29]; Ezek 11:5; Acts 1:16.

12. See, for example, Gary Edward Schnittjer, *Old Testament Use of Old Testament: A Book-by-Book Guide* (Grand Rapids: Zondervan, 2021).

13. See the use of the verb συγκρίνω ("to draw a conclusion, interpret") in 1 Cor 2:13 and the noun ἐπίλυσις ("explanation, interpretation") in 2 Pet 1:20.

14. See Zephaniah's Use of Scripture in the introduction.

King Josiah to his father Amon's dark days (2 Kgs 21:19–26), which stresses the need for Zephaniah's message. The temporal phrase "in the days of" (בִּימֵי) linked with the name of the reigning king signals the time of the original prophecy. Similar historical signals are common in preexilic books (cf. Isa 1:1; Jer 1:2; Amos 1:1; Mic 1:1) and probably fix the prophecy's original temporal setting before Jerusalem's downfall and characterize the whole as a merciful message of divine warning.

Explanation of the Text

1. The Nature and Source (1:1)

Like many prophetic writings (e.g., Hos 1:1; Joel 1:1; Jonah 1:1; Mic 1:1; Hag 1:1; Zech 1:1; Mal 1:1), the book of Zephaniah opens with a title that characterizes the divine origin and authority of the book as a whole: "YHWH's word" (דְּבַר־יְהוָה). YHWH is Israel's covenant Lord (Exod 3:14–15; 6:6–8; 34:6–7), but because he also made the universe, he holds claim not only to Israel but also to everything (Exod 20:11; Deut 10:14; Neh 9:6). In Zephaniah, the uncaused One speaks a comprehensible "word" that contains words. Just as the Bible connects law with the priest and counsel with the sage, so it associates God's "word" with the prophet (Jer 18:18), which he receives as an ambassador of the divine council (23:18; Amos 3:7) for his audience (Jer 23:22, 28; cf. Deut 18:20–22).

After the superscription, Zephaniah declares words of reproof, direction, caution, and hope, but God is the source of every letter and thus gives the revelation canonical authority. The prophet's message flows from the great King's unified will; failing to heed this message makes one a spiritual traitor. Fulfilled prophecy, such as Babylon destroying Jerusalem in 586 BC (e.g., Zeph 1:10–13), initially

demonstrated that Zephaniah's words were God's "word" (Deut 18:22). Such events validated Zephaniah as one of YHWH's prophets, led others to recognize the book of Zephaniah's divine authority, and emphasized the certainty of the prophet's future predictions.[15]

2. The Messenger (1:1)

God's mouthpiece for his message is named "Zephaniah" (צְפַנְיָה, "YHWH has hidden"), a figure known in Scripture only from this book.[16] The superscription does not specify his vocation (cf. Jer 1:1; Ezek 1:3; Amos 1:1), designate him as a "prophet" (נָבִיא; cf. Hab 1:1; Hag 1:1; Zech 1:1), or identify his place of origin (cf. Jer 1:1; Amos 1:1; Mic 1:1; Nah 1:1). However, the larger context demonstrates that Zephaniah is one of YHWH's prophets (i.e., a covenant-mouthpiece; cf. 2 Kgs 17:13; Zech 7:11–12).[17] Additionally, his association with "Josiah . . . Judah's king" (ca. 640–609 BC) clarifies that he prophesied to the southern kingdom after the northern kingdom's fall (ca. 723 BC) and just before Babylon invaded and destroyed Jerusalem (605, 597, 586 BC). The Babylonian Talmud (b. Meg. 15a) asserts that Zephaniah was

---

15. Gowan, *Theology of the Prophetic Book*, 8–9; Gentry, *How to Read and Understand the Biblical Prophets*, 32–37.

16. See Zephaniah's Title and Authorship in the introduction and Berridge, "Zephaniah (Person)," *ABD* 6:1075.

17. Cf. 2 Chr 36:15; Jer 23:21–22; Hos 12:9–10; Zech 7:11–12; Mal 3:1.

from Jerusalem and that his father, Cushi, was a prophet.

Zephaniah's five-member genealogy[18] draws attention to the earliest member, Hezekiah, who is likely the godly reformer and thirteenth king of Judah who reigned from 729–686 BC (see 2 Kgs 18–20; Isa 36–39).[19] Some question this connection because the text does not name Hezekiah as "king," but this is probably because "Josiah" was already reigning. Furthermore, if the author referred to a different "Hezekiah," why would he include him in the genealogy at all and why does he not explicitly distinguish him from King Hezekiah? Finally, four generations could pass between Hezekiah (age twenty-five in 729, 2 Kgs 18:1) and Zephaniah (likely between twenty and thirty around 622 BC) given the early ages of fathers in Judah's royal house: Amon at age sixteen (2 Kgs 21:19; 22:1), Josiah at age fourteen (22:1; 23:36), and Jehoiakim at age eighteen (24:8). Even if we assume each man was twenty-five years old when he fathered his son, Zephaniah would be thirty-two in 622 BC.[20] It is chronologically probable, therefore, that the Hezekiah in the book's heading is the Judean king.

Such a connection with Hezekiah, the royal reformer, places the prophet's own role as spiritual and social reformer in context, perhaps even justifying his ministry.[21] The link with the royal family would also explain Zephaniah's awareness of both the royal court (1:8; 3:3–4) and the international scene (2:4–15) and establish his Judean royal heritage. Specifically, it highlights how God, in alignment with his Davidic kingdom promises (2 Sam 7:12–16), had preserved a faithful remnant in the Davidic line, even amid an age of spiritual darkness. The inclusion of God's name in three of Zephaniah's forefathers likely accents this generational faith: Gedaliah ("Yah[weh] is great"), Amariah ("Yah[weh] has spoken"), and Hezekiah ("Yah[weh] is my strength" or "Yah[weh] has strengthened me").

The only name of the five generations that is not theophoric (i.e., bearing God's name) is "Cushi" (כּוּשִׁי), Zephaniah's father, who may be identified with the great-grandfather of Jehudi (Jer 36:14), who served as a royal official during the reign of Jehoiakim (609–598 BC). The name appears related to the ethnic title "Cushite" (כּוּשִׁי) and the

---

18. Outside superscriptions to prophetic books, see 2 Chr 20:14 for a five-member genealogy; Jer 36:14 for four; Zech 1:1 for three; see also Tob. 1:1 for seven; and Bar 1:1 for six. For non-prophets, see Num 27:1 (//Josh 17:3); 1 Sam 1:1; 9:1.

19. For arguments that "Hezekiah" in Zeph 1:1 is indeed the godly reformer and thirteenth king of Judah who reigned from 729–686 BC (2 Kgs 18–20; Isa 36–39), see, e.g., J. M. P. Smith, "Book of Zephaniah," 182–83; Motyer, "Zephaniah," 898; David W. Baker, *Nahum, Habakkuk and Zephaniah: An Introduction and Commentary*, TOTC 27 (Downers Grove, IL: InterVarsity Press, 1988), 91; Robertson, *Books of Nahum, Habakkuk, and Zephaniah*, 253; Renz, *Books of Nahum, Habakkuk, and Zephaniah*, 455–57. Both Berlin and Sweeney review the question but make no conclusions (Berlin, *Zephaniah*, 65–66; Sweeney, *Zephaniah*, 48). Roberts, Ben Zvi, and Shepherd question the plausibility (Roberts, *Nahum, Habakkuk, and Zephaniah*, 166; Ben Zvi, *Book of Zephaniah*, 47; Shepherd, *Commentary on the Book of the Twelve*, 353). Shepherd asserts that the extended genealogy is there only to distinguish the prophet from others bearing his name, but this insufficiently accounts for the fact

that Zephaniah is the only prophet to include a five-member genealogy. While Zephaniah's spelling of "Hezekiah" (חִזְקִיָּה) is used of figures other than the king (see 1 Chr 3:23; Neh 7:21; 10:18[17]), and while his spelling is not identical to the spelling of the king's name in other prophetic superscriptions (יְחִזְקִיָּהוּ in Isa 1:1; cf. 2 Kgs 20:10; Jer 15:4; יְחִזְקִיָּה in Hos 1:1; Mic 1:1), it is a common spelling of the king's name elsewhere (e.g., 2 Kgs 18:1, 10, 13–16), along with חִזְקִיָּהוּ (e.g., 16:20; 18:9, 17, 19, 22, 29–32, 37), which always refers to the king except in 2 Chr 28:12.

20. For example, if Hezekiah fathered Amariah in 729, and he fathered Gedaliah in 704, and he fathered Cushi in 679, and he fathered Zephaniah in 654, Zephaniah could have been thirty-two in 622 BC. Manasseh fathering Amon at age forty-five (21:1, 19) explains why Josiah is but three generations from Hezekiah. Cf. J. M. P. Smith, "Book of Zephaniah," 183; Gene Rice, "The African Roots of the Prophet Zephaniah," *JRT* 36 (1979): 21–22; Berlin, *Zephaniah*, 68–69; contrast R. Smith, *Micah–Malachi*, 125.

21. Cf. Berlin, *Zephaniah*, 65.

geographical designation "Cush" (כּוּשׁ), which stand prominently in the book's respective declarations of punishment and restoration (Zeph 2:12; 3:10).[22] Cush was the center of black Africa in the region of modern Sudan (cf. Jer 13:23) and one of the most southern and western kingdoms of the OT age (see Esth 1:1).[23] Because the mention of the "Cushites" (Zeph 2:12) and "Cush" (3:10) are both distinctive in the flow of Zephaniah's oracle, the author is likely anticipating the book's international restoration theme by including "Cushi" in the superscription (see esp. Zeph 2:9, 11; 3:9–10; cf. 2:12).

We know that a colony of Cushite mercenaries was located in Gerar of the northern Negeb between the tenth and eighth centuries BC (see 1 Chr 4:39–41; 2 Chr 12:3; 14:9–15; 21:16).[24] We also know that Jerusalem's leaders worked with Cushites (2 Sam 18:21; Jer 38:7; 39:16)[25] and that Judah made political alliances with the nation of Cush, including one in the period prior to the birth of Zephaniah's father (Isa 18:1–2; 20:5–6; 37:9//2 Kgs 19:9).[26] Zephaniah, therefore, was likely biracial, bearing both Judean royal and Cushite ancestry (potentially via Cushi's mother, Gedaliah's wife).[27]

---

22. Gene Rice writes of the name "Cushi": "As in the case of Gadi, King Menahem's father (2 Kgs 15:14), Hachmonie (1 Chr 27:32; cf. Job 32:2,6; Jer 25:32), it is a gentilic that has become a proper name. Just as Buzi transparently designates a man of Buz, or a Buzite, so Cushi inevitably suggests a man of Cush, or a Cushite" (Rice, "African Roots of the Prophet Zephaniah," 22). Rather than simply meaning "Cushite," "Cushi" could also endearingly mean something like "my black one" or "my piece of Cush," thus expressing his parents' delight in this part of their son's ethnic heritage.

23. See Robert Houston Smith, "Ethiopia (Place)," *ABD* 2:665–67; Donald B. Redford, "Kush (Place)," *ABD* 4:109–11; J. Daniel Hays, "The Cushites: A Black Nation in Ancient History," *BSac* 153 (1996): 270–80; cf. J. Daniel Hays, *From Every People and Nation: A Biblical Theology of Race*, NSBT 14 (Downers Grove, IL: InterVarsity Press, 2003), 87–103. Properly speaking, it is only in the Hellenistic period that the title "Ethiopia" was associated with ancient Cush; more properly, Cush, known from Egyptian material as "Nubia," was the most significant black African nation and was centered south of Egypt in modern Sudan (Roger W. Anderson Jr., "Zephaniah Ben Cushi and Cush of Benjamin: Traces of Cushite Presence in Syria-Palestine," in *The Pitcher Is Broken: Memorial Essays for Gösta W. Ahlström*, ed. Steven W. Holloway and Lowell K. Handy, JSOTSup 190 [Sheffield: Sheffield Academic, 1995], 60).

24. See W. F. Albright, "Egypt and the Early History of the Negeb," *JPOS* 4 (1924): 146–48. For alternative views regarding the identification of these groups, see Robert D. Haak, "'Cush' in Zephaniah," in *The Pitcher Is Broken: Memorial Essays for Gösta W. Ahlström*, ed. Steven W. Holloway and Lowell K. Handy, JSOTSup 190 (Sheffield: Sheffield Academic, 1995), 238–51.

25. Cf. Ps 7:1; Jer 36:14, 21, 23. See Gene Rice, "Two Black Contemporaries of Jeremiah," *JRT* 32 (1975): 101–8. In contrast to Berlin (Berlin, *Zephaniah*, 67), I see no reason why "Cush, the Benjamite" in Ps 7:1 could not be both a personal name given by his father and *also* a signal of a biracial heritage.

26. Rice, "African Roots of the Prophet Zephaniah," 25–27. Cf. Isa 30:1–7; 31:1–3 (where "Egypt" likely refers to the Twenty-fifth [Cushite] Egyptian Dynasty); Ezek 29:16; 30:5. There are two other potentially significant connections between ancient Cush and Israel's leadership. First, Moses married a "Cushite" woman (כֻּשִׁית; Num 12:1) (see David Tuesday Adamo, "The African Wife of Moses: An Examination of Numbers 12:1–9," *African Theological Journal* 18.3 (1989): 230–37; J. Daniel Hays, "A Biblical Perspective on Interracial Marriage," *CTR* 6.2 (2009): 12–19). For the alternative view that the text in Numbers is more properly read "Cushanite" (כֻּשָׁנִית), which would allow the wife mentioned in Num 12:1 to actually be Zipporah the "Midianite" (Exod 2:15–22; cf. Hab 3:7), see W. F. Albright, *Archaeology and the Religion of Israel*, OTL (Louisville: Westminster John Knox, 2006), 205n49; Martin Noth, *Numbers: A Commentary*, OTL (Philadelphia: Westminster, 1968), 98; Smith, "Ethiopia (Place)," *ABD* 2:666. Second, the Queen of Sheba visited Solomon to discern his wisdom (1 Kgs 10:1; 2 Chr 9:1a), and the OT associates Cush with both Seba and Sheba (Gen 10:7; 1 Chr 1:9; cf. Ps 72:10). Jesus referred to her as "the queen of the South" (Matt 12:42; Luke 11:31), Josephus called her the "Queen of Egypt and Ethiopia" (*A.J.* 8.165–75), and Ethiopia's national saga titled *Kebra Nagast* ("Glory of the Kings") claims her as their former queen and asserts that her visit to Solomon resulted in her adopting his religion and even having a son by him. Most scholars today place Sheba in the southwest corner of the Arabian Peninsula, and its placement just across from ancient Cush's known center raises the possibility that the Cushite kingdom stretched across the Red Sea into this region. See Stephen D. Ricks, "Sheba, Queen of," *ABD* 5:1170–71.

27. So Rice, "African Roots of the Prophet Zephaniah," 21–31. cf. Anderson Jr., "Zephaniah Ben Cushi and Cush of Benjamin," 45–70; Robert A. Bennett, "The Book of Zephaniah: Introduction, Commentary, and Reflections," in *NIB*, ed. Leander E. Keck (Nashville: Abingdon, 1996), 659, 670–72;

Joseph Blenkinsopp agrees that "Cushi" is a gentilic proper name, but he proposes that the superscription's genealogy mentions King Hezekiah (1) to establish Zephaniah's necessary Jewish heritage as a YHWH prophet (see Deut 18:15, 18) and (2) to curb any potential concerns that "Cushi" linked Zephaniah with ancient Cush (see Amos 9:7).[28] Deuteronomy 23:7–8 insist that only third-generation Egyptians could enter YHWH's assembly, and Scripture commonly ties Egypt and Cush together. As such, in contrast to Blenkinsopp, the extended genealogy back to King Hezekiah may have served to substantiate Zephaniah's ministry as a YHWH-prophet even though his father was a Cushite.[29] Regardless, there seems no good reason why the prophet could not bear both Judean royal blood and a Cushite lineage, and the way the rest of the book highlights Cush supports this link in 1:1.

3. The Historical Context (1:1)

Zephaniah ministered in the days of "Josiah . . . Judah's king," who was Hezekiah's great-grandson. Josiah was Judah's last good king (2 Kgs 23:25), who assumed the throne at age eight after the murder of his wicked father Amon (642–640 BC). During his three-decade reign (640–609 BC), Josiah accomplished religious reform by reestablishing YHWH worship at the Jerusalem temple (2 Kgs 22:1–23:30; cf. 2 Chr 34:3–35:19). It is not clear at what point in Josiah's reign that Zephaniah prophesied. However, numerous factors suggest Zephaniah ministered before Josiah's reform movement had fully begun but after he initially cleansed the land of religious defilement in 628 BC and found the Torah Scroll in 622 BC (see Zephaniah's Date and Occasion in the introduction). We know that Josiah explicitly targeted many of the problems Zephaniah confronted (e.g., the eradication of practices and persons associated with "Baal" worship, Zeph 1:4–5 with 2 Kgs 23:4–5, 10, 24).[30] Hence, following the horrific reigns of Manasseh (696–642 BC) and Amon (642–640 BC) (see 2 Kgs 21), Zephaniah probably assisted Josiah's reformation.

Canonical and Theological Significance

Consider Some Implications of the Book of Zephaniah Being "YHWH's Word"

Since the book of Zephaniah comes from God, we must take it seriously and surrender to its authority. The book distinguishes itself from the utterances of any other deity or mere human since it is "YHWH's word." The Judeans preserved the book as Scripture because they recognized that Jerusalem's 586 BC destruction validated the prophet's message (Deut 18:21–22). Since then, the punishment and restoration

---

Hays, "The Cushites," 396–409. Anderson provides the most detailed engagement with the primary and secondary sources, but he also views the biblical data as less important than the Egyptian sources for shaping a proper understanding a Cushite presence within the Levant in the days of Zephaniah.

28. Joseph Blenkinsopp, *A History of Prophecy in Israel*, 2nd ed. (Louisville: Westminster John Knox, 1996), 113, 263n1.

29. Cf. J. Heller, "Zephanjas Ahnenreihe: Eine Redaktionsgeschichtliche Bemerkung Zu Zeph. I.1," *VT* 21 (1971): 102–4.

30. Cf. 2 Kgs 21:3, 5–6, 21.

that God wrought through Christ's death and resurrection and the church's growth inaugurated the ultimate day of YHWH and only reinforced the book's canonicity. Zephaniah was among those who "spoke from God while being carried along by the Holy Spirit" (2 Pet 1:21). Though the original audience of the prophet was Judah in the days of Josiah, since his words are in the canon of Scripture, his primary audience is those in every age who now hear the words in this context instructing them in a way that nurtures endurance and encouragement leading to hope (Rom 15:4; cf. 1 Pet 1:10–12).

Zephaniah is part of the Christian Scriptures that Jesus designated as God's "word" (Mark 7:13; 12:36), viewed as authoritative (Matt 4:3–4, 7, 10; 23:1–3), and called people to embrace in order to avoid doctrinal error and hell (Mark 12:24; Luke 16:28–31; 24:25; John 5:46–47). As the "word" of YHWH, the book is "true" (1 Kgs 17:24; Ps 119:160), "upright" (Ps 33:4), a guide (Ps 119:105), fixed and lasting (Ps 119:89; Isa 40:8), and powerful (Ps 147:18; 148:8; Heb 1:3). Zephaniah is one of "all the prophets" through whom God foretold the good news of Christ (Acts 3:18, 24; 10:43).[31] These predictions "cannot be nullified" (John 10:35) and will be completely fulfilled (Matt 5:17–18; Luke 24:44; Acts 13:32–33). Because we can only enjoy life by obeying God's word (Matt 4:4; cf. Deut 8:3; 32:47) and by encountering Jesus (John 6:35; 11:25), Zephaniah's message is imperative for the church. The question for us, therefore, is, "Will we listen?" Will we glorify God by heeding the Savior's exhortation to pursue him together in hope both to avoid punishment and to enjoy salvation?

Celebrate How God Uses and Preserves a Remnant Without Partiality

Here we rejoice in two truths. First, Zeph 1:1 orients sinners to treasure God as one who redeems and calls people without discrimination (Deut 10:17–18; Acts 10:34–35). Zephaniah was likely biracial, being a descendant of the black African Cushites and Judah's Jewish royal line. Therefore, God chose to write some of his Bible through a man with African-Israelite descent in anticipation of his Babel-reversing restoration blessings (Zeph 3:9–10; cf. Gen 11:7–9) that would culminate in an international bride of worshipers (Rev 5:9–10; 7:9–10; cf. Gen 12:3; 22:18). As a Caucasian American growing up after the Holocaust of World War II with children adopted from Africa and in a land that has often practiced racial prejudice and violence against African Americans, I celebrate God's beautiful purpose in choosing Zephaniah. Furthermore, within Zephaniah's book, YHWH willingly redeems any who call on his name. YHWH could have brought immediate punishment on the rebels from Judah and the world. Instead, he sent a prophet to motivate sinful people to repent by recalling the covenant curses and blessings. Indeed, our God is

---

31. See also Luke 24:27, 46–47.

"compassionate and gracious, slow to anger, and abounding in steadfast love and faithfulness" (Exod 34:6).

Second, Zeph 1:1 displays YHWH's commitment to perpetuate hope in the Davidic kingdom promises. Zephaniah's link to Judah's King Hezekiah places the prophet in the line of David to whom YHWH promised an everlasting throne (2 Sam 7:16). Zephaniah's own name and the names of three of his forefathers include in them an abbreviated form of the name YHWH. These names likely bear witness to a multigenerational trust in God as provider, protector, and ultimate fulfiller of his kingdom promises for Israel and all nations (Gen 12:3; Zeph 3:10). Despite Manasseh and Amon's sinister reigns (see 2 Kgs 21:1–26; cf. Jer 7:31), some fathers and mothers perpetuated hope in YHWH's promises. Like Moses, they regarded "the reproach for the sake of Christ as greater wealth than the treasures of Egypt" (Heb 11:26). They also heeded God's call to pass on a passion for YHWH's supremacy to the next generation (Deut 6:7, 20–25; cf. Judg 2:10; Ps 78:4–8). Today we live in the age of fulfillment, and Jesus continues to capture the affections of men and women, boys and girls from every tongue, tribe, and people group.

PART II

Zephaniah 1:2–18

The Setting of the Savior's Invitation to Satisfaction: *A Call to Revere YHWH in View of His Coming Day*

Main Idea of Zephaniah 1:2–18

Mankind in general and Judah in particular must revere YHWH in view of the gravity of his impending judgment.

Literary Context of Zephaniah 1:2–18

The body of the book presents itself as the prophet's single, unified oracle (Zeph 1:2–3:20b), which the superscription in 1:1 tells us, constitutes God's very "word." The initial section addressed here (1:2–18) provides the setting for the Savior King's invitation to satisfaction that shapes the heart of the book's message (2:1–3:20). To help motivate his listeners patiently to pursue YHWH as the means to the satisfied life (2:1, 3; 3:8, 14), Zephaniah opens by calling for divine reverence in view of YHWH's coming punishment against Judah and the world (1:2–18).[1] As Sweeney notes, by describing the consequences that will befall the corrupt and rebellious, Zephaniah seeks to persuade his yet unnamed audience "to distinguish its behavior from the wicked who will be punished and thus identify with the righteous."[2] Only those who

---

1. Sweeney too believes Zeph 1:2–18 "functions as an introduction to the formal parenetic address in 2:1–3:20" by preparing "the audience to think of the Day of YHWH as a time when YHWH will unleash punishment against the wicked . . .

[and] to respond positively to the exhortation to seek YHWH in 2:1–3:20" (Sweeney, *Zephaniah*, 51).

2. Sweeney, "Form-Critical Reassessment," 388–408, here 393.

70   *Part II: The Setting of the Savior's Invitation to Satisfaction*

pause to take seriously how their sin has offended God's holiness have the possibility of delighting in salvation.

We will see that the autumn Israelite Feast of Ingathering/Booths at the transition of the agricultural calendar (Exod 23:16; 34:22) supplies a likely historical context for Zephaniah's oracle. The prophet utilizes not only the harvest imagery (Zeph 1:2–3; 2:1–2; cf. 3:8, 18) but also the sacrifices related to the temple altar dedication (1:7, 18; cf. 3:8) to highlight the end of one era and the beginning of a new one.

I. The Superscription of the Savior's Invitation to Satisfaction (1:1)

➡ **II. The Setting of the Savior's Invitation to Satisfaction: A Call to Revere YHWH in View of His Coming Day (1:2–18)**

III. The Substance of the Savior's Invitation to Satisfaction: Charges to Seek YHWH Together and to Wait (2:1–3:20b)

     III.1 Stage 1: The Appeal to Seek YHWH Together to Avoid Punishment (2:1–3:7)

     III.2 Stage 2: The Appeal to Wait for YHWH to Enjoy Salvation (3:8–20b)

IV. The Subscription of the Savior's Invitation to Satisfaction (3:20c)

Structure and Outline of Zephaniah 1:2–18

Following the superscription in 1:1, the asyndetic אָסֹף אָסֵף ("I will surely gather") in 1:2 opens the book's body. Scholars disagree whether the first main section runs through 1:18 or 2:3. Those arguing for 2:3 do so for two reasons. First, the theme of the day of YHWH that is so evident in 1:2–18 (see esp. 1:4–6, 8–13) still controls 2:1–3. Second, the mention of the Philistines in 2:4 leads some to see a topic shift away from judgment on Judah (1:2–2:3) to punishment of the foreign nations (2:4–15).[3] However, these two arguments are not persuasive. The note of coming punishment on the broader world occurs first in 1:2–3 and 1:14–20 rather than 2:4, and it is YHWH's day against both Judah and the foreign nations that shapes the "decree" (חֹק) of punishment in 2:2. For this reason, the mention of foreign nations in 2:4–15 is not as distinctive as some assert. Also, the causal "for" (כִּי) in 2:4 suggests a close relationship between 2:4 and what precedes it. Thus, interpreters should not understand 2:4 to indicate a new major unit.

Other good arguments exist for seeing the first main section running through

---

3. E.g., Roberts, *Nahum, Habakkuk, and Zephaniah*, 162–63; Motyer, "Zephaniah," 162–63; Vlaardingerbroek, *Zephaniah*, v–vi, 25–27.

1:18. The group of imperatives in 2:1 bear no syntactic link with what precedes and, therefore, mark 2:1 as initiating the main hortatory section of the oracle. This exhortation section continues through the imperatives in 2:3 and 3:8 to the book's closure in 3:20. Additionally, only at 2:1 is a particular audience addressed. Though YHWH's wrath and its effects appear in 1:2–18, only at 2:1 and following does the "day" of YHWH serve as explicit motivation for change. As Floyd notes: "The point of 1:2–18 is to realize what the nature of the present situation is. Ch. 2 begins to deal with what should then be done and also explains why."[4] It is best, therefore, to treat 1:2–18 as the oracle's introduction, which provides a motivational setting for the subsequent primary parenesis.[5] (For an expansion on these arguments, see the discussion of Structure and Outline in the Part III macrounit overview of 2:1–3:20.)

As noted, in 1:2–18 Zephaniah operates as YHWH's prophetic messenger who urges his audience to revere God in the light of the nearness and nature of his day of wrath. Throughout the section, first-person verbs mark YHWH's voice as primary at 1:2–6, 8–13, 17, whereas the prophet's voice is evident where the text refers to YHWH with third-person subjects or verbs (1:7, 18) or where one such text is echoed (1:14–16 echoing 1:7).[6] Thus YHWH and Zephaniah have three speeches that alternate back and forth (Y→Z→Y→Z→Y→Z).

Figure Part II.1: YHWH's vs. Zephaniah's Speeches in Zephaniah 1:2–18	
YHWH	**Zephaniah**
1:2–6	1:7
1:8–13	1:14–16
1:17	1:18

Nevertheless, the lack of introductory speech formulas and the sustained coherence and cohesion of the whole indicate that the frequent shift in person neither governs the flow of the argument nor distinguishes levels of authority. The dramatic antiphonal character switching constitutes a single "word" (1:1) *as if* a single voice is speaking. (For further discussion, see Critiquing Alternative Proposals to Zephaniah's Macrostructure and Thought Flow in the introduction.)

---

4. Floyd, *Minor Prophets, Part 2*, 186.

5. Cf. Sweeney, "Form-Critical Reassessment," 392–93.

6. See also Wendland and Clark, "Zephaniah," 5–7. They note that because the third-person references to YHWH in Zeph 1:5–6 are still clearly part of God's speech begun in 1:2, "the occurrence of third-person references to YHWH is not diagnostic of an utterance of the prophet except when they happen to occur in the subject position (1:7b; 2:11; 3:5, 15, 17)" (ibid., 6). As such, the third-person references to God in 1:5,

6, 8, 12, 17; 2:5, 9, 10; 3:8, 9, 12, 20 do not cancel the fact that YHWH is the primary speaker in those texts. Wendland and Clark attribute 1:11 to Zephaniah in view of its imperative plus vocative structure, which they parallel to 2:1, 3; 3:14 (Wendland and Clark, "Zephaniah," 7). However, as the commentary notes, 1:11 functions quite differently from the other texts; without other formal signals, it is best seen as continuing YHWH's speech act begun in 1:8.

The section has two units, the first (1:2–6) supplying a framework and context for the subsequent call to revere YHWH (1:7–18). The oracle opens in 1:2–6 with predictive discourse announcing an impending punishment that will impact the whole world (1:2–3), including Judah and Jerusalem (1:4–5). Verse 7 then designates this time of wrath as "the day of YHWH" (יוֹם יְהוָה), and the following verses repeat the term "day" (יוֹם), thus signaling the thematic unity of the whole (1:8–10, 14–16, 18). The use of the onomatopoeic exclamatory Hebrew interjection הַס ("Hush!/Silence!") in 1:7a signals the start of a new unit and shifts the discourse from anticipation to a form of directive speech, urging the audience to revere God. The reason for this dreadful silence is then unpacked, first by detailing YHWH's sanctions against Jerusalem (1:7b–13) and then by expounding the destruction that awaits the whole earth (1:14–18). While many scholars treat 1:2–18 simply as announcing and describing YHWH's coming wrath, Floyd is correct that "this theme . . . is completely subordinate to the hortatory elements of the text."[7] The announcement of coming devastation in 1:2–6 provides a context for the appeal to hushed reverence in 1:7a, and the causal conjunction "for/because" (כִּי) in 1:7b shows that the following announcement of God's imminent day of punishment serves only to motivate the silent awe for which 1:7a calls.[8]

Each of the two units in 1:2–18 declares a coming destruction of the world in general and Jerusalem in particular. In chiastic fashion (A–B–B′–A′)[9] the global punishment (1:2–3, 14–18) encircles the local punishment (1:4–6, 7b–13), stressing that none will escape God's wrath. Judah and the world must take seriously that YHWH's fury against the wicked is inescapable.[10]

---

7. Floyd, *Minor Prophets, Part 2*, 185.

8. While the interjection הַס ("Hush!") signals that directive speech is the primary discourse-type that governs 1:7–18, the lack of a true imperative distinguishes this material from what follows in 2:1–3:20, wherein imperatives in 2:1, 3 and 3:8, 14 set the section apart as the primary hortatory portion of the oracle. Zephaniah 1:2–18 prepares the reader to hear the book's main exhortations that follow (see Structure and Literary Form at 1:7–18).

9. So too Floyd, *Minor Prophets, Part 2*, 186.

10. For a synthesis of the message of Zeph 1:1–18, see De-Rouchie, "Revering God," forthcoming.

Zephaniah 1:2–6

A. The Context of the Call to Revere YHWH: Coming Punishment

Main Idea of the Passage

YHWH commits to gather and punish the idolatrous peoples of the wider world in general (1:2–3) and of Judah and Jerusalem in particular (1:4–6).

Literary Context

Following the superscription in 1:1, Zephaniah begins his prophecy with YHWH's promise to judge the entire earth (1:2–3), including Judah and Jerusalem (1:4–6)—all because of rampant wickedness and idolatrous rebellion. The unit in 1:2–6 provides the context for God's call to revere him in view of his coming day of wrath (1:7–18). The asyndetic Hebrew interjection הַס ("Hush!"; 1:7a) marks this call. Together, 1:2–18 establish the setting of the parenetic heart of the book (2:1–3:20), which is an urgent exhortation to pursue YHWH in hope.

II. The Setting of the Savior's Invitation to Satisfaction: A Call to Revere YHWH in View of His Coming Day (1:2–18)

→ **A. The Context of the Call to Revere YHWH: Coming Punishment (1:2–6)**
    1. Global Punishment Against the Rebels of Humanity (1:2–3)
    2. Local Punishment Against the Rebels of Judah and Jerusalem (1:4–6)
  B. The Content of the Call to Revere YHWH (1:7–18)

Translation and Exegetical Outline

(See pages 75–76.)

Structure and Literary Form[1]

The opening unit (1:2–6) announces YHWH's intent to punish the wicked based on a list of indictments.[2] The unit has two parts, distinguished by content and form. Concerning content, the discourse begins broadly with YHWH announcing global punishment against the world's rebels (1:2–3). The text's focus then narrows, addressing the local punishment of Judah and Jerusalem's rebels (1:4–6).[3] The repetition of the phrase "to cut off" (כרת) in 1:3c and 1:4b also signals an A–B–A′–B′ topical pattern within the unit, with both parts displaying a progression of two parallel divine actions:

Part 1: "Gathering" (1:2–3b) → "cutting" (1:3c)
Part 2: "Stretching out" (1:4a) → "cutting" (1:4b)

Concerning form, the unit's lack of syntactic connection with what precedes (i.e., the asyndeton at the head of 1:2) sets it apart from the introductory superscription in 1:1. Additionally, the exclamation "Hush!" (הַס) at the head of 1:7a distinguishes 1:2–6 from what follows. Furthermore, the oracular formula "the utterance of YHWH" (נְאֻם־יְהוָה)[4] at the end of 1:2 reinforces the unit's opening, and its repetition at the end of 1:3c climaxes and closes the first of the two parallel parts.[5]

Six first-person verbs all point to YHWH as the main speaker in the unit. The initial three are *yiqtols* (1:2–3b), and the next three are *weqatals* (1:3c–4b). Though God addresses himself in third-person in 1:5–6, he remains the primary speaker, for the prophet's voice is shown primary only where third-person references to YHWH occur in the subject position (e.g., 1:7b; 2:11; 3:5, 15, 17).[6] Nevertheless, the oracular formula "the utterance of YHWH" in 1:2, 3c reminds the reader that the entire message comes through Zephaniah,[7] who operates as the covenant ambassador heralding the message of the great King (1:1; cf. 1:15). Thus, the divine and human voices speak as one.[8]

---

1. This section was first published in Jason S. DeRouchie, "Confronting Idolatry in Zephaniah 1:4–6 and the Twenty-First Century," *MJT* 22.2 (2023): 19–24.

2. See Sweeney, *Isaiah 1–39*, 529–31.

3. The same shift from a global perspective to a focus on God's people in seen in at least Amos 1:2–2:16 and Mic 1:2–16.

4. Sweeney, *Isaiah 1–39*, 546.

5. Wendland and Clark, "Zephaniah," 6. The oracular for-

mulas in 1:2–3 do not distinguish oracular from non-oracular speech (Floyd, *Minor Prophets, Part 2*, 191).

6. Wendland and Clark, "Zephaniah," 6; contra Sweeney, *Zephaniah*, 56.

7. So too Sweeney, *Zephaniah*, 56, 58.

8. Thus, the prophet's personality is implicitly acknowledged even when he speaks words as if from the very mouth of God.

Zephaniah 1:2–6[1]

II. The Setting of the Savior's Invitation to Satisfaction: A Call to Revere YHWH in View of His Coming Day (1:2–18)

A. The Context of the Call to Revere YHWH: Coming Punishment (1:2–6)

  1. Global Punishment against the Rebels of Humanity (1:2–3)

    a. YHWH's Ingathering of Everything for Judicial Assessment (1:2–3b)

      (1) The Declaration of the Ingathering (1:2)

      (2) The Details of the Ingathering (1:3a–b)

        (a) Human and Beast (1:3a)

        (b) Bird and Fish and Idols (1:3b)

    b. YHWH's Punishment of Rebellious Humanity (1:3c)

	Hebrew	English
2 [Y]	אָסֹף אָסֵף כֹּל מֵעַל פְּנֵי הָאֲדָמָה נְאֻם־יְהוָה:	I will surely gather everything from on the face of the ground—the utterance of YHWH.
3a	אָסֵף אָדָם וּבְהֵמָה	I will gather human and beast;
3b	אָסֵף עוֹף־הַשָּׁמַיִם וּדְגֵי הַיָּם וְהַמַּכְשֵׁלוֹת אֶת־הָרְשָׁעִים	I will gather the bird of the heavens and the fish of the sea and the stumbling blocks with the wicked.
3c	וְהִכְרַתִּי אֶת־הָאָדָם מֵעַל פְּנֵי הָאֲדָמָה נְאֻם־יְהוָה:	And I will cut off humanity from on the face of the ground—the utterance of YHWH.

Continued on next page.

1. For information on the guidelines used for tracing the argument, see The Method in the introduction, pp. XX.

Continued from previous page.

			2. Local Punishment against the Rebels of Judah and Jerusalem (1:4–6)
4a	וְנָטִיתִי יָדִי עַל־יְהוּדָה וְעַל כָּל־יוֹשְׁבֵי יְרוּשָׁלָ͏ִם	So, I will stretch out my hand against Judah and against all the inhabitants of Jerusalem.	a. YHWH's Extension of His Hand against Judah and Jerusalem (1:4a)
			b. YHWH's Punishment of Remaining Paganism in Judah and Jerusalem (1:4b–6)
4b	וְהִכְרַתִּי מִן־הַמָּקוֹם הַזֶּה אֶת־שְׁאָר הַבַּעַל	And I will cut off from this place the remnant of the Baal—	(1) The Declaration and Object of Punishment (1:4b)
			(2) The Composition of the Object of Punishment (1:4c–6)
[4c]	אֶת־שֵׁם הַכְּמָרִים עִם־הַכֹּהֲנִים:	the name of the illegitimate priests with the priests,	(a) The Identities of the Illegitimate Priests with the Priests (1:4c)
[5a]	וְאֶת־הַמִּשְׁתַּחֲוִים עַל־הַגַּגּוֹת לִצְבָא הַשָּׁמָיִם	and those who bow down on the roofs to the host of the heavens,	(b) The Star-Worshipers (1:5a)
[5b]	וְאֶת־הַמִּשְׁתַּחֲוִים הַנִּשְׁבָּעִים לַיהוָה וְהַנִּשְׁבָּעִים בְּמַלְכָּם:	and those who bow down, who swear to YHWH but swear by their king,	(c) The Syncretistic Hypocrites (1:5b)
[6]	וְאֶת־הַנְּסוֹגִים מֵאַחֲרֵי יְהוָה וַאֲשֶׁר לֹא־בִקְשׁוּ אֶת־יְהוָה וְלֹא דְרָשֻׁהוּ:	and those who turn away from YHWH and who have neither sought YHWH nor inquired of him.	(d) The Self-Ruled, Self-Dependent (1:6)

The common *yiqtol* plus *weqatal* pattern in Zeph 1:2–6 marks the discourse as anticipatory.[9] Part one (1:2–3) marks the predictive context by an indicative *yiqtol* in non-first position (1:2) that announces YHWH's intent to gather everything for judicial assessment, adding emphasis at the end using the oracular formula. But before proclaiming the divine punishment in 1:3c, two asyndetic *yiqtol* clauses (1:3a–b) explicate YHWH's gathering in 1:2. He gathers human and beast (1:3a) and then bird and fish and idols (1:3b). The *weqatal* in 1:3c then announces the consequence of the worldwide ingathering, building on the initial action stated in 1:2 and concluding part one with another use of the oracular formula.[10] After stating this global perspective, part two continues with two *weqatal* clauses detailing how God's punishment against the world will also reach Jerusalem. In the first clause, God declares that he will extend his strong hand even against Judah (1:4a). In the second, he notes what this means: he will destroy every hint of Baal worship in the land (1:4b–6).

This targeting of a holdout of Baal followers is the first in a complex collection of direct objects in 1:4–6. The definite direct object marker אֶת־ fronts each object, but some object markers lack the Hebrew connector וֹ (gloss "and"). When two or more adjacent noun phrases are linked by וֹ, the phrases bear equal syntactic value and function (e.g., a compound subject or direct object). In contrast, the lack of connection (i.e., asyndeton) marks the second in apposition to the first.[11]

The above translation of 1:4–6 indicates that there is one primary direct object that YHWH promises to "cut off"—"the remnant of the Baal," which is signaled by the definite direct object marker (אֶת־) in 1:4b. In the series of four more object markers that follow, the first (1:4c) is asyndetic, and then this is conjoined to the following three (1:5–6) by the repeated connector "and" (וֹ). The resulting pattern is: אֶת . . . . וְאֶת . . . וְאֶת . . . וְאֶת . . . The residue of Baal worship still in the land is defined by four different, though at times overlapping, groups: (1) various priests *and* (2) star worshipers *and* (3) syncretistic oath takers *and* (4) apostate rebels, including those who fail to pursue YHWH in any way. Most translations skew this pattern by *adding* connection where it is not present and/or by *removing* connection where it is present, thus altering the prophet's meaning. Of the translations consulted, Young's Literal Translation (1898) alone represents the MT precisely, following this pattern: Ø→Ø→and→and→and. Every other version alters the meaning in one of five ways:

---

9. Duane A. Garrett and Jason S. DeRouchie, *A Modern Grammar for Biblical Hebrew* (Nashville: Broadman & Holman, 2009), 312–14; DeRouchie, *How to Understand and Apply*; cf. Robert E. Longacre, *Joseph—A Story of Divine Providence: A Text Theoretical and Textlinguistic Analysis of Genesis 37 and 39–48*, 2nd ed. (Winona Lake, IN: Eisenbrauns, 2003), 105–10.

10. Sweeney skews this unit's structure by failing to see that (1) the asyndeton (i.e., lack of connection) at 1:3a–b can signal explication, and (2) the וֹ (*waw*) of the *weqatal* in 1:3c connects to 1:2 rather than 1:3b (Sweeney, *Zephaniah*, 62).

11. For an overview of the role of *waw* and asyndeton in the OT, see DeRouchie, *How to Understand and Apply*, 103–9.

Part II: The Setting of the Savior's Invitation to Satisfaction

Figure 2.1: Translational Patterns in Zephaniah 1:4–6		
MT	Ø→Ø→waw→waw→waw	A single direct object with four-part compound appositive (MT; cf. YLT [1898])
	Pattern	**Meaning (Versions)**
1.	Ø→and→and→and→and	A five-part compound direct object (LXX, Geneva Bible [1599], Douay-Rheims [1610], KJV [1611], Webster Bible [1833], RV [1885], ASV [1901], UASV [2022], Bible in Basic English [1965], NASB20 [2020])
2.	Ø→and→Ø→Ø→Ø	A two-part compound direct object with three-part appositive in unlinked series (NRSVue [1989], ESV [2001], CEB [2011])
3.	Ø→Ø:→Ø→Ø→Ø	A single direct object with a single appositive, which itself is clarified by a three-part appositive in unlinked series (NKJV [1982], WEB [1997], NIV [2011])
4.	Ø→Ø:→Ø→Ø→and	Same as #3 but with last member of three-part appositive conjoined (NET [1996])
5.	Ø→Ø→Ø→Ø→and	Unclear, but potentially a single direct object with a four-part appositive with only the last member conjoined (CSB [2016])

Interpreters most commonly consider "the remnant of the Baal" and "the names of the illegitimate priests with priests" as two *different* groups, with some translations treating the star worshipers, syncretistic oath takers, and rebels as descriptive of the religious leaders (e.g., NRSVue, ESV, CEB) and others viewing them as additional groups (e.g., LXX, KJV, NASB20). Other interpreters rightly recognize that the various priests describe the Baal-followers, but then they view the last three clusters as identifying the makeup of the religious leaders (NKJV, NIV, NET). In contrast to these approaches, the prophet views "the remnant of Baal" as the larger category and the four following clusters as the sub-categories that shape the overarching residue of Baal-influence in Jerusalem. Baal's sway was affecting far more in Jerusalem than just the priests, and YHWH's indictment was against not only the cultic heads but also everyone who worships creation, lives hypocritically, or fails to depend wholly on YHWH.

Explanation of the Text

1. Global Punishment Against the Rebels of Humanity (1:2–3)

Zephaniah's oracle opens with a threat of encroaching judgment that will result in mankind's global destruction. After a comprehensive judicial assessment in Zephaniah 1:2–3b, God declares the resulting punishment for all the wicked of humanity. Three elements highlight the passage's unity: (1) the four-fold repetition of the consonants אסף (1:2–3b), (2) the wordplay between הָאָדָם ("humanity / the man," 1:3c) and הָאֲדָמָה ("the ground," 1:2, 3c), and

(3) the use of *inclusio*. The repeated prepositional phrase "from on the face of the ground" (מֵעַל פְּנֵי הָאֲדָמָה) and the repeated oracular formula—"the utterance of YHWH" (נְאֻם־יְהוָה)—mark this *inclusio*.[12] The oracular formulas provide an authoritative punch at the beginning of the message emphasizing the certainty of coming punishment (1:2a, 3c).[13]

a. YHWH's Ingathering of Everything for Judicial Assessment (1:2–3b)

(1) The Declaration of the Ingathering (1:2)

While the Hebrew phrase אָסֹף אָסֵף (ESV = "I will utterly sweep away") that initiates the oracle in 1:2 has often challenged interpreters, both forms likely derive from the root אסף ("to gather"), the first being a *qal* infinitive absolute and the second most likely a *hiphil yiqtol* first common singular with the I-א dropped, as is normal when two *alephs* come together.[14] The root אסף appears to have originated in the context of harvest. From early times the noun אָסִיף designates the Feast of "Ingathering" (Deut 16:13), which celebrates the completion of one agricultural cycle and the start of another (Exod 23:16; 34:22).[15] Sweeney notes that this feast bore three associations: (1) beginning the new agricultural year (cf. Lev 23:23–25;

Num 29:1–6); (2) celebrating the world's creation on the first of the seventh month and the Day of Atonement (Lev 23:26–32; Num 29:7–11); (3) asking forgiveness and seeking spiritual cleansing on the tenth day of the seventh month.[16] Roberts and Sweeney suggest that the Feast of Ingathering provides the most likely context for the prophet's proclamation.[17] This link would explain Zephaniah's choice and repetition of the verb אסף ("to gather") and connect directly to the book's theme of the day of YHWH, which stresses one era's end and another's beginning.[18]

The prophets use forms of the verb "to gather" (אסף) to speak of two eschatological realities. First, YHWH can "gather" the faithful remnant through a second exodus unto restoration (Mic 2:12).[19] Second, YHWH can "gather" the world's rabble for battle (Zech 14:2) and punishment (Isa 24:22; cf. Hos 4:3). This latter "ingathering" appears in Zeph 1:2–3b. Zephaniah 3:8 then anticipates God pouring out his wrath by reemploying "to gather" (אסף) in this same way, paralleling it with the verb "to assemble" (קבץ) (cf. Mic 4:11–12). Significantly, Zephaniah later uses the same two verbs to speak of the global "ingathering" for salvation (Zeph 3:18, 19–20).[20] This suggests that the various "ingatherings" are a single future event

---

12. Sweeney, *Isaiah 1–39*, 546.

13. Cf. De Vries, *From Old Revelation to New*, 63.

14. GKC, §68g–h. For a defense of this view, see DeRouchie, "YHWH's Future Ingathering in Zephaniah 1:2," 173–91.

15. Cf. Lev 23:33–43; Num 29:12–38; Deut 16:13–15. See Carl E. Armerding, "Festivals and Feasts," *DOTP* 300–313, esp. 311–12. The Feast of Ingathering became the major festival signaling the start of the civil new year.

16. Sweeney, *Zephaniah*, 108; cf. David J. A. Clines, "The Evidence for an Autumnal New Year in Pre-Exilic Israel," *JBL* 93 (1974): 22–40.

17. Roberts, *Nahum, Habakkuk, and Zephaniah*, 169; Sweeney, *Zephaniah*, 62.

18. See at Zeph 1:5, 7, and 3:18 for more comments on the book's potential "festival" background.

19. Cf. e.g., Isa 11:10–12; Jer 23:5–8; Zech 10:10–11; John 11:51–52.

20. Cf. Zeph 3:9–10; Mic 4:6. Zephaniah 3:18 contains interpretive challenge; see the commentary for my assessment and conclusions. Vlaardingerbroek rightly categorized this judgment as "eschatological" and as one that would affect "the whole creation" (Vlaardingerbroek, *Zephaniah*, 37), yet he interprets the language rhetorically and asserts that in Zeph 1:2–2:3 "there is actually nothing that points to a world judgment" (Vlaardingerbroek, *Zephaniah*, 50; cf. Renz, *Books of Nahum, Habakkuk, and Zephaniah*, 464). In contrast, nothing in Zephaniah's immediate historical context completely fulfills the universal scope of this part of his oracle.

with two purposes, both associated with the day of YHWH.[21]

The similar content and the repetition of "to gather" (אסף) in 1:2–3b and 3:8 suggest the two texts point to the same event. English translations often skew this link because interpreters read the repeated verb אָסֵף in 1:2–3b as the *hiphil yiqtol* first common singular of סוּף ("to bring to an end"), which when preceded by אָסֹף, the *qal* infinitive absolute of אסף, results in a combined meaning like "sweep away" (NRSVue, WEB, ESV, NIV, CSB), "consume" (KJV, ASV, NKJV), "remove" (NASB20, UASV), "destroy" (NET), or "take away" (BBE). However, normal Hebrew grammar does not allow for such a change in verbal root.[22] It seems more likely that Zephaniah is following the common pattern of strengthening the verbal sense of the *yiqtol* verb by preceding it with an infinitive absolute of the same root.[23]

This results in distinguishing God's act of "ingathering" in 1:2–3b from his "cutting off" in 1:3c. As in 3:8, where Zephaniah distinguishes God's assembling from his outpouring of wrath, so too in 1:2–3 he differentiates between the collection for punishment (1:2–3b) and the punishment itself (1:3c). Similarly, in the very next verses the prophet applies the ingathering unto judgment pattern to Judah and Jerusalem. Zephaniah 1:4a parallels the theme of ingathering by mentioning the "stretching out" of God's strong hand, and then 1:4b deals with the divine "cutting off" of the rebels.[24]

Zephaniah's "gathering" is comparable to reapers gathering or processing grapes or olives while removing the spoiled.[25] YHWH probably alludes to this harvest context when he promises to "surely gather" (אסף) his earthly creatures for judicial assessment (Zeph 1:2; cf. 3:8b, 18) and then to "cut off humanity from on the face of the ground" (1:3).[26]

A statement clarifying the covenantal action's scope accompanies the divine ingathering's initial announcement: God will draw together "everything from on the face of the ground" (1:2). The use of "ground" (אֲדָמָה) rather than "earth/land" (אֶרֶץ) recalls the original sphere of the curse (Gen 3:17–19) and adds to the harvest context. אֲדָמָה "designates agricultural land that sustains a sedentary population in contrast to barren land," whereas אֶרֶץ includes the latter (see e.g., Gen 2:5; 3:23; Isa 28:24).[27] The entire phrase "from on the face of the ground" (מֵעַל פְּנֵי הָאֲדָמָה; Zeph 1:2–3) consistently occurs in contexts of divine punishment (e.g., Exod 32:12; 1 Kgs 13:34; Amos 9:8).[28] It is possible that Zephaniah uses this phrase to echo the vast extent of the flood-judgment (Gen 6:7; 7:3–4, 23; 8:8), but the mention of "fish" (Zeph 1:3) expands the scope of YHWH's action,

---

21. Cf. Ezek 34:17, 20–22; Joel 4:12–16[3:12–16]; Mal 3:19–20[4:1–2]. See also Matt 3:12; 13:30, 40–42; 25:32–33.

22. GKC, §113w.

23. GKC, §113, l–r; *IBHS*, §35.3.1b; Joüon, §123d–q; *BHRG*, §20.2.1.

24. Vlaardingerbroek stands out in his affirmation, "It would seem more natural to assume that the verb [אסף in 1:2] denotes an act of bringing together to a specific place and with a specific purpose" (Vlaardingerbroek, *Zephaniah*, 49).

25. See the repeated use of אסף in Jer 8:13 with 2:21; 5:1, 10; 6:9. Holladay argues that Jer 8:13 builds off Zeph 1:2–3. See William L. Holladay, "Reading Zephaniah with a Concordance: Suggestions for a Redaction History," *JBL* 120 (2001): 672–73.

26. An associated use of the harvest imagery is where YHWH tramples his gathered grapes in a winepress of wrath (see Isa 63:3–6; Rev 14:14–20).

27. Michael A. Grisanti, "אֲדָמָה (*'ǎdāmâ* I)," *NIDOTTE* 1:271; for a more extended assessment see Daniel I. Block, "The Foundations of National Identity: A Study in Ancient Northwest Semitic Perceptions" (DPhil thesis, University of Liverpool, 1982), 300–19. Cf. Gen 3:17; 4:2–3, 12; Exod 23:19; 34:26; Deut 26:2, 10, 15; Isa 1:7; Jer 7:20.

28. Gen 4:14; Deut 6:15; 1 Kgs 9:7; Jer 28:16. While the prepositional phrase usually functions adverbially modifying explicit destruction verbs (as in Zeph 1:3c), such is not always the case in Zeph 1:2 and other texts (cf. Gen 8:8).

for the great deluge never explicitly targeted marine life. The prophet does not subvert, replace, or even qualify God's earlier promise never again to "strike down every living creature as I have done" (Gen 8:21).[29] Not only does YHWH later qualify his words by asserting, "Never again shall all flesh be cut off *by the waters of the flood*" (9:11; cf. Isa 54:9–10), but also in Zeph 1:2–3 he promises to "gather" *all* creatures but only to "cut off" mankind (cf. 1:18; 3:8).[30]

(2) The Details of the Ingathering (1:3a–b)

After his broad statement in 1:2 that he will gather "everything" (כֹּל), YHWH specifies in 1:3a–b what he means. Through two asyndetic explication clauses that begin with the verb אָסֵף ("I will gather"; cf. 1:2), he promises to "gather human and beast . . . the bird . . . and the fish . . . and the stumbling blocks with the wicked" (1:3a–b). The humans and beasts represent the animate land creatures, whereas the fish and birds represent animate sea and air creatures respectively (cf. Job 12:7–8; Ps 69:35[34]).[31] Zephaniah probably places mankind upfront to stress humanity's representational headship over creation (see Gen 1:26, 28; Ps 8:6–8). Additionally, his listing of the initial four

creatures in reverse order to their creation in Genesis (Gen 1:20–28; cf. Hos 4:3) probably implies "the reversal of creation."[32] That is, the ingathering of the various creatures prepares the way for the old age to give rise to the new.

The inclusion of the phrase "and the stumbling blocks with the wicked" (וְהַמַּכְשֵׁלוֹת אֶת־הָרְשָׁעִים) is unexpected and difficult, leading some to view it as a later gloss.[33] However, its unforeseen inclusion and contextual agreement with YHWH's judgment against rebellious humanity (cf. 1:18) supports its originality. The general meaning of the first word is "rubble" (Isa 3:6), but Ezekiel later speaks of idols as a "stumbling block" (using a related masculine noun מִכְשׁוֹל) to the house of Israel (Ezek 7:19–20; 14:3–4). This use fits the present context. By using the similar feminine plural noun (מַכְשֵׁלוֹת), Zephaniah likely refers to idols, which God promises to collect along with the sinful who worship them (cf. 2 Chr 28:23).[34]

The prophet's list of objects that God will gather, therefore, begins and ends with mankind, but here the text focuses only on a subset of the whole—"the wicked" (הָרְשָׁעִים). These are the covenant rebels who contrast with the righteous remnant that emerges in chapters 2–3. The next clause declares

---

29. Contra Watts, *Books of Joel, Obadiah, Jonah, Nahum, Habakkuk, and Zephaniah*, 156; DeRoche, "Zephaniah 1:2–3," 105–6; Berlin, *Zephaniah*, 82; Patterson, *Nahum, Habakkuk, Zephaniah*, 270.

30. See DeRouchie, "YHWH's Future Ingathering in Zephaniah 1:2," 173–91. My reading casts doubt on Bailey's claim that "the totality of destruction is hyperbolic" (Waylon Bailey, "Zephaniah," in *Micah, Nahum, Habakkuk, Zephaniah*, by Kenneth L. Barker and Waylon Bailey, NAC 20 [Nashville: Broadman & Holman, 1999], 411). Zephaniah himself provides enough qualifiers to show what he intends. He does not deny that the animals can be guilty of violence (Gen 6:13; cf. 7:21) nor does he assert that they will be preserved; instead, his focus is only on YHWH's punishment of human sinfulness shown in idolatry (Zeph 2:3, 18; cf. 3:8).

31. Ben Zvi, *Book of Zephaniah*, 56.

32. DeRoche, "Zephaniah 1:2–3," 106; cf. David A. R. Clark, "Reversing Genesis: A Theological Reading of Creation Undone in Zephaniah," *ExpTim* 123 (2012): 166–70. See also Deut 4:17–18; Ps 8:7–8.

33. E.g., DeRoche, "Zephaniah 1:2–3," 105; Roberts, *Nahum, Habakkuk, and Zephaniah*, 170; Sweeney, *Zephaniah*, 65. The phrase does not occur in the LXX at all, but it is found in the later Greek witnesses like Symmachus, which reads τα σκανδαλα συν [τοις] ασεβεσι ("the stumblings with the wicked") (cf. Matt 13:41).

34. So, too, Robertson, *Books of Nahum, Habakkuk, and Zephaniah*, 259. While unattested elsewhere in this spelling, the form could also be a *hiphil* feminine plural participle of כשל with the *hireq-yod* written as *tsere*, meaning "to cause to stumble." The result would be a rendering, "and those who cause the wicked to stumble" (cf. Sweeney, *Zephaniah*, 64).

that YHWH will "cut off" just these people rather than every person.[35]

If indeed God focuses his punishment on wicked humans and their idols, why then does he gather *all* humans and beasts, birds and fish? It is probably because the carved images themselves (= מַכְשֵׁלוֹת) were formed in the likeness of these various animate creatures (see Deut 4:16–18), and therefore these creatures would serve as witnesses to mankind's debauchery.[36]

b. YHWH's Punishment of Rebellious Humanity (1:3c)

The language of "cutting off" (*hiphil* כרת) in 1:3c works with the harvest imagery of 1:2–3b and often occurs in contexts of punishment where the act refers to the ultimate covenant curse of death (see esp. 1 Kgs 9:7; Isa 14:22; Ezek 14:13).[37] In these contexts, "to cut" means "to eradicate, set aside, or exterminate."[38] Zephaniah develops the curse-context through the wordplay between הָאָדָם ("humanity / the man") and הָאֲדָמָה ("the ground") (Zeph 1:3c), which recalls YHWH's words to Adam after the fall, "For you are dust, and to dust you will return" (Gen 3:19). As DeRoche notes, mankind will be separated from the very substance from which he was created and upon which he depends (2:7; 3:17–19), and this ultimately means he will be separated from God.[39] *All* humans

stand accountable to God, who is the covenant Lord of all things through creation (9:9–10; cf. Isa 24:5–6; Jer 25:30–33), and he will punish all disloyalty in the world (see Deut 30:7). This new punishment will come not with flood but with fire (Zeph 1:18; 3:8).[40]

2. Local Punishment Against the Rebels of Judah and Jerusalem (1:4–6)[41]

Significantly, even God's special covenant people are not immune to this global reprimand of YHWH. Just as his worldwide "ingathering" will give rise to a global excision (Zeph 1:2–3), two conjoined *weqatal* clauses in 1:4a–b tell us that the "stretching out" of his disciplining hand against Judah will equally result in his "cutting off" the idolaters from among his people. YHWH's execution of wrath against Jerusalem in 1:4, 12 contrasts with her restoration in 3:14, 16.

a. YHWH's Extension of His Hand Against Judah and Jerusalem (1:4a)

YHWH will "stretch out" (נטה) his hand against his enemies from among his own people. Bailey notes that God's extended hand "symbolized omnipotent power (Jer 32:17) and God's sovereign direction of history (Isa 14:26–27; Jer 27:5)."[42] This imagery frequently occurs in contexts of divine

---

35. Vlaardingerbroek, *Zephaniah*, 56.

36. Ben Zvi has observed that the text's purview includes only humans and animals and does not address plants or any other created elements (Ben Zvi, *Book of Zephaniah*, 272–73). Ben Zvi's note supports the view that Zeph 1:2–3b is *not* addressing *universal* destruction. Alternatively, Ben Zvi proposes that it suggests the author lived and worked in an urban rather than rural environment. On the connection between Zeph 1:3 and Deut 4:16–18, see Berlin, *Zephaniah*, 73.

37. E.g., Gen 9:11; 1 Kgs 14:10; Ezek 14:17; Amos 1:5, 8; Mic 5:9–12; Nah 2:14; Zech 9:6, 10. At times "cutting off" explicitly refers to the death penalty (Exod 31:14; Lev 20:3–6). Note how

the "cutting" ritual that ratified ancient covenants (Gen 15:18; Jer 34:18) was itself most likely a self-maledictory oath sign (see Peter J. Gentry and Stephen J. Wellum, *Kingdom through Covenant: A Biblical-Theological Understanding of the Covenants*, 2nd ed. [Wheaton, IL: Crossway, 2018], 286–94).

38. Eugene E. Carpenter, "כָּרַת (*kārat*)," *NIDOTTE* 2:722.

39. DeRoche, "Zephaniah 1:2–3," 106.

40. Cf. 2 Pet 3:5–7.

41. This exposition of Zeph 1:4–6 expands material first published in DeRouchie, "Confronting Idolatry," 24–35.

42. Bailey, "Zephaniah," 417.

retribution (Isa 5:25; Ezek 14:13),[43] and here God pledges to work against Judah in the same manner that he will work against the foreign nations (Zeph 2:13). At the exodus, God's outstretched hand was originally a gesture of destruction for Egypt and a "gesture of salvation" for Israel (Exod 3:20; 7:5; 9:15; cf. 15:6, 12), but in this text it "is now one of judgment" for Judah.[44] "Judah" was all that remained under Israelite control after the Assyrians ransacked and exiled the northern kingdom in 723 BC. Nevertheless, in the century that followed leading up to Zephaniah's ministry, Judah failed to learn from her sister's fate and even grew worse. Thus, "the soul of backslider Israel is more righteous than traitor Judah" (Jer 3:11). The disposition of many of those associated with the capital city "Jerusalem" remained no different than their evil neighbors.

b. YHWH's Punishment of Remaining Paganism in Judah and Jerusalem (1:4b–6)
(1) The Declaration and Object of Punishment (1:4b)

Thus, God promised to "cut off from this place the remnant of the Baal" (1:4b), reemploying the covenant excision language (כרת) used in 1:3c.[45] The term "place" (מָקוֹם) can designate a broad space (e.g., Jer 16:2–3, 9; 22:11–12). However, its regular association with the central sanctuary (Deut 12:5; 1 Kgs 8:29; Jer 27:22) suggests that part of what is at stake in bringing punishment on "Jerusalem" may be cultic purification.[46] YHWH is holy, and Jerusalem was to stand as a beacon of

his holiness to the world with both the center of the Davidic kingdom and God's temple in its midst (1 Kgs 11:13, 36; Jer 17:25). Yet, the sinful inhabitants increasingly contaminated the city. Such wickedness necessitated the death of the guilty (Lev 15:31) or the sacrifice of a substitute (17:11).[47] Prohibited, unaddressed uncleanness would result in God's completely removing the people from the land (Lev 18:26–30; 20:22–24).

Within Jerusalem, the object of God's wrath was "the remnant of the Baal" (שְׁאָר הַבַּעַל). Because in Scripture, the terms for "remnant" never denote a deity, Zephaniah here likely refers to a subset and perhaps even a majority in Jerusalem's populace illegitimately worshiping this false god. This wicked "remnant," which Zephaniah describes with the masculine noun (שְׁאָר), contrasts with the remnant of the faithful and humble that Zephaniah will refer to with the feminine noun (שְׁאֵרִית) and that YHWH will preserve in his impending ordeal (Zeph 2:7, 9; 3:13).[48]

"Baal" (בַּעַל I) in Hebrew bears a common meaning of "lord, owner" and as such frequently developed into a title and then a proper name for gods.[49] It is associated even with YHWH (2 Sam 5:20), but its common connection with "Baal"-Hadad, the false Canaanite/Aramean deity of storm and fertility, pushed Hosea to prohibit any association of the term "Baal" with YHWH (Hos 2:18–19[16–17]; cf. 1 Kgs 18:21) for it too often led to insidious syncretism.[50] The storm god, Baal, provided the most enduring threat to exclusive YHWH worship in Israel, especially because

---

43. See also Isa 23:11; Jer 51:25; Ezek 14:9; 16:27; 25:7, 13, 16; 35:3.

44. Motyer, "Zephaniah," 912.

45. Ezekiel 14:13 and 25:13 use the language of the "outstretched hand" and "cutting off" to target humans and animals (Ben Zvi, Book of Zephaniah, 61).

46. Sweeney, Zephaniah, 58, 66. Cf. Deut 12:3, 11, 21, 26; 1 Kgs 8:30, 35; 2 Chr 6:20, 21, 26; Ezek 42:13.

47. Cf. Heb 9:22.

48. For more on "remnant," see the discussion at Zeph 2:7.

49. J. C. de Moor and M. J. Mulder, "בַּעַל ba'al," TDOT 2:2:184; cf. 186.

50. Roberts, Nahum, Habakkuk, and Zephaniah, 172.

the Levant was so dependent on rain (see 1 Kgs 17–18).[51] The Bible consistently adds the definite article before "Baal" (e.g., הַבַּעַל), but extrabiblical discoveries from Ras Shamra and elsewhere clearly use Baal as a proper name, so most scholars today affirm that "*baʿal* with the article belongs to the category of common nouns and adjectives which can be regarded as proper names when referring to a specific individual."[52] Nevertheless, it is also possible that the definite article points to a specific physical idol of Baal (i.e., *the* Baal-idol) in Jerusalem that the Judeans worshiped.

The statement "the remnant of the Baal" in Zeph 1:4 means not a part of Baal proper but rather a holdout of the cult of Baal as a group. Trusting counterfeit gods like Baal for help was always evil in YHWH's sight (see Deut 5:7; Judg 3:7). Such folly brought destruction to the northern kingdom (2 Kgs 17:16–18), and the same activity during the reigns of Manasseh and Amon (22:3, 21) rendered Judah's destruction imminent (21:11–15; cf. 23:26–27; 24:3–4). That a hold-out of such paganism and apostasy continued in Zephaniah's day was deeply concerning, especially because it reached all the way up to the religious and political leadership (Zeph 1:4; 3:3–4; cf. Jer 11:13). God would act, eradicating Baalism not only from Israel but from the entire world (cf. 2 Kgs 10:28).

(2) The Composition of the Object of Punishment (1:4c–6)

English translations differ in their view of the number of groups that receive judgment. The

Structure and Literary Form section argued that "the remnant of the Baal" included four groups:[53]

1. Legitimate and illegitimate clergy practicing idolatry (1:4c)
2. Those revering the stars as gods (i.e., star-worshipers, 1:5a)
3. Those paying lip service to YHWH but retaining in practice other "higher authorities" (i.e., syncretistic hypocrites, 1:5b)
4. Those going their own way and failing to pray for guidance and help (i.e., the self-ruled and self-dependent, 1:6)

[4c] Among "the remnant of the Baal," the first group Zephaniah lists as God's target is "the name of the illegitimate priests along with the priests" (Zeph 1:4c). Israelite "priests" (כֹּהֲנִים) of YHWH were supposed to be Levites who taught God's Torah, guarded knowledge, and preserved what was holy (Lev 10:10–11), but some in Zephaniah's day were corrupt, having "treated torah violently" (Zeph 3:4; cf. Ezek 22:26; Mal 2:7–9). They were also serving in Jerusalem alongside the כְּמָרִים (rendered "illegitimate priests"), a term occurring only twice elsewhere in the OT (2 Kgs 23:5; Hos 10:5) but which appears to connote the non-Levitical clerics that Jeroboam I and later kings ordained to serve at the unlawful high places throughout the land (1 Kgs 12:31–32 and 13:33–34 with 2 Kgs 23:5).[54]

כֹּמֶר is a loanword in biblical Hebrew and served as the most common term for "priest" outside

---

51. The text may also suggest Mesopotamian influence on the Jerusalem cult, because Assyria was the major superpower of the day (see Zeph 2:12–15) and also had a deity named *bēl* (= Baal) (Baker, *Nahum, Habakkuk and Zephaniah*, 93). For more on this topic, see Vlaardingerbroek, *Zephaniah*, 70–72.

52. De Moor and Mulder, "בַּעַל (*baʿal*)," *TDOT* 2:192.

53. The "remnant of Baal" is the main group, which has four distinct subgroupings. The first begins with an asyndetic direct

object marker (אֶת־) plus noun construction. The next three connect to it through a *waw* plus direct object marker (וְאֶת־) plus substantival participle construction.

54. Cf. 2 Kgs 17:32; 2 Chr 10:13–15; 13:9. So too Carl F. Keil, "The Books of the Kings," trans. James Martin in *Commentary on the Old Testament* (1872; repr. in 10 vols., Peabody, MA: Hendrickson, 1996), 3:342 (433–34), on 2 Kgs 23:5; cf. Ben Zvi, *Book of Zephaniah*, 68.

Israel.[55] Because biblical authors do not hesitate to apply the term כֹּהֵן to priests of other regions like Egypt (Gen 47:22), Midian (Exod 2:16), and Philistia (1 Sam 6:2) and to priests of foreign gods like Dagon (1 Sam 5:5), Baal (2 Kgs 11:18), Chemosh (Jer 48:7), and Milcom (Jer 49:3), Zephaniah's use of כְּמָרִים is probably a rhetorical jab aimed at illegitimate Israelite priests.

In contrast to this interpretation, Sweeney posits that the כְּמָרִים in Zeph 1:4c were only "Judean priests of YHWH who were engaged in—or accused of engaging in—illegitimate Yahwistic worship."[56] His view, however, does not distinguish this group from the כֹּהֲנִים "with" (עִם־) whom the כְּמָרִים are associated and who are clearly legitimate (though idolatrous) priests equally included in "the remnant of the Baal."[57] Cogan and Tadmor prefer the idea that the כְּמָרִים in Scripture were actually non-native priests designated to certain

pagan deities, whereas the כֹּהֲנִים were Israelite priests.[58] This distinction is attested in the fifth-century BC Aramaic Jewish Elephantine papyri, which designates the Egyptian priests כמריא but the Jewish priests כהניא.[59] However, the explicit inner-biblical link in Kings between Jeroboam's appointment of illegitimate priests (1 Kgs 12:31–32; 13:33–34) and the unnamed seer's prophecy that a king named Josiah would burn the bones of those Jeroboam ordained (13:2 with 2 Kgs 23:15–16, 20) suggests that the כְּמָרִים were indeed not foreigners but non-Levitical Israelites serving as priests. Furthermore, the sly nature of oath taking (see the discussion at Zeph 1:5) suggests that idolatry in Jerusalem during the days of Josiah was likely *not* so forthright as to have actual foreign priests of Milcom from Bene-Ammon or Baal from Canaan serving at the Jerusalem temple.[60]

---

55. See "I כֹּמֶר," *HALOT* 482; P. Jenson, "כֹּמֶר (kōmer)," *NIDOTTE* 2:654–55; see, for example, the mention of "the priests [kmr] of Khnub the god" in the "Petition for Reconstruction of Temple," trans. Bezalel Porten (ca. 410 BC, *COS* 3.50:123n10). The root meaning of כֹּמֶר is associated either (1) with rising heat (כמר in the *niphal*, of emotions: Gen 43:40; 1 Kgs 3:26; Hos 4:8; or of skin, Lam 5:10) that can result in darkness (cf. כִּמְרִירֵי in Job 3:5; also Sir 11:4) or (2) with a trap/snare (cf. מִכְמָר in Ps 141:10; Isa 51:20; מִכְמֶרֶת in Isa 19:8; Hab 1:16; cf. 1QHod 3:26; 5:8). Both images aptly fit spiritual deceivers.

56. Sweeney, *Zephaniah*, 68.

57. Contra Ben Zvi, who asserts that the כֹּהֲנִים are not necessarily part of "the remnant of the Baal" (Ben Zvi, *Book of Zephaniah*, 71), and contra Berlin, who tries to make עִם־ mean "among" rather than "with" in a way that equates rather than aligns the two parties (Berlin, *Zephaniah*, 75).

58. Mordechai Cogan and Hayim Tadmor, *II Kings: A New Translation with Introduction and Commentary*, AB 11 (New Haven: Yale University Press, 2008), 285; cf. Jenson, "כֹּמֶר (kōmer)," *NIDOTTE* 2:654–55.

59. E.g., Bezalel Porten and Ada Yardeni, *Textbook of Aramaic Documents from Ancient Egypt*, 4 vols. (Winona Lake, IN: Eisenbrauns, 1986), A4.7:1, 5, 18; A4.8:1, 4, 17; see Ben Zvi, *Book of Zephaniah*, 69–70; Jenson, "כֹּמֶר (kōmer)," *NIDOTTE* 2:654.

60. Recognizing the distinction between the כְּמָרִים and

the כֹּהֲנִים in 1:4c, Calvin compared the former group to the "monks" of his day, "who did not themselves offer sacrifices, but were a sort of attendants, who undertook vows and offered prayers in the name of the whole people" (John Calvin, "Habakkuk, Zephaniah, Haggai," in *Commentaries on the Twelve Minor Prophets*, trans. John Owen, 500th anniversary., vol. 15 of *Calvin's Commentaries* [Grand Rapids: Baker Books, 2009], 193). His interpretation fails to account for 2 Kgs 23:5, which explicitly says that the kings appointed the כְּמָרִים "to make offerings on the high places." The LXX does not render כְּמָרִים עִם־ ("illegitimate priests with") but instead simply reads "the names of the priests" (τὰ ὀνόματα τῶν ἱερέων), a pattern adopted by the RSV, NRSVue, and NET. The latter follows Roberts seeing עִם־הַכֹּהֲנִים ("with the priests") as a later gloss that defines the rare word that precedes (Roberts, *Nahum, Habakkuk, and Zephaniah*, 167–68). This approach seems unlikely, however, for two reasons: (1) The LXX actually translates כֹּהֲנִים but drops כְּמָרִים עִם־, probably due to not knowing its meaning (as is also apparent in the LXX of 2 Kgs 23:5 and Hos 10:5; see Ivan Jay Ball Jr., *A Rhetorical Study of Zephaniah* [Berkeley: BIBAL, 1988], 25). This strongly suggests that כֹּהֲנִים was not a later gloss and that כְּמָרִים was also original. (2) If כֹּהֲנִים was designed to define כְּמָרִים, the prophet would have marked its appositional function by asyndeton. In contrast, the use of the preposition עִם־ ("with") demands that the two clerical classes be in some way distinct.

While not fully eradicated at the time of Zephaniah's oracle, King Josiah's religious reforms would cleanse the land of all the idolatrous priests, whether illegitimate or legitimate in biological heritage (2 Kgs 23:5, 8–9, 20).[61] The fact that their "name" is "cut off" not only points to complete annihilation but also suggests that a core problem among the cult leaders was concern for their own renown rather than for God's (see Gen 11:4 vs. 4:26). In the future, God would grant his restored remnant a great and everlasting name that would ultimately point to his great renown and glory (Zeph 3:19–20; cf. Isa 56:4–5).

[5] Second, alongside the religious leadership in the remnant of the Baal (1:4) are the star-worshipers (1:5a). The phrase "the host of the heavens" (צְבָא הַשָּׁמַיִם) can refer to the spiritual armies of YHWH (e.g., 1 Kgs 22:19; cf. 1 Sam 17:45; Isa 13:4), but more commonly, as here, it denotes the stars, perceived as divine beings (cf. Amos 5:26; Acts 7:42–43).[62] The *hishtaphel* of II חוה means "to prostrate, bow down" and always expresses an action or attitude directed toward a superior, be it human or divine.[63] Normally the word expresses an external gesture of greeting, respect, submission, or worship

aligned with an inner attitude, though hypocrisy was possible; other times, it simply expresses one's disposition (e.g., a posture of prayer with hands outstretched) and does not require prostration.[64] In Israel, only YHWH was to receive such worship (Deut 4:19; 5:9; 26:10), and the penalty for worship of other gods was death (8:19; 11:16).

Like the ancients of Babel, who built a high temple to gain easier access to the gods (Gen 11:4), some in Zephaniah's audience were climbing to their roofs to worship the astral bodies (cf. Jer 19:13; 32:29).[65] The Canaanite god Baal was regularly associated with "the heavens," so worshiping luminaries was natural.[66] The plural "roofs" (גַּגּוֹת) suggests private worship,[67] and because the homage was to the stars, the acts were done at night in secrecy. And because many ancients believed that the most powerful gods slept in the evening, these would also be times of desperation.[68] YHWH never sleeps (Ps 121:4), and he apportioned the sun, moon, and stars "to all the peoples under all the heavens" not as legitimate objects of worship (Deut 4:19; cf. 17:3; Jer 44:25–27) but as providential signs (Gen 1:14) that point to the certainty of his kingdom promises (Gen 15:5; Jer 33:22) and power (Neh 9:6; Ps 8:4–5[3–4]; Isa

---

61. Cf. 2 Chr 34:5; Jer 48:7; 49:3.

62. "The queen of the heavens" (הַשָּׁמַיִם מְלֶכֶת) cult is probably associated with this same problem (Jer 7:18; 44:15–25; cf. 8:2; 19:13; Roberts, *Nahum, Habakkuk, and Zephaniah*, 172). As anticipated by Moses's condemnations of astral worship (Deut 4:19 and 17:3), the presence of preconquest place names like Jericho (יְרֵחוֹ "moon city," e.g., Num 22:1), En-Shemesh (עֵין שֶׁמֶשׁ, "the spring of the sun [god]," e.g., Josh 15:7), Beth-Shemesh (בֵּית־שֶׁמֶשׁ "the house of the sun [god]," e.g., Josh 15:10), Har-heres (הַר־חֶרֶס "the mount of the sun [god]," e.g., Judg 1:35), and Timnath-heres (תִּמְנַת־חֶרֶס "the area of the sun [god]," Judg 2:9) show how bound up Canaanite worship was with heavenly bodies (J. M. P. Smith, "Book of Zephaniah," 188; Motyer, "Zephaniah," 3:913). In the days of Assyrian supremacy this type of Israelite idolatry appears most prevalent, both in the north (e.g., Amos 5:26) and in the south—especially during the reigns of Manasseh and Amon (2 Kgs 21:3, 5, 21) and into the time of Josiah (23:5, 12).

63. "חוה II," *HALOT* 295–96.

64. Terence E. Fretheim, "חָוָה (ḥāwâ II)," *NIDOTTE* 2:43.

65. Holladay believes Jer 19:13 is directly dependent on Zeph 1:5. See Holladay, "Reading Zephaniah with a Concordance," 673.

66. Cross, *Canaanite Myth and Hebrew Epic*, 7–8; cf. Patterson, *Nahum, Habakkuk, Zephaniah*, 273.

67. Vlaardingerbroek, *Zephaniah*, 75.

68. The Old Babylonian "Prayer to the Gods of the Night," trans. Ferris J. Stevens (ANET 390–91), portrays a petitioner calling upon the constellations to witness his act of homage and guarantee his petitions. He believes the stars are lesser gods, but he is also convinced that the great gods who ordinarily control world affairs sleep in the evening. Though the text is dated to around a thousand years before Zephaniah, it represents a typical worldview among the ancients.

40:25–26).[69] Punishment had already fallen on the northern kingdom for venerating the creation as if it were divine (2 Kgs 17:16), and now YHWH declares comparable punishment on the south due to their sustained idolatry (cf. 2 Kgs 21:3, 5–6, 21; Jer 19:13). And when this chastisement came, the Judean rebels would not be gathered or buried but would be spread out like dung under the very luminaries they once revered (Jer 8:2).[70]

Mesopotamian astral deities appear to have influenced Israel since the days of Amos (Amos 5:26).[71] De Moor has also observed a potential link between Israel's roof worship and the autumn New Year Festival for Baal. During this seven-day feast, the king organized sacrificial meals to honor Baal, and on the first day of the feast, he offered sacrifices and drink offerings on the roof of the temple.[72] Not only were many Israelites in Zephaniah's day engaged in similar acts (Zeph 1:5),[73] but this harvest festival for Baal bore a striking thematic and temporal similarity to Israel's Feast of Ingathering (Deut 16:13; cf. comments at Zeph 1:2).[74] Again, Zephaniah may be using the timing and content of this specific feast to call his audience to Godward

allegiance. Josiah's reforms included the destruction of at least one roof-altar designated for astral worship, along with two others that Manasseh had set up in the temple-courts (2 Kgs 23:12; cf. 21:5).

The third subset of Baal followers are the syncretistic hypocrites—"those who bow down, who swear to YHWH but swear by their king" (Zeph 1:5b). Some scholars question the originality of the repeated substantival participle הַמִּשְׁתַּחֲוִים ("those who bow down") due to an alleged syntactic awkwardness with the asyndetic substantival participle that follows and due to the fact that the LXX does not include the phrase.[75] The repetition could simply be dittographic (accidental scribal repetition). Nevertheless, the MT is readable, and such a structure is known elsewhere in biblical Hebrew—even in Zephaniah (Zeph 1:12c; cf. Jer 23:2; Song 3:3; 5:7).[76]

The prophet clearly asserts that Jerusalem's Baal worship included a form of syncretism that combined devotion to YHWH with that of another. The MT renders the second party מַלְכָּם, which naturally means "their king," as translated in the LXX (τοῦ βασιλέως αὐτῶν; cf. NET). However, following the

---

69. Cf. 1 Kgs 22:19; Job 38:31; 147:4; Isa 45:12; Amos 5:8. Daniel I. Block, *Deuteronomy*, NIVAC (Grand Rapids: Zondervan, 2012), 130. This view of God's purpose for the luminaries runs counter to how astrologers seek to discern the future or a god's will in the present. YHWH mocks such acts (see Isa 47:13; Jer 10:1–3; cf. Dan 2:27; 5:7–12) and condemns all forms of divination or omens (Lev 19:26; Deut 18:10; cf. b. Sanh. 65b–66a). Heiser insists that Moses uses the sun, moon, and stars in Deut 4:19 as a cipher for the "sons of God" in 32:8 and that they are indeed illegitimate objects YHWH appointed for the nations to worship so as to ensure their punishment (Michael S. Heiser, *The Unseen Realm: Recovering the Supernatural Worldview of the Bible* [Bellingham, WA: Lexham, 2015], 112–15). Yet why would a disguised message be necessary in Deut 4:19 if he was free to speak of the "sons of God" in 32:8?

70. King Josiah sought to eradicate star-worship (2 Kgs 23:5, 12), but it apparently returned quickly in subsequent generations (cf. Jer 7:18; 8:2; 19:13; 44:17–25; Roberts, *Nahum, Habakkuk, and Zephaniah*, 172).

71. Vlaardingerbroek identifies the most important to be Shamash, Sin, Ishtar, and "the seven" (Vlaardingerbroek, *Zephaniah*, 69).

72. De Moor and Mulder, "בַּעַל *baʿal*," *TDOT* 2:190. See also "Ugaritic Rites for the Vintage," trans. Baruch A. Levine, Jean-Michel de Tarragon, and Anne Robertson (*COS* 1.95:301), for the most extensive depiction of the annual fall celebration of the grape harvest at the temple of Baal in Ugarit including mention of the king's roof worship. See also the description of pagan roof worship in "The Kirta Epic," trans. Dennis Pardee (*COS* 1.102:334).

73. Cf. 2 Kgs 21:5; 23:12; Jer 19:13; 32:29.

74. De Moor and Mulder, "בַּעַל *baʿal*," *TDOT*, 2:191.

75. E.g., Knud Jeppesen, "Zephaniah I 5B," *VT* 31.1 (1981): 372–73; Sweeney, *Zephaniah*, 70.

76. GKC, §§120g–h, 154a n1. See also 1 Kgs 14:17//2 Chr 12:10 and Ball, *Rhetorical Study of Zephaniah*, 26–30. The lack of the phrase in the Greek text may only arise from carelessness or deliberate abbreviation.

path of the Greek Lucianic recension, the Peshitta, and the Vulgate, some find it more satisfying contextually to revocalize the MT as מִלְכֹּם ("Milcom"), the national god of Bene-Ammon (1 Kgs 11:5, 33; 2 Kgs 23:13).[77] Still, others leave the MT form as מַלְכָּם but see it either as a variant spelling or at least a reference to "Milcom" (Jer 49:1, 3)[78] or "the Molech-god" (הַמֹּלֶךְ; see Lev 18:21; 2 Kgs 23:10; Jer 32:35),[79] a Canaanite deity some have questionably proposed is only a local manifestation of Milcom (1 Kgs 11:5, 7).[80] Israel's historians and Jeremiah appear to apply the title "king" to Milcom (2 Sam 12:30//1 Chr 20:2; Jer 49:1, 3), and Josiah's reformation did explicitly confront "Milcom" worship (2 Kgs 23:13). However, because the king's reforms also targeted Ashteroth of the Sidonians and Chemosh of the Moabites (23:13), it is difficult to know why Zephaniah would have narrowed his focus here on Milcom. Furthermore, the text addresses the remnant of the *Baal*, not Milcom (Zeph 1:4).

In view of the parallel with "YHWH" in the clause of Zeph 1:5, "their king" was probably an epithet for a divine rather than human being (i.e., "Baal" of 1:4).[81] At least five lines of evidence support this conclusion. First, Berlin rightly notes that swearing *by* a human "king" or any other human personage is otherwise unknown in Scripture (though it does occur in extrabiblical texts and perhaps is anticipated in some biblical texts).[82] Second, unlike his two royal predecessors, Josiah, as leader of the reform movement, "turned to YHWH with all his heart and with all his being and with all his substance" (2 Kgs 23:25). He would not have affirmed or received such veneration. Third, the ancients outside the Bible regularly applied the title "king" to deities,[83] God uses the term to refer to Leviathan (Job 41:26[34]), both Amos and Isaiah may refer to a foreign god with it (Isa 57:9; Amos 5:26), and Jeremiah applies it to Milcom (Jer 49:1, 3).[84] Fourth, Scripture frequently designates YHWH as "king," and Zephaniah does so with the title "Israel's King" (מֶלֶךְ יִשְׂרָאֵל) in Zeph 3:15 (cf. Isa 44:6).[85] YHWH is "the great King above all gods" (Ps 95:3), but for the logic in Zeph 1:5 to work, the "king" must be some figure other than YHWH. Fifth, when Zephaniah later stresses that YHWH and no other is Israel's sovereign, saving,

---

77. See Douay-Rheims, NASB20, NRSVue, NKJV, ESV, CEB, CSB. Bene-Ammon is the full proper name of Israel's "cousins" to the east, who are commonly tagged the Ammonites. For more, see the comments at Zeph 2:8 and Daniel I. Block, "*bny 'mwn*: The Sons of Ammon," *AUSS* 22.2 (1984): 197–212.

78. See Geneva, Bishop's, KJV, Darby, YLT, Webster, RV, UASV, WEB.

79. See NLT, NIV.

80. The union of "Milcom" and "Molech" is questionable for at least three reasons: (1) Josiah destroyed distinct holy sites for the two (2 Kgs 23:10–13), (2) Scripture only indicates children being offered to Molech, and (3) Molech's origins were Canaanite (see Emile Puech, "Milcom מלכם," *DDD* 575–76; George C. Heider, "Molech מלך," *DDD* 581–85). Significantly, the title "Molech" usually includes the definite article in the OT (= הַמֹּלֶךְ, "the Molech-god"), and the spelling is likely a derogatory form of מֶלֶךְ ("king"), using the vowels of "shame" (בֹּשֶׁת) (see "מֶלֶךְ," *HALOT* 592; Judith M. Hadley, "מֶלֶךְ (*mōlek*)," *NIDOTTE* 2:956. Molech was likely "a netherworld deity to whom children were offered by fire for some divinatory purpose" (Heider, "Molech," *DDD* 585).

81. So too Keil, "Twelve Minor Prophets," 10:441 (2:128); Patterson, *Nahum, Habakkuk, Zephaniah*, 275; contrast Nicholas R. Werse, "Of Gods and Kings: The Case for Reading 'Milcom' in Zephaniah 1:5bß," *VT* 68.3 (2018): 505–13. The Tg. Neb. renders the phrase וְיָמָן בְּשׁוּם פָּתַכְרֵיהוֹן ("and those who swear by the name of their idols"). For similar applications of the title "king" to foreign deities, see Job 18:14; Hos 10:7; Amos 5:26.

82. See Exod 22:27; 1 Sam 17:55; 1 Kgs 21:10; Isa 8:21. Berlin, *Zephaniah*, 76.

83. Philip J. Nel, "מֶלֶךְ (*mālak* I)," *NIDOTTE* 2:951.

84. The reference to the Ammonite king in 2 Sam 12:30 // 1 Chr 20:2 may refer to the same if the LXX is followed.

85. For more on YHWH as "king," see the discussion at Zeph 3:15.

and satisfying "King" (Zeph 3:15), he is most likely intentionally confronting the common use of the title מַלְכָּם ("their king") from 1:5 as applied to Baal or any from among a host of other competing deities over which he bore authority.[86] From the perspective of the prophet, the *gods* of the nations were the source of the problem, and destroying them would result in the undoing of every earthly rebellion (2:11).

As Vlaardingerbroek hypothesizes, the prophet is most likely intentionally confronting a certain form of oath-taking that allowed the inhabitants of Jerusalem to invoke inconspicuously the authority of other gods under the title "king" while still sounding like they were remaining faithful to YHWH.[87] Such hypocritical syncretism demanded bold confrontation. Akin to the days of Samuel when Israel wanted a human king to replace YHWH (1 Sam 8:7; 10:19; 12:12), some in Zephaniah's audience were giving their highest allegiance to a being other than the true God. In the ancient world, the worldviews of polytheism (many gods) and henotheism (a chief god of many others) allowed for "the remnant of the Baal" to affirm YHWH as Israel's national god outwardly while inwardly expressing higher allegiance to Baal and the numerous other deities over which he exercised

authority. But true Mosaic Yahwism, as affirmed by Zephaniah, condemned the worship of any rivals to YHWH (see Zeph 2:11 with 1:18 and 3:8).[88]

Significantly, the remnant of Baal made oaths "to" (לְ) YHWH but did so "by" (בְּ = under the highest authority of) "their king."[89] The former action involves a vow or promise to a given party, whereas the latter action invokes the power of a higher authority to witness the vow and to hold one accountable, thus guaranteeing the promise.[90] When humans invoke a deity as witness to an oath, they treat the deity as a chief authority and place themselves under the potential judgment of that god (see 1 Sam 28:10; 1 Kgs 1:29–30 where the whole oath formula is present).[91] Those who swear "by YHWH" in an honorable way can rejoice (Ps 63:12[11]), but those who swear "by YHWH" and then pursue ungodliness profane God's name (Lev 19:12) and place themselves under covenant curse. Moses directed Israel to swear only *by* YHWH (Deut 6:13; 10:20), and Joshua charged them never to swear *by* the false gods of the nations (Josh 23:7; cf. Deut 32:21). Nevertheless, the people of Judah were doing just this underhandedly (see also Jer 5:7), and Zephaniah's preaching and Josiah's reform sought to end it (e.g., 2 Kgs 23:6, 10, 12–15, 24).

---

86. Ben Zvi helpfully compares the use of "their king" (מַלְכָּם) in Zeph 1:5 to the use of "your God" (אֱלֹהֶיךָ) in Jer 2:28 (Ben Zvi, *Book of Zephaniah*, 77). For an argument in favor of מַלְכָּם meaning "their Molech-god," see Berlin, *Zephaniah*, 77.

87. So Vlaardingerbroek, *Zephaniah*, 40–41, 70.

88. Cf. Exod 34:14; Deut 4:35, 39; 5:7; 6:4; 1 Sam 2:2; 2 Sam 22:32; Isa 45:5, 18, 22; 46:9. For a developed description of Mosaic Yahwism in relation to other "gods" (אֱלֹהִים), see Michael S. Heiser, "Monotheism, Polytheism, Monolatry, or Henotheism? Toward an Assessment of Divine Plurality in the Hebrew Bible," *BBR* 18 (2008): 27–30. In contrast to Heiser, we can affirm the divine council without affirming a *pantheon*; Mosaic Yahwism affirmed only *one* Savior, Sovereign, and Satisfier in the throne room of heaven. See John H. Walton, "Interpreting the Bible as an Ancient Near Eastern Document," in *Israel: Ancient*

Kingdom or Late Invention?, ed. Daniel I. Block (Nashville: Broadman & Holman, 2008), 305–9; Jason S. DeRouchie, "Making the Ten Count: Reflections on the Lasting Message of the Decalogue," in *For Our Good Always: Studies on the Message and Influence of Deuteronomy in Honor of Daniel I. Block*, ed. Jason S. DeRouchie, Jason Gile, and Kenneth J. Turner (Winona Lake, IN: Eisenbrauns, 2013), 421–25.

89. The LXX misses the change in preposition, and the Tg. Neb., Peshitta, and Vulgate do something similar. Some English versions express the distinction (e.g., the RV, Darby, YLT, UASV, NRSVue, NASB20, ESV).

90. Cf. similar preposition shifts in Josh 2:12; 9:18; 1 Sam 24:21; 28:10; 1 Kgs 1:17, 30; 2:8.

91. Cf. Matt 23:16–22.

[6] The fourth group aligned with the remnant of the Baal are the self-ruled, self-dependent, who outrightly reject YHWH (Zeph 1:6). To "turn away back" (*niphal* of I סוג) from YHWH always depicts covenant disloyalty (e.g., Pss 44:19[18]; 78:56–57; Isa 59:12–13). The nature of this apostasy is then defined negatively by the subsequent *waw* plus relative clause (וַאֲשֶׁר). Specifically, the rebellion was manifest through failure to "seek" (*piel* בקש) and "inquire" (דרש). These verbs often act as synonyms and denote reliance on God through prayerful repentance, request for help, or worship (e.g., Deut 4:29; Ps 105:3–4; Jer 29:13).[92] The terms can also refer to the dependent pursuit of knowing God's will or word (1 Kgs 22:5; Amos 8:12). While the two verbs have overlapping semantic ranges, Vlaardingerbroek notes that, when YHWH is the object, בקש more commonly means "to pray," whereas דרש usually means "to inquire" via an oracle or recognized Scripture.[93] The rebels, therefore, would be those who reject prayer and God's word in their daily approach to life, and turning from Baal would require acceptance of both. In Zeph 2:3, a quest for "righteousness" and "humility" before God explicate the call for all the faithful remnant to "seek [בַּקְּשׁוּ] YHWH." Only pursuing God in this way will allow one to avoid divine punishment and to experience lasting joy. Practical atheism, in which God is irrelevant for daily living, can only result in destruction.

Canonical and Theological Significance

Zephaniah's Confrontation of Idolatry Then and Now[94]

Zephaniah opens his oracle strongly confronting idolatry, stressing how YHWH would soon overturn "the stumbling blocks with the wicked" (Zeph 1:3) and eradicate from Judah "the remnant of the Baal" (1:4). An idol is "an illegitimate object of worship," and idolatry is a false or improper form of worship "involving reverential human acts of submission and homage before beings or objects in the place of the one true God."[95] YHWH had stressed: "There should never be to you other gods beside me. You should never make for yourself a graven image, any likeness that is in the heavens above or that is at the earth beneath or that is in the waters under the earth. You should never worship them or serve them" (Deut 5:7–9). Yet as Moses foresaw (4:25–26; 31:16–17), Israel secured their own punishment (8:19–20) by going after foreign gods in the land and following the customs of the nations (Judg 2:12; 2 Kgs

---

92. Chhertri suggests that, "when used together, *bqš* denotes seeking in a general sense while *drš* denotes inquiring of God with a view to repentance" (Chitra Chhetri, "בָּקַשׁ [*bāqaš*]," *NIDOTTE* 1:725). For a comparable synonymous use of בקש and דרש, see 1QS III, 11.

93. Vlaardingerbroek, *Zephaniah*, 77.

94. The material in this section abridges DeRouchie, "Confronting Idolatry," 35–41.

95. Daniel I. Block, *For the Glory of God: Recovering a Biblical Theology of Worship* (Grand Rapids: Baker Academic, 2014), 29; cf. G. K. Beale, *We Become What We Worship: A Biblical Theology of Idolatry* (Downers Grove, IL: InterVarsity Press, 2008), 17.

17:7–8). As Zephaniah stressed, the fate of the wicked in Judah would resemble the fate of the nations, because "against YHWH they have sinned" (Zeph 1:17).

Idolatry remains pervasive in our world today, whether in the fashioned idols of Hinduism of India or the more sophisticated practical atheism, materialism, and superstar veneration of the West. Paul charged those in Corinth professing allegiance to Christ, "Do not be idolaters" (1 Cor 10:7), and he warned them not to think "idolaters . . . will inherit the kingdom of God" (1 Cor 6:9–10).

What made and makes idolatry so attractive? At least seven features clarify why this false and dangerous worldview entices so many.[96]

1. *Guaranteed.* Do you ever pray and feel that God is not there? Are you ever tempted to hope in more tangible things like people (Pss 118:9; 146:3) or money (Ps 49:5–6; 1 Tim 6:17)? An idol was a visible, physical representation that was considered to transmit the presence of a deity. Yet the one true God declared that idols are controlled by demons and that such gods are worthless nothings, being made of mere wood and holding no ultimate power (Deut 32:17).[97] God created and creates all things and therefore knows all, guides all, and is present and active in all (Gen 1:1; Isa 45:7; Dan 2:21; Heb 1:3; Acts 17:24–28).[98]

2. *Works-oriented and covetous.* Are you ever prone toward self-righteousness or tempted with materialism? By offering food sacrifices to idols, people believed they obligated the gods to multiply their crops, fertility, cattle, etc. Paul called covetousness idolatry (Eph 5:5; Col 3:5), and this is because idolatrous "worship" is at its core a pursuit of prosperity or health as an earned wage for works done (Hos 2:12; 9:1; Mic 1:7; Rom 4:4). In contrast, true worship excludes self-exalting boasts (Jer 9:23–24; Rom 3:27; 1 Cor 4:7)[99] and considers God to be the supreme treasure of reality who alone is worthy of worship (Matt 13:44–46; Rev 4:11).

3. *Easy.* Do you ever find it easier to please men rather than God or to love yourself over others? Idolatry called for frequent and generous outward sacrifices yet did not demand a true love for God or neighbor. It was not tied to covenantal obligations, as is clear in the way many in Judah remained prayerless, oppressed the weak, failed to heed God's word, and lived in self-reliance (Zeph 1:6; 3:1–2). It was the easy way, but it led to destruction (Matt 7:13–14).

---

96. Stuart originally listed nine attractions, which I have here adapted and developed. See Douglas K. Stuart, *Exodus*, NAC 2 (Nashville: Broadman & Holman, 2006), 450–54. For a fuller description, see DeRouchie, "Confronting Idolatry," 35–41.

97. Cf. Isa 41:24, 29; 44:14–20; Jer 10:14–15; 1 Cor 8:4; 10:19–20.

98. Cf. Exod 4:11; Deut 32:39; 1 Sam 2:6–8; Jer 10:11–13; Isa 42:5; 44:24; 46:9–10; 48:12–13; Rom 11:36; Eph 1:11; 4:6; Col 1:16; Heb 1:3)

99. Cf. Rom 4:2; Eph 2:9; Jas 4:16.

Zephaniah calls his listeners to seek YHWH in righteousness and humility and to wait upon the only true God to act (Zeph 2:3; 3:8). This kind of lifestyle is not just hard; it is impossible (Rom 8:7; 1 Cor 2:14), apart from God's grace (Matt 19:26; Phil 2:12–13).[100]

4. *Convenient.* Do you ever find that following God gets in the way of your own agenda? While frequent and generous offerings were expected, such "worship" of idols could be performed whenever and wherever one so chose—"on every hill and under every green tree" (1 Kgs 14:23; 2 Kgs 17:10). But true worship of Yahweh demanded that Israel value YHWH over self, regardless of the cost (e.g., Deut 12:2–14; 16:16; 22:1–4). Today, God-dependent and God-exalting lifestyle is not always convenient (Luke 14:26–28; 2 Cor 12:10). Nevertheless, it is right, good, and necessary and it is the only path to life (Matt 16:24–25).

5. *Normal.* Are you ever prone to follow the crowd and give in to peer pressure, even when you know the majority is wrong? Idolatry was *the* normal way of life in the ancient world, usually being characterized by *polytheism* (many gods) (2 Kgs 17:16; Zeph 1:4), *syncretism* (blending worldviews) (2 Kgs 17:33; Zeph 1:5), and *pantheism* (God and the universe are one) (Jer 8:2; Zeph 1:5). Against *polytheism*, Christians must affirm "'that an idol is nothing in the world,' and that 'there is no God but one'" (1 Cor 8:4, 6; cf. Deut 32:39; Isa 45:21–22). Contrary to *syncretism*, "no one can serve two masters" (Matt 6:24; cf. John 3:18; Rom 8:13; 1 John 3:10). And in contrast to *pantheism*, Yahweh God is eternally and wholly distinct from his creation yet sovereign over it (Gen 1:1; Isa 45:7; Heb 1:3; Acts 17:24–28).

6. *Logical.* When you are sick, would you rather see a specialist or a general practitioner? Ancient peoples believed that most gods of the nations specialized in aspects of the world or nature—e.g., Baal, weather (Judg 2:11, 13); Ashtoreth, love and fertility (2:13); Chemosh, war (11:24); Dagon, grain (16:23).[101] This made it logical for people to seek "expert" help rather than go to YHWH, who had to manage all spheres of life. While some today find it more desirable to heed "the experts" over God's Word or to follow the culture's priorities and scheduling patterns instead of God's values and instructions, Yahweh alone sits

---

100. Cf. Ezek 36:26–27; 1 Cor 15:10; Col 1:28–29.

101. They also distinguished personal, family, and national gods, the latter of whom bore limited geographical sovereignty (see 1 Kgs 20:23, 28; 2 Kgs 5:15, 17; Jonah 1:3). While all Israelites would have affirmed Yahweh as their national god (because he created the nation and redeemed them from Egypt), many did not hesitate to pay homage to other deities in family or personal worship. Zephaniah, thus, pointed to those who "swear *to* YHWH but *by* their king [e.g., Baal]" (Zeph 1:5). On the three categories of gods, see H. A. Frankfort, John A. Wilson, and Thorkild Jacobsen, *Before Philosophy: The Intellectual Adventure of Ancient Man: An Essay on Speculative Thought in the Ancient Near East*, Pelican Books A198 (Harmondsworth: Penguin Books, 1951), 22, 87, 107, 123, 128–29, 218–33; Karel van der Toorn, *Family Religion in Babylonia, Syria, and Israel: Continuity and Change in the Forms of Religious Life*, SHCANE 7 (Leiden: Brill, 1996).

on the throne of the universe (Deut 4:35, 39; 32:39), and he calls his people to let this truth inform all their lives (5:7; 6:4–5).

7. *Sensuous.* How often are you tempted to turn away from God to satisfy ungodly desires? Sexual immorality and impurity of all sorts are forms of idolatry. In Scripture, it included bowing down and kissing idols (1 Kgs 19:18), visual images and smells (Ezek 8:10–12), cutting the body, loud cries (1 Kgs 18:28; Ezek 8:14), heavy feasting and drunkenness (Amos 2:8; Acts 15:20–21; 21:25; 1 Cor 8:4–13), and immoral sex (Amos 2:7–8; Mic 1:7; cf. the close association in Acts 15:20; Eph 5:5; Col 3:5). Paul stressed that those who live "in the passions of the flesh" are "by nature children of wrath" (Eph 2:3; cf. 1 Cor 6:9–10; 1 John 3:16). Yet having been cleansed (1 Cor 6:11), we must "make no provision for the flesh" (Rom 13:14), while still celebrating God's good gifts in their proper context and measure (1 Tim 4:4–5).

John urged his fellow believers, "Little children, keep yourselves from idols" (1 John 5:21), and he also warned that idolaters will end up "in the lake burning with fire and sulfur, which is the second death" (Rev 21:8). Idolatry will result in ruin. Zephaniah opens his oracle warning against such evil, urging his listeners to embrace YHWH's supremacy over all and to seek and inquire of him (Zeph 1:4–6), knowing that he will ultimately put an end to "all the gods of the earth" (2:11). May we be among the remnant who heeds his voice.

Zephaniah's Message within Redemptive History

Zephaniah's oracle exists within the framework of Scripture's history of redemption. The prophet's message stands within a long line of canonized revelation detailing divine acts of judgment, promise, and warning. Because of the first man's rebellion, God cursed the whole world (Gen 3:14–24; Isa 24:4–6; 43:27), made it crooked beyond human repair (Eccl 7:13–14), and enslaved it to corruption in hope that he would free it (Rom 8:20–21; cf. Gen 6:11–13). YHWH would restore all things through Eve and Abraham's offspring (Gen 3:15; 12:3; 26:4).[102] God anticipated this restoration when he planted the nation of Israel in the promised land (15:13–14, 18; 17:8), but he realized it ultimately through their royal representative (22:17–18; 24:60; 49:8–10), the one whom we know as Jesus Messiah.

YHWH's covenant with Abraham has two stages by which God would restore all things. The first is the old covenant, wherein the patriarch's descendants become a

---

102. For this view of Gen 3:15, see C. John Collins, "A Syntactical Note (Genesis 3:15): Is the Woman's Seed Singular or Plural?," *TynBul* 48 (1997): 139–47; T. Desmond Alexander, "Further Observations on the Term 'Seed' In Genesis," *TynBul* 48 (1997): 363–67; Jonathan Cheek, "Recent Developments in the Interpretation of the Seed of the Woman in Genesis 3:15," *JETS* 64.2 (2021): 215–36.

nation in the promised land (Gen 12:1–2d; 17:7–8). The second is the new covenant through which Abraham becomes the father of many nations through the blessing of the male offspring (12:2e–3; 17:4–6; 22:18).[103] During the old covenant, YHWH called Israel to be "a kingdom of priests and a holy nation" (Exod 19:6), by which they would mediate and display God's holiness to the world (cf. Deut 4:5–8). Yet as God's corporate "son" (Exod 4:22–23; cf. Gen 5:1–3), Israel failed in their calling much like Adam did before. Thus, YHWH would exile them from the promised land (Deut 4:25–28; 31:16–18), as the old covenant worked out its "ministry of condemnation" (2 Cor 3:9).

For Zephaniah and his audience, history was proving this true. The Assyrians had already destroyed the Northern Kingdom because of Israel's covenant infidelity (2 Kgs 17:13–15), and now YHWH's wrath was "near" Judah (Zeph 1:7) and the rest of the world (1:14). Babylon's progressive overthrow of Jerusalem in 605, 597, and 586 BC initiated Judah's destruction that Zephaniah foretold in 1:4–6 and 1:10–13. Nevertheless, Zephaniah associated the *global* destruction of the wicked (1:2–3, 14–18) with the *local* devastation YHWH would bring on Jerusalem's idol worshipers. This link underscores that Babylon's defeat of Jerusalem typologically anticipated YHWH fulfilling his global and antitypical predictions. Thus, we must read Zeph 1:2–6 eschatologically and see it as pointing to the final divine punishment that will reconcile to God all things in the heavens and on the earth.[104]

At least one OT text and a series of NT texts support this typological interpretation. Most of the passages even use harvest imagery to speak of the final judgment; they likely allude to Zeph 1:2–6. Recall that Zephaniah frequently uses the root אסף ("to gather") (1:2–3; 3:8, 18) to portray the day of YHWH as ending one era and beginning another. This portrayal associates the prophet's message with the Feast of Ingathering (cf. Lev 23:33–43; Num 29:12–38; Deut 16:13–15), which likely provided a context for his oracle. As the culminating feast to Judah's agricultural cycle (Exod 23:16; 34:22), this feast reminded the people "to look forward as well as back,"[105] and it is this reality that apparently gripped Zechariah, who explicitly associated the Feast of Ingathering with the day of YHWH.

Zechariah writes, "Look, a day is coming for YHWH when your spoil will be divided in your midst, and I will *gather* [וְאָסַפְתִּי] all the nations against Jerusalem for the battle, and the city will be taken. . . . And it will come about that all who remain from all the nations who came against Jerusalem will go up year after year to bow

---

103. For more on this, see Jason S. DeRouchie, "Counting Stars with Abraham and the Prophets: New Covenant Ecclesiology in OT Perspective," *JETS* 58.3 (2015): 459–60; DeRouchie, *How to Understand and Apply*, 109–11.

104. This stands against both Vlaardingerbroek and Renz

who view the eschatological language only as a rhetorical device (Vlaardingerbroek, *Zephaniah*, 50; Renz, *Books of Nahum, Habakkuk, and Zephaniah*, 464). In my view, the allusion to Zeph 1:2–3 in 3:8 speaks directly against this interpretation.

105. Armerding, "Festivals and Feasts," *DOTP*, 312.

before King YHWH of hosts and to keep the Feast of Booths" (Zech 14:1–2, 16). For Zechariah, YHWH's day includes an ingathering for *the* great battle at the end of the age when YHWH restores right order in his world (cf. Rev 11:7; 16:14; 19:19; 20:8). In that day, the ingathered remnant from the nations will perpetually celebrate the Feast of Ingathering/Booths, commemorating God's kingship, victory, and the new creation he has established.[106] Both Zephaniah and Zechariah were hoping for the same future universal ingathering.

Matthew's Gospel uses the verb συνάγω ("to gather") in three passages to refer to the great ingathering of the nations at the end of the age (Matt 3:12; 13:30; 25:32). This is the same verbal root that one of the LXX Naḥal Ḥever manuscripts uses to render the Hebrew verb אסף ("to gather") in Zeph 1:2.[107] These texts all depend upon Zephaniah's ingathering theme, but the second bears the strongest link.

First, John the Baptist declares that Jesus is one "whose winnowing fork is in his hand, and he will clear his threshing floor and gather [συνάξει] his wheat into the barn, but the chaff he will burn with inextinguishable fire" (Matt 3:12). Importantly, he declares this in a context announcing the day of YHWH's intrusion (Matt 3:11 with Isa 4:2–4; Mal 3:1–3; 23–24[4:5–6]). The Baptist's words portray a single future harvest, wherein the grain is "gathered up," and the wheat is separated from the chaff. While Zephaniah does not mention "fire" in 1:2–3b, he employs the language in 1:18 and 3:8 after introducing in 1:7–8 the sacrificial nature of YHWH's day of wrath.

Second, Jesus compared the kingdom of heaven to a field mixed with wheat and weeds. At harvest time, reapers should "gather [συλλέξατε] first the weeds, and bind them into bundles for burning them; but gather [συναγάγετε] the wheat into my barn'" (Matt 13:30). While explaining the parable, Jesus said, "Therefore, just as the weeds are gathered [συλλέγεται] and fire burns, so will it be at the end of the age. The Son of Man will send his angels, and they will gather [συλλέξουσιν] out of his kingdom all the causes of sin and all the lawbreakers [πάντα τὰ σκάνδαλα καὶ τοὺς ποιοῦντας τὴν ἀνομίαν], and they will throw them into the fiery furnace" (13:40–42). Two parallels with Zephaniah exist. First, Matthew speaks of "ingathering" using the verbs συλλέγω ("to gather by plucking or picking") and συνάγω ("to gather up"). Both verbs adequately render the Hebrew אסף in Zeph 1:2–3b (cf. 1 Kgs 10:26; Deut 16:13), but the latter appears in the Greek version from Naḥal Ḥever. Second, the Hebrew text of Zeph 1:3 mentions the σκάνδαλα ("stumbling blocks"; ESV = "causes of sin") and the ἀνομίαν ("lawless"). The LXX lacks the phrase "the stumbling blocks with the wicked" in 1:3, but Symmachus contains it, using the wooden τὰ σκάνδαλα σὺν

---

106. Sweeney, *Zephaniah*, 108; cf. Armerding, "Festivals and Feasts," *DOTP*, 312.

107. 8ḤevXII gr, XX, 25–26.

[τοῖς] ἀσεβέσι ("the stumbling blocks with the wicked"). Jesus alluded to Zephaniah's Hebrew text to speak of the great eschatological ingathering.[108]

Third, when the Son of Man comes in his glory with the angels and sits on his glorious throne, "before him will be gathered [συναχθήσονται] all the nations, and he will separate people one from another as a shepherd separates the sheep from the goats" (Matt 25:32). Jesus again employs the verb συνάγω to speak of the great ingathering of the nations at the end of the age. God will gather all peoples together for a single judgment that will differentiate the righteous from the wicked. The latter "will go away into eternal punishment, but the righteous into eternal life" (25:46).

A Context for Response

Zephaniah's opening words supply no hint of potential deliverance. God will gather "everything" for judicial assessment, and he will destroy all the "wicked" (1:2–3). Indeed, even in Judah and Jerusalem, God will wash away every trace of idolatry (1:4). This being affirmed, Zephaniah *is* preaching (cf. 2 Kgs 17:13), which raises the possibility of hope since "preaching becomes futile" in "a judgment without any possibility of escape."[109] Clearly, God intends to vanquish "the wicked" and "the remnant of the Baal" (1:3c, 4b). Already, therefore, Zephaniah's rhetoric anticipates the question, "What must I do to be saved? Is there hope of deliverance?"

The prophet will begin to address such aspects directly in 2:1–4 and then again in 3:8. In 1:2–6, he simply sets before his audience the reality of impending divine wrath. Still, one expects that some would recall the ancient promises that after Israel's punishment God would display unmatched compassion in the latter days (Deut 4:30–31; 30:1–14). In this future age, Abraham and David's expected son would definitively serve as the agent of blessing to the world (Gen 22:17b–18; Ps 72:17; Isa 49:6). His perfect life of faithful loyalty would bring salvation (Gen 12:2–3; Deut 17:14–20; Isa 55:3) through a substitutionary, victorious death and resurrection (Isa 52:13–53:12). His global rule would establish eternal peace (2 Sam 7:16; Isa 9:7). Zephaniah anticipates God's future compassion by recalling many of these promises later in his book.

A Proper Response

How then were the humble who depended on God to respond to Zephaniah's words, and how are we to respond today? Three points merit comment.

---

108. So too Robertson, *Books of Nahum, Habakkuk, and Zephaniah*, 259–60; "σκάνδαλον," BDAG 926, §§2, 3; R. T. France, *The Gospel of Matthew*, NICNT (Grand Rapids: Eerd-mans, 2007), 536; D. A. Carson, "Matthew," in *Matthew–Mark*, 2nd ed., EBC (Grand Rapids: Zondervan, 2010), 9:374.

109. Vlaardingerbroek, *Zephaniah*, 73.

Take Seriously the Warning of God's Coming Judgment

Whether consciously or unconsciously, we often live as if God's punishment will not reach us. Such was true at the time of the flood, and Zephaniah faced the same in his day, as the remnant of the Baal declared, "YHWH will neither do good nor do ill" (Zeph 1:12). Yet YHWH demands that we take his holiness and supremacy seriously. He will bring "everything" into judgment (1:2) and punish all the wicked (1:3c). This includes not only mankind in general (1:3a–b), but even people who claim to belong to God but have rebellious rather than surrendered hearts (1:4).

When Christ returns, opportunity for repentance will cease. Then the wicked "will go away into eternal punishment, but the righteous into eternal life" (Matt 25:46; cf. 13:41–42).[110] Heed Zephaniah's warning regarding the impending time of divine wrath. Let God's kind forbearance and patience move you to repentance before it is too late (Rom 2:4; cf. 11:22).

Flee *Pluralism* and Syncretism, and Follow YHWH on the Only Path That Leads to Life

To ensure fertility and productivity, people worshiped the god Baal, who exemplified all that is hostile to YHWH. Even in Jerusalem, the very epicenter of God's power and presence on earth, a remnant of the Baal-worshipers spurned YHWH's name (Zeph 1:4; cf. 3:5; 2 Kgs 21:5). This group included idolatrous Judeans—the biological seed of Abraham with membership in the Mosaic covenant. Their idolatry was syncretistic, still naming YHWH as *a* god but not treating him as such. This problem started with the religious leaders and spread to the community, making a mockery of YHWH's uniqueness (Zeph 1:4; 3:4).

Like a teacher of wisdom, Zephaniah depicts syncretistic covenant unfaithfulness as going one's own way rather than following God (1:6; cf. Ps 1:6; Prov 15:9). And as was true for those in Jerusalem, our prayerlessness and self-dependence reveal our true loyalty. Additionally, the comfort and power that wealth creates still tempt us, even if we do not outwardly associate such temptations with the Baal (John 6:24).[111] Apart from Jesus, we cannot seek or inquire of the Father (John 14:6), and only in the path of Christ will we find life (Matt 7:13–14). All who minimize sin and fail to seek the Savior will reap sure destruction (John 3:36).

Pray for Perseverance in Holiness and for Restorative Grace

Calvin's prayer at the end of his meditation of Zeph 1:4 is helpful at this point:

Grant, Almighty God, that as we are so prone to corruptions, and so easily turn from the right course after having commenced it, and so easily degenerate from the truth

---

110. Cf. Isa 30:33; 34:10; 66:24; Dan 12:2.

111. Motyer, "Zephaniah," 912.

once known,—O grant, that, being strengthened by thy Spirit, we may persevere to the end in the right way which thou showest to us in thy word, and that we may also labor to restore the many who abandon themselves to various errors; and though we may effect nothing, let us not yet be led away after them, but remain firm in the obedience of faith, until having at length finished all these contests, we shall be gathered into that blessed rest which is prepared for us in heaven, through Christ our Lord. Amen.[112]

112. Calvin, "Habakkuk, Zephaniah, Haggai," 194.

Zephaniah 1:7–18

B. The Content of the Call to Revere YHWH

Main Idea of the Passage

Zephaniah calls his audience to revere YHWH in view of the nearness and nature of his day of wrath.

Literary Context

Zephaniah 1:7–18 is the second of two units introducing the book's main hortatory portion: the Savior's call to seek YHWH and wait on him (2:1–3:20). The first unit announced impending doom against the broader world in general and Judah and Jerusalem in particular (1:2–6). This unit opens with a low-level parenetic call to revere God in hushed awe (1:7a), and then it grounds this call in one of Scripture's most detailed foreshadowings of the day of YHWH (1:7b–18). The rising heat from the fires of YHWH's jealousy and the thorough nature of his retribution should cause all in the yet-unnamed audience to turn from wickedness to worship, beginning with silent surrender.

II. The Setting of the Savior's Invitation to Satisfaction: A Call to Revere YHWH in View of His Coming Day (1:2–18)

    A. The Context of the Call to Revere YHWH: Coming Punishment (1:2–6)

➡   **B. The Content of the Call to Revere YHWH (1:7–18)**

       1. The Call to Revere YHWH (1:7a)

       2. A Reason to Revere YHWH Related to Jerusalem (1:7b–13)

       3. Another Reason to Revere YHWH Related to the Whole World (1:14–18)

Translation and Exegetical Outline

(See pages 101–103.)

Structure and Literary Form

Both content and form signal this unit's textual boundaries.[1] As for content, the fourteen times that 1:7–18 repeats language of "the day"/"the day of YHWH" (יוֹם יְהוָה; 4x in 1:7–10 and 10x in 1:14–16, 18) solidifies the general vision of coming wrath in 1:2–6. Formally, clear grammatical markers frame the whole. Specifically, the asyndetic exclamatory interjection "Hush!" (הַס) at the front of 1:7a sets apart what follows as its own unit, and the syntactic disjunction created through the asyndetic imperative "Bind yourselves together" (הִתְקוֹשְׁשׁוּ) in 2:1 shows that 1:18 completes the book's introduction. Just as the prophet's announcement of punishment that precedes in 1:2–6 confronted the world in general (1:2–3) and then Judah and Jerusalem in particular (1:4–6), this unit in 1:7–18 threatens the same groups but in reverse order, targeting first Jerusalem's wicked (1:7b–13) and then those of the wider world (1:14–18). Therefore, the two major divisions of chapter 1 together exhibit an A–B–C–B′–A′ pattern:[2]

> A Global punishment (1:2–3)
> > B Local punishment on Judah and Jerusalem (1:4–6)
> > > C Hush! (1:7a)
> > B′ Jerusalem's fall (1:7b–13)
> A′ The world's destruction (1:14–18)

Because this unit clarifies the imminent and cataclysmic character of the day of YHWH (1:7b–18), many scholars treat it as no more than another prophetic judgment speech.[3] But the causal conjunction "because/for" (כִּי) in 1:7b shows that the subsequent prophetic announcement of punishment[4] in 1:7b–18 supports the unit's primary purpose, marked by the exclamatory "Hush!" (הַס) in 1:7a.[5]

---

1. Cf. Sweeney, *Zephaniah*, 75.
2. So too Floyd, *Minor Prophets, Part 2*, 186.
3. E.g., Sweeney, *Zephaniah*, 75.
4. For a definition, see Sweeney, *Isaiah 1–39*, 529.

5. So too Floyd, *Minor Prophets, Part 2*, 185–86, though even he sees 1:7–18 as merely extending the prophetic announcement of punishment in 1:2–6 and therefore defines all of 1:2–18 as "a prophecy of punishment" (187).

Zephaniah 1:7–18

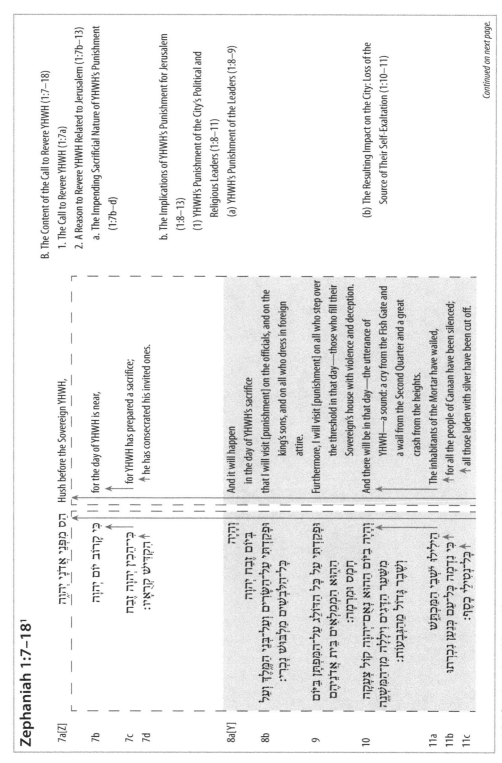

Continued on next page.

1. For information on the guidelines used for tracing the argument, see The Method in the introduction, pp. XX.

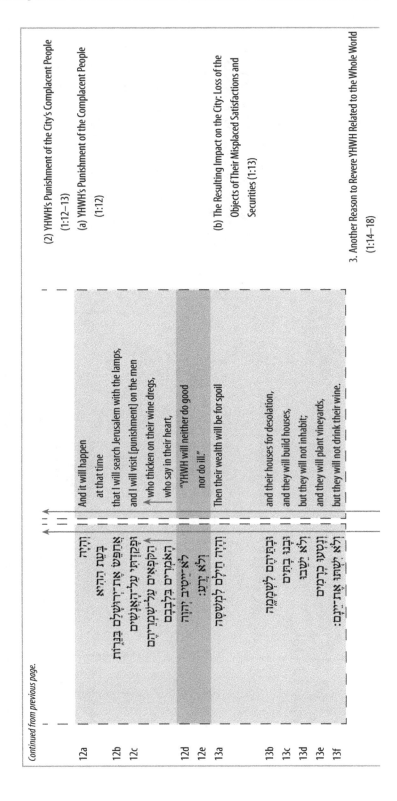

a. The Characteristics of the Coming Day of Punishment (1:14–16)
- (1) The Imminence of the Day (1:14a)
- (2) The Torturous Sound of the Day (1:14b–c)
- (3) The Terror of the Day (1:15–16)

b. The Effects of the Coming Punishment (1:17–18)
- (1) Humanity's Distress (1:17)
  - (a) The Promise (1:17a)
  - (b) The Content (1:17b–d)
    - • Inflicted Disability (1:17b–c)
    - • Sacrificial Dismemberment (1:17d)
- (2) Humanity's Destruction (1:18)
  - (a) The Impossibility of Deliverance (1:18a)
  - (b) The Complete Destruction of Every Inhabitant (1:18b–c)

	English	Hebrew
14a [Z]	The great day of YHWH is near—near and hastening fast.	קָרוֹב יוֹם־יְהוָה הַגָּדוֹל קָרוֹב
14b	The sound of the day of YHWH is bitter;	וּמַהֵר מְאֹד קוֹל יוֹם יְהוָה
14c	a Mighty One is shouting there.	מַר צֹרֵחַ שָׁם גִּבּוֹר
15a	That day is a day of wrath—	יוֹם עֶבְרָה הַיּוֹם הַהוּא
[15b]	a day of distress and anguish,	יוֹם צָרָה וּמְצוּקָה
[15c]	a day of ruin and devastation,	יוֹם שֹׁאָה וּמְשׁוֹאָה
[15d]	a day of darkness and gloom,	יוֹם חֹשֶׁךְ וַאֲפֵלָה
[15e]	a day of cloud and thick darkness,	יוֹם עָנָן וַעֲרָפֶל
[16]	a day of trumpet blast and battle cry against the unassailable cities and against the high battlements.	יוֹם שׁוֹפָר וּתְרוּעָה עַל הֶעָרִים הַבְּצֻרוֹת וְעַל הַפִּנּוֹת הַגְּבֹהוֹת
17a [Y]	Surely, I will bring distress to humanity,	וַהֲצֵרֹתִי לָאָדָם
17b	with the result that they will walk as the blind,	וְהָלְכוּ כַּעִוְרִים
17c	for against YHWH they have sinned.	כִּי לַיהוָה חָטָאוּ
17d	Indeed, their blood will be poured out like dust and their belly like dung pellets.	וְשֻׁפַּךְ דָּמָם כֶּעָפָר וּלְחֻמָם כַּגְּלָלִים
18a [Z]	Also, their silver—even their gold—will not be able to deliver them in the day of the wrath of YHWH.	גַּם־כַּסְפָּם גַּם־זְהָבָם לֹא־יוּכַל לְהַצִּילָם בְּיוֹם עֶבְרַת יְהוָה
18b	And in the fire of his jealousy all the earth will be consumed,	וּבְאֵשׁ קִנְאָתוֹ תֵּאָכֵל כָּל־הָאָרֶץ
18c	for a complete, even terrifying, end he will deal against all the inhabitants of the earth.	כִּי־כָלָה אַךְ־נִבְהָלָה יַעֲשֶׂה אֵת כָּל־יֹשְׁבֵי הָאָרֶץ

*the dashed-line boxes (vv. 7b–13 and 14–18) mark two reasons that those related to Jerusalem should revere Yahweh (v. 7a).

† The grayed squares mark the two parallel groups who should heed v. 7a: the leaders (vv. 8–11) and the general populace (vv. 12–13). The darker gray marks embedded speech.

‡ The long innermost arrows show that the two units, vv. 7b–13 and vv. 14–18, provide parallel reasons to heed v. 7a.

104 Part II: The Setting of the Savior's Invitation to Satisfaction

This interjection expresses less hortatory force than the explicit imperatives in Zephaniah's main section.[6] Nevertheless, we should still view 1:7–18 as a low-level prophetic exhortation[7] that calls listeners to revere YHWH in silence (1:7a) and that provides further motivation[8] for this call (1:7b–18).

Content and form also indicate that the overall unit has two main parts—exhortation (1:7a) and rationale (1:7b–18), the latter of which has two halves. Following the hortatory appeal in 1:7a (הַס), the prophet uses a motive clause (כִּי) to base his call to honor God in the imminence of God's punishment: "the day of YHWH is near" (קָרוֹב יוֹם יְהוָה, 1:7b). He then describes the divine retribution against Jerusalem (1:7b–13). At both 1:8 and 1:12 the climax marker "and it will happen . . . that" (וְהָיָה) signals development from the motive clause in 1:7b and introduces two discrete paragraphs. Each paragraph includes a divine action plus result—the first addressing YHWH's punishment on Jerusalem's political and religious leaders (1:8–11) and the second describing the divine condemnation of all in the city who are complacent (1:12–13). YHWH declares punishment against the various parties through two first-person verbs (two *weqatal* forms in 1:8b, 9//a *yiqtol* and *weqatal* in 1:12b–c). Following the judgments, the form וְהָיָה occurs again, this time functioning as a regular verb (1:10, 13a)[9] and describing the implications for the city (1:10–11//1:13).

The lack of conjunction at the head of 1:14 suggests a disjunction from what precedes, but the focus on the day of YHWH continues. Asyndeton in Hebrew usually signals either a fresh beginning or explication,[10] and in 1:14a the repetition "the day of YHWH is near" (קָרוֹב יוֹם יְהוָה) from 1:7b suggests that 1:14–18 expands the reason for heeding the call to revere God with the focus now being impending doom for the entire world.[11] The prophet graphically describes the characteristics of the coming day (1:14–16) and then develops the effects, noting both humanity's distress (1:17) and destruction (1:18).

Significantly, 1:15–16 contain five of Longacre's six proposed markers for surface structure peak.[12] By heightening attention to the characteristics of YHWH's "day,"

---

6. The imperatives appear in Zeph 2:1 [2x]; 2:3 [3x]; 3:8 [1x]; 3:14 [4x].

7. So too Floyd, *Minor Prophets, Part 2*, 195, 199. For definitions, see Sweeney, *Isaiah 1–39*, 520.

8. See Sweeney, *Isaiah 1–39*, 524–25.

9. וַיְהִי ("and it happened that") or וְהָיָה ("and it will happen that") operates as a transition/climax marker when it lacks a clear subject (or antecedent) that agrees in number and gender and often when it introduces a protasis-apodosis construction (see DeRouchie, *How to Understand and Apply*, 117–19; *BHRG* §40.24–25). The occurrences of וְהָיָה in Zeph 1:8, 12 fit this definition, but the instances in both 1:10 and 1:13 have explicit subjects and are not found in two-element syntactic constructions.

10. Garrett and DeRouchie, *A Modern Grammar for Biblical Hebrew*, 284–85 (§37.C); DeRouchie, *How to Understand and Apply*, 103–9.

11. Motyer actually treats the phrase קָרוֹב יוֹם יְהוָה ("the day of YHWH is near") in 1:14a as an *inclusio* with similar wording in 1:7b, seeing the final unit of ch. 1 beginning in 1:14b and running through 1:18 (Motyer, "Zephaniah," 917). It is more natural, however, to see both phrases in 1:7b and 14a as *introducing* what follows.

12. Robert E. Longacre, *The Grammar of Discourse*, 2nd ed. (New York: Springer, 1996), 38–48. The feature not included is "concentration of participants."

Zephaniah creates a "zone of turbulence" in the text that further emphasizes the need to revere YHWH (1:7a).

1. *Rhetorical underlining:* The repetition of "day" (יוֹם) seven times in 1:15–16 calls attention to the central place of YHWH's day in this unit.
2. *Heightened vividness:* The prophet uses five pairs of nouns that graphically and arrestingly develop the portrayal of YHWH's day of "wrath" (עֶבְרָה) (1:15–16): "distress and anguish" (צָרָה וּמְצוּקָה), "ruin and devastation" (שֹׁאָה וּמְשׁוֹאָה), "darkness and gloom" (חֹשֶׁךְ וַאֲפֵלָה), "clouds and thick darkness" (עָנָן וַעֲרָפֶל), "trumpet blast and battle cry" (שׁוֹפָר וּתְרוּעָה).
3. *Change of pace:* The asyndetic construction along with five pairs of staccato-like outburst in 1:15–16 slows the oracle's pacing and by this brings tension into the text.
4. *Change of vantage point and/or orientation:* The shift from "the day of YHWH is near" (1:7b) to "the *great* day of YHWH is near" (1:14a) suggests a change in scope from local punishment to global punishment and perhaps also a shift from immediate to eschatological disaster.
5. *Incidence of particles and onomatopoeia:* The presence of prose particles
6. (הַ/אֲשֶׁר/אֶת־) helps formally distinguish prose from poetry.[13] Not one of the absolute nouns in the five construct pairs is definite, and this poetic flow draws attention to the brief unit.

Floyd and Renz disagree with this understanding of 1:7–18's discourse structure. They parallel the interjection in 1:7a with the possible sense of an imperative in 1:11. For Floyd, the whole unit exhorts people to prepare for the day of YHWH as for both a festival day of sacrifice (1:7–10) and a day of solemn lamentation (1:11–18).[14] Renz treats 1:7–10 and 1:11–18 as successive movements that share the same general structure, portray the coming threat at YHWH's day, and focus on God as the agent of destruction.[15] Both scholars fail to grasp the full significance of (1) the asyndeton (i.e., lack of connection) marking a fresh beginning at verse 14, (2) the repetition of "the day of YHWH is near" (קָרוֹב יוֹם יְהוָה) in 1:7b and 1:14a, and (3) the forms of וְהָיָה ("and it will happen that") in 1:8a and 12a used as discourse markers to introduce parallel units. They also inadequately account for 1:7a being an interjection and *not*

---

13. See Francis I. Andersen and A. Dean Forbes, "'Prose Particle' Counts of the Hebrew Bible," in *The Word of the Lord Shall Go Forth: Essays in Honor of David Noel Freedman in Celebration of His Sixtieth Birthday*, ed. Carol L. Meyers and M. O'Connor, vol. 1 of *American Schools of Oriental Research,* *Special Volume Series* (Winona Lake, IN: Eisenbrauns, 1983), 165–83.

14. Floyd, *Minor Prophets, Part 2*, 184–86.

15. Renz, *Books of Nahum, Habakkuk, and Zephaniah*, 485, 512.

an imperative[16] and that הֵילִ֫ילוּ in 1:11a is more likely an indicative *hiphil qatal* ("they have wailed") than a *hiphil* imperative ("Wail!").[17] Regardless of the latter point, 1:11a is best understood as an inner-paragraph comment directly related to what precedes; it does not start a new section.

Explanation of the Text

1. The Call to Revere YHWH (1:7a)

Building on the prophetic announcement of punishment in 1:2–6, Zephaniah now captures his yet-undefined audience's attention by calling them to "reverential silence at the approach of YHWH."[18] Like a herald, he prepares his listeners for the king's arrival through the arousing onomatopoeic exclamatory interjection הַס ("Hush!").[19] The ancients employed this term to signal a solemn announcement (Deut 27:9), to call courtiers to respectfully quiet themselves in an earthly king's presence (Judg 3:19), or to move potential worshipers of YHWH to turn their attention reverently to the great King (Hab 2:20; Zech 2:17[13]).[20] Caleb quieted the ten spies with a verbal form of the same root (Num 13:30), and then the Levites used a comparable term to silence weeping and grieved worshipers in the presence of God's holi-

ness (Neh 8:11). Combining the interjection with the spatial, compound, and idiomatic preposition "from before" (מִפְּנֵי, lit., "from the face of") suggests that YHWH's presence was near and deserves reverence (cf. Zech 2:17[13]). Like God's revelation at Sinai, encountering YHWH should evoke fear that leads to holiness (Exod 20:20). It should generate a disposition that says with Isaiah, "Woe to me, for I am ruined! . . . For the King, YHWH of hosts, my eyes have seen!" (Isa 6:5). Zephaniah had already used God's personal name "YHWH" (יְהוָה) in the superscription (Zeph 1:1) and twice in the oracular formula (1:2–3). Now, the name adds force to the main body with the title "Lord/Sovereign" (אֲדֹנָי) preceding it.[21] "Sovereign" highlights God's supreme, authoritative status, perhaps as covenant lord,[22] and may intentionally contrast with "Baal" (בַּעַל) in 1:4, a term that also means "master" but depicts ownership.[23]

---

16. Floyd refers to the interjection as a "command" but recognizes the form "is based on a noun rather than an imperative verb" (Floyd, *Minor Prophets, Part 2*, 193). Renz wrongly considers the interjection as an imperative and then follows Floyd in relating the interjection to the form he tags an imperative in 1:11a (Renz, *Books of Nahum, Habakkuk, and Zephaniah*, 485).

17. Although formally the same, the context suggests that הֵילִ֫ילוּ in Zeph 1:11a is more likely a *hiphil qatal* third masculine plural of ילל ("they have wailed") than a *hiphil* masculine plural imperative of ילל ("Wail!") (against Renz, *Books of Nahum, Habakkuk, and Zephaniah*, 498).

18. Vlaardingerbroek, *Zephaniah*, 82.

19. The LXX uses εὐλαβεῖσθε ("Beware!"), which equally captures the call to trusting awe.

20. Shepherd sees הַס ("Hush!") in Zeph 1:7 as a catchword that ties the book to Habakkuk within the Book of the Twelve (Shepherd, *Commentary on the Book of the Twelve*, 36).

21. As a title for YHWH, the noun אָדוֹן is always plural with a "fossilized" first common singular suffix (so "אָדוֹן," *HALOT* 12–13); this is an instance of the intensive or honorific plural (GKC, §124i; *IBHS*, §7.4.3.c). Thus, we should just read "Lord" and not "my Lord(s)."

22. The prophet will explicitly designate YHWH as "king" (מֶלֶךְ) in Zeph 3:15.

23. So Patterson, *Nahum, Habakkuk, Zephaniah*, 277; Gordon H. Johnston, "אָדוֹן (ʾādôn)," *NIDOTTE* 1:255.

2. A Reason to Revere YHWH Related to Jerusalem (1:7b–13)

a. The Impending Sacrificial Nature of YHWH's Punishment (1:7b–d)

The particle "for" (כִּי) in 1:7b marks the reason why listeners should silently revere God: the Sovereign YHWH (אֲדֹנָי יְהוִה) is about to arrive for his day of judgment. Royal inscriptions from the ancient world combined the language of "sovereignty" with "a day of conquest," asserting that a true sovereign could achieve his victory in a single day.[24] While such a background could have influenced YHWH's prophets, "day" (יוֹם) in the biblical phrase "the day of YHWH" (יוֹם יְהוָה) seems to mean a discrete yet undefined occasion. Indeed, as Achtemeier notes, "day" in Zephaniah "designates not a definite *extent* of time but a definite *event* in time, whose nature is to be determined entirely by the Lord."[25] Therefore, "the day of YHWH" could entail multiple fulfillments escalating to a climax.[26]

Within the Book of the Twelve, the Joel-Amos-Obadiah sequence supplies the initial descriptions of YHWH's day, and the Zephaniah-Haggai-Zechariah-Malachi sequence develops it.[27] God's major and minor prophets apply "the day of YHWH" (יוֹם יְהוָה) and its abbreviated parallels (e.g., "the day," "that day") in two ways: (1) the ultimate day when YHWH will punish and restore/re-create the world and (2) the periodic penultimate days that anticipate it.[28] The day of YHWH is the climactic future event when God will finally establish his sovereignty, eradicate evil, and bring the world lasting peace (e.g., Zeph 1:14–18; 3:8; Ezek 39:8).[29] But Scripture also links it with YHWH's various typological intrusions into space and time to reconstitute right order through punishing wickedness—both against the wider world

---

24. Stuart, "The Sovereign's Day of Conquest," 159–64.

25. Elizabeth Achtemeier, *Nahum–Malachi*, Interpretation (Atlanta: John Knox, 1986), 66. See also Patterson, *Nahum, Habakkuk, Zephaniah*, 286–87.

26. Similarly, De Vries, *From Old Revelation to New*, 60; A. Joseph Everson, "The Days of Yahweh," *JBL* 93 (1974): 331.

27. Shepherd, *Commentary on the Book of the Twelve*, 355.

28. Scholars have defined the core of Israel's "day of YHWH" tradition in various ways—e.g., a vision of YHWH's enthronement (Mowinckel), anticipations of YHWH's future work on behalf of Israel (Černý), holy war and conquest (von Rad), treaty curses (Fensham), theophany (Hoffman), or various blends of these options (Cross, Weiss, Everson). In my perspective, we must take a more eclectic approach to the day of YHWH. As Motyer writes, on the one hand, "The Hebrew word *day* (*yôm*) is used idiomatically for a decisive event or series of events, a moment or period in which destiny is settled. . . . [The day of YHWH is] the climax alike of history, sin, and the purposes of God" (Motyer, "Zephaniah," 3:917–18). On the other hand, "In some sense the prophets saw significant historical events as the day of the Lord. . . . The prophets simply had in mind that these were events of such a dire nature that they exemplified a reality that would be fully demonstrated when the day finally came" (Motyer, "Zephaniah," 3:918; cf. Greg A. King, "The Day of the Lord in Zephaniah," *BSac* 152 [1995]: 16–32). See Sigmund Mowinckel, *He That Cometh:*

The Messiah Concept in the Old Testament and Later Judaism, trans. G. W. Anderson, The Biblical Resource Series (Oxford: Blackwell, 1956); L. Černý, *The Day of Yahweh and Some Relevant Problems* (Prague: University of Karlova, 1948); von Rad, "The Origin of the Concept of the Day of Yahweh," 97–108; F. Charles Fensham, "A Possible Origin of the Concept of the Day of the Lord," in *Biblical Essays: Proceedings of the Ninth Meeting of Die Ou-Testamentiese Werkgemeenskap in Suid-Afrika, and Proceedings of the Second Meeting of Die Nuwe-Testamentiese Werkgemeenskap van Suid-Afrika*, ed. A. H. Van Zyl (Stellenbosch: Potchefstroom Herald, 1966), 90–97; Yair Hoffman, "The Day of the Lord as a Concept and a Term in Prophetic Literature," *ZAW* 93 (1981): 37–50; Frank Moore Cross, "The Divine Warrior in Israel's Early Cult," in *Biblical Motifs: Origins and Transformations*, ed. Alexander Altmann (Cambridge, MA: Harvard University Press, 1966), 11–30; Meir Weiss, "The Origin of the 'Day of the Lord'—Reconsidered," *HUCA* 37 (1966): 29–63; Everson, "Days of Yahweh," 329–37. For some recent surveys of the issue, see Hiers, "Day of the Lord," *ABD* 2:82–83; LaRocca-Pitts, "The Day of Yahweh as a Rhetorical Strategy among Hebrew Prophets"; Barker, "Day of the Lord," *DOTPr*, 132–43.

29. See the Canonical and Theological Significance in this Chapter for how Christ's first coming inaugurated this reality but his second coming consummates it (cf. 2 Thess 1:9–10; 5:2–6; 2 Pet 3:10).

(Isa 13:1–22)[30] and Israel/Judah (Amos 5:18).[31] The ultimate result is a new creation where God's remnant people exalt YHWH through his messianic Davidic king, enjoy God's presence and peace, and are holy (e.g., Isa 4:2–6; 11:1–10; Zech 14:1–21).[32]

The OT statements regarding this "day" are often ambiguous, leaving the reader unclear whether they refer to proximate events or ultimate (eschatological) events. The passage of time clarifies the difference, however, and initial, partial fulfillments establish the certainty that complete fulfillment is coming.

Many in OT Israel likely perceived each historical intrusion of divine wrath as potentially the consummate judgment of the ages (e.g., against Judah [Lam 2:21] or Babylon [Isa 13:13, 19]). However, in time the faithful recognized them as foreshadowings of when YHWH would "make a definite end of all previous history of the whole world, and from this day onwards in the new world there begins an everlasting Kingdom of Yahweh never experienced anywhere before."[33] In Ezek 38:17, YHWH queries of the one named "Gog," "Are you he of whom I spoke in former days by the hand of my servants the prophets of Israel, who in those days prophesied

for years that I would bring you against them?" (cf. Rev 20:7–10). YHWH then declares, "Behold, it is coming, and it will come about.... That is the day that I have spoken" (Ezek 39:8; cf. Jer 6:22–23). Zephaniah is one of the voices God used to anticipate this "day" of his just anger, which is initially directed toward Jerusalem (Zeph 1:7b–13) in anticipation of his wrath against the whole world (1:14–18).[34] For Zephaniah, the ultimate day of global judgment appears to dominate his mind. However, he was likely also anticipating Babylon destroying Jerusalem. This event would have substantiated his message and bolstered confidence that YHWH would later bring universal devastation.[35] While it is possible that the prophet himself may not have distinguished the two events, the shift from "the day of YHWH is near" (1:7a) to "the *great* day of YHWH is near" (1:14a) suggests otherwise.

We know YHWH's day is imminent "for" (כִּי) he has already "prepared a sacrifice" (הֵכִין . . . זֶבַח, 1:7c).[36] If Zephaniah originally proclaimed his message during the Feast of Ingathering (see the comments at 1:2, 5), some may have thought he only spoke about some sacrificial rite in that festival,[37] which had more animal offerings than any

---

30. Cf. Isa 2:10–22; Jer 46:10–12; Ezek 30:1–9; Joel 2:1–11; 3:4[31]; 4:9–16[3:9–16]; Obad 15.

31. Cf. Isa 3:1–4:1; Ezek 13:5; Joel 1:15; Zech 14:1; Mal 3:23[4:5].

32. Cf. Joel 3:1–5[2:28–32]; Amos 9:11–15; Zeph 3:11–20.

33. Černý, *Day of Yahweh and Some Relevant Problems*, 84. Cf. Mowinckel, *He That Cometh*, 145.

34. Some scholars treat Zephaniah's "day of YHWH" language as secondary, believing that eschatological dread and hope arose only later in Israel's history (e.g., Seybold, *Satirische Prophetie*, 23–25; Seybold, *Nahum, Habakuk, Zephanja*, 89–90; Vlaardingerbroek, *Zephaniah*, 80–82). Such views neither take Scripture at face value nor respect Zephaniah's coherence and cohesion. Also, the book contains literary links to 2 Kgs 21–23, which chronicles the very period of which Zephaniah attests to have been a part (Zeph 1:1).

35. The prophets regularly stress the "nearness" of YHWH's retributive justice (using the infinitive absolute form קָרוֹב as an

adjective) when speaking against both Israel and the nations (Zeph 1:7, 14; cf. Isa 13:6; Ezek 30:3; Joel 1:15; 4:14[3:14]; Obad 15). Fulfilled short-term prophecies (like the destruction of Jerusalem in 586 BC) would have substantiated the prophets' claims of eschatological and universal destruction (like Zephaniah apparently predicts in 1:2–3, 14–18; cf. Deut 18:22; Ezek 33:32–33). These factors should have aroused both dread and hope, awakening some people out of their spiritual slumber.

36. Sweeney treats 1:7c as a second reason (alongside 1:7b) for the demand for silence in 1:7a (Sweeney, *Zephaniah*, 75, 78). Had Zephaniah intended this, he would have likely conjoined the second parallel ground clause by *waw* (= וְכִי "and for") (cf. Gen 33:11; Josh 7:15; 1 Sam 19:4; 22:17; 1 Kgs 2:26; Job 31:25; Isa 65:16).

37. So Roberts, *Nahum, Habakkuk, and Zephaniah*, 177. Throughout Israel's history, the Feast of Ingathering provided the context for the temple altar's dedication (see 1 Kgs 8:2, 65; 2 Chr 5:3; 7:8–9; Ezra 3:4; cf. 1 Kgs 12:25–33; 1 Macc 4:36–59),

annual feast (see Num 28–29, esp. 29:12–40). The prophets commonly use sacrificial language to portray YHWH's day of wrath against Jerusalem (Isa 22:5, 12–14; Jer 12:3) and her evil neighbors (Isa 34:1–2, 5–6; Jer 46:10; Ezek 39:17, 20–21). Floyd sees a combination of cultic ("day of sacrifice") and non-cultic ("day of slaughter") imagery here.[38] The Bible always portrays the "day of sacrifice" as a "day of slaughter"—a divine war against heaven's enemies resulting in death and anticipating YHWH's ultimate day of righting all wrongs and reconciling all things.[39] Zephaniah intentionally ties together God's future fury on the wicked with the Torah's vision of penal substitutionary atonement as the only means of escape. Here, however, as Motyer aptly observes, "Zephaniah takes the word of grace (the provision of a sacrifice for sin) and makes it the vehicle of the message of wrath: those who have long despised the sacrifice that God provides become the sacrifice their sin merits" (cf. Jer 12:3).[40]

Where rebellion has created a breach in the covenant relationship, God must execute sovereign justice. Only the substitute or sinner's death can secure atonement (Lev 17:11; Isa 22:12–14). And when faith fails to secure atonement in the provided proxy (see Isa 52:13–53:12; Heb 9:22), God's fiery wrath will ultimately consume the offenders (see Zeph 1:18; 3:8). Zephaniah here echoes Isaiah's assertion regarding atonement: "Surely this wrong [of Jerusalem] will not be atoned for you *until you die*" (Isa 22:14).

That 1:7d is asyndetic suggests that the clause further describes the statement that "YHWH has prepared a sacrifice" in 1:7c. However, this does not help us know if YHWH's "invited ones" (קְרֻאָיו) that he has "consecrated" (הִקְדִּישׁ) in 1:7d are (1) the sacrificial victims themselves[41] or (2) those who will "eat" the sacrifice.[42] This latter group may be the birds and wild animals that will feast upon the dead's carcasses (see Ezek 39:17–20; cf. Deut 28:26)[43] or, more likely, the enemy invaders that YHWH set apart to destroy his adversaries (e.g., Isa 13:3–5; cf. Deut 28:49–52; Jer 10:25; 22:7).[44]

Elsewhere the biblical authors apply related forms of the root קדשׁ ("to be/make holy, to consecrate") to both the agents of slaughter (*pual* in Isa 13:3; *piel* in Jer 22:7) and the sacrifice itself, whether substitute animal (*hiphil* in Exod 28:38; *hithpael* in 2 Chr 30:17) or human rebel (*hiphil* in Jer 12:3, ESV = "set them apart"). After assessing these and related texts, de Jong argued that, unlike the *piel*, the *hiphil* form of קדשׁ in the OT never refers "to bringing something or someone into a temporary state of holiness to participate in cultic activity" (option 2). He, therefore, concluded that הִקְדִּישׁ in Zeph 1:7d means "irrevocably dedicated to Yahweh" as the sacrifice (option 1).[45]

---

which may further clarify Zephaniah's treatment of the day of YHWH as *sacrifice*.

38. Floyd, *Minor Prophets, Part 2*, 194.

39. Sweeney has rightly noted that with every sacrifice Israel's cultic calendar conceptualized "YHWH's creation and de-creation through the defeat of enemies" (Sweeney, *Zephaniah*, 81).

40. Motyer, "Zephaniah," 917.

41. E.g., Seybold, *Satirische Prophetie*, 25; Baker, *Nahum, Habakkuk and Zephaniah*, 95; Sweeney, *Zephaniah*, 78; John Hans de Jong, "Sanctified or Dedicated? הקדיש in Zephaniah 1:7," *VT* 68 (2018): 94–101; Renz, *Books of Nahum, Habakkuk, and Zephaniah*, 490.

42. E.g., Robertson, *Books of Nahum, Habakkuk, and Zephaniah*, 270–71; Ben Zvi, *Book of Zephaniah*, 83; Roberts, *Nahum, Habakkuk, and Zephaniah*, 178.

43. See also Luke 17:37; Rev 19:17–18. Ben Zvi believes the "invited ones" are intentionally ambiguous to generate uneasiness in the audience (Ben Zvi, *Book of Zephaniah*, 85–86).

44. Luther, "Lectures on Zephaniah," 325–26; Calvin, "Habakkuk, Zephaniah, Haggai," 206–7; Keil, "Twelve Minor Prophets," 10:441 (2:130); Patterson, *Nahum, Habakkuk, Zephaniah*, 279–80.

45. De Jong, "Sanctified or Dedicated?," *VT* 68 (2018): 94–101, quotes from 97 and 100.

In contrast, three reasons suggest that the ones "consecrated" are likely the agents of slaughter (option 2). First, de Jong's observation is too restrictive to cultic contexts and fails to appreciate that Zephaniah is blending images of the cult and covenantal curse. The biblical authors do employ the *hiphil* when designating individuals for a sacred covenantal purpose, whether as prophetic agents (Jer 1:5, "Before you came forth from a womb *I consecrated you* [הִקְדַּשְׁתִּיךָ]") or as a cursed sacrifice (Jer 12:3, "*And consecrate them* [וְהַקְדִּשֵׁם] for a day of slaughter"). Second, as Muraoka observed, some verbs like קדש have "scarcely discernible difference in meaning or nuance" when occurring in both *piel* and *hiphil* forms.[46] For example, in Exod 29:44 God declares that he will "consecrate" (*piel* of קדש) the tent of meeting, the altar, and the priests, but in 1 Kgs 9:3 YHWH asserts that he has "consecrated" (*hiphil* of קדש) the Solomonic temple. Third, de Jong fails to account for the relevant occurrences of the *qal* passive participle form for "invited ones" (קְרֻאִים or קְרוּאִים). These occurrences refer to either the instruments carrying out God's punishment (Ezek 23:23, ESV = "men of renown") or those feasting on a sacrifice (e.g., 1 Sam 9:13; 1 Kgs 1:41).

As such, the "guests" are most likely (1) the scavenging birds and beasts that will eat the slaughtered carcasses and/or (2) the invaders whom YHWH previously sent to destroy Judah. These destroyers

would then feast on the meat (i.e., spoil) like priests would during the sin or guilt offerings.[47] The second option seems most likely for two reasons: (1) enemies bring climactic devastation within Deuteronomy's list of curses (Deut 28:49–52); (2) Jerusalem's cleansing in Zeph 3:11b probably alludes to Isa 13:3–5, which refers to enemy invaders (see below). The Babylonians would be the most immediate referent for Zephaniah's "guests" (Jer 34:21–22; Hab 1:6).[48] Significantly, in a parallel text, YHWH uses similar language to announce that Babylon will serve as his instrument of slaughter against Judah: "As for me, I have commanded to those consecrated by me [לִמְקֻדָּשָׁי]; also I have invited [קָרָאתִי] my warriors for my anger—those exultant in my eminence" (Isa 13:3; cf. Jer 22:7).

If Zephaniah speaks about the Babylonians, he likely never names them because they are only agents and YHWH remains Judah's biggest threat. Also, the Babylonians would function as types for the ultimate priestly destroyers of evil— King YHWH working through his royal Son and his godly remnant. These would execute God's wrath on the nations (Ps 149:5–9).[49] This godly remnant may legitimately be part of Zephaniah's understanding. Thus, 1:7d could provide the book's first explicit clue that YHWH would preserve an unpunished remnant (Zeph 2:7, 9; 3:9–10, 12; cf. Jer 1:5) who would witness and even participate in the chastisement of the wicked.[50]

---

46. Joüon, 144n1.

47. For more on God's use of the other nations to chasten Israel, see Isa 10:5–10; Jer 5:15–17; 49:37; Ezek 5:16; Hos 8:14; Joel 2:25; Amos 6:14; Hab 1:12.

48. Schmidt notes how the prophets regularly refer to YHWH's agent of destruction, characterizing the perpetrator as (1) coming from afar (Deut 28:49; Isa 5:26; Jer 4:16; Hab 1:8) in the north (Isa 14:31; Jer 4:6; 51:48; Ezek 38:6, 15), (2) speaking an incomprehensible language (Deut 28:49; Isa 28:11; 33:19; Jer 5:15), (3) moving as fast as the wind (Deut 28:49; Isa 5:26;

Jer 6:26; Ezek 38:9, 16; Hab 1:8) on horses or chariots (Isa 5:28; Jer 6:23; Ezek 38:4, 15; Joel 2:4; Hab 1:8), (4) showing no mercy (Deut 28:50; Jer 6:23; Joel 2:3), and (5) besieging or destroying cities (Deut 28:52; Isa 14:31; Jer 4:16; Joel 2:7) (Werner H. Schmidt, "צָפוֹן *ṣāpôn* North," *TLOT* 3:1096).

49. Cf. 1 Cor 6:2 and Rev 2:26–27 with Ps 2:9; Rev 12:5; 19:15.

50. Cf. Dan 7:22; Joel 4:8–16[3:8–16]; Zech 14:5; Mal 3:21[4:3]; Matt 19:28; Rom 16:20; Rev 20:4.

b. The Implications of YHWH's Punishment for Jerusalem (1:8–13)

Two small paragraphs (1:8–11; 1:12–13) follow the "for" (כִּי) clause in 1:7b. Both paragraphs include stated actions followed by result. They each begin with a fronted וְהָיָה ("and it will happen that") functioning as a climax marker. They then use וְהָיָה again but this time as a full verb to express the result of God's punishment (1:10, 13a).[51] The day of YHWH will come against Jerusalem's political and religious leaders (1:8–11) and her complacent citizens (1:12–13). The prophet alludes to the temple in 1:9, mentions known city-locations in 1:10–11, and explicitly names the capital "Jerusalem" in 1:12. The initial phrase "in the day of YHWH's sacrifice" (בְּיוֹם זֶבַח יְהוָה) in 1:8 stands as the referent for the temporal statements "at that time" (בָּעֵת הַהִיא) and "in that day" (בַּיּוֹם הַהוּא) in 1:9, 10, 12. Thus, one should read all the events in this unit as happening approximately at the same time.[52]

(1) YHWH's Punishment of the City's Political and Religious Leaders (1:8–11)

YHWH's punishment against "the remnant of the Baal" in Judah (1:4) would reach as far as the nation's debauchery and idolatry extended. This included Jerusalem's political and religious leaders (cf. 3:3–4) but not the king who led the reform (2 Kgs 22–23; cf. 2 Chr 34–35).[53] With two fronted *weqatal* forms, God declares that he will discipline the nobles and cultic personnel "in the very day of YHWH's sacrifice."[54] The repetition of the phrase "And I will visit [punishment]" (וּפָקַדְתִּי) in 1:8b and 1:9 both distinguishes the groups and emphasizes that "the day of YHWH's sacrifice" (יוֹם זֶבַח יְהוָה) is, in part, a retributive event of serious proportions.[55] YHWH has appointed a day of "visitation" (Isa 10:3; 29:6; cf. Dan 9:24) that will bring chastisement to some (Zeph 1:12; Isa 24:22; Jer 6:15; 10:15)[56] and salvation to others (Zeph 2:7).[57] Furthermore, as Sweeney highlights, the verb choice is ironic. The ones whom God "appointed" (פקד) to bring justice (e.g., Num 31:48; Deut 20:9; 2 Kgs 11:15) are the very ones whom he will "visit" (פקד) with judgment.[58] That Zephaniah was aware of such high-level corruption suggests his place in the royal house (see Zeph 1:1). His very peers were causing the problems in the land, and his love for YHWH compelled him to speak up.

(a) YHWH's Punishment of the Leaders (1:8–9)

The first group that YHWH says he will punish are the political overseers—the aristocracy. He divides them into three parties and introduces them with "on ... and on ... and on" (וְעַל ... וְעַל ... עַל, 1:8). The "officials" (שָׂרִים) were public leaders who helped oversee government and military operations on the king's behalf (Jer 26:10; 36:12, 21; 43:5). The "king's sons" (בְּנֵי־הַמֶּלֶךְ) were likely the royal princes (2 Kgs 10:13; Jer 36:26; 38:6)—perhaps

---

51. On the distinction between וְהָיָה as climax marker and full verb, see Structure and Literary Form for Zeph 1:7–18.

52. So De Vries, *From Old Revelation to New*, 52; cf. 44, 47.

53. Smith, Roberts, and Bailey think that Zephaniah's oracle omits mention of King Josiah because he was a minor lacking influence (2 Kgs 22:1) (J. M. P. Smith, "Book of Zephaniah," 196; Roberts, *Nahum, Habakkuk, and Zephaniah*, 178; Bailey, "Zephaniah," 429). However, Josiah likely needed no correcting because he obeyed God and led the reform movement (2 Kgs 23:25; cf. 23:3, 21). So too Keil, " Twelve Minor Prophets," 10:442 (1:130).

54. Many scholars assert that this phrase is secondary (e.g.,

J. M. P. Smith, "Book of Zephaniah," 196; Seybold, *Satirische Prophetie*, 25–26; Seybold, *Nahum, Habakuk, Zephanja*, 96; Roberts, *Nahum, Habakkuk, and Zephaniah*, 178; Vlaardingerbroek, *Zephaniah*, 85). This view fails to recognize how sacrificial imagery intentionally frames this unit (see 1:7–8, 17–18).

55. The verb פקד generally means "to visit" (cf. Zeph 2:7d) but can mean "to avenge, afflict, bring punishment" when the verb is intransitive, as here (cf. 1:9a, 12c; see also Isa 10:12; 27:1; Jer 9:24; 11:22). "פקד," *HALOT* 955, under *qal*, §5.

56. Cf. Luke 19:44.

57. Cf. 1 Pet 2:12.

58. Sweeney, *Zephaniah*, 83.

multiple generations of royal offspring (e.g., sons of Manasseh, Amon, and Josiah), who partnered with the officials and together with them made up the royal court.[59] The phrase "all who dress in foreign attire" (כָּל־הַלֹּבְשִׁים מַלְבּוּשׁ נָכְרִי) could designate a societal class or an office. Israel had requirements for dress related to the pursuit of holiness (Num 15:38–40; cf. Deut 22:11–12). The OT regularly treats certain clothing as a sign of importance (e.g., 1 Kgs 10:5; Job 27:16; Ezek 16:13).[60] We know that both in ninth-century Israel (2 Kgs 10:22) and in Zephaniah's seventh-century Judah (2 Kgs 22:14 // 2 Chr 34:22) there were individuals designated as keepers of "the wardrobe/garments" (הַבְּגָדִים/הַמֶּלְתָּחָה) in both political and religious spheres. At the least, this foreign dress means some Judean nobles had the financial means to wear imported garments to formal events. They highly valued the world's self-image and by this implicated themselves.[61]

Robertson, however, has noted how types of clothing possibly distinguished those worshiping foreign gods from YHWH's faithful. Specifically, Jehu ordered the keeper of the wardrobe to secure "the vestments for all the worshipers of the Baal" and then charged the worshipers themselves to ensure that there were no servants of YHWH among them (2 Kgs 10:22–23). Robertson writes, "In the vast throng assembled for sacrifice, recognition of the priests of Baal in distinction from the priests of Yahweh may have hinged on a difference in clothing."[62] From this perspective, the different priestly groups of Zeph 1:4 or those worshiping "the host of the heavens" in 1:5 could have worn different attire.[63]

From God's perspective, the nobles' outer garb associated them with the nations and testified to their inner corruption.[64] Hence, Zephaniah confronted them. Indeed, Josiah's reform efforts were attempting to curb "the nations' abominations" that his predecessors followed (2 Kgs 21:2; cf. 21:20).

The phrase "all who step over the threshold" (כָּל־הַדּוֹלֵג עַל־הַמִּפְתָּן) in Zeph 1:9 likely targets the

---

59. Cf. Renz, *Books of Nahum, Habakkuk, and Zephaniah*, 491. The LXX read τὸν οἶκον τοῦ βασιλέως ("the house of the king" = הַמֶּלֶךְ בֵּית), broadening the punishment to the entire royal family perhaps because the king's sons would be too young for the prophet's castigation. If Zephaniah preached in 622 BC, Josiah's oldest son, Eliakim (born around 634 BC and renamed Jehoiakim), would have only been around twelve years old (cf. 2 Kgs 23:34, 36). Brin suggests that the title "the son of the king" may have referred to non-biological, administrative personnel with a close tie to the monarch; here "son" would express membership in a social class, as it may in relation to the army (1 Sam 14:52; 2 Chr 25:13), the prophets (2 Kgs 2:3; Amos 7:14), the priests (Ezra 10:18; 1 Chr 9:30), the sages (Isa 19:11), people of importance (Neh 11:14), and servants of a household (Eccl 2:7) (Gershon Brin, "The Title ה]בן[מלך and Its Parallels: The Significance and Evaluation of a Cultic Title," *AION* 29 [1969]: 432–65; cf. Sweeney, *Zephaniah*, 84). Sabottka suggests that "the king" (הַמֶּלֶךְ) in 1:8 refers to the Baal, thus making "the sons of the king" not Jerusalem's princes but all those associated with "the remnant of the Baal" (Zeph 1:4a) (Liudger Sabottka, *Zephanja*, BO 25 [Rome: Biblical Institute Press, 1972], 36–38). Two reasons make Sabottka's proposal unlikely: (1) The mention of "officials" in 1:8b proves that the

prophet is drawing attention to the corruption of the city's elite. (2) The pair הַשָּׂרִים . . . בְּנֵי הַמֶּלֶךְ ("the officials . . . the king's sons") points elsewhere to Jerusalem's political leaders (Jer 52:10; cf. 2 Kgs 25:7).

60. Cf. Matt 11:8.

61. As Renz notes, "Typifying people as *clothed in foreign clothing* first of all characterizes them as parading their wealth, but it likely also portrays them here as being at home in an alien culture or at least as being unconcerned about preserving a distinct identity" (Renz, *Books of Nahum, Habakkuk, and Zephaniah*, 492).

62. Robertson, *Books of Nahum, Habakkuk, and Zephaniah*, 276.

63. Building on 2 Kgs 10:22, Roberts proposes that the prophet may have been targeting a certain form of "religious syncretism, in which foreign apparel was donned for religious purposes" (Roberts, *Nahum, Habakkuk, and Zephaniah*, 178; cf. Robertson, *Books of Nahum, Habakkuk, and Zephaniah*, 276).

64. See 1 John 2:15–16. Smith notes how closely national distinctiveness was tied to loyalty to one's god in the ancient world (J. M. P. Smith, "Book of Zephaniah," 198). See also Vlaardingerbroek, *Zephaniah*, 86; Keil, " Twelve Minor Prophets," 10:442 (2:131).

priests who regularly passed through the temple doorway.[65] The other seven occurrences of "threshold" (מִפְתָּן) all refer to a temple's entrance,[66] and all but six of the twenty-two occurrences of the parallel term for "threshold" (סַף) relate to Jerusalem's temple.[67] We know of three "keepers of the threshold" (שֹׁמְרֵי הַסַּף) who participated in Josiah's temple renovation and worship reform. They were high ranking temple-personnel (after the chief priest and second priests, 2 Kgs 25:18; Jer 52:24) who received contributions (2 Kgs 22:4; cf. 12:10) and removed pagan cult-instruments (23:4). There were also many other lower-level cult-workers known as "guardians of the thresholds" (שֹׁעֲרֵי הַסִּפִּים); they served as porters or entry guards at the gates in the large temple complex (1 Chr 9:22; 2 Chr 23:4). However, because Zephaniah refers to a singular, specific threshold (הַמִּפְתָּן), he is likely referring to the priests entering the temple-building itself rather than to various common worshipers coming in and out of the temple-courtyard and broader precinct.

The four other occurrences of the verb דלג are all in the *piel* and mean "leap."[68] The *qal* in our passage likely retains the same basic meaning,[69] though perhaps with less intensity (e.g., "to step").[70] The only potential biblical parallel for leaping a threshold comes in 1 Sam 5:3–5. There the priests of Dagon would not tread on his temple's threshold (= מִפְתָּן) after finding his idol's head and hands lying cut off upon it. No link between Zephaniah and Samuel is apparent, but the similar imagery could suggest that the activity in Zeph 1:9 is superstitious. Furthermore, we know that Judah at times borrowed religious practices from the Philistines (Isa 2:6), and, as we will see in the commentary at Zeph 1:11, the Philistines (= "the people of Canaan," cf. 2:5) were directly influencing Zephaniah's Judah.[71] While the activity's precise significance remains unclear, someone would likely not want to touch the threshold because they recognized it to be a spiritually-symbolic border between the realm of the divine and the outside world.[72] Such a view would be an affront to proper worship of YHWH.

Many commentators follow this interpretation,[73] but Sweeney is correct that this possibility only seems apparent if we translate the verb דלג as "to leap"—thus expressing an unexpected way to move through a doorway. If, however, the verb

---

65. Cf. Sweeney, *Zephaniah*, 85. In contrast, Luther and Calvin think Zephaniah keeps addressing the servants of government leaders (cf. Renz, *Books of Nahum, Habakkuk, and Zephaniah*, 493–94). They "leap" to do their masters' corrupt desires (Luther, "Lectures on Zephaniah," 18:328), or they triumphantly "danced on the threshold" of the weak (Calvin, "Habakkuk, Zephaniah, Haggai," 15:209–10); cf. Keil, " Twelve Minor Prophets," 10:442 (2:131).

66. See 1 Sam 5:4–5; Ezek 9:3; 10:4, 18; 46:2; 47:1.

67. In four occurrences, סַף appears to refer to the threshold in a royal building (1 Kgs 14:17; Zeph 2:14; Esth 2:21; 6:2), and two others involve private dwellings (Judg 19:27; Ezek 43:8). The distinction between מִפְתָּן and סַף is not clear. Some call them "synonyms" (Carol L. Meyers, "Threshold," *ABD* 6:544); others propose that סַף is the threshold as viewed from inside the building, whereas מִפְתָּן is the name when viewed from without ("סַף II," *DCH* 6:177). Cognates to סַף outside the Bible can denote parts of a doorway other than its threshold (Meyers, "Threshold," *ABD* 6:544). Thus, סַף in Scripture is likely a general term related to an entrance in numerous contexts,

but מִפְתָּן always relates specifically to the temple's threshold. The denominative verb ספף seems to mean "to stand at the threshold" (Ps 84:11[10]).

68. See 2 Sam 22:30//Ps 18:30; Song 2:8; Isa 35:6.

69. In a recent thorough study of the D-stem in biblical Hebrew, Beckman has argued that if the *qal* is fientive, then the *piel* has a similar meaning to the *qal*. See John C. Beckman, "Toward the Meaning of the Biblical Hebrew Piel Stem" (PhD diss., Harvard University, 2015), iv, xiii, 50, 243, 252–53.

70. So Sweeney, *Zephaniah*, 87.

71. The Tg. Neb. supplies the interpretive rendering כָּל דִּמְהַלְכִין בְּנִמּוֹסֵי פְּלִישְׁתָּאֵי ("all who walk according to the customs of the Philistines").

72. Meyers, "Threshold," *ABD* 6:545; cf. J. M. P. Smith, "Book of Zephaniah," 197–98; Joel F. Drinkard Jr., "Threshold," *NIDB* 5:589.

73. Cf. Roberts, *Nahum, Habakkuk, and Zephaniah*, 179; Seybold, *Nahum, Habakuk, Zephanja*, 97; Berlin, *Zephaniah*, 79–80; Vlaardingerbroek, *Zephaniah*, 87–89; Patterson, *Nahum, Habakkuk, Zephaniah*, 280.

means only "to step," then Zephaniah would simply be using a descriptive phrase for the priests without any derogatory sense. They simply are the ones who "step over the threshold," thus distinguishing them from the commoner who could not do so.[74] Regardless, the following appositional phrase starkly reveals a key component of their sinful activity.

As recognized by most translations (contra the ESV), the phrase "those who fill their Sovereign's house with violence and deception" (הַמְמַלְאִים בֵּית אֲדֹנֵיהֶם חָמָס וּמִרְמָה) in 1:9 begins without a conjunction. This suggests that, no matter how one renders דלג, the common sins of cruelty and falsehood characterized the religious leaders of the temple-precinct.[75] The phrase "their Sovereign's house" (בֵּית אֲדֹנֵיהֶם) very naturally reads as an allusion to Lord (אֲדֹנָי) YHWH's temple because of the prior focus on the temple threshold in 1:9 and YHWH being called as "Sovereign/Lord" (אֲדֹנָי) in 1:7a.[76] God set the priests apart to teach God's instruction authoritatively (Lev 10:10–11) and to

care for the temple and its sacrifices (1 Chr 23:13). But King Manasseh had led them astray, building in the temple altars to foreign deities, setting up a carved image of Asherah, and engaging in child sacrifice, witchcraft, and sorcery (2 Kgs 21:4–7). Then his son Amon repeated his sins (21:20–21). Such was Judah's state when Josiah inherited it. The religious leaders were filling the temple of God with "violence" (חָמָס), oppressing the sojourner, the fatherless, and the widow, and shedding innocent blood (Jer 6:7; Hab 1:2–3). As "violence" instigated the flood punishment (Gen 6:11, 13), it now resulted in the temple's and its leadership's destruction.[77] Furthermore, the very priests who were supposed to be working for justice practiced "deception" or "fraud" (מִרְמָה; cf. Jer 5:27 with 5:28, 31), and the community followed their pattern (9:8 with 9:4–6).[78] Thus, Yahweh would punish because the very house called by his name had become "a den of robbers" (7:11).[79]

To summarize, in Zeph 1:8–9 the prophet claims

---

74. Sweeney, *Zephaniah*, 87–88.

75. For similar prophetic confrontations, see Amos 3:10; Isa 3:14–15; Mic 2:2; Ezek 22:27–29.

76. So too Sweeney, *Zephaniah*, 88; Motyer, "Zephaniah," 3:919; contra Seybold, *Nahum, Habakuk, Zephanja*, 97; Ben Zvi, *Book of Zephaniah*, 100–102. The LXX read it as a reference to YHWH's temple: τοὺς πληροῦντας τὸν οἶκον κυρίου τοῦ θεοῦ αὐτῶν ἀσεβείας καὶ δόλου ("those who fill the house of the Lord their God with impiety and fraud"). The term אֲדֹנָי is formally the plural noun אֲדֹנִים plus first common singular suffix (= "my lords"). This leads some to believe Zephaniah is referring to either the homes of various government officials (Patterson, *Nahum, Habakkuk, Zephaniah*, 280) or temples of pagan deities (Baker, *Nahum, Habakkuk and Zephaniah*, 96). However, because אֲדֹנָי commonly refers to YHWH and also stands as a common *qere* of nearly every occurrence of the divine name, grammarians tag it a "plural of majesty" whose suffix often appears emptied of its original force—thus "Sovereign/Lord" rather than "my Sovereign/Lord" (GKC, §§87g; 135q; cf. §102m). While אֲדֹנֵיהֶם in Zeph 1:9a is formally plural, it most likely bears a singular referent because בֵּית ("house") that precedes it is singular—"the *house* of their sovereign." It would be strange for many human "masters" or distinct divine "lords"

to have a single house. Moreover, since אֲדֹנָי clearly refers to the "Sovereign" YHWH in 1:7a, the context supports אֲדֹנָי in 1:9a as being YHWH. In 1:9 the "house" refers to YHWH's temple.

77. So too Robertson, *Books of Nahum, Habakkuk, and Zephaniah*, 278.

78. Holladay proposes Jer 5:27 is directly dependent on Zeph 1:9 (Holladay, "Reading Zephaniah with a Concordance," 674). The verb II רמה (cf. "II רמה," *HALOT* 1239) occurs only eight times in the OT and commonly refers to some kind of deceit, treachery, or betrayal carried out against another (e.g., Gen 29:25; Josh 9:22; 1 Sam 28:12; Prov 26:19). This related noun מִרְמָה occurs forty times and always describes crafty, treacherous dealings with others (e.g., Gen 34:13; 2 Kgs 9:23), whether through deceitful lips (Ps 17:1; 52:6[4]), false witness (Ps 24:4; Prov 12:17), false scales (Prov 11:1; Amos 8:5), or the like.

79. Cf. Matt 21:13; Mark 11:17; Luke 19:46. Even if "their master" refers not to YHWH but to King Josiah, the point of the violence and fraud remains similar since (1) Jerusalem's preexilic temple complex attached to the royal palace (2 Kgs 16:18; Ezek 43:6–9) and (2) the king controlled the treasures deposited in both the temple and palace (Roberts, *Nahum, Habakkuk, and Zephaniah*, 179).

Jerusalem's political and religious leaders instigated Judah's covenant rebellion and were a fundamental cause of its destruction (see Zeph 3:3–4).[80] Where selfishness, power, money, and pagan influence reign, abuse, oppression, and fraud prevail (see Zeph 3:1, 3–4, 19).[81] Eventually, YHWH would crush this wickedness and eliminate injustice and falsehood (see Zeph 3:13).

(b) The Resulting Impact on the City: Loss of the Source of Their Self-Exaltation (1:10–11)

The text now switches from discussing the initial victims of God's punishment to the resulting impact on the city (1:10–11). It emphasizes this impact by using the oracular formula "the utterance of YHWH" (נְאֻם־יְהוָה).[82] The third masculine singular קוֹל ("sound") serves as the subject of וְהָיָה ("And he/it will be"),[83] thus showing that it is a true verb expressing result and not a macrosyntactic signal. A collective "sound" (קוֹל) will accompany the "punishment" promised in 1:8–9.[84] It will take the form of a "cry" (צְעָקָה), a "wail/lament" (יְלָלָה),

and "a great crash" (שֶׁבֶר גָּדוֹל) amid Jerusalem's environs (cf. Jer 25:36; 48:3).[85] A locative prepositional phrase (= מִן "from") follows the latter three audible noises and suggests they all work together, most likely in apposition to "sound" (קוֹל). The varied noises describe the din of war when YHWH appears,[86] bringing with him pain, grief, and destruction.[87]

A shriek would rise from "the Fish Gate" (שַׁעַר הַדָּגִים), which was Jerusalem's main northwest entrance (2 Chr 33:14; Neh 3:38–39) and which was likely associated with the fish market (13:16).[88] Similarly, howling would come from "the Second Quarter" (הַמִּשְׁנֶה), the city section just west of the Temple Mount and City of David, where at least some influential people resided (2 Kgs 22:14).[89] Zephaniah probably mentions these locations and "the heights" to clarify that God would begin his punishment of Jerusalem from the direction that would first destroy the district housing many of its leaders (Zeph 1:8–9).[90] "The heights" (הַגְּבָעוֹת) likely refers to some particular higher areas within

---

80. Cf. Jer 32:32; 34:18–19.

81. Cf. Isa 1:23; Amos 3:10.

82. See De Vries, *From Old Revelation to New*, 62.

83. My translation renders as the impersonal "and there will be" to preserve more closely the Hebrew word order.

84. Against Vlaardingerbroek, *Zephaniah*, 92; cf. Sweeney, *Zephaniah*, 89. קוֹל functions as an interjection meaning "Listen!" only when it stands with a following genitive at *the beginning* of a sentence (GKC, §146b; Joüon, §162e).

85. The phrase "a great crash" (שֶׁבֶר גָּדוֹל) occurs elsewhere only in Jer 4:6; 6:1; 14:17; 48:3; 50:22; 51:54, and Holladay thinks Jeremiah is building on Zeph 1:10 (Holladay, "Reading Zephaniah with a Concordance," 674). For comparable use of קוֹל, צְעָקָה, and יְלָלָה, see Jer 25:36. שֶׁבֶר refers to a "breaking" ("I שֶׁבֶר," *HALOT* 1404–5), but in Zeph 1:10 the focus appears clearly on the audible nature and could refer to the devastating sounds of human destruction (e.g., Isa 15:5; 65:14; Prov 15:4; so Vlaardingerbroek, *Zephaniah*, 93) or to reverberation of buildings collapsing.

86. For a curse with similar language, see "The Inscriptions of Bar-ga'yah and Mati'el from Sefire," trans. Joseph A.

Fitzmyer (*COS* 2.82:214). Cf. "The Treaty Between *KTK* and Arpad," trans. Franz Rosenthal (*ANET*, 660).

87. Shepherd rightly suggests that Jeremiah's use of similar language to describe Moab's destruction signals that "this Day of the LORD is not limited to the historical judgment of Judah" (Shepherd, *Commentary on the Book of the Twelve*, 357). However, Zephaniah may blur these two judgments so that Judah's historical punishment foreshadows the eschatological global judgment. Shepherd virtually states this himself: "The Day of the LORD is an eschatological day of worldwide judgment, which Judah's historical judgment merely prefigures" (Shepherd, *Commentary on the Book of the Twelve*, 356).

88. Dale C. Liid, "Fish Gate," *ABD* 2:797–98. The LXX's rendering πύλης ἀποκεντούντων ("the gate of those who pierce") apparently reflects reading הַדָּגִים ("of the fish") as הֹרְגִים ("the slayers," 2 Kgs 17:25; cf. Hos 9:13) (so Roberts, *Nahum, Habakkuk, and Zephaniah*, 175).

89. Philip J. King, "Jerusalem," *ABD* 3:755. Nehemiah 11:9 may also refer to this area.

90. Whereas the Hinnom and Kidron Valleys surround Jerusalem's west, southern, and eastern boundaries and the

Part II: The Setting of the Savior's Invitation to Satisfaction

the city rather than to hills surrounding Jerusalem in the north and west since Zephaniah lists them after geographical locations *within* Jerusalem.[91]

Floyd notes that Zephaniah's wailing language could refer either to mourning accompanying "irrecoverable loss (e.g., Mic 1:8–16) or a public complaint ritual in which people pray for deliverance from some communal crisis (e.g., Joel 1:13–14).[92] Verse 11 describes an economic collapse, which Floyd suggests logically supports (כִּי "for") the latter option (cf. Amos 5:16–17). The prophet responds to the leaders' wickedness by targeting their source of self-exaltation—both wealth and foreign influence will be no more. However, a "great crash" (שֶׁבֶר גָּדוֹל; cf. Jer 50:22; 51:54) accompanies the sounds, and this points to something greater than a public mourning rite. Zephaniah envisions Jerusalem under siege, and the wailing relates not only to deprivation but also to destruction and death!

The head of 1:11 lacks a connector. This suggests that the statement develops the assertion in 1:10 that YHWH would first target Jerusalem's northwest environs. The verb "to wail" (from the root ילל) in 1:11a echoes the noun "wail" (יְלָלָה) in 1:10, further suggesting a link between verses 10–11. Verse 11 begins with הֵילִילוּ, and its initial position supports reading it as a *hiphil* imperative masculine plural ("*Wail*, O inhabitants of the Mortar!") (e.g., NASB20, ESV, NLT, NET, NIV, CSB).[93] Read

this way, verse 11 becomes a temporary directive intrusion, adding rhetorical force to the prediction in verse 10 that cries of pain would rise.[94] While possible, we can also parse הֵילִילוּ as *hiphil qatal* third common plural, so that the clause is indicative: "The inhabitants of the Mortar *have wailed*" (cf. NRSVue, CEB). This reading seems more likely for several reasons. (1) Verse 10 expresses the horrific sounds of war and sets a descriptive context that is carried on in verse 11.[95] (2) Zephaniah commonly uses the *qatal* rhetorically in his predictions, treating what is future as if it is already accomplished (see 2:11, 15; 3:15), thus indicating its certainty. (3) The placement of the *qatal* verb before its subject in 3:15 provides precedent for this syntax in Zephaniah.[96] (4) The prophet apparently uses imperatives to guide the book's main argument (2:1, 3; 3:8, 14), so an imperative here seems out of place. Regardless of how we parse הֵילִילוּ, 1:11 is an embedded inner-paragraph comment that is not part of the book's primary hortatory thrust.

Those who have wailed are "the inhabitants of the Mortar" (יֹשְׁבֵי הַמַּכְתֵּשׁ). This region or precinct's location is not clear. The meaning of מַכְתֵּשׁ as "mortar" (from the root כתש "to pound") implies a flat depression within Jerusalem.[97] Also, the Mortar's position was probably associated with the Fish Gate or Second Quarter on Jerusalem's northwest side since verse 11 likely expands on verse 10

Tyropoeon Valley runs north-south down the middle of the city, the north has no valley and therefore is most vulnerable to outside attack.

91. So J. M. P. Smith, "Book of Zephaniah," 199; Baker, *Nahum, Habakkuk and Zephaniah*, 97; Motyer, "Zephaniah," 920.

92. Floyd, *Minor Prophets, Part 2*, 198.

93. Similarly, the LXX, Tg. Neb., and Peshitta all take הֵילִילוּ as an imperative.

94. Renz reads an imperative here. He also wrongly assumes that Isa 23:6, 14 and Jer 51:8 require it (Renz, *Books of Nahum, Habakkuk, and Zephaniah*, 498n162), but they do not. See Tachick, *Use of Zephaniah 3 in John 12*, 89.

95. Both Sweeney and Vlaardingerbroek note that the de-

scriptive context supports reading הֵילִילוּ as a *qatal*. Following Wolff, however, Vlaardingerbroek still interprets it as an imperative since he believes it is part of the prophetic genre "The Call to Public Complaint" (cf. Isa 14:31; Jer 6:26; Ezek 21:17) (Vlaardingerbroek, *Zephaniah*, 91–92, 94; Sweeney, *Zephaniah*, 90; see Hans Walter Wolff, "Der Aufruf Zur Voksklage," *ZAW* 76 [1964]: 48–56; cf. Sweeney, *Isaiah 1–39*, 544).

96. Contra Roberts, *Nahum, Habakkuk, and Zephaniah*, 175.

97. "מַכְתֵּשׁ,"*HALOT* 583. מַכְתֵּשׁ might refer to the whole city of Jerusalem, which Jer 21:13 calls "the valley" (see J. M. P. Smith, "Book of Zephaniah," 200). But the grammar of Zeph 1:11 makes this unlikely, and "the mortar" probably refers to

(due to the asyndeton). Archaeologists suggest the probable location is the Tyropoeon Valley, situated between the Western Hill and the City of David/Temple Mount and stretching northward through the Second Quarter to the Fish Gate.[98]

People wail because (כִּי "for") God will have destroyed all the foreign traders of goods. The Hebrew text again stresses the certainty of punishment by treating it as if it had already occurred. It uses two divine-passive *niphal qatal* verbs, first of II דמה ("have been silenced") and then of כרת ("were cut off").[99] Switching from future prediction to accomplished fact would have forced readers to feel more keenly the seriousness of the prophet's call.

The context associates the Mortar with "the people of Canaan" and "those laden with silver," suggesting that the Mortar was the market district wherein "foreign" influence and "violence and fraud" commonly flourished (cf. 1:8–9). The term "Canaan" (כְּנַעַן) or "Canaanite" (כְּנַעֲנִי) is often a general noun meaning "merchant" or "trader" (Job 40:30; Prov 31:24; Isa 23:8). Many interpreters fol-

low this rendering here (e.g., NRSVue, ESV, NET, NIV, CEB, CSB), likely because the following appositional statement speaks of "all those laden with silver" (כָּל־נְטִילֵי כָסֶף)—those associated with trade who make money off sold goods.[100] But Zephaniah speaks of "*the people* of Canaan" (עַם כְּנַעַן). This phrase makes little sense as "a people of a trader." Additionally, the prophet associates the same term "Canaan" (כְּנַעַן) with the Philistines in 2:5.

Others propose that "the people of Canaan" refers to the Israelites whose business dealings made them "become Canaanite."[101] This approach would potentially echo "the remnant of the Baal" (the Canaanite's chief god) motif from 1:4. There the Israelites associated with foreigners so much that they took on their character (1:4–6, 8; cf. Ezek 16:3). While this is possible, at least three reasons suggest that YHWH will destroy non-Israelite traders associated with the Judeans: (1) Zephaniah 2:5 treats "Canaan" as the land of the Philistines (cf. Num 13:29; Deut 1:7). (2) The prophet is confident that God's wrath is universally "against all the

---

a specific location, despite Luther thinking that Zephaniah uses the term to stress that God would grind down Jerusalem's citizens as though they were in a mortar (cf. Prov 27:22; Luther, "Lectures on Zephaniah," 18:330). Keil believes Zephaniah uses the term to refer to a specific location while employing judgment imagery (Keil, " Twelve Minor Prophets," 10:443 (1:133).

98. See Amihai Mazar, *Archaeology of the Land of the Bible, Volume 1: 10,000–586 B.C.E.*, AYBRL (New York: Doubleday, 1990), 424.

99. In Zeph 1:11, the parallel with כרת ("cut off") shows that death is in view. The LXX misses this parallel by translating 1:11b ὡμοιώθη πᾶς ὁ λαὸς Χανάαν ("all the people who were made like Canaan"), apparently reading I דמה ("to be like, resemble"). Distinguishing between the *niphal* of II דמה ("be silenced") and III דמה ("be destroyed") is often difficult, perhaps because the two roots are actually one (cf. Ps 49:13, 21[12, 20]; Isa 15:1; Jer 47:5; Hos 4:5; Obad 5; see "II דמה" and "III דמה," *HALOT* 225–26).

100. The Hebrew verb נטל means "to lay upon" (*qal*, Lam 3:28) and "to lift up" (*piel*, Isa 63:9). Most contemporary translations and one ancient version render the noun נָטִיל in Zeph 1:11 actively ("who weigh out," NRSVue, NASB20, ESV;

Peshitta) rather than passively ("those laden with," KJV, CSB; LXX, Tg. Neb., Vulgate). Elsewhere, the Hebrew Bible communicates the active sense with the verb (שׁקל "to weigh") followed by כֶּסֶף ("silver") (e.g., Gen 23:15; Isa 55:2; Jer 32:9; Zech 11:12). While Isa 40:13 may contain an intransitive meaning of "have weight," the verb נטל elsewhere never bears the transitive meaning of "weigh out." Vlaardingerbroek unjustifiably views the grammatical form as active but helpfully assigns a passive meaning and affirms that the passive rendering "captures the essence of the meaning" (Vlaardingerbroek, *Zephaniah*, 96; cf. Berlin, *Zephaniah*, 87). Unlike minted coins that a government or religious authority stamped to certify that they met weight standards, the "silver" (כֶּסֶף) in Zeph 1:11 likely refers to money in the form of bullion (by weight), for coinage did not become the standard money until the mid-fifth century (though it is apparent much earlier; see 1 Chr 29:7; cf. Ezra 2:69; Neh 7:69–71). See John Wilson Betlyon, "The Provincial Government of Persian Period Judea and the Yehud Coins," *JBL* 105 (1986): 633–42; John Wilson Betlyon, "Coinage," *ABD* 1:1076–89.

101. Contra Luther, "Lectures on Zephaniah," 330; Keil, " Twelve Minor Prophets," 10:443 (2:133); Motyer, "Zephaniah," 920; Patterson, *Nahum, Habakkuk, Zephaniah*, 281.

inhabitants of the earth" (Zeph 1:18), including the Philistines (2:5). (3) The contrast between "wailing" (*hiphil* of ילל) and "silence" (*niphal* of II דמה) in 1:11 suggests *two* different groups in 1:11. The Judean elite inhabiting the Mortar cry out because God has eradicated ("silenced/cut off") the source of their superiority (i.e., the Philistine traders).

Therefore, Zeph 1:11 probably refers to a negative Philistine influence comparable to a statement of Isaiah a century earlier: "They fill up from the east and are interpreting signs like the Philistines, and with the children of foreigners they clap hands. His [Jacob's] land is filled with silver and gold, . . . with horses, . . . with empty idols" (Isa 2:6–8; cf. Hos 12:8[7]).[102] The Philistines' location on the Mediterranean coast made them important merchants who engaged in foreign trade.[103] In this reading, YHWH promises to end the source of the Judean leaders' pride and to eradicate those becoming rich at the poor's expense (cf. Zeph 1:8, 13, 18).[104]

(2) YHWH's Punishment of the City's Complacent People (1:12–13)

Paralleling 1:8a, the fronted climax marker וְהָיָה ("and it will happen that") in 1:12a begins to further explain the devasting nature of Jerusalem's divine chastisement. In 1:13a, וְהָיָה has an explicit subject (חֵילָם "their wealth"), so it functions as a full verb rather than a discourse marker. It signals that what follows is the consequence of the divine search-and-destroy-mission that 1:12b–c details (וּפָקַדְתִּי . . . אֲחַפֵּשׂ "I will search . . . and I will

visit [punishment]").[105] Zephaniah's line of vision certainly includes Jerusalem's leaders but likely expands beyond them to include all in the city who were uncritically self-reliant and secure.

[12] YHWH will "search" (*piel yiqtol* of חפשׂ) the city "with the lamps" (בַּנֵּרוֹת), seeking the rebels who dwell in the shadows. The lamps signify both the thoroughness of YHWH's hunt (see Luke 15:8) and the inescapable nature of God's fury (Isa 24:17–18; Amos 5:18–20; 9:2–4; cf. Ps 139:11–12). They also imply Jerusalem's spiritual darkness and the relative hiddenness of her sin (cf. Zeph 1:15)[106] and may even hint that God's wrath would come like a thief in the night (Joel 2:9).[107] Thus, Moses's ancient assertion that "your sin will find you out" will prove true (Num 32:23).

Zephaniah uses the definite article to highlight *the* lamps. This could be an example of imperfect determination, wherein biblical authors make objects specifically determinate because they are used for a specific purpose (e.g., Exod 16:32 of "a full omer"; 21:7 "with *an* awl"; 21:20 "with *a* rod").[108] However, the definiteness may point to *the* seven "lamps" found on each of the ten temple lampstands in Jerusalem's temple, from which "the eyes of YHWH . . . roam through all the earth" (Zech 4:2, 10).[109] From Moses's day forward, the lampstand light was to burn from evening to morning (e.g., Exod 27:20–21; Lev 24:3; 2 Chr 13:11) lest God's people incur his wrath (cf. 2 Chr 29:7–8). The lamps' continual illumination testified that YHWH was "home" at the central sanctuary and

---

102. So too Wendland and Clark, "Zephaniah," 9; cf. Calvin, "Habakkuk, Zephaniah, Haggai," 241.

103. See H. J. Katzenstein and Trude Dothan, "Philistines," *ABD* 5:326–33.

104. Cf. Baker, *Nahum, Habakkuk and Zephaniah*, 97. Vlaardingerbroek rightly observes that societies based on trade and riches always produce situations "where one human is dependent on another" (Vlaardingerbroek, *Zephaniah*, 42).

105. On the use of פקד, see the note at Zeph 1:8.

106. Using comparable vocabulary, we read elsewhere that "a man's breath is the lamp [I נֵר] of YHWH, which searches [חֹפֵשׂ] all chambers of a belly" (Prov 20:27; cf. Ps 139:12).

107. Cf. 1 Thess 5:2; Rev 3:3.

108. So Vlaardingerbroek, *Zephaniah*, 98 following Joüon, §137m.

109. Sweeney, *Zephaniah*, 94. Moses's tabernacle had only one lampstand (Exod 25:37; 39:37), but Solomon's temple had ten (1 Kgs 7:49; 2 Chr 4:7).

invited worshipers into fellowship with him. If the prophet is indeed envisioning these lamps in Zeph 1:12, the temple is now dark, and YHWH's enflamed presence has departed in a just fury of torment to seek his enemy (cf. Isa 66:6). Ezekiel would later see the departure of YHWH's glory from the temple (Ezek 8–11), and it was this move that opened the city up for Babylon to destroy it.

Next, parallel definite participle phrases characterize the rebel objects of divine fury in two ways. First, they are "the men who thicken on their wine dregs" (הָאֲנָשִׁים הַקֹּפְאִים עַל־שִׁמְרֵיהֶם, Zeph 1:12). This phrase points either to maturation or spoilage of wine.[110] Bad things often happen in the dark. Here the prophet portrays Jerusalem's citizens in a drunken state, and in the Prophets, this often implies poor mental and ethical judgment and disengagement with reality (e.g., Isa 5:11–13; Jer 51:7–8; Hab 2:5).[111] English versions commonly translate the whole dynamically as those "who are complacent" (e.g., ESV, NIV84; cf. NRSV), "who settle down comfortably" (CSB), "who are stagnant in spirit" (NASB20), or "who are entrenched in their sin" (NET). The context certainly supports the idea that they were unhealthily and foolishly at "ease" (cf. Jer 48:11–12) and that their commercial flourishing was only the result of a developing inner

corruption.[112] YHWH would soon pour them out as a drink offering.

The *second* characteristic, which may explain the first, is that they are "the men . . . who say in their heart, 'YHWH will neither do good nor do ill'" (הָאֹמְרִים בִּלְבָבָם לֹא־יֵיטִיב יְהוָה וְלֹא יָרֵעַ, Zeph 1:12; cf. Ps 10:11, 13). While recognizing YHWH's existence, they lived as deists, believing God was removed and would never fulfill his promises of blessing and curse, "good" and "ill" (cf. Jer 5:12–13; Amos 9:10; Mic 3:11).[113] In Jer 10:5, we learn that the idols of the nations were like scarecrows in a cucumber field, having no real life and not having in them the power to do evil or good (cf. Isa 41:23).[114] Thus, Zephaniah's contemporaries were treating YHWH as an idol, as if he were one who does not care for people or account for their actions. In this regard, Calvin perceptively noted:

> It is what peculiarly belongs to God, to govern the world, and to exercise care over mankind, and also to make a difference between good and evil, to help the miserable, to punish all wickedness, to check injustice and violence. When anyone takes away these things from God, he leaves him an idol only. . . . [A]ll who deny God to be the governor of the world entirely extinguish, as much as they can, his glory.[115]

---

110. David J. Clark, "Wine on the Lees (Zeph 1:12 and Jer 48:11)," *BT* 32.2 (1981): 241–43. No manuscript supports emending the Hebrew הָאֲנָשִׁים ("the men") to הַשַּׁאֲנַנִּים ("those at ease," Ps 123:4; Isa 32:9, 11; Amos 6:1; Zech 1:15) as some scholars suggest (e.g., J. M. P. Smith, "Book of Zephaniah," 201). The LXX translated שִׁמְרֵיהֶם ("their wine dregs") with τὰ φυλάγματα αὐτῶν ("their ordinances"), apparently mistaking the root for I שמר ("to keep, watch"), in the sense of keeping God's Torah (e.g., Deut 4:6; 5:1; 6:3).

111. Cf. Prov 4:14–16; 20:1; 23:29–35; 31:4–7. Sweeney, *Zephaniah*, 94. Baker is correct that Zephaniah is condemning apathy and not the use of alcohol (Baker, *Nahum, Habakkuk and Zephaniah*, 98).

112. So Floyd, *Minor Prophets, Part 2*, 198; cf. Vlaardingerbroek, *Zephaniah*, 100.

113. See also Ezek 8:12; 9:9. The good and ill here are "likely not ethical but material: to bring advantage or to do harm" (Vlaardingerbroek, *Zephaniah*, 100; cf. 41; J. M. P. Smith, "Book of Zephaniah," 202). Luther notes that in asserting YHWH's own indifference, the Judeans were also mocking Zephaniah as he declared their coming end (Luther, "Lectures on Zephaniah," 18:332). Yet as would be true in the days of Ezekiel, Yahweh would fulfill Zephaniah's prophecies and "they will know that a prophet has been in their midst" (Ezek 33:33).

114. Holladay thinks Jer 10:5 directly depends on Zeph 1:12 (Holladay, "Reading Zephaniah with a Concordance," 674).

115. Calvin, "Habakkuk, Zephaniah, Haggai," 217.

Psalm 73:10–11 closely parallels this portrayal of Jerusalem's population, for Asaph bemoans of God's people: "And waters of a full cup are slurped for them, and they will say, 'How has God known, and is there knowledge in the Most High?'" (cf. Job 21:12–13; Mal 3:13–14). YHWH declares, "I will visit [punishment]" on such people (Zeph 1:12).[116]

YHWH's delayed judgment should have prompted the people to humility, gratitude, and repentance (cf. 2 Pet 3:9). Instead, they failed to fear punishment or desire blessing. Yet such "functional atheism" is foolish (Ps 14:1//53:2[1]; cf. 10:4), for YHWH's patience does not mean that he will automatically clear the guilty (Exod 34:6–7).[117] Jerusalem's complacent sinners would soon meet their end. Indeed, YHWH would remove false securities ("wealth . . . houses . . . vineyards") and cleanse the land of its defilements (cf. Zeph 2:4, 9, 13, 15; 3:6).

[13] Zephaniah 1:13a–b declares that YHWH's punishment would deplete Jerusalem's goods and dwellings, leaving the Judeans' "wealth" (חֵילָם, Gen 34:29; Deut 8:17) for "spoil" (מְשִׁסָּה, 2 Kgs 21:14; Isa 42:22; Jer 30:16) and their houses for "desolation" (שְׁמָמָה, Lev 26:33; Isa 62:4; Jer 6:8). The text implies that YHWH's unnamed destroying agents

(initially the Babylonians) would claim all moveable property and destroy all that was immovable, leaving the land a waste.

Verse 13c–e then supplies two pairs of positive-negative statements. The initial lines each use an indicative future *weqatal* (וּבָנוּ "and they will build"; וְנָטְעוּ "and they will plant"). These suggest that the "nearness" of YHWH's day of punishment (1:7b) was still far enough off, for individuals would build more houses and plant more vineyards. Nevertheless, the text is stressing that those who build and plant would *not* enjoy the benefits of their labors (וְלֹא יֵשֵׁבוּ "and they will not inhabit"; וְלֹא יִשְׁתּוּ "and they will not drink"). Zephaniah draws on the wording in Deut 28:30, 39 and declares that God's curse would sweep them all away (cf. Amos 5:11; Mic 6:15), just as he had intended to do with the Canaanites so many years before (Deut 6:10–11).[118]

The imagery strongly suggests that the prophet relates the rebel Judeans with the "people of Canaan" (see Zeph 1:11b) and believes that through his day of wrath YHWH was purifying a new promised land in which to establish his presence and kingdom (see Canonical and Theological Significance section below).

---

116. For this phrase, see the comments at Zeph 1:8–9.

117. Cf. Deut 32:4; Hab 1:13. See Motyer, "Zephaniah," 921; Dever, "The Message of Zephaniah," 868. Cf. Calvin, "Habakkuk, Zephaniah, Haggai," 221; J. M. P. Smith, "Book of Zephaniah," 202; Vlaardingerbroek, *Zephaniah*, 100.

118. Futility curses were common in the ancient world (see K. A. Kitchen, *On the Reliability of the Old Testament* [Grand Rapids: Eerdmans, 2003], 291–94; cf. Melissa Ramos, "A Northwest Semitic Curse Formula: The Sefire Treaty and Deuteronomy 28," *ZAW* 128 [2016]: 205–20; Laura Quick, *Deuteronomy 28 and the Aramaic Curse Tradition*, Oxford Theology and Religion Monographs [Oxford: Oxford University Press, 2018]). For the loss of houses and agriculture, see, e.g., the early 2nd millennium BC legal compilation, "The Code of Hammurabi," trans. Theophile J. Meek (*ANET*, 178–80 [rev. xxvi:68, 78]), later translated as "The Laws of Hammurabi," trans. Martha Roth (*COS* 2.131:352-53). See also Gary M. Beckman's

translation of the late 2nd millennium BC text, "Hittite Treaty 18B Between Hattusili III of Hatti and Ulmi-Teshshup of Targhuntassa," §9 (rev. 5-7), in *Hittite Diplomatic Texts*, ed. Hary Hoffner Jr., 2nd ed., WAW 7 (Atlanta: Scholars Press, 1999), 112; the early first millennium BC "Inscriptions of Bar-ga'yah and Mati'el from Sefire," trans. Joseph A. Fitzmyer (*COS* 2.82:214; and the post-700 BC Assyrian text entitled, "The Vassal Treaties of Esarhaddon," trans. Erica Reiner (*ANET*, 538). Nevertheless, Zephaniah most likely alludes to Deut 28 since (1) he frequently cites Deuteronomy (see Zephaniah's Use of Scripture in the introduction) and (2) the prophets regularly allude to the old covenant curses and restoration blessings (see Douglas Stuart, *Hosea–Jonah*, WBC 31 [Dallas: Word, 1987], xxxi-xli; Douglas K. Stuart, "Malachi," in *The Minor Prophets: An Exegetical and Expository Commentary*, ed. Thomas Edward McComiskey, 3 vols. [Grand Rapids: Baker Academic, 1992], 1259–60; cf. DeRouchie, *How to Understand and Apply*, 46–51).

Figure 3.1: Scriptural Allusions in Zephaniah 1:13	
Zeph 1:13	**Deut 28:30, 39**
וּבָנוּ בָתִּים וְלֹא יֵשֵׁבוּ וְנָטְעוּ כְרָמִים וְלֹא יִשְׁתּוּ אֶת־יֵינָם And they will build houses, **but they will not inhabit**; and they will plant vineyards, **but they will not drink** their wine.	בַּיִת תִּבְנֶה וְלֹא־תֵשֵׁב בּוֹ כֶּרֶם תִּטַּע וְלֹא תְחַלְּלֶנּוּ . . . כְּרָמִים תִּטַּע וְעָבָדְתָּ וְיַיִן לֹא־תִשְׁתֶּה וְלֹא תֶאֱגֹר A house you will build, **but you will not dwell** in it; a vineyard you will plant, but you will not begin [to drink] it. . . . Vineyards, you will plant and serve, but wine **you will not drink**, and you will not gather.
Amos 5:11	**Mic 6:15**
בָּתֵּי גָזִית בְּנִיתֶם וְלֹא־תֵשְׁבוּ בָם כַּרְמֵי־חֶמֶד נְטַעְתֶּם וְלֹא תִשְׁתּוּ אֶת־יֵינָם: Houses of stone you have built, **but you will not dwell** in them. Vineyards of desire you have planted, **but you will not drink** their wine.	אַתָּה תִזְרַע וְלֹא תִקְצוֹר אַתָּה תִדְרֹךְ־זַיִת וְלֹא־תָסוּךְ שֶׁמֶן וְתִירוֹשׁ וְלֹא תִשְׁתֶּה־יָּיִן: You will sow, but you will not reap. You will tread olive, but you will not anoint with oil, and [your will tread] grape juice, **but you will not drink** wine.

3. Another Reason to Revere YHWH Related to the Whole World (1:14–18)

Zephaniah 1:14 echoes the motive clause in 1:7b (כִּי קָרוֹב יוֹם יְהוָה "for the day of YHWH is near") and opens a new unit that builds on the previous reason to hush before God in 1:7b–13. Those listening to Zephaniah should revere YHWH because of the nature of the encroaching punishment (1:14–16) and its devastating global effects (1:17–18).

a. The Characteristics of the Coming Day of Punishment (1:14–16)

Zephaniah again stresses the nearness of YHWH's day (1:7b) but now adds that the coming day of wrath is "great" (הַגָּדוֹל) (cf. Joel 2:11;

3:4[2:31]; Mal 3:23[4:5]).[119] As Zeph 1:17–18 makes clear, this adjective adds emphasis but also signals a shift in scope from local to global punishment and likely also a shift in time from immediate to long-range retribution. In hindsight, Zeph 1:7–13 appears to address Jerusalem's immediate punishment in 586 BC, but time has proven that 1:14–18 refer to the final judgment associated with the end of the age (cf. Mal 3:23[4:5]).[120] To speak of this latter day as "near and hastening fast" (קָרוֹב וּמַהֵר מְאֹד) is to see history with respect to eternity and God's timeline.[121]

(1) The Imminence of the Day (1:14a)

The imminent timing (Zeph 1:14a), the torturous sound (1:14b–c), and the sheer terror of the day

---

119. See also Hos 2:2[1:11]. Note also the "*great* tribulation" in Matt 24:21; Rev 2:22; 7:14.

120. Zephaniah 1:16 will allude to Isa 2:12, 15, an eschatological passage about YHWH punishing the world. Vlaardingerbroek asserts, "הַגָּדוֹל underscores the all-inclusive and eschatological character of the Day of Yahweh" (Vlaardingerbroek, *Zephaniah*, 106).

121. Specifically, the final period associated with Christ's first and second comings (Acts 2:20; Rev 6:17; 16:14; cf. Matt 24:32–33; Rom 13:11; Phil 4:5; Rev 1:3; 22:10). מַהֵר ("hastening") is either a *piel* participle without preformative *mem* (מְ, see GKC, §52s) or a *piel* infinitive construct functioning adverbially. Later biblical authors recognize that Zephaniah was among the prophets "serving not themselves but you" and that

(1:15–16) make an immediate response imperative (cf. Isa 13:6; Ezek 30:3).[122] Because (כִּי, Zeph 1:7b) "the great day of YHWH is near," Zephaniah's audience must revere God (1:7a).

(2) The Torturous Sound of the Day (1:14b–c)

Assuming that the prophet intended 1:14b to stand as a clause, the present study follows the pattern of the NKJV, NRSVue, ESV, and NIV in treating the form מַר ("bitter, potent") as the predicate adjective in 1:14b: "The sound of the day of YHWH *is bitter.*"[123] Zephaniah 1:14c then associates this unpleasant, torturous ring with the shouting of a "Mighty One"—a warrior (גִּבּוֹר). In contrast, the Masoretic cantillation links the term "bitter" with 1:14c.[124] It apparently treats 1:14b as an interjection and מַר in 1:14c as an adverb (i.e., "bitterly"; cf. Isa 33:7; Ezek 27:30).[125] The resulting translation of 1:14b–c would be something like: "The sound of the day of YHWH! A warrior is bitterly shouting there" (cf. YLT, CSB, NASB20).

Regardless of what מַר modifies, the "sound" (קוֹל) in 1:14b recalls the "sound" (קוֹל) of the day

in 1:10, where it is associated with the "cries" and "wails" of the victims of YHWH's war of judgment (cf. Isa 5:26–30).[126] This connection probably led the ESV translators to treat the "mighty one" of Zeph 1:14 (ESV = "mighty man") as a valiant soldier crying in defeat. In contrast, 1:14c probably points to YHWH's war cry for at least four reasons: (1) In 1:10–11 the terms for "cry" (צְעָקָה), "wail" (יְלָלָה), and "wailing" (ילל) differ from the term for "shouting" (צרח) in 1:14c. (2) YHWH is the only explicit attacker (see the first-person speech in 1:2–4, 8, 12, 17).[127] (3) Zephaniah 3:17 uses the same substantival adjective "Mighty One" (גִּבּוֹר) to designate YHWH as the Warrior (cf. Deut 10:17). The NIV agrees and renders the clause in Zeph 1:14c, "The Mighty Warrior shouts his battle cry" (cf. Pss 29:4; 68:33).[128] (4) Zephaniah likely is alluding to Isaiah, who proclaimed: "YHWH *like a mighty man* [כַּגִּבּוֹר] goes forth, like a man of war he arouses zeal; he cries out, even he *shouts aloud* [יַצְרִיחַ]; against his enemies he *will prove himself mighty* [יִתְגַּבָּר]" (Isa 42:13, italics added).

YHWH's "voice" (קוֹל) was prominent in the

---

he wrestled Scripturally with "what person or time the Spirit of Christ in [him] was indicating when he predicted the sufferings of Christ and the subsequent glories" (1 Pet 1:11–12). We, therefore, should not say conclusively that Zephaniah "did not foresee a history continuing for centuries" (Vlaardingerbroek, *Zephaniah*, 83). See Ben Zvi, *Book of Zephaniah*, 117–18, for a solid argument against Sabottka's repointing of the MT's וּמַהֵר מְאֹד as וּמַהֵר מָאַד with the meaning "and as a grand soldier himself" (Sabottka, *Zephanja*, 50–52; cf. Anson F. Rainey, "The Soldier-Scribe in Papyrus Anastasi I," *JNES* 26 [1967]: 58–60).

122. Cf. Joel 2:1; 4:14[3:14]; Obad 15.

123. The adjective מַר derives from the root מרר, which can mean "to be bitter, potent," whether of strong drink (Isa 24:9) or of trials/punishment (Ruth 1:13; Jer 4:18). Elsewhere, מַר carries the sense of "fierce" (Judg 18:25; 1 Sam 22:2; 2 Sam 17:8; Hab 1:6). The sound in Zeph 1:14 thus bears a painful, torturous ring. Other texts convey similar realities with מַר (Amos 8:10) and without it (Isa 13:7–8; Jer 30:5–7).

124. מַר follows the *zaqeph qaton* (i.e., a major disjunctive accent that stands over יְהֹוָה) and includes a *munaḥ* (מַר, i.e., a common conjunctive accent) that links it to what follows.

125. Biblical Hebrew can render adjectives as adverbs, especially those that are feminine (GKC, §100d).

126. Some scholars treat the קוֹל ("sound, voice") as an interjection, meaning, "Listen!" (e.g., Ben Zvi, *Book of Zephaniah*, 118–19; Berlin, *Zephaniah*, 189; Vlaardingerbroek, *Zephaniah*, 106–7; CSB; NASB20). Grammarians posit this reading only when קוֹל *begins* a sentence and a genitive follows it (GKC, §146b; Joüon, §162e). Retaining the normal sense of קוֹל is both possible and natural.

127. See Motyer, "Zephaniah," 3:922–23. The mention of "spoil" (מְשִׁסָּה) in 1:13a suggests that some human agents will claim booty, but the impersonal nature of the declaration keeps the focus on YHWH as the main warrior.

128. Many support this reading (e.g., Achtemeier, *Nahum-Malachi*, 71–72; Ball, *Rhetorical Study of Zephaniah*, 42; Ben Zvi, *Book of Zephaniah*, 120; M. O'Connor, *Hebrew Verse Structure*, 2nd ed. [Winona Lake, IN: Eisenbrauns, 1997], 246; Motyer, "Zephaniah," 922–23; Renz, *Books of Nahum, Habakkuk, and Zephaniah*, 505).

theophany at Sinai (Deut 4:12; 8:20; 18:16), and it will be prominent on the day of his wrath. The word order of Zeph 1:14c focuses on the "shouting," which the offending parties view as "bitter," for they realize that God's fury is against them.[129] From this perspective, the particle "there" (שָׁם) in 1:14c would refer to the location of YHWH's nearness, from which his cry goes forth.[130]

(3) The Terror of the Day (1:15–16)

Zephaniah 1:15–16 may describe YHWH's day of wrath and the horror of his punishment more ominously than any other OT passage.[131] As noted under Structure and Literary Form above, these verses signal the surface structure peak in chapter 1 and heighten the urgency of the call to revere YHWH (1:7a). The seven occurrences of "day" in these two verses (six in construct as "a day of . . ." and standing as the predicate of "that day") may portray de-creation (6 + 1), following the allusion

to de-creation in 1:3.[132] YHWH's sudden, coming day of fury will be unbearable for his adversaries.

Here Zephaniah summarizes the time as one of "wrath" (עֶבְרָה), and he reemploys this term in 1:18, as the prophets tend to do (e.g., Isa 13:9, 13; Ezek 38:19).[133] The Hebrew fronts "a day of wrath" before the subject to orient the reader to the context.[134] Five word-pairs in construct follow. Each pair adds to the terrifying nature of the divine retribution and begins with the term "day" (יוֹם). This repetition rhetorically intensifies YHWH's punishment.[135]

The terms "distress and anguish" (צָרָה וּמְצוּקָה) echo YHWH's prospective curses against Israel in Deuteronomy (Deut 28:53, 55, 57). However, Zephaniah applies these curses to the whole world (cf. Jer 16:19; Obad 12, 14; Hab 3:16), just as God promised would happen to all Mosaic covenant curses during the new era after exile (Deut 30:7). Heightening the dramatic effect of Zephaniah's

---

129. Normal word order for verbless clauses is subject-predicate (GKC, §141, l; Joüon, §154f), but communicators can place the predicate up front to orient the reader to the greater context (i.e., a contextualizing constituent) or to highlight prominent material (i.e., focus). See Randall Buth, "Word Order in the Verbless Clause: A Generative-Functional Approach," in *The Verbless Clause in Biblical Hebrew: Linguistic Approaches*, ed. Cynthia L. Miller, LSAWS 1 (Winona Lake, IN: Eisenbrauns, 1999), 79–108.

130. The versions struggled with the particle שָׁם ("there"). The LXX appears to read שָׁם as the inflected verb שָׂם ("he placed, appointed"): "The sound of the day of the Lord is bitter and harsh; it has worked powerfully [τέτακται δυνατή]" (Zeph 1:14). Ben Zvi and Berlin render שָׁם temporally as "then/at that time" (Ben Zvi, *Book of Zephaniah*, 120; Berlin, *Zephaniah*, 89; cf. IBHS, §39.9.1h). This is unlikely since translating every possible parallel as "there" seems to work best (e.g., Job 35:12; Pss 14:5//53:6[5]; 36:13[12]; 132:17; Prov 8:27).

131. Von Rad wrote, "Zephaniah contains the most comprehensive proclamation of the day of judgment" (Gerhard von Rad, "ἡμέρα, 'Day' in the OT," TDNT 2:945). Patterson notes how no less than six of the features of Zeph 1:14–18 occur in Joel 2:1–11 (Patterson, *Nahum, Habakkuk, Zephaniah*, 287).

132. So, too, Peter C. Craigie, *Twelve Prophets: Volume 2: Micah, Nahum, Habakkuk, Zephaniah, Haggai, Zechariah, and*

Malachi, DSBS (Louisville: Westminster John Knox, 1985), 116; Baker, *Nahum, Habakkuk and Zephaniah*, 100–101; Renz, *Books of Nahum, Habakkuk, and Zephaniah*, 506. Motyer even suggests that each of the six occurrences of the construct form "day" recall a particular day of the original creation week (Motyer, "Zephaniah," 923).

133. Cf. Isa 9:18; Lam 2:22; Ezek 22:21, 31.

134. When two nominals stand side by side, the most defined is the subject (see Janet W. Dyk and Eep Talstra, "Paradigmatic and Syntagmatic Features in Nominal Clauses," in *The Verbless Clause in Biblical Hebrew*, 133–86, esp. 152; cf. DeRouchie, *How to Understand and Apply*, 212–14). For more on the role of the contextualizing constituent, see the resources in the note on word order at 1:14c.

135. For Scripture's use of the various terms, see Ball, *Rhetorical Study of Zephaniah*, 84–88; Ben Zvi, *Book of Zephaniah*, 122–24. Vlaardingerbroek suggests these verses had "a more or less independent existence or stem from another context" (Vlaardingerbroek, *Zephaniah*, 103), and Ball posits that Zeph 1:15–16 represents an ancient hymn (Ball, *Rhetorical Study of Zephaniah*, 84). Such is unlikely, however, for the verses fail to express hope in God as is common throughout the Psalter. Zephaniah simply uses rhythm and repetition to heighten the gravity of YHWH's day and to emphasize the need to revere God (1:7a).

words, the initial two-word pairs include an assonantal wordplay in Hebrew ("distress and anguish," צָרָה וּמְצוּקָה *ṣārâ ûmĕṣûqâ*, Job 15:24; Jer 30:7; Obad 14; "ruin and devastation," שֹׁאָה וּמְשׁוֹאָה *šōʾâ ûmĕšôʾâ*, Job 38:27; Isa 10:3; Ezek 38:9).[136]

Furthermore, "darkness . . . gloom . . . cloud . . . thick darkness" (חֹשֶׁךְ . . . אֲפֵלָה . . . עָנָן . . . עֲרָפֶל) are all cataclysmic images that regularly describe YHWH's day.[137] Such images of shadow and night depict what happens when God's fierce, transcendent presence enters space and time.[138] They also express the reversal of creation (from life to death, from light to darkness) for those he is punishing (cf. Gen 1:2). In Egypt, the Israelites enjoyed the light of YHWH's favor while the enemies experienced a deep darkness (Exod 10:22–23); now all the world had become God's enemies, and his "day" would bring night to their existence (cf. Amos 5:18, 20). People often associate darkness with war and death, so it is difficult to know whether the biblical authors envisioned actual atmospheric changes or were simply depicting the personal experience of those dying.[139]

"Trumpet blast and battle cry" (שׁוֹפָר וּתְרוּעָה) refer to sounds of alarm that ready people for war in reference to both offense (e.g., Num 10:9) and defense (e.g., Amos 3:6). They are often associated with God's immediate or future judgments, whether from offense—as in Zeph 1:16 (Jer 51:27; Zech 9:14)—or defense (Jer 6:1; Joel 2:1).[140] God inaugurated the old covenant at Mount Sinai with darkness and trumpet call (Exod 19:16–20; 20:18; Deut 4:11; 5:22), and Zephaniah applies both images here. Thus, Zephaniah may view the foreboding images at Mount Sinai as anticipating the covenant's curses and end and may here be anticipating that God would establish a new covenant through his day of wrath.[141]

Two prepositional phrases beginning with "against" (עַל) and highlighting the objects of YHWH's anger conclude the subunit in Zeph 1:16: "against the unassailable cities and against the high battlements" (עַל הֶעָרִים הַבְּצֻרוֹת וְעַל הַפִּנּוֹת הַגְּבֹהוֹת). Using almost identical vocabulary in Deuteronomy's curses, YHWH had declared of his people's enemy: "And he will bring distress to you in all your

---

136. Bailey, "Zephaniah," 440.

137. The OT uses the imagery of darkness to describe the day of YHWH's proleptic and ultimate manifestations, both against Israel (Isa 5:30; 8:22; Joel 2:2 3:3–4[2:30–31]; Amos 5:18, 20; 8:9) and the foreign nations (Isa 13:10; Ezek 30:3; Joel 4:15[3:15]). The NT similarly describes the outpouring of God's wrath, both with respect to Jesus's death on the cross and to the final judgment (Matt 24:29; Acts 2:20; Rev 6:12; 8:12). The "Lamentation over the Destruction of Sumer and Ur" comparably depicts a god's punishment as a violent storm (ca. 2004 BC). Lines 388–392 read, "Woe! Storm after storm swept the Land together. The great storm of heaven, the ever roaring storm, The malicious storm which swept through the Land—The city-ravaging storm, the house-ravaging storm, The stable-ravaging storm, the sheepfold-burning storm" ("Lamentation over the Destruction of Sumer and Ur," trans. Jacob Klein [*COS* 1.166:535–39]). The Sumerian word translated as "storm" is UD, which usually means "day" or "weather" and therefore could be rendered "stormy-day" (*COS* 1.166:538n31).

138. Cf. 1 Kgs 8:12 // 2 Chr 6:1; Nah 1:3; Ps 97:2.

139. Recognizably, because YHWH dwells in "thick darkness" (1 Kgs 8:12), the association of darkness with war and death is specifically in relation to what happens when YHWH's transcendent presence enters space and time.

140. Isaiah associates the blowing of a great trumpet with the ingathering of the redeemed at the future second exodus (Isa 27:12–13; cf. 11:11). Zephaniah believes this ingathering of the saved will happen concurrently with the ingathering of the wicked for judgment (cf. Zeph 1:2–3; 3:8, 18–20). The NT connects such sounds with God's punishment (Rev 8:7; 11:15) and with Christ's second appearing and ingathering of the elect (1 Thess 4:16; cf. Matt 24:31).

141. For a similar understanding, see Robertson, *Books of Nahum, Habakkuk, and Zephaniah*, 283–84. Texts depicting the new covenant also associate cloud and theophany (Matt 17:5; 24:30; 26:64; Acts 1:9, 11; 1 Thess 4:17; Rev 1:7; 14:14–16).

Zephaniah 1:7–18   125

gates until the coming down of your high and un-assailable walls [חֹמֹתֶיךָ הַגְּבֹהוֹת וְהַבְּצֻרוֹת], in which you were trusting" (Deut 28:52). Now, as promised in Deut 30:7, YHWH extends this curse to all his enemies. Citing Zeph 1:16 with Isa 2:12, 15, Sweeney posits that Zephaniah may also be drawing on Isaiah and highlighting that "the previously threatened Day of YHWH from the time of Isaiah is about to take place."[142]

Vlaardingerbroek suggests that the "trumpet," "battle cry," "unassailable cities" (הֶעָרִים הַבְּצֻרוֹת), and "high battlements" in 1:16 allude to the capture of Jericho during the first conquest.[143] While the only significant linguistic parallel to this particular text is the mention of the "trumpet" (שׁוֹפָר, Josh 6:5, 20), the fact that the conquest motif is prevalent in 1:11, 13 makes this possibility feasible (for more, see the Canonical and Theological Significance section below). Furthermore, many accounts of Israel's conquest speak of the Canaanite's "unas-sailable cities" (Num 13:28; Deut 1:28; 9:1) that Israel overpowered (Deut 6:10–11; cf. Neh 9:25). As such, Zephaniah pictures the day of YHWH as a new and more complete conquest where neither Jerusalem's rebels nor any unrepentant sinner of the world will survive.[144] The Sovereign One easily overcomes humanity's false securities and the pride that produces them since human pride consistently incurs God's fury (Zeph 2:8, 15; 3:6).[145]

b. The Effects of the Coming Punishment (1:17–18)

With Zeph 1:17–18, the prophet brings the book's introductory section to a close. Here he summarizes the lasting effects of YHWH's coming punishment, noting both humanity's distress (1:17) and complete destruction (1:18). The reference to "humanity" (אָדָם) in 1:17 and the breadth of "all the inhabitants of the earth" (כָּל־יֹשְׁבֵי הָאָרֶץ) in 1:18 signal a shift from Jerusalem's localized punishment in 1:7–13 to a universal destruction in 1:14–18, which echoes the broader use of "human/humanity" (אָדָם) and "ground/tilled soil" (אֲדָמָה) in 1:2–3.[146]

(1) Humanity's Distress (1:17)

Based on his declaration that the day of chastisement was fast approaching (1:14a), God now promises to "bring distress [וַהֲצֵרֹתִי from צרר] to humanity" (1:17a) and clarifies the content of that distress (1:17b–d). While he will use human and natural agents, YHWH himself is always the decisive mover in punishment.[147]

[17a] The "distress" in 1:17a recalls YHWH's day as one of "distress" (צָרָה) from 1:15b by using a related root (צרר; cf. Jer 10:18). This day comes against אָדָם. Several contextual elements suggest that אָדָם refers to "humanity" in general (הָאָדָם, lit., "the human [population]") and not to a subset

---

142. Sweeney, *Zephaniah*, 101.

143. Vlaardingerbroek, *Zephaniah*, 110; cf. Berlin, *Zephaniah*, 90.

144. Similarly, Sweeney believes the use of the phrase הַבְּצֻרוֹת הֶעָרִים ("unassailable cities") in Zeph 1:16 suggests that "Judah has taken the role played by Canaan in the time of Joshua" (Sweeney, *Zephaniah*, 101). However, instead of just Judah, I have argued for the entire world.

145. Cf. Isa 2:6–21, esp. 2:12, 15, 17; Hos 8:14.

146. Ben Zvi says the general announcements of judgment frame chapter 1 with a "minor" *inclusio*. Unfortunately, he interprets them only as hyperbole (Ben Zvi, *Book of Zephaniah*,

285; cf. Roberts, *Nahum, Habakkuk, and Zephaniah*, 185). But unlike exaggeration, which misleads, hyperbole illuminates truth. Hence, the prophet would still be stressing that God's just wrath would judge every sinner apart from a penal substitute's work (Rom 2:9–10; 5:9–10; 6:3–5).

147. Vlaardingerbroek treats 1:17 as secondary (Vlaardingerbroek, *Zephaniah*, 104). But 1:17 contributes to the overall argument and is tied to the immediate literary context, making a later editor's interpolation unnecessary. Why could Zephaniah have not stressed that the people would suffer due to their sin against YHWH?

of "humanity" against whom God's fury will fall.[148] First, with echoes of the global flood, Zeph 1:2–3 pairs "human/humanity" (אָדָם) with "ground/tilled soil" (אֲדָמָה) to highlight the sphere and object of YHWH's encroaching wrath, which would apparently be worldwide. Second, the use of the word "great" (גָּדוֹל) in 1:14a signals that YHWH's day in 1:14–18 is more expansive than Judah's destruction in 1:7b–13. Third, as will be seen, 3:8 repeats language from 1:18 and connects the "land/earth" (אֶרֶץ) in 1:18 to the world's "nations" and "kingdoms."

[17b–d] Having promised to bring anguish on humanity, YHWH now clarifies the makeup of and reason for this distress. Two descriptions that are mainly figurative disclose the depth of the impending pain (Zeph 1:17b–d).[149] A ground clause comes between them and serves as the basis for this pain by highlighting the immensity of humanity's violation (1:17c).

Human blindness is the first evidence of YHWH's coming distress (1:17b). This covenant curse (Deut 28:28–29; cf. 28:65) refers to physical blindness but implies a spiritual inability to see God's beauty, understand his word, and recognize one's need (cf. 29:3[4]; Job 5:14; 12:25; Isa 59:10).[150] In context, the blindness relates to the darkness of the day (Zeph 1:15).[151]

Zephaniah then explicitly states the reason for the blindness: *because* (כִּי "for") "against YHWH they have sinned" (1:17c; cf. 2 Kgs 18:14). Within Zephaniah, this reason most clearly explains why YHWH pours out his wrath (cf. Jer 50:14), and it parallels the reasoning of other prophets (cf. Isa 13:9, 11; 24:5–6; Jer 50:14). Zephaniah's assertion highlights the act-consequence nexus that controls God's covenantal blessings and curses, and it supplies a reason for any who may question God's justice in bringing such punishment (cf. Jer 3:25; 8:14). Zephaniah's words serve as a warning. Acts of idolatry (Zeph 1:5), disloyalty (1:6), oppression (1:9), and complacency (1:12) are not just unloving to one's neighbor; they are direct affronts to YHWH. And since one man's sin results in God justly punishing the entire nation (e.g., Achan in Josh 7:11), then certainly the whole earth's sustained rebellion demands a corporate judgment. Furthermore, Zephaniah envisions sin as not only being worthy of punishment but as a punishment itself.[152] The objects of God's wrath will experience spiritual inability that God's arm alone can mercifully overcome (cf. Isa 53:1; 59:16).

The next manifestation of divine chastisement is the pouring out of the victims' "blood [and] belly" (דָּם [and] לְחֻם), as if they were "dust [and] dung pellets" (עָפָר [and] גְּלָלִים) (Zeph 1:17d).[153] Three points deserve mention. First, the prophet again uses images of sacrifice (1:7c) and war (esp. 1:15–

---

148. Cf. Jer 25:30–33; 32:20. Many follow a similar approach—e.g., Keil, "Twelve Minor Prophets," 10:445 (2:136); Achtemeier, *Nahum–Malachi*, 72–73; Berlin, *Zephaniah*, 90; Motyer, "Zephaniah," 922, 924. For the alternative view, see, e.g., Luther, "Lectures on Zephaniah," 335–37; J. M. P. Smith, "Book of Zephaniah," 205–6; Ben Zvi, *Book of Zephaniah*, 127–28; Roberts, *Nahum, Habakkuk, and Zephaniah*, 182, 184; Sweeney, *Zephaniah*, 102. Inconsistently, Smith does believe that Zeph 1:18 refers to universal judgment (J. M. P. Smith, "Book of Zephaniah," 207).

149. While usually occurring with a singular verb (e.g., Deut 8:3; 1 Sam 25:9; Isa 2:20), the singular אָדָם does at times use a plural verb, as here (Job 36:25; Jer 47:2).

150. Hence, Jesus's giving sight to the blind (e.g., Mark 8:22–26; 10:46–52) signified both the curse's removal and the coming of God's new covenant kingdom (Isa 42:7; cf. 35:5; 42:16; 49:9). King Nebuchadnezzar's blinding of Zedekiah (one of Judah's princes, see Zeph 1:8) likely represents God's curse against Judah's rebellion (see Jer 25:6–7).

151. Renz, *Books of Nahum, Habakkuk, and Zephaniah*, 509.

152. Cf. Rom 1:24, 26, 28.

153. The meaning of לְחֻם (= לֶחֶם) is unclear. Here it is rendered "belly." Elsewhere it can refer to either the abdominal area (Isa 47:14) or the stomach (Job 20:23; 30:4; cf. the related verb II לחם (see also "II לחם," *HALOT* 526), meaning "to eat," Ps 141:4; Prov 23:6; Obad 7). God's wrath being against *all* mankind

16).[154] YHWH required that in the slaughtering process, priests were to empty out the blood and the worthless and repulsive parts of the sacrificial victims (Lev 1:9, 15; Mal 2:3).[155] Similarly, in war, the victims were often dismembered with small body parts scattered over the landscape like fertilizer (see Jer 16:4; 25:33; cf. Job 20:7).[156] Accordingly, Berlin writes, "The massacre will be so great that corpses will not be left intact; the remains will be in small fragments—specks and clumps—scattered over the landscape" (cf. Ps 18:43[42]).[157] YHWH's day of fury will result in complete destruction. Second, the Bible usually associates the verb "to pour out" (שׁפך) with liquids (e.g., 79:3), but in Lev 14:41 it refers to the emptying of plaster "dust" (עָפָר) in an unclean place outside the city after being removed from the inside of an infected house (cf. Ps 18:43[42]). This association suggests that Zephaniah sees sinners as unclean and that God will treat them as such (cf. Ezek 36:17–18).[158] Third, the mention of "dust" (Zeph 1:17) once again suggests creation's reversal (cf. 1:2–3). Humanity came from the "dust" (Gen 2:7) and now returns to "dust," experiencing God's curse (3:19).[159]

(2) Humanity's Destruction (1:18)

YHWH now repeats the particle גַם (here with a negative = neither . . . nor)[160] and echoes Zeph 1:15 by describing the coming punishment as one of divine "wrath" (עֶבְרָה). Verse 18 again synthesizes the effects of YHWH's justice both negatively and positively.

[18a] First, deliverance from God's judgment will be impossible. Whether "silver" and "gold" refer to wealth (Zeph 1:11; cf. Prov 3:14)[161] or expensive idols (Zeph 1:5; 2:11; Isa 30:22),[162] no form of earthly or spiritual power can rescue the rebel from God's wrath (see 1 Sam 12:20–21).[163] As the sage said, when dealing with YHWH, "wealth does not profit in a day of wrath" (Prov 11:4). This is so because he "is not partial and takes no bribe" (Deut 10:17; cf. Isa 13:17). Ezekiel would later allude to Zephaniah's prophecy when anticipating Jerusalem's destruction, thus showing that he too read Jerusalem's downfall typologically (Ezek 7:19).[164]

Figure 3.2: Comparison of Zephaniah 1:18 with Ezekiel 7:19	
Zeph 1:18	**Ezek 7:19**
גַּם־כַּסְפָּם גַּם־זְהָבָם לֹא־יוּכַל לְהַצִּילָם בְּיוֹם עֶבְרַת יְהוָה	כַּסְפָּם וּזְהָבָם לֹא־יוּכַל לְהַצִּילָם בְּיוֹם עֶבְרַת יְהוָה
Also their silver—even their gold—will not be able to deliver them in the day of the wrath of YHWH.	Their silver and their gold will not be able to deliver them in the day of the wrath of YHWH.

(men and women alike) may have dissuaded the prophet from using the more common term בֶּטֶן ("belly"), which often refers to a woman's "womb" (e.g., Isa 44:2, 24; 49:1, 5; Jer 1:5).

154. So too R. L. Smith, *Micah–Malachi*, 132, referring to Zeph 1:15–18.

155. For the burnt offering, see Lev 1:9, 11, 13, 15; for the peace offering, see 3:2–4, 8–10, 13–15; for the sin offering, see 4:7–10, 18, 25, 34; 4:9; for the guilt offering, see 6:2–4.

156. Job 20:7 uses the same term גֵּלֶל for "dung," but Jer 16:4; 25:33; and Mal 2:3 use a different term (דֹּמֶן). See also Pss 79:3; 83:11[10]; Jer 8:1–2; 9:21[22]; 25:33.

157. Berlin, *Zephaniah*, 91.

158. Motyer, "Zephaniah," 924.

159. Daniel C. Timmer, *The Non-Israelite Nations in the*

Book of the Twelve: Thematic Coherence and the Diachronic-Synchronic Relationship in the Minor Prophets, BibInt 135 (Leiden: Brill, 2015), 152, 154; Renz, *Books of Nahum, Habakkuk, and Zephaniah*, 509.

160. See *BHRG*, §40.20(3); cf. GKC, §154a n1(c).

161. So Ben Zvi, *Book of Zephaniah*, 131.

162. So Sabottka, *Zephanja*, 58.

163. In contrast to Ben Zvi, the prophet does not limit הָאָדָם in 1:17 to the wealthy (Ben Zvi, *Book of Zephaniah*, 131). Zephaniah is stressing that money, regardless of amount, will never be able to save one from YHWH's punishment.

164. Walther Zimmerli, *Ezekiel 1: A Commentary on the Book of the Prophet Ezekiel, Chapters 1–24*, trans. Ronald E. Clements, Hermeneia (Philadelphia: Fortress, 1979), 199;

[18b–c] Second, building on the early statements and images of sacrifice (Zeph 1:7, 17), YHWH's punishment means complete destruction for every earthly rebel, all because "the fire of [God's] jealousy" was aroused (1:18; cf. 3:8).[165] Scripture often associates YHWH's jealousy with his blazing desire to be worshiped as the only God (e.g., Deut 4:23–24; Ps 79:5; Ezek 23:25).[166] Like a just judge committed to what is right, YHWH's consuming passion for his name's honor will soon burst forth in fiery wrath against the earth's ungodly (Isa 66:15–16; Mal 3:19[4:1]).[167] Speaking of Jerusalem's 586 BC destruction that occurred soon after Zephaniah, Lamentations draws attention to the "fire" of YHWH that consumed Jerusalem (Lam 1:13; 2:3–4; 4:11). Such historical destruction anticipates a greater conflagration to come.

Zephaniah declares that YHWH's fires will consume כָּל־הָאָרֶץ, a reference to "all the earth" and not to "all the land" of Judah.[168] While אֶרֶץ is restricted to a particular geopolitical "land" in 2:3 and 5 (see below), a more global use seems operative in 1:18; 2:11; 3:8, 19, echoing the broader use of אָדָם ("human/humanity") and אֲדָמָה ("ground/tilled

soil") in 1:2–3. This is especially clear in 3:8, which speaks of YHWH pouring out his wrath on the world's "nations" (גּוֹיִם) and "kingdoms" (מַמְלָכוֹת) and which recalls the wording of 1:18 when it declares, "In the fire of my jealousy all the earth will be consumed" (בְּאֵשׁ קִנְאָתִי תֵּאָכֵל כָּל־הָאָרֶץ).

Zephaniah's statement that "all the earth will be consumed" recalls 1:2–3 and parallels the coming punishment with the great deluge.[169] However, the reason that follows (כִּי "for") limits the destruction to the earth's *human* population. All seven other occurrences of the verb ישׁב ("to dwell, inhabit") in Zephaniah include human subjects.[170] This judgment contrasts with the deluge brought about by the corruption and violence of "all flesh" (Gen 6:12–13). That flood was against both humans and beasts,[171] but Zephaniah limits his focus of eschatological destruction to mankind and the material goods in which they find security (see comments on Zeph 1:2–3).

Recalling the "greatness" of the day in 1:14a, Zephaniah declares that the encroaching destruction will be "complete" (כָּלָה = ESV "full") (cf. Isa 10:23; 28:22; Jer 46:28),[172] reinforcing the truth

---

Block, *Book of Ezekiel: Chapters 1–24*, 264; Berlin, *Zephaniah*, 91; Sweeney, *Zephaniah*, 104.

165. See also Ezek 36:5 for the same phrase (cf. Ps 79:5; Ezek 38:19). Some scholars see Zeph 1:18 representing a major stylistic and syntactic shift that suggests the verse is secondary (e.g., Seybold, *Satirische Prophetie*, 34; Vlaardingerbroek, *Zephaniah*, 113). In contrast, 1:18 is solidly grounded in its context by (1) the coordinating particle גַּם ("also") fronting 1:18, (2) the sacrificial imagery associating 1:18 with 1:7, 17 and 3:8, (3) the echo of 1:15 in the description of the coming judgment as "the day of the wrath of YHWH," (4) the echoes of Zephaniah's confrontation of material securities (1:11, 13; cf. 8–9), and (5) the close verbal tie with 3:8.

166. Cf. Exod 33:3, 5; 34:14; Deut 5:7–10; 6:15; 32:21–22. YHWH's holy fires will either ignite and fuel holiness in the redeemed (Exod 20:20; Deut 9:3 with 10:12–13; Heb 12:28–29) or consume the wicked (Num 11:1; 16:35; Deut 9:3; 2 Kgs 1:10; Jude 7; Rev 20:9). Leviticus 9:24–10:3 is one text that combines both images.

167. Cf. 2 Thess 1:7–8; Heb 10:27; 2 Pet 3:7.

168. Against Vlaardingerbroek, *Zephaniah*, 113; Renz, *Books of Nahum, Habakkuk, and Zephaniah*, 511–12. The arguments in 1:17a that אָדָם refers to humanity at large and not to a subset equally apply to this discussion. For some supporters of the universal reading, see the note at 1:17.

169. Cf. 2 Pet 3:5–7; cf. Jer 25:30–33. See also Deut 32:21–22; Jer 4:4; Matt 25:41; 1 Cor 3:13; Heb 10:27; 2 Pet 3:10–13; Rev 16:8–9; 20:14–15. Already in Scripture, YHWH rained fire from heaven on Sodom and Gomorrah (Gen 19:24, 28) in a way that alluded to the deluge (7:4), but only on a local scale. Cf. Michael B. Shepherd, *The Textual World of the Bible*, StBibLit 156 (New York: Lang, 2013), 6–7.

170. See Zeph 1:4, 11, 13; 2:5 [2x], 15; 3:6. *DCH* records only six of the total 1090 occurrences of ישׁב in the OT as including animals as the subject: Deut 3:19; Josh 1:14; Jer 50:39; Ps 17:12; Job 38:40 ("יֹשֵׁב," *DCH* 4:320).

171. God destroying "all flesh" in the flood included "everything on the dry land in whose nostrils was a breath of a spirit of life" (Gen 7:21–22).

172. Elsewhere YHWH declares that he will *not* make a

of 1:12a that YHWH will find and punish *every* rebel—no person will escape. Furthermore, the prophet stresses that the coming end will also be נִבְהָלָה (the *niphal* participle of בהל), which the English versions take to mean either "terrifying" (e.g., NASB20, NRSVue, NET, CSB) or "sudden" (e.g., YLT, NKJV, ESV, NIV). The immediate context supports both options. Zephaniah 1:14b–17d expresses the day's horror, and 1:12d–e, 14a

expresses its sudden nature. However, this verb in the *niphal* elsewhere means "sudden" only in wisdom texts (Prov 28:22; Eccl 8:3). Furthermore, twenty-one of its total twenty-four *niphal* verb forms mean "to be scared, horrified, dismayed, panicked, out of one's senses" before expected turmoil (e.g., Isa 13:8; Jer 51:32; Ezek 7:27). Zephaniah probably emphasizes the terrifying nature of the great day.[173]

Canonical and Theological Significance

Zephaniah's Day of YHWH within Its Biblical Context[174]

In 1:7–18, Zephaniah urges his readers to revere YHWH in view of his coming fury against sin. Here the prophet portrays the day of YHWH as sacrifice (1:7–8), cataclysm (1:15), and conquest (1:16). He further suggests that the day will also bring restoration, though he makes this explicit only later (see esp. 3:9–20). The very concept of YHWH's day seems to derive from the Bible's discussion of both creation and covenant, and it is also linked to sacrifice and YHWH's wars of punishment, by which he reestablishes right order in his world.

Echoes of Canaan's Downfall: Zephaniah's Day of YHWH as Conquest in 1:7–18

Zephaniah portrays the day of YHWH with images of conquest. Often in 1:7–18 the prophet alludes to the original conquest of Canaan, suggesting that he envisioned YHWH's day to be a greater, more ultimate divine conquest by which God would atone for sin and establish a new promised land on a global scale.

Originally, YHWH declared that Israel needed to carry out the conquest against the Canaanites lest Israel imitate their sinful ways (Deut 20:18; cf. Judg 2:3). When Israel obeyed the covenant and the command of conquest, God would bless them, and they would enjoy "great and good cities that you did not build, and houses full of all good things that you did not fill, and hewn cisterns that you did not dig, vineyards and olive trees that you did not plant" (Deut 6:10–11; cf. Jer 29:5–7). But instead of

---

"complete end" (כָּלָה) of his people but will preserve a remnant (Jer 5:18; 46:28; cf. Ezek 11:13; 20:17).

173. See Gen 45:3; Exod 15:15; Judg 20:41; 1 Sam 28:21; 2 Sam 4:1; Isa 13:8; 21:3; Jer 51:32; Ezek 7:27; 26:18; Psa 6:3–4,

11; 30:8; 48:6; 83:18; 90:7; 104:29; Job 4:5; 21:6; 23:15; Prov 28:22.

174. See also Zephaniah's Vision of the Day of YHWH in the introduction.

overcoming those opposing YHWH, Israel worshiped their gods and became like the Canaanites, thus becoming God's enemy (Deut 8:19–20).

Judah lost sight of YHWH's greatness and attributed their strength and affluence to the Canaanite traders (Zeph 1:11). These foreigners had reshaped Judah's worship (1:4–5), dress (1:8), and lifestyle (1:6, 9) so much that Zephaniah could call the rebel Judeans "the remnant of the Baal" (i.e., the chief god of the Canaanites, 1:4b).

For this reason, YHWH would reverse Israel's covenant blessing with covenant curse, exiling them from the land.[175] Directly recalling Moses's predictions (Deut 28:30, 39), Zephaniah stresses that Judah "will build houses, but they will not inhabit; and they will plant vineyards, but they will not drink their wine" (Zeph 1:13; cf. Amos 5:11; Mic 6:15).[176] This wording shows that the prophet associates God's punishment of Judah's rebels with the Canaanites, and Zephaniah calls this new conquest the day of YHWH.

And yet God's conquest against the new "Canaanites" goes beyond Judah (1:7b–13) and applies to the entire world (1:14–18), "for against YHWH they have sinned" (1:17). In Zeph 1:15–16, the images of war and cataclysmic destruction prevail. The mention of "unassailable cities" (הֶעָרִים הַבְּצֻרֹת) in 1:16 recalls the Canaanite strongholds and casts the entire world as being the new promised land (Num 13:28; Deut 3:5). The mention of "trumpet" (שׁוֹפָר) recalls Israel's overpowering of the Canaanites (Josh 6:5, 20; cf. Neh 9:25) and indicates that YHWH's day is indeed a new conquest that will cleanse the earth of its defilements.

But God's conquest is not the end. Just as Israel's conquest would have included their inhabiting the land (Deut 6:10–11), so too we will see later in Zephaniah's oracle that YHWH would restore blessing for "the remnant of the house of Judah" (Zeph 2:7; cf. 2:9; 3:13). In fulfillment of Isaiah's prediction (Isa 61:4; 65:21–22; cf. Ezek 28:26), the faithful remnant would survive YHWH's day of wrath and experience the blessings of the conquest. On the tracts of shorelines that once belonged to the Philistines, "the remnant of the house of Judah . . . will pasture. In the houses of Ashkelon at evening they will lie down" (Zeph 2:7). The day of YHWH will prove to be not only a new conquest that cleanses God's earth but also a time of restoration for the world, whose fruitfulness and blessing will last forever (3:8–20).

Features of the Day of YHWH as Punishment

Zephaniah echoes many of his predecessors and contemporaries in the way he portrays YHWH's day as one of wrath, and his own representation likely supplied fuel for later authors' depictions of the divine fury. Figure 3.3 overviews many common features in biblical portraits of YHWH's day as punishment:

---

175. So, too, Shepherd, *Commentary on the Book of the Twelve*, 357–58.

176. Cf. Lev 26:16; Deut 28:30–31, 38–42; Hos 4:10; 5:6; 8:7; 9:12, 16; Amos 4:8; 8:12; Hag 1:16; Mal 1:4. Comparable curses

Figure 3.3: Common Features of the Day of YHWH as Punishment	
Feature	**Description**
Like a thief (Zeph 1:12)	The day of YHWH is near (Zeph 1:7, 14) and will come at night (1:12) like a thief to find complacent sinners who are spiritually asleep and not expecting judgment (Joel 2:9–10, Amos 5:18; Zeph 1:15).[176] Therefore, people must be awake spiritually, taking both God and sin seriously (Joel 1:5; Rom 13:11–14; Eph 5:14).[177]
Darkness, gloom, and clouds (Zeph 1:15)	The prophets regularly use darkness, gloom, and clouds as images of YHWH's wrath. The ominous shadows portray the reversal of creation (Gen 1:2–3) and punishment on individuals (2 Sam 22:12; Job 15:22), nations in general (Isa 13:10; Ezek 30:3; Zeph 1:15), and Israel (Joel 2:2; Amos 5:18, 20). Such cataclysmic features accompanied Christ's death (Mark 15:33; cf. Acts 2:20; Rev 12:4) and will appear at his victorious return (Matt 24:29–30; 1 Thess 4:17; Rev 6:12–13).
Trumpet (Zeph 1:16)	A trumpet blast was a common signal in war (Num 10:9; 2 Chr 13:14; Amos 3:6). The OT authors regularly link such sounds of alarm with God's offensive activity on that day (Jer 51:27; Zeph 1:16; Zech 9:14) and with the objects of destruction themselves (Ezek 7:14; Hos 5:8; Joel 2:1). The NT authors also note God's trumpet signals both Christ's return (Matt 24:31; 1 Thess 4:16) and numerous eschatological judgments.[178]
Destruction by fire (Zeph 1:18; 3:8)	Fire's association with both sacrifice (Zeph 1:7) and war (1:14–16) makes it an ideal image to depict YHWH's day of retribution. God's flame will torch his enemies in Jerusalem[179] and in the whole world.[180] In the NT, Christ's second coming signals the final and ultimate day of YHWH. Then, he will be revealed "from heaven . . . in flaming fire" to carry out God's justice (2 Thess 1:7–8).[181]
A lion's roar	Though lacking in Zephaniah, Scripture often depicts YHWH as a lion.[182] Lions stalk in silence so as not to alarm their prey. Thus, YHWH roars on his day to call near his "pride" and to frighten his foes (Amos 1:2) rather than to hunt (Hos 11:10; Joel 4:16[3:16]; 2 Pet 3:10). The lion is also a royal image associated with the tribe of Judah and the Messiah (Gen 49:9–10; Num 24:9; 2 Chr 9:18–19). It is this "Lion of the tribe of Judah, the Root of David," who will conquer on YHWH's day (Rev 5:5).

Christ and the Ultimate Fulfillment of the Day of YHWH

The NT declares that Jesus's death and resurrection initiated the day of YHWH as both punishment and renewal. Christ first appeared as the *object* of God's wrath for those he would save, and with his resurrection he initiated the new creation. Yet when he returns, he will be the *agent* of God's wrath against his enemies and fully save those waiting for him. For those without Christ, YHWH's day of fury is all future. But for the believing remnant, Christ's first coming realized YHWH's day,

---

related to efforts that fail to produce are found throughout the ancient world, as in (1) the treaty inscriptions of Bar-gaʾyah of *KTK* and Matiʾel of Arpad from Sefire (ca. 750 BC), "The Treaty Between *KTK* and Arpad," trans. Franz Rosenthal (*ANET*, 659); "The Inscriptions of Bar-gaʾyah and Metiʾel from Sefire," trans. Joseph A. Fitzmyer (*COS* 2.82:214), and (2) Neo-Assyrian King Ashurbanipal's annals regarding his campaign against the Arabs (ca. mid-600s BC), "Texts from Hammurabi to the Downfall of the Assyrian Empire," trans. A. Leo Oppenheim (*ANET*, 300).

177. Cf. Matt 24:43, 50; Luke 12:46; 17:30; 1 Thess 5:2, 4–5; 2 Pet 3:10; Rev 3:3; 16:20.

178. Cf. Matt 24:42–44; Mark 13:33–37; Luke 12:37–38; 21:34–36; 1 Thess 5:6; Rev 3:2–3; 16:15.

179. See Rev 8:2, 6–8, 10, 12, 13; 9:1, 13–14; 10:7; 11:15.

180. See Isa 29:6; 30:30; Hos 8:14; Joel 2:3, 5; 3:3[2:30]; Amos 5:6; Obad 18; Mic 1:7; Nah 1:6; 3:15.

181. See Mic 1:4; Nah 1:6; 3:15; Zeph 1:18; 2:2; 3:8; Mal 3:19[4:1].

182. Cf. Matt 3:12; 13:40; Luke 3:17; 12:49; Heb 10:27; 2 Pet 3:7, 10; Rev 18:8; 20:9.

A Proper Response

Allow the Gravity of the Day of YHWH to Move You to Revere God

Zephaniah 1 portrays a God who demands reverence (1:7), whose justice shows no prejudice (1:8–9), whose just jealousy judges with flames of wrath (1:18; cf. 3:8), and who punishes all affronts to his holiness (1:7, 12–13) in ways both terrible and complete (1:11, 15–18). Whereas some may minimize certain types of sins, believing them to be insignificant, Zephaniah asserts that any sin demands the full vent of YHWH's anger.[184] How could some continue to treat God as both passive and distant, declaring, "YHWH will neither do good nor do ill" (1:12)?[185]

Smith has noted that "no prophet has made the picture of the day of Yahweh more real" than Zephaniah.[186] The words the prophet uses to describe the outbreak of divine anger are staggering—a day of "wrath, distress, anguish, ruin, devastation, darkness, gloom, cloud, thick darkness, trumpet, and battle cry" (1:15–16). Can the situation be more ominous? The book of Lamentations graphically unpacks the horrors of God's judgment against Jerusalem in 586 BC: hunger and thirst (Lam 2:11–12, 19; 4:4–5, 9); cannibalism (2:20; 4:10); slaughter (2:20–22); affliction, tribulation, hopelessness (3:1–18); divine distance (3:8, 44); lack (4:5); famine and heat (4:7–8; 5:10); rape (1:4; 5:11); humiliation (5:12); and forced labor (5:13). Yet Judah's devastation would only be a foretaste of God's greater retribution to come in Christ (2 Thess 1:8–9; 2 Pet 3:10). How dreadful to have the source of all power and the upholder of all life working against you!

Having learned that the living God is approaching in anger, we must reverently quiet our speech, hearts, and activity before the sovereign God! As "sons of light and sons of day," Christians must "be sober, having put on a breastplate of faith and love and a helmet—the hope of salvation. For God has not appointed us for wrath but for obtaining salvation through our Lord Jesus Christ" (1 Thess 5:5, 8–9). Furthermore, as we wait "for our blessed hope" (Titus 2:13), we must "consider one another for proving love and good deeds, not forsaking the assembly of ourselves, as is the custom of some, but encouraging, and all the more as you see the Day drawing near" (Heb 10:23–25).

---

183. E.g., Isa 38:13; Jer 25:38; 49:19; Hos 5:14; 13:7–8; Amos 1:2; 3:8; Lam 3:10.

184. Motyer, "Zephaniah," 924. Idolatry (Zeph 1:3–4), syncretism (1:5), lack of dependence (1:6), violence and deception (1:9), and complacency (1:12) are all among the "sins" that demand sacrificial atonement to appease YHWH's just wrath (1:7, 17–18; cf. Isa 22:14).

185. Cf. Motyer, "Zephaniah," 922.

186. J. M. P. Smith, "Book of Zephaniah," 176.

Another way we can revere God is by recalling the dread of YHWH's day in our corporate worship, for what we fear tomorrow will change how we live in the present.[187] In AD 1250, Thomas of Celano vividly captured the ominous gravity of Zeph 1:15–16 in his Latin *Dies Irae* ("Day of Wrath"), the hymn that Robertson says the church has translated into more languages than any other.[188]

> That day of wrath, that dreadful day
> When heav'n and earth shall pass away!
> What pow'r shall be the sinner's stay?
> How shall he meet that dreadful day?
> When, shriveling like a parched scroll,
> the flaming heav'ns together roll;
> When louder yet, and yet more dread,
> Swells the high trump that wakes the dead;
> O on that day, that wrathful day
> When man to judgment wakes from clay
> Be though the trembling sinner's stay,
> Though heav'n and earth shall pass away.[189]

May such poetry resound again from the lips of YHWH's gathered saints, both to warn of danger and to call people to revere the living God.

Celebrate YHWH's Gift of a Substitute Sacrifice

In Zephaniah, YHWH portrays his war of judgment against sin as a "sacrifice" (Zeph 1:7). That is, atonement is God's reconstituting right order by means of war (cf. Isa 22:14). The offerings of animals in Leviticus were a means by which the heavenly Warrior engaged in a conquest against evil to reestablish peace, punishing a substitute rather than a sinner. Similarly, at the cross, God's war against evil manifests itself in his cursing Christ on behalf of the elect (Isa 53:11; Gal 3:13). "And he was pierced on account of our transgressions; he was crushed on account of our iniquities; the discipline that brought us peace was on him" (Isa 53:5).[190] His substitutionary act of love secured our right standing with God (Rom 5:1, 18–19), so that we no longer need to fear the future day of YHWH's wrath (5:9–11).

For those in Christ, YHWH's future day will bring eternal salvation, not harm

---

187. For more on how belief in God's promises of blessing and curse change our present action, see Jason S. DeRouchie, "Is Every Promise 'Yes'? Old Testament Promises and the Christian," *Them* 42 (2017): 16–45; DeRouchie, *Delighting in the Old Testament*, 131–89.

188. Robertson, *Books of Nahum, Habakkuk, and Zepha-*

niah, 283. See Paul Haupt, "The Prototype of the Dies Irae," *JBL* 38.2–3 (1919): 142–51.

189. Translated from the Latin by Sir Walter Scott, as found in *The Trinity Hymnal* (Philadelphia: Great Commission, 1961), No. 242.

190. Cf. Rom 4:25; 2 Cor 5:21; 1 Pet 2:24.

(see Zeph 3:8–20; 1 Thess 5:9; 2 Tim 4:8).[191] We have good news worth celebrating! Though we were a people bound to encounter the full heat of "the fire of [YHWH's] jealousy" (Zeph 1:18), "our savior Christ Jesus . . . destroyed death and brought to light life and immortality through the gospel" (2 Tim 1:10). He is "the Lamb of God, who takes away the sin of the world!" (John 1:29).

While There Is Still Hope, Call Others to Take Sin Seriously and to Revere God

The great day of God's wrath is nearer to us than it was to Zephaniah. And this wrath "remains" on everyone who fails to surrender to Jesus (John 3:36; cf. Rom 2:8; Eph 2:3; 5:6). For those still under divine condemnation (Rom 8:1), the future day of YHWH remains ominous, for God will at that time destroy his enemies (2 Thess 1:8–9; cf. Isa 66:15–16; Heb 10:27).[192] As such, before "the day of vengeance of our God" (Isa 61:2), the church must join Zephaniah in calling others to "hush before the Sovereign YHWH" (Zeph 1:7). We must take sin seriously and revere the One who will come in blazing wrath against his adversaries.

---

191. Cf. Rom 5:9; 1 Cor 1:8; 5:5; 2 Cor 5:10; Phil 1:6, 10; 2:16; 1 Pet 2:12; 1 John 4:17.

192. Cf. Rom 2:5; 1 Thess 5:1–3; 2 Pet 2:9; 3:7.

PART III

Zephaniah 2:1–3:20b

The Substance of the Savior's Invitation to Satisfaction: *Charges to Seek YHWH Together and to Wait*

Main Idea of Zephaniah 2:1–3:20b

The faithful remnant should patiently pursue YHWH together to avoid punishment and to enjoy salvation.

Literary Context of Zephaniah 2:1–3:20b

Basic Overview

The book's primary exhortation section (Zeph 2:1–3:20b) builds on the call to revere YHWH because of his encroaching day of wrath (1:2–18).[1] In sum, 2:1–3:20b charges the faithful remnant of Judah and other lands to seek YHWH together and to wait for him, both to avoid punishment and to enjoy salvation. The six main imperatives are masculine plural and appear in two groupings: (1) in 2:1a, 3a: "*Bind yourselves together, and become a sheaf! . . . Seek* YHWH . . . *Seek* righteousness; *seek* humility!*" (הִתְקוֹשְׁשׁוּ וָקוֹשּׁוּ . . . בַּקְּשׁוּ אֶת־יְהוָה . . . בַּקְּשׁוּ־צֶדֶק בַּקְּשׁוּ עֲנָוָה); (2) in 3:8a: "Therefore, *wait* for me!" (לָכֵן חַכּוּ־לִי). The two groupings of imperatives (2:1, 3; 3:8)

---

1. The strong syntactic disjunction in Zeph 2:1 (through the asyndetic imperative) and the forceful parenetic thrust of the commands in 2:1, 3, and 3:8 mark 2:1–3:20 as the book's hortatory core and distinguish it from the preceding setting (1:2–18).

initiate the two stages of Zephaniah's primary exhortation: seek YHWH together (2:1–3:7) and wait for him (3:8–20).

The listeners must, therefore, look and long, hunger and hope, entreat and trust. The prophet motivates this twofold exhortation in two ways. First, to call people to avoid punishment, he highlights the impending curse YHWH will bring on the rebels of the world (2:4, 2:5–3:7). Second, to encourage people toward salvation, he draws attention to joyous blessings reserved for the remnant who persevere through judgment (3:8b–10, 11–20).[2]

Significantly, 3:14 includes three groupings of four additional imperatives, the first feminine singular (רָנִּי, "Sing aloud!"), the second masculine plural (הָרִיעוּ, "Shout!"), and the third and fourth both feminine singular (שִׂמְחִי וְעָלְזִי, "Be merry, and exult!"). These imperatives do not begin a new unit. Though providing the book's rhetorical climax, they offer positive motivation for heeding God's charge to "Wait for me!" in 3:8a (see below).[3]

The Prophet and His Audience

The superscription (Zeph 1:1) and setting (1:2–18) sections established Zephaniah's noble position in the Davidic line (1:1) and his awareness of foreign influence (cf. 1:11b–c) and the corruption of the royal court (1:8b) and religious elite (1:9a). This unit further reflects the prophet's awareness of international affairs (2:4–15, 3:6–7), even referring to events far removed in both space and time (esp. 2:12–15) and suggesting not only his divinely-empowered awareness but also "the availability of diplomatically reported information."[4]

While 1:2–18 has both local (1:4–13) and global foci (1:2–3, 14–18), these verses do not specify an audience. In the book's main section, however, Zephaniah directly designates his listeners. First, attached to the initial main imperatives, he addresses "the nation not longing" (הַגּוֹי לֹא נִכְסָף, 2:1) and "all the humble of the land" (כָּל־עַנְוֵי הָאָרֶץ, 2:3). The former most likely refers to the inhabitants of Judah in general ("the nation") and the latter to the humble remnant minority among Judah who have "hushed" before YHWH (1:7) and "bundled" together before his coming

---

2. For similar approaches to how the charges to seek YHWH together (2:1, 3) and wait for YHWH (3:8) function within Zephaniah, see Robert B. Chisholm Jr., *Interpreting the Minor Prophets* (Grand Rapids: Zondervan, 1990), 202–3; E. Ray Clendenen, "The Minor Prophets," in *Holman Concise Bible Commentary*, ed. David S. Dockery (Nashville: Broadman & Holman, 1998), 377–79.

3. Though Floyd understands the function of 2:1, 3 and 3:8 similarly, he thinks the imperatives in 3:14 signal another

major movement in the book (Floyd, *Minor Prophets, Part 2*, 165–66). His interpretation fails to account enough for (1) the way 3:14–15 falls within two future-oriented addresses that serve to motivate the charge to "Wait!" in 3:8 (3:11–13, 16–20) and (2) the way 3:15 serves to motivate the commands in 3:14 and treats *future* realities as certainties through its use of *qatal* verbs in 3:15a–b. For more, see below.

4. Floyd, *Minor Prophets, Part 2*, 228.

day of wrath (2:1; cf. 2 Kgs 22:19–20). Judah and its remnant initially appear to be the primary audience of the exhortations in Zeph 2:1, 3. However, Zephaniah may intentionally use imprecise language because he believed foreign peoples beyond Judah could also experience protection on the day of YHWH (see below).[5]

Second, using vocative speech, Zephaniah addresses both the Philistines (2:5) and the "Cushites" (כּוּשִׁים, 2:12). That he addresses foreign peoples directly suggests that the book's main exhortations reach beyond Judah and its remnant to the broader world.[6] Because all humanity has sinned against YHWH (1:17), all humanity must "seek YHWH" together to avoid punishment and must "wait on YHWH" to enjoy salvation.

Third, the last group of vocatives addresses a transformed Jerusalem that includes a unified remnant from both Judah and the world. God identifies his worshipers from all the nations as "the daughter of my scattered ones" (3:10). He directly associates them with "the remnant of the house of Judah" (2:7a) and "the remnant of my people . . . and the remainder of my nation" (2:9c–d) in the cleansed new Jerusalem and its environs. YHWH and his prophet now address this new community as "the remnant of Israel" (שְׁאֵרִית יִשְׂרָאֵל, 3:13a), the "daughter of Zion" (בַּת צִיּוֹן, 3:14a), "Israel" (יִשְׂרָאֵל, 3:14b; cf. 3:12), the "daughter of Jerusalem" (בַּת יְרוּשָׁלָם, 3:14d), and "Zion" (צִיּוֹן, 3:16a). Based on 3:9–10, peoples from both Israel and non-Israelite nations constitute the one people of God and are Jerusalem's members (3:15; cf. 3:10).

> I. The Superscription of the Savior's Invitation to Satisfaction (1:1)
>
> II. The Setting of the Savior's Invitation to Satisfaction: A Call to Revere YHWH in View of His Coming Day (1:2–18)
>
> ➡ **III. The Substance of the Savior's Invitation to Satisfaction: Charges to Seek YHWH Together and to Wait (2:1–3:20b)**
>
> **III.1 Stage 1: The Appeal to Seek YHWH Together to Avoid Punishment (2:1–3:7)**
>
> **III.2 Stage 2: The Appeal to Wait for YHWH to Enjoy Salvation (3:8–20b)**
>
> IV. The Subscription of the Savior's Invitation to Satisfaction (3:20c)

---

5. For more on this question, see DeRouchie, "Addressees in Zephaniah 2:1, 3," 183–207. Many factors support Zephaniah's target audience including some of Judah's neighbors, most notably that Zephaniah speaks directly to Canaan (Zeph 2:5) and the Cushites (2:12), using second person address. With this, the Philistines exercised influence within Jerusalem (Zeph 1:11; 2:5; cf. Isa 2:6), Jerusalem and likely Zephaniah (see Zeph 1:1) had strong ties with many Cushites, and YHWH's prophets sometimes engaged foreign peoples on their turf (e.g., 2 Kgs 8:7–15; Jer 27:3; 51:61–64; Jonah 3:4–5; cf. Jer 1:5).

6. Renz maintains that Zephaniah never addressed the foreign nations directly but used the vocative address for mere rhetorical purposes (Renz, *Books of Nahum, Habakkuk, and Zephaniah*, 552–53). Zephaniah's vision of international hope suggests otherwise.

Structure and Outline of Zephaniah 2:1–3:20b

Unit Beginning?

Some scholars believe 2:1–3 concludes 1:2–18 and the mention of foreign nations in 2:4 signals a topic shift from Judah's judgment to her neighbor's punishment.[7] However, such a view fails to account for both the book's grammar and actual content (see also Zephaniah's Macrostructure in the introduction).[8]

At least three *grammatical* reasons cast doubt on 2:1–3 concluding 1:2–18: (1) In the cline of volitional intensity, imperatives mark the highest level of positive rhetorical force in directive speech.[9] Thus, by their very nature, the five imperatives in 2:1, 3 ("Bind yourselves together, and become a sheaf. . . . Seek. . . . Seek . . . seek") highlight this shift. (2) The imperative in 2:1a (הִתְקוֹשְׁשׁוּ, "Bind yourselves together") signals a syntactic break, creating a strong disjunction in the text. Disjunction marked by asyndeton usually initiates a new thought unit or explicates what precedes, whether by restating, clarifying, or explaining.[10] The imperative at the head of 2:1 does not explain what precedes. So, it likely marks a fresh beginning in the book that shifts focus away from the announcement of impending punishment in 1:2–6 and the demand to revere God in 1:7–18 to the beginning of the main exhortations (noted by the use of imperatives).[11] (3) The causal conjunction "for" (כִּי) in 2:4 makes the punishment against the nations that follows inseparable from the preceding exhortation in 2:3.[12]

As for *content*, several factors indicate that 2:1–3 introduces what follows rather

---

7. E.g., Roberts, *Nahum, Habakkuk, and Zephaniah*, 162–63; Motyer, "Zephaniah," 162–63; Vlaardingerbroek, *Zephaniah*, v–vi, 25–27. Against Vlaardingerbroek, 1:2–3, 14–18 and 3:8 focus on *global* judgment rather than Judah's. This undercuts his claim that the international scope in 2:4–15 came from a different time period in Zephaniah's ministry and originally supported Josiah's reform politics, whereas 1:2–2:3 and 3:1–8 did not (Vlaardingerbroek, *Zephaniah*, 25).

8. Cf. Ball, *Rhetorical Study of Zephaniah*, 114–22; Sweeney, "Form-Critical Reassessment," 392–93; Daniel Hojoon Ryou, *Zephaniah's Oracles against the Nations: A Synchronic and Diachronic Study of Zephaniah 2:1–3:8*, BibInt 13 (Leiden: Brill, 1995), 283–85; Sweeney, *Zephaniah*, 106.

9. Longacre, *Joseph*, 121; DeRouchie, *How to Understand and Apply*, 112–13; cf. Garrett and DeRouchie, *A Modern Grammar for Biblical Hebrew*, 331.

10. See Stephen G. Dempster, "Linguistic Features of Hebrew Narrative: A Discourse Analysis of Narrative from the Classical Period" (PhD diss., University of Toronto, 1985), 42–47; DeRouchie, *How to Understand and Apply*, 103–4; Jason S.

DeRouchie, "*Waw* and Asyndeton as Guides to Macrostructure in Biblical Hebrew Prose," in *Like Nails Firmly Fixed: Essays on the Text and Language of the Hebrew and Greek Scriptures, Presented to Peter J. Gentry on the Occasion of His Retirement*, ed. Jonathan Kiel, Phillip Marshall, and John Meade, BET 115 (Leuven: Peeters, 2023), 129–50.

11. Cf. Sweeney, *Zephaniah*, 51, 106, though he fails to recognize the imperative in 3:8 as joining with those in 2:1–3 to capture "the fundamental premise of the entire book."

12. Motyer begins a section in 2:4, despite believing it explains "the foregoing proclamation of judgment" (Motyer, "Zephaniah," 902). Wendland and Clark treat 2:4 as a Janus construction that works both directions—rhetorically beginning a new unit but also presenting "a strong motivation for people to heed the preceding divine warning-appeal (2:1–3)" (Wendland and Clark, "Zephaniah," 24nn8, 36). For more on this commentary's approach, see the explanation at 2:4. Cf. Ryou, *Zephaniah's Oracles*, 203–4; Renz, *Books of Nahum, Habakkuk, and Zephaniah*, 485, 520nl, 521–22.

than concludes what precedes. (1) The global concerns in 1:2–3 and 1:14–18 provide a literary frame for the initial section,[13] suggesting that all of 1:2–18 shapes a literary unit. (2) The vocative address in 2:1, 3 marks the first instances of the prophet addressing a particular audience ("the nation not longing," 2:1; "all the humble of the land," 2:3). Before this, the prophet announces coming punishments and calls for reverence, but he does so without explicitly stating his target. Something new begins in 2:1. (3) Whereas Zeph 1:2–18 speaks of YHWH's day in relation to God's actions, 2:1–3 brings it up in relation to the people's needed response.[14] Furthermore, the explicit use of the "day" (יוֹם) of YHWH language employed in 2:2–3 is only picked up again in 3:8 and then continued in 3:11 and 16. This thematic tie at the two points where the imperatives lie upholds the view that 2:5–3:7 supports the primary line of exhortation. Therefore, strong internal evidence shows that 2:1–3 goes with what follows rather than what precedes.

Argument Flow and Outline

Zephaniah 2:1–3:20b presents a logically cohesive, powerful, and sustained argument that lacks introductory speech formulas. As in 1:2–18, a unified argument exists regardless of whether Zephaniah refers to God with third-person subjects or verbs[15] or whether YHWH refers to himself with first-person verbs or pronouns.[16] Overall, the pattern moves from Zephaniah to YHWH seven times. Nevertheless, in the book's final section (3:8–20b), YHWH has adjacent speeches both at 3:8–10 and 3:11–13 and at 3:18 and 3:19–20b; Zephaniah has back-to-back speeches at 3:14–15 and 3:16b–18. Hence, each character has seven groupings of speech acts. But Zephaniah has eight actual speeches, and YHWH has nine, with 3:19–20b ending the whole oracle.

---

13. So too Sweeney, "Form-Critical Reassessment," 393n13.

14. Sweeney, "Form-Critical Reassessment," 393. One may add: (4) Judah and the world's coming punishment (1:2–18) provides only the setting for the book's main exhortations to seek YHWH together (2:1, 3) and to wait for YHWH (3:8). (5) YHWH regularly declares punishment beyond Judah throughout the book, including in 1:2–18 (e.g., 1:2–3, 14–18; 2:4–15; 3:6, 8). Hence, calling 1:2–2:3 "Judgment against Judah and Jerusalem" in distinction from "Oracles against the foreign nations" in 2:4–15 fails to capture Zephaniah's intent (Roberts, *Nahum, Habakkuk, and Zephaniah*, 162). (6) The parallel units (each beginning with "woe!" [הוֹי] in 2:5 and 3:1) that lament the state and fate of the foreign nations (2:5–15) and Jerusalem (3:1–7) supply unmarked reasons why Zephaniah's listeners must seek God together (2:1, 3) and wait for him (3:8). Thus, the foreign nation material in 2:5–15 provides a natural rationale for what precedes.

15. See Zeph 2:1–4, 6–7, 11; 13–15; 3:5, 7e–f, 14–17.

16. See Zeph 2:5, 8–10, 12; 3:6–7d, 8–13, 18–20. As noted, Wendland and Clark argue conclusively that a third-person reference to YHWH only determines the prophet is speaking when it occurs "in the subject position (1:7b; 2:11; 3:5, 15, 17)" (Wendland and Clark, "Zephaniah," 6). Thus, the third-person references to God in 1:5, 6, 8, 12, 17; 2:5, 9, 10; 3:2, 8, 9, 12, 20 do not cancel YHWH from being the primary speaker of those texts. One should read 3:1 -4 as YHWH's speech since the "Woe!" statement in 3:1 -4 parallels YHWH's clear "Woe!" statement in 2:5. This conclusion differs from Wendland and Clark ("Zephaniah," 11 -12) but uses their same logic of attributing 1:14 -16 to the prophet based on their parallel with 1:7 ("Zephaniah," 7).

Figure Part III.1: YHWH's Speeches vs. Zephaniah's in Zephaniah 2:1–3:20b	
YHWH	**Zephaniah**
2:5 2:8–10 2:12 3:1–4 3:6–7d	2:1–4 2:6–7 2:11 2:13–15 3:5 3:7e–f
3:8–10 3:11–13 3:18 3:19–20b	3:14–15 3:16–17

Zephaniah 2:1–3:20b is the book's main literary unit, and second masculine plural address frames the whole (2:1; 3:20). The book's formal exhortations come in the masculine plural imperatives of 2:1a, 3a ("Bind yourselves together, and become a sheaf! . . . Seek YHWH. . . . Seek righteousness; seek humility!") and 3:8a ("Therefore, wait for me!"). On these, everything depends.[17] They thus show that Zephaniah's highest level discourse is directive,[18] and the possibility for blessing and curse based on one's response gives the whole a parenetic thrust.[19] By the commands, the prophet sought to persuade his audience to seek YHWH together and to wait on him for the day when he would overcome all evil and secure for them a delight-filled deliverance.[20]

As is common in directive speech, Zephaniah urged his audience to obey his exhortations by using marked and unmarked motive clauses. Two large sections containing negative (2:5–3:7) and positive (3:11–20b) reasons explain why the remnant should heed God's voice. Yet all announcements of punishment and salvation are "subordinated to commands."[21]

---

17. While recognizing the role of the imperatives in 2:1, 3, Sweeney misses both the discourse significance of the imperative in 3:8, which is central to Zephaniah's message, and that לָכֵן ("therefore") in 3:8 draws an inference from 2:4–3:7 and not just 3:1–7 (Sweeney, *Zephaniah*, 111). Both Ryou and Floyd correctly recognize the link between 2:1, 3 and 3:8 (Ryou, *Zephaniah's Oracles*, 284–85; Floyd, *Minor Prophets, Part 2*, 203). Ryou, however, treats the two texts as an opening and closing frame rather than as parallel beginnings of two stages of an extended argument. Floyd does not carry the exhortation unit begun in 3:8 to its necessary completion at 3:20 but instead ends it at 3:13. The parallel "in that day" (בַּיּוֹם הַהוּא) statements

in 3:11 and 3:16 suggest that the unit beginning in 3:8 extends to the end of the book and that the imperatives in 3:14 are part of the overall motivation to wait in 3:8a. For more on this, see below.

18. See DeRouchie, *How to Understand and Apply*, 112–13.

19. See Sweeney, *Isaiah 1–39*, 527. Floyd characterizes 2:1–3:20 as "Prophetic Exhortation" (Floyd, *Minor Prophets, Part 2*, 213, cf. 203), with 2:1–3 specifically supplying a "Prophetic Call to Repentance" (p. 217).

20. For an overview of the main imperative sections in Zeph 2:1–4 and 3:8–10, see DeRouchie, "Seeking God and Waiting."

21. Floyd, *Minor Prophets, Part 2*, 203, cf. 213.

First, the charges themselves in 2:1, 3, and 3:8 frame 2:5–3:7, which highlights the lamentable state and fate of the rebels from the foreign nations (2:5–15) and Jerusalem (3:1–7). Zephaniah 2:5 and 3:1 both begin with parallel asyndetic "Woe" [הוֹי] statements and start units giving reasons why the people of Judah and other lands should seek YHWH together (2:1–4).[22] As Waldemar observes, "The woe of 3:1 represents the transition from the series of foreign nations oracles to prophecies concerning Jerusalem, . . . a transition that links the two series more than it divides. . . . Jerusalem is not contrasted with the foreign nations, but is drawn perhaps editorially, into their list and threatened with the same prospect, namely the Day of the Lord."[23] The inferential "Therefore" (לָכֵן) in 3:8 shows that 2:5–3:7 also gives reasons for the following command. Because of the encroaching punishment against Judah's neighbors and Jerusalem, the God-fearing remnant of Judah and other lands must seek YHWH together *and* wait on him.

Second, 3:8b–20b provides the book's greatest motivation to maintain a unified hope. People must "wait" for YHWH "for" (כִּי in 3:8b and 3:9a) God promised to punish his enemies and to transform a preserved remnant from the earth at judgment time (3:8b–10). The text then expounds in glorious detail the remnant's all-satisfying salvation (3:11–20b). The book's motivational climax begins in 3:14–15 with an intrusive flood of joy that uses four imperatives of celebration (רָנִּי . . . . הָרִיעוּ . . . שִׂמְחִי וְעָלְזִי, "Sing aloud! . . . Shout! . . . Be merry, and exult!"). These imperatives treat God's coming restoration as if it has already begun, thus stressing its certainty. Then, partially through the most extensive reported speech in the book (3:16–18), the passage continues to beautifully portray the greatness of God's work on behalf of his redeemed (3:16–20b).[24]

---

22. So, too, Ryou, *Zephaniah's Oracles*, 284. הוֹי is preceded by *waw* in only three of its fifty-one occurrences (see Jer 22:18 [2x]; 34:4), and many of the forty-eight asyndetic forms are parallel with another הוֹי. E.g., (1) Isa 5:8, 11, 18, 20, 21; (2) Isa 10:1, 5; (3) Isa 28:1; 29:1; 29:15; 30:1; 31:1; 33:1; (4) Isa 45:9, 10; (5) Amos 5:18; 6:1; (6) Hab 2:6, 9, 12, 15, 19.

23. Cited by Christensen, "Zephaniah 2:4–15," 682, from Janzen Waldemar, "'*Ašrê* and *Hoi* in the Old Testament" (PhD diss., Harvard University, 1969), 234. Both VanGemeren and Motyer observe this and include 2:4–15 with 3:1–7 under a common heading (Willem A. VanGemeren, *Interpreting the*

Prophetic Word: An Introduction to the Prophetic Literature of the Old Testament [Grand Rapids: Zondervan, 1990], 174; Motyer, "Zephaniah," 901). In apparent tension, Wendland and Clark state that 3:1 begins the final division of the book but that "the exclamatory *hôy* . . . suggests significant continuity with what has gone before (cf. 2:5)" (Wendland and Clark, "Zephaniah," 12, 28; quote from 28).

24. For an overview of the motivation section in Zeph 3:11–20 with extended mediation on YHWH's singing (3:17) that was not included in this commentary, see DeRouchie, "Rejoicing Then and Now."

III.1 Zephaniah 2:1–3:7

Stage 1: *The Appeal to Seek YHWH Together to Avoid Punishment*

Main Idea of Zephaniah 2:1–3:7

The faithful remnant from Judah and other lands must seek YHWH together to avoid punishment.

III. The Substance of the Savior's Invitation to Satisfaction: Charges to Seek YHWH Together and to Wait (2:1–3:20b)

➡ **III.1 Stage 1: The Appeal to Seek YHWH Together to Avoid Punishment (2:1–3:7)**
    A. The Charge to Unite in Submission to YHWH (2:1–2)
    B. The Charge to Seek YHWH in Righteousness and Humility (2:3–4)
    C. Further Reasons to Seek YHWH Together (2:5–3:7)
III.2 Stage 2: The Appeal to Wait for YHWH to Enjoy Salvation (3:8–20b)

Literary Context of Zephaniah 2:1–3:7

The imperatives and vocative address in Zeph 2:1 and 3 signal the shift from the setting (1:2–18) to the substance of the book's primary exhortations, which come in two stages. In stage 1, Zephaniah appeals to those in Judah and other lands to seek YHWH together to avoid punishment (2:1–3:7). Stage 2, then, includes his appeal to wait for YHWH so as to enjoy salvation (3:8–20b). For more, see the "Literary Context" discussion at the introduction to Part III.

Zephaniah 2:1–2

CHAPTER 4

A. The Charge to Unite in Submission to YHWH

Main Idea of the Passage

Those in the nation recognized for its lack of desire for YHWH must unite in surrender under God to avoid punishment.

Literary Context

Having stressed the coming onslaught of divine fury and the need to revere God (Zeph 1:2–18), Zephaniah opens the book's main body (2:1–3:20b) with the first of two stages of the Savior's invitation to satisfaction (2:1–3:7). The five imperatives in 2:1–2, 3–4 supply the main hortatory thrust of this section: "*Bind yourselves together, and become a sheaf!* . . . *Seek* YHWH. . . . *Seek* righteousness; *seek* humility!" (הִתְקוֹשְׁשׁוּ וָקוֹשּׁוּ . . . בַּקְּשׁוּ אֶת־יְהוָה . . . בַּקְּשׁוּ־צֶדֶק בַּקְּשׁוּ עֲנָוָה). Two reasons to seek YHWH together follow these commands (2:5–15, 3:1–7). Both reasons begin with "Woe!" (הוֹי) and concern avoiding punishment. The prophet then adds stage 2 of his exhortation. This exhortation initially calls the present and future remnant from Judah and other lands to "wait" (חַכּוּ) for YHWH (3:8a). It then motivates this call by focusing on the future salvation awaiting those who surrender to God (3:8b–20b).

III. The Substance of the Savior's Invitation to Satisfaction: Charges to Seek YHWH Together and to Wait (2:1–3:20b)

    III.1 Stage 1: The Appeal to Seek YHWH Together to Avoid Punishment (2:1–3:7)

➡   **A. The Charge to Unite in Submission to YHWH (2:1–2)**

          1. The Need to Unite (2:1)

          2. The Time to Unite (2:2)

      B. The Charge to Seek YHWH in Righteousness and Humility (2:3–4)

      C. Further Reasons to Seek YHWH Together (2:5–3:7)

    III.2 Stage 2: The Appeal to Wait for YHWH to Enjoy Salvation (3:8–20b)

Translation and Exegetical Outline

(See page 147.)

Structure and Literary Form

Stage 1 of YHWH's call to long for him expectantly includes three main units. The initial two give the primary charges and the third provides two unmarked reasons to heed the exhortations. The first and second units (2:1–2, 3–4) include five masculine plural imperatives that drive the primary line of argumentation and signal the whole as directive speech.[1] That is, the main body of the book is prophetic exhortation, whose content has various positive and negative motivations.[2] In the third unit (2:5–3:7), the prophet motivates obedience by declaring either future punishment or protection based on obedience. These motivations mainly consist of two statements of "Woe!" with dramatic extensions (2:5–15; 3:1–7) that decry Jerusalem and her neighbors' sinful ways and announce their coming downfall.[3]

The section's first unit of 2:1–2 opens with two conjoined masculine plural imperatives from the same root (קשש, "to bind/bundle"). The first lacks any syntactic connection to what precedes and opens the book's main hortatory portion. Together the imperatives call any awakened Judeans to "bind themselves together" like sheaves to be preserved (2:1). They must quickly repent before the winds of divine wrath come and blow them away like chaff (2:2). The prophet probably proclaimed his message at the Feast of Ingathering that celebrated YHWH's provision throughout the

---

1. See DeRouchie, *How to Understand and Apply*, 112–13; cf. Garrett and DeRouchie, *A Modern Grammar for Biblical Hebrew*, 330–33.

2. See Sweeney, *Isaiah 1–39*, 527.

3. Sweeney, *Isaiah 1–39*, 543; cf. Westermann, *Basic Forms of Prophetic Speech*, 190–98.

Zephaniah 2:1–2[1]

III. **The Substance of the Savior's Invitation to Satisfaction: Charges to Seek YHWH Together and to Wait (2:1–3:20b)**

III.1 **Stage 1: The Appeal to Seek YHWH Together to Avoid Punishment (2:1–3:7)**

A. The Charge to Unite in Submission to YHWH (2:1–2)

1. The Need to Unite (2:1)

2. The Time to Unite (2:2)

1a [Z]	הִתְקוֹשְׁשׁוּ	Bind yourselves together,
1b	וָקוֹשּׁוּ הַגּוֹי לֹא נִכְסָף׃	and become a sheaf, O the nation not longing—
2a	בְּטֶרֶם לֶדֶת חֹק	before a birthing of a decree
2b	כְּמֹץ עָבַר יוֹם	(like chaff, a day has passed),
2c	בְּטֶרֶם לֹא־יָבוֹא עֲלֵיכֶם חֲרוֹן אַף־יְהוָה	before the fury of YHWH's anger surely comes on you,
2d	בְּטֶרֶם לֹא־יָבוֹא עֲלֵיכֶם יוֹם אַף־יְהוָה׃	before the day of YHWH's anger surely comes on you.

1. For information on the guidelines used for tracing the argument, see The Method in the introduction, pp. XX.

Part III.1: Stage 1: The Appeal to Seek YHWH Together to Avoid Punishment

agricultural year.[4] This setting adds to the rhetorical force of his words and stresses that God was ready to begin a new era of salvation history by ending the present one.

Explanation of the Text

Zephaniah 1 described Judah's idolatry and complacency (1:4–6, 12), their impending horrific punishment (1:7–13), and the rest of the world's coming punishment (1:2–3, 14–18) due to sin against YHWH (1:17). Zephaniah now transitions to a message of instruction and further warning for all in Judah and her neighbors who have ears to hear. This transition includes two conjoined commands (הִתְקוֹשְׁשׁוּ וָקוֹשּׁוּ, "Bind yourselves together, and become a sheaf!") and the book's first vocative address (הַגּוֹי לֹא נִכְסָף, "O the nation not longing").

1. The Need to Unite (2:1)

Building on the harvest celebration associated with the Feast of Ingathering,[5] Zephaniah opens this exhortation section with an asyndetic *hithpolel* imperative followed by a conjoined *qal* imperative, both from the root קשש.[6] The verb derives from the noun for "straw, stubble" (קַשׁ) and likely means something like "bundle" or "heap," resulting in a translation like, "Bind yourselves together, and become a sheaf!"[7] The prophet first declares what the hearers are to do to themselves, and then he clarifies the resulting condition.[8] Texts associate the *polel* form of this verb with collecting straw (Exod 5:7, 12) or sticks (Num 15:32–33; 1 Kgs 17:10, 12). The noun often appears in judgment contexts against rebellious Israel (Isa 5:24; Joel 2:5) or their neighbors (Exod 15:7; Isa 47:14; Obad 18), highlighting how quickly God burns his enemies: "[God's enemies] are consumed *like straw* fully dried" (Nah 1:10; cf. Mal 4:1).[9] Sweeney hears echoes of Zeph 1:7 in 2:1 and believes that the prophet is "portraying the gathering of the people as the gathering of the very sticks that are to be burned up as part of

---

4. See the comments at Zeph 1:2, 5, 7.

5. See the comments at Zeph 1:2, 5, 7.

6. Some scholars propose that the second imperative is a *qal* (קוֹשּׁוּ) from either קוש ("ensnare") or יקש ("lay a trap") (e.g., Sabottka, *Zephanja*, 60–62; Rudolph, *Micha, Nahum, Habakuk, Zephanja*, 271). Others see the second verb as deriving from קשה ("to be hard") (e.g., Gillis Gerleman, *Zephanja: Textkritisch und Literarisch Untersucht* [Lund: Gleerup, 1942], 24). Most scholars parse the forms either as they are here (e.g., J. M. P. Smith, "Book of Zephaniah," 221; Kapelrud, *Message of the Prophet Zephaniah*, 31; A. Vanlier Hunter, "Seek the Lord!: A Study of the Meaning and Function of the Exhortations in Amos, Hosea, Isaiah, Micah, and Zephaniah" [ThD diss., St. Mary's Seminary and University, 1982], 267; Berlin, *Zephaniah*, 97; Ryou, *Zephaniah's Oracles*, 17–20) or with the second imperative being a *polel* of קשש, perhaps with a more active rather than stative meaning (i.e., "make a sheaf"; e.g., Ball, *Rhetorical Study of Zephaniah*, 97; Ben Zvi, *Book of Zephaniah*, 137n386; Roberts, *Nahum, Habakkuk, and Zephaniah*, 186–87; Sweeney, *Zephaniah*, 114). For a summary of the discussion, see

Ben Zvi, *Book of Zephaniah*, 137–39. Haupt proposed reading Zeph 2:1a–2b: "Bow yourselves and bend to the Lord, O sinful people! Before Fate descend upon you like a passage hawk" (Paul Haupt, "The Peregrine Falcon," *JBL* 38.4 [1919]: 152–56). However, his conclusions are unlikely and unnecessary. Renz's translation fails to keep the ingathering context: "Act like those who scrape together and scrape up" (Renz, *Books of Nahum, Habakkuk, and Zephaniah*, 517).

7. The relationship of קשש with the verb קשה ("to be hard") supports this rendering. See "קשש," *HALOT* 1154–55; "I קשש," "II קשש," "III קשש," *DCH* 7:338. Connecting the verb to harvest fits the context of Zephaniah far better than a link with building (contra John Gray, "Metaphor from Building in Zephaniah II 1," *VT* 3.4 [1953]: 404–7).

8. Hunter, "Seek the Lord!," 267. Gesenius notes that the second of two coordinate imperatives (commonly joined by *waw*) usually supplies the initial imperative's consequent state or action (GKC, §110f). Cf. Isa 29:9; Hab 1:5.

9. Cf. Berlin, *Zephaniah*, 96.

the sacrifice on the Day of YHWH."[10] Similarly, Ben Zvi notes that ingathering regularly happens on the eve of punishment (e.g., Lev 26:25; Jer 4:5; Joel 1:14).[11] However, Zephaniah's imagery is more positive, for he urges the people to defend themselves from the coming inferno. In short, they are to be straw, *not* chaff, bundling themselves in unity and by this separating themselves from all that God's just, fiery wrath will consume.[12] In Judah's history, both kings and prophets called for God's people to gather as an expression of repentance (2 Chr 20:4; Joel 1:14–15).

The prophet uses the book's first vocative address to identify his audience "the nation not longing" (הַגּוֹי לֹא נִכְסָף). The *niphal* of the verb כסף in its two other occurrences is followed by the preposition לְ ("to, for"), which together mean to "be in a state of longing for" something.[13] In the present context, "YHWH" is the missing center in the people's existence (see Zeph 1:17; 2:3), so he is probably the implied object.[14] In contrast, some treat the verb as passive rather than active, meaning "not desired [by YHWH]"—i.e., under his wrath.[15] They do so because the preposition לְ with object is not explicit. While possible, the active rendering is more likely for several reasons: (1) We have no examples of the passive meaning of this verb in Scripture, and we must infer the prepositional phrase "by YHWH" (בֵּיהוָה) or "for YHWH" (לַיהוָה) either way. (2) After assessing similar derogatory vocatives in explicit and implicit calls to repentance, Ben Zvi notes that "they tend to refer to the people's attitude and not to the (real or deserved) attitude of others toward the people."[16] (3) In Zeph 2:1–2, YHWH desires the audience's repentance. This suggests the focus is on their lack of desire for him rather than on God not desiring them. Thematically, the text echoes 1:12, where the prophet referred to the complacency and functional atheism common in Jerusalem. Furthermore, the relationship of the verb כסף to the noun for "silver" (כֶּסֶף) also ironically links the verse to both 1:11 and 1:18, where God emphasizes the transience of wealth and its impotence to save.[17] While the prophet's audience entertains

---

10. Sweeney, *Zephaniah*, 115; cf. Robertson, *Books of Nahum, Habakkuk, and Zephaniah*, 290, 292, who compares the text to Mal 3:19[4:1].

11. Ben Zvi, *Book of Zephaniah*, 138.

12. Cf. Calvin, "Habakkuk, Zephaniah, Haggai," 229; Patterson, *Nahum, Habakkuk, Zephaniah*, 294, 296; Renz, *Books of Nahum, Habakkuk, and Zephaniah*, 524.

13. See Gen 31:30; Ps 84:3; cf. Ps 17:12; Job 14:15. Some English translations render the phrase הַגּוֹי לֹא נִכְסָף in Zeph 2:1 as "shameless nation" (NRSVue, ESV) or "shameful nation" (NIV), following an Aramaic cognate that means "to be ashamed." (Cf. Akkadian *kuspu* ["shame"] and Arabic *kasafa* ["to be dark, gloomy, pale"]; see also כֶּסֶף "silver" = "pale money"). However, at least three reasons make this interpretation questionable: (1) No other Scriptural occurrences of כסף employ this meaning. (2) The Tg. Neb. reads כסף as "desiring" (Aramaic = *peal* participle חמיד). (3) The other ancient versions supply no clear support. See Ben Zvi, *Book of Zephaniah*, 141.

14. So Hunter, "Seek the Lord!," 261–62; Ben Zvi, *Book of Zephaniah*, 142; Renz, *Books of Nahum, Habakkuk, and Zephaniah*, 523. This seems more probable than the interpretation of the Tg. Neb., which understands the missing object as "to return to the Torah" of God (אוֹרַיְתָא = Hebrew הַתּוֹרָה). In contrast, Sabbottka unpersuasively stretches the meaning of the negative לֹא to mean "nothing" and views it as object of the verb כסף, thus referring to the people's idols (= "the nation longing for nothing") (Sabottka, *Zephanja*, 62–63).

15. Calvin, "Habakkuk, Zephaniah, Haggai," 230; Kapelrud, *Message of the Prophet Zephaniah*, 105; Roberts, *Nahum, Habakkuk, and Zephaniah*, 187, 189. In contrast, both Irsigler and Motyer treat the verb in an absolute sense, the former proposing "no aspirations, indifference" and the latter suggesting "insensitive, devoid of feeling" (Hubert Irsigler, *Gottesgericht und Jahwetag: Die Komposition Zef 1,1–2,3, untersucht auf der Grundlage der Literarkritik des Zefanjabuches*, ATSAT 3 [St. Ottilien: Eos, 1977], 62; Motyer, "Zephaniah," 3:926). Nevertheless, Motyer still summarizes the meaning as "unresponsive to the Lord."

16. Ben Zvi, *Book of Zephaniah*, 142. For example, we read, "Return, O apostasy—Israel" (Jer 3:12), and "Return, O apostate sons" (3:14, 22).

17. Cf. Sweeney, *Zephaniah*, 115.

misdirected longings (cf. Matt 6:24), YHWH still longs for their surrender and mercifully calls them to humble themselves and repent while there is still hope.

The previous context in general and the specific links with Zeph 1:11–12 point to "Judah" as the most likely referent to "the nation" (הַגּוֹי). The prophet has just spoken judgment and warning against Judah for their rebellion (Zeph 1:4–6 and 1:7b–13), as he did for the rest of the world (1:2–3, 14–18). After 2:1–4, he will again forecast doom against other nations (2:5–15) and Jerusalem (3:1–7).[18] But Wendland and Clark propose this "nation" is Philistia since (1) Zeph 1:11 already vaguely mentioned Philistia's people, (2) their cities in 2:4 "retrospectively" identify the nation in 2:1, and (3) God directly confronts them in 2:5–7.[19] However, 2:4 most likely provides a reason (signaled by כִּי) only for 2:3 and not also 2:1–2 since (1) the imperative "seek!" (בַּקְּשׁוּ) at the beginning of 2:3 lacks explicit connection with what precedes and (2) the subordinate conjunction כִּי ("for") normally does not cross sentence-boundaries in Hebrew.[20] Thus,

the mention of Philistia's cities in 2:4 should not inform our reading of 2:1–2, and this conclusion leaves Judah as the best option for "the nation not longing."

2. The Time to Unite (2:2)

Zephaniah now repeats the preposition "before" (בְּטֶרֶם) three times to highlight his urgency and the fleeting opportunity to repent. We first learn that Zephaniah's audience must "bundle" themselves "before a birthing of a decree" (בְּטֶרֶם לֶדֶת חֹק) (Zeph 2:2a). In this context of warning, this phrase most likely portrays God as a woman in labor, who will soon bring forth wrath against the world's rebels. YHWH the Rock birthed (ילד) his people through great travail (Deut 32:18; cf. Isa 51:1–2), but now he would soon birth their destruction.[21]

None of the versions reflect a parent text different from the Hebrew Masoretic tradition. Nevertheless, some scholars have proposed emendations because the language of "birthing a decree" is strange and unique to this passage.[22] But the text

---

18. Some scholars are too confident that the text negatively portrays Judah by calling it a "nation" (גּוֹי) instead of a "people" (עַם) (Watts, *The Books of Joel, Obadiah, Jonah, Nahum, Habakkuk, and Zephaniah*, 164; cf. Baker, *Nahum, Habakkuk and Zephaniah*, 102; Bailey, "Zephaniah," 446). Of the 108 instances of *singular* גּוֹי in the OT, 52 refer to Israel (48.15 percent). This fairly high percentage cautions against seeing intentional derogation here. Also, several positive examples of Israel being a "nation" (גּוֹי) exist (e.g., Gen 12:2; Exod 19:6; 2 Sam 7:23; Ps 33:12; Isa 9:3; Jer 31:36; Ezek 37:22; Mic 4:7). Ezekiel 2:3 is the sole example of plural "nations" referring to Israel. Thus, 53 of the total 504 occurrences of גּוֹי (10.52 percent) refer to God's people. Cody helpfully distinguishes between עַם and גּוֹי: "While 'am through the Old Testament refers to a people or nation in its aspect of centripetal unity and cohesiveness, *gôy* is linked inseparably with territory and government and what we would today call foreign relations" (Aelred Cody, "When Is the Chosen People Called *gôy*?," *VT* 14.1 [1964]: 5). Similarly, Block notes that עַם ("people") is a "warm, kinship term" whereas גּוֹי bears "a distinctly political nature" as reflected in its frequent pairing with מֶלֶךְ/מַמְלָכָה (Daniel I. Block, "Nations/

Nationality," *NIDOTTE* 4:4:965; cf. Daniel I. Block, "Nations," *ISBE* 3:492–96).

19. Wendland and Clark, "Zephaniah," 8–9. Smith has a similar position but only after omitting large portions of 2:2–3 and 7 as secondary (J. M. P. Smith, "Book of Zephaniah," 211–21).

20. Contra Floyd, *Minor Prophets, Part 2*, 216; Sweeney, *Zephaniah*, 112; Wendland and Clark, "Zephaniah," 8.

21. The travail in Deut 32:18 most likely refers to YHWH's bearing the punishment for Israel's sin in Exod 17:1–7. See Jesse R. Scheumann, "A Biblical Theology of Birth Pain and the Hope of the Messiah" (Bethlehem College and Seminary, ThM thesis, 2014), 26–29; cf. Edmund P. Clowney, *The Unfolding Mystery: Discovering Christ in the Old Testament*, 2nd ed. (Phillipsburg, NJ: P&R, 2013), 120–28.

22. For an overview of the different suggestions, see Sweeney, *Zephaniah*, 116; cf. Dominique Barthelemy et al., eds., *Preliminary and Interim Report on the Hebrew Old Testament Text Project: Prophetical Books II* (New York: United Bible Societies, 1980), 5:374–75. See below for many of Sweeney's examples including the Hebrew negative לֹא.

makes sense as it stands, and Scripture elsewhere uses the language of birth figuratively,[23] even in association with YHWH's eschatological actions with his people (Isa 42:14–16).[24]

God usually appoints or prescribes חֹק as a legal "statute" for humans (e.g., Exod 12:24; Josh 24:25; 1 Sam 30:25), but the term also refers more broadly to a "decree" that specifies nature's rules (e.g., Ps 148:6; Job 28:26) or God's purposes in the world (e.g., Ps 2:7).[25] This latter category applies here, referring to the covenant curses embodied in YHWH's day (cf. Lev 26:14–39; Deut 28:15–68). Later the prophet will speak of "all that [YHWH has] purposed against [Jerusalem]" (Zeph 3:7), and then YHWH will declare, "My judgment" (מִשְׁפָּטִי) is to gather nations, to assemble kingdoms, to pour out on them my indignation" (3:8).

An intrusive asyndetic parenthetical clause (2:2b) follows the initial prepositional phrase. While the meaning would shift slightly, the subject of the verb עָבַר ("it has passed") could be either מֹץ ("chaff"; cf. Isa 29:5) or יוֹם ("day"; Gen 50:4). The result would be either "Like chaff has passed, *so* a day!" or "Like chaff, a day has passed!" Most English versions see 2:2b as unpacking the "decree" (חֹק) in 2:2a and thus treat the combination of "day" and "chaff" as referring to how quickly *the* day of YHWH will come and go (e.g., NASB20, ESV, NIV, CSB). Isaiah sometimes used "chaff" in this way

(e.g., Isa 17:13–14; 29:5–6). In minor contrast, the NET associates "day" not with the day of YHWH proper but with Judah's quickly passing window of opportunity to repent: "before God's decree becomes reality and the day of opportunity disappears like windblown chaff." In support of the NET reading, "day" here lacks the article. This contrasts with the book's nineteen other references to *the* day of YHWH, all of which are either explicitly definite[26] or have this day as their specific referent in context (1:15 [5x], 16). For Zephaniah, the time for those viewing themselves as wheat to "bundle" is now (2:1). The opportunity is quickly fleeting, and those failing to join in unity will soon blow away like the chaff.

Zephaniah now fronts two more temporal prepositional phrases with "before" (בְּטֶרֶם), each of which extends his urgency (2:2c–d).[27] He employs "the anger of YHWH" (אַף־יְהוָה) twice to recall "YHWH's wrath" (עֶבְרַת יְהוָה) from 1:18 and to emphasize further the gravity of his charge. Associating this anger with "fury" (חֲרוֹן) also recalls its fiery nature (cf. 1:18; 3:8), and connecting it with "the day" (יוֹם) explicitly links it with chapter 1's fourteen occurrences of YHWH's "day" of wrath (1:7–10, 14–16, 18). However, here the prophet's warning supports his charge for united surrender (2:1) and sets up the more primary exhortation in Zeph 2:3.

---

23. "Wind" (Isa 26:18), "stubble" (Isa 33:11), "frost" (Job 38:29), "evil" (Job 15:35), "deception" (Ps 7:15), and various events (Prov 27:1) are all birthed.

24. Many keep the text as it is including Gerleman, *Zephanja*, 25; Rudolph, *Micha, Nahum, Habakuk, Zephanja*, 272; Hunter, "Seek the Lord!," 263–64; Ball, *Rhetorical Study of Zephaniah*, 98–100; Ben Zvi, *Book of Zephaniah*, 143; Berlin, *Zephaniah*, 97; Ryou, *Zephaniah's Oracles*, 23–24; Motyer, "Zephaniah," 926; Sweeney, *Zephaniah*, 116.

25. The noun חֹק derives from the verb חקק, meaning "to engrave" (Ezek 4:1) or "inscribe" (Isa 30:8) (so Motyer, "Zephaniah," 3:926).

26. See Zeph 1:7b, 8a, 9, 10, 14a–b, 15, 18a; 2:2d, 3d; 3:8a, 11a, 16a. Most of the definite forms occur in construct with a definite absolute noun.

27. Zephaniah 2:2c–d uniquely places לֹא ("not") after בְּטֶרֶם ("before"). In English, this would be a double negative, but in Hebrew "two negatives in the same sentence . . . make the negation more emphatic" (GKC, §152y; cf. Joüon, §160p). Others try to interpret the construction as a purpose: "*in order that* the fury/day of the anger of God *not* come on you" (so Gerleman, *Zephanja*, 28; Ball, *Rhetorical Study of Zephaniah*, 118).

Canonical and Theological Significance

See the next chapter for Canonical and Theological Significance for Zeph 2:1–4.

Zephaniah 2:3–4

B. The Charge to Seek YHWH in Righteousness and Humility

Main Idea of the Passage

The remnant from Judah and other lands must seek YHWH in righteousness and humility to avoid punishment.

Literary Context

The main exhortation in Zephaniah (2:1–3:20b) opens with the first of two stages of the Savior's invitation to satisfaction (2:1–3:7). Five masculine plural imperatives in two groupings (2:1–2, 3–4) shape the primary hortatory thrust of this section: "*Bind yourselves together, and become a sheaf!* . . . *Seek* YHWH. . . . *Seek* righteousness; *seek* humility!" (הִתְקוֹשְׁשׁוּ וָקוֹשּׁוּ . . . בַּקְּשׁוּ אֶת־יְהוָה . . . בַּקְּשׁוּ־צֶדֶק בַּקְּשׁוּ עֲנָוָה). In short, the remnant from Judah and other lands must seek the Lord together to avoid punishment. What follows are two unmarked reasons for seeking YHWH together, both of which relate to seeing God's wrath turned away (2:5–15, 3:1–7). Stage 2 of the prophet's exhortation then calls the remnant in Judah and other lands to "wait" (חַכּוּ) for YHWH (3:8a) and motivates this by promising future salvation (3:8b–20b).

> III. The Substance of the Savior's Invitation to Satisfaction: Charges to Seek YHWH Together and to Wait (2:1–3:20b)
>
> III.1 Stage 1: The Appeal to Seek YHWH Together to Avoid Punishment (2:1–3:7)
>
>   A. The Charge to Unite in Submission to YHWH (2:1–2)
>
> → **B. The Charge to Seek YHWH in Righteousness and Humility (2:3–4)**
>
>   **1. The Charge to Seek YHWH (2:3)**
>
>   **2. An Initial Reason to Seek YHWH: The Devastation of Philistia (2:4)**
>
>   C. Further Reasons to Seek YHWH Together (2:5–3:7)
>
> III.2 Stage 2: The Appeal to Wait for YHWH to Enjoy Salvation (3:8–20b)

Translation and Exegetical Outline

(See page 155.)

Structure and Literary Form

Stage 1 of the Savior's invitation to satisfaction includes three units: two masculine plural commands for listeners to unite in surrender to YHWH (2:1–2), three masculine plural commands for the remnant to seek YHWH (2:3–4), and two unmarked reasons for heeding all the commands (2:5–15; 3:1–7). The second unit in 2:3–4 appears to narrow the addressees from the unlonging nation in general to the humble, faithful remnant of the land.[1] Three identical masculine plural *piel* imperatives (בַּקְשׁוּ, "seek!") urge this group to "seek YHWH" while he may be found (2:3). The initial command to "seek YHWH" is asyndetic, marking its independence from the previous commands and highlighting it as the main thrust of the stage 1 exhortation.[2] The next two disconnected imperatives explicate it, specifying the righteousness and humility necessary for authentically seeking God. The prophet initially motivates this call to pursue YHWH with a hopeful comment: "Perhaps you may be hidden at the day of YHWH's anger" (2:3d).

---

1. אֶרֶץ here could mean either "earth" or "land"; elsewhere in the book it refers to the "earth" as a whole (1:18; 2:11; 3:8, 19–20), except in 2:5b, where it refers to the "the land of the Philistines." Already the book has shifted focus from the world in general (1:2–3) to Judah and Jerusalem in particular (1:4–6, 7–13) and then back to the whole world (1:14–18). The emphasis on "the nation" in 2:1b suggests that we should read הָאָרֶץ in

2:3a in a more restrictive sense, referring to "the land" of Judah. For more on Zephaniah's audience, see DeRouchie, "Addressees in Zephaniah 2:1, 3," 183–207.

2. Joüon, §177e, f; Jason S. DeRouchie, *A Call to Covenant Love: Text Grammar and Literary Structure in Deuteronomy 5–11*, (Pascataway, NJ: Gorgias, 2014), 123.

Zephaniah 2:3–4[1]

B. The Charge to Seek YHWH in Righteousness and Humility (2:3–4)

1. The Charge to Seek YHWH (2:3)

3a	בַּקְּשׁוּ אֶת־יְהוָה כָּל־עַנְוֵי הָאָרֶץ אֲשֶׁר מִשְׁפָּטוֹ פָּעָלוּ	Seek YHWH, all the humble of the land who have heeded his judgment.	a. The Charge Voiced (2:3a)
3b	בַּקְּשׁוּ־צֶדֶק	Seek righteousness;	b. The Charge Explicated (2:3b–c)
3c	בַּקְּשׁוּ עֲנָוָה	seek humility!	
3d	אוּלַי תִּסָּתְרוּ בְּיוֹם אַף־יְהוָה:	(Perhaps you may be hidden at the day of YHWH's anger.)	c. A Parenthetical Motivation for the Charge (2:3d)

2. An Initial Reason to Seek YHWH: The Devastation of Philistia (2:4)

4a	כִּי עַזָּה עֲזוּבָה תִהְיֶה	For Gaza will be abandoned,	a. The Desertion of Gaza and Desolation of Ashkelon (2:4a–b)
4b	וְאַשְׁקְלוֹן לִשְׁמָמָה	and Ashkelon for a desolation.	
4c	אַשְׁדּוֹד בַּצָּהֳרַיִם יְגָרְשׁוּהָ	As for Ashdod, by the noonday they will drive her out,	b. The Expulsion of Ashdod and Uprooting of Ekron (2:4c–d)
4d	וְעֶקְרוֹן תֵּעָקֵר:	and Ekron will be uprooted.	

1. For information on the guidelines used for tracing the argument, see The Method in the introduction, pp. XX.

He then immediately grounds (כִּי, "for/because") the call by predicting Philistia's destruction, which shows that God's fiery wrath is at Judah's doorstep (2:4). Only by wholly surrendering to YHWH is there any possibility of escaping his blazing fury (2:3d).

Many scholars group 2:1–3 together and treat 2:4 as introducing a different focus on the foreign nation (2:5–15).[3] However, 2:4 begins with the subordinate conjunction "for" (כִּי), signaling its close syntactic connection to the three imperatives in 2:3.[4] Furthermore, 2:5 directly addresses the Philistines with both vocatives and second-person speech, but the cities are in third person in 2:4. Finally, the Masoretes put a closed paragraph marker after 2:4 (ס= *setumah*), suggesting that 2:5 begins a new unit. Thus, the grammar and cantillation support 2:4 being a *reason* why those in the land who depend on God must seek YHWH. His global punishment is imminent against those nearest Judah.[5] Specifically, 2:4 presents the destruction of four key Philistine cities as a sample of future worldwide destruction. Zephaniah had already predicted the Philistines' devastation in 1:11b–c and noted its negative effect on Jerusalem's nobility. The Philistine's destruction would also lead to the ruining of all rebels in Judah's capital city (1:12–13). The Philistine's negative influence on Judah in Zephaniah's day and the nearness of their immediate desolation by Egypt and Babylon likely led the prophet to focus on them here.

Explanation of the Text

1. The Charge to Seek YHWH (2:3)

Zephaniah first addressed the whole rebellious nation of Judah in 2:1–2. He now narrows his focus to the faithful remnant who have heeded his initial call, giving them a more ultimate challenge. He repeats the masculine plural imperative "seek!" (בַּקְּשׁוּ) three times, urging those submitted to God to "seek YHWH" together (Zeph 2:3a). Zephaniah then explains that to "seek YHWH" means to seek "righteousness" and "humility" (2:3b–c).[6] Only by seeking YHWH may one find deliverance from the day of punishment (2:3d).[7]

---

3. E.g., J. M. P. Smith, "Book of Zephaniah," 211–15; Kapelrud, *Message of the Prophet Zephaniah*, 27–30; Ball, *Rhetorical Study of Zephaniah*, 114–20; Ben Zvi, *Book of Zephaniah*, 150, 295–98; Seybold, *Nahum, Habakuk, Zephanja*, 102–4; Sweeney, "Form-Critical Reassessment," 399; Vlaardingerbroek, *Zephaniah*, 214–16; Floyd, *Minor Prophets, Part 2*, 215–18; Irsigler, *Zefanja*, 189–93.

4. E.g., Berlin, *Zephaniah*, 99, 101–2; Ryou, *Zephaniah's Oracles*, 186–207; Floyd, *Minor Prophets, Part 2*, 215–16; Sweeney, *Zephaniah*, 111; Wendland and Clark, "Zephaniah," 8; Renz, *Books of Nahum, Habakkuk, and Zephaniah*, 520n1. Floyd, Sweeney, and Wendland and Clark believe כִּי grounds all of Zeph 2:1–3. This interpretation is unlikely since (1) the initial imperative in 2:3 lacks syntactic connection with the

imperatives in 2:1 and (2) כִּי is an inner-clausal connector that does not normally extend beyond the borders of a sentence. As such, 2:4 gives an initial reason to seek YHWH, with no direct reference to the imperatives in 2:1.

5. Cf. Ball, *Rhetorical Study of Zephaniah*, 122. The syntax, rhetorical function, and third-person nature of 2:4 support this reading, and no manuscript evidence exists to suggest that 2:4 originally followed 2:5 (so Roberts, *Nahum, Habakkuk, and Zephaniah*, 196) or 2:6 (so Holladay, "Reading Zephaniah with a Concordance," 678).

6. The threefold use of the imperative "seek!" (בַּקְּשׁוּ) in Zeph 2:3 may counter the threefold note of urgency expressed through "before" (בְּטֶרֶם) in 2:2 (so Motyer, "Zephaniah," 3:927).

7. Sweeney has persuasively argued that the Greek trans-

a. The Charge Voiced (2:3a)

Earlier the prophet said those in Jerusalem had "neither *sought* [בִּקְשׁוּ] YHWH nor inquired of him" (1:6; cf. 3:2). Their syncretism meant that they had turned from YHWH, though they might still swear to him (1:4–6). Zephaniah now reemploys the *piel* verb בקשׁ as an imperative, urging his listeners to "seek" YHWH alone (2:3a; cf. Ps 105:4). Oh, that his listeners would respond like the psalmist, "Your face, O YHWH, will I seek" (Ps 27:8).

YHWH is the object of בקשׁ in the OT thirty times, fourteen of which occur in the Latter Prophets.[8] Those who "seek" YHWH will find him (e.g., Jer 29:13; Hos 5:15; cf. 2 Chr 7:14),[9] but God's people regularly turned from him (e.g., Hos 7:10; cf. 2 Chr 15:4). YHWH did pledge that one day after the curse of exile his great compassion would reverse this downward pattern, moving his people to turn from sin and to "seek" him permanently (e.g., Deut 4:29–31; Jer 50:4; Hos 3:5). Zephaniah now urges his listeners to respond accordingly.

In 2:3a, he uses the second occurrence of vocative address in the book (cf. 2:1), naming his target recipients "all the humble of the land who have heeded his judgment." Identifying this audience demands understanding each part of this statement.[10]

First, the term עָנָו speaks of one broken in spirit (i.e., "bowed, bent" under life's pressures). Only the "humble" (עֲנָוִים) can repent by earnestly depending on God (Ps 37:11; Isa 11:4) and entirely submitting to him (cf. Ps 76:9–10[8–9]; Isa 51:1; Amos 5:6).[11] Some restrict the humiliation to what the economically "poor" feel in contrast to the "rich" (cf. Ps 10:12, following the *qere*).[12] However, the term is usually broader (e.g., Job 24:4; Amos 8:4) as seen in Psalms where the "humble" contrast with the wicked and oppressive (e.g., Pss 9:18–19[17–18]; 10:12–13; 37:10–11).[13] Likewise, Zephaniah's context shows that the prophet focuses less on economics and more on disposition.[14] While his concerns reach the financially vulnerable, he targets his message against the abuse of power and the failure to value those made in God's image. He confronts the strong and influential who act cruelly and corruptly, exploiting the weak (Zeph 1:9, 11, 18; 3:1, 3). By the book's end, God promises to preserve the "afflicted (עָנִי) and needy" and contrasts them with the arrogant rather than the wealthy (3:11–12).[15] Therefore, the "humble" in 2:3 are all

---

lator read a Hebrew text like the MT, despite the significant translational differences: ζητήσατε τὸν κύριον, πάντες ταπεινοὶ γῆς· κρίμα ἐργάζεσθε καὶ δικαιοσύνην ζητήσατε καὶ ἀποκρίνεσθε αὐτά ("Seek the Lord, all you humble of the earth; work justice, and seek righteousness, and answer them"). The LXX translator apparently made a series of changes resulting from him reading the pausal *qatal* form פָּעֲלוּ (usually פָּעֲלוּ "they have carried out") as the imperative פַּעֲלוּ ("carry out/work!"), which would read פָּעֲלוּ in pause. The result is that the LXX does not view the audience as having heeded God's word yet, but it holds out hope that they will. See Sweeney, *Zephaniah*, 119–20.

8. Chhetri, "בָּקַשׁ (*bāqaš*)," *NIDOTTE* 1:708. Cf. Isa 45:19; 65:1; Hos 3:5; 5:6; Zeph 1:6; 2:3.

9. See also 2 Chr 15:2; Prov 8:17; Isa 55:6, though with different verbs for "seek."

10. For fuller treatment, see DeRouchie, "Addressees in Zephaniah 2:1, 3," 183–207.

11. The adjective עָנָו in Zeph 2:3 means "humble," and the adjective עָנִי in 3:12 means "afflicted, needy." Dumbrell writes, "עָנִי means to have been humbled, afflicted by necessity or circumstances, stressing difficulty of the condition and implying ... some kind of disability present.... עָנָו means, basically, bent over (under the pressure of circumstances) and consequently, as affliction does its proper work, humble" (William J. Dumbrell, "עָנִי, עָנָו ['ānāw; 'ānî]," *NIDOTTE* 3:451–52).

12. Sabottka, *Zephanja*, 65–66; Norbert Lohfink, "Zephaniah and the Church of the Poor," *TD* 32.2 (1985): 113–18. Cf. Kapelrud, *Message of the Prophet Zephaniah*, 32–33; Renz, *Books of Nahum, Habakkuk, and Zephaniah*, 525–26.

13. Cf. Ben Zvi, *Book of Zephaniah*, 149n423.

14. Cf. Hunter, "Seek the Lord!," 268–69.

15. While Renz initially emphasizes socioeconomic class distinctions (Renz, *Books of Nahum, Habakkuk, and Zephaniah*, 525–26, 557, 561, 614, 618–19), Zeph 3:12–13 later forces him to affirm that what Zephaniah commends "is not

peoples who, in view of the coming judgment (1:7), repent of their sin (1:17) and seek YHWH (2:3), regardless of economic status.[16]

Second, Zephaniah says the "humble" are those "of the land" (הָאָרֶץ). Elsewhere in Zephaniah, the term rendered "land" usually refers to the whole "earth/world" and not just Judah's territory.[17] Thus, some scholars see verse 3 addressing not only Judah's righteous remnant but also a remnant from the entire world (see 3:9; cf. 2:9, 11).[18] While Zephaniah retains a global vision concerning both punishment (1:2–3, 14–18; 2:4, 5–15; 3:6, 8, 15, 19) and salvation (2:9, 11; 3:9–10), the context's primary audience is Judah, "the nation not longing" (2:1). Furthermore, the second masculine plural imperatives in 2:3 and 3:8, 14 apparently address the righteous remnant that begins in Judah. Hence, the reference to הָאָרֶץ is likely more restrictive, indicating "the land" of Judah, similar to "the land of the Philistines" (אֶרֶץ פְּלִשְׁתִּים) in 2:5b. Nevertheless, as noted below, Zephaniah's broader literary context indicates that some from other nations will join "the humble" from Judah in the new Jerusa-

lem, and this allows the unspecified vocative in 2:3 to include a larger group.[19]

Third, the prophet describes the humble of the land as those "who have heeded his [i.e., YHWH's] judgment" (אֲשֶׁר מִשְׁפָּטוֹ פָּעָלוּ). Nearly thirty times elsewhere in the OT, the singular מִשְׁפָּט ("judgment, verdict, just decree, sentence") is the object of the verb עשׂה ("to do, make") and refers to living according to God's rule of justice, usually as defined in the Mosaic instruction[20] and often associated with "righteousness" (צְדָקָה).[21] Many scholars read the statement in 2:3 in just this way.[22] Accordingly, English translations tend to render the singular מִשְׁפָּט as if the text refers to covenant stipulations (e.g., "ordinances," NASB20; "commands," NRSVue, ESV, NET, NIV, CSB). But, long ago Ehrlich rightly observed that only in Zeph 2:3 does the singular object מִשְׁפָּט complement the verb פעל ("to do, carry out"); this strongly suggests a different meaning for the clause in 2:3.[23] Additionally, the prophet has placed the object מִשְׁפָּט in focus before the verb,[24] highlighting its direct relationship to the immediate context. Those "who have heeded

---

a low socioeconomic status as such but a certain attitude and lifestyle" (p. 620; cf. p. 602).

16. Robertson's proposal that "all the humble of the land" (כָּל־עַנְוֵי הָאָרֶץ) may be "the people of the land" (עַם־הָאָרֶץ), who set up young Josiah as king in Judah (2 Kgs 21:24), is too narrow (Robertson, *Books of Nahum, Habakkuk, and Zephaniah*, 294). However, Zephaniah's words may well allude to all who followed King Josiah's example in repentance after the priests discovered the Torah Scroll. After Josiah heard the scroll's words and humbly responded (2 Kgs 22:13), YHWH promised the king that he would delay disaster against Jerusalem because "you were humbled [וַתִּכָּנַע] from before YHWH" (22:19).

17. See Zeph 1:18; 2:11; 3:8, 19–20; cf. 2:5.

18. E.g., Motyer titles the unit, "An appeal to readiness—to Judah (2:1–2) *and to the world* (2:3) (Motyer, "Zephaniah," 925). While viewing 2:3 as secondary, Smith sees the phrase referring to "the pious community of Israelites the world over" (J. M. P. Smith, "Book of Zephaniah," 214).

19. See DeRouchie, "Addressees in Zephaniah 2:1, 3," 183–207. See also Floyd, *Minor Prophets, Part 2*, 216.

20. E.g., Gen 18:19; 1 Kgs 3:28; Jer 5:1; Ezek 18:8; Mic

6:8; Ps 149:9. For texts with YHWH acting this way, see, e.g., Deut 10:18; 1 Kgs 8:45; Ps 9:5[4]; 146:7; Ezek 39:21; Mic 7:9. Cf. Ben Zvi, *Book of Zephaniah*, 148. The singular מִשְׁפָּט is the implied object of the verb "to keep" (שׁמר) only in the construct phrase "keepers of judgment" (מִשְׁפָּט שֹׁמְרֵי) in Ps 106:3.

21. E.g., 2 Sam 8:15; 2 Chr 9:8; Ps 119:121; Prov 21:3; Jer 22:3; 23:5; 33:15; Ezek 18:5, 19, 21, 27. For texts with YHWH acting this way, see 1 Chr 18:14; Ps 103:6; Jer 9:23[24].

22. E.g., Calvin, "Habakkuk, Zephaniah, Haggai," 236; Keil, " Twelve Minor Prophets," 10:447 (2:139); Baker, *Nahum, Habakkuk and Zephaniah*, 103; Robertson, *Books of Nahum, Habakkuk, and Zephaniah*, 294; Berlin, *Zephaniah*, 98; Motyer, "Zephaniah," 927; Vlaardingerbroek, *Zephaniah*, 122; Sweeney, *Zephaniah*, 118; Patterson, *Nahum, Habakkuk, Zephaniah*, 295; Renz, *Books of Nahum, Habakkuk, and Zephaniah*, 526. See also the NET notes (under Zeph 2:3 n9).

23. Arnold B. Ehrlich, *Randglossen zur Hebräischen Bibel: Textkritisches, Sprachliches und Sachliches—Fünfter Band, Ezechiel und die kleinen Propheten*, vol. 5 (Hildesheim: Olms, 1968, orig., 1901 Hebrew), 311–12.

24. So too Berlin, *Zephaniah*, 98.

his judgment" are principally the individuals in Judah who have (1) "hushed" before YHWH (1:7), (2) already turned their hearts from their idolatry, self-rule, oppression, and complacency (1:4–6, 8–9, 12), and (3) heeded the declarations of chapter 1's coming global punishment and the "decree's" (חֹק) coming fury in 2:2.

The breadth of how פעל is used outside Zephaniah renders such an interpretation possible, and the specific application of the singular of the noun מִשְׁפָּט within Zephaniah supports this reading. Beyond the book, the action expressed through פעל can include doing deeds (e.g., Num 23:23; Isa 26:12; Ps 11:3), executing "all that [YHWH] commands" (Job 37:12) or "what is right" (Ps 15:2), and engaging in "iniquity, wrong" (Job 36:23; Ps 58:3; 119:3), "wrong" (Job 34:32), "evil" (Prov 30:20), and "falsehood" (Hos 7:1). Therefore, it is possible that the "doing" or "executing" of the "judgment" captured in the clause אֲשֶׁר מִשְׁפָּטוֹ פָּעָלוּ refers to "heeding" or "rightly responding to" God's judicial decree to punish sin.

Moreover, the singular form of מִשְׁפָּט occurs twice more in Zephaniah. Both instances appear to refer to God's just decision to punish worldwide human rebellion (3:5c, 8b; cf. 3:15a). Zephaniah 3:5c speaks of YHWH setting forth "his judgment" (מִשְׁפָּטוֹ) every day, which likely describes repeated and various declarations of his final verdict against sin.

Then YHWH summarizes in 3:8b his judicial ruling: "My judgment [מִשְׁפָּטִי] is to gather nations, to assemble kingdoms, to pour out on them my indignation—all the fury of my anger." In view of YHWH's strong pronouncements of retribution in chapter 1, the most natural "judgment" associated with YHWH in 2:3 is his "decree" to punish sinners.[25]

In directive discourse, two syntactically disconnected imperatives commonly stand side by side (here, groups of imperatives in 2:1 and 3) with the first expressing a preliminary command of physical motion and the second stating the main charge.[26] For example, the priests in Josiah's day needed initially to "go" away from him to then "inquire" of YHWH on behalf of the nation (2 Kgs 22:13; cf. Exod 8:21[25]). Likewise, Zephaniah charged his Judean contemporaries to "bind" themselves together first so they could "seek" YHWH as one (Zeph 2:1, 3). Only those who heeded the first command could fulfill the second. The pattern resembles how Jer 50:4 and Zech 8:21–22 anticipate a day when diverse groups of meek people will come together and journey to a restored Jerusalem so they can there "seek" YHWH and entreat his favor together.[27]

b. The Charge Explicated (2:3b–c)

Zephaniah knows that others from Judah will join him in paying homage to YHWH (see Zeph

---

25. For Floyd, the remnant showed "humility" and "heeded" the specific "judgment" by obeying the initial call in 2:1 to gather together to YHWH (Floyd, *Minor Prophets, Part 2*, 216; cf. Michael Weigl, *Zefanja und das "Israel der Armen": Eine Untersuchung zur Theologie des Buches Zefanja*, ÖBS 13 [Klosterneuburg: Österreichisches Katholisches Bibelwerk, 1994], 103–4). While possible, this approach requires an unlikely time lapse between 2:1 and 2:3 where none is suggested and fails to account for the arguments above. The interpretation followed here allows Zephaniah to have made the commands in 2:1 and 3 within the same message, it keeps all the book's singular uses of "judgment" (מִשְׁפָּט) referring to the same reality, and it allows for a disposition of surrender following the interjection

"Hush!" in 1:7 and the whole depiction of coming punishment in chapter 1 to suffice for the "humility" and "heeding" already accomplished in 2:3.

26. Joüon, §177e–f; DeRouchie, *Call to Covenant Love*, 123. Cf., e.g., Gen 44:25; Exod 10:8; Lev 10:4; Deut 2:24; Josh 2:1; Ruth 4:1; 1 Sam 9:10; 1 Kgs 1:12; Isa 55:1; Jer 12:9; Ezek 20:39.

27. Hezekiah's reforms are another possible parallel, though different word groups occur. In those days, people from the Northern Kingdom first "humbled themselves" (*niphal* of כנע instead of the adjective עָנָו) and came to Jerusalem (2 Chr 30:11). Only then did they "seek" (דרש instead of בקשׁ; cf. Zeph 1:6) YHWH (1 Chr 30:19) through the Passover feast.

2:7, 9; 3:11–13; cf. 1 Kgs 19:18), disassociating from "the remnant of Baal" (Zeph 1:4). He now explicates his call to "seek YHWH" from two angles.

First, having spurned the chaos of injustice and rebellion, those humbled before God should "seek righteousness" (בַּקְּשׁוּ־צֶדֶק). YHWH is "righteous" (צַדִּיק, 3:5). His "righteousness" (צֶדֶק) is his right regard for his infinite value and his commitment both to act according to this value and to align everything with it, both in the cosmos (Pss 89:14; 119:75) and community (Deut 16:20; Ps 15:2). A "righteous" (צַדִּיק, Ezek 18:5–9; Hab 1:4) person, in turn, does "righteousness" (צְדָקָה) by mirroring God's righteousness (Hos 14:10) through valuing him and those he made in his image (Gen 18:19; Deut 6:25).[28] Thus, righteousness regularly involves just acts, especially for the marginalized (cf. Ps 52:5[3]; Isa 1:21–23). Though Zephaniah's Judah had quickly departed from this type of righteousness (Zeph 1:9; 3:1–5), truly seeking YHWH requires it.[29]

Second, turning from elevating self to exalting YHWH, the humble of the land must "seek humility" (בַּקְּשׁוּ עֲנָוָה), depending on God at even deeper levels. The sage associated "humility" with "the fear of YHWH" (Prov 15:33), contrasted it with the "haughty" (18:12), and viewed it as the sole path to "honor" (22:4; cf. Zeph 3:11–12).[30] Some scholars have questioned if Zephaniah would call those who were already "humble" (עָנָו) to "seek humility" (בַּקְּשׁוּ עֲנָוָה) even further.[31] However,

this quest accords with Scripture's stress on the dangers of hardening one's heart and on the need to persevere in faith (Ps 95:7–8; Prov 28:14).[32] From this perspective, Calvin noted that divine discipline rouses even the most loyal of saints "to seek true religion with greater ardor than they had before done. . . . When calamities arise and God appears as judge, we ought to be stimulated to greater care and diligence."[33]

c. A Parenthetical Motivation for the Charge (2:3d)

While YHWH will find and destroy every rebel on his day of wrath (Zeph 1:12, 18; cf. Deut 7:20; Amos 9:3), heeding Zephaniah's threefold charge opens the possibility of being "hidden" (*niphal* of סתר) from God's anger—that is, protected or sheltered by YHWH from his rage (cf. Pss 27:5; 31:20; see also Jer 36:26).[34] In the period after punishment, the citizens of the transformed Jerusalem will "take refuge in the name YHWH" (Zeph 3:12). Therefore, the call to "seek YHWH" here is the beginning of a reality that will continue through judgment and beyond.

The prophets regularly use qualifiers like "perhaps" (אוּלַי) to warn their hearers not to presume divine favor (Joel 2:14; Amos 5:15; Jonah 3:9).[35] Surviving judgment comes only by surrendering to God and aligning one's life with his definition of right order (cf. Isa 33:14–16). As Shepherd notes,

---

28. See "צֶדֶק," *HALOT* 1004–5; cf. David J. Reimer, "צדק (ṣādaq)," *NIDOTTE* 3:741–66.

29. See Canonical and Theological Significance below for how Zephaniah's call to "seek righteousness" fits within a larger biblical framework.

30. Ben Zvi states that "ענוה is a (or the) human attitude that leads to the establishment of the correct relationship between YHWH and human beings" (Ben Zvi, *Book of Zephaniah*, 148).

31. E.g., Ehrlich, *Randglossen zur Hebräischen Bible*, 5:311–12; Rudolph, *Micha, Nahum, Habakuk, Zephanja*, 273–74; Ben Zvi, *Book of Zephaniah*, 144; Vlaardingerbroek, *Zephaniah*, 115.

32. Cf. 1 Thess 4:9–10.

33. Calvin, "Habakkuk, Zephaniah, Haggai," 235.

34. Reading תִּסָּתְרוּ as a *niphal yiqtol* of סתר is more probable than Patterson's understanding that it is a *hithpael yiqtol* of סור ("turn") with metathesis of the ת, resulting in the meaning "turn oneself aside"—i.e., "escape, be delivered" (Patterson, *Nahum, Habakkuk, Zephaniah*, 297).

35. Cf. Exod 32:30; 2 Sam 16:12; Dan 4:27; Acts 8:22; 2 Tim 2:25.

the prophet's words make "refuge in the Day of the LORD contingent upon demonstration of genuine faith (see Nah 1:7)."[36] The text does not intend to signal Zephaniah's limited knowledge or uncertainty about God's response toward repentance. YHWH's merciful character is unchanging (Exod 34:6–7), his promises are sure, and Zephaniah elsewhere emphasizes both that the people can be reconciled with God (Zeph 3:7) and that YHWH will preserve a humble remnant (2:7, 9; 3:11–20).[37] Nevertheless, he also stresses the certainty of his coming wrath against wicked humanity.

2. An Initial Reason to Seek YHWH: The Devastation of Philistia (2:4)

God now promises to eliminate the foreign rebels from nearby Philistia. The causal conjunction "for" (כִּי) at the head of 2:4 shows that this pledge gives one reason why the remnant from Judah should seek YHWH.[38] The main point is that the punishment is near and will reach them if they fail to seek YHWH permanently (cf. Zeph 3:6–7).[39]

Ordered from southwest to northeast geographically, "Gaza . . . Ashkelon . . . Ashdod . . . Ekron" were four of the five Philistine cities/capitals located west of Israel along the Mediterranean Sea. Gath's absence from the list (cf. Josh 13:3) is common among the prophets (see Jer 25:20; Amos 1:6–8; Zech 9:5–7) and is likely due either to its present weakened state (see Amos 6:2)[40] or to its more positive association with Israel throughout history (e.g., 1 Sam 27:1–7).[41] Zephaniah conjoins the towns into two pairs, with the first and last towns including a wordplay. The first pair of Gaza and Ashkelon focuses on the forsaken state of the cities themselves. "Gaza" (עַזָּה, 'azzâ) will be "abandoned" (עֲזוּבָה, 'azûbâ) by its inhabitants and Ashkelon will be "for a desolation" (לִשְׁמָמָה). The second grouping of Ashdod and Ekron draws attention to the inhabitants. Some unknown agents will quickly (i.e., "by the noonday"; cf. Jer 15:8)[42]

---

36. Shepherd, *Commentary on the Book of the Twelve*, 362.

37. Baker notes, "'Perhaps' safeguards God's sovereign freedom." Nevertheless, "the fullness of who he is [as a God who grants forgiveness in the face of true repentance] relieves this 'perhaps' of any anxiety or uncertainty" (Baker, *Nahum, Habakkuk and Zephaniah*, 104; cf. Calvin, "Habakkuk, Zephaniah, Haggai," 239; Motyer, "Zephaniah," 3:928; Vlaardingerbroek, *Zephaniah*, 122–23). Contrast J. M. P. Smith, "Book of Zephaniah," 215; Kapelrud, *Message of the Prophet Zephaniah*, 88.

38. Many scholars recognize the way the subordinate conjunction כִּי ties together Zeph 2:3–4 (e.g., Ryou, *Zephaniah's Oracles*, 186–207; Floyd, *Minor Prophets, Part 2*, 215–18; Sweeney, *Zephaniah*, 120; Renz, *Books of Nahum, Habakkuk, and Zephaniah*, 520nl; cf. Berlin, *Zephaniah*, 99, 101). Others, however, join v. 4 with the oracle against Philistia in 2:5–7 (e.g., Ben Zvi, *Book of Zephaniah*, 150; Roberts, *Nahum, Habakkuk, and Zephaniah*, 195–96; cf. Rudolph, *Micha, Nahum, Habakuk, Zephanja*, 279). For an argument against this latter approach, see the discussion of Structure and Literary Form above.

39. A secondary element may also be that only through seeking YHWH can they benefit from their enemy's destruction (see Zeph 2:7, 9).

40. Contra Smith and Ball (J. M. P. Smith, "Book of Zeph-

aniah," 216; Ball, *Rhetorical Study of Zephaniah*, 121), Gath existed during Zephaniah's day since Assyrian King Sargon II (ca. 721–705) claims to have defeated it in the eleventh year of his reign (ca. 712–711 BC), *after* Zephaniah's ministry (see "Annals of Tiglath-pileser III," trans. D. D. Luckenbill [*ANET*, 286]). Others propose that Gath may have been under Judah's control at this time (Rudolph, *Micha, Nahum, Habakuk, Zephanja*, 3:279; Roberts, *Nahum, Habakkuk, and Zephaniah*, 197), but Haak assessed all the archeological evidence and claims it was not under Judah's control but only in a disabled state (Haak, "Zephaniah's Oracles against the Nations," 12n12; cf. Berlin, *Zephaniah*, 99).

41. Keil proposes that Zephaniah limits the list to four cities because Philistia here represents the world and because in the next unit the four groupings of nations are used to highlight the whole earth, according to the four quarters of the globe (Keil, "Twelve Minor Prophets," 10:448 [2:140]).

42. Cf. J. M. P. Smith, "Book of Zephaniah," 215; Vlaardingerbroek, *Zephaniah*, 136–37. This timing assumes that battles commonly began at sunrise (Job 4:20; Isa 38:12; cf. Josh 10:12–13; see also the "Moabite Stone," ca. 835 BC, lines 15–16 [*ANET*, 320; cf. 293]) rather than noon, the common midday break from all business (see Jer 6:4; 15:8; cf. 2 Sam 4:5;

expel (i.e., "they will drive her out") Ashdod's inhabitants.[43] In another wordplay, "Ekron" (עֶקְרוֹן ʿeqrôn) will "be uprooted" (תֵּעָקֵר teʿāqer) like a plant (cf. Eccl 3:2). Each of the four lines begins with the city's name, creating a sense of repetitive pounding as the hammer of God's judgment strikes.[44] Together, the four describe the totality of YHWH's punishment of Philistia.[45]

According to Zalcman, in order to portray Philistia's utter devastation, Zephaniah intentionally chose verbs associated elsewhere with "four of the most bitter fates a woman can endure": abandonment (עֲזוּבָה, Isa 54:6; cf. 60:15; 62:4), spinsterhood (שְׁמָמָה, 2 Sam 13:20; Isa 54:1; cf. Isa 62:4), divorce (גרש, Lev 21:7; Num 30:10[9]; Ezek 44:22), and barrenness (עקר, y. Ber. 6:3; b. ʿAbod. Zar. 22a).[46] Consequently, Sweeney argues for an intentional contrast between devastated Philistia in Zeph 2:4 and restored, joy-filled Jerusalem, the "daughter of Zion," in 3:14–20.[47]

Thus, the prophet may be portraying Philistia as a rejected woman, unprotected by her gods (cf. Isa 47:8–9). She may even represent the wicked of the world who "have sinned" against YHWH (Zeph 1:17) and who will experience YHWH's day of wrath (Ezek 30:3; Obad 15; cf. Isa 24:5).[48] Zephaniah 2:4 motivates Judah to repent lest she also be without a husband (cf. Isa 50:1; Jer 3:8; 31:32). Yet instead of "abandoning" (עזב) his future remnant, YHWH will be present in their midst (Zeph 3:15). Rather than being a "desolation" (שְׁמָמָה), the new people of God will rejoice (3:14) as YHWH saves and transforms his lame and banished bride (3:19; cf. Isa 64:4).

Significantly, extrabiblical texts indicate the burning relevance of Zephaniah's prophecy in 2:3–4. Herodotus testifies to Egypt's extended twenty-nine-year siege of Ashdod (640–611 BC) (Hist. 157.1), which was contemporary with Zephaniah's ministry. The same source states that Pharoah Neco conquered Gaza in 609 BC (Hist. 2.159.2). We also know that, following the 605 BC defeat of the Egyptians at Carchemish along the Euphrates,[49] the Babylonians invaded the south, at least destroying Ashkelon in 604 BC. Finally, Egypt attacked Gaza in 601 BC. Zephaniah may have intended all or any of these events to call the remnant from Judah to seek YHWH. More likely, however, the contemporary events only pointed to a more total and global destruction anticipated in these words.

The prophet uses a third masculine *plural* verb to speak of a group (the Egyptians?) rather than an individual (YHWH) driving out Ashdod's population (יְגָרְשׁוּהָ "they will drive her out").

---

1 Kgs 20:16). Muraoka notes צָהֳרַיִם ("noon") could be dual due to the convergence of two time lines as noon, but he thinks it is more likely *not* a genuine dual (see Joüon, §91g).

43. It is unlikely that Zephaniah here uses a pun on the name "Ashdod" (אַשְׁדּוֹד). Contra David Winton Thomas, "A Pun on the Name of Ashdod in Zephaniah 2:4," *ExpTim* 74.2 (1962): 63.

44. Cf. Berlin, *Zephaniah*, 98. Berlin further notes that the first letters of the various city names create a chiasm of sound (A, Gaza: עַזָּה [ʿazzâ] / B, Ashkelon: אַשְׁקְלוֹן [ʾašqlôn] // B′, Ashdod: אַשְׁדּוֹד [ʾašdôd] / A′, Ekron: עֶקְרוֹן [ʿeqrôn]) (p. 99).

45. Cf. Ben Zvi, *Book of Zephaniah*, 150–51.

46. Lawrence Zalcman, "Ambiguity and Assonance at Zephaniah II 4," *VT* 36.3 (1986): 367. Gordis discerns that "desolation" better translates שְׁמָמָה than "spinsterhood" for the second category and that Zephaniah portrays an ascending scale of suffering: deserted as a betrothed woman; desolate as a deserted wife; driven out as a divorced woman; uprooted as a barren woman (Robert Gordis, "A Rising Tide of Misery: A Note on a Note on Zephaniah II 4," *VT* 37.4 [1987]: 487–90).

47. Sweeney, *Zephaniah*, 123.

48. Keil proposes that Philistia may stand as "representatives of the heathen world by which Judah was surrounded" (Keil, " Twelve Minor Prophets," 10:447 [2:139]). In this sense, God's words against Philistia in Zeph 2:4 anticipate his punishment against the great prostitute, Babylon the great, at the end of the age in Rev 18:7–8.

49. Pharaoh Neco was going to this battle when he killed King Josiah (2 Kgs 23:29–30; 2 Chr 35:20–24).

Nevertheless, the group operates as YHWH's agents of wrath. That they will drive Ashdod out by noon may even contrast with the Egyptian's extended attempt to overtake the city, thus distinguishing between "the height of human military endeavor" and "the ease and speed of the Lord's victory."[50] Judah's remnant needed to realize that a God-instigated death loomed on the horizon, and their only hope was to surrender in trust and allegiance to YHWH.[51]

Canonical and Theological Significance

Seeking Righteousness in Its Biblical Context

Zephaniah's call to "seek righteousness" (בַּקְּשׁוּ־צֶדֶק, Zeph 2:3) exhorts those who have revered God (1:7), affirmed their sin (1:17), and gathered together (2:1) to conform their lives wholly to God's will as the fruit of a right standing already enjoyed by faith. Habakkuk's placement in the Twelve encourages this reading. Prior to Zeph 2:3, the reader has already learned that only "one righteous [צַדִּיק] by his faith will live" through YHWH's coming fury (Hab 2:4).[52] Thus, for any to survive YHWH's judgment day (Zeph 2:4), they must already enjoy right standing by faith.

The prophet apparently alludes here to Isa 51:1, one of only two other verses in Scripture that include the terms בקשׁ ("seek"), יהוה ("YHWH"), and צֶדֶק ("righteousness") (cf. Isa 45:19).[53] Reading the charge in Deut 16:20 through a redemptive-historical lens (צֶדֶק צֶדֶק תִּרְדֹּף, "Righteousness, righteousness you must pursue"), Isaiah said, "Listen to me, pursuers of righteousness [רֹדְפֵי צֶדֶק], who seek YHWH [מְבַקְשֵׁי יהוה]: Look to a Rock from which you were hewn and to a quarry from which you were dug. Look to Abraham your father and to Sarah who bore you. When [he was only] one [man], I called him so that I might bless him and multiply him" (Isa 51:1–2). Those seeking righteousness and YHWH in Isa 51:1 follow the patriarch's example when he was but one (51:2, i.e., not yet with offspring). The link between "righteousness," "YHWH," and "Abraham" recalls Gen 15:6. There, the

---

50. Motyer, "Zephaniah," 932. Motyer correctly understands that the prophecy about Philistia moved from the immediate to the eschatological future, but he likely overstates matters when he says that Zephaniah "is not thinking of Philistia as the historical entity of his own day" (Motyer, 931).

51. For more on the historical background to Zephaniah's vision of Philistia's devastation, see Ben Zvi, *Book of Zephaniah*, 303–4; Sweeney, *Zephaniah*, 121–22; cf. William W. Hallo and William Kelly Simpson, *The Ancient Near East: A History*, 2nd ed. (New York: Harcourt, Brace, 1998), 285–93.

52. For this rendering of Hab 2:4b and reading אֱמוּנָה as "faith" rather than "faithfulness," see Shepherd, *The Twelve*

Prophets in the New Testament, 47–54; Clendenen, "Salvation by Faith or by Faithfulness in the Book of Habakkuk?," 505–13; Shepherd, *The Text in the Middle*, 30–36. For the way Paul contrasts this text with Lev 18:5 in Gal 3:11–12, see Jason S. DeRouchie, "The Use of Leviticus 18:5 in Galatians 3:12: A Redemptive-Historical Reassessment," *Them* 45.2 (2020): 240–59. For the widely accepted view that אֱמוּנָה in Hab 2:4 means "faithfulness," see, e.g., R. W. L. Moberly, "אָמַן (āman I)," *NIDOTTE* 1:424–25.

53. I thank my doctoral fellow Brian Verrett for this observation and for reflecting with me on Isa 51:1–2.

patriarch "believed [הֶאֱמִן] in YHWH, and it was reckoned to him righteousness [צְדָקָה]" after hearing God affirm his promise of the Messiah.[54] Isaiah's point was that those pursuing righteousness should follow Abraham's example by placing their faith in YHWH and his messianic promise and by responding to their right standing with righteous deeds (cf. Gal 2:20; 1 John 3:7). This corresponds to James's statement about how the patriarch's works "fulfilled" the earlier declaration of righteousness and "completed" his faith (Jas 2:23). Hence, Isaiah's hearers were those already fearing YHWH and "obeying the voice of his [righteous] servant" (Isa 50:8, 10); they trusted in YHWH and relied on him (50:10), and they knew righteousness, having YHWH's Torah in their heart (51:7). Thus, they experienced the realities promised in the new covenant (Jer 31:33).

Since Isaiah expects salvation to come through faith in the Messiah, he asks in the messianic prophecy, "Who has believed [הֶאֱמִין] our report?" (Isa 53:1). Those who place their faith in the Messiah as Abraham did become righteous (53:11) since the Messiah is himself the "righteous one" (53:11; cf. 50:8) of whom "no deceit was in his mouth" (53:9; cf. 50:8–9). He will bear righteous offspring (53:11) who as his servants will carry on his mission by making others righteous in him (54:13–14; 56:1; cf. Dan 12:3). When Zephaniah later says, "And in their mouth will never be found a tongue of deceit" (Zeph 3:13), he recalls Isaiah's messianic servant (Isa 53:9). In this way, Zephaniah presents God's eschatological people who seek righteousness from Zeph 2:3 and 3:13 as Isaiah's remnant who became righteous (Rom 5:1) and remain righteous by faith in Jesus (cf. Gal 5:6 → Rom 13:10 → Rom 2:13).

Zephaniah's command to "seek righteousness" resembles Jesus's charge to his disciples: "But seek first the kingdom [of God] and his righteousness" (Matt 6:33). As in Matt 5:6, 10, 20, and 6:1, the "righteousness" to which Jesus refers is not foundational justification. It is right living that is the fruit of an inward change (see 1 John 3:7) that will ultimately be the external evidence of Christ's justifying work in us (Rom 2:6, 13).[55] For Zephaniah, to "seek righteousness" is to desire the proper fruit of faith and surrender. It is to endeavor with God's help to align our lives with YHWH's definition of right order, increasingly prizing God in Christ as king and valuing those made in his image (cf. 2 Tim 2:22).[56]

---

54. For this reading of Gen 15:6, see Jason S. DeRouchie, "Lifting the Veil: Reading and Preaching Jesus' Bible through Christ and for Christ," *SBJT* 22.3 (2018): 171–77; cf. Brian Vickers, *Justification by Grace through Faith: Finding Freedom from Legalism, Lawlessness, Pride, and Despair*, Explorations in Biblical Theology (Phillipsburg, NJ: P&R, 2013), 58–61.

55. See John Piper, *The Future of Justification: A Response to N. T. Wright* (Wheaton, IL: Crossway, 2007); G. K. Beale, "The Role of Resurrection in the Already-and-Not-Yet Phases

of Justification," in *For the Fame of God's Name: Essays in Honor of John Piper*, ed. Sam Storms and Justin Taylor (Wheaton, IL: Crossway, 2010), 190–214; A. B. Caneday, "Judgment, Behavior, and Justification According to Paul's Gospel in Romans 2," *JSPHL* 1 (2011): 153–92.

56. See Benno Przybylski, *Righteousness in Matthew and His World of Thought*, SNTSMN 41 (Cambridge: Cambridge University Press, 2004), 89–91; cf. Carson, "Matthew," 217.

A Proper Response

Commune Regularly with Other Believers to Aid One Another's Perseverance

The masculine plural imperatives in Zeph 2:1 [2x], 3 [3x] and 3:8 [1x] stress individual responsibility for heeding God's commands. Yet those heeding Zephaniah's charges should fulfill them *together*. No believer is to "seek YHWH" alone (2:3). Therefore, Zephaniah's initial charge opens by calling those who will listen to "bind" themselves and "make a sheaf" (2:1). God's coming punishment will explode on the earth like a nuclear bomb, and in his love, YHWH wants people to seek him together and to find strength in united surrender. The writer of Hebrews urged his readers to "exhort one another every day" (Heb 3:13) and to "consider one another for the arousal of love and good deeds . . . and all the more as you see the Day drawing near" (10:24–25). "The Day" is the ultimate "day of YHWH's anger" to which Zephaniah points (Zeph 2:2–3). Partnership with other believers, seen especially through active local church membership, helps us continue to grow in holiness, which properly prepares us to see YHWH (Heb 12:14).

Continue Seeking YHWH, Pursuing Righteousness and Humility

Motyer noted, "In the Bible the only way to flee *from* God is to flee *to* him."[57] Zephaniah yearns for his audience to be free from the fear of death (cf. Heb 2:15) and to experience "the holiness without which no one will see the Lord" (12:14). He thus urges his audience to hunger for YHWH with a proper disposition of heart (humility) and a proper orientation of life (righteousness).

First, to seek YHWH by seeking humility (Zeph 2:3), we must first turn from self-reliance and self-exaltation to radical God-dependence and God-exaltation. With John the Baptizer, we must say, "He must increase, but I must decrease" (John 3:30). In our piety and ministry, we must serve in God's strength, not our own, and seek divine rather human approval (Matt 10:28; Acts 5:29; 1 Pet 4:11). In our suffering, instead of being anxious (Matt 6:34), we must humble ourselves by "casting all . . . anxieties upon [God], because he cares" (1 Pet 5:7; cf. Phil 4:6–7). In our victories, we ought to declare, "By the grace of God I am what I am" (1 Cor 15:10). And when we boast, we should only "boast in the Lord" (1 Cor 1:30–31; 2 Cor 10:17–18). It is the impoverished not the proud who engage in prayer and praise, and only in humbly seeking YHWH is there any hope for protection on the day of his wrath (Jas 4:6; 1 Pet 5:5).[58]

Second, to seek YHWH by seeking righteousness (Zeph 2:3) requires living impartial and loving lives rather than abusive ones. We must image God's character

---

57. Motyer, "Zephaniah," 927.

58. Cf. Lev 26:19; Job 20:6–7; 40:12; Prov 16:18.

(Deut 10:17–19)[59] and value others made in his image (Gen 9:6; Jas 3:9). Too easily, our God-given proficiency, power, or possessions move us to forget YHWH as the great giver (Deut 8:14, 17; Hos 13:5–6) and to elevate ourselves over others at their expense. In Zephaniah's day, outsiders "reproached and became haughty against the people of YHWH of armies" (Zeph 2:10). Insiders, especially leaders, shamelessly engaged in "violence and deception" and like wild beasts oppressed others (1:9; 3:1, 3–5). In contrast, "YHWH is righteous. . . . He never does wrong. Morning by morning he gives his judgment for the light" (3:5; cf. Deut 32:4). YHWH is one "who practices steadfast love, justice, and righteousness in the earth" (Jer 9:24),[60] and knowing him means that we will also delight in such things (cf. 2 Tim 2:22).

When we truly seek YHWH (Zeph 2:3), we will always find ourselves confronting the world and caught up in radical love, especially for the broken and despised. Our experience of God's goodness and love compels us to display this same love to others and to help them savor it for themselves (Exod 22:20[21]; John 13:34–35; 1 John 4:10–11).[61] "Religion that is pure and undefiled before God, the Father, is this: to visit orphans and widows in their affliction, and to keep oneself unstained from the world" (Jas 1:27; cf. 1 John 3:16–18). This is what Zephaniah meant by "seeking YHWH . . . righteousness . . . humility" (Zeph 2:3).

Learn from YHWH's Disciplining Hand

Zephaniah intends his audience to learn from YHWH's discipline against others. Thus, God's promise to destroy Philistia in the near future grounded his charge to "seek YHWH" (Zeph 2:3–4). Judah was too friendly with this nearby nation (1:11; cf. Isa 2:6). They needed to see that, because God was punishing the Philistines, Judah's end was near.

YHWH's revealed purpose in disciplining humans is to generate repentance and worship—whether they receive the discipline (Lev 26:18, 21, 23–24, 27–28) or only witness it (Deut 13:10–11; 17:12–13; 19:19–20; 21:21). When the Siloam tower fell and killed eighteen people, Jesus asked the crowd about the victims, "Do you think that they were worse offenders than all the others who live in Jerusalem?" He then answered, "No, I tell you; but unless you repent, you will all likewise perish" (Luke 13:4–5). For those who have eyes to see, YHWH's disciplining hand against us and others serves as a means of grace to move us to greater holiness.

YHWH wanted to punish Philistia so Jerusalem would fear him. However, most in Judah were hard-hearted (Zeph 3:6–7; cf. Jer 2:30; 3:3) and rejected the warnings

---

59. Cf. 2 Chr 19:7; Job 34:19; Acts 10:34; Rom 2:11; Gal 2:6; Eph 6:9; Col 3:25; 1 Pet 1:17.

60. Cf. Deut 10:17–18; Pss 33:5; 89:15[14]; Isa 5:16; Hos 2:19.

61. Cf. Exod 23:9; Lev 19:33–34; Deut 10:19; Rom 13:8.

like their fathers (e.g., Isa 42:25; Amos 6:6–12). Still, the prophet was confident that the remnant would see sin's gravity, respond with deeper humility, and desire YHWH. "Now all discipline for a moment seems to be . . . painful, but afterward it yields a peaceful fruit of righteousness to those who have been trained by it" (Heb 12:11). May God grant us hearts that increasingly seek him when we encounter sin's negative results.

6

CHAPTER

Zephaniah 2:5–3:7

C. Further Reasons to Seek YHWH Together

Main Idea of the Passage

The faithful remnant from Judah and other lands should seek YHWH together because of the lamentable state and fate of the rebels from both the foreign nations and Jerusalem.

Literary Context

Basic Overview

Stage 1 of the Savior's invitation to satisfaction continues in Zeph 2:5–3:7. Two units begin with an asyndetic "Woe" (הוֹי) and address the state and fate of the rebels from the foreign nations (2:5–15) and Jerusalem (3:1–7). Together the units clarify why the faithful remnant from Judah and other nations must seek YHWH together (2:1–4). An inferential particle "Therefore" (לָכֵן) follows in 3:8, showing that 2:5–3:7 also give a logical reason for "waiting" on YHWH (3:8), which shapes the primary exhortation in stage 2 of Zephaniah's message (3:8–20).

The Role of the Prophecies against Foreign Nations

Biblical prophets often prophesied against foreign nations (e.g., Isa 13–23; Jer 46–51; Ezek 25–32), and similar statements appear in Zeph 2:5–15. Such retributive words assume YHWH's universal authority (Exod 9:29; 19:5; Deut 10:14).[1]

---

1. See also Job 41:11; Pss 24:1 50:12; 89:12[11]; 1 Cor 10:26. Cf. Berlin, *Zephaniah*, 117; Sweeney, *Isaiah 1–39*, 214; Vlaardingerbroek, *Zephaniah*, 126.

Earlier, the prophet declared that God intended to destroy the earth's peoples "for against YHWH they have sinned" (Zeph 1:17c). This rationale recalls why YHWH previously destroyed the Canaanites (Deut 9:4–5). Elsewhere we learn that sometimes God chastised Israel's neighbors to evoke awe in his universal authority (Mal 1:5). Such punishment both stressed that he was Israel's only Savior and shamed Israel for looking for another (Isa 20:6). In Zeph 3:6–7, God says that he destroyed Judah's neighbors to move Jerusalem to repent and thus escape their encroaching doom. But Zephaniah's contemporaries would not listen.

Many scholars doubt that YHWH ever intended his prophets to confront foreign peoples with their words.[2] However, YHWH's prophets did engage the outside world (e.g., 2 Kgs 8:7–15; Jer 27:3; 51:61–64; Jonah 3:1–5), and YHWH through Zephaniah at times addresses Israel's neighbors in the second person (Zeph 2:5, 12), thus suggesting a direct confrontation, perhaps to foreign emissaries or local traders (cf. 1:8, 11). It may also be that Zephaniah anticipated his book would be read by foreigners (cf. 1 Pet 1:12), even if he spoke directly only to Judah. Zephaniah's outside audiences may be only hypothetical, the prophet using the second person speech rhetorically to motivate his fellow Judeans. Yet such a proposal seems unnecessary, and the universal thrust of the book's message makes it unlikely.

Several scholars argue that these prophecies inspired Judah to hope in imminent restoration.[3] Oracles of punishment can certainly function this way,[4] and the prophet announcing that YHWH would "restore [the] circumstance" of "the remnant of the house of Judah" (2:7) would have comforted the faithful few. Furthermore, in 3:8, the certainty of YHWH's day of wrath against the world grounds his call for the faithful remnant to keep waiting for him (using both לָכֵן, "Therefore," and כִּי, "For/because").

Nevertheless, within the flow of 2:1–3:7, the nations' prophetic judgments mainly encouraged Zephaniah's listeners to reject sin and together seek YHWH; instilling hope was only secondary (2:1, 3). Judah would share their neighbors' fate; only "the *remnant* of the house of Judah" would enjoy protection.[5] Within stage 1 (2:1–3:7) of the book's main exhortation section, God intended that his fury would awaken sinners (1:17) from their slumber, be they from Judah (1:4–13; 2:1–4; 3:1–7) or other nations (1:2–3, 14–18; 2:5–15). The idolatrous and syncretistic (1:4–5), self-reliant

---

2. E.g., John H. Hayes, "The Usage of Oracles against Foreign Nations in Ancient Israel," *JBL* 87.1 (1968): 81–92, esp. 81; Roberts, *Nahum, Habakkuk, and Zephaniah*, 197; Berlin, *Zephaniah*, 117; Sweeney, *Isaiah 1–39*, 213; Vlaardingerbroek, *Zephaniah*, 126; Sweeney, *Zephaniah*, 126, 146.

3. E.g., R. L. Smith, *Micah–Malachi*, 135; Baker, *Nahum, Habakkuk and Zephaniah*, 105; House, *Zephaniah*, 71; Roberts, *Nahum, Habakkuk, and Zephaniah*, 197; Floyd, *Minor Prophets, Part 2*, 220, 227–28, 232; Sweeney, *Zephaniah*, 107.

4. For example, Ezekiel's oracles against the nations are "negative messages of hope" in the book's second half that is

devoted to highlighting "hope and restoration for Judah/Israel" (Daniel I. Block, *Book of Ezekiel: Chapters 25–48*, NICOT [Grand Rapids: Eerdmans, 1998], 3).

5. So also Kapelrud, *Message of the Prophet Zephaniah*, 77; cf. Ben Zvi, *Book of Zephaniah*, 171. Similarly, Timmer distinguishes between "my people" (i.e., historical Judah) in texts like Zeph 2:8, 10 and "the remnant of the house of Judah" (2:7), "the remnant of my people," and "the remainder of my nation" (2:9) (i.e., a future group living after universal punishment) (Timmer, *Non-Israelite Nations*, 155).

(1:6), violent and deceptive (1:9), complacent and falsely secure (1:11–13, 18; 2:1b), verbally abusive and proud (2:8b–c, 10b–c, 15a–c), and rebellious and defiled (3:1–4, 7) from Judah and other lands, both in Zephaniah's present and in the future, needed to take their sin seriously, for God certainly would.

III. The Substance of the Savior's Invitation to Satisfaction: Charges to Seek YHWH Together and to Wait (2:1–3:20b)

    III.1 Stage 1: The Appeal to Seek YHWH Together to Avoid Punishment (2:1–3:7)

        A. The Charge to Unite in Submission to YHWH (2:1–2)

        B. The Charge to Seek YHWH in Righteousness and Humility (2:3–4)

➡   **C. Further Reasons to Seek YHWH Together (2:5–3:7)**

           1. The Lamentable State and Fate of the Rebels from Foreign Nations (2:5–15)

           2. The Lamentable State and Fate of the Rebels from Jerusalem (3:1–7)

    III.2 Stage 2: The Appeal to Wait for YHWH to Enjoy Salvation (3:8–20b)

Translation and Exegetical Outline

(See pages 171–174.)

Structure and Literary Form

This extended section contains prophecies about foreign nations (2:5–15) and announces punishment against Judah (3:1–7).[6] It contains literary features like metaphor and simile (2:5–7, 9; 3:3), irony (2:12), synecdoche (2:13; 3:6), thematic repetition (3:1), wordplay (2:7), literary allusion (2:9), hendiadys (3:7), and substitution (3:7).[7]

Having used sequences of imperatives in 2:1, 3 and having commented on a foreign nation's destruction in 2:4, Zephaniah now develops and extends the scope of judgment in this section's final unit. He cites two reasons why his listeners must seek YHWH together. Each reason begins with a "Woe!" (הוֹי) speech (2:5–7; 3:1–4) and includes lament, castigation, and foretelling of doom addressing the state and fate of the rebels from the foreign nations (2:5–15) and Jerusalem (3:1–7).[8]

---

6. For these categories with descriptions, see Sweeney, *Isaiah 1–39*, 528–30.

7. Patterson, *Nahum, Habakkuk, Zephaniah*, 299.

8. Cf. Ryou, *Zephaniah's Oracles*, 284, 334–43; Floyd, *Minor Prophets, Part 2*, 202, 219, 231; Renz, *Books of Nahum, Habakkuk, and Zephaniah*, 546. Floyd describes the prophecies

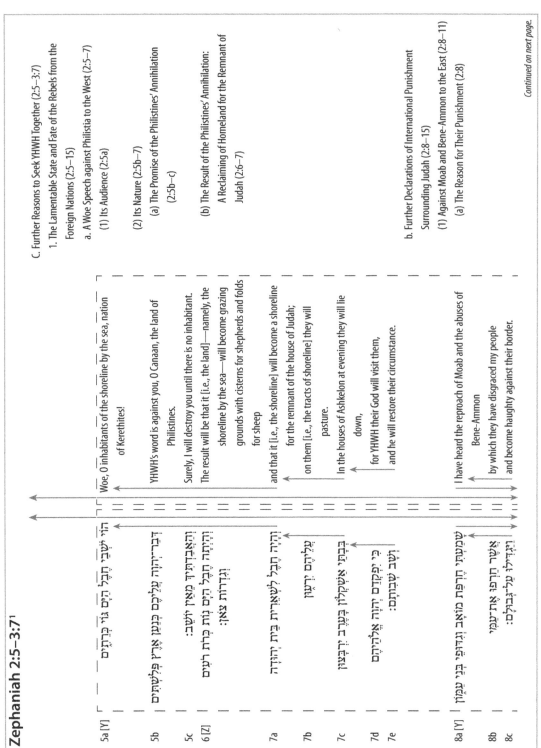

172 Part III.1: Stage 1: The Appeal to Seek YHWH Together to Avoid Punishment

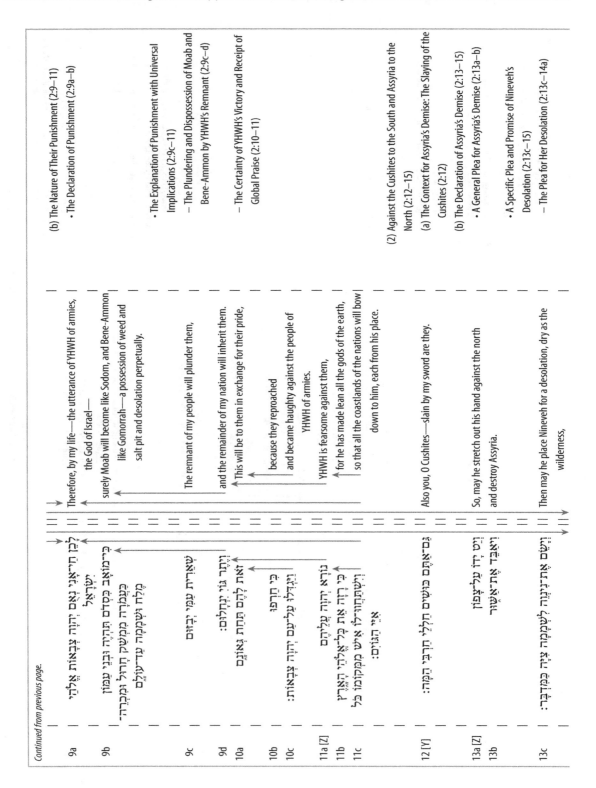

Line	Hebrew	English	Outline
14a	וְרָבְצ֨וּ בְתוֹכָ֜הּ עֲדָרִ֗ים כָּל־חַיְתוֹ־ג֔וֹי	with the result that in her midst herds will lie down—every beast of a nation.	– The Plea for Her Desolation (2:13c–14a) *cont.*
14b	גַּם־קָאַת֙ גַּם־קִפֹּ֔ד בְּכַפְתֹּרֶ֖יהָ יָלִ֑ינוּ	Even an owl, also a bustard, will lodge at her capitals.	– The Promise of Her Desolation (2:14b–e)
14c	ק֣וֹל יְשׁוֹרֵ֣ר בַּֽחַלּ֗וֹן	A sound will sing at the window.	
14d	חֹ֙רֶב֙ בַּסַּ֔ף	Devastation will be at the threshold,	
14e	כִּ֥י אַרְזָ֖ה עֵרָֽה׃	when he has exposed her cedar work.	
15a	זֹ֠את הָעִ֤יר הָעַלִּיזָה֙ הַיּוֹשֶׁ֣בֶת לָבֶ֔טַח הָאֹֽמְרָה֙ בִּלְבָבָ֔הּ	This is the exultant city—the one dwelling in security, the one saying in her heart,	– The Appraisal of Her Desolation (2:15)
15b	אֲנִ֖י	"I am,	
15c	וְאַפְסִ֣י ע֑וֹד	and my limit is still [unreached]."	
15d	אֵ֣יךְ ׀ הָיְתָ֣ה לְשַׁמָּ֗ה מַרְבֵּץ֙ לַֽחַיָּ֔ה	How she has become a desolation, a resting place for the beast.	
15e	כֹּ֚ל עוֹבֵ֣ר עָלֶ֔יהָ יִשְׁרֹ֖ק	Each one passing over her will hiss;	
15f	יָנִ֥יעַ יָדֽוֹ׃	he will shake his fist.	
3:1 [Y]	ה֥וֹי מֹרְאָ֖ה וְנִגְאָלָ֑ה הָעִ֖יר הַיּוֹנָֽה׃	Woe, O rebellious and defiled one—the oppressive city!	2. The Lamentable State and Fate of the Rebels from Jerusalem (3:1–7) a. Jerusalem's Characteristics (3:1)
2a	לֹ֤א שָֽׁמְעָה֙ בְּק֔וֹל	She has not listened unto a voice;	b. Jerusalem's Fundamental Failures (3:2–7) (1) An Overview of Her Fundamental Failures (3:2) (a) Her Initial Resistance (3:2a–b)
2b	לֹ֥א לָקְחָ֖ה מוּסָ֑ר	she has not received instruction.	
2c	בַּֽיהוָה֙ לֹ֣א בָטָ֔חָה	In YHWH she has not trusted;	(b) Her Resulting Unresponsiveness (3:2c–d)
2d	אֶל־אֱלֹהֶ֖יהָ לֹ֥א קָרֵֽבָה׃	unto her God she has not drawn near.	
3a	שָׂרֶ֣יהָ בְקִרְבָּ֔הּ אֲרָי֖וֹת שֹֽׁאֲגִ֑ים	Her officials in her midst are roaring lions.	(2) An Elaboration of Her Fundamental Failures (3:3–7) (a) Her Crooked Leaders (3:3–5) • Their Tendencies (3:3–4) – The Political Leaders (3:3)
3b	שֹׁפְטֶ֙יהָ֙ זְאֵ֣בֵי עֶ֔רֶב	Her judges are evening wolves;	
3c	לֹ֥א גָרְמ֖וּ לַבֹּֽקֶר׃	they have not gnawed to the morning.	
4a	נְבִיאֶ֙יהָ֙ פֹּֽחֲזִ֔ים אַנְשֵׁ֖י בֹּֽגְד֑וֹת	Her prophets are reckless, men of treacheries.	– The Religious Leaders (3:4)
4b	כֹּהֲנֶ֙יהָ֙ חִלְּלוּ־קֹ֔דֶשׁ	Her priests have profaned what is holy;	
4c	חָמְס֖וּ תּוֹרָֽה׃	they have treated Torah violently.	

Continued on next page.

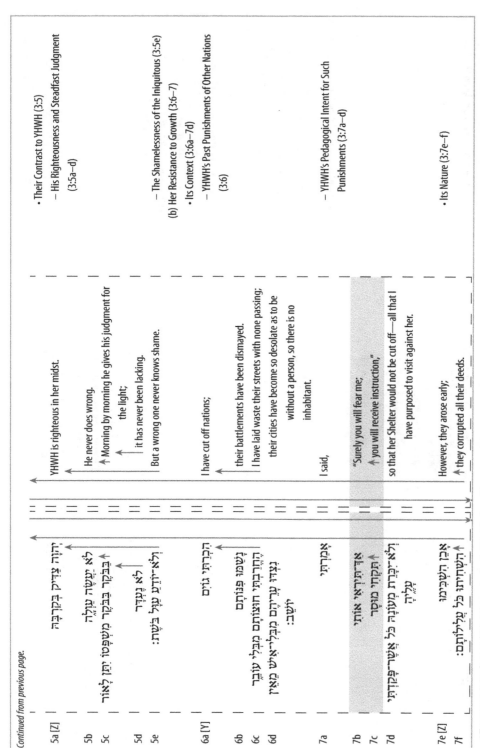

While causal conjunctions do not formally mark these two reasons, the opening use of asyndeton allows them to function rhetorically as a basis for the commands in 2:1 and 3 (and 3:8, see below).[9] Zephaniah's audiences must seek YHWH together because their wickedness would soon result in universal punishment. At its core, this evil is human pride and oppression. Those in Judah and the surrounding nations elevated themselves above YHWH and those made in his image.[10] Ultimately, YHWH's day would remove all the arrogance deriving from the tower of Babel (Gen 11:4, 8). In Zeph 3:9–10, the cleansing judgment from the outside to the inside will transform a multiracial community of worshipers (see below).[11]

The first reason why listeners must seek YHWH together is because of the coming universal punishment oriented around the four points of the compass with Judah at the center (2:5–15). YHWH will encircle Jerusalem ominously before destroying her.[12] The opening paragraph in 2:5–7 contains the first formal "Woe!" speech and focuses on Philistia to the West. God addresses them directly (2:5a–b) and then declares their destruction in no uncertain terms: "I will destroy you until there is no inhabitant" (2:5c). God then states that the result of Philistia's annihilation will include "the remnant of the house of Judah" possessing the territory of Philistia (2:7). The text does not state why YHWH's wrath will fall on the Philistines, but it likely pertains to their lack of humility (2:3–4)[13] and anti-YHWH influence on Judah (see the comments at 1:11; cf. Isa 2:6). The unit opens by declaring Philistia's coming doom, which thematically links with YHWH's declared punishment in 2:4. As Renz notes, this link "helps identify the oracles about nations as a further, expanded rationale for the exhortation to repent."[14]

After the initial statements of woe against proud Philistia (2:5–7), YHWH declares doom on some of Judah's other neighbors (2:8–15).[15] Besides this shift in subject matter, the text returns to syntactically independent first-person speech. God initially confronts Moab and the Bene-Ammon to the east for their arrogant

---

against the nations as "the motivation of the call to repentance in 2:1–3" (Floyd, *Minor Prophets, Part 2*, 220, 224, 228; cf. 232). He sees the "Woe!" in 2:5 and 3:1 less introducing "a 'woe' oracle" and more "evoking a mood of lamentation and establishing a parallel between the prophecies concerning foreign nations in 2:2–15 and the prophecy concerning Judah in 3:1–7" (Floyd, 219; cf. 231).

9. Because the units are extensive, the prophet could not use the inner-clausal subordinate conjunction כִּי ("for/because") to signal the rationale. In such cases, asyndeton signals that the unit generally explicates what precedes, leaving one to discern the specific rhetorical function from context. Here, each unit beginning with "Woe!" gives an independent but related reason why the audience should heed the commands in 2:1, 3. The inference marker לָכֵן in 3:8 then emphasizes that 2:5–3:7 also supplies the reason for heeding the command in 3:8.

10. See Zeph 2:3a–c, 8b–c, 10b–c, 15a–c; 3:2–4, 11b–12a. For a similar conclusion, see Floyd, *Minor Prophets, Part 2*, 209.

11. See Floyd, *Minor Prophets, Part 2*, 211–13. Floyd notes, "In this section of Zephaniah Judah's international seventh-century context is viewed through a mythic lens as the antitype of Babel" (Floyd, *Minor Prophets, Part 2*, 210). For more on this, see the discussion at Zeph 2:12 and 3:9–10.

12. So too Keil, "Zephaniah," 140; Robertson, *Books of Nahum, Habakkuk, and Zephaniah*, 296; Ryou, *Zephaniah's Oracles*, 323–25; Floyd, *Minor Prophets, Part 2*, 204. For other prophecies in Scripture that use a four-directional arrangement, see Patterson, *Nahum, Habakkuk, Zephaniah*, 300.

13. So too Floyd, *Minor Prophets, Part 2*, 209.

14. Renz, *Books of Nahum, Habakkuk, and Zephaniah*, 522.

15. For prophecies against foreign nations, see Sweeney, *Isaiah 1–39*, 528–29.

mocking of the Judeans (2:8).[16] He then concludes (לָכֵן, "therefore") that he will make them like Sodom and Gomorrah (2:9–10). Zephaniah then adds an extended oracular formula for dramatic effect—"the utterance of YHWH of armies, the God of Israel" (2:9a).[17] It enhances the likelihood that Zephaniah intended his sermon for an audience broader than Judah. It also shows that YHWH is both able and committed to work justice for his faithful ones. The prophet then adds a comment on YHWH's fierceness against Moab and Bene-Ammon and asserts that all spiritual and earthly forces will pay homage to YHWH (2:11).

Among those submitting to YHWH (גַּם, "also") are the Cushites to the south. YHWH addresses Cush directly, although they appear to have already suffered defeat (2:12, see below). The book gives no reason for Cush's demise and assumes the reader already knows.[18] Their defeat adds proof (via the connector וְ "and") that God will fully destroy the northern megapower Assyria (2:13–15). The summary appraisal in 2:15 implies that the nature of Assyria's sin was pride, and it would lead to her downfall since Nineveh was "the exultant city—the one dwelling in security, the one saying in her heart, 'I am, and my limit is still [unreached].'"[19]

That YHWH will confront Jerusalem is the second reason listeners must seek YHWH together (3:1–7). The punishment YHWH brings around Judah will implode in Jerusalem. This reason begins with another "Woe!" statement (3:1–4), paralleling the one in 2:5–7. God first characterizes Jerusalem as a "rebellious and defiled one—the oppressive city" (3:1). Both YHWH and Zephaniah then describe her populace. YHWH first notes her failures of resistance and unresponsiveness (3:2). Then the two relate these failures to Jerusalem's crooked leaders (3:3–5) and resistance to fear God (3:6–7). Each of these subunits (3:1–5, 6–7) is syntactically independent and clarifies the nature of Jerusalem's wickedness. Nevertheless, repeating "instruction" (מוּסָר) in 3:2, 7 and continually addressing Jerusalem in the third feminine singular signals that 3:1–7 is a coherent unit. The final verses mention that God disciplined the nations (e.g., Cush in 2:12) so Jerusalem would repent and live, but it only became more corrupt.

At 3:8 two shifts suggest that the inferential particle "therefore" (לָכֵן) at the head of 3:8 concludes a unit larger than 3:1–7, moving the overall argument into stage 2 (3:8–20) of the Savior's invitation:[20] (1) the shift in person from feminine singular (see 3:1–7) back to the masculine plural forms (see 2:1 and 3) and (2) the switch from declaring Jerusalem's wickedness and coming destruction (3:1–7) to YHWH's

---

16. On the preference for "Bene-Ammon" over "Ammon," see Zeph 2:8.

17. On the oracular formula, see Sweeney, *Isaiah 1–39*, 546.

18. So too Bennett, "Book of Zephaniah," 691; Floyd, *Minor Prophets, Part 2*, 226.

19. Sweeney, *Zephaniah*, 150. On the summary appraisal, see Sweeney, *Isaiah 1–39*, 539.

20. For more on this, see the discussion in Structure and Literary Form at 3:8–20.

positively exhorting a broader group to "wait for me!" (3:8). Stage 1 of Zephaniah's two-stage exhortation comes to an end in 3:7.

The initial imperatives address Judah in general (2:1–2) and then its remnant (2:3–4), but the addressees' ambiguity allows for broader application.[21] The declarations of woe and punishment move from Judah's neighbors (2:5–15) to Jerusalem (3:1–7), setting up a rhetorical flavor akin to how Amos declares punishment against seven nations before finally pronouncing judgment against Israel (1:2–2:16).[22] As was true of 1:2–18, the content in stage 1 of the prophet's sermon follows a chiastic pattern, but in an inverse order with Judah/Jerusalem operating at the frame.

Figure 6.1: Topical Framing in Zephaniah 1:2–18 and 2:1–3:7	
The Setting (1:2–18)	The Substance, Stage 1 (2:1–3:7)

A. Global punishment (1:2–3)
  B. Local punishment on Judah and Jerusalem (1:4–6)
    C. Be silent! (1:7a)
  B'. Jerusalem's fall (1:7b–13)
A'. The world's destruction (1:14–18)
	A. Judah's remnant must humble themselves
	  together (2:1–4)
	  B. YHWH will destroy Judah's neighbors (2:5–15)
	A'. YHWH will destroy Jerusalem (3:1–7)

Explanation of the Text

1. The Lamentable State and Fate of the Rebels from the Foreign Nations (2:5–15)

Zephaniah now supports his charge to "seek YHWH" together in 2:1–4 by giving the first of two unmarked reasons. He builds a four-point compass of punishment around Judah, starting with the neighboring rival Philistines to the west (2:5–7) and Moab and Bene-Ammon to the east (2:8–11) and then the imperial powers of the Cushites (probably as the former controllers of Egypt) and Assyria to the south and north, respectively (2:12–15). The text implies that God's judgment on Judah's surrounding nations will implode on

her (cf. Hab 2:16–17). Joining with the remnant by repenting is the only possible hope of preservation (see Zeph 2:3, 7, 9).

The universal scope of this book's punishment (1:2–4; 14–18) and renewal (3:8–20) and the statement of YHWH's supremacy over "all the gods of the earth" in 2:11 strongly suggest that Zephaniah uses these five nations to represent the whole world, which stands under God's wrath.[23] Nevertheless, Zephaniah's contemporary context most certainly influenced his choice of these particular people groups. As Sweeney notes, all are "nations bordering Judah/Israel that held portions of the Israelite/Judean population or its territory

---

21. See DeRouchie, "Addressees in Zephaniah 2:1, 3."

22. Cf. Robertson's comparable comments on Zeph 1:4 (Robertson, *Books of Nahum, Habakkuk, and Zephaniah*, 260).

23. Berlin, *Zephaniah*, 117–19; Motyer, "Zephaniah," 931; contra Sweeney, *Zephaniah*, 17.

(Philistia, Moab, and Ammon), or nations whose demise, whether past or impending, demonstrates YHWH's efficacy in the world (Cush, Assyria)."[24] Furthermore, Haak observes that Zephaniah's oracles against the nations "are directed only against areas which specifically were under strong Assyrian domination" in his day.[25] Zephaniah likely did not mention peoples like Edom, Egypt, and Babylon, all of whom frequent foreign nation oracles in other prophetic books, because they did not fit these criteria.[26] He may also have listed Assyria last both because they were the greatest political force of the day and, of all those listed, they were Judah's most sinister contemporary foe.[27]

Many scholars claim that Zephaniah mainly denounced these nations for political reasons. Christensen says Zephaniah denounced them to give "a theological basis for Josiah's program of political expansion" at Assyria's expense.[28] Berlin claims it was to "revive and support Judean nationalism and stir up anti-Assyrian sentiment."[29] But the historical data give little support for Josiah expanding

territory,[30] and the biblical authors portray Josiah's spiritual reform as calling for surrender to YHWH rather than to an earthly king.[31] Zephaniah himself presents YHWH as Israel's highest "King" (3:15), who would establish a transformed Jerusalem as the center of a new, multiethnic world order (3:8–20). Zephaniah's oracles against foreign nations seek to establish YHWH's reign and not Josiah's in the listeners' ears.[32]

a. A Woe Speech against Philistia to the West (2:5–7)

The term rendered "Woe" (הוֹי, 2:5) is an emotive introductory particle that the prophets often use to show angst over covenant rebellion and idolatry (e.g., Hab 2:12, 19) and/or dismay over approaching doom (e.g., Jer 30:7).[33] Both seem operative here. Lamenting the state and fate of the nations surrounding Judah (Zeph 2:5; cf. Nah 3:1) and of Jerusalem herself (Zeph 3:1; cf. Isa 5:8–22; Hab 2:9–19), the prophet employs the particle twice to introduce his two reasons for Judah's patient

---

24. Sweeney, *Zephaniah*, 14.

25. Haak, "Zephaniah's Oracles against the Nations," 19. For the important role that historical knowledge played in determining which nations a prophet targeted, see Ben Zvi, *Book of Zephaniah*, 299–300. However, YHWH's ability to foretell the future (e.g., Isa 43:8–13; 45:20–21; 46:8–11; 48:3–8) means that a prophet could speak of a nation or its leader that was outside the prophet's own historical setting. Thus, Isaiah could speak of Babylon (e.g., Isa 13; 14:3–23; 21:1–10; 47) and King Cyrus of Persia (Isa 44:24–28; 45:1–7).

26. See Ben Zvi, *Book of Zephaniah*, 306.

27. J. M. P. Smith, "Book of Zephaniah," 232; Robertson, *Books of Nahum, Habakkuk, and Zephaniah*, 296; Roberts, *Nahum, Habakkuk, and Zephaniah*, 195, 203; Patterson, *Nahum, Habakkuk, Zephaniah*, 313.

28. Christensen, "Zephaniah 2:4–15," 669–82, quote from 678. Cf. Sweeney, *Zephaniah*, 14–18.

29. Berlin, *Zephaniah*, 119–24, quote from 120; Berlin, "Zephaniah's Oracle against the Nations," 175–84, quote from 177.

30. See Berlin's critique of Christensen in Berlin, *Zephaniah*, 119–20; Berlin, "Zephaniah's Oracle against the Nations," 177.

31. Haak mistakenly *assumes* that Zephaniah's message "served a political purpose—to manipulate public opinion in the direction of royal policy," unless by "policy" we mean King Josiah's *religious* reforms (see Haak, "Zephaniah's Oracles against the Nations," 6–7).

32. For a discussion of how some materials from the early chapters in Genesis probably influenced the shaping and message of Zeph 2:5–15, see the section on Canonical and Theological Significance following the explanation of 3:1–7.

33. Sweeney, *Isaiah 1–39*, 543. In Scripture, though הוֹי occurs only in prophetic contexts of judgment, Roberts rightly notes that the particle is merely exclamatory, designed to get the attention of hearers like the English "hey!" (e.g., Isa 55:1; Roberts, *Nahum, Habakkuk, and Zephaniah*, 114, 118). See also Richard J. Clifford, "The Use of *hôy* in the Prophets," *CBQ* 28.4 (1966): 458–64; Delbert R. Hillers, "*hôy* and *hôy*-Oracles: A Neglected Syntactic Aspect," in *The Word of the Lord Shall Go Forth: Essays in Honor of David Noel Freedman in Celebration of His Sixtieth Birthday*, ed. Carol L. Meyers and M. O'Connor, vol. 1 of *American Schools of Oriental Research, Special Volume Series* (Winona Lake, IN: Eisenbrauns, 1983), 185–88.

pursuit of YHWH (Zeph 2:5–15; 3:1–7). In the first instance, however, the "woe" speech itself is limited to the prophet's condemnation of the Philistines in 2:5–7. The words of punishment against the other foreign nations that follow reflectively extend beyond the actual statement of "woe."

(1) Its Audience (2:5a)

Through a verbless declaration, YHWH recognizes the target of his "woe" as "the Kerethites" (Zeph 2:5a). The subsequent explanatory unit identifies them as the "Philistines" (2:5b; cf. Ezek 25:16), whose four key cities the prophet sentenced in 2:4.[34] These people originated from Caphtor, known today as Crete (Amos 9:7; cf. Deut 2:23; Jer 47:4), and they dwelt just west of Judah on the Mediterranean's eastern "shoreline by the sea" (Zeph 2:5a).[35]

(2) Its Nature (2:5b–7)

Zephaniah 2:5b–7 details the "woe" oracle's essence. The unit opens with an asyndetic clause in 2:5b and continues through a chain of three *weqatal* clauses in 2:5c–7a. Zephaniah 2:7b–e then further specifies the claims in 2:6–7a.

(a) The Promise of the Philistines' Annihilation (2:5b–c)

While all of Zephaniah's oracle is "YHWH's word" (דְּבַר־יְהוָה) (1:1), in 2:5b YHWH directs a particular "word" of curse against Judah's western

neighbors.[36] He addresses these neighbors using a second masculine plural suffix ("against *you*").

YHWH gives no explicit reason for his punishment, but the context gives two clues. First, God's declaration of punishment against the four Philistine cities grounded Zephaniah's call to "seek humility" in 2:3c. This suggests that the Philistines too would experience divine wrath because they arrogantly denied YHWH as the universal King. Second, the prophet describes "the land of the Philistines" as "Canaan" (כְּנָעַן). Only here does the title "Canaan" designate Philistia alone.[37] However, the Former Prophets state that "all the regions of the Philistines" were accounted "to the Canaanite" (Josh 13:2–3; cf. Num 13:29). God originally allotted this region to Judah (Josh 15:12), but they had failed to acquire it (Judg 3:1–3). YHWH left the Philistines and the other surviving nations to "test Israel" (3:1, 4); these foreigners would confine them, and their foreign gods would "ensnare" Israel in sin (2:3). Significantly, in Zeph 1:11, the prophet already said "the people of Canaan" negatively influenced Jerusalem.[38] A century earlier, Isaiah also claimed that the Philistine wares and divination had infiltrated Jerusalem (Isa 2:1, 6). Therefore, along with the Philistines' prideful failure to seek the true God (Zeph 2:3–4), YHWH intended to judge them for their insidious influence on Judah within the promised land.[39] Indeed, as in all his wars of punishment (even against Jerusalem,

---

34. Rather than reading כְּרֵתִים ("Kerethites") as a proper name, both Tg. Neb. and the Vulgate relate it to the verb כרת ("to cut") (so too Luther, "Lectures on Zephaniah," 341), an intentional word play that may have actually incited Zephaniah to use the term alongside "Philistines" (so Gerleman, *Zephanja*, 29).

35. On the origins of the Philistines, see Daniel M. Master, "Piece by Piece: Exploring the Origins of the Philistines," *BAR* 48.1 (2022): 30–39.

36. As Ben Zvi notes, "The phrase X – על ה' דבר in Zeph 2:5 has a contextual meaning of 'decreed doom'" (Ben Zvi, *Book of Zephaniah*, 154).

37. J. M. P. Smith, "Book of Zephaniah," 217; Ben Zvi, *Book of Zephaniah*, 155; Vlaardingerbroek, *Zephaniah*, 139.

38. This stands against Motyer's claim that the use of "Canaan" in Zeph 1:11b "has no bearing on the context" of 2:5b (Motyer, "Zephaniah," 932). The book mentions this location in only these two places, and this ties the texts together and suggests that "the people of Canaan" at least included the Philistines (cf. Isa 2:6). Cf. Roberts, *Nahum, Habakkuk, and Zephaniah*, 197.

39. So also Roberts, *Nahum, Habakkuk, and Zephaniah*, 197.

3:6–7; cf. Deut 20:16–18; Josh 6:21), God promises in Zeph 2:5c to remove the evil ones "until there is no inhabitant" (מֵאֵין יוֹשֵׁב). This phrase points to a nation's utter decimation (e.g., Jer 4:7; 34:22; 51:29), but it does not require the absence of any remnant (44:22).[40] Zechariah later envisioned that YHWH's triumph over the Philistines would result in some of them becoming part of God's righteous remnant (Zech 9:6–8). Thus, "no inhabitant" will be left because they will receive new identities. Similarly, the psalmist declared that some from Philistia would receive new birth certificates, claiming they were born in Jerusalem (Ps 87:4; cf. 60:10[8]; 108:10[9]).

(b) The Result of the Philistines' Annihilation:
A Reclaiming of Homeland for the Remnant of Judah (2:6–7)

Due to three supposed grammatical irregularities, translators have struggled with Zeph 2:6–7. First, in 2:6, most English translations treat חֶבֶל ("shoreline")[41] as a feminine subject of the feminine verb וְהָיְתָה ("and it shall be"),[42] even though the noun elsewhere is always masculine, as in 2:7 where it agrees with the masculine singular verb וְהָיָה ("and it shall be").[43] In contrast, "the shoreline by the sea" is likely an appositive phrase with the actual antecedent subject of the verb in 2:6 being the feminine noun אֶרֶץ from 2:5a (= "the *land* of the Philistines").[44] The resulting translation in 2:6 is, "And it [the land]—that is, the shoreline by the sea—will become grazing grounds."

Second, in 2:7a, the verb וְהָיָה is masculine, but if the subject were חֶבֶל that follows, one would expect the noun to be definite just as it is within the construct chain in the previous clause.[45] The definite appositive phrase of 2:6 does indeed serve as the antecedent subject of 2:7a, and חֶבֶל in 2:7a is a predicate nominative: "And it [the shoreline] will become a shoreline for the remnant of the house of Judah." Also, the use of חֶבֶל in 2:7a may also bear a double meaning that anticipates Judah's possession, since elsewhere the term can mean an allotted "portion" (e.g., 1 Chr 16:18//Ps 105:11; Ezek 47:13).[46]

Third, in 2:7b, because no masculine plural antecedent is apparent for the pronominal suffix on עֲלֵיהֶם ("on *them*"), some scholars emend the text

---

40. J. M. P. Smith, "Book of Zephaniah," 218. Zephaniah 2:5c uses the strong causative וְהַאֲבַדְתִּיךְ ("And I will destroy you"). The second feminine singular suffix ("you") likely addresses the feminine אֶרֶץ ("land") of 2:5b in a personal way.

41. The NIV renders חֶבֶל simply as "land" in both Zeph 2:6 and 7a, but most English versions translate it as "seacoast," whether it is in construct with הַיָּם ("the sea") or not (e.g., NRSVue, NASB20, ESV, NET, CSB). The majority approach is a fine contextual rendering, but the form "shoreline" is here used to indicate that the term expresses something long and narrow, whether as a cord that fastens (Esth 1:6) or binds (Job 36:8), a rope that measures (Zech 2:5) or surrounds to apportion (Ezek 47:13), or a long, narrow strip of land (Deut 3:4). The last use occurs in Zeph 2:7, for the strip of ground that shapes the Mediterranean coastline is indeed long and narrow.

42. Cf. NASB20, NET, NIV, CSB; the NRSVue and ESV treat Zeph 2:6 as direct address with חֶבֶל as a vocative and the verb as if it were second person.

43. Clines explicitly notes that the noun is masculine but then treats Zeph 2:6 as an exception (I "חֶבֶל," *DCH* 3:151).

44. So too Motyer, "Zephaniah," 932.

45. Andersen and Forbes highlight how Hebrew poetry often limits its use of prose particles, including the definite article, and how Zeph 2–3 show prose particle counts similar to those in poetic texts (7.66 percent in ch. 2 and 7.25 percent in ch. 3); as such, the lack of an article on חֶבֶל in 2:7 could be due simply to the text's poetic nature (Andersen and Forbes, "'Prose Particle' Counts of the Hebrew Bible," 165–83, see esp. 166 and 175). However, they also note that "there are quite a few chapters of prose with a score less than 10%." Closely examining Zeph 2:1–3:7 reveals that every other time an intended definite noun occurs independently or as the absolute of a definite construct chain, the definite article is always present (2:1a, 3a, 5a, 11b–c, 15a; 3:1a; cf. preposition plus article combinations in 2:4c, 7c, 13c, 14c–d, 15d; 3:3c, 5c). Thus, Zephaniah's pattern suggests that a lexicalized article would occur at 2:7a if חֶבֶל were the subject.

46. Roberts, *Nahum, Habakkuk, and Zephaniah*, 192; Berlin, *Zephaniah*, 106; Vlaardingerbroek, *Zephaniah*, 132; Sweeney, *Zephaniah*, 130.

to עַל־הַיָּם ("by the sea").[47] However, no emendation is necessary. The antecedent could be the singular noun "shoreline" (חֶבֶל) in 2:7a, for a pronoun referring to a collective is often in the plural.[48] The antecedent could also be the feminine plural noun "grazing grounds" (נְוֹת) in 2:6, for suffixed pronouns commonly take the masculine in the third plural, even when one expects the feminine.[49]

In 2:6–7, Zephaniah uses the pastoral imagery of "grazing grounds" (נְוֹת), "cisterns" (כְּרֹת),[50] "shepherds" (רֹעִים), "folds" (גְּדֵרוֹת),[51] "sheep" (צֹאן), and "pasturing" (רעה) to depict fertility and peace for God's people (cf. 3:13).[52] The prophet specifically asserts that once God eradicates the Philistines, their land would be "for the remnant of the house of Judah" (לִשְׁאֵרִית בֵּית יְהוּדָה) (2:7a). This is the first explicit reference in the book to a preserved remnant on the other side of global punishment. Zephaniah already anticipated such a possibility

by his command for Judah to gather in submission "before the fury of the YHWH's anger comes on you" (2:2c) and with his claim, "Perhaps you may be hidden on the day of YHWH's anger" (2:3d).[53] Elsewhere, YHWH's prophets use the masculine and feminine forms for "remnant" interchangeably (שְׁאֵרִית/שְׁאָר). These forms may refer neutrally to a group remaining after some event, negatively to nations or parts of nations that YHWH will destroy, or positively to a faithful group remaining after YHWH's fury. This final group constitutes those who are preserved and represents hope for humanity's future under God.[54] Zephaniah restricts the masculine form to the negative context (1:4) and uses the feminine form (2:7, 9; 3:13) and related verb (3:12) to highlight the positive, eschatological uses.

Significantly, while here Zephaniah admonishes the foreign nations, his use of "remnant" language

---

47. E.g., GKC, §135p; Roberts, *Nahum, Habakkuk, and Zephaniah*, 192; NET.

48. "כְּרֹת," *HALOT* 501; cf. GKC, §135p.

49. Joüon, §149b. Cf. Gerleman, *Zephanja*, 34; Ben Zvi, *Book of Zephaniah*, 161.

50. The NRSVue and ESV translate the feminine plural כְּרֹת as "meadows." They link it with the noun כַּר ("pasture, meadow"), but elsewhere this noun is only masculine in both singular (Isa 30:23) and plural (Ps 65:14[13]) (cf. "כְּרֹת," *HALOT* 501). The NASB95 and CSB render the form "caves" and the NIV "wells" based on the probable link with a supposed feminine noun כָּרָה related to the verb כרה ("to dig, hew") (so "I כרה," *DCH* 4:458–59). Some propose כְּרֹת is dittography from the previous נְוֹת (so "כְּרֹת," *HALOT* 501), but only the Vulgate supports this by rendering the collocation נְוֹת כְּרֹת with the single verb *rĕquiēs* ("respite"). The LXX apparently struggled with כְּרֹת and rendered it Κρήτη ("Crete"), echoing the "Kerethites" (כְּרֵתִים) of the previous verse.

51. Ben Zvi writes, "It seems likely that 'enclosure for flock' stands as an equivalent for the 'enclosure for human beings,' i.e., cities. The land of cities will be a land of flock enclosures (and of pastures for the shepherds)" (Ben Zvi, *Book of Zephaniah*, 158). Similarly, Berlin notes that the usage of pastoral imagery "may be metaphorical: the remnant of the House of Judah, like a flock, will graze and bed down in what once were the cities of Philistia" (Berlin, *Zephaniah*, 107).

52. See the Canonical Significance of Zeph 2:5–15 below

for how Zephaniah's statements about shepherds fit within the Bible's larger use of shepherd imagery.

53. See too the discussion of "his invited ones" at Zeph 1:7.

54. Gerhard F. Hasel, "Semantic Values of Derivatives of the Hebrew Root ŠʾʾR," *AUSS* 11 (1972): 152–69; R. E. Clements, "שָׁאַר šāʾar," *TDOT* 14:272–86; H. Wildberger, "שאר šʾr to Remain," *TLOT* 3:1283–92; Sang Hoon Park, "שָׁאַר (šāʾar)," *NIDOTTE* 4:11–17. For a neutral use of שְׁאָר in the Prophets, see Mal 2:15; for שְׁאֵרִית, see Jer 39:3; 40:11; 41:10, 16; 42:2; 43:5; Ezek 36:3, 4; Hag 1:12, 14; 2:2. For a "remnant" bound for destruction in the Prophets, שְׁאָר is used negatively of Babylon (Isa 14:22), Moab (16:14), Syria (17:3), Kedar (21:17), and Jerusalem's remnant of Baal (Zeph 1:4), whereas שְׁאֵרִית is used negatively of Philistia (Isa 14:30; Jer 25:20; 47:4–5; Ezek 25:16; Amos 1:8), Moab (Isa 15:9), Babylon (Jer 50:26), the nations in general (Ezek 36:5), and Israel/Judah (Jer 6:9; 8:3; 11:23; 15:9; 24:8; 40:15; 52:15, 19; 44:7, 12, 14, 28; Ezek 5:10; 9:8; 11:13). For the "remnant" of God's reconstituted people in the Prophets, שְׁאָר is used positively of Israel/Judah (Isa 10:20–22; 11:11, 16; 28:5), whereas שְׁאֵרִית has a broader positive usage relating to Edom (Amos 9:12) and Israel/Judah (Isa 37:4, 32; 46:3; Jer 23:3; 31:7; Amos 5:15; Mic 2:12; 4:7; 5:7–8; 7:18; Zech 2:7, 9; 3:13; 8:6, 11–12). In the Prophets, we also find the *niphal* participle of שאר, used substantivally to express similar realities, neutrally (Zech 11:9; 12:14), negatively of the nations (Ezek 6:12) and of Israel/Judah (Jer 21:7; Ezek 17:21), and positively of Israel/Judah (Isa 4:3; 37:31).

in relation to Judah still warns the prophet's community. This is so because "only in the context of a prophecy of doom . . . can there be an authentic remnant theme."[55] The phrase "the remnant of the house of Judah" (שְׁאֵרִית בֵּית יְהוּדָה) appears in the OT only here at Zeph 2:7a, but elsewhere comparable phrases occur, most notably "the remnant of my people" (שְׁאֵרִית עַמִּי) in 2:9c and "the remnant of Israel" (שְׁאֵרִית יִשְׂרָאֵל) in 3:13a.[56] Zephaniah retains hope only for Judah's remnant and not the nation as a whole. Only those heeding his prophetic call to "bind" together and "seek YHWH" (2:1a, 3a) may survive the fires of YHWH's wrath (2:3d). The "Judah" of Josiah's reforms included many from the northern tribes who rejected the northern paganism, emigrated to Judah after Samaria's destruction (723 BC), and turned to YHWH (2 Chr 34:6–9; cf. 2 Kgs 23:16, 19).[57] This was the group that Babylon exiled, that later returned to Jerusalem and its environs, and that produced the Messiah who reconstituted a new Israel. Thus, we see that Zephaniah's "remnant of the house of Judah" is at least a purged yet reunified "Israel" (cf. Zeph 3:13a), growing out of the purifying fires of punishment (see 3:11–13). But the prophet envisioned the composition of this protected people as

more diverse, including some preserved and now "adopted" foreigners.[58] As we will see in Zeph 2:9, 11 and 3:9–13, God associates his remnant with Judah, Jerusalem, and Israel, yet this people will be a multiethnic community, all of whom have surrendered themselves to YHWH and who have joined for worship as God's people in the new Jerusalem.

In Zeph 2:6–7a, the prophet predicted that Philistia's destruction would produce positive results for Judah's remnant. He further specifies these advantageous results in the next two clauses, both of which begin with prepositional phrases (2:7b–c). Zephaniah then grounds the latter of these two prepositionally fronted clauses with two additional clauses (2:7d–e).

First, the prophet asserts that Judah's remnant will "pasture" (רעה) on the various tracts of the shoreline (עֲלֵיהֶם "on them").[59] The ambiguous verb "pasture" is fitting because in English it can refer to both a sheep herd "grazing" or a shepherd-leader "tending." Both meanings are intentional since in 2:6 Judah's remnant includes both "shepherds" and "sheep."[60]

Second, the same group that "pastures" will inhabit the houses of Ashkelon (Zeph 2:7c; cf. 2:4b) because (כִּי) YHWH would visit (פקד) and restore

---

55. George W. Anderson, "The Idea of the Remnant in the Book of Zephaniah," in *Festschrift Gillis Gerleman*, ed. Sten Hidal et al., ASTI 11 (Leiden: Brill, 1978), 12; cf. Andrew M. King, "A Remnant Will Return: An Analysis of the Literary Function of the Remnant Motif in Isaiah," *JESOT* 4 (2015): 155–59.

56. In Isa 46:3 "the remnant of the house of Israel" (שְׁאֵרִית בֵּית יִשְׂרָאֵל) has a similar referent to Zeph 2:7a. "The remnant of Judah" (שְׁאֵרִית יְהוּדָה) also occurs many times in Jeremiah (e.g., Jer 40:15; 42:15; cf. 40:11), but it only refers to Gedaliah's community and not to an eschatological remnant. The title "the remnant of Israel" (שְׁאֵרִית יִשְׂרָאֵל) is most common and can refer to a general group of ethnic Israelites (1 Chr 12:39 [with שְׁרִית]; 2 Chr 34:9), a future community of ethnic Israelites set apart for judgment (Jer 6:9; Ezek 9:8; 11:13), or an eschatological group of preserved ones identified with Israel and likely including saved and "adopted" foreigners (Jer 31:7;

Mic 2:12; Zeph 3:13). The genitive relationship in the phrase "the remnant of X" is likely one of origin, meaning "the remnant *deriving from* X" (see GKC §128g; Joüon §129d–f).

57. See also 2 Chr 11:13–17; 15:9; 30:1, 5, 10–11, 25.

58. See, e.g., Ps 87; Isa 2:2–4; 54:3; Jer 12:16; Zech 8:22–23.

59. The referent of the masculine plural verb יִרְעוּן ("they will pasture") in Zeph 2:7b is the collective feminine singular noun שְׁאֵרִית ("remnant") of 2:7a. Collective singular nouns, even when feminine, can have masculine plural predicates when they represent "exclusively or at least generally, masculine persons" (e.g., Amos 1:8; GKC, §145b, e; cf. Ben Zvi, *Book of Zephaniah*, 160).

60. The meaning of רעה changes dependent on whether the subject is livestock (= "graze, feed") or humans (= "lead to feed, shepherd") (see "רעה I," *HALOT* 1258–59).

them (2:7d–e). In 1:8b–9 and 12, YHWH had promised to "visit" punishment (פקד) on Jerusalem's leaders (cf. Isa 10:3); now in Zeph 2:7d, we learn that his day of "visitation" will also bring favor to "the remnant of the house of Judah."[61] The third masculine plural suffixes on יִפְקְדֵם ("he will visit *them*," 2:7d) and שְׁבוּתָם ("*their* circumstance," 2:7e) supports reading the subject of the third masculine plural verbs יִרְעוּן ("*they* will pasture," 2:7b) and יִרְבָּצוּן ("*they* will lie down," 2:7c) as the remnant of Judah, whether among the people in general or their leaders.[62] Of the four Philistine cities mentioned in 2:4, only Ashkelon nestled directly on the Mediterranean Sea's shores. By mentioning Ashkelon, Zephaniah shows that the remnant would reach the coast and completely conquer Philistia.[63] The combined images of the "shoreline" being "grazing grounds" (2:6) and Philistia still including houses that humans inhabit (2:7c) indicate the text's figurative nature.

Significantly, the original Mosaic covenant blessings included Israel's dwelling in "Canaanite" houses within the promised land (Deut 6:10–11; cf. notes at Zeph 1:13; 2:5). Similarly, this text anticipates God's people reclaiming land he once promised to Judah (see Josh 15:12; Judg 1:18) and dispossessing those peoples who tested Israel for centuries since Israel failed to eradicate them (cf.

Josh 11:22; 13:2–3; Judg 3:1–3).[64] Zephaniah envisions God's terrestrial sovereignty expanding to include the whole earth, as was the goal from the beginning in garden of Eden (Gen 1:28; 2:15).[65] All this will come about after God's punishment falls on the world and "for" (כִּי) YHWH would visit his faithful few.

The divine "visitation" (פקד) here points to YHWH's redemptive care for his remnant (cf. Jer 27:22). Elsewhere in the book this verb points to God punishing Jerusalem (Zeph 1:8b, 12c; 3:7). Therefore, the same "visitation" at the day of YHWH will result in both curses on the rebels and blessing on the faithful (cf. 3:8–10).[66] The consequence of his visitation is that "he will restore their circumstance" (lit., "and he will turn their turning," וְשָׁב שְׁבוּתָם). This phrase points to the reversal of a previous move downward and regularly appears with restoration promises that refer to a return to a state once enjoyed, whether economic or spiritual and whether dealing with a remnant of Israel/Judah or of specific other nations.[67] The translation of שְׁבוּת as "prosperity" (= NET) or "fortune(s)" (= NRSVue, NASB20, ESV, NIV, CSB) is possible (cf. Job 42:10). However, the more general rendering of "circumstance" allows the various contexts to clarify whether the restoration is economic or a broader well-being that includes

---

61. Cf. 1 Pet 2:12. See also Robertson, *Books of Nahum, Habakkuk, and Zephaniah*, 301. For more on YHWH's "visitation," see the comments at Zeph 1:8–9.

62. In contrast, Smith can only distinguish the Jewish remnant from the shepherds and flocks and argue that Zephaniah envisioned actual livestock living in the houses of Ashkelon by treating 2:7d–e as secondary (cf. 2:14–15; J. M. P. Smith, "Book of Zephaniah," 219). Calvin saw the mention of a remnant in 2:7 as "a striking divergency from the flocks of shepherds to the tribe of Judah" (Calvin, "Habakkuk, Zephaniah, Haggai," 243).

63. Cf. Vlaardingerbroek, *Zephaniah*, 142.

64. Cf. Floyd, *Minor Prophets, Part 2*, 212.

65. Cf. Gen 22:17–18; 26:3–4; Jer 3:16–17; Matt 5:5; Rom 4:13; Rev 21:2, 10–27.

66. See DeRouchie, "YHWH's Future Ingathering in Zephaniah 1:2," 173–91. So too Floyd, *Minor Prophets, Part 2*, 219.

67. שָׁבִית/שְׁבוּת refers to the restoration of Israel/Judah in Deut 30:3; Pss 14:7; 53:7[6]; 85:2[1]; 126:4; Jer 29:14; 30:3, 18; 31:23; 32:44; 33:7, 11, 26; Ezek 16:53; 39:25; Hos 6:11; Joel 4:1[3:1]; Amos 9:14; Zeph 2:7; 3:20. As to the other nations, it refers to Moab in Jer 48:47, Bene-Ammon in Jer 49:6, Elam in Jer 49:39, Sodom in Ezek 16:53, and Egypt in Ezek 29:14. Cf. Elmer A. Martens, "Motivations for the Promise of Israel's Restoration to the Land in Jeremiah and Ezekiel" (PhD diss., Claremont Graduate School, 1972).

the reestablishment of a new covenant with God.[68] The present context supports the latter focus.

These words against the Philistines included words of divine favor for a future remnant associated with Judah (2:7). Still, for Judah as a whole, the prophet intended that Philistia's foreseen desolation would motivate those from Judah and other lands to "seek YHWH" (2:3–4). Apart from heeding this call, there would be no hope for a future beyond God's wrath.

In Zephaniah's day, Philistia was gradually being conquered. This would continue to the end of the seventh century BC, leaving demolished all four of the cities in 2:4. Nevertheless, the scope of Zephaniah's vision pushes beyond anything realized in his present time. Philistia's immediate desolations were mere foretastes of a greater punishment that would precede the transformed remnant of Judah dwelling in a transformed land. (For an overview of the historical context and the way it anticipates the eschatological future, see the commentary discussion at the end of Zeph 2:4.)

b. Further Declarations of International Punishment Surrounding Judah (2:8–15)

(1) Against Moab and Bene-Ammon to the East (2:8–11)

The asyndetic *qatal* verb שָׁמַעְתִּי ("I have heard") in Zeph 2:8 signals a shift in both content and voice (from the prophet's to YHWH's). Thus, 2:7 concludes the formal "woe" speech, but the larger section continues now by declaring judgment on Moab and Bene-Ammon, Judah's "cousins" to the east (see Gen 19:36–38).[69] They opposed Israel at the conquest (Deut 23:3–4) and regularly raided and oppressed Israel thereafter (2 Kgs 13:20; 2 Chr 20:1), at times as God's explicit agents of curse (Judg 3:12; 10:7; 2 Kgs 24:2). Their elevated, protected location on the Gilead Plateau east of the Jordan River often prompted a superiority complex that delighted in others' destruction (cf. Isa 16:6; Jer 48:27–30; Ezek 25:3, 6), but YHWH had taken note. Zephaniah requires humble dependence on God (Zeph 1:6; 2:3; 3:2, 12–13) and speaks much against arrogance in all forms (2:7, 9, 15; 3:11). Pride always results in ruin (Prov 16:18)—especially when one directs it against YHWH's people (see Gen 12:3; Deut 32:35–36).

(a) The Reason for Their Punishment (2:8)

Unlike YHWH's punishment of the Philistines (but see Zeph 1:11; 2:3–4), the text now explicitly states the reasons for the judgment of Judah's eastern neighbors: they directed "reproach" (חֶרְפָּה) and "abuses" (גִּדּוּפִים) against the Judeans (2:8a–b; cf. Isa 51:7; Ezek 5:15). These acts were common among Judah's enemies (cf. Ps 44:17[16]). Nevertheless,

---

68. The KJV renders וְשָׁב שְׁבוּתָם as "and return their captives" at Zeph 2:7e and follows many versions (LXX, Vulgate, Tg. Neb., and Peshitta) and the Masoretic *Qere* (= שְׁבִיתָם) in reading the substantive as שְׁבִית derived from the verb שׁבה ("take captive, deport, carry away"; cf. Isa 14:2; 61:1; Jer 50:33). The meaning of the phrase would then relate to the reversal of the remnant of Judah's exile or imprisonment. However, Job 42:10 probably identifies that the form שְׁבוּת is both extant and derived from the verb שׁוב, for in that context a link to captivity or exile is unlikely (see שְׁבוּת, שְׁבִית, *HALOT* 1385–86). In Bracke's words, the phrase "is a technical term indicating a restoration to an earlier time of well-being," whether as "Yahweh's reversal of his judgment" (most common) or, at the very least (as with Job), "the alleviation of affliction and a return to a cir-

cumstance even more prosperous than . . . originally enjoyed" (John M. Bracke, "*šûb šebût*: A Reappraisal," *ZAW* 97.2 [1985]: 233–44, quotes from 244 and 242, respectively).

69. The joining together of Moab and Bene-Ammon into a single pronouncement of punishment occurs only here in Zeph 2:8–11 and in Ezek 25:8–11 (cf. Amos 1:13–2:3; Jer 48:1–49:6). While often translated "Ammonites," "Bene-Ammon" (בְּנֵי עַמּוֹן) is the normal proper name for Israel's western neighbors, although the abbreviation עַמּוֹן is also used (e.g., 1 Sam 11:11; Ps 83:8). Genesis 19:38 notes that Lot's youngest daughter bore a son and called his name בֶּן־עַמִּי ("the son of my people"). The text then tells us that "he is the father of Bene-Ammon [בְּנֵי־עַמּוֹן] to this day." For more on this rendering, see Block, "*bny 'mwn*," 197–212.

as Shepherd notes, this is a significant offense since "a reproach against God's people is a reproach against the God whose name they bear."[70] Judah's foreigners even became "haughty against their border" (וַיַּגְדִּילוּ עַל־גְּבוּלָם, 2:8b–c), using the common *hiphil* of גדל plus the preposition עַל (הִגְדִּיל עַל, lit., "he made great over"), which refers to mere boasting or mocking (Ps 35:26; Ezek 35:13; cf. Zeph 2:10c).[71] Moab and Bene-Ammon's "making great" is specifically "against [the Judeans'] border" (עַל־גְּבוּלָם), suggesting that these foreigners' harassment and pride includes intrusion into the promised land (see NEB; cf. Ezek 35:12–13).[72] Territorial disputes against Moab and Bene-Ammon dotted Israel's tenth–eighth centuries (e.g., 2 Sam 8:2, 11–12; 12:26–31; 2 Kgs 3),[73] and the same can likely be said of Moab down to Josiah's day (cf. 2 Kgs 13:20). The prophet may be referring to these border encroachments in Zeph 2:8c.[74]

(b) The Nature of Their Punishment (2:9–11)

Having stated the basis for the punishment (2:8), YHWH now clarifies this punishment's nature. He promises to destroy Moab and Bene-Ammon in 2:9 and then clarifies the nature of the punishment with universal implications in 2:9c–11.

• The Declaration of Punishment (2:9a–b)

"Therefore" (לָכֵן), because of Moab and Bene-Ammon's insults and arrogance, YHWH vows to act on behalf of his own (2:9).[75] He guarantees his oath in three ways: (1) He swears upon his own life ("by my life"; cf. e.g., Gen 22:16; Num 14:21; Isa 45:23), stressing that his vow was as guaranteed as his existence and declaring a curse upon himself should he fail to fulfill his promise.[76] (2) He notes that he bears supreme power ("YHWH of armies") and cares uniquely for his people ("the God of Israel"; cf. 1 Sam 2:30; Isa 17:6). (3) He uses the particle כִּי asseveratively, meaning "surely" (Zeph 2:9b).

YHWH begins by declaring that he would make Moab and Bene-Ammon "like Sodom and . . . like Gomorrah" (Zeph 2:9b). God destroyed these cities in the days of Lot (Gen 19:24–26), the forefather

---

70. Shepherd, *Commentary on the Book of the Twelve*, 363.

71. According to Vlaardingerbroek, the preposition עַל with הִגְדִּיל signifies "higher than" and a "hostile threatening sense" (Vlaardingerbroek, *Zephaniah*, 146).

72. So too many scholars—e.g., Calvin, "Habakkuk, Zephaniah, Haggai," 246; R. L. Smith, *Micah–Malachi*, 134; Robertson, *Books of Nahum, Habakkuk, and Zephaniah*, 304; Ben Zvi, *Book of Zephaniah*, 165–66; Roberts, *Nahum, Habakkuk, and Zephaniah*, 200; O'Connor, *Hebrew Verse Structure*, 251; Motyer, "Zephaniah," 934; Vlaardingerbroek, *Zephaniah*, 146; Sweeney, *Zephaniah*, 136; Patterson, *Nahum, Habakkuk, Zephaniah*, 307. Instead of saying Moab and Bene-Ammon violated "their [i.e., Judah's] border" (גְּבוּלָם), the LXX emphasizes that they arrogantly claimed *YHWH's* land ("my borders" [τὰ ὅριά μου]).

73. With 2 Kgs 3:4, see the Moabite Stone from ca. 835 BC ("The Moabite Stone," [*ANET*, 320–21]; "The Inscription of King Mesha," [*COS* 2.23:137–38]).

74. Cf. Keil, " Twelve Minor Prophets," 10:449–50 (2:143).

75. The particle לָכֵן commonly introduces prophetic judgment (e.g., 1 Sam 3:14; 2 Kgs 19:32; Amos 3:11), and it is directly followed by a surety oath in Ezek 5:11; 35:6, 11; Zeph 2:9.

76. So too Robertson, *Books of Nahum, Habakkuk, and Zephaniah*, 304. On divine self-maledictory oaths, see Meredith G. Kline, *By Oath Consigned: A Reinterpretation of the Covenant Signs of Circumcision and Baptism* (Grand Rapids: Eerdmans, 1968), 16–17, 42; Dennis J. McCarthy, *Treaty and Covenant: A Study in Form in the Ancient Oriental Documents and in the Old Testament*, 2nd ed., Analecta Biblica 21 (Rome: Biblical Institute Press, 1981), 91–96, 255; Gordon P. Hugenberger, *Marriage as a Covenant: Biblical Law and Ethics as Developed from Malachi* (Grand Rapids: Baker Books, 1994), 193–97. In the OT, only YHWH uses the phrase חַי־אָנִי ("the life of me"). Greenberg notes that it is the deity's equivalent to an Israelite vowing חַי יְהוָה ("by the life of YHWH," e.g., Judg 8:19; 1 Sam 14:39, 45; Hos 4:15). Nevertheless, it is an odd grammatical pattern wherein the pronoun אָנִי ("I") replaces the Tetragrammaton in first-person contexts, serving as the absolute form in a construct chain (lit., "by the life of I," cf. e.g., Num 14:21; Ezek 5:11; Zeph 2:9) (Moshe Greenberg, "The Hebrew Oath Particle *ḥay/ḥē*," *JBL* 76.1 [1957]: 34–39). In such cases, חַי־אָנִי is equivalent to "YHWH of armies has sworn by his soul" (נִשְׁבַּע יְהוָה צְבָאוֹת בְּנַפְשׁוֹ, Jer 51:14; cf. Ps 89:36[35]). On the likelihood of translating חַי in the phrase חַי־יְהוָה or חַי־אָנִי as a noun meaning

of Moab and Bene-Ammon.[77] Whereas Philistia would become "grazing grounds," YHWH would devastate and depopulate this once agrarian society. He will counter fertility with ground abounding with weeds,[78] salt pit, and waste (cf. Isa 7:23–25; Jer 17:6). Each of these images relates directly to the Sodom and Gomorrah episode (vegetation [Gen 19:25; Deut 29:23], salt [Gen 19:26; Deut 29:23], and extended desolation [Isa 13:19–20; Jer 50:39–40]).[79] Here, the text echoes God's curse of the ground (Gen 3:18) and again stresses the reversal of the created order (see note at Zeph 1:3).[80]

God would confront the highlanders' "boasts" (2:8) and "pride" (2:10). In the days just before Zephaniah, ancient sources reveal many examples of Arabs from the western Arabian desert encroaching on the Assyrian-controlled territories of Moab and Bene-Ammon. Sweeney suggests that we should assume such clashes continued and that seventh-century readers would have interpreted these conflicts as fulfilling Zephaniah's predictions.[81] Josephus also notes that Nebuchadnezzar

subjugated the Moabites and Ammonites in his twenty-third year (ca. 582/1 BC), and Ben Zvi thinks this fulfills Zephaniah's predictions.[82] But the destructive scope that the prophet envisions seems far greater and more eschatological in nature. We should view any Arab or Babylonian activity in this region as a foretaste of greater worldwide punishment to come.[83]

- The Explanation of Punishment with Universal Implications (2:9c–11)

Zephaniah 2:9c–11 now explains the punishment with universal implications. As with Philistia's judgment sentence (Zeph 2:6–7), YHWH begins by tempering his portrayal of complete desolation by noting that a remnant of survivors from Judah will both "plunder" (בזז) and "inherit" (נחל) Moab and Bene-Ammon (2:9c–d). The ones who will claim these nations are "the remnant of my people [שְׁאֵרִית עַמִּי] . . . and the remainder of my nation [וְיֶתֶר גּוֹי]." These phrases recall "the remnant of the house of Judah" (שְׁאֵרִית בֵּית יְהוּדָה) in 2:7a and

---

"life," see also Helmer Ringgren, "חָיָה chāyāh," *TDOT* 4:339–40; Jerzy Woźniak, "Bedeutung Und Belege Der Schwurformel *ḥaj Jahwe*," *BZ* 28.2 (1984): 249.

77. Biblical authors make similar comparisons elsewhere when addressing God's judgment against the ungodly (2 Pet 2:6; Rev 11:8) from Israel (e.g., Deut 29:23; Lam 4:6; Amos 4:11; Matt 10:15; cf. Isa 1:9–10; Jer 23:14; Ezek 16:46–56) or the nations (Isa 13:19; Jer 49:18; 50:40).

78. The LXX rendered the *hapax legomenon* מִמְשָׁק ("possession") in the phrase מִמְשַׁק חָרוּל (lit., "a possession/ground of weed") as "Damascus," likely drawn from Gen 15:2, where מֶשֶׁק, a related *hapax* occurs: "And as for the son of the possession of my house [וּבֶן־מֶשֶׁק בֵּיתִי]—he is the Damascene Eliezer [דַּמֶּשֶׂק אֱלִיעֶזֶר, i.e., Eliezer of Damascus]." We must derive the meaning of "possession" solely from the context, and the LXX's approach, while affirming Zephaniah's interest in the foreign nations' relationship to YHWH, is most likely a corruption (so too, e.g., Gerleman, *Zephanja*, 37–38; Rudolph, *Micha, Nahum, Habakuk, Zephanja*, 277; Berlin, *Zephaniah*, 109; Ryou, *Zephaniah's Oracles*, 38; Sweeney, *Zephaniah*, 139–40). See also Greenfield, who argues the phrase means "a place for harvesting nettles" (Jonas C. Greenfield, "A Hapax Legomenon, ממשק חרול," in

Studies in Judaica, Karaitica, and Islamica: Presented to Leon Nemoy on His Eightieth Birthday, ed. Sheldon R. Brunswick [Ramat Gan: Bar Ilan University Press, 1982], 79–85).

79. Baker, *Nahum, Habakkuk and Zephaniah*, 107; cf. Floyd, *Minor Prophets, Part 2*, 222–23. As is clear from Sodom and Gomorrah's destruction (Gen 13:10; 19:24–26), Scripture (cf. Deut 29:22–23; Judg 9:45; Job 39:6; Jer 17:6) and extrabiblical materials ("The First Soldier's Oath," trans. Billie Jean Collins [*COS* 1.66:166]; "The Bukān Inscription," trans. K. Lawson Younger, Jr. [*COS* 3.89:219]) often associate "salt" with a curse of infertility. See F. Charles Fensham, "Salt as Curse in the Old Testament and the Ancient Near East," *BA* 25.2 (1962): 48–50.

80. Cf. Floyd, *Minor Prophets, Part 2*, 223.

81. Sweeney, *Zephaniah*, 135–36. See, e.g., "Texts from Hammurabi to the Downfall of the Assyrian Empire," *ANET*, 297–301.

82. Josephus, *A.J.* 10.180–85; cf. Ben Zvi, *Book of Zephaniah*, 304. This was the same year Babylon deported some 745 Judeans (Jer 52:30), and the two events are likely related. So J. Maxwell Miller and John H. Hayes, *A History of Ancient Israel and Judah* (Philadelphia: Westminster, 1986), 425.

83. So also Keil, " Twelve Minor Prophets," 10:450 (2:144).

characterize them as those who will enjoy the post-war creation by surviving YHWH's wrath (2:3d).[84]

– The Plundering and Dispossession of Moab and Bene-Ammon by YHWH's Remnant (2:9c–d)

But what will they plunder and inherit? The third masculine plural pronominal suffixes rendered "them" (יִנְחָלוּם . . . יְבָזּוּם) (. . . יִנְחָלוּם יְבָזּוּם) in 2:9c–d could refer to Moab and Bene-Ammon as land, people, or both.[85]

The focus on the territory's state in 2:9b suggests, at the very least, that claiming land is in view. Unlike the Philistines (2:7), God did *not* originally promise Israel these peoples' territory (Deut 2:9, 19). Thus, the remnant dispossessing them partially fulfills God's original commission that those made in his image fill and subdue the earth while operating as royal priests and displaying his glory (Gen 1:28; 2:15).[86] Keil proposes that Moab and Bene-Ammon's territories cannot be in view, for "a land turned into an eternal desert and salt-steppe would not be adapted for a *nachălâh* (possession) for the people of God."[87] However, Zeph 3:8–20 implicitly and Isaiah explicitly indicate that after God's curse the redeemed remnant will rebuild and enjoy creational renewal: "And they [who were delivered by the Spirit-empowered anointed one] will build

the ancient ruins. The former devastations they will raise up, and they will repair the wasted cities, the devastations of many generations" (Isa 61:4; cf. 35:6; 58:12).[88] Abraham's remnant offspring will fulfill YHWH's ancient promise by claiming the territory once linked with Lot (Gen 13:12–17).[89]

Furthermore, the remnant's possession of Moab and Bene-Ammon also includes incorporating some of these foreign peoples into God's newly transformed people. The strongest evidence for this comes from the immediate context in two forms. First, Zeph 2:11 highlights the nature of YHWH's work of power against the peoples of the world and their gods in a way that opens the door for not only prisoners of war but also servants from the nations prostrating themselves in worship before God (see below). Second, Zephaniah later envisions a global salvation arising out of the fires of wrath, with an ethnically mixed group of peoples gathering to worship YHWH in the new Jerusalem (Zeph 3:9–10).[90]

– The Certainty of YHWH's Victory and Receipt of Global Praise (2:10–11)

Zephaniah 2:10–11 gives a two-part summary appraisal of God's judgment against Moab and Bene-Ammon.[91] "This" (זֹאת) at the head of verse 10 refers

---

84. YHWH can indeed allow his prophets to foresee the future, so there is no need to identify the mere mention of a remnant with the postexilic era when a remnant was present (cf. Zech 8:6, 11–12; against, e.g., Rudolph, *Micha, Nahum, Habakuk, Zephanja*, 281–82; Seybold, *Satirische Prophetie*, 48; Seybold, *Nahum, Habakuk, Zephanja*, 107).

85. Cf. Ben Zvi, *Book of Zephaniah*, 169–70.

86. Cf. Exod 19:5–6; 1 Pet 2:9; see also Num 14:21; Ps 72:17–19; Isa 11:9–10; Hab 2:14.

87. Keil, " Twelve Minor Prophets," 10:450 (2:143).

88. Thus, Ezra-Nehemiah's rebuilding after YHWH's wrath foreshadows the rebuilding God's saints will do after the worldwide judgment.

89. See also Gen 22:17–18; 26:3–4; Rom 4:13; Heb 11:10. Cf. Robertson, *Books of Nahum, Habakkuk, and Zephaniah*, 305.

90. See the Canonical Significance of Zeph 2:5–15 below

for more reasons to believe that God will incorporate former enemies into a newly transformed people.

91. Some scholars regard all or part of Zeph 2:10–11 to be secondary (e.g., J. M. P. Smith, "Book of Zephaniah," 228; Rudolph, *Micha, Nahum, Habakuk, Zephanja*, 281–82; Seybold, *Satirische Prophetie*, 48; Seybold, *Nahum, Habakuk, Zephanja*, 107; Ryou, *Zephaniah's Oracles*, 302). However, the common use of the summary appraisal in oracles against both Israel (Jer 13:25) and the foreign nations (Isa 14:26–27; 17:14) along with the common association of universal homage with the day of YHWH (see below) suggest the unit's originality. See, e.g., Ball, *Rhetorical Study of Zephaniah*, 136–37; Roberts, *Nahum, Habakkuk, and Zephaniah*, 201; Floyd, *Minor Prophets, Part 2*, 223; Sweeney, *Zephaniah*, 141. Zephaniah will use a comparable summary appraisal against Assyria in 2:15a. For more on the summary appraisal, see Sweeney, *Isaiah 1–39*, 539.

specifically to the divine punishment in 2:9.[92] The retribution will come "in exchange for their pride" (תַּחַת גְּאוֹנָם), in which they "reproached" (חֵרְפוּ) and "became haughty against" (וַיַּגְדִּלוּ עַל־) God's people.[93] YHWH's retribution recalls the indictments in 2:8. "Pride" (גָּאוֹן) precedes destruction (Prov 16:18), for YHWH hates it (8:13) and will eliminate it from the world (Isa 13:11; 23:9; cf. Isa 16:6; Jer 48:29). Like Sodom before them (Ezek 16:49–50), YHWH would remove them from their high position. Designating God as "YHWH of armies" reinforces his ability to do so (Zeph 2:10c; cf. 2:9a).

With a verbless clause, Zeph 2:11a opens by declaring YHWH's present disposition toward Moab and Bene-Ammon: He is "fearsome" (נוֹרָה) toward them.[94] The most natural referent for the prepositional object suffix "them" is Moab and Bene-Ammon to whom all third-person references point in the previous verse.[95] YHWH's "fearsomeness" or "awesomeness" is that overwhelming quality associated with his incomparable character (Deut 10:17; Ps 99:3) and actions (Exod 34:10; 2 Sam 7:23).[96] It manifests itself in his wars of judgment (Exod 15:11; Deut 7:21), and it defines

the nature of his day of wrath (Joel 2:11, 31; Mal 3:23[4:5]). God willed for his people to "fear" him (Zeph 3:7) more than other gods (1 Chr 16:25; Ps 96:4), and he promised that the saved remnant would not need to "fear" evil (Zeph 3:15–16). In this context, YHWH will direct his "fearsome" quality against Moab and Bene-Ammon.

What follows in 2:11b–c is a reason why (כִּי) the hearts of Moab and Bene-Ammon should fear God in terror or worship: "He has made lean *all* [כָּל] the gods of the earth, so that *all* [כָּל] the coastlands of the nations will bow down to him, each from his place" (emphasis added).[97] Motyer notes, "All false worship will be starved out and all true worship offered."[98] The LXX and most English translations render these clauses as parallel future predictions (e.g., NRSVue, NASB20, NET, ESV).[99] However, the Hebrew uses a *qatal* verb followed by a *weyiqtol*, which commonly portrays a past-time action as complete, followed by its purpose or result.[100] The context suggests that Zephaniah uses the *qatal* as he does elsewhere to present a *future* event as being irrevocable and certain in God's mind (e.g., Zeph 1:11; 2:2, 15; 3:15, 18).[101] YHWH will have "made

---

92. Against Sabottka, Watts, and Vlaardingerbroek (Sabottka, *Zephanja*, 88–89; Watts, *The Books of Joel, Obadiah, Jonah, Nahum, Habakkuk, and Zephaniah*, 170–71; Vlaardingerbroek, *Zephaniah*, 149), rendering זֹאת as "shame" is unlikely, for its role as a demonstrative meaning "this" is firmly established, and it is commonly used in summary appraisals.

93. For the meaning of תַּחַת as "in exchange for, in return for, as payment for," see, e.g., Gen 44:4; Exod 21:25; 1 Sam 25:21; Job 28:15; Ps 35:12; Prov 17:13; Jer 18:20 ("תַּחַת I," *DCH* 8:625, §2.d).

94. Whereas the MT reads נורא as נוֹרָא ("fearsome," the *niphal* participle of ירא "to fear"), the LXX apparently read either נִרְאָה ("appeared," the *niphal* participle masculine singular of ראה "to see"), or יֵרָאֶה ("he will appear," the *niphal* yiqtol third masculine singular of ראה), for it renders the form ἐπιφανήσεται ("[the Lord] will appear," a future passive indicative third masculine singular of ἐπιφαίνω "to appear").

95. Contra Ball, *Rhetorical Study of Zephaniah*, 138.

96. Cf. Pss 65:6[5]; 66:3; 106:22; 145:6.

97. A similar logical move from lesser to greater appears in Obad 15–16.

98. Motyer, "Zephaniah," 936; cf. Baker, *Nahum, Habakkuk and Zephaniah*, 108.

99. It is possible that an initial *yod* (י) before רזה could have been lost due to haplography after כִּי (= *piel* יְרַזֶּה, "he will make lean"). However, the *qatal*→*weyiqtol* pattern found in the Masoretic Text is common and fits the context (see below). The NIV and CSB treat the כִּי clause in Zeph 2:11b as temporal and future (= "when") and 2:11c as expressing the result of the prediction in 2:11a; however, the *qatal* plus *weyiqtol* pattern is common enough to suggest that 2:11c provides the purpose or result of 2:11b.

100. The structure *qatal* plus *weyiqtol* occurs around fifty-five times in the Hebrew OT. For the clause groupings preceded by כִּי, see Gen 29:21; Job 3:13; Pss 55:14[13]; 91:14; Isa 10:13; 51:2; Jer 23:18; Lam 1:19, Ezek 47:9; Hos 4:6; 6:1.

101. This interpretation diminishes the need to emend (against, e.g., J. M. P. Smith, "Book of Zephaniah," 228–29, 31;

lean" (רָזָה) the gods of the world, in some way "starving" them of praise, perhaps by removing the worshipers who gave them food (cf. Ps 50:12–13; Ezek 44:7).[102] Also, Berlin thinks the imagery of YHWH constricting or shrinking the gods predicts him reducing the gods' territories through conquest, which is possible since the ancients closely associated gods with specific regions.[103] Regardless, YHWH will shame and defeat these spiritual forces (cf. Jer 50:2; 51:44; 51:52), depriving them of reputation, respect, and rule, as he did to Egypt's gods (cf. Exod 12:12; 15:11; 18:11).[104] By this he will show the world that no being like Baal (Zeph 1:4–5) or idols or the spiritual forces behind them (Deut 32:17; Ps 106:37)[105] is worthy of worship or trust.

Scripture portrays YHWH as the Lord of heaven and earth (Gen 14:22; Ezra 5:11),[106] the only sovereign Creator of all things visible and invisible (Exod 20:11; Ps 115:15; Isa 45:7).[107] He has no peers (Exod 20:3; Ps 89:7, 9[6, 8]), and he does not share power, authority, or jurisdiction with any other.[108] He stands not as the head of a pantheon of rival deities but as the decisive and ultimate overseer of the universe. Nevertheless, he acts within a heavenly council (Job 1:6; Ps 82:1; Jer 23:18).

The Bible refers to the members of this council variously as "gods" (אֱלֹהִים), "the sons of the gods" (בְּנֵי־הָאֱלֹהִים), "messengers/angels" (מַלְאָכִים), and "holy ones" (קְדֹשִׁים). None of them rival YHWH but are instead subordinate and subservient to him. They serve (1 Kgs 22:19), bow to (Ps 29:2), obey (103:20–21), and praise him (148:2–5). Thus, he is "the God of the gods" (Deut 10:17) and "the great King above all gods" (Ps 95:3; cf. 96:4–5). When Zephaniah declares that YHWH has famished "all the gods of the earth," he refers to these beings' representative idols or to the fallen beings themselves—spiritual beings who were never worthy of worship.

The ultimate evidence that "YHWH [will be] fearsome" against Moab and Bene-Ammon (Zeph 2:11a) is that the human inhabitants from the earth's most distant shores ("the coastlands of the nations") will turn away from their pitiful objects of worship and pay homage to the only true God (2:11c). For the first time in the book, we learn that "worship of the living God shall extend to the uttermost extremities of the earth."[109] By associating the "coastlands" (אִיִּים) with "the nations" (הַגּוֹיִם), Zephaniah focuses on the "inhabited lands" at the far-reaches of the globe.[110] The logic seems

---

Rudolph, *Micha, Nahum, Habakuk, Zephanja*, 278; Roberts, *Nahum, Habakkuk, and Zephaniah*, 193).

102. Contra Sabottka, who translates רזה here as *beherrscht* ("controlled, ruled, have dominion over," this verb most likely means "make lean, starve, famish" (cf. Isa 17:4), being related to the adjective רָזֶה ("thin, gaunt," Ezek 34:20) and the noun I-רָזוֹן ("emaciation, leanness," Isa 10:16) ("רזה I," *DCH* 7:458; cf. Sabottka, *Zephanja*, 90–91). The English versions use several translations: "shrivel" (NRSVue), "starve" (NASB20, CSB), "weaken" (NET), "famish" (ESV), "destroy" (NIV).

103. Berlin, *Zephaniah*, 110.

104. Cf. Renz, *Books of Nahum, Habakkuk, and Zephaniah*, 566.

105. Cf. 1 Cor 10:19–20.

106. Cf. Matt 11:25; Acts 17:24.

107. Cf. Rom 11:36; Eph 3:9–10; Rev 14:7; see also Col 1:16; Heb 1:2; 2:10.

108. See Walton, "Interpreting the Bible as an Ancient Near Eastern Document," 305–9; DeRouchie, "Making the Ten Count," 421–25. Heiser has similar conclusions but unhelpfully speaks of YHWH standing in a pantheon of gods (Heiser, "Monotheism, Polytheism, Monolatry, or Henotheism?," 27–30).

109. Robertson, *Books of Nahum, Habakkuk, and Zephaniah*, 302.

110. Ben Zvi suggests that context demands that we not restrict the meaning of אִיִּים to "coastlands" but should instead apply to it a more general meaning like "habitable lands" (Ben Zvi, *Book of Zephaniah*, 175; cf. Keil, " Twelve Minor Prophets," 10:451 (2:145); Ball, *Rhetorical Study of Zephaniah*, 109). While some texts like Isa 41:1, 5; 42:4; 49:1; and 51:1 could refer only to "habitable lands," the term commonly refers to a subset of the inhabited world, especially regions associated with the sea (e.g., Isa 11:11; 23:2; 24:15; 42:10; Jer 25:22; Ezek 26:18;

to be that the proof of YHWH's triumph over all the world's gods will be that even the most distant regions of the globe will recognize YHWH's greatness.[111] As Renz notes, "Those who are predicted to *offer obeisance* to YHWH in this verse do so in the knowledge that the gods to whom they used to bow down are not worthy of their worship."[112]

No nation or people should seek help from "gods" that cannot save (Isa 43:10–11; Hos 13:4) since everyone will behold God's glory and revere YHWH in that future day.[113] As YHWH swore, "To me every knee shall bow, every tongue shall swear allegiance" (Isa 45:23).[114] This act will come on a day of global judgment (Zeph 3:8) during which all peoples will honor YHWH. The text has

already mentioned the presence of a worshiping remnant who will stand in contrast to those receiving YHWH's wrath (see 2:3, 7, 9). Thus, some of those kneeling will be rebels admitting their defeat (3:15, 19; cf. Ezek 39:6; Mic 7:16–17),[115] but others will be servants praising their glorious Redeemer (Zeph 3:9–10; cf. Pss 22:28–30[27–29]; 86:9; Isa 49:7).[116]

In Zephaniah's vision, venerating YHWH on this day will not be restricted to a single place or a people. Most interpret the vision of coastal peoples bowing "each from his place" (Zeph 2:11c) to mean that Zephaniah does not restrict the praise of YHWH to either a single people or place (cf. 3:9; Isa 19:19–25; Mal 1:11, 14).[117] Some interpreters

---

27:3). Motyer suggests the term came to refer to "distant lands, especially those reached only by the sea" (Motyer, "Zephaniah," 936). Genesis links the "coastlands" (אִיִּים) to Japheth's descendants (Gen 10:5), some of whom would ultimately dwell in the tents of Shem, the peoples from whom the Messiah would rise (9:26–27). Scripture elsewhere calls those from the "coastlands" to worship YHWH (Ps 97:1; Isa 24:15; 42:10) and characterizes them as longing for his justice (Isa 42:4; 51:5) and as objects of his redeeming love (Isa 11:11; 41:5) and wrath (Jer 47:4; Ezek 26:15, 18; 39:6). Zephaniah simply states that *all* these distant lands will bow to YHWH (Zeph 2:11c).

111. Sweeney links Zeph 2:12–15 with 2:11 by identifying both Cush and Assyria among the "coastlands" (Sweeney, *Zephaniah*, 144) and by pointing to a well-known ancient world map from the eighth or seventh century BC (see Wayne Horowitz, *Mesopotamian Cosmic Geography*, Mesopotamian Civilizations [Winona Lake, IN: Eisenbrauns, 1998], 20–42, the map is on 21; cf. Eckhard Unger, "From the Cosmos Picture to the World Map," *Imago Mundi* 2 [1937]: 1–7). The map, however, suggests a cosmic reconstruction that differs from Scripture's (e.g., Gen 2 and 10), and Sweeney fails to account enough for the "also" (גַּם) at the head of 2:12, which introduces an additional unit (2:12–15) that stands paired with 2:8–11. These two work with the "woe" speech of 2:5–7 to provide four compass points around Jerusalem (*west* = Philistia, 2:5–7; *east* = Moab and Bene-Ammon, 2:8–11; *south and north* = Cush and Assyria, 2:12–15).

112. Renz, *Books of Nahum, Habakkuk, and Zephaniah*, 568.

113. Cf. Vlaardingerbroek, *Zephaniah*, 127, 150. Timmer questionably limits the mention of "the nations" in Zeph 2:11 to non-Israelites (Timmer, *Non-Israelite Nations*, 155nn9, 160).

However, the global scope of the book (e.g., Zeph 1:18; 3:8) seems to make Judah a subset of the rest of the world, allowing God's judgment against the world (1:2–3, 14–18) to fall on them (1:4–6, 8–13). Thus, Philistia's fall in 2:4 clarifies why the faithful remnant from Judah and other lands must seek YHWH (2:3).

114. Cf. Rom 14:11; Phil 2:10.

115. See also Isa 66:24; 2 Thess 1:9; Rev 21:8. Ben Zvi presents a false dichotomy regarding Zeph 2:11 when he writes, "YHWH's purpose is not to destroy nation after nation—as the series of announcements of judgement may suggest—but to bring them to bow to YHWH" (Ben Zvi, *Book of Zephaniah*, 313; cf. Berlin, *Zephaniah*, 124). *Both* rebel and remnant can bow before YHWH.

116. See also Ps 66:4; 2 Thess 1:10. Furthermore, at the cross Christ *already* "disarmed the rulers and authorities . . . by triumphing over them" (Col 2:15). The OT names these spiritual powers "gods," against which Christians today battle (Eph 6:12). Yet, these very powers and rulers were created *by* (i.e., "in") Christ and *for* Christ, so that in conquering them on our behalf God might display his Son's preeminence (Col 1:15–18). The Father's worship is inseparable from the praise offered to his royal Son (Phil 2:10–11; Rev 5:8–14; cf. Ps 2:7–12; Heb 2:6–9). For God's salvation of some from Judah and the nations and his destruction of others, see Daniel C. Timmer, "The Non-Israelite Nations in Zephaniah: Conceptual Coherence and the Relationship of the Parts to the Whole," in *The Book of the Twelve and the New Form Criticism*, ed. Mark J. Boda, Michael H. Floyd, and Colin M. Toffelmire (Atlanta: SBL Press, 2015), 253.

117. Cf. John 4:21–24.

believe this image contrasts with those texts that envision some from the nations gathering to YHWH's presence at the newly extended mountain of God (Zeph 3:10; cf. Isa 2:3; Jer 3:16–17).[118] Keil, on the other hand, proposes that the preposition מִן ("from") on מִמְּקוֹמוֹ ("from his place") implies the peoples going to Jerusalem.[119] Such may be the case. However, the prophets affirm both realities, and Zephaniah elsewhere seems to retain both images side by side (Zeph 3:9–10), which suggests they may refer to the same truth from different vantage points. Thus, the prophets likely foresaw a time when YHWH's presence, symbolized in the image of a new Jerusalem, would fill the whole earth, making Jerusalem and the new creation co-terminous.[120] In such a setting, people could both "come" to meet YHWH's presence while remaining where they were.

Hope existed for a remnant from Moab and Bene-Ammon. For the majority, though, Isaiah's earlier words express Zephaniah's expectation: "And [YHWH] will humble the haughtiness of the human, and he will bring down the pride of men. And YHWH alone will be exalted in that day" (Isa 2:17). Since God would devastate these proud neighbors to the east, Judah herself should expect to receive YHWH's fury unless they "seek humility" (2:3c)![121]

(2) Against the Cushites to the South and Assyria to the North (2:12–15)

The "also" (גַּם) at the head of 2:12 indicates that the text-block running from 2:12–15 is distinct from yet complementary to the preceding discussion of Moab and Bene-Ammon.[122] Having confronted peoples west and east of Judah, Zephaniah's compass of judgment continues by highlighting the Cushites to the south and the Assyrians to the north.

(a) The Context for Assyria's Demise: The Slaying of the Cushites (2:12)

Zephaniah 2:12 opens with YHWH directly addressing the Cushites with a second person plural pronoun plus vocative phrase ("Also *you*, O Cushites"). He spoke to the Philistines in the second person plural (2:5b), but here he immediately turns and declares the Cushites' destruction using a third-personal plural pronoun ("slain by my sword are *they*").

Scholars do not agree on the "Cushites" identity here. Some consider them Egyptians,[123] though perhaps referring to Egypt's Twenty-fifth Cushite Dynasty, which fell in 663 BC.[124] Viewing the Cushites as "Egyptians" is questionable for (1) the OT never equates Cush with Egypt, (2) Cush normally cannot mean Egypt,[125] and (3) the only text

---

118. Cf. Isa 45:14; 56:6–7; 66:20; Mic 4:1; Zech 8:20–23; 14:16. See also Baker, *Nahum, Habakkuk and Zephaniah*, 108; Robertson, *Books of Nahum, Habakkuk, and Zephaniah*, 308; Roberts, *Nahum, Habakkuk, and Zephaniah*, 202; Vlaardingerbroek, *Zephaniah*, 150.

119. Keil, " Twelve Minor Prophets," 10:451 (2:145).

120. Cf. Isa 4:2–6; 65:17–19; Jer 3:16–18; Rev 21:1–2, 9–27.

121. Cf. Robertson, *Books of Nahum, Habakkuk, and Zephaniah*, 307.

122. Most scholars agree with this conclusion. However, Ball's view that גַּם is an emphatic particle introducing a phrase dependent on the previous one results in this translation: "so that all the coastlands of the nations will bow down to him . . . Even you, O Cushites" (Ball, *Rhetorical Study of Zephaniah*,

140). This interpretation is doubtful since it (1) understands the "them" of Zeph 2:11a as "the gods" rather than Moab and Bene-Ammon and (2) connects "slain by my sword are they" to the subsequent Assyrians rather than to the more immediate Cushites (see pp. 140–43).

123. J. M. P. Smith, "Book of Zephaniah," 232, 236; Christensen, "Zephaniah 2:4–15," 677; Baker, *Nahum, Habakkuk and Zephaniah*, 108; Sweeney, "Form-Critical Reassessment," 390; Vlaardingerbroek, *Zephaniah*, 129, 152; Patterson, *Nahum, Habakkuk, Zephaniah*, 311–12.

124. So, e.g., Christensen, Sweeney, and Patterson (see below).

125. E.g., Gen 10:6; Isa 20:3, 4; 43:3; Ezek 29:10; 30:5.

mentioning a Cushite king of Egypt names him "Cush's king," not Egypt's (2 Kgs 19:9//Isa 37:9).[126] Others suggest the "Cushites" are the Kassites of Mesopotamia,[127] whom Berlin describes as "the descendants of the forebearer of the Assyrian empire."[128] However, Haak correctly comments that the Mesopotamian Kassite kingdom ended around 1160 BC toward the close of the Late Bronze Age[129] and that there is no clear reason why Zephaniah would refer to them here.[130]

Haak himself equates the "Cushites" of Zeph 2:12 with nomadic peoples living in Arabia and southern Judah in the Judean monarchy's latter days.[131] We know a colony of "Cushite" mercenaries existed in Gerar of the northern Negeb between the tenth and eighth centuries BC (1 Chr 4:39–41; 2 Chr 12:3; 14:9–15; 21:16). But Sweeney is correct in saying that these nomadic peoples were probably not significant enough to warrant mentioning, especially when compared to the Edomites, who also go unmentioned.[132] Moreover, the "Cushites" of 2:12 are most naturally associated with the region of "Cush" in 3:10, whose rivers are probably

the White and Blue Nile rather than any waters of the Sinai or northern Arabia.[133] Thus, Zephaniah probably associated the "Cushites" with the African kingdom centralized south of ancient Egypt in the region of modern Sudan.[134]

These Cushites descended from Noah's son Ham, along with Egypt, Put, and Canaan (Gen 10:6). This kingdom of Cush was one of the ancient world's most southern and western empires (see Esth 1:1).[135] If Zephaniah was indeed biracial with mixed Judean and Cushite ancestry (see Zeph 1:1), his mention of Cush here would show his unwillingness to shy away from their guilt, though he would later celebrate the redemption of their remnant (3:9–10).[136] At times Israel looked to these Cushites rather than to God for help (Isa 20:5–6),[137] but YHWH here declares their judgment and with that his sufficiency (cf. Isa 18:1–6; 20:3–4; Ezek 30:4–5).

After initial direct address, the unit opens with YHWH describing the state of the Cushites as "slain by my sword" (חַלְלֵי חַרְבִּי).[138] This predicate adjective phrase is a construct chain that includes

---

126. Ben Zvi, *Book of Zephaniah*, 176–77.

127. Ball, *Rhetorical Study of Zephaniah*, 141, 244–52; Berlin, *Zephaniah*, 112–13; Berlin, "Zephaniah's Oracle against the Nations," 179–80.

128. Berlin, *Zephaniah*, 113; Berlin, "Zephaniah's Oracle against the Nations," 180.

129. See Hallo and Simpson, *The Ancient Near East*, 98, 103–6.

130. Haak, "'Cush' in Zephaniah," 242.

131. Haak, "'Cush' in Zephaniah," 238–51. Both Berlin and Sweeney state that Haak identifies the southern "Cushites" with the Midianites (Sweeney, *Zephaniah*, 147; cf. Berlin, *Zephaniah*, 112; Berlin, "Zephaniah's Oracle against the Nations," 179), but Haak explicitly rejects this equation (Haak, "'Cush' in Zephaniah," 243n16).

132. Sweeney, *Zephaniah*, 147; cf. Berlin, *Zephaniah*, 112; Berlin, "Zephaniah's Oracle against the Nations," 179. In contrast to Haak and with Berlin and Sweeney, Hab 3:7 likely equates the peoples of "Cushan" with the Midianites since other sources locate a district known as Kushan in the same region as Midian (Albright, *Archaeology and the Religion of Israel*,

205n49) and Moses's wife mentioned in Num 12:1 could have been a "Cush[an]ite" (rather than a "Cushite") and therefore be the same as the "Midianite" Zipporah (Exod 2:15–22) (so Noth, *Numbers*, 98; Smith, "Ethiopia (Place)," *ABD* 2:666). For more on Moses's marriage to a Cush[an]ite, see the footnote in the exposition of Zeph 1:1.

133. So too Sweeney, *Zephaniah*, 148.

134. See David O'Connor, "The Locations of Yam and Kush and the Their Historical Implications," *JARCE* 23 (1986): 27–50.

135. See Smith, "Ethiopia (Place)," *ABD* 2:665–67; Redford, "Kush (Place)," *ABD* 4:109–11.

136. Rice, "African Roots of the Prophet Zephaniah," 29.

137. For a historical overview of Judah's alliance with the Twenty-fifth Cushite Dynasty of Egypt, see Rice, "African Roots of the Prophet Zephaniah," 25–27.

138. To keep all of Zeph 2:12 in third person, O'Connor proposes that חַרְבִּי ("my sword") may be better read חֶרֶב י, with the *yod* (י) being a rare abbreviation for the name YHWH (יְהוָה) (O'Connor, *Hebrew Verse Structure*, 253). However, because similar switches in person occur elsewhere both in and outside Zephaniah (e.g., Ezek 28:22; see GKC, §141g–h), and because

an adjective and possessive noun. Its fronted placement before the subject "they" (הֵמָּה) highlights their horrific state, likely to provide a contextual backdrop for the following confrontation against Assyria (see below). The idea of being "slain by sword" is common in the Prophets,[139] but only this text associates this phrase directly with YHWH (cf. Isa 66:16; Jer 25:33). Nevertheless, Scripture commonly portrays YHWH as a warrior who uses his "sword" (חֶרֶב) to deliver his people (Deut 33:29) and to punish his enemies (32:25, 41–42; Ps 17:13).[140] Often the sword imagery is figurative for curses like plague (1 Chr 21:12). Other times it refers to a physical sword wielded either by the angel of YHWH (Josh 5:13; 1 Chr 21:30; cf. Gen 3:24) or by human agents of God's wrath (e.g., Ezek 21:24; 32:11). Here YHWH neither clarifies the nature of or reason for the Cushites' destruction. We simply know they are slain.

Most English versions render the verbless clause in Zeph 2:12 as future (e.g., NRSVue, NASB20, NET, ESV, NIV, CSB). With this reading, Zephaniah could envision Saite Egyptian Pharoah Psammetichus II's campaign against

the Cushites in 593/592 BC, Nebuchadnezzar of Babylon's invasions into the south in 568/67 BC (see Jer 43:10–13; Ezek 29:19; 30:25; 32:11), or Cambyses II of Persia's defeat of both Cush and Egypt around 525 BC.

However, both the disjunctive nature of 2:12 (brought about by the גַּם, "also") and its lack of verbal specificity suggests the verse instead functions transitionally and refers "to a present condition or even to a status that originated in the past."[141] On this reading, the slaying of the Cushites would have *already* happened, most likely when the Twenty-fifth Cushite Dynasty of Egypt fell in 663 BC, one generation *prior* to Zephaniah's preaching (see Isa 20:3–6). The Cushites controlled Egypt from ca. 715–663 BC, but the Assyrians overthrew them under Assurbanipal's rule.[142] Their relatively recent downfall explains the prophet's brevity since the audience would be familiar with the event.[143]

Zephaniah uses Cush's past demise by YHWH's sword as proof that the superpower Assyria, highlighted in the following verses, would also fall (Zeph 2:13–15). As Christensen notes, "Assyria's greatest military achievements were attained under the

---

the divine name is never abbreviated elsewhere in the book, the need for emendation is unlikely (so too Roberts, *Nahum, Habakkuk, and Zephaniah*, 193n19; Berlin, *Zephaniah*, 113).

139. E.g., Isa 22:2; Jer 14:18; Ezek 31:17–18; 32:20–21; Zeph 2:12; cf. Num 19:16; Lam 4:9.

140. God directs his sword against Assyria (Isa 31:8), Edom (Isa 34:5–6), Philistia (Jer 47:6), Cush (Zeph 2:12), and Israel (Jer 9:16; 12:12; Ezek 21:8[3]; cf. Ezek 32:11).

141. Ben Zvi, *Book of Zephaniah*, 179, 304. Renz is right that Zeph 2:12 is "a statement about status rather than about an event," though an event that caused the situation is implied (Renz, *Books of Nahum, Habakkuk, and Zephaniah*, 569).

142. For this interpretation, see, e.g., Watts, *The Books of Joel, Obadiah, Jonah, Nahum, Habakkuk, and Zephaniah*, 172; Christensen, "Zephaniah 2:4–15," 681; Floyd, *Minor Prophets, Part 2*, 212–13; Sweeney, *Zephaniah*, 146; Renz, *Books of Nahum, Habakkuk, and Zephaniah*, 569. On the composition and fall of the Twenty-fifth Cushite Dynasty in Egypt, see Hallo and Simpson, *The Ancient Near East*, 287–90; Anthony Spal-

inger, "Egypt, History of: 3rd Intermediate–Saite Period (Dyn. 21–26)," *ABD* 2:359–60.

143. At least six observations support reading Zeph 2:12 as a reference to the fall of Egypt's Twenty-fifth Cushite dynasty and as transitioning into a unit focused principally on Assyria's demise. First, one must explain why Zephaniah's words against the Cushites are the briefest among his oracles against the foreign nations. Furthermore, 2:12 is the only statement that is not explicitly future. Instead, by nature the verbless clause gives only background information and gets its tense from the context; in this case, the historical event was well-known. Within the literary flow, 2:12 is a rhetorical aside that describes the present (cf. Floyd, *Minor Prophets, Part 2*, 226). Second, fronting the predicate adjectival phrase ("slain by my sword") before the subject "they" (הֵמָּה) focuses attention on the dreadful state of Cush. It also naturally provides a setting for understanding the subsequent confrontation against Assyria. Third, Zephaniah's argument seems to parallel that of his potential contemporary, Nahum. He highlighted Assyria's 663 BC destruction of the

providence of Yhwh."[144] Though they once served as his "rod of . . . anger," he would bring them down (Isa 10:5–12; Zeph 2:13–15).[145] Within the flow of the book, this southern kingdom's overthrow signals "that a great transformation has already begun, one that will eventually include his overthrow of a northern nation also."[146] And if Assyria falls, what would it mean for Judah?

(b) The Declaration of Assyria's Demise (2:13–15)

The connector *waw* (וֹ) at the head of 2:13 indicates "the thematic connection" linking the Cushites' fall (at the hand of the Assyrians) and Assyria's future defeat.[147] The Cushites' downfall in 2:12, therefore, signals Assyria's demise in 2:13–15. The prophet uses a chain of three *weyiqtols* (2:13a–c) and a *weqatal* (2:14a). First position *weyiqtol* forms usually are non-indicative, expressing the speaker's wish, will, or a purpose for a previous activity, and they appear to function this way here.[148] Instead of rendering all four verbs as future like most English versions and commentators do, the *weyiqtols* are more likely volitional, conveying the prophet's prayerful plea, and the *weqatal* signals the result of Zephaniah's hopes. Specifically, the prophet first provides a general plea for Assyria's demise (2:13a–b) and then expresses a specific plea for Nineveh's desolation (2:13c–15): "So may he [YHWH] stretch out his hand against the north and destroy Assyria. Then may he place Nineveh for a desolation, dry as the wilderness, with the result that in her midst herds will lie down—every beast of a nation" (2:13–14a).[149] In Motyer's words, "It is as if Zephaniah were himself caught up in the divine program and was urging it on to completion."[150] Following the specific appeal comes a promise of the certainty of destruction (2:14b–15).

• A General Plea for Assyria's Demise (2:13a–b)

Echoing the imprecatory psalms[151] and YHWH's promised actions against Judah (Zeph 1:4), Zephaniah opens with a general but passionate plea for

---

Cushite Egyptian capital "Thebes" to stress how YHWH would destroy Assyria as well (Nah 3:8–13) (cf. Floyd, *Minor Prophets, Part 2*, 210, 212–13). Fourth, Zephaniah gives no reason for God's anger with the Cushites. This silence suggests the event is in the past, needing no rationale. In contrast God is punishing Philistia for negatively influencing Judah (Zeph 1:11) and not depending on YHWH (2:3–4), Moab and Bene-Ammon for their pride (2:10), and Assyria for her proud boasts (2:15). Fifth, whereas *future* prospects of divine fury against the nations fill the book, the prophet notes that YHWH had already "cut off nations" but that Judah had failed to fear (3:6–7). The reference to the Cushites' demise in 2:12 would refer to one such defeat, suggesting that "YHWH has already begun his campaign against the nations" (Timmer, *Non-Israelite Nations*, 156). Sixth, the stress of 2:5–15 on God's passion to punish the world's pride (2:8, 10, 15; cf. 2:3) starting possibly with Cush in the south (2:12) and moving northward to Mesopotamia (2:13–15) aligns with 3:9–10's vision. There God would begin reversing the tower of Babel episode (which human pride initiated, Gen 11:4) by creating a group of worshipers from beyond the region of Cush. Zephaniah apparently focuses on universal restoration arising from this kingdom center (3:9–10) because God started the world's spiritual cleansing in Cush (2:12)

(Floyd, *Minor Prophets, Part 2*, 211–13). Therefore, based on grammar and literary flow (1–2), biblical-historical context (3), literary-historical context (4–5), and literary-theological context (6), Zeph 2:12 most likely refers to the Twenty-fifth Egyptian Cushite Dynasty's past destruction.

144. Christensen, "Zephaniah 2:4–15," 681.

145. For more on God's use of the other nations to chasten Israel, see Jer 5:15–17; 49:37; Ezek 5:16; Hos 8:14; Joel 2:25; Amos 6:14; Hab 1:12.

146. Floyd, *Minor Prophets, Part 2*, 226.

147. Renz, *Books of Nahum, Habakkuk, and Zephaniah*, 571.

148. See GKC, §109b; Joüon, §114g–h; S. R. Driver, *A Treatise on the Use of the Tenses in Hebrew*, 3rd ed. (Oxford: Clarendon, 1892), §172.

149. A first-position *yiqtol* can function like an indicative future (GKC, §109k; Joüon, §114, l), but the more common volitional use is likely here.

150. Motyer, "Zephaniah," 936; cf. Keil, "Twelve Minor Prophets," 10:452 (2:147); Robertson, *Books of Nahum, Habakkuk, and Zephaniah*, 312.

151. See, e.g., Pss 10:15; 28:4; 35:4–6; 109:6–15; 137:8–9; 139:19–22. See also John N. Day, "The Imprecatory Psalms and Christian Ethics," *BSac* 159 (2002): 166–86.

God to "stretch out his hand" of vengeance into the north and to destroy Assyria (2:13a–b).[152] The term commonly rendered "the north" (צָפוֹן) usually has no article, stands as the top compass point, and marks the region from which God's agents of destruction usually originate.[153] Assyria invaded the region of Israel from the north (Isa 14:31), and from here Babylon would overtake Judah (Jer 25:9; cf. 27:5–8) and her neighbors (Ezek 26:7; cf. Jer 43:10–13).[154] The north is also the center of Baal's reign in Canaanite mythology (*spn* = Hebrew צָפוֹן),[155] which suggests that Zephaniah may have seen Assyria as the infecting source of much of Judah's troubles (see Zeph 1:4–6).

The superpower Assyria controlled the Near East from 870–626 BC and had conquered Israel's capital Samaria in 723 BC, resulting in the northern kingdom's exile (2 Kgs 17; cf. Isa 10:5). Their barbaric war tactics were notorious throughout the world, and the prophet Nahum devoted his entire book to Assyria's impending doom.[156] In the past, YHWH had employed them as "the rod of my anger" against Israel (Isa 10:5). He had also promised that when he finished his work with Assyria, he would "visit [punishment] on the fruit of the greatness of the heart of Assyria's king and on the splendor of the height of his eyes" (10:12). Now, Zephaniah pleaded with YHWH to fulfill his earlier declaration.

- A Specific Plea and Promise of Nineveh's Desolation (2:13c–15)

– The Plea for Her Desolation (2:13c–14a)

Indeed, Zephaniah next focuses on Nineveh, Assyria's capital in the empire's last few decades.[157] He entreats YHWH to destroy it (Zeph 2:13c–14a), promises its desolation (2:14b–e), and then gives a summary appraisal (2:15). Nineveh was rich in agriculture, nestled on the Tigris River's east bank just downstream from the Kurdish mountains' foothills.[158] Zephaniah uses the pattern set at the garden of Eden, where mankind's sin moved God to curse the ground (Gen 3:17–18).[159] He initially asks YHWH to make Nineveh like a dry wasteland

---

152. Context alone determines whether the name אַשּׁוּר (*'aššûr*) refers to the city, the land, the empire, and even the chief Assyrian deity. So far, Zephaniah has only mentioned cities that represent named nations (e.g., Jerusalem for Judah; Gaza, Ashkelon, Ashdod, and Ekron for Philistia). Thus, אַשּׁוּר here probably refers to the nation of "Assyria" and not the former capital "Assur" (cf. Berlin, *Zephaniah*, 114; contra Roberts, *Nahum, Habakkuk, and Zephaniah*, 203).

153. Though Assyria is northeast of Judah, most Mesopotamian movements related to trade or war came from the north since they had to circle the intervening northern Arabian desert.

154. The Hebrew Bible seldom names God's northern agents of punishment, but history's progress has disclosed at least the most immediate referents—e.g., Assyria (Isa 14:31), Babylon (Jer 46:10, 20, 24; 47:2), and Persia (50:3, 9, 42; 51:48). Still, the northern enemy's frequent anonymity (e.g., Isa 41:25; Jer 1:13–15; cf. Amos 3:11) allows these nations to anticipate a greater, unidentified final enemy (Ezek 38:6, 15; 39:2; cf. Rev 20:7–10), whom God would crush (Ezek 39:1–6; cf. Isa 14:25; Joel 2:20). Also, against the Babylon king's claim to sovereignty in the "north" (Isa 14:13), the biblical authors polemicized Bab-

ylon by figuratively locating YHWH's throne at Mount Zion in the "north" (Ps 48:3[2]) and portraying his glorious theophanic presence as coming from there (Job 37:22; Isa 2:12–17; Ezek 1:4). See Schmidt, "צָפוֹן *ṣāpôn* north," *TLOT* 3:1094–95.

155. See Richard J. Clifford, *The Cosmic Mountain in Canaan and the Old Testament* (Eugene, OR: Wipf & Stock, 2010), 58–97.

156. Assyria often terrorized small communities with horrific brutality to encourage submission to its rule. For a discussion, see A. Kirk Grayson, "Assyrian Rule of Conquered Territory in Ancient Western Asia," in *CANE*, ed. Jack M. Sasson (Peabody, MA: Hendrickson, 2001), 1:959–68, esp. 1:959–61). For an example from the annals of Assurnasirpal II (ca. 884–858 BC), see A. Kirk Grayson, *Assyrian Rulers of the Early First Millennium BC: I [1114–859 BC]*, The Royal Inscriptions of Mesopotamia: Assyrian Periods 2 (Toronto: University of Toronto Press, 1987), 201.

157. Because he mistakenly dated Nineveh's fall, Luther was convinced that this entire unit pointed to Babylon's downfall rather than Nineveh's (Luther, "Lectures on Zephaniah," 346).

158. A. Kirk Grayson, "Nineveh (Place)," *ABD* 4:1118–19.

159. Cf. Motyer, "Zephaniah," 937.

(cf. Nah 3:7), so that "herds" (עֲדָרִים) would "lie down" in her midst, replacing humans (Zeph 2:13–14a; cf. Jer 51:43).[160] The noun "herd, flock" (עֵדֶר) normally refers to domesticated animals like sheep or goats (e.g., Gen 29:8; Isa 32:14), but the larger context suggests a difference from the "grazing lands" predicted for Philistia (Zeph 2:6).[161] Instead, the prophet adds the appositional phrase "every beast of a nation" (כָּל־חַיְתוֹ־גוֹי) to broaden the scope to include both domesticated (e.g., Num 35:3; Isa 46:1) and wild (e.g., Ps 104:11; Isa 43:20) animals.[162] Berlin rightly sees here "a certain irony in the picture of Assyria being overrun by other nations' wildlife, even as Assyria overran and gained control of many of its neighbors."[163]

– The Promise of Her Desolation (2:14b–e)

The vision of an arid and untamed wilderness then continues in three statements clarifying Nineveh's complete devastation (Zeph 2:14b–d).[164] Together, these statements depict the tops (capitals), middles (windows), and bottoms (thresholds)

of structures. The prophet shifts from plea to promise, adding with fresh certainty various evidences of Nineveh's coming destruction. The particle "even" (גַּם) begins 2:14b showing that the clause builds on the previous statements by noting two types of animals that will dwell at the ornamental capitals atop the pillars.

Scholars are unsure about the identity of the creatures, but the desert-like setting after God's curse (2:13c) limits the options. Most of the versions (Tg. Neb., Peshitta, Vulgate) render קָאַת as "pelican," the LXX translates it "chameleon," and others suggest "goose," "jackdaw," "hawk," or "owl."[165] Only the latter three are possible since this term refers to unclean winged creatures (Lev 11:18; Deut 14:17), relates to the verb "vomit" (קָא, קִיא, i.e., regurgitate),[166] and occurs in a dry environment (Zeph 2:13c; cf. Ps 102:7[6]; Isa 34:10–11).[167] In a poetic historical turn, the presence of such a bird in Nineveh's ruins also shows how this once glorious city had become the residence for the ceremonially defiled.[168]

---

160. On the enormity of such transformation, see J. M. P. Smith, "Book of Zephaniah," 233.

161. Cf. Floyd, *Minor Prophets, Part 2*, 227.

162. The phrase כָּל־חַיְתוֹ־גוֹי ("every beast of a nation") is a construct chain with the paragogic וֹ in חַיְתוֹ being the remains of an early accusative case ending (GKC, §90o; Joüon, §93r; cf. e.g., Gen 1:24; Pss 50:10; 104:11; Isa 56:9). The use of "nation" (גּוֹי) here is unique, with Joel 1:6 being the only other place where גּוֹי occurs in relation to animals. There it means something like "swarm," which suggests to some that meaning here (= "all the beasts [living in] *flocks*"; see, e.g., Keil, "Twelve Minor Prophets," 10:452 (2:147); Barthelemy et al., *Prophetical Books II*, 5:378). As such, scholars have proposed many emendations. The *BHS* suggests that גּוֹי arose through confusion with the following גַּם and that we should insert הַשָּׂדֶה ("the field"), as in Ps 104:11. Others replace גּוֹי with שָׂדַי ("my field," J. M. P. Smith, "Book of Zephaniah," 236–37; Roberts, *Nahum, Habakkuk, and Zephaniah*, 193); נָוֶה ("field, meadow," Rudolph, *Micha, Nahum, Habakuk, Zephanja*, 276, 278; Roberts, *Nahum, Habakkuk, and Zephaniah*, 193); גַּיְא ("valley," Seybold, *Satirische Prophetie*, 53); or בְּגֵוָה ("in her self," Vlaardingerbroek, *Zephaniah*, 157), among others. Yet, the concept of "nation" commonly included factors like ethnicity, theology, kingship, language, and *territory* (see Block, "Nations," *ISBE* 3:492–96; Block, "Nations/Nationality," *NIDOTTE* 4:966–69; R. E. Clements and G. Johannes Botterweck, "גּוֹי *gôy*," *TDOT* 2:428–29), so no need exists for emendation (so too Sweeney, *Zephaniah*, 153).

163. Berlin, *Zephaniah*, 115.

164. Motyer, "Zephaniah," 937.

165. See "קָאַת, קָאַת," *HALOT* 1059–60; "קָאַת I" and "קָאַת II," *DCH* 7:169.

166. Cf. Prov 26:11. So G. R. Driver, "Birds in the Old Testament: I. Birds in Law," *PEQ* 87 (1955): 16.

167. Cf. Isa 34:11; Zeph 2:14; Ps 102:7[6]. Driver's proposal of a "scops owl" fits these criteria (Driver, "Birds in the Old Testament: I. Birds in Law," 16). Haupt's identification with a "pelican" seems unlikely since Nineveh would be "dry as the wilderness" (Zeph 2:13c) and the pelican does not regurgitate its food (Paul Haupt, "Pelican and Bittern," *JBL* 39.3–4 [1920]: 158–61).

168. Robertson, *Books of Nahum, Habakkuk, and Zephaniah*, 313.

Similarly, most ancient versions (LXX, Tg. Neb., Vulgate) render קפֹד as "hedgehog," but the Peshitta translates it "owl," and others propose "porcupine," "bittern," or "bustard."[169] The hedgehog would likely not dwell atop a column, but the porcupine could. However, in a similar context describing Edom's destruction (Isa 34:11), the term appears in a list of four creatures including three birds, which suggests קפֹד is also a bird. The most likely candidates are an owl or the bustard, not only because of the dry environment but also because the root meaning "roll up" (קפד) likely points to the way the animal's neck can get thick or bunched up.[170]

Regardless, in the absence of humans, hoots and howls from unclean animals will now ring from the windows of buildings (Zeph 2:14c).[171] Moreover, by using a descriptive verbless clause with a summative sense, the prophet envisions "devastation" (חֹרֶב)[172] resting at the entrance threshold (סַף) when (כִּי) YHWH lays bare the strong, imported cedar fram-

ing (cf. 2 Kgs 19:23).[173] The imagery highlights the devastation of a former sign of grandeur and security (Zeph 2:14d–e; cf. Ezek 31:3; Jer 22:4–15). This destruction may arise from the removal of its gold overlay (e.g., 1 Kgs 6:20–22) or, more likely, exposure to the elements due to destroyed doors.[174] The definite nature of "*the* threshold" (הַסַּף) may suggest that the city's main gate, palace, or center of city government is in view. If the threshold refers to the entrance to Nineveh's main temple, Zephaniah could be alluding to the pagan gods' demise (see Zeph 2:11).[175] However, the prophet likely used the parallel form מִפְתָּן ("threshold") in 1:9 to refer to Jerusalem's *temple* threshold, so the alternative term here likely points in another direction.[176]

– The Appraisal of Her Desolation (2:15)

The prophet now gives a summary appraisal of Nineveh's end (Zeph 2:15), much as he did for Moab and Bene-Ammon (2:10–11).[177] The demonstrative pronoun "This" (זֹאת) refers to

---

169. See "קפֹד" *HALOT* 1117; "קפֹד I" and "קפֹד II," *DCH* 7:274.

170. Driver reasonably claims the קפֹד as a "ruffed bustard" (G. R. Driver, "Birds in the Old Testament: II. Birds in Life," *PEQ* 87 [1955]: 137). Haupt's link with the "bittern" is unlikely since its neck lacks thickness and it is drawn to water (Haupt, "Pelican and Bittern," 160–61).

171. Elsewhere the verb שִׁיר refers only to human singing, but Scripture does speak of birds "giving sound/voice" (Ps 104:12), of "the sound of the bird" (Eccl 12:4), and of spring being "the time of the song" when "the sound of the turtledove is heard in our land" (Song 2:12). After extensive assessment, Renz concludes that the singer must be from "among the animals" (Renz, *Books of Nahum, Habakkuk, and Zephaniah*, 574).

172. The LXX, Vulgate, and some contemporary versions (e.g., NRSVue, NJPS) and scholars read עֹרֵב ("raven") instead of חֹרֶב ("devastation") (cf. Vlaardingerbroek, *Zephaniah*, 155). The gutturals ע and ח are at times confused on oral grounds, and reading "raven" fits the context. Yet, the shift to חֹרֶב seems more difficult to explain, thus giving priority to the MT as it stands (so too Ben Zvi, *Book of Zephaniah*, 181–82). Following Aquila and Symmachus, Sabottka and O'Connor read חֶרֶב ("sword") instead of חֹרֶב ("devastation"), but this is a minority

tradition and there is no need to deviate from the MT (Sabottka, *Zephanja*, 92; O'Connor, *Hebrew Verse Structure*, 254).

173. See also 1 Kgs 5:6; 7:2; Ezra 3:7.

174. Cf. Sweeney, *Zephaniah*, 154.

175. In this reading, the כִּי could be causal (= "for/because") allowing the exposed cedar work to prove that YHWH has defeated Assyria's gods, thus bringing "devastation . . . at the threshold."

176. For more on the relationship of מִפְתָּן and סַף, see the commentary at Zeph 1:9. Many Assyrian palaces, especially in the days of Ashurbanipal, had reliefs depicting hunting raids against wild animals. Thus, Berlin suggests 2:13–14 is "playing on the artistic menagerie in Assyrian palaces and turning it into a vision of destruction and ruin" (Berlin, *Zephaniah*, 116).

177. For the integral role 2:15 plays in the unit, see Ryou, *Zephaniah's Oracles*, 303–4; Floyd, *Minor Prophets, Part 2*, 227. The LXX's versification has 3:1 at what is 2:15 in the MT, suggesting that 2:15 starts the statements of punishment against Jerusalem. The use of הוֹי ("Woe!"), however, at the head of 2:5 and 3:1 in the MT marks each unit's beginning. Vlaardingerbroek believes 2:15 gives the words of the "song" from 2:14c (Vlaardingerbroek, *Zephaniah*, 161), but three reasons make this unlikely. (1) It is strange that a bird would "sing" words

Zephaniah's description of Nineveh (2:13–14). The whole clause marks the city's proud delight as basis for her destruction: "This is the exultant city [הָעִיר הָעַלִּיזָה]—the one dwelling in security,[178] the one saying in her heart, 'I am, and my limit is still [unreached]'" (2:15a–c).

The Hebrew אֲנִי וְאַפְסִי עוֹד occurs in Zeph 2:15b–c and Isa 47:8, 10. Traditionally, scholars have rendered it, "I am/exist, and there is no one else/besides me" (e.g., NRSVue, NASB20, ESV, CSB; cf. NET, NIV), which may capture the sense.[179] My approach follows Isaiah's use of אֶפֶס, which likely influenced Zeph 2:15. Building on the noun's basic meaning of "end," Isaiah consistently applies אֶפֶס in the sense of "limit" or "terminus" of (1) space (Isa 45:22; 52:10), (2) God's greatness (45:14), (3) God's existence (45:6; 46:9), (4) God's purposes (46:9; 54:14), or (5) human life or activity (34:12; 40:17; 41:12, 29).[180] In this light, the use of אֶפֶס in Zeph 2:15c and Isa 47:8, 10 recalls Isa 45:14 ("God is in you [Jerusalem], and there is not still an end of God['s greatness]"), so that Nineveh is claiming, "I am, and my limit [of greatness] is still [unreached]." Like Babylon after her (Isa 47:8, 10),

Nineveh perceived no end of her magnificence, yet God would not tolerate such pride (42:8; 45:5; cf. 46:9).[181]

YHWH detests triumphal arrogance that trusts human might instead of him (Pss 118:8–9; 146:3; Isa 2:22)[182] and elevates self at others' expense (Deut 24:14; Prov 18:5; 22:16).[183] Motyer notes, "In Moab pride looked outward and denigrated others; in Assyria pride looks inward and finds everything to delight: personal uniqueness, superiority, complacency, security."[184] Isaiah earlier declared that "exultant" (עַלִּיז) Jerusalem (Isa 22:2; 32:13) and Tyre (23:7) were objects of God's wrath, and he also noted that YHWH's curse on the world would end such self-"exultation" (24:8; cf. 2:17; 10:12; 47:8). Zephaniah already showed how rejoicing in self-security is dangerous (Zeph 2:8, 10),[185] and the prophet would later emphasize how YHWH would remove those exulting (עַלִּיז) in Jerusalem's pride (3:11; cf. 3:14). Nineveh's confidence was a false-security, and their destruction was both certain and imminent with such a disposition.

By using a *qatal* form of היה ("to be, become"), Zephaniah talks as if Nineveh's punishment were

---

comprehended by humans. (2) The form of 2:15 naturally aligns with that of a summary appraisal. (3) Zephaniah 2:14d separates 2:15 from 2:14c. Even if one reads "raven" (עֹרֵב) instead of "devastation" (חֹרֶב) in 2:14d, as Vlaardingerbroak does, the song comes from the window (2:14c) and not the threshold (2:14d), suggesting that the raven does *not* sing the song. Indeed, ravens croak or caw and do not sing.

178. Reading לָבֶטַח as "in security" treats the preposition as a לְ of accompaniment, meaning "in, with" (so "בֶּטַח I," *DCH* 2:141). Roberts aligns with the NJPS, suggesting we should read this entire clause as an unmarked question: "Is this the exultant city ... ?" (Roberts, *Nahum, Habakkuk, and Zephaniah*, 194n28, 204).

179. Gesenius proposed a similar translation, believing that the *hireq-yod* (י) on וְאַפְסִי was an old accusative ending and that אַפְסִי was in construct with עוֹד (GKC, §§90, l, 152s). In contrast, Muraoka sees אֶפֶס as a negative and views the *hireq-yod* as a genuine first common singular pronominal suffix and not an archaic ending. He translates the whole, "Me, and *my exclu-*

sivity still (is)," which he believes means, "I, and I exclusively (= I alone), I exist!" (Joüon, §160n).

180. The basic meaning of אֶפֶס as "end" could, by extension, mean "nothing, no longer, there is no more" (see GKC, §152s; Joüon, §160n). Still, אֶפֶס in Isa 46:9 aligns better with the more general meaning of "end" found elsewhere in the book (= "[I am] God, and the end is like me"—i.e., continuing forever) than a negative (אֱלֹהִים וְאֶפֶס כָּמוֹנִי "[I am] God, and there is none like me").

181. Cf. Deut 4:35, 39; 1 Kgs 8:60; Mark 12:32. Similarly, Calvin noted that "the cause of the ruin of Nineveh is ... that it had promised to itself a perpetuity in the world. But ... God cannot endure the presumption of men" (Calvin, "Habakkuk, Zephaniah, Haggai," 257).

182. See also Zeph 1:18; cf. 2 Chr 32:8.

183. See also Zeph 3:1; cf. Lev 19:15; Isa 1:17.

184. Motyer, "Zephaniah," 937.

185. See Jas 4:6; 1 Pet 5:5. Cf. Lev 26:19; Job 20:6–7; 40:12; Prov 16:18.

already accomplished. Thus, he writes, "How she *has become* a desolation—, a resting place for the beast." Again, he stresses the untamed nature of the environment to show how far Nineveh will have declined. Those passing by will express both horror and affirmation as they observe how the brutal oppressor has fallen (see Jer 19:8; Nah 3:19).[186] The Medes and Babylonians accomplished this destruction in 612 BC,[187] and this ensures that Zephaniah's other promises will come to pass.[188]

Baker notes how the shaking of the "hand" (יָד) in Zeph 2:15 shapes an inclusion with 2:13a around the words against Assyria: "The message starts with God's hand raised in judgment and closes with a hand raised in amazement at the judgment wrought."[189]

Canonical Significance of Zeph 2:5–15

The commentary will address the practical significance of Zeph 2:5–3:7 after explaining 3:1–7. Here I reflect specifically on aspects of the canonical significance of 2:5–15.

The Beginning Reversal of Babel in Zeph 2:5–15

Zephaniah casts the day of YHWH as a climactic de-creation and re-creation that will both echo and reverse all negative effects of the primeval curses associated with the garden of Eden, the flood, and the tower of Babel. Zephaniah proves this by alluding to early chapters in Genesis to highlight the themes of sin, punishment, and restoration. Already in Zeph 1:2–3, the prophet alluded to the flood narrative of Gen 6. In Zeph 3:9–13 he will describe returning to God's mountain/garden of Gen 2:10–14, reversing the tower of Babel debacle of Gen 11:7–9, and fulfilling the Abrahamic promises of Gen 12:3. Furthermore, historical factors and some of these early chapters serve as a conceptual and literary guide for Zephaniah's shaping of 2:5–15, and these features inform the text's message.

First, Floyd notes many features in Zeph 2 that portray "Judah's international seventh-century context . . . as the antitype of Babel."[190] Floyd shows why Cush, not Egypt, provides the southern pole of Zephaniah's compass. According to the global geography of Gen 2, "Ethiopia [i.e., Cush], not Egypt, stands opposite Mesopotamia

---

186. Cf. 1 Kgs 9:8; Jer 49:17; 50:13; Ezek 27:36.

187. For a description of Nineveh's fall, see Babylonian Chronicles 3 ("The Neo-Babylonian Empire and Its Successors," trans. A. Leo Oppenheim [*ANET*, 303–5]). There we also read (3.1.66) the final reference to any Assyrian king—Ashuruballit (609 BC). Xenophon claims that by 401 BC the desert sands had all but eradicated any evidence of Nineveh's existence (Xenophon, *Anabasis* 3.4.8–12). Similarly, Lucian (AD 120–190), declared how Nineveh had perished, leaving no trace of its previous existence (*Charon*, 23). Cf. J. M. P. Smith, "Book of Zephaniah," 235; Robertson, *Books of Nahum, Habakkuk, and Zephaniah*, 312; Ben Zvi, *A Historical-Critical Study of the Book of Zephaniah*, 302; Patterson, *Nahum, Habakkuk, Zephaniah*, 315.

188. So also Motyer, "Zephaniah," 937.

189. Baker, *Nahum, Habakkuk and Zephaniah*, 110; cf. Berlin, *Zephaniah*, 114.

190. Floyd, *Minor Prophets, Part 2*, 210.

on the world axis. . . . In this cosmological scheme Ethiopia ('Cush') and Assyria stand poles apart."[191] Furthermore, the movement from Cush's downfall (Zeph 2:12) to Assyria's destruction (2:13–15) is both natural and expected for two reasons. To begin, it was Cush's son Nimrod (נִמְרֹד, from מרד "rebel") who built both Babel (connected to the tower) and Nineveh (Gen 10:10–11). Additionally, God scattered the Cushites a "pole" away from their northern counterpart. In Floyd's words, "It is singularly appropriate that Yahweh's reversal of the scattering and linguistic confusion that began at Shinar [i.e., the location of the tower of Babel] would culminate with the destruction of Nineveh."[192]

Zephaniah 2:5–15 contributes to the book's portrayal of the reversal of Babel's tower judgment. This reversal culminates in YHWH's regathering descendants of those he once scattered (3:9–10). This multiethnic worshiping community will gather with transformed speech to the new Jerusalem. Floyd writes:

> If Yahweh is about to "change the speech of the peoples to a pure speech" (3:9a), his action would begin at some place on the outward perimeter of the primeval dispersion from Babel and extend back to the place where human speech first became confused. It would thus begin at a place that from a Judeocentric perspective could represent the southern end of the world; and it would extend back to Shinar in Mesopotamia, a place that from the same perspective could represent the northern end of the world. In 2:12–15 the action of Yahweh is described as having begun in Cush (2:12) and as eventually extending to Nineveh in Assyria (2:13). As a result of Yahweh's worldwide action the primal unity of the human race will finally be restored through universal worship of Yahweh.[193]

Second, Zeph 2:5–15 addresses the spread of arrogance springing from Babel (Gen 10:1–11:9). By smiting Cush (2:12), God began eradicating humanity's pride that spread from Babel's tower (Gen 10:32–11:9). God's destruction of Cush anticipated the worldwide restoration that would follow his cleansing the world of its arrogance and all other forms of sin. During this time, the prophet holds out hope, but it is only for the faithful remnant from Judah (2:3, 7, 9) and the foreign nations (2:9, 11; 3:9–10). God would gather a worshiping remnant from the world's "peoples" who descended from those he once scattered at Babel. Representatives of this group are located "beyond the rivers of Cush," and all the worshipers will assemble before YHWH's presence in the new Jerusalem (Zeph 3:9–10) and will constitute the transformed "remnant of Israel" whom YHWH has joined together (3:13a). Two elements in the immediate context point to this remnant's international nature: (1) Foreign

---

191. Floyd, *Minor Prophets, Part 2*, 213.
192. Floyd, *Minor Prophets, Part 2*, 213.

193. Floyd, *Minor Prophets, Part 2*, 211.

nations will be part of the remnant's inheritance: "The remainder of my nation will inherit them" (2:9d). (2) The peoples from the farthest reaches of the planet will "bow down" to YHWH in either worship or defeat (2:11c).

God Incorporating Enemy Peoples in Its Biblical Context

In the commentary above, I presented two reasons from Zephaniah that the remnant possessing Moab and Bene-Ammon likely included not only claiming their territory but also incorporating some of these former enemies into God's newly transformed people (2:9c–d). Numerous reasons from the broader biblical context further support this view that God's transformed people will include some of these nations:

1. Abraham's singular offspring who will "possess the gate of his enemies" will be the agent through whom "all the nations of the earth" regard themselves as blessed (Gen 22:17b–18). This implies that some from the nations who were once his foes have become his followers.
2. In keeping with Zephaniah's many allusions to Isaiah,[194] Zeph 2:9–11 may allude to Isa 11:14. It uses the same verb for "plunder" (בזז) and envisions an eschatological ingathering of some from the nations including Edom, Moab, and Bene-Ammon along with the banished of Israel. Furthermore, with the same verb Zephaniah uses for "inherit," Isaiah anticipates how Israel's restored house will "inherit" (*hithpael* of נחל) some of the world's other peoples as servants (Isa 14:2; cf. 61:5; 66:20–21). He also anticipates "the outcast of Moab" sojourning in Zion's midst when the Davidic king reigns uprightly (16:3–5; cf. 9:7; 11:4–5). The eschatological incorporation of these groups into God's people must mean he transforms their identities. After all, YHWH had barred any Ammonite or Moabite from entering the assembly of YHWH (Deut 23:3) and told Israel, "You shall not seek their peace or their good . . . forever" (23:6).
3. A remnant of survivors from Judah will "inherit" (נחל) Moab and Bene-Ammon (Zeph 2:9c–d). YHWH elsewhere uses the nominal form of the root נחל to promise his royal anointed one that the nations would be his "inheritance" (נַחֲלָה-I) and the ends of the earth his "possession" (אֲחֻזָּה) (Ps 2:8). Korah's sons later interpret this when they sing that various non-Israelite peoples gain new birth certificates declaring, "This one was born there [i.e., in the new Jerusalem]" (Ps 87:4; cf. Gal 4:26–27).

---

194. For a list, see the discussion of Zephaniah's use of Scripture under Zephaniah's Hermeneutic and Theology in the introduction.

4. Jeremiah notes that while YHWH will destroy the Moabites and Bene-Ammon, he will also "restore [the] circumstance" of both Moab and Bene-Ammon in the latter days (Jer 48:47; 49:6).[195] He also declares that some who were once Israel's evil neighbors would be "built up into the midst of" God's people (12:16). Those foreigners once serving with Babylon would now serve "YHWH their God and David their king" (30:9), a phrase parallel to one Hosea earlier used when speaking of the restored remnant of Israel after exile (Hos 3:5). God will accomplish these goals even as "he will make an end in all the nations" (Jer 30:11). That YHWH preserves the surrendered foreigners but destroys the nations suggests that YHWH no longer counts the former among the latter.

5. Using a conceptually related verb, Amos envisioned those who are a part of the restored Davidic kingdom "possessing" (ירש) nations called by God's name (Amos 9:11–12). James uses this text to support Peter's conviction that the time to include Gentiles in God's one people had arrived (Acts 15:16–18). Similarly, Isaiah charges the new Jerusalem, as YHWH's bride, to "enlarge the place of your tent" because "your offspring will possess [ירש] the nations" (Isa 54:2–3). This suggests her numbers will expand. This expansion will occur because the righteous, suffering Servant's atonement will "sprinkle many nations" and "declare many righteous" (52:15; 53:11).

God's Shepherds in Their Biblical Context

Zephaniah 2:6–7 used the pastoral imagery of "grazing grounds" (נְוֹת), "cisterns" (כְּרֹת), "shepherds" (רֹעִים), "folds" (גְּדֵרוֹת), "sheep" (צֹאן), and "pasturing" (רעה) to depict fertility and peace for God's people (cf. Zeph 3:13). In the Prophets this symbolism depicts the eschatological age (e.g., Isa 5:17; 65:10). Such hopes contrast with the days of the old covenant prophets. Back then, the self-serving "shepherd-leaders" mistreated God's "sheep-people" (Jer 23:1; 50:6; Ezek 34:2, 8; cf. Zech 10:2). Even in Zephaniah, Jerusalem's haughty and oppressive leaders (e.g., Zeph 1:8–9; 3:1, 3–4, 11) lead the populace to be complacent, aimless, unjust, and impious (1:4–6, 12; 2:3; 3:1–2, 5, 7).

However, YHWH promised that he would rise as the chief shepherd, stand against the evil shepherds, and rescue his sheep (Ezek 34:10, 12, 15), all by sending "one shepherd, my servant David," who would feed them (34:23). This servant-king-priest (Zech 3:8–9; 6:12–13; 9:9–11) would be a good shepherd—forgiving, saving, and establishing a universal covenant by his own blood through substitutionary

---

195. Zephaniah 2:7 uses the same phrase ("restore [the] circumstance") for Judah's remnant.

suffering.[196] Through this servant-shepherd-king-priest, God would "remove the wrong of this land in a single day" (Zech 3:8–9), and his leader would "build YHWH's temple/palace" from which he would reign on God's behalf (6:13) and rule with peace "from sea to sea, and from the River to the ends of the earth" (9:10). In the day that this shepherd's own people from the house of David and Jerusalem would pierce him to death, God would pour out on his people "a spirit of grace and pleas for mercy," and he would generate a river of life "to cleanse them from sin and uncleanness" (12:10; 13:1; cf. 14:7). Those whom God has purified would call upon his name, then he would identify his shepherd's representative role, and the shepherd would declare his loyalty to God: "They will call upon my name, and I will answer them. I will say, 'He is my people,' and he will say, 'YHWH is my God'" (13:9).[197]

The one shepherd from David's line will lead (e.g., Jer 23:1–8; Mic 5:2–4; Zech 13:7–9) and work through his under-shepherds. In Zeph 2:6, the prophet refers to the under-shepherds by mentioning "shepherds" and "sheep." These shepherd-leaders would enjoy every supply ("cisterns") and the sheep-people every protection ("folds"). As YHWH foretold through Jeremiah with similar language: "And I will give to you shepherds [רֹעִים] according to my heart, and they will shepherd [וְרָעוּ] you with knowledge and prudence" (Jer 3:15). And again, "And I will gather the remnant of my sheep [צֹאנִי] from all the land that I have driven them there, and I will return them unto their fold [נְוֵהֶן], and they will be fruitful and multiply. And I will establish over them shepherds [רֹעִים], and they will shepherd them [וְרָעוּם], with the result that they will neither fear nor be dismayed any more nor shall they be punished—the utterance of YHWH" (23:3–4).

The NT points to Jesus as the one great or chief shepherd who has, through his sacrificial death and triumphant resurrection, already initiated the awaited rest for all who believe in him, whether Jew or Gentile.[198] As chief shepherd, Jesus supplies and empowers "pastors" (= "shepherds," Eph 4:11), serving as elders/overseers, who in the present age "shepherd" God's people by feeding them, protecting them from wolves, and giving oversight.[199] Finally, in the age to come, "the Lamb . . . will shepherd them, and he will guide them to living springs of water, and God will wipe away every tear from their eyes" (Rev 7:17).

---

196. See Zech 11:7; 13:7, 9; cf. 12:10; 13:1; 14:7; Isa 9:6–7; 11:1–5; 42:1–9; 49:1–13; 50:4–11; 52:13–53:12; 61:1–4.

197. This translation contrasts with all major translations that change the singular forms to plurals.

198. See John 10:11–16, 27–30; Heb 13:20; 1 Pet 2:25; 5:1–4; Rev 7:15–17.

199. See John 21:16; Acts 20:27–29; 1 Pet 5:2.

Explanation of the Text

2. The Lamentable State and Fate of the Rebels from Jerusalem (3:1–7)

The prior lament against the rebels of foreign nations (Zeph 2:5–15) moved from Judah's borders to the ends of the inhabited world (i.e., Philistia to Moab and Bene-Ammon to Cush and Assyria). This movement implied Judah's coming destruction, but 3:1–7 explicitly highlights Jerusalem's doom (3:5–7). The recurrence of "Woe!" (הוֹי) in 3:1 marks the unit's start (3:1–7) paralleling the one begun at 2:5 (2:5–15). While the previous woe statement specifically marked Philistia as YHWH's target (2:5–7), here the text gradually characterizes Jerusalem as "the oppressive city" (הָעִיר הַיּוֹנָה) without explicitly mentioning its name. Keeping the city unnamed is intended as a rhetorical device to delay full disclosure only to later shock Judeans who would think that Nineveh is the target of the oracle.[200] Renz may also be right that omitting the city's name represents an "erasure of sacred identity: Jerusalem (the holy) has become like Nineveh (the profane, the wicked)."[201] Several factors indicate Jerusalem is in focus: (1) "YHWH" is "her God" (3:2). (2) Her leaders neglect the "Torah" (3:4). (3) YHWH is "in her midst," dwelling in his temple as the people's "Shelter" (3:5; cf. 3:7d). (4) The second feminine singular audience ("you") contrasts with other "nations" (3:6–7).

YHWH is the speaker in 3:1–4 since he has the main voice in 2:5, which parallels the woe speech in 3:1–4.[202] YHWH being in the third person in 3:5 marks it as the prophet's voice, but the return to first-person speech in 3:6–7 signals that YHWH is again the primary speaker.

The prophet bemoans Jerusalem's wickedness in 3:1. He then clarifies her fundamental failures in 3:2–7. Initially he notes these failures (v. 2). Then he elaborates on them by characterizing her leaders (vv. 3–5) and her intransigence (vv. 6–7). Together, the verses provide a further reason why the remnant from Judah and other lands should indeed pursue YHWH together ("bind . . . together" and "seek," 2:1–3) with patient trust ("wait," 3:8).

a. Jerusalem's Characteristics (3:1)

Zephaniah opens by strongly expressing grief and warning (הוֹי "Woe!"), after which he makes clear that God's punishment overviewed in 2:5–15 will ultimately implode on Judah, resulting in her ruin. The prophet begins by depicting the state of the capital city using three stative participles. The initial two are conjoined and independent (מֹרְאָה וְנִגְאָלָה "rebellious and defiled"), and the third is attributive, characterizing the city as "oppressive" (יוֹנָה).[203] In this single statement, the prophet addresses Jerusalem's "relationship to God [= rebellious], to self [= defiled], and to other

---

200. So also Baker, *Nahum, Habakkuk and Zephaniah*, 111. For more details, see the initial footnote in the explanation of Zeph 3:1.

201. Renz, *Books of Nahum, Habakkuk, and Zephaniah*, 587.

202. For a further defense that God is speaking in 3:1–3, see the Argument Flow and Outline footnotes within the Structure and Outline section in the Part III macro unit overview of Zeph 2:1–3:20, pp. 135–36.

203. Some propose that the verse's three participles were

intentionally ambiguous "word games," designed to delay the reader's sense of the prophet's intent (e.g., B. Jongeling, "Jeux de Mots En Sophonie III 1 et 3?," *VT* 21 (1971): 541–47; Ben Zvi, *Book of Zephaniah*, 184–87; Vlaardingerbroek, *Zephaniah*, 170–71; Sweeney, *Zephaniah*, 157–61). The versions struggled with the meaning and significance of 3:1. (1) Some ancient versions read the *qal* feminine singular participle מֹרְאָה ("rebellious," from the verb מרה "rebel") as "fearful, awesome," relating it to the masculine participle form מוֹרָא מֹרָא from ירא ("fear") (see

people [= oppressive]."[204] We could construe the whole of 3:1 as a verbless clause with a descriptive subject and compound predicate adjective. In this reading, God fronts the compound phrase to place the features in focus ("Woe, the oppressive city is *rebellious and defiled!*"). However, my translation above has rendered the words merely as vocative address in view of the comparable parallel structure in 2:5 (cf. NRSVue). The verbal root מרא of the first participle is irregular. While it could mean "fattened" (cf. Isa 11:6), perhaps alluding to one more way Judah is living complacently (cf. Zeph 1:12),[205] most scholars treat it as a biform of the verb מרה meaning "rebellious, recalcitrant." The parallel with the *niphal* participle of the verb גאל ("defiled") makes this likely.[206]

Zephaniah initially portrays YHWH's bride-city as "rebellious and defiled" (מֹרְאָה וְנִגְאָלָה, 3:1). These scathing words characterize her as both insubordinate to her covenant Lord and impure from not keeping his precepts. The prophet then calls the city "oppressive" (יוֹנָה). This term indicates that she manifested her disobedience and contamination by abusing the vulnerable. Zephaniah already said that the religious elite were filling YHWH's temple with "violence and deception" (1:9), and this oppressive activity spanned Judah's entire ruling class (3:3–4; cf. Isa 3:13–15; Jer 22:1–3). Swart notes that the

verbal root ינה "expresses exploitation, extortion, and despoliation," a meaning most clear in texts employing the causal *hiphil* stem (e.g., Ezek 18:7, 12, 16; 22:29; 46:18).[207]

God had prohibited the Israelites from oppressing the sojourner, widow, orphan (Exod 22:20[21]; Lev 19:33), and even the runaway slave (Deut 23:16–17[15–16]). He also urged his people to save the voiceless from the oppressor (Jer 22:3). Zephaniah had charged the faithful remnant from Judah and the other nations to "seek righteousness" (Zeph 2:3b). Ezekiel later clarifies that a "righteous" man (Ezek 18:5, 9) is one "who is not oppressing [לֹא יוֹנֶה]: He restores his pledge with respect to the debt; he does not commit robbery; he gives his bread to a hungry person; and he clothes naked persons with a garment" (18:7).

Far from displaying pure and undefiled religion by imaging God's impartiality and justice, especially toward the marginalized (Deut 10:17–18; Jas 1:27; cf. Ezek 18:5–9), the Jerusalem that Josiah inherited was disobedient, corrupt, and abusive. In many ways it resembled Nineveh, "the exultant city" (Zeph 2:15; cf. 3:11). Zephaniah's audience needed to humble themselves, heeding the prophet's charge to "bind themselves together" with the other repentant sinners (2:1) and to "seek YHWH" and his "righteousness," attempting with YHWH's

---

LXX, Peshitta). (2) All the major versions consistently read the *niphal* feminine singular participle וְנִגְאָלָה as coming not from II גאל (= "and defiled") but from I גאל (= "and redeemed") (see LXX, Tg. Neb., Peshitta, Vulgate; so too Luther, "Lectures on Zephaniah," 349). (3) Some versions read the participle הַיּוֹנָה not as "the oppressive [city]" but as either the noun יוֹנָה ("dove") (see LXX, Peshitta; so too Luther, "Lectures on Zephaniah," 349) or the proper name יוֹנָה ("Jonah") (see Vulgate). The latter clearly links 3:1 to the previous discussion of Nineveh. In contrast to the versions' readings, the הוֹי ("Woe!") shows that 3:1 begins a new unit focused on punishment and requires reading the verbals negatively, and 3:2–5 exposes Jerusalem as the prophet's focus.

204. Motyer, "Zephaniah," 941. I added the words in brackets.

205. So Sabottka, *Zephanja*, 102–3; O'Connor, *Hebrew Verse Structure*, 255.

206. See "I מרא," *HALOT* 630. Gesenius notes how III-ה verbs sometime follow the pattern of III-א verbs (GKC, §75rr). Cf. J. M. P. Smith, "Book of Zephaniah," 244; Gerleman, *Zephanja*, 47; Rudolph, *Micha, Nahum, Habakuk, Zephanja*, 284–85; R. L. Smith, *Micah–Malachi*, 137; Ball, *Rhetorical Study of Zephaniah*, 150; Ben Zvi, *Book of Zephaniah*, 184.

207. Ignatius Swart, "יָנָה (yānâ)," *NIDOTTE* 2:463. Roberts also compares our text to Isa 1:2–20 due to Jerusalem's stubborn disobedience (1:2–9), pollution from violence (1:15), and oppressive character (1:16–17) (Roberts, *Nahum, Habakkuk, and Zephaniah*, 212).

help to prize God as king and to value those made in his image (2:3).

b. Jerusalem's Fundamental Failures (3:2–7)

(1) An Overview of Her Fundamental Failures (3:2)

At her core, Jerusalem was both resistant to YHWH's word and work and unresponsive to his promises and presence. Zephaniah accents these facts in 3:2, using a series of four negative *qatal* clauses that together characterize the city's failures, which started in the past and continued into the present.[208] He then elaborates on these sins in 3:3–7.

(a) Her Initial Resistance (3:2a–b)

In 3:2, Zephaniah notes Jerusalem's basic failures. He first targets her initial resistance (3:2a–b) and then notes her resulting unresponsiveness (3:2c–d). The prophet characterizes Jerusalem as resistant in 3:2a–b. She is both willingly deaf and unwilling to learn ("she has not listened unto a voice [לֹא שָׁמְעָה בְּקוֹל]; she has not received instruction [לֹא לָקְחָה מוּסָר]"). In context, Jerusalem appears to oppose YHWH most flagrantly.[209] Zephaniah accuses the city's leaders of violating YHWH's instruction and character (3:4–5). Moreover, he portrays the nations' divine punishment as some of the "instruction/correction" (מוּסָר) from which those in Judah's capital should have

learned (3:6–7). Thus, with a potential allusion to Zephaniah, Jeremiah would assert, "This is the nation whose [people] have not listened to the voice [לוֹא־שָׁמְעוּ בְּקוֹל] of YHWH its God and have not received correction [וְלֹא לָקְחוּ מוּסָר]; the trustworthiness has perished and has been cut off from their mouth" (Jer 7:28; cf. 2:30; 25:4).[210] Zephaniah 3:2a–b portrays resistance to YHWH's "voice" and "instruction." Yet the object of the words is more than antecedent Scripture/Torah (cf. Zeph 3:4c) since God continued speaking through both his prophets (Deut 18:20–22; 2 Kgs 17:13; Hos 12:10) and providence (Jer 27:5–6; Dan 2:21; Eph 1:11). However, Jerusalem remained deaf (cf. Isa 29:9–12; 30:8–12; Jer 22:21).[211]

Concerning Judah's deafness, the great command to love YHWH began with a call to "hear" (שְׁמַע, Deut 6:4–5).[212] In Scripture, effective hearing is the necessary and initial human response to God's word; it generates fear and faith that leads to obedience and enjoyment of lasting relationship with him (31:12–13).[213] Nevertheless, like the exodus generation (Num 14:22), YHWH's covenant people had refused to listen (Jer 7:28; 22:21) and, therefore, refused to obey. Thus, Judah became deaf much like their idols (Zeph 1:4–5; see Deut 4:28) that had ears but could not hear (Ps 115:4–8; cf. Isa 43:8; Jer 5:21; Ezek 12:2).[214] As the covenant curses stressed, their deafness could only result in destruction (Deut 28:45, 62).

---

208. This study treats the *qatal* verbs in Zeph 3:2 as persistent perfects, expressing past action with ongoing results or present significance. See DeRouchie, *How to Understand and Apply*, 194–95. This approach differs somewhat from Berlin, who treats all as gnomic perfectives expressing present, habitual action (Berlin, *Zephaniah*, 127; cf. Luther, "Lectures on Zephaniah," 349).

209. So too Robertson, *Books of Nahum, Habakkuk, and Zephaniah*, 318n6; Motyer, "Zephaniah," 942; Sweeney, *Zephaniah*, 157, 161.

210. Holladay claims that Jeremiah clearly uses Zeph 3:2.

See Holladay, "Reading Zephaniah with a Concordance," 680–81.

211. So too Sweeney, *Zephaniah*, 161.

212. Cf. Mark 12:29–30.

213. Cf. John 5:24–25; 6:44–45; Rom 10:17; Gal 3:2, 5.

214. Scripture teaches that this spiritual disability (1) brought about the need for Jesus and (2) could only be altered by divine grace (Deut 29:4; Isa 6:9; Matt 13:14; Rom 11:8). For a whole-Bible development of this principle, see Beale, *We Become What We Worship*.

The city had also failed to learn from God's "instruction/correction" (מוּסָר, Zeph 3:2b). This term addresses training in behavior rather than acquiring knowledge. As Merrill notes, the base meaning of the root for מוּסָר relates to "the instilling of values and norms of conduct by verbal (hortatory) means or, after the fact, by rebuke or even physical chastisement."[215] The English versions render the word variously as "instruction" (NASB95), "discipline" (CEB, NASB20), and "correction" (NKJV, NRSVue, NET, NLT, ESV, NIV). The same term in 3:6–7 indicates how Jerusalem should have learned from the divine punishment of her neighbors, but to no avail.

God wounds to heal (Hos 6:1). The Bible notes this as a common pattern. YHWH disciplines those he loves (Deut 8:5; Prov 3:12; Jer 31:18),[216] and he curses to move the recipients and the witnesses from rebellion to loyalty (Lev 26:18, 27–28; Deut 21:21). In keeping with Leviticus and Deuteronomy's warnings, YHWH's covenant people had experienced numerous curses. More than a century earlier, Amos noted how God had made scarce Israel's bread and water and brought both agricultural disaster and foreign invasion, yet the covenant people had not returned to YHWH (Amos 4:6–12; cf. Isa 9:12[13]; 42:25).[217] Similarly, Zephaniah's contemporary Jeremiah would emphasize how YHWH struck Judah in various ways, but they refused to be ashamed of their sin (Jer 2:30; 5:3; cf. Hag 2:17).[218]

Jerusalem's failure to receive instruction certainly would have related to their unresponsiveness to God's corrective hand. But Zeph 3:6 also asserts that Judah had witnessed others' destruction, and 3:7 says that these acts of divine punishment should have also helped Judah grow. In 663 BC, God had overcome the Egyptian Cushite dynasty (Zeph 2:12), beginning his global cleansing at the ends of the inhabited world. Even earlier, in 723 BC, YHWH used Assyria to defeat Israel, yet Jerusalem had not responded by fearing God (Jer 3:8, 10). If Jerusalem would have learned from these case studies in divine discipline, Zeph 3:7 declares that "her Shelter would not be cut off." However, Judah would encounter divine fury for continually resisting God's word and work (Zeph 3:1, 7).

(b) Her Resulting Unresponsiveness (3:2c–d)

Next, Zeph 3:2 notes how Jerusalem's internal resistance resulted in lacking any response to God's promises or presence (3:2c–d). Zephaniah suggests a shift from action to result by reversing the word order of 3:2a–b in 3:2c–d. He now fronts modifying prepositional phrases before the negations, both of which focus on God and thus heighten the gravity of the offence ("*In YHWH* she has not trusted [בַּיהוָה לֹא בָטָחָה]; *unto her God* she has not drawn near [אֶל־אֱלֹהֶיהָ לֹא קָרֵבָה]"). In resisting God's word and work, the rebel majority refused to trust in YHWH or draw near to him in faith.

God calls his people to "trust [בִּטְחוּ] in him at all times" since "he is their help and their shield" (Pss 62:9[8]; 115:9–11). The psalmists regularly make divine deliverance contingent on "trusting" God (e.g., 22:5–6[4–5]; 25:1–2), and it was King Hezekiah's "trust" in YHWH that saved Jerusalem

---

215. Eugene H. Merrill, "יסר (*Yāsar* I)," *NIDOTTE* 2:471.
216. Cf. Heb 12:6; Rev 3:19.
217. For starvation and famine, see Lev 26:26, 29, 45; Deut 28:53–56; 32:24. For agricultural disaster and non-productivity, see Lev 26:19–20; Deut 28:17–18, 22–24, 38–42; 29:23. For

illness, pestilence, and contamination, see Lev 26:16; Deut 28:21–22, 27–28, 35, 59–61; 29:22; 32:24, 39). For occupation and oppression by enemies and aliens, see Lev 26:16–17, 32; Deut 28:31, 33, 43–44, 48, 68; 32:21.
218. Cf. Rev 16:8–9.

from Assyria a century earlier (2 Kgs 18:5; 19:20). Yet unlike Hezekiah, Zephaniah's Judah had refused to "trust," turning from peace and strength (Isa 26:3–4; 30:15; cf. Jer 7:8) and choosing curse over blessing (Jer 17:5–8; cf. 39:18).

With this, Jerusalem had failed to "draw near" (קרב) to God. In Zeph 1:6 we learned that some turned from YHWH and neither sought nor inquired of him. These actions are the opposite of "drawing near." Also, when paired with "trust" and the sacrificial imagery introduced earlier (Zeph 1:7–8, 17–18; cf. 3:8), Zephaniah's emphasis on Jerusalem's not "drawing near" indicates the city's failure properly to approach YHWH with sacrificial substitutes.[219] The sacrificial substitute was the only means for having God's fiery zeal against sin ignite passions for holiness rather than incinerate the sinner (see esp. Lev 9:24–10:3).[220] Israel kept bringing offerings, but they did so without the right heart (1 Sam 15:22; Ps 51:18–19[16–17]; Mic 6:6–8), and so YHWH rejected them (Isa 1:11; Jer 6:20; Mal 1:10). Despite their vows to YHWH (Zeph 1:5), they became abominable, false, and unclean to God by worshiping other gods and making contrary allegiances (1:4–6; cf. Prov 15:8; Hag 2:14). In remaining unresponsive to the great King's invitation into his presence, Zephaniah's audience refused shelter and help (Ps 73:28; cf. Heb 4:16), consigning themselves to punishment.[221]

(2) An Elaboration of Jerusalem's Fundamental Failures (3:3–7)

Having noted the "oppressive city's" fundamental failures in Zeph 3:2, the prophet describes Jerusalem's sins in more detail and highlights the certainty of her coming destruction (3:3–7). This development in lamenting the state and fate of Jerusalem's rebels adds weight to the second reason why those in Judah and other lands must seek YHWH together (2:1–4).

Content more than form guides this subunit's structure since every clause lacks a connector, save 3:5e and 7d, which contrasts the political and religious elite's lifestyles with YHWH's characteristics. The terse structure slows the pace and highlights Jerusalem's wickedness and YHWH's righteousness. The passage opens by targeting the ruling political and religious leaders for their evil tendencies (3:3–4) and dissimilarity to YHWH (3:5). The subunit then reinforces the prior claim of Jerusalem's unteachability (3:2), stating both the context (3:6a–7d) and nature (3:7e–f) of her opposition.

(a) Her Crooked Leaders (3:3–5)

YHWH's voice continues to dominate in 3:3–4 (see above), but the placement of YHWH as third-person subject in 3:5 suggests the prophet's voice leads there. The first-person verbs in 3:6–7 signal the return of YHWH's voice. Sweeney contends that 3:5–7 goes with what follows and not what pre-

---

219. See Exod 40:32; Lev 9:5, 7, 8; Ezek 42:14; 44:15–16.

220. Cf. Exod 3:5; Lev 21:17–18; Num 16:40; 18:22. Some doubt this cultic interpretation. Ben Zvi notes that the general statement of failing to "trust" in Zeph 3:2c pairs the clause in question, and the context lacks relation to temple service (Ben Zvi, *Book of Zephaniah*, 188–89). Sweeney adds that the *hiphil*, rather than the *qal* from here, is generally "the technical term for approaching the altar to offer sacrifice" (see, e.g., Exod 29:4; 40:12; Lev 3:6; 7:35; 8:6; Num 8:9; 16:5; Ezek 40:46; 45:4) (Sweeney, *Zephaniah*, 162). In contrast, as noted above, the

portrayal of YHWH's day as "sacrifice" in Zeph 1:7 anticipates this reading. Zephaniah also focuses on the failure of the people to "draw near" to God with a pure heart (e.g., Lev 9:5, 7, 8), both personally and through priestly representatives. Cf. Motyer, "Zephaniah," 942.

221. In the new covenant, Christians draw near to God only through Jesus's blood and righteousness (Eph 2:13; Heb 7:19; cf. 10:1, 22; 11:6; 1 Pet 3:18). For the collective sense of "drawing near," see Heb 12:22–24 (cf. 10:22 with 24–25 and 3:12–14).

cedes.[222] However, many factors suggest that 3:1–7 forms a unit paralleling 2:5–15: (1) Both 3:3 and 3:5 use "in her midst" (בְּקִרְבָּה) to refer to oppressive Jerusalem. (2) YHWH's "righteous" character in 3:5 intentionally contrasts with the impropriety of the leaders in 3:3–4. (3) The shameful one of 3:5d recalls the wicked leaders of 3:3–4. (4) Both 3:2 and 3:7 affirm that Jerusalem does not "receive instruction." (5) The mention of the nations' ruin in 3:6 recalls YHWH's destroying Cush in 2:12 and his promise to destroy others in 2:5–15. (6) 3:1–7 consistently portrays rebellious Jerusalem in third feminine singular, whereas 3:8–10 returns to the second masculine plural address found in 2:1–4.

• Their Tendencies (3:3–4)

God had previously pronounced judgments against Jerusalem's political and religious rulers (1:8–9). In 3:3–4, YHWH adds that the capital's civil and religious leaders had influenced the city's oppressive character (cf. Isa 3:14–15). With two groupings of three clauses each, the text designates the object of God's judgment by fronting each unit's first two clauses with a particular ruling class's title (שָׂרֶיהָ "her officials"; שֹׁפְטֶיהָ "her judges" // נְבִיאֶיהָ "her prophets"; כֹּהֲנֶיהָ "her priests"). Each unit's third clause expands on the second party's negative actions. Unlike righteous King Josiah who led the reform and whom Zephaniah need not mention,[223]

– The Political Leaders (3:3)

The former group included both Jerusalem's "officials" (שָׂרִים, Zeph 3:3a) and "judges" (שֹׁפְטִים, 3:3b). Rather than serving as shepherds guarding their sheep, they had become like wild beasts, devouring their prey and threatening all opposition (cf. Isa 56:11; Jer 23:1–4; Ezek 34:7–16).[224] The "officials" were supposed to help the king righteously oversee government and military activity while also bearing influence on religion from within Jerusalem's "midst" (see Zeph 1:8; Jer 26:10; 36:12). However, like lions (אֲרָיוֹת) after a hunt, they were roaring (שֹׁאֲגִים), glorying in the flesh of their prey and warding off all who would seek to oppose (Amos 3:4, 8; cf. Jer 5:6). Ezekiel would later speak comparably of Jerusalem's prophets, likening them to "a roaring lion [אֲרִי שׁוֹאֵג] tearing the prey" and characterizing them as those who "eat [human] flesh" and "take treasure and what is precious" (Ezek 22:25; cf. Mic 3:1–3).[225] The lion symbolized royalty in Judah (Gen 49:9–10; Num 24:9) and pointed to the strength of both the nation (Num 23:24) and her God (Hos 11:10–11; Joel 4:16[3:16]; Amos 1:2).[226] Yet now, as Sweeney notes, comparing the leaders to a lion taking prey "conveys the image of an official who feeds off of the

---

these leaders sought to supplant YHWH's authority with their own.

---

222. Sweeney, *Zephaniah*, 167.

223. So too Sweeney, *Zephaniah*, 162.

224. See also Jer 2:8; 10:21; 12:10; 50:6. Holladay notes that Jer 5:6 is the only other place in Scripture where "lions" and "wolves" together represent a threat; therefore, he believes Jeremiah has Zeph 3:3 in mind (Holladay, "Reading Zephaniah with a Concordance," 681).

225. Ben Zvi suggests that Ezekiel's not mentioning the judges of Zeph 3:3–4 "indicates they both may have depended on a third source" (Ben Zvi, *Book of Zephaniah*, 204–5). However, Sweeney correctly observes that the "judges" were chosen from the "officials," so Ezekiel may not have distinguished them

but still used Zephaniah (Sweeney, *Zephaniah*, 163). For more on this option with some questioning its feasibility, see D. H. Müller, "Der Prophet Ezechiel entlehnt eine Stelle des Propheten Zephanja und glossiert sie," *WZKM* 19 (1905): 263–70; Rudolph, *Micha, Nahum, Habakuk, Zephanja*, 287; Zimmerli, *Ezekiel 1*, 466–67; Ben Zvi, *Book of Zephaniah*, 197–205; Block, *Book of Ezekiel: Chapters 1–24*, 725–26; Vlaardingerbroek, *Zephaniah*, 169; Michael Fishbane, *Biblical Interpretation in Ancient Israel* (Oxford: Clarendon, 2004), 461–63.

226. Patrick D. Miller, "Ugaritic ǴZR and Hebrew 'ZR II: Animal Names as Designations in Ugaritic and Hebrew," *UF* 2 (1970): 177–78.

very people whom he is charged to protect."[227] And when a nation devours itself, its life-expectancy will be short.

Next the prophet notes the corrupt activity of the "judges" (Zeph 3:3b–c), whom God appointed from among the officials to settle legal disputes on his behalf (Deut 1:7; 16:18–19; cf. Zech 7:9). The judges were supposed to be "men of strength, fearing God," and "men of truth, hating [unjust] gain [שֹׂנְאֵי בָצַע]" (Exod 18:21). Indeed, representing, reflecting, and resembling YHWH himself (Zeph 3:5c; Ps 101:8), they were supposed to "judge at the morning [לַבֹּקֶר] . . . and deliver one who has been robbed from the hand of one who exploits" (Jer 21:12). However, Judah's judges had become like "evening wolves" (זְאֵבֵי עֶרֶב), moving in packs as vicious fighters, devouring their prey quickly under the cover of night, and regularly satisfying their appetites by the morning's dawn (cf. Gen 49:27; Job 24:14; Hab 1:8).[228] Having worked so hard in the dark, they lacked energy to carry out their judicial responsibilities in the light.[229]

Psalm 59 uses similar imagery. There the psalmist compares his enemies to wild dogs seeking to devour him in the "evening" (עֶרֶב), but he commits to singing his divine protector's praises in the "morning" (בֹּקֶר) (Ps 59:7–8, 15–17[6–7,

14–16]).[230] Later, Ezekiel would compare Judah's "officials" to "wolves" (זְאֵבִים) who "destroy souls for the ultimate purpose of profiting [unjust] gain [בְּצֹעַ בָּצַע]" (Ezek 22:27). Oh, how horrific, when shepherds shift from providing and protecting their flocks to devouring them! Our text shows that the highest Judge knows the wrongdoing that Judah's judiciary has done in the shadows (Zeph 3:3b; cf. Ps 139:12). And a dawn will come when he will give his judgment for the light and ultimately end their leaders' violence (Zeph 3:5c). As God would later promise, "I will deliver my sheep from their mouth, so that they will no longer be food for them" (Ezek 34:10).

– The Religious Leaders (3:4)

Matching the political elite's sin (Zeph 3:3), the religious leaders led God's people astray (3:4). True "prophets" (נְבִיאִים) were God's mouthpieces and covenant ambassadors; having stood in his council, they reminded the people of the covenantal instruction and declared to them indictment, warning, and hope (2 Kgs 17:13; Jer 23:22).[231] Instead, these prophets were "reckless, men of treacheries" (פֹּחֲזִים אַנְשֵׁי בֹּגְדוֹת, Zeph 3:4a; cf. Jer 3:7, 10),[232] who made the people "empty" by speaking "visions of their mind not from YHWH's mouth"

---

227. Sweeney, *Zephaniah*, 163; cf. Roberts, *Nahum, Habakkuk, and Zephaniah*, 213; Vlaardingerbroek, *Zephaniah*, 175.

228. The contrast between "evening" (עֶרֶב) and "morning" (בֹּקֶר) highlights the judges' corruption. Cf. Meinrad Stenzel, "Zum Verständnis von Zeph. 3 3b," *VT* 1 (1951): 303–4; cf. Ben Zvi, *Book of Zephaniah*, 192–93. The LXX read the phrase זְאֵבֵי עֶרֶב ("evening wolves") as זְאֵבֵי עֲרָב ("wolves of Arabia" = λύκοι τῆς Ἀραβίας), but Zephaniah likely characterizes them as "wolves of evening" since they fail to eat "to the morning" (לַבֹּקֶר) (cf. the same phrase in Hab 1:8). Without textual support, some scholars emend עֶרֶב ("evening") to עֲרָבָה ("desert, steppe") or עֲבָרוֹת, following the comparable construction זְאֵב עֲבָרוֹת ("wolf of deserts") in Jer 5:6 (Karl Elliger, "Das Ende der 'Abendwölfe' in Zeph 3,3 Hab 1,8," in *Festschrift für Alfred Bertholet*, ed. Walter Baumgartner and Otto Wilhelm Hermann

Leonhard Eissfeldt [Tübingen: Mohr, 1950], 158–75; Roberts, *Nahum, Habakkuk, and Zephaniah*, 207n6).

229. Cf. Ben Zvi, *Book of Zephaniah*, 194. The specific verb "gnaw" (*qal* גרם) occurs only here, though it appears in the *piel* elsewhere (Num 24:8; cf. Ezek 23:34). Because both forms convey activity, they probably mean the same thing. For a discussion of fientive verbs in both the *qal* and *piel* generally with a similar meaning, see Beckman, "Toward the Meaning of the Biblical Hebrew Piel Stem," iv, xiii, 50, 243, 252–53.

230. Cf. Stenzel, "Zum Verständnis von Zeph. III 3b," 303–5.

231. Cf. Hos 12:10; Zech 7:11–12. See DeRouchie, *How to Understand and Apply*, 46–51.

232. The stative verb פחז occurs elsewhere only in Judg 9:4. Both contexts suggest a meaning like "be reckless." The noun

(Jer 23:16).[233] Having never stood in God's council, they divined lies and tickled ears with destructive words (Jer 23:16–22, 32; Ezek 13; 22:25, 28) and, thus, received YHWH's disapproval (Ezek 13:9).

The "priests" (כֹּהֲנִים) failed in their two main tasks of defining holiness and teaching God's Torah (Lev 10:10–11; Deut 33:10; Mal 2:5–7) and led others into sin. King Manasseh led Israel away from Moses's Torah by replacing the worship of YHWH with idolatry at the central sanctuary and throughout the land (2 Kgs 21:2–9). His godlessness infected the priests in Zephaniah's day, such that they forgot the known "Torah" (תּוֹרָה).[234] Consequently, YHWH was "profaned in their midst" (Ezek 22:26). With a verb used elsewhere for harshly treating individuals like the sick (Job 21:27) and vulnerable (Jer 22:3; Lam 2:6), Zephaniah asserts that these religious leaders had "treated violently" (*qal* חמס) God's instruction (cf. Ezek 22:26), though "a priest's lips should guard knowledge, and [people] should seek Torah from his mouth" (Mal 2:7). Zephaniah's contemporary Habakkuk rightly characterized the result: "Torah will turn cold, and judgment will never go forth,

for evil is surrounding the righteous person. Therefore, judgment will go forth perverted" (Hab 1:4). When the prophet asserts, "[They] profaned what is holy" (חִלְּלוּ־קֹדֶשׁ) (Zeph 3:4), he refers to their contempt for YHWH's holy presence at the temple and the associated rituals of worship.[235]

Jeremiah summarized well Judah's state when he said that both prophet and priest had "become defiled" (חָנֵפוּ, Jer 23:11), "profiting [unjust] gain" (בּוֹצֵעַ בָּצַע) (6:13; 8:10; cf. 2:8). Nevertheless, "what will they do" when God brings an end to the land (5:30–31; cf. Lam 4:13)?[236] Instead of complacently thinking that "YHWH will neither do good nor do ill" (Zeph 1:12d–e; cf. Mic 3:11), they should have heeded Isaiah's charge, "To Torah and to testimony! If they will not speak according to this word, then to him there is no dawn!" (Isa 8:20).

• Their Contrast to YHWH (3:5)

With strong contrast to the corrupt tendencies of Jerusalem as a whole and her human rulers in particular, Zeph 3:5 magnifies God's nature and work and provides hope for a change in Judah's state and fate.[237] The prophet opens with a verb-

---

פַּחַז in Gen 49:4 also seems to mean "recklessness." Holladay says the *hapax legomenon* פַּחֲזוּת ("recklessness") in Jer 23:32 depends on the usage in Zeph 3:4 (Holladay, "Reading Zephaniah with a Concordance," 682). Though the noun בֹּגְדוֹת occurs only here, it basically means "acts of treachery, disloyalty, or faithlessness" based on the related verb בגד, e.g., Jer 3:8; Mal 2:14), noun (בֶּגֶד, Isa 24:16; Jer 12:1), and adjective (בָּגוֹד, Jer 3:7, 10).

233. Cf. Isa 30:10; Jer 5:31; Lam 2:14; Ezek 13:2; 22:28; Mic 3:5; Zech 13:3.

234. While Hag 2:11 and Mal 2:6–9 use the term Torah (תּוֹרָה) to refer to a priestly ruling, Renz notes that the Minor Prophets' other uses of תּוֹרָה "are best understood as a reference to a publicly known, probably written, divine standard" (Thomas Renz, "Torah in the Minor Prophets," in *Reading the Law: Studies in Honour of Gordon J. Wenham*, ed. J. G. McConville and Karl Möller, LHBOTS 461 [London: T&T Clark, 2007], 91). The use of "Torah" in Zeph 3:4 could specifically refer to Deuteronomy's Torah Scroll, which Josiah's reform

movement sought to implement after Hilkiah the priest discovered it (cf. 2 Kgs 22:8–20; 2 Chr 34:8–21).

235. See "the sanctuary" in NKJV, NASB20, NIV, CSB. Cf. Calvin, "Habakkuk, Zephaniah, Haggai," 269; Baker, *Nahum, Habakkuk and Zephaniah*, 112.

236. Cf. Isa 28:7; Mic 3:11.

237. Cf. Ben Zvi, *Book of Zephaniah*, 208. Motyer marks general contrasts between YHWH's depiction in Zeph 3:5 with the city in 3:2 and the political and religious leaders in 3:3–4 (Motyer, "Zephaniah," 941): Whereas the city would not listen (3:2a), rejected correction (3:2b), failed to trust (3:2c), and did not draw near (3:2d), YHWH was speaking and never absent (3:5d), constantly made his decisions known (3:5c), is totally trustworthy (3:5b), and was always available (3:5a). Whereas the officials failed in their duty (3:3a), the judges selfishly satisfied themselves (3:3b), the prophets were treacherous (3:4a), and the priests defiled the holy (3:4b), YHWH was never away from his post (3:5d), was constantly making his judgments known (3:5c), was free from deviancy (3:5b), and set the standard (3:5a).

less clause that describes both YHWH's character and his proximity to the depravity in Jerusalem: "YHWH is righteous in her midst" (יְהֹוָה צַדִּיק בְּקִרְבָּהּ, Zeph 3:5a).[238] Verse 3:3a stated that the corrupt "officials" were "in her midst" (בְּקִרְבָּהּ), and now the prophet implies that their sins were contaminating YHWH's very habitation. To declare God "righteous" (צַדִּיק) is to acquit him of any of the wrongs Jerusalem's nobility were exercising.[239] It also means that the one enthroned at Jerusalem's temple is unswerving in his passion to preserve and display right order—committed to seeing his own supremacy and justice upheld and those made in his image respected (cf. comments at 2:3).[240]

– His Righteousness and Steadfast Judgment (3:5a–d)

This God, the prophet says, "never does wrong" (לֹא יַעֲשֶׂה עַוְלָה, Zeph 3:5b; cf. 2 Chr 19:7; Ps 92:16[15]). Thus, YHWH's actions and character directly oppose the beastly practices of Jerusalem's elite (cf. Ps 37:1). That (1) YHWH's righteousness is a present reality in Jerusalem (Zeph 3:5a), (2) he works "morning by morning" (3:5c), and (3) his judgment "has never been lacking" (3:5d) all suggest that the dynamic *yiqtol* in 3:5b signifies present, continuous action: "[YHWH] never does wrong." Nevertheless, because most *yiqtols* in the

book are future, the statement may be a promise for the immediate and distant future with continuous implications: "[YHWH] will never do wrong." Regardless, the testimony affirms to both victims and violators the truth of Moses's previous words: "All his ways are judgment [מִשְׁפָּט]—a God of faithfulness and without wrong [עָוֶל]; righteous [צַדִּיק] and upright is he" (Deut 32:4; cf. Job 34:10; Ps 18:30). But how does YHWH's constant uprightness align with Zephaniah's present reality in Judah?

YHWH's steadfast love is new every morning (Lam 3:22–23). Yet Zeph 3:5 adds that YHWH's judgment is fresh every dawn: "Morning by morning he gives his judgment for the light [בַּבֹּקֶר בַּבֹּקֶר מִשְׁפָּטוֹ יִתֵּן לָאוֹר]" (Zeph 3:5c).[241] The adverbial phrase בַּבֹּקֶר בַּבֹּקֶר (lit., "in the morning, in the morning") is distributive, meaning "every morning."[242] It emphasizes that YHWH proclaims his judgment against sin and for holiness as constantly as light overcomes night.[243] As YHWH elsewhere declared, "At the mornings [לַבְּקָרִים] I will destroy all evil ones of earth, to cut off from the city of YHWH all those doing wickedness" (Ps 101:8). An explanatory clause using an unexpected *qatal* verb then emphasizes that his judgment "has never been lacking" (לֹא נֶעְדָּר, Zeph 3:5d), which should move all to think, the hurting to hope, and

---

238. Cf. Exod 9:27; Deut 32:4; 2 Chr 12:6; Ezra 9:15; Neh. 9:8; Pss 119:137; 129:4; Jer 12:1.

239. For this use of "righteousness" language, see, e.g., Exod 23:7–8; Deut 16:19; 25:1; 1 Kgs 8:32; 2 Chr 6:23; Isa 5:23; 29:21; 50:7–9. Cf. Ben Zvi, *Book of Zephaniah*, 207–8; Sweeney, *Zephaniah*, 172. See also George W. Ramsey, "Speech Forms in Hebrew Law and Prophetic Oracles," *JBL* 96 (1977): 45–58.

240. Cf. Judg 5:11; 1 Sam 12:7; Pss 36:7[6]; 50:6; 98:9; 99:4; 143:1; Isa 51:5–8; 56:1; Jer 9:24; 11:20; Hos 2:19; 10:12; Mic 6:5; Zech 8:7–8. Motyer writes: "The Lord's righteousness is his consistency of character (Ps. 11:7), reliability in relation to his stated purposes (Neh. 9:8), and correctness in all his actions (Ps. 145:17)" (Motyer, "Zephaniah," 944).

241. Cf. Ps 37:28. O'Connor renders the whole: "The evil one does not act in the morning. In the morning he is given his

judgment" (O'Connor, *Hebrew Verse Structure*, 256). This reading struggles since he treats the feminine noun עַוְלָה ("wrong, injustice, badness") as the masculine noun עַוֶּל ("wrong one, sinner," cf. 3:5e), divides the common idiom בַּבֹּקֶר בַּבֹּקֶר (see below), applies a rare pointing to יתן, and opposes the Masoretic pointing and cantillation, while the MT makes sense.

242. See GKC, §123c. The phrase is used elsewhere for Israel daily gathering manna in the wilderness (Exod 16:21), the daily rituals and worship at the tabernacle or temple (30:7; Lev 6:21; 1 Chr 23:30; Ezek 46:13), a royal noble's daily lustful torment (2 Sam 13:4), repeated divine punishment (Isa 28:19), and YHWH's sustained instruction of his royal Servant (50:4).

243. The expression "give judgment" (נתן מִשְׁפָּט) occurs only Zeph 3:5, Job 36:6, and Ezek 23:24.

the oppressor to dread. Then comes one whose entire lifestyle is characterized by wrongdoing (= עַוָּל "a wrong one, sinner") and who "never knows shame" (3:5e). In strong contrast, God "will never do wrong" (3:5b). We'll now consider each line of this important verse in more detail.

Many contemporary English versions and commentators read the phrase לָאוֹר ("for/to/at the light") temporally, paralleling it with בַּבֹּקֶר בַּבֹּקֶר ("morning by morning") and fronting the following phrase (= "Morning by morning he gives his judgment; *at the light* it has never been lacking") (cf. NRSVue, NET, ESV, NIV, CSB).[244] By this reading, Zeph 3:5c–d offers an effective parallel, and the noun's definiteness ("*the* day") makes the temporal reading quite natural. Elsewhere, other prepositions with אוֹר ("light") express temporal meanings (e.g., עַד־הָאוֹר "unto the dawn/day light," Judg 19:26; מִן־הָאוֹר, "from the dawn/day light," Neh 8:3).

Nevertheless, I follow the MT, LXX, and Vulgate in treating the prepositional phrase לָאוֹר ("for/to/at the light") as an adverbial modifier of the verb "to give" (נתן) in Zeph 3:5c. The preposition is likely the common "לְ of reclassification or product," meaning that the prepositional phrase either portrays God's judgment from a specific angle or expresses the state or condition that results from God's act of his justice (cf. KJV, NASB20).[245] Following similar usage elsewhere in the literary prophets (e.g., Isa 59:9; Hos 6:5; Mic 7:8–10), "the light" is neither a

temporal marker (i.e., "at dawn") nor a reference to "the sun."[246] Rather it is a metaphor for "that which guides to the right way."

The daily "judgment" (מִשְׁפָּט) in Zeph 3:5 serves as "*the* light" (הָאוֹר) for all victims and violators dwelling in Jerusalem's darkness. That is, God manifests his final verdict against sin to direct Zephaniah's audience to the only means of enduring the day of YHWH. In 2:3, the singular noun מִשְׁפָּטוֹ ("his judgment") referred to the "decree" of YHWH's day of wrath. In 3:8, the singular noun מִשְׁפָּטִי ("my judgment") similarly refers to YHWH's ultimate judicial decision to punish all opposing his ways (cf. Isa 5:16; Ps 9:9[8]). The "judgment" in Zeph 3:5c–d seems to refer to a preemptive declaration of God's future judgment-sentence in Zephaniah's day.[247]

The prophet has made clear that in his time injustice reigned among Jerusalem's leaders, resulting in improper worship (Zeph 1:4–6; 3:2) and oppressing the poor (1:9; 3:1, 3–4). To what then was Zephaniah referring when he spoke of God's "giving his judgment for the light" every morning? The joining of the verb "give" (נתן) with "judgment" (מִשְׁפָּט) is relatively rare in the OT. It appears when YHWH judges in favor of the oppressed (Job 36:6) and allows Babylon to punish Judah for their sins (Ezek 23:24). Close parallels also appear when he works justice for the downtrodden by giving them food (Ps 146:7) and when he displays (gives)

---

244. The temporal use of the preposition לְ occurs in phrases like לַמּוֹעֵד הַזֶּה ("at this appointed time," Gen 17:21; 2 Kgs 4:16), לַיּוֹם הַשְּׁלִישִׁי ("by the third day," Exod 19:11), לַבֹּקֶר ("by the morning," Exod 34:2), and לָעֶרֶב ("by the evening," Ps 90:6). Cf. J. M. P. Smith, "Book of Zephaniah," 241; Gerleman, *Zephanja*, 51; Kapelrud, *Message of the Prophet Zephaniah*, 107; R. L. Smith, *Micah–Malachi*, 137; Ball, *Rhetorical Study of Zephaniah*, 161–62; Ben Zvi, *Book of Zephaniah*, 210–11; Roberts, *Nahum, Habakkuk, and Zephaniah*, 205; O'Connor, *Hebrew Verse Structure*, 256; Motyer, "Zephaniah," 944; Vlaardingerbroek, *Zephaniah*, 178.

245. For more on these categories, see Ronald J. Williams and John C. Beckman, *Williams' Hebrew Syntax*, 3rd ed. (Toronto: University of Toronto Press, 2007), §278; *BHRG*, §39.11(4a). Cf. Luther, "Lectures on Zephaniah," 352; Calvin, "Habakkuk, Zephaniah, Haggai," 273; Keil, " Twelve Minor Prophets," 10:454–55 (2:151); Sabottka, *Zephanja*, 107–8; House, *Zephaniah: A Prophetic Drama*, 124; Robertson, *Books of Nahum, Habakkuk, and Zephaniah*, 315; Berlin, *Zephaniah*, 130; Sweeney, *Zephaniah*, 167.

246. Contra Berlin, *Zephaniah*, 125, 130.

247. So too Vlaardingerbroek, *Zephaniah*, 178.

his glory among the nations by judging them (Ezek 39:21). Irsigler helpfully sees Zeph 3:5 as referring to every instance of Yahweh's "judging and saving help 'in the morning.'"[248] This "judgment" would manifest itself in the prophet's immediate future in at least the following five ways:

1. *Through the prophetic indictment and curse.* Hosea declared, "Therefore, I have hewn them by the prophets; I have slain them with the words of my mouth, and my judgment goes forth as the light [*properly* וּמִשְׁפָּטִי כָאוֹר יֵצֵא]" (Hos 6:5).[249] God's words through the prophets "slew" the hearers, cutting them down with covenant indictments and curses and showing that only by repenting could they hope to survive YHWH's great and imminent day of wrath (cf. Isa 33:14–16; Joel 2:11–14; Zeph 2:1–4).[250]

2. *Through just rulings of judges.* While most of the city's leaders were corrupt (Zeph 1:8–9; 3:3–4), when judges heeded God's call to "judge at the morning with judgment (Jer 21:12; cf. Ps 101:8) and to "render a judgment of truth" and "peace" and to "show loyalty and compassion" (Zech 7:9; 8:16), they displayed

the just decree of the unchanging God (Deut 1:16–17; 10:17–18).[251]

3. *Through YHWH's punishing nations.* One way YHWH displayed his judgment for the light was by destroying neighboring nations around Judah and thus signaling that he alone was their surest shelter (Zeph 3:6–7; cf. Isa 20:6; Ezek 29:16).[252] Sadly, those in Jerusalem resisted growth by failing to repent after seeing YHWH punish their neighbors.

4. *Through daily substitutionary sacrifices.* YHWH proclaimed his holiness and his final guilty verdict against sinners through the daily rituals at the temple.[253] The daily burnt sacrifices manifested the sinner's guilty verdict each morning and evening (Exod 29:38–46; Num 28:1–8), thus testifying to God's overflowing mercy. Israel's daily sacrifices pictured this greater, more ultimate sacrifice, which God would enact either on his sacrificial substitute[254] or on the sinners themselves (Zeph 1:7–8).[255]

5. *YHWH's sustaining common graces.* Smith and Roberts both propose that YHWH's "judgment" in Zeph 3:5 refers to how God daily orders and sustains the created natural world

---

248. See, e.g., Pss 5:4[3]; 30:6[5]; 46:6[5]; 59:17[16]; 90:14; 143:8; cf. Exod 14:27; Isa 17:14; 33:22) Irsigler, *Zefanja*, 335; cf. Joseph Ziegler, "Die Hilfe Gotten 'Am Morgen,'" in *Alttestamentliche Studien. Friedrich Nötscher Zum Sechzigsten Geburtstage 19. Juli 1950*, ed. Hubert Junker, BBB 1 (Bonn: Hanstein, 1950), 281–88.

249. The MT of Hos 6:5 has וּמִשְׁפָּטֶיךָ אוֹר יֵצֵא ("and your judgments are as light going forth"), but the context demands that the "judgments" be YHWH's, and translating יֵצֵא ("it will go forth") is awkward. In contrast, the LXX, Peshitta, and Tg. Neb. all read וּמִשְׁפָּשִׁי כָאוֹר יֵצֵא ("and my judgment will go forth as the light"). This approach divides the words differently, seeing the *yod* as a first common singular suffix on a singular noun and the *kaph* as a preposed preposition כְּ ("like, as") on a definite noun. So Wolff, *Hosea*, 105n.g; Stuart, *Hosea–Jonah*, 99n5d.

250. So too Calvin, "Habakkuk, Zephaniah, Haggai," 273–74;

Keil, "Twelve Minor Prophets," 10:545–55 (2:151); Patterson, *Nahum, Habakkuk, Zephaniah*, 320.

251. Cf. Ziegler, "Die Hilfe Gotten 'Am Morgen,'" 285–86; Sabottka, *Zephanja*, 107; Irsigler, *Zefanja*, 355. By such acts, they were also supplying a foretaste of the future, when YHWH would "render to each one according to his deeds" (Matt 16:27; cf. John 5:29; Rom 2:6).

252. Cf. Calvin, "Habakkuk, Zephaniah, Haggai," 273–74; Patterson, *Nahum, Habakkuk, Zephaniah*, 320.

253. See Seybold, *Satirische Prophetie*, 111; Irsigler, *Zefanja*, 335; Sweeney, *Zephaniah*, 173–74. Sweeney limits Zephaniah's perspective to this context alone, but Irsigler reads the reference more broadly, including all examples of God helpfully judging and saving in the morning.

254. See Ps 22; Isa 52:13–53:12; Hos 14:4–8; Zech 13:7–9.

255. Cf. Isa 34:6; Jer 46:10; Ezek 39:17.

(Gen 8:22; Jer 33:20).[256] For example, each day the sun's light overcomes darkness and metaphorically testifies that YHWH will establish right order by overcoming all evil one day.[257] Furthermore, the mere presence of the sun rising on the evil and the good (Matt 5:45) recalls a grace purchased through substitutionary sacrifice (Gen 8:20–22), meaning that every experience of common grace in this age testifies to God's just judgment.

These expressions of justice emphasized sin's seriousness and initially manifested "the light," guiding Judah in the righteous way and showing that God would triumph over all darkness and evil (e.g., Isa 9:1[2]; 42:6; Mic 7:8–10).[258] These daily portraits of judgment should have aroused Judah's sinners to repent, the flashes of light burning away the shadows of their hearts. However, at the time of Zephaniah's sermon, most of Jerusalem remained unresponsive. And so long as they continued unwilling to follow "the light," YHWH's day would be for them "darkness" and not "light" since their deeds were evil (Isa 59:9; Amos 5:18, 20).[259]

– The Shamelessness of the Iniquitous (3:5e)

Having described YHWH's righteous character and sustained upright actions, Zephaniah concludes this subunit by contrasting the God who "never does wrong" (3:5b) with a wrongdoer (= עַוָּל "a wrong one") who "never knows shame" (3:5e). Anticipating a parallelism between 3:5b and 3:5e (וְלֹא . . . לֹא), some scholars try to make YHWH, and not the iniquitous one, the subject of 3:5e.[260] This view, however, fails in at least three ways: (1) It does not account for the change in predicate from *yiqtol* (3:5b) to participle (3:5e). (2) It creates an awkward repetition, wherein we learn first that YHWH never does wrong (עַוְלָה) and then that he never knows a sinner (עַוָּל). (3) It creates a very unnatural double object, with "shame" (בֹּשֶׁת) restating "wrong one" (עַוָּל) (= "And he [i.e., YHWH] is never knowing wrong, shame").[261] As such, 3:5b and 3:5e most likely stand in contrast, with the latter adding emphasis to how distinct YHWH is from the common leader in Jerusalem.[262]

A person who "never knows shame" fails to feel proper regret over his actions and therefore does not repent. In Motyer's words, "Constant attention to deviancy sears the conscience."[263] Yet Berlin rightly notes that the meaning may be more profound since elsewhere (1) the negative verbal expression "not know" (לֹא יָדַע) can mean "ignore" (Isa 42:25) and (2) the noun and verb associated with the root בשת can express "reproach, disgrace, condemnation" (Zeph 3:11, 19).[264] Thus, she renders the final clause, "But the wrongdoer ignores condemnation."[265]

---

256. Cf. Job 38:12, 31–33; Ps 104:28–30; Isa 40:26. J. M. P. Smith, "Book of Zephaniah," 240; Roberts, *Nahum, Habakkuk, and Zephaniah*, 214; cf. Patterson, *Nahum, Habakkuk, Zephaniah*, 320.

257. Cf. Berlin, *Zephaniah*, 125, 130; Renz, *Books of Nahum, Habakkuk, and Zephaniah*, 591; see also Rudolph, *Micha, Nahum, Habakuk, Zephanja*, 284, 286, 288–89.

258. Cf. Isa 49:6; 51:4; John 1:4–5, 9; 3:19–21; 8:12; 12:35–36, 46.

259. Cf. John 3:19. For more on Zeph 3:5, see Jason S. DeRouchie, "YHWH's Judgment Is New Every Morning: Zephaniah 3:5 and the Light of the World," *TJ* 43NS (2022): 131–46.

260. E.g., Sweeney, *Zephaniah*, 167n.d, 174–75.

261. Furthermore, while secondary, the Masoretic accents demand that the "wrong one" (עַוָּל) stand as the subject and that "shame" (בֹּשֶׁת) be the object.

262. This contrast does not mean that Zeph 3:5e is secondary. It merely emphasizes the contrast between YHWH and Jerusalem's leaders already present in the context (cf. Ball, *Rhetorical Study of Zephaniah*, 164–65; House, *Zephaniah: A Prophetic Drama*, 124; contra J. M. P. Smith, "Book of Zephaniah," 241; Irsigler, *Gottesgericht und Jahwetag*, 164, 188; Ben Zvi, *Book of Zephaniah*, 213).

263. Motyer, "Zephaniah," 944.

264. Berlin, *Zephaniah*, 131.

265. Cf. Rom 1:18. Berlin, *Zephaniah*, 125.

216 Part III.1: Stage 1: The Appeal to Seek YHWH Together to Avoid Punishment

(b) Her Resistance to Growth (3:6–7)

After synthesizing Jerusalem's fundamental failures in Zeph 3:2, Zephaniah elaborates on them in 3:3–7, with verses 3–5 focusing on her crooked leaders and verses 6–7 describing her resistance to growth. Zephaniah 3:6a–7d supply the context for this resistance, whereas 3:7e–f addresses its nature.[266]

• Its Context (3:6a–7d)

As to the context, Judah's present hardness of heart disregards God's numerous gracious acts toward Jerusalem seen in the punishment of others. These punishments should have warned those in Judah's capital.[267] Specifically, 3:6a opens with an asyndetic narrative thesis statement in first person singular, by which the sovereign, covenant Lord recalls how he has "cut off nations" (הִכְרַתִּי גוֹיִם).[268] The same verb (כרת) occurs in the weqatal in 1:3–4 promising sinful humankind and rebellious Judah's eventual judgment. Here it occurs in the qatal and may only stress the certainty of future alienation or decimation (e.g., 1:11; 2:2, 11, 14–15).[269] However, it probably points to past activities[270] since 3:7 clar-

ifies how God *has acted* to motivate Jerusalem's repentance, but that Zephaniah's contemporaries had, *in response*, grown more corrupt. Thus, the echo of 1:3–4 in 3:6a suggests that YHWH had already set forth destructive foretastes of his encroaching fury against the whole world by Zephaniah's time. Such is God's just retribution for human sin (1:17), whether linked to the covenant with creation through Adam and Noah (Gen 9:9–10; Isa 24:5–6; 43:27) or the Mosaic covenant that reflects it (Deut 28:15–68; cf. Isa 54:9–10; Hos 6:7).

– YHWH's Past Punishments of Other Nations (3:6)

YHWH refers to specific divine acts against the "nations" (גוֹיִם). These acts might include Egypt's defeat at the exodus. However, this frequent motif in the prophets normally focuses on Israel's deliverance from or return to slavery and not on God's punishing Egypt (e.g., Jer 7:22; Hos 11:1; Mic 6:4).[271] As such, YHWH is more likely referring to instances where he had already used Assyria as "the rod of my anger" (Isa 10:5; cf. 13:5),[272] like the Northern Kingdom's fall in 723 BC (2 Kgs 17:5; cf. Hos 13:16) and like the Cushite Egyptian dy-

---

266. Some scholars create a sharper division between Zeph 3:5 and 3:6 due to (1) the change from referring to YHWH in third person to his speaking in first person and (2) the supposed change in focus from Jerusalem to the nations (e.g., J. M. P. Smith, "Book of Zephaniah," 241, 243; Watts, *The Books of Joel, Obadiah, Jonah, Nahum, Habakkuk, and Zephaniah*, 176–77; Kapelrud, *Message of the Prophet Zephaniah*, 35–36; R. L. Smith, *Micah–Malachi*, 140; Renz, *Books of Nahum, Habakkuk, and Zephaniah*, 582–86). However, switching YHWH's character from third person to first person is common within the book and in no way signals a major break (cf. 2:4–7 and 2:13–15 in third person with 2:8–12 in first person). Also, 3:6 mentions the nations to develop the topic from 3:2 that Jerusalem has not "received instruction." YHWH has sought to train them through numerous international case studies, but his people failed to heed and repent. We must treat 3:1–7 as its own unit standing parallel to 2:5–15 (cf. e.g., Ben Zvi, *Book of Zephaniah*, 314–17; Roberts, *Nahum, Habakkuk, and Zephaniah*, 214; Ryou, *Zephaniah's Oracles*, 305–8; Floyd, *Minor Prophets, Part 2*, 230–31; Sweeney, *Zephaniah*, 401–2).

267. Motyer treats all the qatal verbs in Zeph 3:6 as perfects of certainty, thus focused on *future* activity, but the statements in 3:7 he leaves as past (Motyer, "Zephaniah," 947; cf. J. M. P. Smith, "Book of Zephaniah," 241). The flow of thought, however, requires that the Judean's *persistent* rebellion in 3:7e–f provides a direct response to the *past* divine discipline in 3:6 and the past divine intent expressed in 3:7a–d.

268. Roberts repoints גוֹיִם ("nations") to גוֹיָם ("their nation") and reads the verse as a reference to Assyria devastating Judah during Hezekiah's time (Roberts, *Nahum, Habakkuk, and Zephaniah*, 214; cf. 208–9n12; Holladay, "Reading Zephaniah with a Concordance," 682). However, every ancient version follows the MT, suggesting that Judah should have learned from YHWH devastating others.

269. Cf. Carpenter, "כָּרַת (kārat)," *NIDOTTE* 2:722.

270. Cf. Zeph 1:6–7, 17; 2:3, 8, 10; 3:2.

271. But see Isa 11:15–16. Watts never mentions any references, allusions, or echoes of the exodus in Zephaniah (see Rikk E. Watts, "Exodus Imagery," *DOTPr* 205–14).

272. So too Vlaardingerbroek, *Zephaniah*, 181.

nasty's end in 663 BC (see Isa 20:1–6), the latter of which Zephaniah referenced in Zeph 2:12.[273]

Three explicatory asyndetic clauses now follow God's assertion (Zeph 3:6b–d), thus continuing his choppy syntax that both slows the pace and draws attention to the content. Each clause uses a third person plural pronominal suffix to refer to the "nations" ("*their* battlements," "*their* streets," "*their* cities"). Together these clauses clarify the results of YHWH's destructive activity. The first and third include third-person *niphal* passives, whereas the middle one is a first-person *hiphil* active and causative (A–B–A′). The centrality of the first-person speech highlights that God ultimately ruined the nations (Amos 3:6; cf. Isa 42:24; Zeph 2:12), though he used Assyria in the downfall of both northern Israel and Cushite Egypt (2 Kgs 17:6; Isa 20:4).

These nations' "battlements have been dismayed" (נָשַׁמּוּ פִּנּוֹתָם). The noun "battlements" (פִּנּוֹת) fundamentally means "corners." As in 1:16, it likely refers to the enemy cities' corner towers that now lie empty (cf. 2 Chr 26:15).[274] Reading פִּנּוֹתָם as "their battlements" parallels the physical locations of "their streets" and "their cities" in Zeph 3:6c–d. However, some read the plural noun figuratively as pointing to the downfall of the various national leaders (= symbolic "cornerstones") since the mention of "battlements" is abrupt and the preceding context confronts Judah's political and religious elite (Zeph 3:3–4).[275] Though this term is used figuratively in the Prophets,[276] the first interpretation seems more likely since the immediate context and

Zeph 1:16 already referred to city "battlements." The use of the *niphal* verb שמם, rendered here as "have been dismayed," favors neither option, for it can refer to the humiliation of both places (e.g., Lev 26:22; Isa 54:3; Zech 7:14) and people (e.g., Job 21:5; Jer 4:9; Ezek 4:17).

Next, YHWH declares, "I have laid waste their streets" (הֶחֱרַבְתִּי חוּצוֹתָם) and then adds that no one journeys over them anymore (Zeph 3:6c). The noun חוּץ generally means "outside," but in the plural it can refer to "open fields" (Ps 144:13; Job 5:10), city "streets" (2 Sam 1:20; Isa 10:6; Lam 2:21), and even to "marketplaces" (1 Kgs 20:34). The options are all possible here, but the present focus on cities with buildings and the lack of economic imagery suggest the meaning relates to "streets." The lack of people highlights the utter devastation God has wrought, but it does not negate the possibility that future travelers may pass over the ruins in amazement (see Zeph 2:15).

Finally, YHWH clarifies what he has hinted at in the two previous declarations in 3:6b–c. The nations' "cities" that he has cut off "have become so desolate as to be without a person," leaving no inhabitant (3:6d). As with the reference to humanity in 1:17, אִישׁ here generically refers to any person, whether male or female. Just as YHWH's day of vengeance will come against "all the inhabitants of the earth" (כָּל־יֹשְׁבֵי הָאָרֶץ, 1:18), so God leaves the cities "without a person, so there is no inhabitant" (מִבְּלִי־אִישׁ מֵאֵין יוֹשֵׁב) in each nationally focused foreshadowing of this day. When YHWH punishes, he does so convincingly.

---

273. Renz wrongly concludes that the wording of 3:6 recalls the future destructions in ch. 2 (Renz, *Books of Nahum, Habakkuk, and Zephaniah*, 584). Thus, he claims that 3:6–7 must date later than 1:2–3:5 (Renz, *Books of Nahum, Habakkuk, and Zephaniah*, 582–86, 595–97). But 3:6 leaves unnamed those nations that collapsed, and Judah's witnessing of the conquest of the Cushites (2:12), the Philistines' progressive destruction (2:4; 2:5–7), and other unnamed nations' defeats (e.g., Israel in 723 BC) sufficiently clarify YHWH's claim. The book's final

form treats all of Zeph 1:2–3:20 as a single oracle, and Renz's proposal adds unnecessary discontinuity.

274. The LXX translator rendered the noun γωνίαι from γωνία ("corner, cornerstone"), suggesting a reference to "battlements." See also the references to Jerusalem's northwest "corner gate" in 2 Kgs 14:13; 2 Chr 26:9; Jer 31:38; cf. Zech 14:10. Cf. "פִּנָּה," *DCH* 6:708–9, esp. §§1, 3.

275. "פִּנָּה," *HALOT* 944–45.

276. See Judg 20:2; 1 Sam 14:38; Isa 19:13; Zech 10:4.

Significantly, Jeremiah uses similar language to describe Judah's destruction: "And I will make Jerusalem for a heap, a lair of jackals, and the cities of Judah I will make a desolation *without inhabitant* [מִבְּלִי יוֹשֵׁב]" (Jer 9:10[11]; cf. 2:15; 4:7).[277] If Jeremiah is alluding to Zeph 3:6, he is associating Jerusalem's coming ruin with that of the nations.

– YHWH's Pedagogical Intent for Such Punishments (3:7a–d)

In 3:7a–d, YHWH continues the context of Jerusalem's resistance to growth by stating his pedagogical intent for punishing other nations: motivating those in Jerusalem to take sin seriously and to fear him lest they experience the covenant curses. Like 3:6a, 3:7a opens with an asyndetic first-person *qatal* verb. This *qatal* introduces a reported "speech" of God (אָמַרְתִּי "I said"), which he addresses directly to Jerusalem with second feminine singular forms, thus clarifying how the city should have responded when he disciplined others.[278] "Surely you will fear me; you will receive instruction" (3:7b–c).[279] "Fearing" (ירא I) God is the proper human disposition of respect or worship toward him.[280] It arises from awe of

his sovereignty (Isa 8:13; Eccl 3:14) and "fearsomeness" (נוֹרָא, Zeph 2:11). Such fear should never be directed toward other gods (2 Kgs 17:35–36); it opposes evil (Prov 3:7; 8:13; 16:17), results in blessing (Pss 15:14; 103:11; Prov 10:27), and precedes all God-honoring living.[281] Godward fear is evident when people magnify God's greatness and ability (Mal 1:5; cf. Deut 32:26–27; Ezek 36:20–21) and resist looking to created powers for ultimate help (Isa 20:5–6; Ezek 29:16). Failure to fear YHWH brought the northern kingdom's collapse (2 Kgs 17:7), as it would for Judah.

Having asserted his desire that Jerusalem fear him (Zeph 3:7b), YHWH explicates this wish by noting his intent that she "receive instruction" (תִּקְחִי מוּסָר). Every encounter with YHWH's curses, whether experienced personally or by others, is intended to lead us to repentance (cf. Lev 26:18, 21, 23–24, 27–28). God intended that his discipline of Judah's neighbors rectify Jerusalem's ways; as the inhabitants observed how YHWH treated others they should have adjusted their own course, humbling themselves before YHWH and heeding his voice. But as 3:2b already asserted, to date the city had "not received instruction" (לֹא לָקְחָה מוּסָר).[282]

---

277. The LXX's translation may refer to both Judah and the nations, for it reads "arrogant, proud ones" (ὑπερηφάνος = גֵאִים, cf. Zeph 3:11) in the place of "nations" (גּוֹיִם) (cf. Isa 2:12). However, the other versions (Tg. Neb., Peshitta, Vulgate) all follow the MT. Furthermore, Isaiah stresses how God's destruction of other nations to whom Israel/Judah once looked for help should awaken his people to recognize him alone as their source of strength (Isa 20:6). This compares to Zephaniah's point in 3:6–7.

278. As already seen Zeph 1:12 and 2:15, the verb אמר can be used of an internal speech act—a thought. While sometimes accompanied by a modifier like "in your heart" (בִּלְבָבְךָ, e.g., Deut 8:17; Isa 14:13; Ps 14:1; Eccl 2:1), this is not always the case (e.g., Gen 20:11; Exod 2:14; Num 24:11; Deut 12:20; Josh 22:33; 2 Sam 12:22; 2 Kgs 5:11; 20:19; Ruth 4:4; 2 Chr 13:8). So Ben Zvi, *Book of Zephaniah*, 214; Vlaardingerbroek, *Zephaniah*, 182.

279. For a similar logic, see Isa 5:4. I have read the adverb אַךְ as an asseverative, expressing certainty = "surely" (cf. Gen

44:28; 1 Sam 16:6; 1 Kgs 22:32; Ps 85:10; Williams and Beckman, *Williams' Hebrew Syntax*, §389; *BHRG*, §40.8[2]; cf. Calvin, "Habakkuk, Zephaniah, Haggai," 279; J. M. P. Smith, "Book of Zephaniah," 242; Ball, *Rhetorical Study of Zephaniah*, 293; House, *Zephaniah: A Prophetic Drama*, 124; Vlaardingerbroek, *Zephaniah*, 182–83; Sweeney, *Zephaniah*, 167).

280. On the range of meaning of ירא, see Daniel I. Block, "The Fear of YHWH: The Theological Tie That Binds Deuteronomy and Proverbs," in *The Triumph of Grace: Literary and Theological Studies in Deuteronomy and Deuteronomic Themes* (Eugene, OR: Cascade, 2017), 283–311. He notes a semantic spectrum that includes "terror, fright, anxiety, awe, reverence, submission, allegiance, trust."

281. See Exod 20:20; Deut 5:29; 6:24; 10:12; Job 28:28; Ps 128:1; Prov 9:1; Eccl 12:13; cf. Matt 10:28; Eph 6:5; Phil 2:12; Heb 12:28–29.

282. See the comments at Zeph 3:2 for more on the meaning of מוּסָר ("instruction, correction").

If Jerusalem softened her heart, then "her Shelter would not be cut off" (וְלֹא־יִכָּרֵת מְעוֹנָהּ). Numerous features need comment. First, if Judah would seek YHWH (2:3) and respond to his correction (3:7), she would be protected from the same fate that had already occurred to some nations (כרת, "cut off," 3:6a) and that all others soon would also experience (כרת, "cut off," 1:3). This fate included "all that I have purposed to visit against her." Zephaniah uses the verb "visit" (פקד) to signal God's coming judgment on Judah (1:8, 12) and the blessing he pledged for her remnant (2:7). Here it refers to the covenant curses (Lev 26:14–33; Deut 28:15–68) that YHWH had appointed against Judah for covenant violation.[283]

Second, the verb "cut off" (כרת) indicates that the city's rebellion would result in the same fate that God had already begun working against others. As he had "cut off" (כרת) nations (3:6a), so he would "cut off" (כרת) Jerusalem (3:7d), unless she repented (cf. 2:4; Jer 18:7–10).

Third, YHWH's point is far greater than the collapse of the city. When used for personal dwellings, "shelter" (מָעוֹן) refers only to God as the Shelter of his people (Deut 33:27; Pss 71:3; 91:9)[284] or to his abode, whether in heaven (Deut 26:15; 2 Chr 30:27;

Jer 25:30) or at his earthly sanctuary (1 Sam 2:29; 2 Chr 32:15; Ps 76:3). The other main use is of a "den" or "lair" for wild animals.[285] God declared through Jeremiah that he would make Judah a den if they continued to rebel (e.g., Jer 9:10; 10:22; 49:22). Ironically, in view of her beastly leadership (Zeph 3:3–4), Jerusalem was already a lair for beasts while also being God's dwelling place (3:5). His presence was their Shelter, yet their sustained disobedience had destined them to lose this treasure, which finally happened as stated in Ezek 11:23 (cf. Ezek 8:4; 10:4, 18–19).[286]

• Its Nature (3:7e–f)

Heeding God's "instruction" would have resulted in forgiveness and life, but the prophet uses a strong disjunctive "however" (אָכֵן) to signal the inhabitants of Judah's response: "They arose early; they corrupted all their deeds" (Zeph 3:7e–f).[287] The initial verb rendered "they arose early" (הִשְׁכִּימוּ) emphasizes the people's eagerness to sin (3:7e) and contrasts with YHWH's commitment to work his judgment "morning by morning" (3:5). The next clause clarifies this point and indicates the nature of Judah's resistance to growth (3:7f). The *hiphil* of the verb שחת means "to ruin,

---

283. On the certainty of Israel/Judah's lasting covenant disloyalty and destruction, see Deut 4:25–28 and 31:16–18, 27–29. But God's promise of restoration blessing was just as certain as the curse (Deut 4:30–31; 30:1–14; cf. Lev 26:40–45). O'Connor links כל with what precedes and renders the whole: "Nothing shall be cut off from her dwelling when I take notice of her" (O'Connor, *Hebrew Verse Structure*, 257). This reading misses the passage's punishment context, separates the subject irregularly from the verb, treats the noun מְעוֹנָה ("her shelter") as if it had a preposed מִן preposition ("from"), and fails to account for the regularity of כֹּל אֲשֶׁר ("all that") in the OT (occurring some 426 times).

284. In these texts, "shelter" (מָעוֹן) often parallels "rock" (סֶלַע, צוּר) and/or "fortress" (מְצוּדָה).

285. See Ps 104:22; Job 37:8; 38:40; Song 4:8; Amos 3:4; Nah 2:12–13.

286. Both Ben Zvi and Berlin miss the proper referent of

"shelter" when they claim that the "dwelling" this "person" will lose is the city (Ben Zvi, *Book of Zephaniah*, 217; Berlin, *Zephaniah*, 132). Many contemporary scholars, along with the RSV and NRSVue, follow the LXX and Peshitta here, which read מֵעֵינֶיהָ ("from her eyes" = ἐξ ὀφθαλμῶν αὐτῆς) instead of מְעוֹנָה ("her shelter"). House follows this reading, which "fits the context of Yahweh's correction of the city better than the MT" (House, *Zephaniah: A Prophetic Drama*, 132, on Zeph 3:7[b]; cf. J. M. P. Smith, "Book of Zephaniah," 242; Rudolph, *Micha, Nahum, Habakuk, Zephanja*, 286; R. L. Smith, *Micah–Malachi*, 68; Roberts, *Nahum, Habakkuk, and Zephaniah*, 205). However, as shown, losing YHWH as "shelter" perfectly fits both the immediate literary context and the broader focus on the day of YHWH.

287. For examples of אָכֵן as a strong adversative, see Ps 82:6–7; Isa 49:4; 53:3–4; Jer 3:19–20.

destroy,"[288] the effected product of which is marked by the direct object "all their deeds" (כֹּל עֲלִילוֹתָם).[289] Moses had predicted that stubborn Israel would "act corruptly" (*hiphil* שחת) in the promised land, ultimately resulting in the covenant curses (Deut 31:16–18). Thus, following the pattern of the fool (cf. Ps 14:1; 53:2[1]) and of those in the days of the flood (Gen 6:11–12), the Judeans "corrupted" *all* their actions (cf. Deut 32:5; Isa 1:4; Hos 9:9), resulting in disaster (cf. Zeph 1:2–4, 18; 3:11).[290]

Canonical and Theological Significance

The Eschatological Realization of YHWH's Judgment as the Light in Zephaniah 3:5[291]

Zephaniah 3:5 contrasts the sinful tendencies of Jerusalem's leaders with YHWH's righteousness and notes how God daily gives foretastes of his final verdict to punish sin (i.e., "his judgment," מִשְׁפָּטוֹ, κρίμα αὐτοῦ). In Zephaniah's day, people encountered such typological glimpses through five ways: (1) the prophets' indictments and curses, (2) judges' upright decisions, (3) YHWH punishing neighboring nations, (4) the daily temple sacrifices, and (5) YHWH forbearing with rebellious people. Each just act stressed sin's gravity and preemptively manifested the "light" (אוֹר, φῶς) to lead Judah in the right path and to show that God would triumph over all darkness and evil.

Scripture commonly associates light with God's overcoming darkness and judging sin. Light's triumph over darkness at creation first sets the pattern (Gen 1:3). It appears again in Sodom and Gomorrah's destruction (19:15, 23), the plagues against Egypt and the exodus (Exod 10:22–23; 14:19–20, 24, 27), and in Jericho's ruin (Josh 6:15). Both Testaments commonly associate the coming of light with God's new creation that overcomes the old order.[292]

Within this biblical context, Zephaniah declares that "morning by morning [YHWH] gives his judgment for the light" (Zeph 3:5), and other prophets spoke parallel truths. After noting YHWH's commitment to "let linger my judgment for a light

---

288. "פָּנָה," *HALOT* 1470–71.

289. In rare instances a direct object can act as the action's agent (see *BHRG*, §32.2.1[4]), which here would mean that "all their deeds" were the means by which they "destroyed" others. However, it is likely that the direct object simply identifies the verb's effected patient or product.

290. In contrast to the majority of scholars (e.g., R. L. Smith, *Micah–Malachi*, 139–40; Ball, *Rhetorical Study of Zephaniah*, 167–70; Seybold, *Nahum, Habakuk, Zephanja*, 112; Vlaardingerbroek, *Zephaniah*, 183), Sweeney unpersuasively reads Zeph 3:7 as pointing to Judah's humbling rather than

destruction since he thinks 3:6–7 provides "the basis for the following call . . . to wait for YHWH (v. 8)" (Sweeney, *Zephaniah*, 176–78). As argued below, 3:8 draws an inference from the whole unit running from 2:5–3:7, includes Judah among the nations that YHWH will destroy, and calls the faithful remnant within it to wait on YHWH rather than the entire rebellious nation (cf. 2:3).

291. The discussion that follows is significantly drawn from DeRouchie, "YHWH's Judgment Is New Every Morning," 131–46.

292. See Isa 9:2; 58:8, 10; 60:1, 3, 19–20; Mal 4:2; Eph 5:8, 14.

to peoples" (Isa 51:4), Isaiah noted how the remnant of his day hoped "for the light" but only experienced darkness (59:9). They longed for God to right all wrongs, and this he would do when his "light"—the messianic King, Servant, and Conqueror—would arrive, bringing God's light-giving judgment.[293] Similarly, YHWH noted that through prophetic speech "my judgment goes forth as the light" (Hos 6:5). This judgment included Israel's exile and a third-day resurrection/second exodus that, as "certain as dawn" (6:3), both YHWH and his Messiah would effect.[294] Finally, righteous YHWH himself will render his "judgment" and stand as "the light" (Mic 7:8–9) as he works for his remnant people's salvation (vv. 18–19), ultimately through his shepherd King (5:2–5; 7:14–17).

Within this biblical framework that includes Zeph 3:5, John 3 addresses similar realities with similar vocabulary by contrasting the coming divine wrath with the light of God's Son that leads to eternal life.

> Whoever believes in him [i.e., God's Son] is not judged [κρίνεται]. But the one who does not believe in him is already judged [κέκριται], because he has not believed in the name of the only Son of God. And this is the judgment [ἡ κρίσις]—that the light [τὸ φῶς] has come into the world, and the humans have loved the darkness rather than the light [τὸ φῶς] because their works were evil. For everyone who is doing wicked things hates the light [τὸ φῶς] and does not come to the light [τὸ φῶς], in order that his works will not be exposed. (John 3:18–19).

John 3 speaks of Christ's incarnation as the intrusion of "light" into the world and associates it with God's "judgment." Both Zephaniah and John speak of "judgment" and "light," both speak of judgment as the light, and both speak of this judgment operating as the light in the *present* yet in a way that anticipates a greater *future* illumination. John regularly portrays Jesus as God's "light"[295] and believes that God the Father granted Jesus his Son authority to judge and that he would do so on the final day (5:26–29). Whether consciously thinking of Zeph 3 or not, this implies that John would have viewed Zephaniah's motif of God's "judgment as the light" as a predictive foretaste that both clarifies and anticipates Christ's final judgment. Nevertheless, those who now fail to come to the light that God has revealed in the person of his Son are already condemned, with God's wrath remaining on them (John 3:36). Indeed, for fear that others will both recognize and condemn their shameful deeds, they remain in the darkness, just like the shameful political and religious leaders of Zephaniah's day (Zeph 3:2–5).

---

293. See Isa 9:2, 6; 42:6; 49:6; Matt 4:15–16; Luke 1:79; John 1:4–5, 9; 8:12; Rev 21:23–25.

294. See Hos 1:10; 3:5; 6:2; 11:10–11; 14:4–8; cf. Rom 9:26.

295. See John 1:4–5, 7–8, 9; 3:19–21; 8:12; 9:5; 11:9–10; 12:35–36, 46.

Corresponding to the five ways God gave "his judgment for the light" in Zephaniah's day, we see comparable expressions linked with Jesus in John's gospel. First, Jesus is the ultimate prophet who proclaimed the seriousness of sin and the need for repentance before God (John 4:19, 44; 6:14; 7:40; 9:17). Second and third, he is the decisive judge who judges justly and truly and who provides the only means of passing from death to life; he is also the one who will execute final judgment against the unrepentant on the last day (5:22–24, 27–30; 8:16; 9:39; 12:31, 48; 16:8–11). Fourth, he is God's Lamb who came to take away the sins of the world (1:29, 36; 3:15–16); he did this by bearing God's wrath as he served as a sacrificial substitute for his sheep. These are the believers from the Jews and others scattered throughout the earth (10:16–18; 11:51–52; cf. Rev 5:9; 7:9). Fifth, even before the sun ever rose upon the earth, Jesus was the source of all life (John 1:1–3), and his life became the light leading to life for mankind—a light that darkness cannot overcome (1:4–5). His sacrifice paved the way for sinners today to see the sunrise rather than wake up to a flood of judgment (see Gen 8:20–22; cf. Matt 5:45; Acts 14:27). And each glimmer of such heavenly glories should nurture humility at YHWH's mercy for letting darkness dissipate and should move one to consider how a just God could let light overcome night.

One day, the glory of God shining through the Lamb will be the only light. Those redeemed from the nations will walk in it, and night will be no more (Rev 21:23–25). This is the ultimate hope to which Zeph 3:5 points. May we celebrate that his judgment is new every morning! Great is your faithfulness, O God!

A Proper Response to 2:5–3:7

Turn from Pride and Oppression to Humility and Righteousness While There Is Hope

Zephaniah equates the state and fate of Jerusalem's faithless Israelites whom he earlier called "the remnant of the Baal" (Zeph 1:4) with that of their pagan neighbors. Like the nations who elevated themselves at the expense of others (2:8, 10, 15), Jerusalem had become oppressive and unjust to its own people (3:1, 3–4). And just as YHWH promised to destroy the nations for their sin (2:5, 9, 13), he would also cut off Jerusalem, destroying the city (3:7). In famishing the gods of the earth, YHWH promises to remove every false security in which people trust, resulting in every human bowing to him, whether as believing remnant or defeated rebel (2:11; cf. Phil 2:10–11; Rev 5:8–14). He "will clear his threshing floor and gather his wheat into the barn, but the chaff he will burn with unquenchable fire" (Matt 3:12; cf. Zeph 2:1–2).

Convinced of the fleeting nature of the world and its desires, we must "not love the world or the things in the world" (1 John 2:15, 17). Indeed, knowing that "salvation is nearer to us now than when we first believed," we must "put on Christ, and make no provision for the flesh, to gratify its desires" (Rom 13:11, 14). If it was foolish in Zephaniah's day to trust in foreign powers, whether spiritual or earthly (Zeph 2:11; 3:6–7), how much more foolish is it today since Christ has *already* "disarmed the rulers and authorities . . . by triumphing over them" (Col 2:15)? "Before a birthing of a decree" (Zeph 2:2; i.e., before the decree takes effect), turn from pride and oppression to seek YHWH, humility, and righteousness. Only in such a context is there hope for being part of the remnant, whom God will save (2:3, 7, 9).

Fear YHWH and Learn from His Merciful Discipline

Zephaniah stresses that our righteous God (Zeph 3:5) is ever ready to pardon and restore any who "fear" him and "receive correction" (3:7). Sinners should be awed by a merciful God whose revealed purpose in discipline is to redeem rebels (Lev 26:14–16, 18, 21, 23–24, 27–28). Rather than bringing immediate death, YHWH often bestows kindness, forbearance, and patience to generate repentance (Rom 2:4) and to awaken new or sustained faith in his future grace (11:20–22). Thus, God says, "Those whom I love, I reprove and discipline, so be zealous and repent" (Rev 3:19). The majority in Judah remained deaf to God's voice and were unreceptive to his instruction; they did not trust YHWH or draw near to him (Zeph 3:2, 7). YHWH intended his discipline to lead Judah to repentance (cf. Amos 4:6–12; Rev 16:8–10) by seeing their sin as a serious offense and by recognizing that he alone was their sure Shelter (Zeph 3:6–7; cf. Isa 20:1–6; Mal 1:4–5). Nevertheless, the people remained unresponsive, living in the darkness rather than following the light God supplied (Zeph 3:5).[296] Will we do the same? May we be a people who fear God, resting in his new covenant promise that he will enable for his elect the very fear and passionate following that he commands (Jer 32:40).

Take Comfort, Saints, Knowing YHWH Will Justly Destroy All Persecutors.

Zephaniah 2:5–3:7 laments the state and fate of rebels from both Judah's neighboring nations (2:5–15) and Jerusalem itself (3:1–7). Included in these verses are many strong warnings to sinners, which should ultimately give hope to the redeemed. YHWH will decisively punish all who infect God's people with worldliness (i.e., the Philistines, 1:11), who disgrace and persecute them (i.e., the Moabites and Ammonites, 2:8, 10), or who flaunt themselves as superior (i.e., the Assyrians, 2:15). YHWH is "righteous" and "never does wrong" (3:5), and the daily light of judgment will ultimately come to its rightful end (3:8). He will "destroy" (2:5), "plunder" (2:9), and desolate (2:13, 15) all his enemies, and every false source of strength and security he will famish (2:11). Afterward, he will reapportion goods and turf as a lasting

---

296. For the ultimate reason behind their unresponsiveness, compare Deut 29:3[4] and Rom 11:7–8 with Rom 9:22–24.

supply for his remnant people (2:7, 9). Then, they will worship him as those freed and redeemed (2:11).

Paul clarifies the implications of this coming judgment for believers today, for it is this future hope of justice that empowers us to resist retaliation and to love in the present: "If possible, as far as it depends on you, be living at peace with everyone. Never be avenging yourselves, beloved, but give place to the wrath, for it is written, 'Vengeance is mine, I will repay, says the Lord.' On the contrary, 'if your enemy is hungry, feed him; if he is thirsty, give him something to drink.' . . . Do not be overcome by evil, but overcome evil with good" (Rom 12:18–21). With Zephaniah's declaration of punishment against Assyria in view, Calvin reflected on how Christians can hope for the day when God will fully eradicate evil:

> If, then, our enemies triumph now, and their haughtiness is intolerable, let us know, that the sooner the vengeance of God will overtake them; if they are become insensible in their prosperity, and secure, and despise all dangers, they thus provoke God's wrath, and especially if to their pride and hardness they add cruelty, so as basely to persecute the Church of God, to spoil, to plunder, and to slay his people, as we see them doing. Since then our enemies are so wanton, we may see as in a mirror their near destruction, such as is foretold by the Prophet: for he spoke not only of his age, but designed to teach us, by the prophetic spirit, how dear to God is the safety of his Church; and the future lot of the ungodly till the end of the world will no doubt be such as Nineveh is described here to have been—that though they swell with pride for a time, and promise themselves every success against the innocent, God will yet put a stop to their insolence and check their cruelty, when the proper time shall come.[297]

---

297. Calvin, "Habakkuk, Zephaniah, Haggai," 259.

Zephaniah 2:1–3:20b   225

III.2 Zephaniah 3:8–20b

Stage 2: *The Appeal to Wait for YHWH to Enjoy Salvation*

Main Idea of Zephaniah 3:8–20b

The faithful remnant from Judah and other lands must wait for YHWH to enjoy salvation.

> III. The Substance of the Savior's Invitation to Satisfaction: Charges to Seek YHWH Together and to Wait (2:1–3:20b)
> III.1 Stage 1: The Appeal to Seek YHWH Together to Avoid Punishment (2:1–3:7)
> → **III.2 Stage 2: The Appeal to Wait for YHWH to Enjoy Salvation (3:8–20b)**
>   **A. The Charge to Wait for YHWH to Act (3:8–10)**
>   **B. Promises to Motivate Waiting for YHWH: The Remnant's Satisfying Salvation (3:11–20b)**

Literary Context of Zephaniah 3:8–20b

The use of the masculine plural imperative in YHWH's call "wait for me" in 3:8 signals the start of stage 2 of the prophet's primary exhortations. In stage 1 (2:1–3:7), Zephaniah charged the remnant from Judah and other lands to seek YHWH together to avoid punishment. Now he urges this same remnant to wait for YHWH to enjoy salvation (3:8–20b). The particle לָכֵן ("therefore") at the head of 3:8 highlights that the need for the remnant to patiently trust God (3:8) is inferred from the truth that God will punish both Judah's neighbors (2:5–15) and Jerusalem herself (3:1–7). The call to wait is also motivated by a series of promises related to the remnant's satisfying salvation (3:11–20b). For more, see the "Literary Context" discussion at the introduction to Part III.

Zephaniah 3:8–10

A. The Charge to Wait for YHWH to Act (3:8–10)

Main Idea of the Passage

The faithful remnant from Judah and beyond must wait for YHWH because he still intends to destroy his global enemies and to transform a community of global worshipers.

Literary Context

Zephaniah has already charged the believing remnant of Judah and other lands to seek YHWH together to avoid punishment (2:1–4). Now he adds stage 2 of his invitation to satisfaction. Those following YHWH must also "*wait*" (חַכּוּ) for him (3:8) to enjoy the coming deliverance. Amid the suffering associated with the day of YHWH, joyous salvation comes through looking and longing, heeding and hoping, entreating and trusting—patiently pursuing God together.

Zephaniah included two units in 2:5–15 and 3:1–7 that each begin with parallel uses of asyndetic "Woe" (הוֹי). These two units (1) detail the sad state and fate of Judah's neighbors and of Jerusalem herself, (2) divide the imperatives that give the first and second stages of his prophetic exhortation, and (3) indicate why the remnant should seek YHWH together. Now, the inferential particle "Therefore" (לָכֵן) in 3:8 further shows that 2:5–3:7 functions as the basis for the imperatives in 2:1, 3 and 3:8. Thus, 2:5–3:7 explains why Judah's remnant must not only pursue God together (2:1, 3) but also do so patiently (3:8).

Following the charge to "wait" for YHWH in 3:8a, the prophet encourages persistent trust by highlighting the faithful's future hope. Initially, a dual basis for heeding his charge to "wait" is God's future judgment on the nations (3:8b–c) and his promise of global restoration (3:9–10). Zephaniah then explains his highest motivation for the remnant's obedience (3:11–20b). Those who seek and wait for YHWH together will experience deliverance that will entail God removing their shame (3:11–13), climaxing their joy (3:14–15), and consummating their rescue (3:16–20b), all for his joy (3:17) and glory (3:19–20).

> III. The Substance of the Savior's Invitation to Satisfaction: Charges to Seek YHWH Together and to Wait (2:1–3:20b)
>   III.1 Stage 1: The Appeal to Seek YHWH Together to Avoid Punishment (2:1–3:7)
> ➡ **III.2 Stage 2: The Appeal to Wait for YHWH to Enjoy Salvation (3:8–20b)**
>   **A. The Charge to Wait for YHWH to Act (3:8–10)**
>   B. Promises to Motivate Waiting for YHWH: The Remnant's Satisfying Salvation (3:11–20b)

Translation and Exegetical Outline

(See page 229.)

Structure and Literary Form

Scholars disagree on the role of the inferential particle "therefore" (לָכֵן) plus imperative "wait" (חַכּוּ) in Zeph 3:8. This produces different understandings of the meaning and role of 3:8 along with the book's overarching structure. OT prophets commonly employ לָכֵן to mark a divine verdict following an accusation of covenant (dis)loyalty (e.g., Zeph 2:9; Hos 2:6; Ezek 5:10–11).[1] Thus, many scholars assume that Zephaniah draws a negative inference from at least part of the indictments in 3:1–7. For some, this means 3:8 is a threat that contrasts with the restoration material in 3:9–20b.[2] That is, *because* those in Jerusalem have oppressed the weak and shamefully despised YHWH (3:1–5) and/or have not feared YHWH and received instruction (3:7), they must *therefore* await coming destruction (3:8). Irsigler claims that 3:8 infers from 3:6–7 and announces YHWH's coming punishment against the wicked Jerusalemites, sarcastically urging them to "just wait!" for God's judgment.[3]

---

1. Wolff notes, "In the older prophets, לכן almost always marks the transition from the proof of guilt to the threat of punishment" (Wolff, *Hosea*, 35–36).

2. Rudolph, *Micha, Nahum, Habakuk, Zephanja*, 289–90; Vlaardingerbroek, *Zephaniah*, 184, 190; Irsigler, *Zefanja*, 342, 343–44; Renz, *Books of Nahum, Habakkuk, and Zephaniah*, 582–86, 595–97. For the prophetic judgment speech, see Sweeney, *Isaiah 1–39*, 533–34.

3. Irsigler, *Zefanja*, 342, 353; cf. Vlaardingerbroek, *Zephaniah*, 184.

Zephaniah 3:8–10[1]

III.2 Stage 2: The Appeal to Wait for YHWH to Enjoy Salvation (3:8–20b)

A. The Charge to Wait for YHWH to Act (3:8–10)

1. The Charge to Wait for YHWH (3:8a)

2. Two Reasons to Wait for YHWH (3:8b–10)

a. YHWH's Intent to Punish All the Wicked of the Earth (3:8b–c)

b. YHWH's Promise to Create a Community of Worshipers from the Whole Earth (3:9–10)

(1) The Details of the Promise (3:9)

(2) The Exposition of the Promise (3:10)

8a [Y][2] Therefore, wait for me —the utterance of YHWH—for the day of my rising as witness.

לָכֵן חַכּוּ־לִי נְאֻם־יְהוָה לְיוֹם קוּמִי לְעַד

8b For my judgment is to gather nations, to assemble kingdoms, to pour out on them my indignation—all the fury of my anger,

כִּי מִשְׁפָּטִי לֶאֱסֹף גּוֹיִם לְקָבְצִי מַמְלָכוֹת לִשְׁפֹּךְ עֲלֵיהֶם זַעְמִי כֹּל חֲרוֹן אַפִּי

8c for in the fire of my jealousy all the earth will be consumed.

כִּי בְּאֵשׁ קִנְאָתִי תֵּאָכֵל כָּל־הָאָרֶץ

9 For then I will change for peoples a purified lip so that all of them may call on the name YHWH, to serve him with one shoulder.

כִּי־אָז אֶהְפֹּךְ אֶל־עַמִּים שָׂפָה בְרוּרָה לִקְרֹא כֻלָּם בְּשֵׁם יְהוָה לְעָבְדוֹ שְׁכֶם אֶחָד

10 From the region of the rivers of Cush, my supplicants, the daughter of my scattered ones, will carry my offering.

מֵעֵבֶר לְנַהֲרֵי־כוּשׁ עֲתָרַי בַּת־פּוּצַי יוֹבִלוּן מִנְחָתִי

---

1. For information on the guidelines used for tracing the argument, see The Method in the introduction, pp. XX.

2. According to the Masoretes, Zeph 3:8 is the only verse in the Hebrew Bible that includes all the letters of the alphabet (שׁ stands for both שׁ and שׂ) including final letters.

*The inside arrows pointing upward mark 3:8b–20b as a unit subordinate to 3:8a, with v. 8b–c and vv. 9–10 marked with a conjunction כ indicating the grounds for the imperative in v. 8a, and vv. 11–20b unmarked and supplying motivation for v. 8a.

Renz observes that 3:8 "does not seem to fit with the preceding," for "the verse speaks of judgment on nations and kingdoms, but the preceding verses accuse Jerusalem." Therefore, the charge to "wait" and the declaration of punishment in 3:8 conclude the statements of disaster running from all of 2:5–3:7.[4]

Others rightly recognize that the command in 3:8 does not initiate a judgment speech because elsewhere the verbal root in the imperative "wait" (חַכּוּ) of 3:8 never introduces negative threats.[5] Rather, the verb functions either neutrally (e.g., 2 Kgs 7:9; Job 3:24; Hos 6:9) or to urge positive anticipation, like waiting for God's judgment to pass (Isa 8:17) or his deliverance to come (e.g., Ps 33:20; Isa 64:4; Hab 2:3). Some affirm the positive nature of the verb "wait" but believe Zephaniah speaks sarcastically in 3:8.[6] Renz sees prophetic "irony" at work yet believes the command to "wait" is still a threat.[7] However, grammatical and macro-structural features suggest that 3:8 is positive, calling the remnant to wait for YHWH in hope.

First, two grammatical features support reading Zeph 3:8 positively.

(1) In 3:1–7, the prophet refers to Jerusalem in third feminine singular (Zeph 3:1–5, 7) and its rebellious inhabitants in third masculine plural (3:7), but the imperative "wait" in 3:8 is in second masculine plural.[8] This latter formation links 3:8 with the book's only other earlier imperatives at 2:1 and 3, which are all second masculine plural. This connection supports reading 3:8 as supplying stage 2 of the Savior's invitation to satisfaction and addressing the faithful remnant from Judah and other lands who have heeded the call to seek YHWH together.[9] As such, 3:8 infers (לָכֵן, "therefore") from the state and fate of the rebels from both the surrounding nations and Jerusalem (2:5–15; 3:1–7). As noted above, the unit in 2:5–3:7 provides two reasons why the remnant should seek YHWH together (2:1–4). The remnant

---

4. Renz, *Books of Nahum, Habakkuk, and Zephaniah*, 596; cf. 598–99. Renz believes that "Zeph 1:2–3:5 offers a coherent message," which originally concluded with 3:8. In contrast, he claims 3:6–7, 9–20 are later additions, suggesting that these speeches treat the judgments as having already occurred (Renz, *Books of Nahum, Habakkuk, and Zephaniah*, 582–86, 595–97, 605–7, 623–27, 637–38). Renz fails to consider seriously the unity of 1:2–3:20. He also unnecessarily treats 3:6–7 as viewing as past what 2:5–15 treated as future, strains the syntax in 3:8–10, fails to appreciate the way 3:11–13 parallels 3:16–20, and misses the imperatives' role in 3:14–15.

5. Keil, " Twelve Minor Prophets," 10:456 (2:153); J. M. P. Smith, "Book of Zephaniah," 244; Motyer, "Zephaniah," 948; Robertson, *Books of Nahum, Habakkuk, and Zephaniah*, 326; Roberts, *Nahum, Habakkuk, and Zephaniah*, 215; Floyd, *Minor Prophets, Part 2*, 202–3; Sweeney, *Zephaniah*, 179–80; Patterson, *Nahum, Habakkuk, Zephaniah*, 326.

6. Irsigler, *Zefanja*, 342, 353; Larry L. Walker, "Zephaniah," in *Daniel-Malachi*, 2nd ed., EBC 8 (Grand Rapids: Zondervan, 2008), 685.

7. Renz, *Books of Nahum, Habakkuk, and Zephaniah*, 598–99; cf. Ball, *Rhetorical Study of Zephaniah*, 231.

8. Both the LXX and Vulgate modified the Hebrew to singular imperatives (Greek = ὑπόμεινόν με; Latin = *expecta me*), likely to link Zeph 3:8 more clearly to the singular forms in 3:1–7. Renz claims the MT's masculine plural imperative in 3:8 must address the inhabitants of Jerusalem at the end of 3:7 (Renz, *Books of Nahum, Habakkuk, and Zephaniah*, 594nl).

9. Floyd recognizes the similarity in form and content between 3:8 and 2:1–3 and also affirms that these texts are "the two main structural poles around which the rest of the material is organized" (Floyd, *Minor Prophets, Part 2*, 203; cf. Ryou, *Zephaniah's Oracles*, 284–85). For others who link 3:8 and 2:3, see Keil, " Twelve Minor Prophets," 10:456 (2:153); J. M. P. Smith, "Book of Zephaniah," 244; Chisholm, *Interpreting the Minor Prophets*, 210; Roberts, *Nahum, Habakkuk, and Zephaniah*, 215; Bailey, "Zephaniah," 484; Tachick, *Use of Zephaniah 3 in John 12*, 92–93.

should do so (2:1–4) *because* of the impending doom on Judah's neighbors (2:5–15) and on Jerusalem (3:1–7). Furthermore, *because* of this coming destruction (2:5–3:7), they must also wait for YHWH to rise as covenant witness (3:8–10).

In contrast, some affirm that 3:8 draws an inference from 3:1–7 (or 3:6–7), but they explain the logic differently. Roberts concludes that the "them" upon whom YHWH will pour his wrath must be those in Jerusalem who corrupted their deeds (3:7) and not the nearer "nations" and "kingdoms" in the very clause of 3:8b.[10] From an opposite perspective, Sweeney contends that the nations in 3:8 do not include Judah and that God pours out his wrath on them so that they may in turn affirm his long-term commitment to Jerusalem despite her prior judgment.[11] Similarly, Motyer recognizes that חכה ("wait") never communicates punishment but claims 3:8 gives hope to the very nation against which YHWH declared doom in 3:7.[12]

None of these approaches work, for Zephaniah is clear that God will vindicate only the remnant seeking YHWH (2:3, 7, 9; 3:12–13) and not Judah as a whole (1:4–6, 7–13; 3:1–7, 11). Also, Jerusalem is included among "all the earth" and the "nations" and "kingdoms" that YHWH intends to consume (3:8; cf. 1:18).[13] In 3:7, YHWH hopes that Jerusalem would heed his discipline with fear so he could relent from his purposed disaster, but instead "they arose early; they corrupted all their deeds" and thereby ensured coming doom (cf. 2 Kgs 21:11–15; 23:26–27). Hope exists only for the remnant who will seek YHWH together and wait for him.

(2) This leads to the next grammatical element justifying an optimistic reading of 3:8. After the initial imperative "wait!," YHWH declares two reasons why those he charges must patiently trust him. Both reasons begin with the causal particle "for" (כִּי) and the second can only apply to a hopeful people. The remnant must endure in faith *because* YHWH will punish all the earth's wicked during his great eschatological ingathering (3:8b–c) and *because* at the time of this ingathering (כִּי־אָז "for then") God will create a body of worshipers from the whole earth (3:9–10). Smith's dismissal of כִּי־אָז as having "no meaning" suggests that he has not understood the passage.[14] Vlaardingerbroek admits that the conjunction "for" (כִּי) at the head of 3:9 "is hard

---

10. Roberts, *Nahum, Habakkuk, and Zephaniah*, 216.

11. Sweeney, *Zephaniah*, 178–79. Sweeney affirms that "the particle לָכֵן . . . does express consequentiality" and that Zephaniah refers "to Jerusalem's past wrongdoing" in 3:7 as "an important basis for the calls to wait for YHWH (3:8) and to seek YHWH before it's too late (2:1–3)." However, the consequentiality "must be of a different nature" (Sweeney, *Zephaniah*, 178–79). See also J. M. P. Smith, "Book of Zephaniah," 246–47. Vlaardingerbroek asserts that the global elements of 3:8 are secondary (Vlaardingerbroek, *Zephaniah*, 179–80), but this inadequately attempts to resolve apparent exegetical tensions and fails to explain a later editor's contradiction of Zephaniah's oracle.

12. Motyer, "Zephaniah," 948; cf. Ben Zvi, "Understanding the Message of the Tripartite Prophetic Books," 94, 100.

13. Motyer and Sweeney link YHWH's cutting off nations in 3:6 to his punishing nations in 3:8 (Motyer, "Zephaniah," 948; Sweeney, *Zephaniah*, 179). However, in 3:6 YHWH had already encouraged Jerusalem's repentance by destroying nations, and the inference in 3:8 predicts the world's complete and future decimation, in which Judah participates.

14. George Adam Smith, *The Book of the Twelve Prophets*, 2nd ed. (New York: Doubleday, 1930), 2:69.

to pin down," especially "without a preceding clause."[15] Irsigler attempts to read the כִּי־אָז in 3:9 contrastively as "however, then,"[16] but an adversative rendering for כִּי requires at least an understood preceding negative, which this context lacks.[17] Renz initially notes that כִּי־אָז "always has a close relationship with what preceded" and that the clause expresses the "ultimate result" [apparently of 3:8],[18] but he contradicts this logic when he later claims that כִּי only adds emphasis ("surely then") and that כִּי־אָז signals only a temporal transition.[19] Wendland and Clark designate the כִּי as "emphatic consequential" with a translation of "so, indeed."[20] Because the כִּי־אָז clause in 3:9 indicates an event temporally posterior to the main clause in 3:8a, 3:9 does indeed signal the consequence of what precedes.[21] However, the result functions rhetorically to motivate the faithful remnant to wait, thus justifying the translation "for then." As Sweeney observes, "The expanded particle כִּי־אָז points to vv. 9–10 as the climactic elements in the reasons given for the basic exhortation of the passage in v. 8a, 'wait for me.'"[22]

Second, reading 3:8 as a positive appeal and as the beginning of stage 2 of Zephaniah's invitation to satisfaction manifests remarkable and apparently intentional symmetry within the book's main exhortation section. Note the right column in figure 7.1 below. Both stages 1 and 2 follow the same basic pattern: One or more second masculine plural imperatives are grounded in one or more כִּי ("for") clauses followed by two extended parallel sections (each beginning the same way) that provide unmarked motivation for the command(s). The balance enhances the book's harmony and justifies reading 3:8 as part of Zephaniah's central exhortation to the remnant.

The positive use of the imperative in 3:8 identifies the unit as directive or parenetic speech.[23] The whole is a "prophetic exhortation," which often includes varied types of motivations.[24] In sum, (1) the lexical usage of the verb "wait" in Scripture, (2) the unlikelihood that 3:8 draws an inference only from 3:1–7, (3) the link between the second masculine plural imperatives in 2:1, 3 and 3:8, and (4) the positive reason for waiting supplied in 3:9 all suggest that 3:8 positively charges the remnant rather than negatively warns rebels.

---

15. Vlaardingerbroek, *Zephaniah*, 196.

16. Irsigler, *Zefanja*, 344; so, too, Calvin, "Habakkuk, Zephaniah, Haggai," 283; Ben Zvi, *Book of Zephaniah*, 226n740.

17. GKC, §163a, b; *IBHS*, §39.3.5d; Carl Martin Follingstad, *Deictic Viewpoint in Biblical Hebrew Text: A Syntagmatic and Paradigmatic Analysis of the Particle* כי *(Kî)*, Special Issue, *JOTT* (Dallas: SIL International, 2001), 12, 241–43; 252–57, 280–81; Joüon, §172c; Williams and Beckman, *Williams' Hebrew Syntax*, §447; *BHRG*, §40.29.2.3. Cf. Gen 17:15; 18:15; 19:2; 32:29; Josh 5:14; 17:16–18; 1 Sam 8:7; 15:35; 2 Sam 20:21; 1 Kgs 18:18; 21:15; Amos 7:14.

18. Renz, *Books of Nahum, Habakkuk, and Zephaniah*, 603n.a.

19. Renz, *Books of Nahum, Habakkuk, and Zephaniah*, 607–8.

20. Wendland and Clark, "Zephaniah," 30; cf. Renz, *Books of Nahum, Habakkuk, and Zephaniah*, 603n.a, 608.

21. Barry L. Bandstra, "The Syntax of the Particle 'Ky' in Biblical Hebrew and Ugaritic" (PhD diss., Yale University, 1982), 137.

22. Sweeney, *Zephaniah*, 183; cf. Patterson, *Nahum, Habakkuk, Zephaniah*, 328.

23. See DeRouchie, *How to Understand and Apply*, 112–13; cf. Garrett and DeRouchie, *A Modern Grammar for Biblical Hebrew*, 330–33.

24. Floyd, *Minor Prophets, Part 2*, 203, 213, 235; see Sweeney, *Isaiah 1–39*, 527.

Figure 7.1: The Balanced Structure of Zephaniah's Stage 1 and 2 Exhortations	
Stage 1: The Appeal to Seek YHWH Together to Avoid Punishment (2:1–3:7)	
1. The Charge to Unite in Submission to YHWH (2:1–2)	
2. The Charge to Seek YHWH in Righteousness and Humility (2:3–4)	
a. The Charge to Seek YHWH (2:3)	Commands (2mp imperatives)
b. An Initial Reason to Seek YHWH (2:4)	Initial basis fronted with "for" (כִּי)
3. Further Reasons to Seek YHWH Together (2:5–3:7)	Two unmarked reasons, both beginning with "Woe!" (הוֹי)
a. The Lamentable State and Fate of the Rebels from the Foreign Nations (2:5–15)	
b. The Lamentable State and Fate of the Rebels from Jerusalem (3:1–7)	
Stage 2: The Appeal to Wait for YHWH to Enjoy Salvation (3:8–20)	
1. The Charge to Wait for YHWH to Act (3:8–10)	
a. The Charge to Wait for YHWH (3:8a)	Command (2mp imperative)
b. Two Reasons to Wait for YHWH (3:8b–10)	Two initial bases, both fronted with "for" (כִּי)
2. Promises to Motivate Waiting for YHWH: The Remnant's Satisfying Salvation (3:11–20b)	Two unmarked promises, both introduced by "in that day" (בַּיּוֹם הַהוּא)
a. The Promise that YHWH Will Not Shame Jerusalem (3:11–13)	
b. A Discursive Charge to Rejoice as if the Great Salvation Has Already Occurred (3:14–15)	
c. The Promise That YHWH Will Save Completely (3:16–20b)	

Accordingly, stage 2 of the Savior's exhortation to pursue him patiently consists of two main units (3:8–10, 11–20b). We focus on the first here, which gives the main charge to "wait" for YHWH (3:8a) and then two reasons to do so, each beginning with the causal conjunction "for" (כִּי, 3:8b–c, 9–10). The first reason has its own basis, also signaled by כִּי, and indicates God's intent to gather nations to pour out upon them his fury, *for* he has already purposed that his fiery jealousy will consume the earth (3:8b–c). The second reason promises that, at the time YHWH rises to judge the earth, he will also generate a transformed community of worshipers who will, with unified heart, call upon his name (3:9). He then expands the details with an asyndetic clause, noting that the remnant will be multiethnic and come to serve YHWH from the region of the rivers of Cush, possibly the homeland of Zephaniah's ancestors (3:10; see the discussion at 1:1).

Significantly, Wendland and Clark note that in 3:8–10 "Zephaniah's rhetoric as well as the subject of discussion is clearly reaching a peak in terms of intensity and salience."[25] One feature to which they point is the pronounced use of possessive personal pronouns that clarify YHWH's extensive sphere of influence. YHWH's comment regarding "my rising" (3:8a) leads first to the ominous "*my* judgment," "*my* indignation," "all the fury of *my* anger," and "the fire of *my* jealousy" (3:8b–c),

---

25. Wendland and Clark, "Zephaniah," 31.

which stand against the more positive "*my* supplicants," "the daughter of *my* dispersed ones," and "*my* offering" (3:10). The initial grouping indicates unrepentant objects of his wrath who have sinned against YHWH (1:17–18). The latter grouping concerns those who have sought YHWH and sought righteousness and humility (2:3). These now fear (3:7b) and call (3:9–10) on YHWH, and they take refuge in his name (3:12b). Additionally, Ben Zvi notes that 3:8–10 stands out due to the many textual links with 3:8.[26] Specifically, (1) the second masculine plural command to "wait" links with the similar imperatives in 2:1, 3; (2) the language of "ingathering" reaches back to 1:2–4 and anticipates 3:18–20b; (3) the statement in 3:8 "for in the fire of my jealousy all the earth will be consumed" recalls 1:18; (4) the phrase "the fury of my anger" points back to 2:2; and (5) "my judgment" alludes to both 2:3 and 3:5.

Explanation of the Text

1. The Charge to Wait for YHWH (3:8a)

Zephaniah employs the inferential particle "therefore" (לָכֵן) to mark a significant development in his appeal. The two parallel units in 2:5–15 and 3:1–7 both begin with "Woe!" (הוֹי) and support the charge to "seek YHWH" together in 2:1–4. Now, the prophet returns to his primary exhortation. He uses the same second masculine plural imperative form and allows his description of the global and local rebellion and prospect of punishment (2:5–3:7) to ignite the remnant's trustful endurance in the present. They are patiently to persist in hope for the salvation that God will bring after rising as the righteous judge to punish the guilty.

The Structure and Literary Form section above explained why YHWH's call to "wait for me" (חַכּוּ־לִי) bears a positive rather than threatening

sense. Those looking to God should await his passing punishment (Isa 8:17) and coming salvation (Ps 33:20; Isa 64:4). YHWH himself pours forth grace upon those waiting for him, who persevere through trials with trust (Isa 30:18).[27]

The oracular formula, "the utterance of YHWH" (נְאֻם־יְהוָה), is intrusive and points to the unit's climactic nature (cf. Zeph 1:2–3, 10; 2:9).[28] The text first refers to a specific "day" (יוֹם), which is "the day of YHWH" that Zephaniah has already mentioned (see 1:7–10, 14–16, 18; 2:2–3). Specifically, through an extended construct chain, YHWH names this encounter "the day of my rising" (יוֹם קוּמִי). Next, the MT has לְעַד ("for prey/plunder"), which fits the context of war in 3:8 (cf. ESV, NET, CSV) and may allude to Jerusalem's leaders' predatory activities in 3:3.[29] However, the term "prey/plunder" is rare, and Scripture nowhere else uses it as some-

---

26. Ben Zvi, *Book of Zephaniah*, 318.
27. Cf. Matt 10:22; 2 Tim 2:12; Heb 12:3; Jas 1:12; 5:11.
28. On the oracular formula, see Sweeney, *Isaiah 1–39*, 546.
29. Cf. Gerleman, *Zephanja*, 55; Motyer, "Zephaniah," 948; Sweeney, *Zephaniah*, 180–89; Renz, *Books of Nahum, Habakkuk, and Zephaniah*, 599; see also Ball, *Rhetorical Study of*

Zephaniah, 172. Keil reads "for prey," but he then takes the prey as the righteous remnant that God plunders from the nations whom he will judge (Keil, " Twelve Minor Prophets," 10:456 (2:154). While lexical usage calls into question this reading, similar imagery appears in Isa 53:12 (cf. 49:7; 52:15), and the link between Zeph 3:8 and 3:9–10 could support it.

thing YHWH claims for himself (see Gen 49:27; Isa 33:23). In contrast, both the LXX and Syriac Peshitta read לְעֵד ("for a witness"; cf. NRSVue, NASB20, NIV), which fits how Scripture commonly portrays YHWH as a "witness" or "accuser" in judgment contexts.[30] The language of a *witness arising* (using both the noun עֵד "witness" and the verb קום "arise") also appears,[31] but עֵד never occurs with קום.[32] As such, the verse probably stresses the remnant's need to look hopefully to when YHWH will rise as a covenant witness.[33] Knowing both the majority's rebellion and the minority's repentance, he will justly sentence by acting as a legal witness and judge.

2. Two Reasons to Wait for YHWH (3:8b–10)

YHWH now clarifies why the remnant from Judah and other lands must continue to "wait" for him to exert his covenant lordship: (1) because he intends to punish the wicked of the earth (Zeph 3:8b–c) and (2) because he will save a remnant from the nations, reversing the effects of the tower of Babel (3:9–10).

a. YHWH's Intent to Punish All the Wicked of the Earth (3:8b–c)

The first reason the remnant of Judah must persist in their hope of salvation is that God will eventually punish the world's rebels: "For my judgment is to gather nations . . . to pour out on them my indignation." With Zephaniah's contemporary Habakkuk, they must take their stand at the watch post, wait for YHWH to act, and live by faith (Hab 2:1–4), taking joy in the God of their salvation and trusting that YHWH will be their strength (3:17–19).[34]

Zephaniah has already explicitly referred to YHWH's great eschatological "judgment" (מִשְׁפָּט) as a warning that the remnant has heeded (Zeph 2:3)[35] and as that which YHWH renders by numerous means each morning (3:5).[36] Like those preparing metal for melting (Ezek 22:19–22) or sheaves for threshing (Mic 4:12–13), YHWH has determined "to gather" (אסף, Zeph 1:2–3; 3:18; Zech 14:2–3) and "assemble" (קבץ, Ezek 16:37; Joel 4:2[3:2]) all people groups (גּוֹיִם, "nations") and political powers (מַמְלָכוֹת, "kingdoms") for judicial sentencing.[37] The prophet foretold the same great

---

30. See, e.g., Gen 31:50; 1 Sam 12:5–6; 20:12; Job 16:19; Jer 42:5; Mic 1:2; Mal 3:5.

31. See Deut 19:15–16; Job 16:8; Pss 27:12; 35:11.

32. With the Vulgate, Seybold and Berlin take לְעֵד in a temporal sense meaning "forever" or "once and for all" (Seybold, *Satirische Prophetie*, 112–13; Berlin, *Zephaniah*, 133; cf. Calvin's disagreement with this view: Calvin, "Habakkuk, Zephaniah, Haggai," 281). This interpretation fails to account for the many texts where עֵד ("witness") either appears in relation to YHWH as judge or in association with the verb קום ("arise"). Ben Zvi believes the meaning includes all three elements—"prey/plunder," "witness," and "forever" (Ben Zvi, *Book of Zephaniah*, 220–23), but such deliberate polysemy is unusual.

33. So too J. M. P. Smith, "Book of Zephaniah," 247; Rudolph, *Micha, Nahum, Habakuk, Zephanja*, 287; R. L. Smith, *Micah–Malachi*, 139; Ball, *Rhetorical Study of Zephaniah*, 172; House, *Zephaniah*, 132; Robertson, *Books of Nahum, Habak-*

kuk, and Zephaniah, 324–25; Roberts, *Nahum, Habakkuk, and Zephaniah*, 209; Ryou, *Zephaniah's Oracles*, 67–68; Vlaardingerbroek, *Zephaniah*, 185–86; Floyd, *Minor Prophets, Part 2*, 233. For Judah's tendency to look to less dreadful gods, see the commentary at Zeph 1:5.

34. On the translation of Hab 2:4, see Shepherd, *The Twelve Prophets in the New Testament*, 48–51; Clendenen, "Salvation by Faith or by Faithfulness in the Book of Habakkuk?," 505–13.

35. On this reading of "judgment" in 2:3, see DeRouchie, "Addressees in Zephaniah 2:1, 3," 192–95, 197–99.

36. See DeRouchie, "YHWH's Judgment Is New Every Morning," 131–46.

37. For similar imagery with אסף, see Isa 13:4; 24:22; with קבץ, see Isa 49:18. Motyer proposes that "nation" may refer to a "political entity" and "kingdom" to a "political system" (Motyer, "Zephaniah," 949).

eschatological ingathering in 1:2–3 with language drawn from the flood account to describe how God would cut off unrepentant sinners from the face of the earth.[38] And as was true there, those whom God will draw together apparently included Judah since they too are destined for punishment (1:4–6, 7–13; 3:1–7) and one of the nations included among "all the earth" (3:8c).[39] The terms "nation" (גּוֹי) and "kingdom" (מַמְלָכָה) commonly pair, especially in the writing prophets.[40] Together they usually act synonymously and describe a large confederation of people united under a single ruler and associated with a common land.[41] But God's strong hand will destroy these various sovereignties.[42]

Specifically, through an infinitive construction expressing purpose, YHWH clarifies that he gathers nations and assembles kingdoms "to pour out" (לִשְׁפֹּךְ) his "indignation" (זַעַם) upon them. YHWH holds a "cup of wrath" (Isa 51:17, 22; Jer 25:15) that he "pours out" (שׁפך) like fire (Lam 2:4) and water (4:11). His "fury" (חָרוֹן, Lam 4:11; Zeph 3:8), "rage" (עֶבְרָה, Hos 5:10), "indignation" (זַעַם, Ezek

22:31; Zeph 3:8), and "wrath" (חֵמָה, Jer 6:11; Ezek 7:8; 14:19) flow forth against Israel, and his "indignation" (זַעַם) and "wrath" (חֵמָה) boil over against his enemies, whether personal (Ps 29:25[24]) or national (Jer 10:25; Ezek 30:15).[43]

The noun "indignation" (זַעַם) refers to intense anger and, at times, curse.[44] In Zeph 3:8, the appositive phrase "all the fury of my anger" (כֹּל חֲרוֹן אַפִּי) clarifies God's "indignation."[45] In 2:2–3, the prophet already spoke of "the day of YHWH's anger" (יוֹם אַף־יְהוָה) and associated it with "the fury of YHWH's anger" (חֲרוֹן אַף־יְהוָה), using the same language. But the addition of "all" (כֹּל) in this context intensifies the dreadful character of the day when YHWH gathers "all" from the earth's face (1:2), stretches his hand against "all" in Jerusalem (1:4), punishes "all" the princes and those influenced negatively by foreigners and superstitious practices (1:8–9), consumes "all" the earth and makes a complete end of "all" its inhabitants (1:18), and emaciates "all" the earth's gods (2:11). On this day, God's enemies will become the sacrifice

---

38. See DeRouchie, "YHWH's Future Ingathering in Zephaniah 1:2," 173–91. In Zeph 3:18 (אסף) and 3:19–20 (קבץ), the prophet will speak of the same ingathering from a more positive perspective—the drawing together of the faithful remnant (cf. 3:9–10) that will happen "on that day" (3:16) and "at that time" (3:19–20).

39. Timmer maintains that "a clear distinction between the nations/kingdoms on the one hand and Israel/Judah on the other is maintained across the book, so that Judah here [in 3:8] is almost certainly *not* referred to with nations-terminology" (Timmer, *Non-Israelite Nations*, 158). Such is unlikely because the phrase "all the earth" in 3:8c, which Timmer admits must include Judah, occurs in a causal clause fronted by כִּי ("for") and thus identifies that YHWH's consuming "all the earth" is merely a restatement of his pouring out his wrath on the "nations" and "kingdoms" (3:8b). Similarly, Judah should be included among all "humanity" and among "all the inhabitants of the earth" upon whom YHWH's day of wrath will fall (1:18). While distinct from her neighbors (2:5–15; 3:1–7), Judah is part of the universal catastrophe that is coming, and this is so throughout the entire book.

40. See, e.g., Isa 13:4; 60:12; Jer 1:10; 51:20; Ezek 29:15; 37:22; Nah 3:5; Hag 2:22.

41. Block, "Nations," *ISBE* 3:492–96; Block, "Nations/Nationality," *NIDOTTE* 4:966–72.

42. Renz unconvincingly claims that this announcement was originally not eschatological but only spoke of a regional judgment ending "the world as Judah knew it" (Renz, *Books of Nahum, Habakkuk, and Zephaniah*, 600). However, Zeph 3:8 indicates that it is indeed "all the *earth*" that "will be consumed" and not just "all the *land*" by linking "nations" and "kingdoms" to הָאָרֶץ ("the earth/land"). Renz himself admits that Zephaniah's immediate context suggests that "the reference to the entire region becomes *the whole earth*" and that "vv. 9–10 pick up the wider, international focus of v. 8" (ibid., 607).

43. For examples with the alternate verb נתך ("to pour out") that include both חֵמָה ("wrath") and אַף ("anger"), see Jer 7:20; 42:18; 44:6.

44. See Num 23:7–8; Mic 6:10; cf. Isa 66:14; Zech 1:12; Mal 1:4.

45. The noun "indignation" (זַעַם) is the object of the verb "pour out" (שׁפך) elsewhere in Ps 69:25[24]); Ezek 21:36; 22:31. Psalm 69:25[24] has the parallel phrase "fury of anger" (חֲרוֹן אַף).

(1:7, 17–18),[46] as his jealousy for the fame of his name consumes all those opposing his rule.[47]

YHWH will punish the earth's sinners and eradicate all evil from the world. This is the first reason the faithful remnant from Judah and other lands must wait for YHWH.

b. YHWH's Promise to Create a Community of Worshipers from the Whole Earth (3:9–10)

Zephaniah now gives his second reason (כִּי, "for") for the remnant of Judah and other lands to continue trusting God.[48] On the very day (אָז, "then") that he arises to execute his sentence on the world (3:8), he will reverse the effects of the tower of Babel episode by drawing together a multiethnic community of worshipers who will serve him in unity (3:9–10).[49] YHWH first announces this promise in general terms (Zeph 3:9) and then expounds upon it in a way uniquely meaningful for Zephaniah himself (3:10).

(1) The Details of the Promise (3:9)

Alongside punishing the world, YHWH now promises to alter speech patterns on behalf of (reading אֶל expressing advantage[50]) a select group of surviving "peoples" (עַמִּים). The plural stands against independent "people" groups (עַם, e.g., 1:11; 2:8–10) and likely points to a new diverse community that YHWH will draw from the "nations" and "kingdoms" that he promises to gather for judicial assessment (3:8).[51] Achtemeier and Vlaardingerbroeck identify these "peoples" with the remnant "people" from Judah (2:7, 9),[52] but Timmer thinks the plural "peoples" are all non-Israelites.[53] In contrast, while the plural signals that these "peoples" are more than the Judean remnant, their association with those from "all the earth" (3:8) signals that they include faithful Judeans and others from the broader world.[54] Together these "peoples" will form a new singular "people" (עַם) (3:12), whom God will exalt as agents of his praise amid the non-delivered "peoples" (עַמִּים) of the earth (3:20b).

The verb rendered "change" (הפך) denotes a complete reversal. The pattern usually involves "changing X *into* Y" (the preposition לְ "to" accompanying the accusative).[55] However, the text here only discloses the final result—that God will give them "a purified lip so that all of them may call

---

46. Marvin A. Sweeney, *The Twelve Prophets*, ed. David W. Cotter, Berit Olam: Studies in Hebrew Narrative and Poetry 2 (Collegeville, MN: Liturgical Press, 2000), 522.

47. Cf. Ps 69:25[24]; Jer 10:25; Ezek 21:36[31]; 22:31; Rev 16:1.

48. For more on כִּי, see the discussion within Structure and Literary Form above.

49. De Vries notes, "Although the 'then' of v 9 is contemporaneous with the 'day' of v 8, in effect it extends this day into something entirely new" (De Vries, *From Old Revelation to New*, 204).

50. *IBHS*, §11.2.2; Williams and Beckman, *Williams' Hebrew Syntax*, §302.

51. Roberts, Vlaardingerbroeck, and Holladay all propose emending "peoples" (עַמִּים) to "their people" (עַמָּם), with focus on the Judeans, since the book has not yet used the plural "peoples" and since they struggle to track Zephaniah's thought flow from 3:1–7 to 3:8–10 (Roberts, *Nahum, Habakkuk, and Zephaniah*, 210, 216–17; Vlaardingerbroeck, *Zephaniah*, 195; Holladay, "Reading Zephaniah with a Concordance," 683).

Emending a text, however, should always be a last resort, and a sound case can be made for leaving the text as it stands.

52. Achtemeier, *Nahum–Malachi*, 83; Vlaardingerbroeck, *Zephaniah*, 192–94. Vlaardingerbroeck actually emends the text from עַמִּים ("peoples") to עַמִּי ("my people") because "in what follows they [the peoples] do not play any role at all" (p. 192). In contrast, the remnant from these plural multiethnic "peoples" become the one "people" who "take refuge in the name YHWH" (Zeph 3:12).

53. Timmer, *Non-Israelite Nations*, 165; cf. Keil, "Twelve Minor Prophets," 10:459 (2:157); House, *Unity of the Twelve*, 149; Robertson, *Books of Nahum, Habakkuk, and Zephaniah*, 327; Berlin, *Zephaniah*, 135; Renz, *Books of Nahum, Habakkuk, and Zephaniah*, 610.

54. So, too, Calvin, "Habakkuk, Zephaniah, Haggai," 284–85; Baker, *Nahum, Habakkuk and Zephaniah*, 115.

55. E.g., Deut 23:6[5] and Neh 13:2 ("curse into blessing"); Pss 30:12[11] ("mourning into dancing"); 66:6 ("the sea into dry land"); Jer 31:13 ("mourning into joy"); Amos 5:8 ("deep darkness into the morning"); 6:12 ("justice into poison").

on the name YHWH" (3:9). The dual form "lips" (שְׂפָתַיִם) commonly refers to an organ of speech, which some use negatively to utter rash oaths (Lev 5:4), sin (Job 2:10), testify against themselves (Job 15:6), deceive (Ps 34:14[13]; Prov 24:28), boast (Prov 27:2), falsely honor God (Isa 29:13), and assert wrong (Mal 2:6). Others use the same organ positively to proclaim good news (Ps 40:10[9]), praise God (Pss 63:4[3]; 119:171), shout for joy (Job 8:21; Ps 71:23), declare YHWH's rules (Ps 119:13), and guard knowledge (Prov 5:2). Here YHWH promises to produce in his remnant a "*purified* lip" (שָׂפָה בְרוּרָה), which employs the less common singular term "lip" (שָׂפָה)[56] and describes the nature of the speech with what is likely the *qal* passive participle of the verb ברר (cf. 1 Chr 16:41; Job 33:3).[57] In the *qal*, the term ברר commonly denotes "purging" (e.g., Ezek 20:38; Eccl 3:18), but by extension it can mean "to select, choose" (Neh 5:18; 1 Chr 7:40; 9:22) and ultimately "to cleanse, purify" (2 Sam 22:27//Ps 18:27[26]; Isa 52:11). This "lip" differs significantly from the remnant of the Baal in Zephaniah's Jerusalem who swore falsely (Zeph 1:5), boasted sinfully (1:12; 2:8, 15; cf. 3:11–12), and instructed deceptively and abusively (3:3–5, 13).[58] The prophet's prediction recalls YHWH's promise through Hosea that in the days of the new creation covenant "I will remove the names of the Baals from her mouth, and they will

no longer be remembered by their name" (Hos 2:19[17]).

Because YHWH associates his new creational work with these peoples' profession (see below) and, by this, their witness, the work itself transforms their identities. Though some previously swore falsely in YHWH's name (Zeph 1:5), now none will "bear his name in vain" (Exod 20:7; Deut 5:11).[59] This parallels Ps 87, where YHWH promises to give some from foreign nations including "Cush" new birth certificates linking them to his city Zion and declaring, "This one was born there" (Ps 87:4, 6). Similarly, Isaiah predicted that in YHWH's eschatological day of wrath "five cities in the land of Egypt will be speaking the lip of Canaan and swearing to YHWH of armies" (Isa 19:18; cf. 19:25). While "speaking the lip of Canaan" could mean that foreigners will speak Hebrew, it more likely signals that they will pledge their allegiance to YHWH.[60]

YHWH's name represents his identity in all its beauty, perfection, and authority (cf. Prov 18:10).[61] This is clear in Exod 34:6–7, where appositive phrases attributing to God both character qualities (nature, ontology) and actions (function) follow the uniquely repeated proper name "YHWH, YHWH" (cf. Num 6:23–27; Deut 32:2–4). Therefore, "to call on the name YHWH" (לִקְרֹא ... בְּשֵׁם יְהוָה, Zeph 3:9), is to express worshipful dependence

---

56. This singular שָׂפָה commonly means "lip" as in the bank of a sea or river (e.g., Gen 22:17; 41:3), the fringe of a curtain or piece of clothing (e.g., Exod 26:4, 10; 28:26), the edge of a territory (e.g., Judg 7:22), the brim of a cup or bowl (e.g., 1 Kgs 7:26; 2 Chr 4:2, 5), or the rim of the altar (Ezek 43:13). It can also refer to "language, speech" (e.g., Gen 11:6–7; Ps 81:6[5]; Isa 28:11) and even the "lip" as the instrument of talking (e.g., Job 12:20; Ps 12:3[2]; Ezek 36:3).

57. So too Richard E. Averbeck, "בָּרַר (*bārar* I)," *NIDOTTE* 1:757–59.

58. For "unclean lips" (טְמֵא־שְׂפָתַיִם), see Isa 6:5–7. For similar imagery of purified lips, though with different terms, see Pss 15:3; 24:4; Prov 10:8, 11, 32; Isa 33:15.

59. For an explanation of this interpretation, see Carmen Joy Imes, *Bearing Yhwh's Name at Sinai: A Reexamination of the Name Command of the Decalogue*, BBRSup 19 (University Park: Pennsylvania State University Press, 2018).

60. Cf. Franz Delitzsch, "Isaiah," trans. James Martin, 2 vols. in *Commentary on the Old Testament*, (1885, 1892; repr. in 10 vols., Peabody, MA: Hendrickson, 1991), 7:236 (1:364–65) (references to the twenty-five-volume edition are given in parentheses). Without basis, the Living Bible renders Zeph 3:9, "At that time I will change the speech of my returning people to pure Hebrew."

61. Douglas K. Stuart, "Names, Proper," *ISBE* 3:483–88; Allen P. Ross, "שֵׁם," *NIDOTTE* 4:147–51.

on the only God who fully and completely reigns, saves, and satisfies (Ps 116:4, 13, 17).[62] In Zeph 3:9, crying out to God in prayer and praise is the initial goal of purified speech. It expresses both what "longing for" and "seeking" YHWH looked like among the faithful remnant (Zeph 1:6; 2:1, 3),[63] and it also would characterize those taking refuge in YHWH's name at the end of the age (3:12).[64]

Significantly, God was promising to create not a single language but a unified profession and commitment among his redeemed (cf. Zech 14:9; Rev 7:9–10). As seen below, the altered speech anticipates the tower of Babel judgment's reversal (Gen 11:1–9) while retaining different languages as a lasting testimony of God's power to reverse the curse. Thus, Motyer rightly observes, "Just as the central motivation of Babel was to organize life without God, so now the unified world centralizes the Lord, using its newfound speech to call on the name the Lord. The Genesis process . . . has gone into reverse, and humanity, which in sin moved ever farther and farther from Eden is brought back [3:13d] into its perfect provision, rest, and security."[65]

Of those for whom God acts, "all of them" (כֻּלָּם) will now use their speech to call upon YHWH's name (Zeph 3:9). God's new democracy in which all participate differs from the old covenant people that included both remnant and rebel. The lan-guage resembles Jeremiah's anticipation that *all* members in the new covenant will know YHWH and be forgiven (Jer 31:34) and Joel's hope that the Spirit's presence would rest on *all* flesh after the day of YHWH comes (Joel 3:1–2[2:28–29]) and that "*everyone* who calls on the name YHWH will be delivered" (כֹּל אֲשֶׁר־יִקְרָא בְּשֵׁם יְהוָה יִמָּלֵט) (3:5[2:32]).[66]

Besides calling on YHWH's name, this community will "serve him with one shoulder" (Zeph 3:9). In Scripture, the verb "serve" (עבד) commonly refers to acts of covenant loyalty or religious worship that magnify God's worth.[67] Since the "shoulder" (שְׁכֶם) commonly bears burdens,[68] the imagery suggests that the community will provide mutual support in a common cause[69] and minister side by side as if one person.[70] Many English versions treat the actions of "calling" and "serving" as two separate goals by inserting the conjunction "and" between them (e.g., NRSVue, ESV, NIV, CSB). However, the Hebrew text connects the verbal phrases with only the preposition "to" (לְעָבְדוֹ "to serve him"). Thus, one "calls" on his name for the purpose of "serving" YHWH in unity (so NASB20). "Calling on YHWH" is like the plug that connects one to the power for "service."[71]

When paired with "offering" (מִנְחָה, 3:10), the verb to "serve" (עבד) commonly relates to acts of homage due a king (cf. 2 Sam 8:2, 6; 1 Kgs 4:21; 17:3), which

---

62. Related to the *beth of instrument*, grammarians at times refer to the function of the preposition ב on שֵׁם ("name") as the *beth of communication*, wherein "the instrument used to communicate with God, i.e., calling on his name, is governed by בְּ" (*BHRG*, §39.6.3.c).

63. Cf. Gen 4:26; 12:8; 13:4; 21:33; 26:25; 1 Kgs 18:24; 2 Kgs 5:11.

64. Cf. Isa 44:5; Joel 3:5[2:32]; Zech 13:9; 14:9.

65. Motyer, "Zephaniah," 951–52.

66. Cf. Acts 2:21; Rom 10:13. See DeRouchie, "Counting Stars with Abraham and the Prophets," 445–85.

67. E.g., Exod 4:23; Deut 6:13; 1 Sam 7:3; Ps 100:2; Jer 2:20; Mal 3:14; cf. Rev 7:9–10.

68. E.g., Gen 9:23; Exod 12:34; Josh 4:5; Judg 9:48; Ps 81:7[6].

69. Cf. Rom 15:1; Gal 6:2; 1 Thess 5:14.

70. Cf. John 17:11; Eph 4:3, 13. It may also imply that any yoke that is carried will be borne together (cf. Isa 9:3[4]; 10:27; 14:25; Matt 11:28–30). An equivalent English phrase is asking people to "shoulder the load."

71. In Paul's words, "everyone who calls on the name of the Lord" through faith (Rom 10:13) encounters the gospel, "the power of God for salvation" (1:16). God's grace enables our work (1 Cor 15:10; Phil 2:12–13), so we must serve "by the strength that God supplies" (1 Pet 4:11).

is YHWH's title later in the chapter (Zeph 3:15). Nevertheless, Isaiah also linked this pair with religious service by speaking of a future day when the Egyptians would "know YHWH . . . and serve [וְעָבְדוּ] with both sacrifice and offering [וּמִנְחָה]" (Isa 19:21; cf. 18:7; 56:6; 66:20–21). Isaiah's usage is significant since his messages influenced Zephaniah.[72] YHWH is both God and king, and his temple is also his palace. Thus, all acts of worship may be both royal and priestly homage, though the latter may also imply in its role a higher sense of mediation to others.

(2) The Exposition of the Promise (3:10)

The lack of connection at the head of Zeph 3:10 helps signal that YHWH now elaborates on his promise in 3:9, referring to those calling on his name as "my supplicants, the daughter of my scattered ones." These will "carry" (*hiphil* יבל) God his "offering" (מִנְחָה) "from the region of the rivers of Cush" (מֵעֵבֶר לְנַהֲרֵי־כוּשׁ),[73] which alludes to Isa 18:1, 7, where the same language is used of the Cushites, though with a different term for "tribute." The noun "supplicants" (עֲתָרִים) occurs only here in the OT, and many of the Medieval Jewish inter-

preters proposed it is was a proper noun referring to a distant unknown people.[74] However, the form is related to the root עתר, which means "to plead, supplicate" (e.g., Gen 25:21; Isa 19:22), a term that probably describes those in Zeph 3:9 who are approaching God with transformed speech that calls on YHWH's name (cf. Zeph 1:6; 3:2).

Through an appositional phrase, YHWH declares that these prayerful ones are "the daughter" (בַּת; i.e., offspring, descendant) of "my scattered ones" (פּוּצַי), the latter being a substantival *qal* masculine plural passive participle of פּוּץ ("to scatter, disperse").[75] YHWH regularly refers to his "scattering" ethnic Israel in exile (e.g., Deut 4:27; Jer 9:15[16]; Ezek 36:19)[76] and to the first or second phase of the eschatological second exodus with comparable dispersion-reversal language (often pairing "scatter" [פּוּץ] with "gather/assemble" [קבץ/אסף], Deut 30:3; Jer 30:11; cf. Zeph 3:8, 18).[77] Nevertheless, at least six reasons exist for believing Zephaniah's vision of restoration involves a reversal of God's universal punishment at the tower of Babel and a multiethnic community of worshipers including a remnant of ethnic Judeans.

---

72. For a list, see the discussion of Zephaniah's use of Scripture under Zephaniah's Hermeneutic and Theology in the introduction.

73. On the likelihood that מֵעֵבֶר means "from the region of" rather than "from beyond," see B. Gemser, "*beʿēber hajjardēn*: In Jordan's Borderland," *VT* 2.4 (1952): 349–55.

74. Ben Zvi lists Ibn Ezra, Radak, Abrabanel, and Alschuler as adherents (Ben Zvi, *Book of Zephaniah*, 227), and Calvin notes this as a common view in his day (Calvin, "Habakkuk, Zephaniah, Haggai," 286).

75. The construction "a/the daughter of X" is frequent in the Latter Prophets, with X referring to persons, peoples, or places. *Persons* = Jeremiah (Jer 52:1), "your mother" (Ezek 16:44–45), "his father" (Ezek 22:11), "a foreign god" (Mal 2:11). *Peoples* = "the Chaldeans" (Isa 47:1, 5), "my people" (e.g., Isa 22:4; Jer 4:11; cf. Lam 2:11), "troops" (Mic 5:1). *Places* = "Zion" or "Jerusalem" (e.g., Isa 1:8; Jer 4:31; Mic 4:8; Zeph 3:14; Zech 9:9), "Gallim" (Isa 10:30), "Tarshish" (Isa 23:10), "Sidon" (Isa 23:12), "Babylon" (e.g., Isa 47:1; Zech 2:11[7]), "Egypt" (Jer 46:11, 19, 24), "Dibon" (Jer 46:18), "Diblaim" (Hos 1:3). Of these, the

most like "the daughter of my scattered ones" in Zeph 3:10 is "my people" (עַמִּי), which includes the first common singular pronominal suffix.

76. With Hebrew *piel* זרה ("to scatter, disperse"), see, e.g., Lev 26:33; 1 Kgs 14:15; Jer 31:10.

77. See also Isa 11:12; Ezek 11:17; 20:34; 28:25; 34:12. Many prophets address the second exodus's two-phase fulfillment (e.g., Deut 30:3–7; Hos 3:1–5; Zech 3:9; 12:10; 13:1; Dan 9:2, 24–27), but Isaiah's specificity is the greatest for certain aspects. Phase 1 includes initial physical restoration to the promised land (Isa 42:18–43:21); phase 2 is spiritual reconciliation with God (43:22–44:23; cf. 11:11). One named Cyrus (Isa 44:24–48:22; cf. 2 Chr 36:20–22) would enact phase 1 (liberation) after "seventy years" of exile (Jer 25:11–12; 29:10). The royal Davidic servant (Isa 49:1–53:12) would secure phase 2 (atonement) to bless the nations (cf. Gen 12:3; 17:4–6; 22:17b–18) after seventy more weeks of years (Dan 9:24). For more on the two-phase second exodus, see Gentry and Wellum, *Kingdom through Covenant*, 491–93.

1. Zephaniah already highlighted that God would assemble the world's nations and kingdoms for punishment (3:8b–c), and later he will mention some whom he will deliver, likely from the same multitude (3:18). Elsewhere prophets describe the great future ingathering not only as God assembling all the wicked for destruction (Isa 24:22; Jer 8:13; Zech 14:2) but also as an eschatological second exodus of salvation unto God's presence for an international community of worshipers.[78] Significantly included among the foreigners are some from Cush who will gain new birth certificates declaring they were born in Zion (Ps 68:32[31]; 87:4; Isa 18:7; 45:14).

2. In Zeph 3:9, YHWH will transform "the peoples" (plural; cf. Zeph 3:20b) and not just "my people" (singular, cf. 2:8–10). This points to a cosmopolitan congregation.

3. Beginning with the tower of Babel debacle, biblical authors use the verb "to scatter" (פּוּץ) to describe God dispersing different types of enemies.[79] Some texts pair it with "assemble" (קבץ) when speaking of reversing the exile of other nations and not just Israel (Ezek 29:13; cf. Jer 12:14–17). John alludes to this reversal in the words of the high priest Caiaphas when he prophesied that "Jesus would die for the [Jewish] nation, and not for the nation only, but also to gather into one the children of God who are scattered abroad [τὰ διεσκορπισμένα]" (John 11:51–52; cf. Isa 49:6).[80]

4. Judeans may have lived in "Cush" (see Isa 11:11; Jer 44:1; Hos 9:3, 6) due to Israel's political alliances (Isa 18:1–2; 20:5–6; cf. Ezek 29:16). However, Zephaniah's possible black African (i.e., Cushite) heritage (Zeph 1:1)[81] and treatment of the Cushites as foreigners (2:12) suggest he sees this region in 3:10 as a source for a non-Israelite remnant.

5. Another reason why YHWH would only mention the region of "Cush" in 3:10 is that Nimrod, great-grandson of Noah and son of "Cush," originally established the arrogant city that came to be known as Babel (Babylon) (Gen 10:6, 10; 11:8–9). It also supports the view that in 3:9–10 God promises to reverse the tower of Babel debacle for the benefit of all peoples. For some of the descendants of the three "families" and seventy "nations" that YHWH "scattered" after the flood (Gen 11:8–9; cf. 10:32), God would now fulfill his promise to Abraham that in him all "the families of the ground will be blessed" (12:3; cf. 18:18; 28:14) and all "the nations of the earth" will "consider themselves blessed" (22:18; 26:4).[82]

---

78. See, e.g., Ps 68:32[31]; Isa 2:2–3; 60:4–5; Jer 3:17; 12:14–17; 30:8–9; Ezek 11:17; Mic 4:1–2, 6; Zech 8:20–23. Cf. DeRouchie, "YHWH's Future Ingathering in Zephaniah 1:2," 183–87.

79. See Gen 10:18; 11:4, 8; 49:7; Num 10:35; Ps 68:2; Isa 24:1; Ezek 29:12; 30:23, 26.

80. While the LXX commonly renders the Hebrew verb פּוּץ with the verb διασκορπίζω ("to scatter"), the Old Greek of Zeph 3:10 omits the phrase "the daughter of my scattered ones." The verb appears in the Washington papyrus, but Vaticanus, Sinaiticus, and Venetus all include the equally common verb διασπείρω ("to scatter").

81. For Zephaniah's heritage, see notes at Zeph 1:1 and

DeRouchie, "Addressees in Zephaniah 2:1, 3," 201–5. Also, reasons 4–6 counter Berlin's claims that in 3:10 (1) "no reason [exists] to single out 'Ethiopia'" and (2) "Cush" refers to a Mesopotamian region (Berlin, *Zephaniah*, 134).

82. For this reading of the *niphal* and *hithpael* forms of ברך in the Abrahamic promises, see Chee-Chiew Lee, "גוים in Genesis 35:11 and the Abrahamic Promise of Blessings for the Nations," *JETS* 52.3 (2009): 467–82, esp. 472; cf. Gentry and Wellum, *Kingdom through Covenant*, 274–77. Presently, no recovered traditions from the ancient world attest to the tower of Babel episode. Nevertheless, a Sumerian epic notes how humanity once had a single language, but the god Enki/ Nudimmud multiplied the world's languages after conflict

6. In Zephaniah's message against the *nations* (Zeph 2:12), Cush was the most substantial, ancient southern empire and at civilization's farthest reaches (cf. Esth 1:1).[83] YHWH's day of wrath would punish and restore, and his global destruction had, in a typological sense, already begun with Cush (Zeph 2:12)—which bore the hereditary namesake of the very one who started Babel (see #5). Thus, it is fitting for God to inaugurate a new creation from Cush to highlight the full reversal of Babel's effects.[84]

Zephaniah's oracles against Israel's foreign neighbors alluded to the Genesis creation account and flood narrative (Zeph 1:2–3; cf. Gen 1:20–28; 6:7; 9:9–11) and drew from the Table of Nations (Zeph 2:5–15; cf. Gen 10). Now, in Zeph 3:9–10 he portrays the new creation. This portrayal both re-calls how Genesis describes the river flowing from the Edenic garden-mountain and dividing into four (see Gen 2:10–14) and emphasizes how God intends to reverse his curse at the tower of Babel (11:1–9) by transforming speech and awakening united global praise.[85]

As noted at Zeph 1:1 and 2:12, "Cush" (כּוּשׁ) was black Africa's ancient power center located in modern-day Sudan. Egyptian records refer to it as "Nubia," but the Greeks later called it "Ethiopia." Cush was also one of the regions where the original rivers of life terminated after flowing from Eden (Gen 2:13).[86] In Zeph 2:10, Cush's "rivers" (נְהָרִים) were likely the White Nile and Blue Nile, the Nile's main tributaries that stretch from modern Uganda and Ethiopia northward toward modern Egypt (see Isa 18:1–2). As if following the rivers of life back up to the garden of Eden for fellowship with the great King,[87] YHWH foretells that some from the

---

with humanity (see "Enmerkar and the Lord of Aratta," trans. Thorkild Jacobsen [*COS* 1.170:547-48; lines 135-55]; cf. Samuel Noah Kramer, "The 'Babel of Tongues': A Sumerian Version," *JAOS* 88 [1968]: 109, 111). Some read this as a prediction of a day when Enki will restore a single language to humanity (see B. Alster, "An Aspect of 'Enmerkar and the Lord of Aratta," *RB* 67 [1973]: 101–9; cf. H. L. J. Vanstiphout, *Epics of Sumerian Kings: The Matter of Aratta*, WAW 20 [Atlanta: Society of Biblical Literature, 2003], 65).

83. The OT writers' term "Put" ("Punt" in Egyptian; e.g., Jer 46:9; Ezek 30:5; Nah 3:9) is the only area potentially south of Cush. See Smith, "Ethiopia (Place)," *ABD* 2:665–67; Redford, "Kush (Place)," *ABD* 4:109–11.

84. Cf. Floyd, *Minor Prophets, Part 2*, 211.

85. See also the discussion of Zephaniah's use of Scripture under Zephaniah's Hermeneutic and Theology in the introduction. For more on Zephaniah's vision of the reversal of the tower of Babel, see Floyd, *Minor Prophets, Part 2*, 209–11. Cf. e.g., R. L. Smith, *Micah–Malachi*, 142; Baker, *Nahum, Habakkuk and Zephaniah*, 115; Ball, *Rhetorical Study of Zephaniah*, 237; Robertson, *Books of Nahum, Habakkuk, and Zephaniah*, 328–29; Motyer, "Zephaniah," 951–53; Sweeney, *Zephaniah*, 183–84.

86. Of the four rivers that Gen 2:11–14 mentions (i.e., the Pishon, Gihon, Tigris, and Euphrates), scholars debate the precise locations of the initial two, with the Pishon flowing around "the whole land of Havilah, where there is gold" and the second flowing around "the whole land of Cush." The challenge only escalates when we consider that the earth's topography would have changed significantly after Noah's flood. The narrator of Genesis identifies the Tigris and Euphrates of his day with the great rivers of old, and he also links the Pishon with "Havilah, where there is gold" and the Gihon with "Cush." Scholars have identified an ancient riverbed running northeast through Saudi Arabia from the Hijaz Mountains near Medina (and the region of ancient Havilah) to the Persian Gulf in Kuwait near the mouth of the Tigris and Euphrates, and this correlates strongly with Scripture's information regarding the Pishon (see James A. Sauer, "The River Runs Dry: Creation Story Preserves Historical Memory," *BAR* 22.4 [1996]: 52–57, 64; John H. Walton, "Eden, Garden of," *DOTP* 204). Significantly, a spring called "Gihon" is associated with Jerusalem, and "Cush" is the title usually linked with the region of the Nile River's headwaters. If the latter connection holds, then Anderson is correct that "Eden would have been the source of all the great freshwater sources known to the ancient Israelite." He further adds, "Because the Gihon Spring flows beneath Jerusalem (and Eden was associated with Jerusalem . . .), the Gihon River may also have been associated with this spring" (Gary A. Anderson, "Eden, Garden of," *NIDB* 2:186). For a similar proposal, see Howard N. Wallace, "Eden, Garden of," *ABD* 2:283.

87. Cf. Gen 2:13; Exod 15:17; Ps 46:4; Ezek 47:1–12; Zech 14:8; Rev 22:1–2.

Figure 7.2: Verbal Correspondences between Genesis 11:1–9 and Zephaniah 3:9–10	
Genesis 11:1–9	**Zephaniah 3:9–10**
[1]And **all** [כָּל] the earth was of **one speech** [שָׂפָה אֶחָת] and **same** [אֲחָדִים] words. [2]And it came about, in their journeying from the east, that they found a plain in the valley of Shinar and settled there. [3]And they said, each to his neighbor, "Come, let us shape bricks, and burn them completely." And they had for themselves the brick for stone, and the tar was to them for the mortar. [4]And they said, "Come, let us build for ourselves a city and a tower–even with its top in the heavens. And let us make for ourselves a **name** [שֵׁם], lest we be **scattered** [נָפוּץ] over the face of the earth. [5]And **YHWH** [יְהוָה] came down to see the city and the tower that the children of the man had built. [6]And **YHWH** [יְהוָה] said, "Look–**one people** and **one speech** to **all** of them [עַם אֶחָד וְשָׂפָה אַחַת לְכֻלָּם]. And this is their start of activity, and now **all** [כֹל] that they purpose to do will not be inaccessible for them. [7]Come, let us go down and let us mix there their **speech** [שְׂפָתָם] so that they will not discern, each the **speech** [שְׂפַת] of his neighbor. [8]And **YHWH scattered** [וַיָּפֶץ יְהוָה] them from there over the face of **all** [כָּל] the earth, and they ceased from building the city. [9]Therefore, he **called** its **name** [קָרָא שְׁמָה] Babel, because there **YHWH** [יְהוָה] mixed the **speech** of **all** [שְׂפַת כָּל] the earth, and from there he **scattered** them [הֱפִיצָם] over the face of **all** [כָּל] the earth.	[9]For then I will change for **peoples** [עַמִּים] a purified **speech** [שָׂפָה] so that **all** of them may **call** on the **name YHWH** [לִקְרֹא כֻלָּם בְּשֵׁם יְהוָה], to serve him with **one** [אֶחָד] shoulder. [10]From the region of the rivers of Cush, my supplicants, the daughter of my **scattered** ones [פוּצַי], will carry my offering.

most distant lands who were severely judged (Zeph 2:11–12) would have a faithful remnant whom God would save on his holy mountain (cf. 3:11–12).

At least eight terms in 3:9–10 appear in Gen 11:1–9: "people(s)" (עַם / עַמִּים); "lip/speech" (שָׂפָה); "call" (קרא); "all" (כֹל); "name" (שֵׁם); "YHWH" (יְהוָה); "one/same" (אֶחָד); "scatter" (פוּץ). In the OT, only Gen 11:1–9 and Zeph 3:9–10 share such language. No other text conjoins "lip" (שָׂפָה) (when signifying speech) with "scatter" (פוּץ) (when signifying exile).[88] Thus, Zephaniah likely portrays YHWH's future reversal of Babel's curse.

These commonalities produce substantive parallels: (1) The "one" "people" with "one" "lip/speech" before Babel, whose "speech" God mixed (Gen 11:1, 6–7), brings forth "peoples" whose "speech" God purifies so that they can serve him in "one" accord (Zeph 3:9). (2) At the place he later "called" Babel, "YHWH" "scattered" those who sought to make a "name" for themselves (Gen 11:4, 8–9), but

now "YHWH" will gather and move some of the descendants of those "scattered" to "call" on his "name" (Zeph 3:9; cf. Gen 4:26).

In Zeph 3:9, YHWH promises harmonious and sustained service (Isa 56:6; Zech 14:9), which includes the saved remnant giving the holy, reigning God his due "offering" (מִנְחָה) and God overturning the idolatrous unity seen at Babel (Gen 11:4, 6). Combining "serve" (עבד) with "offering" denotes a servant/vassal properly respecting YHWH as king (cf. 2 Sam 8:2; 1 Kgs 4:21; 17:3) and a worshiper properly respecting him as God (cf. Isa 19:21; 56:6; 66:20–21). Elsewhere the OT envisions the eschatological age will include enemies gathering as priests[89] to esteem their King[90] in holy worship with tangible gifts of praise.

Some propose that "the daughter of my scattered ones" in Zeph 3:10 is the object rather than the subject of the verb "they will carry" (יוֹבִלוּן) and that the antecedent subject is the plural "peoples" of 3:9 and/

---

88. Ben Zvi fails to see YHWH's promise to reverse the tower of Babel punishment since he restricts his lexical search between Gen 11:1–9 and Zeph 3:9 and does not include 3:10 (Ben Zvi, *Book of Zephaniah*, 225n736).

89. See Isa 66:21; cf. Jer 33:22; Isa 56:6; 60:7.

90. See Isa 18:7; 60:4–7; 66:20; Zech 14:16; cf. Mal 3:3; Ezek 20:40–41.

or "my supplicants" in 3:10: "From beyond the rivers of Ethiopia shall they bring my supplicants, the daughter of my dispersed, for an offering unto me" (RV margin).[91] This would approximate Isa 66:20 where YHWH sends "the survivors of the nations" to the far-off lands to "bring all your brothers from all the nations as an offering [מִנְחָה] to YHWH" (cf. Isa 60:4; 66:12).[92] This parallel is noteworthy given how often Zephaniah's frequent allusions to Isaiah.[93] However none of these Isaiah texts use the verb יבל for "carry," and the proposal strains the Hebrew syntax of Zeph 3:10, forcing the clause structure to be 1st Object–Verb–2nd Object rather than the more natural Subject–Verb–Object.[94]

Whereas Isa 66:20 treats the saved remnant as the "offering" (מִנְחָה), other texts speak of various other kinds of gifts during the great ingathering—e.g., "tribute" (Isa 18:7), "offering" (19:21; Mal 3:3), "gold and frankincense" (Isa 60:6), and "contributions and the choicest of all your gifts with your sacred things" (Ezek 20:40). The connection with Isa 18:7 and 19:21 is significant, because in the former text Isaiah addresses the same ingathering of Cushites, and in 19:21–22 he speaks similarly of Egyptians. Furthermore, these Egyptians will worship YHWH with sacrifice and "offering" (מִנְחָה) and by them "he will be supplicated" (niphal weqatal of עתר), using the verbal form of the noun עָתָר ("supplicant") in Zeph 3:10! Sweeney believes that Zephaniah is alluding to these two texts, which reinforces the notion that the "offering" is something other than people in 3:10.[95]

Carrying gifts to YHWH from a great distance (Zeph 3:10) and the resulting unity that the worshipers will have (3:9) suggests an ingathering to a central location, most likely Jerusalem, where Zephaniah locates God's presence (3:5, 15–17).[96] Zephaniah's vision of new creation on YHWH's day marks a shift in the composition of God's people. From this point forward in the book, those associated with YHWH at his holy mountain are a purified, universal remnant. They have a new identity.

Canonical and Theological Significance

The Initial Fulfillment of Zephaniah's Day of YHWH Restoration

The book of Acts presents the restoration of Zephaniah's day of the YHWH as being initially fulfilled. These findings build on and support the previous Canonical

---

91. So Keil, " Twelve Minor Prophets," 10:458–59 (2:155–57); Patterson, *Nahum, Habakkuk, Zephaniah*, 330–31; see the discussions in David J. Clark and Howard A. Hatton, *A Handbook on the Books of Nahum, Habakkuk, and Zephaniah*, UBS Handbook Series (New York: United Bible Societies, 1989), 193; Ben Zvi, *Book of Zephaniah*, 228; Berlin, *Zephaniah*, 175.

92. See esp. Shepherd, *Commentary on the Book of the Twelve*, 372.

93. The similarities are substantial enough to indicate Zephaniah is portraying the same reality, though perhaps in a different way: "gather/assemble" (אסף/קבץ) "nations" (גּוֹיִם; Isa 66:18; Zeph 3:8); "(show) indignation" (זעם) against God's "enemies/enemy" (אֹיֵב/אֹיְבִים; Isa 66:14; Zeph 3:8, 15); "anger"

(אַף; Isa 66:15; Zeph 3:8); "judge/judgment" (מִשְׁפָּט/שׁפט) with "fire" (אֵשׁ; Isa 66:16; Zeph 3:8); "nations/peoples" (עַמִּים/גּוֹיִם) are "servants" (עֲבָדִים) who "serve" (עבד) YHWH on "the mountain of my holiness" (הַר קָדְשִׁי; Isa 66:14, 19–20; Zeph 3:9, 11); calls to "be merry" (Isa 65:10; Zeph 3:15). In both texts, God's "indignation" and "anger" are against his "enemy/enemies" whom he will "judge" with "fire" after "gathering/assembling" "nations." God's people will be from all the "peoples/nations" and "be merry" and "serve" him on "the mountain of his holiness."

94. On double accusatives, see GKC, §117cc, ff.

95. See Sweeney, *Zephaniah*, 184–85.

96. So also Renz, *Books of Nahum, Habakkuk, and Zephaniah*, 613.

and Theological Significance sections of Zeph 1:2–3, 7, 18, which made the following points:

- Zeph 1:2–3: Jesus alluded to Zephaniah's vision of "ingathering" (cf. 3:8) and associated it with his second coming when God would separate the world's peoples like a farmer distinguishes weeds for burning and wheat for keeping.[97]
- Zeph 1:7: The NT portrays Jesus's crucifixion and resurrection as inaugurating the day of YHWH both as sacrificial punishment on behalf of the faithful remnant and as a new creation.
- Zeph 1:18: The fires of God's wrath to which Zeph 3:8 points (cf. 1:7, 18) are stored up for the unrepentant wicked, but Christ bore them at the cross for all who believe.[98]

Apparently, Luke saw Christ's exaltation and the church's birth and expansion as initial fulfillments of Zeph 3:8–10. This is suggested by many links between God's ingathering of an international group of transformed worshipers in Zeph 3:8–10 and the early chapters of Acts. Both Davis and Keener argue that Luke's account of Pentecost alludes to Gen 11:1–9 and portrays the birth of the church as an initial reversal of the tower of Babel punishment.[99] Butcher goes further by noting ties between the Pentecost account and Zephaniah's vision of punishment-reversal in Zeph 3:8–10 and by suggesting that 3:8–13 supplied a controlling blueprint for the structure of Luke's early chapters.[100] He sees the following three connections, all of which include both lexical and conceptual correspondences: (1) YHWH's rising as witness to the covenant (Zeph 3:8) corresponds to Christ's resurrection and ascension (Acts 1:2–3, 22).[101] (2) The tower of Babel's reversal (Zeph 3:8–10) finds initial fulfillment in the ingathering and events of Pentecost (Acts 2).[102] (3) The pilgrimage of worshipers from the region of Cush (Greek = Ethiopia) (Zeph 3:10) corresponds to God expanding his church to non-Jewish peoples (Acts 8:26–40).[103]

The following seven connections strengthen the idea that Luke believed that

---

97. See Matt 13:24–30; cf. 3:12; 25:32, 46; see also Rev 14:18–20 (cf. Joel 4:13[3:13]), though with different verb forms.

98. Cf. Kline, "Day of the Lord in the Death and Resurrection of Christ," 757–70; Ortlund and Beale, "Darkness over the Whole Land," 221–38.

99. Jud Davis, "Acts 2 and the Old Testament: The Pentecost Event in light of Sinai, Babel and the Table of Nations," CTR 7 (2009): 29–48; Craig S. Keener, Acts, 4 vols. (Grand Rapids: Baker Academic, 2012–2015), 1:840–44.

100. Jerry Dale Butcher, "The Significance of Zephaniah 3:8–13 for Narrative Composition in the Early Chapters of the Book of Acts" (PhD diss., Case Western Reserve University, 1972). Butcher extends Clarke's argument that Luke treats the conversion of the Ethiopian eunuch in Acts 8:26–40 as explicitly fulfilling Zeph 3:10. See W. K. L. Clarke, "The Use of the Septuagint in Acts," in The Beginnings of Christianity: Part I: The Acts of the Apostles, ed. F. J. Foakes-Jackson and Kirsopp Lake, 5 vols. (London: Macmillan, 1920), 2:101–3.

101. Butcher, "Significance of Zephaniah 3:8–13," 53–54.

102. See esp. Acts 2:5–6, 11, 21, 42–47. Butcher, "Significance of Zephaniah 3:8–13," 56–77.

103. Butcher, "Significance of Zephaniah 3:8–13," 77–85.

Jesus's death marked the intrusion of the day of YHWH as punishment and that Jesus's resurrection and ascension inaugurated the day of YHWH as the restoration of the whole cosmos (Zeph 3:8–10).

1. The LXX of Zeph 3:8 has the Lord declaring, "Wait upon me . . . for the day of my rising [*or* resurrection] as a testimony" (ὑπόμεινόν με . . . εἰς ἡμέραν ἀναστάσεώς μου εἰς μαρτύριον). In context, YHWH rises to testify both to the deserved punishment of the world's unrepentant sinners (3:8b–c; cf. 1:17) and to his just pardon of the world's multiracial remnant (3:9–10; cf. 2:3; 3:11–13). Luke opens his narrative alluding both to Jesus's resurrection ("he presented himself alive," Acts 1:3) and ascension ("when he was taken up," 1:2).[104] Luke then highlights how Jesus charged his disciples "to *wait* for the promise of the Father" (περιμένειν τὴν ἐπαγγελίαν τοῦ πατρὸς)—namely, the Holy Spirit (1:4). The link between "waiting upon" (ὑπομένω) in Zeph 3:8 and "waiting for" (περιμένω) in Acts 1:4 is close. Significantly, the outpouring of the Spirit whom Jesus promised resulted in his disciples becoming his "witnesses" (μάρτυρες) (Acts 1:8), using a related term to "testimony" (μαρτύριον) in the LXX of Zeph 3:8.[105] Even more, when replacing Judas as Jesus's apostle, Peter stresses the need to find someone who can join them in being "a witness to his [Jesus's] resurrection" (μάρτυρα τῆς ἀναστάσεως αὐτοῦ) (Acts 1:22).[106] The only verses in Scripture where μάρτυς ("witness") or μαρτύριον ("testimony") occur with ἀνάστασις (rising, resurrection") are Zeph 3:8 and Acts 1:22; 4:33.[107] This increases the likelihood that Luke indeed saw Jesus's resurrection and ascension that give rise to the pouring of the Spirit[108] as partially fulfilling Zephaniah's hope of YHWH's eschatological rise as global Judge and Savior.[109]

---

104. God fulfills the promise of his rising in Zeph 3:8 in a multifaceted way: (1) God will rise as judge at the consummate day of YHWH during Christ's second appearing and decisively pour out his wrath against all unrepentant sinners. (2) God the judge already arose to testify against the sins of the elect from the earth's nations when he cursed Christ at the cross as a substitute wrath-bearer. (3) God has already risen through Christ's resurrection and ascension and by this has inaugurated his new creational work among his redeemed. In Luke-Acts, Luke appears to highlight fulfillments 2 and 3 (on the latter, see Luke 23:44–45; Acts 2:19–20; and the Canonical and Theological Significance discussions at Zeph 1:2–3, 7).

105. For Jesus alluding to Isa 43:10–12 by mentioning "witnesses" in Acts 1:8, see I. Howard Marshall, "Acts," in *Commentary on the New Testament Use of the Old Testament*, ed. G. K. Beale and D. A. Carson (Grand Rapids: Baker Academic, 2007), 528; David G. Peterson, *The Acts of the Apostles*, PNTC (Grand Rapids: Eerdmans, 2009), 110–11. Also, the

prior immediate context in Isa 43 may provide a backdrop for Zeph 3:8–10 and 3:18–20. Like Zephaniah, Isaiah speaks both of God's "assembling" (קבץ) his remnant from the end of the earth (Isa 43:5) and of the nations and peoples "assembling" (קבץ) and "gathering" (אסף) (43:9) to YHWH.

106. Cf. Acts 2:32; 4:33; 10:41; 26:16.

107. By adding the verb ἀνίστημι ("to raise up, rise, arise"), the number of texts grows (Num 23:18; Ruth 4:10; 2 Kgs 23:3; LXX Pss 34:11 [35:11 in Hebrew and English]; 77:5 [78:5 in Hebrew and English]; Job 16:8; Zeph 3:8; Acts 1:22; 2:32; 4:33; 10:41; 26:16). The texts from Psalms and Zephaniah are eschatological in nature.

108. On identifying the "the Holy Spirit" in Acts 1:8 with "the Spirit of Jesus," see Acts 16:7. See also the language of Luke's gospel being only what Jesus "began to do and to teach" (1:1), which makes Acts a record of what he continued to do and to teach by *his* Spirit.

109. Jerome's Vulgate appears to read Zeph 3:8 as a ref-

2. In Zeph 3:8 YHWH declares that his judgment is to gather "nations" (ἐθνῶν) to "pour out" (ἐκχέω) on them—indeed, on "all the earth"—all of the wrath of his anger. In contrast, in Acts 2:4 we learn that Jews and Gentile proselytes "from every nation [ἔθνους] under heaven" had assembled in Jerusalem (Acts 2:40) and that God had promised to "pour out" (ἐκχέω) his Spirit on "all flesh" (2:17–18, 33) to create a people who would be witnesses for Christ "in Jerusalem and in all Judea and Samaria and to the end of the earth" (Acts 1:8). Instead of Luke disagreeing with Zephaniah's portrayal of the day of YHWH as one of vengeance,[110] he uses comparable vocabulary but applies it via his citation of LXX Joel 3:1–2[2:28–29 in English] to the remnant's situation as foretold in Zeph 3:9–10.

3. While Peter cites LXX Joel 3:1–5[2:28–32][111] in Acts 2:17–21, the key term "lip/speech" with γλῶσσα ("tongue") (Acts 2:3–4, 11, 26, always plural) is lacking in Joel but present in the Greek version of both the tower of Babel episode (Gen 11:7; cf. 10:5) and Zeph 3:9. Accordingly, Luke's citation in Acts 2:21 of LXX Joel 3:5[2:32] that "everyone who calls upon the name of the Lord will be saved" (πᾶς ὃς ἂν ἐπικαλέσηται τὸ ὄνομα κυρίου σωθήσεται) closely parallels YHWH's promise in Zeph 3:9 that he would purify the remnant's speech "that all might call upon the name of the Lord" (τοῦ ἐπικαλεῖσθαι πάντας τὸ ὄνομα κυρίου). "Calling on the name YHWH" in Zeph 3:9 not only counters the quest for a name in Gen 11:4, but it also links with Acts 2:21.[112] Thus, both the transformed "speech" and "calling" on the Lord's "name" link Acts 2 with Zeph 3:9–10.

4. With LXX Joel 3:4[2:31 in English] and Acts 2:20, Zeph 3:9 also employs the verb μεταστρέφω ("to turn, cause a change in state or condition") with respect to God's new creation work. Zephaniah, however, uses it with respect to the speech change and not the altering of the atmosphere and heavenly bodies.

5. Pentecost, in association with the Feast of Weeks, is a harvest feast, which conceptually aligns with the ingathering motif in Zephaniah and sets the context for the Feast of Ingathering the book celebrates. (See the comments at Zeph 1:2–3).

6. Zephaniah's image of serving YHWH *in unity* (Zeph 3:9) may have moved Luke to include the comment in Acts 2:42–47 regarding the early saints' corporate surrender and worship.

---

erence to Christ's resurrection (*in die resurrectionis meae in futurum*, "in the day of my resurrection in the future"), and Luther followed this interpretation as well (Luther, "Lectures on Zephaniah," 355). For brief discussion of how the early church father's interpreted Zeph 3:8, see Vlaardingerbroek, *Zephaniah*, 185.

110. So Butcher, "Significance of Zephaniah 3:8–13," 53–56, 67.

111. Note that some editions (e.g., Göttingen) follow Hebrew numbering but also include English numbering.

112. In the 2nd century BC, some Jews anticipated that at the resurrection God would reverse the curse of Babel: "And you shall be one people of the Lord, with one language" (T. Jud. 25:3).

248   *Part III.2: Stage 2: The Appeal to Wait for YHWH to Enjoy Salvation*

7. Luke stresses how God saved devout Jews "from every nation under heaven" (Acts 2:5) to prepare the context for the global ingathering that follows. Nevertheless, strikingly absent from the list of peoples and nations in Acts 2:9–11 are "Ethiopians" (Αἰθίοπες) or residents of "Ethiopia" (Αἰθιοπία), the Greek title meaning "burnt face" and rendering the Hebrew term for "Cush" (כּוּשׁ). Why would Luke not mention any Jews from this region? Perhaps, for Luke, God's saving the Ethiopian eunuch (Acts 8:26–40) directly fulfills Zephaniah's prediction that worshipers from the region of Cush would lead the ingathering of the nations to YHWH at the end of the age (Zeph 3:9–10).[113]

Taken together, the lexical and conceptual parallels found between Zeph 3:8–10 and the early chapters of Acts suggest that Zephaniah's prophecy guided Luke's narration as he described what the ascended Jesus continued to do and to teach by his Spirit through the apostles (see Acts 1:1). These seven observations substantiate that Luke believed that Jesus's death marked the intrusion of the day of YHWH as punishment, and that Jesus's resurrection and ascension inaugurated God's end-time restoration that Zeph 3:8–10 announces.

The Transformed People and YHWH's Eschatological Sanctuary

In 2:11 the prophet announced that "all the coastlands of the nations" would bow down to YHWH as he overcomes the world's "gods." Luther treated 2:11 as a "prelude for the coming kingdom of Christ, which was going to spread not merely among the Jews but into the whole world, throughout all nations."[114] What Zephaniah now envisions in 3:8–10 fulfills this reality.

Specifically, 3:8–10 portrays a centripetal movement of the earth's peoples and powers toward YHWH's judgment seat, where he sits enthroned in sovereign glory. Some whom God gathers from the nations he will destroy (3:8b–c). Still, he will preserve and unify others he calls "my supplicants, the daughter of my scattered ones" (עֲתָרַי בַּת־פּוּצַי, 3:10). These are a globally diverse community of worshipers depending on him (3:9–10). As we shall see in the next Chapter, YHWH then describes the central gathering site as "the mountain of my holiness" (הַר קָדְשִׁי, 3:11c), and those present before YHWH are "the remnant of Israel" (שְׁאֵרִית יִשְׂרָאֵל, 3:13), "the daughter of Zion" (בַּת־צִיּוֹן, 3:14a), "Israel" (יִשְׂרָאֵל, 3:14b), and "the daughter of Jerusalem" (בַּת יְרוּשָׁלָ͏ם, 3:14d). By these statements, the prophet associates the transformed mul-

---

113. Cf. Pss 68:32[31]; 87:4; Isa 18:7; 45:14. Whereas Luke's characterization of the official as "Ethiopian" directly fulfills Zeph 3:10 and related texts, his description of him as a foreigner and a "eunuch" alludes to Isa 56:3–8.

114. Luther, "Lectures on Zephaniah," 344.

tiethnic community with God's people "Israel" and the gathering site with his city "Zion/Jerusalem." How then ought we understand Zephaniah's "Zion/Jerusalem"?

The book has already linked YHWH's presence with Jerusalem (3:5). However, it has also clarified that YHWH would decimate Judah's earthly capital as it was presently known (1:4, 10–13), so that Jerusalem's "Shelter" would be cut off (3:7; cf. 2 Kgs 21:13). But YHWH was never confined to an earthly dwelling (1 Kgs 8:27; Jer 23:24; Acts 17:24). The ark of the covenant in the earthly temple-palace represented and was the step into the heavenly throne room, from which God rules the universe amid his heavenly council (Exod 25:9; Ps 11:4; Isa 66:1).[115] Furthermore, Ezekiel would see that YHWH's presence departing from his earthly residence preceded Jerusalem's downfall, thus opening the door for Babylon's invasion (e.g., Ezek 8:4; 9:3; 11:22–23). For this reason, the initial returnees looked beyond the second temple to the temple's greater eschatological realization. Then YHWH would return to his "temple" in full glory (43:2–5; Hag 2:7, 9; Mic 4:7)[116] and restore his garden paradise in an escalated way (Isa 51:3; 65:17–19; Ezek 36:35).

Thus, one day YHWH would reign from his eschatological temple and new Jerusalem over a renewed Israel, composed of many different people groups (Zeph 3:9–10, 11–13). Elsewhere Zephaniah speaks of these as "the remnant of the house of Judah" (2:7) and "the remnant of my people . . . the remainder of my nation (2:9). The geographical space in which the remnant resides would not only encompass the full promised land, including the territory the Philistines claimed (2:7; cf. Gen 15:18–19; 17:8; Josh 15:12), but the whole earth (Zeph 2:9; cf. Gen 26:3–4), which would become God's expanded mountain (Zeph 3:12; cf. Isa 11:9; Dan 2:44–45).

Additional commentary on the nature of God's eschatological temple/mountain is needed. Besides the anointed king-priest himself being God's Spirit-filled temple (Isa 11:2; 42:1; 59:21; cf. John 2:19–21), he would build the temple-palace with the aid of those far off and also reign from that same place (Zech 6:12–13, 15). As envisioned by Zeph 3:9–10, the nations would gather to this elevated mountain to hear YHWH's Torah (Isa 2:2–4; Mic 4:1–4), which YHWH would deliver through his Servant-King (Isa 42:4; 50:10). Together the nations would become one purified and forgiven family, the new remnant of Israel (Zeph 3:12),[117] serving YHWH their God and their king, the new David (Jer 30:9; Hos 3:5). No longer will YHWH rule from the physical ark of the covenant, which housed his Torah. The entire eschatological Jerusalem will be his throne, as his glory-presence reigns over and through his cosmopolitan, transformed bride (Isa 4:5–6; Jer 3:16–19), in whom will be his Torah (Jer 31:33; cf. 17:1). Thus, the people themselves will become what the ark of the covenant

---

115. Cf. Isa 24:23; Jer 23:18, 22; Matt 5:34–35; Mark 14:58; Acts 7:49; Heb 9:11, 23–24.

116. See also Zech 8:3; Mal 3:1. Many texts associate this

"temple" with God's people (e.g., Isa 4:2–6; Ezek 36:27; 37:26–27; 2 Cor 6:16; Eph 2:20–22).

117. Cf. Ps 87; Isa 19:25; Jer 12:14–16; 31:34.

was, and Jerusalem—in full identity with the people—will be called "YHWH is our righteousness" (33:16; cf. Isa 62:12).

In a very real sense, God is fulfilling today Zephaniah's vision of the eschatological ingathering of a global remnant. The earthly Jerusalem is no longer the locus of God's presence. What Jesus promised the Samaritan woman on Mount Gerizim has come true: "The hour is coming when neither at this mountain nor at Jerusalem will you worship the Father. . . . The hour is coming and is now, when the true worshipers will worship the Father in spirit and truth" (John 4:21, 23). People no longer need to gather to the earthly Jerusalem to meet YHWH, for his presence has become democratized among all who are in Christ by his Spirit. Regardless of geographical location, all who have come to Jesus have already been gathered to and identified with the heavenly new Jerusalem: "You have come to Mount Zion and to the city of the living God, the heavenly Jerusalem" (Heb 12:22; cf. Gal 5:25–26; Rev 21:2).

A Proper Response

Rejoice That the Church Fulfills OT Hopes for a Single Reconciled Community from Every Tribe and Tongue

Within the day of YHWH, Zephaniah envisions God's blessing of reconciliation reaching the nations (Zeph 3:9–10) and fulfilling the Abrahamic covenant (Gen 12:3; 22:18). As argued above,[118] Luke records the initial fulfillment of Zephaniah's anticipated restoration. In Christ's atoning work, God's blessing has moved from "Jerusalem . . . to the end of the earth" (Acts 1:8; cf. Luke 24:47). Zephaniah would have affirmed that the new covenant church consists of Jews and Gentiles in Christ who are now one flock (John 10:16; cf. 11:51–52; 12:19–20), a single olive tree (Rom 11:17–24), and one new man (Eph 2:11–22).

Accordingly, in fulfillment of Zephaniah's hopes for an international remnant of worshipers bringing offerings to God's presence (Zeph 3:10), the NT stresses that the Lord is already forming his church into "a kingdom and priests" "from every tribe and language and people and nation" (Rev 5:9–10; cf. 7:9–10). Already as priests, Christians offer sacrifices of praise (Rom 12:1; Heb 13:15–16; 1 Pet 2:5) at "Mount Zion and . . . the heavenly Jerusalem" (Heb 12:22; cf. Isa 2:2–3; Zech 8:20–23). Nevertheless, we await the day when the "new Jerusalem" will descend from heaven as the new earth (Rev 21:2, 10; cf. Isa 65:17–18). At that time, we will complete our journey to rest in Christ's supremacy and sufficiency (Matt 11:28–29; John 6:35) in a place without the curse (Rev 21:22–22:5).

---

118. See the section above titled The Initial Fulfillment of Zephaniah's Day of YHWH Restoration.

Engage in Missions Since God Saves Worshipers without Prejudice

Zephaniah believes that God's fiery wrath will consume the world's nations and kingdoms (Zeph 3:8b–c). Nevertheless, curse is not his final verdict. Through the blaze, YHWH will preserve and purify a community of multiethnic worshipers from the ends of the earth (3:9–10). Thus, de-creation and death give rise to new creation and life; salvation comes through punishment.

It was Noah's great-grandson through Cush who likely instigated the building project at Babel (Gen 10:10 with 11:8–9). Therefore, Zephaniah's choice of "Cush" as the sample region for global redemption (Zeph 3:9–10) testifies to God's amazing mercy to redeem those whose ancestors once led a rebellion against him. This is even more accented in the way the biblical authors associate "Babel/Babylon" (the same word in Hebrew) with arrogance and God-hostility (e.g., Isa 14:4–23). For them, Babylon symbolizes evil that God will ultimately vanquish in a single hour (1 Pet 5:13; Rev 16:17–18:24). Nevertheless, in Zeph 3:9–10 God promises to reverse the tower of Babel punishment making God's prior "enemies" into those "reconciled to God through the death of his Son" (Rom 5:10; cf. Eph 2:5).

Now, convinced that the fires of God's wrath have already fallen on Jesus for *all* who will call upon YHWH's name, regardless of ethnic heritage (Zeph 3:8–10), we cannot help but desire that all peoples hear of his mercy and grace and cry out for help. Paul's urgency is clear: "'Whosoever calls on the name of the Lord will be saved.' How then may they call with reference to whom they have not believed? And how may they believe of whom they have never heard? And how may they hear without preaching? And how may they preach if they are not sent? . . . So faith is from hearing, and hearing through Christ's word" (Rom 10:13–15, 17). Jesus said, "The harvest is indeed abundant, but the workers are few" (Luke 10:2).

Missions exist today because God is still creating the worshipers Zephaniah describes. The church of Jesus is an increasingly ethnically diverse community that follows the rivers of life back to God's sanctuary. The peoples from the distant lands—whether those who have moved into our own neighborhood or those that still remain in hard-to-reach places—are living in darkness under God's wrath. YHWH's day is at hand, and they will perish under YHWH's just fury unless they believe the good news of Christ's substitutionary sacrifice. We need godly "goers," and we need godly "senders." Today, in the twenty-first century, God is reversing the curse of Babel.[119] Will you join in this mission of seeing the temple-presence of God's Spirit fill the earth with the knowledge of God's glory like the waters cover the sea (Acts 1:8; cf. Num 14:21; Ps 72:19)?[120]

---

119. Jason S. DeRouchie, "By the Waters of Babylon: Global Missions from Genesis to Revelation," *MJT* 20.2 (2021): 6–30.

120. For more on this theme, see Eckhard J. Schnabel, "Israel, the People of God, and the Nations," *JETS* 45 (2002): 35–57;

Eckhard J. Schnabel, *Early Christian Mission*, 2 vols. (Downers Grove, IL: InterVarsity Press, 2004); Kevin DeYoung and Greg Gilbert, *What Is the Mission of the Church? Making Sense of Social Justice, Shalom, and the Great Commission* (Wheaton, IL:

Wait for YHWH

Though creation beautifully displays the grand design of its Creator, it is broken because the Adamic curse affects and infects all things (Rom 8:20–21). Car accidents and cancer temper family celebrations, and marvelous vistas become contexts for mass executions of Christians. Riots and kidnappings occur at city parks designed for child play, and mass shootings devastate schools. Disease runs rampant; people lose jobs; the global economy plummets. The global pandemic of alien guilt[121] continues to produce sinners who sin, leading them to perform injustice against the living God and those made in his image. Believers today live in the foggy transition of the ages—*after* Yahweh has atoned for the sin of his elect through the death of his Son yet *before* he has eradicated all evil and carried out the final judgment (Heb 9:28). The *already* aspects require that we call on his name and serve him together (Zeph 3:9–10). The *not yet* aspects necessitate that we heed Zephaniah's charge to patiently trust YHWH ("wait," 3:8), holding unswervingly to the only God who "acts for one waiting for him" (Isa 64:4).

Waiting is not easy, for great are the temptations to doubt, compromise, fear, or become anxious. Amid trouble, the call is, "Be humbled under the mighty hand of God . . . having cast all your anxiety upon him, because he cares for you" (1 Pet 5:6–7; cf. Phil 4:6–7). "Consider such a one who had endured hostility from sinners against himself, so that you may not become weary in your souls, becoming exhausted" (Heb 12:3). Before us is "the crown of life," and everyone "who endures under trial" will receive it (Jas 1:12). "The Lord knows to deliver godly ones from trial, and to keep unrighteous ones under punishment until the day of judgment" (2 Pet 2:9). So, "let us hold our confession of hope unswervingly, for the one who promised is faithful. And let us consider one another unto the arousal of love and good works, . . . encouraging, and all the more as you see the Day nearing" (Heb 10:23–25). "And after a little suffering, the God of all grace, who has called you unto his eternal glory in Christ, will himself restore, confirm, strengthen, and establish you" (1 Pet 5:10).

Crossway, 2011); Andreas J. Köstenberger, *Salvation to the Ends of the Earth: A Biblical Theology of Mission*, 2nd ed., NSBT 53 (Downers Grove, IL: InterVarsity Press, 2020).

121. By "alien guilt" I refer to the fact that, from fertilization forward, all humans are counted as sinners in Adam, even before they themselves engage in actual sinful acts (Rom 5:12; 18–19). We are "dead in our trespasses and sins" and "by nature children of wrath" (Eph 2:1, 3; cf. John 3:36). Thus, all humans need a savior.

Zephaniah 3:11–20b

B. Promises to Motivate Waiting for YHWH: The Remnant's Satisfying Salvation

Main Idea of the Passage

The hope of satisfying salvation should motivate the faithful remnant from Judah and other lands to wait for YHWH.

Literary Context

The book of Zephaniah's main body shapes the substance of the Savior's charge to hunger and hope for him and includes two stages of prophetic exhortation. In stage 1, Zephaniah urged the humble remnant in Judah and other lands to seek YHWH together to avoid experiencing the fires of God's wrath that he had already begun to pour out upon the world (2:1–3:7). Stage 2 then began in 3:8 with the inferential "therefore," as the prophet called his audience to "wait" for YHWH to enjoy deliverance from his day of fury (3:8–20b).

Previously, two unmarked, extended reasons (both beginning with "Woe!") for why Zephaniah's audience needed to pursue YHWH together followed his masculine plural commands to "gather" and "seek" in 2:1–4 (2:5–15; 3:1–7). Now, Zephaniah follows his masculine plural charge to "wait" for YHWH in 3:8–10 by two extended parallel subunits (3:11–13, 16–20b). Both start with the temporal phrase "in that day," supply promises to motivate unswerving trust, and frame a climactic discursive command to rejoice as if the great salvation had already occurred (3:14–15). Zephaniah's oracle ends at 3:20b. This final unit in 3:11–20b gives the prophet's highest motivation for seeking and waiting for YHWH together (2:1, 3; 3:8).

> III. The Substance of the Savior's Invitation to Satisfaction: Charges to Seek YHWH Together and to Wait (2:1–3:20b)
>
> III.1 Stage 1: The Appeal to Seek YHWH Together to Avoid Punishment (2:1–3:7)
>
> → **III.2 Stage 2: The Appeal to Wait for YHWH to Enjoy Salvation (3:8–20b)**
>
> A. The Charge to Wait for YHWH to Act (3:8–10)
>
> B. **Promises to Motivate Waiting for YHWH: The Remnant's Satisfying Salvation (3:11–20b)**

Translation and Exegetical Outline

(See pages 255–257.)

Structure and Literary Form

Stage 2 of the Savior's exhortation unto life includes two main units (Zeph 3:8–10, 11–20b). After the charge and two reasons to "wait" for YHWH in 3:8–10, 3:11–20b includes three subunits that contain direct and indirect promises to motivate sustained hope in God amid the present and encroaching global turmoil (3:11–13, 14–15, 16–20b). YHWH's voice dominates the outer sections. Each begins with the same fronted, asyndetic prepositional phrase "in that day" (בַּיּוֹם הַהוּא, 3:11, 16), which recalls the future-oriented hope of the "day" of YHWH's rising (3:8a).[1] God's initial promise stimulates persevering trust by pledging that he will not shame Jerusalem but will cleanse her and make his holy mountain a place for his transformed people to flourish (3:11–13). In the latter unit, God promises to save Jerusalem completely, gathering his remnant, fighting for them, restoring them, and raising them up as testaments to his greatness (3:16–20b). A discursive charge to rejoice comes between these units, and it treats the future deliverance as if it had already occurred (3:14–15). In these two verses, Zephaniah reaches his rhetorical motivational peak, but his imperatives do not progress his main exhortations (found in 2:1, 3; 3:8) to another stage. Instead, the intrusive material supports his exhortation to "wait" by making the desire for future joy a present delight.

---

1. Cf. Bailey, "Zephaniah," 487; Patterson, *Nahum, Habakkuk, Zephaniah*, 374.

Zephaniah 3:11–20b

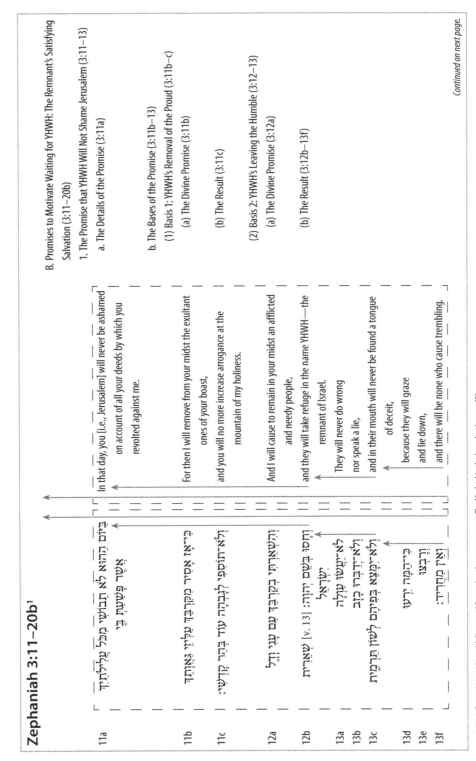

Continued on next page.

1. For information on the guidelines used for tracing the argument, see The Method in the introduction, pp. XX.

Part III.2: Stage 2: The Appeal to Wait for YHWH to Enjoy Salvation

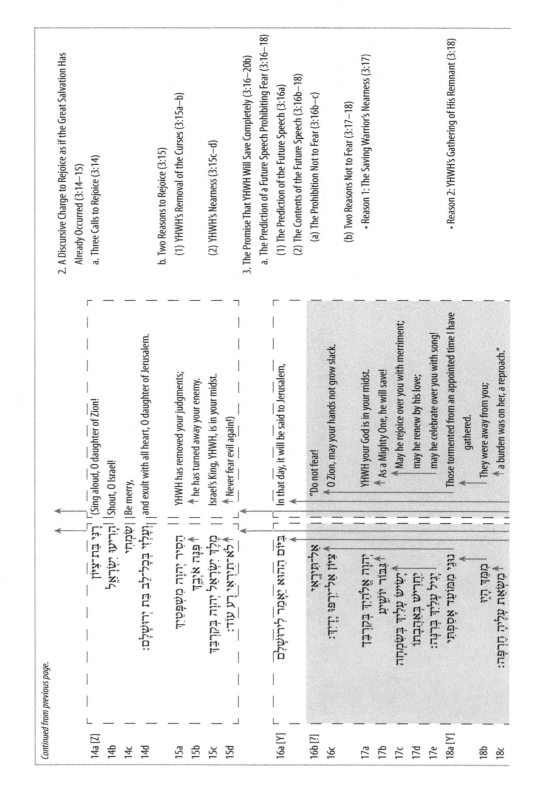

Zephaniah 3:11–20b

19a	הִנְנִי עֹשֶׂה אֶת־כָּל־מְעַנַּיִךְ בָּעֵת הַהִיא	Look, I will be dealing with all who afflict you at that time.
19b	וְהוֹשַׁעְתִּי אֶת־הַצֹּלֵעָה	And I will save the lame one,
19c	וְהַנִּדָּחָה אֲקַבֵּץ	and the banished one I will assemble.
19d	וְשַׂמְתִּים לִתְהִלָּה וּלְשֵׁם בְּכָל־הָאָרֶץ בָּשְׁתָּם	And I will place them for praise and for a name in all the earth, their [place of] shame.
20a	בָּעֵת הַהִיא אָבִיא אֶתְכֶם וּבָעֵת קַבְּצִי אֶתְכֶם	At that time, I will bring you—even at the time of my assembling you,
20b	כִּי־אֶתֵּן אֶתְכֶם לְשֵׁם וְלִתְהִלָּה בְּכֹל עַמֵּי הָאָרֶץ בְּשׁוּבִי אֶת־שְׁבוּתֵיכֶם לְעֵינֵיכֶם	for I will give you for a name and for praise among all the peoples of the earth in my restoring your circumstances before your eyes.

b. The Promissory Implications of the Future Speech (3:19–20b)

(1) Jerusalem's Complete Salvation (3:19)

(2) The Remnant's Complete Participation (3:20a–b)

*The long arrows pointing upward mark 3:8b–20b as a unit subordinate to 3:8a, with v. 8b–c and vv. 9–10 marked with a conjunction כִּי indicating the grounds for the imperative in v. 8a, and vv. 11–20b unmarked and supplying motivation for v. 8a.

†The dotted-line boxes mark vv. 14–15 as a discursive call to rejoice. The dotted-line boxes mark vv. 11–13 and vv. 16–20b in parallel and also mark vv. 14–15 as a discursive call to rejoice.

Is Zephaniah 3:11–20b a Unified Whole?

While scholars generally agree that there are at least minor shifts between the divisions proposed here, many fail to recognize the whole as a discrete unit.[2] For example, Floyd believes 3:8–13 and 3:14–20b belong to different macro-units that he titles "Exhortations to prepare for the Day of Yahweh" (2:1–3:13) and "Exhortations to rejoice in the promise of salvation" (3:14–20).[3] Sweeney fails to recognize the significance of the inference ("therefore") and imperative ("wait!") in 3:8. Like Floyd, he places a substantial break at 3:14 due to "the prophet's syntactically independent direct address to the city of Jerusalem calling for her to rejoice at her impending restoration."[4] Wendland and Clark group 3:1–20 together as the third of the book's three "dialogues" between YHWH and his prophet.[5]

Figure 8.1: YHWH's Speeches vs. Zephaniah's in Zephaniah 3:1–20b	
YHWH	**Zephaniah**
	3:1–5
3:6–7b	3:7c
3:8–13	3:14–17
3:18–20b	

These scholars miss how grammar more than the shift in speaker (i.e., YHWH's voice vs. Zephaniah's) guides the book's argument or how 2:1, 3 and 3:8 provide the rhetorical and structural backbone in the prophet's directive speech.[6] Many features call for reading all of 3:8–20b together—stage 2 of the Savior's invitation to satisfaction.

1. Zephaniah's decision to front both 3:11 and 16 with the asyndetic prepositional phrases "in that day" (בַּיּוֹם הַהוּא) strongly suggests that he intended we read the two subunits together. As Tachick notes, the temporal marker indicates that "3:11–13 and 16–20b emerge as tandem, future-oriented sections."[7] Furthermore, the "day" to which both phrases refer is "the day of my

---

2. Some notable exceptions are F. W. Farrar, *The Minor Prophets* (New York: Revell, 1890), 155–58; Chisholm, *Interpreting the Minor Prophets*, 210–15; Clendenen, "Minor Prophets," 377–79; Tachick, *Use of Zephaniah 3 in John 12*, 86–107.

3. Floyd, *Minor Prophets, Part 2*, 165–66.

4. Sweeney, *Zephaniah*, 170. He further writes, "The shift to a call for rejoicing in v. 14 . . . marks a new rhetorical stage in the prophet's speech" (194).

5. Wendland and Clark, "Zephaniah," 5, 13–14.

6. See E. Ray Clendenen, "Textlinguistics and Prophecy

in the Book of the Twelve," *JETS* 46 (2003): 388; cf. Longacre, *Joseph*, 121; Roy L. Heller, *Narrative Structure and Discourse Constellations: An Analysis of Clause Function in Biblical Hebrew Prose*, HSS 55 (Winona Lake, IN: Eisenbrauns, 2004), 468–69; DeRouchie, *How to Understand and Apply*, 112–13.

7. Tachick, *Use of Zephaniah 3 in John 12*, 100–101; cf. 95–96; see also Patterson, *Nahum, Habakkuk, Zephaniah*, 325, 327; Bailey, "Zephaniah," 490, 495. De Vries notes of the "introductory transitions" in Zeph 3:11 and 16 that "the two events are to be interpreted as roughly synchronous with each other," but

rising as a witness" (יוֹם קוּמִי לְעַד) in 3:8.[8] Thus, all of 3:8–20b is tied together by the mention in 3:8 of "the day"; it alone supplies the back-reference for the temporal phrases that follow.

2. Unlike the four imperatives in 2:1, 3 and single imperative in 3:8, which are all masculine plural, only the second of the four imperatives in 3:14 is masculine plural (הָרִיעוּ, "Shout!"); the others are all feminine singular (רָנִּי . . . שִׂמְחִי וְעָלְזִי, "Sing aloud! . . . Be merry, and exult!"). Zephaniah could have used all masculine plural forms to advance his prophetic exhortations in 2:1, 3 and 3:8 into a further stage. However, this altered pattern suggests that these imperatives function differently than those that precede. The feminine singular nature of the first and third groupings (3:14a, 14c–d) signals that the remnant has become a collective identified with the new, eschatological city of Jerusalem. The masculine plural central imperative (3:14b) then equates the united and restored city with the multiethnic, renewed "afflicted and needy people . . . the remnant of Israel"—the ethnically diverse worshipers who have gathered to YHWH's presence at "the mountain of my holiness" (3:9–12). Zephaniah envisions God having transformed his people and having caused the dawning of salvation history's consummate era.

3. Zephaniah supports his three-part command in 3:14 by employing in 3:15 two *qatal* verbs that speak of YHWH's judgment as if it has already happened. But the rest of the book portrays the day of wrath as still future,[9] though God's destruction of Cush in 2:12 signals that it has in some sense begun, at least typologically. This implies that 3:14–15 does not function like the imperatives in 2:1, 3 and 3:8. Instead, 3:14–15 most likely supplies a rhetorical, celebrative intrusion that supports the call to "wait for me!" in 3:8 by disclosing that YHWH's future salvation is absolutely secure; his faithful remnant can rejoice now as if he has already fully acted.[10] Therefore, the joy of the future creates present satisfaction, as desire gives rise to delight, even in the waiting. (For more on this, see below.)

4. Lexical and conceptual correspondences demonstrate that 3:14–15 links to what precedes and follows. With respect to what precedes, figure 8.2 shows that these connections include the use of בַּת ("daughter"), יִשְׂרָאֵל ("Israel"), *hiphil* of סוּר ("remove"), עָלִיז/עָלַז ("exultant, to exult"), and קֶרֶב ("midst").[11]

---

he sees them functioning in different ways (De Vries, *From Old Revelation to New*, 52; cf. 43–44).

8. Though Wendland and Clark state that "in that day" in 3:11 recalls YHWH's day from 3:8–9, they fail to note the same is true at 3:16. See Wendland and Clark, "Zephaniah," 31, 33.

9. See, e.g., Zeph 1:7, 14; 2:2; 3:8, 11, 19.

10. Floyd is close to this perspective (Floyd, *Minor Prophets, Part 2*, 243–45), but he still fails to see how the imperatives in 3:14 function differently than in 2:1, 3 and 3:8 and how 3:14–15 is actually part of the motivation to "wait" in 3:8.

11. Cf. Ben Zvi, *Book of Zephaniah*, 241; Tachick, *Use of Zephaniah 3 in John 12*, 97n65.

Figure 8.2: Lexical and Conceptual Links between Zephaniah 3:14–15 and 3:8–13

	Zeph 3:8–13	Zeph 3:14–15
1.	"The *daughter* of my scattered ones" (בַּת־פּוּצַי) (3:10)	"O *daughter* of Zion" (בַּת־צִיּוֹן) (3:14a); "O daughter of Jerusalem" (בַּת יְרוּשָׁלָ͏ִם) (3:14d)
2.	"The remnant of *Israel*" (שְׁאֵרִית יִשְׂרָאֵל) (3:13)	"O *Israel*" (יִשְׂרָאֵל) (3:14b)
3.	"I will *remove* . . . the *exultant ones* of your boast" (אָסִיר . . . עַלִּזֵי גַּאֲוָתֵךְ) (3:11b)	"And *exult* with all heart. . . . YHWH has *removed* your judgments . . . your enemy" (וְעָלְזִי בְּכָל־לֵב . . . הֵסִיר יְהוָה . . . מִשְׁפָּטַיִךְ . . . אֹיְבֵךְ) (3:14d–15b)
4.	"I will remove from *your midst* . . . at the mountain of my holiness. And I will cause to remain *in your midst* an afflicted and needy people, and they will take refuge in the name *YHWH*" (אָסִיר מִקִּרְבֵּךְ . . . בְּהַר קָדְשִׁי וְהִשְׁאַרְתִּי בְקִרְבֵּךְ עַם עָנִי וָדָל וְחָסוּ בְּשֵׁם יְהוָה) (3:11b–c, 12a–b)	"O daughter of Jerusalem . . . Israel's king, *YHWH*, is *in your midst*" (בַּת יְרוּשָׁלָ͏ִם . . . מֶלֶךְ יִשְׂרָאֵל יְהוָה בְּקִרְבֵּךְ) (3:14d, 15c)
5.	"There will be none who cause trembling" (אֵין מַחֲרִיד) (3:13f)	"Never fear evil again!" (לֹא־תִירְאִי רָע עוֹד) (3:15d)

With respect to what follows, figure 8.3 shows that the lexical links include צִיּוֹן ("Zion"), יְרוּשָׁלַ͏ִם ("Jerusalem"), רנן/רִנָּה ("sing aloud/song"), שׂמח/שִׂמְחָה ("be merry/merriment"), ירא ("to fear"), יְהוָה ("YHWH"), and קֶרֶב ("midst").[12]

Figure 8.3: Lexical and Conceptual Links between Zephaniah 3:14–15 and 3:16–17

	Zeph 3:14–15	Zeph 3:16–17
1.	The mention of *Zion* (צִיּוֹן) and *Jerusalem* (יְרוּשָׁלַ͏ִם) (3:14a, d)	The mention of *Jerusalem* (יְרוּשָׁלַ͏ִם) and *Zion* (צִיּוֹן) (3:16a, c)
2.	Three-part command to rejoice in YHWH's salvation (3:14) with some lexical correspondence: • *"Sing aloud*!" (רָנִּי) (3:14a) • *"Be merry*!" (שִׂמְחִי) (3:14c)	Threefold note of YHWH's rejoicing in his remnant (3:17c–e) with some lexical correspondence: • "May he celebrate over you with *song*" (יָגִיל עָלַיִךְ בְּרִנָּה) (3:17e) • "May he rejoice over you with *merriment*" (יָשִׂישׂ עָלַיִךְ בְּשִׂמְחָה) (3:17c)
3.	"Never *fear* evil again!" (לֹא־תִירְאִי רָע עוֹד) (3:15d)	"Do not *fear*!" (אַל־תִּירָאִי) (3:16b)
4.	"YHWH has removed your judgments; he has turned away your enemy. Israel's king, *YHWH*, is *in your midst*" (הֵסִיר יְהוָה מִשְׁפָּטַיִךְ פִּנָּה אֹיְבֵךְ מֶלֶךְ יִשְׂרָאֵל יְהוָה בְּקִרְבֵּךְ) (3:15a–c)	"*YHWH* your God is *in your midst*. As a Mighty One, he will save!" (יְהוָה אֱלֹהַיִךְ בְּקִרְבֵּךְ גִּבּוֹר יוֹשִׁיעַ) (3:17a–b)

---

12. Floyd notes elements of nos. 2–4 (Floyd, *Minor Prophets, Part 2*, 243); Ben Zvi, along with Wendland and Clark, lists elements of all four (Ben Zvi, *Book of Zephaniah*, 246; Wend-land and Clark, "Zephaniah," 13). Cf. Robert B. Chisholm Jr., *Handbook on the Prophets* (Grand Rapids: Baker Academic, 2002), 450; Tachick, *Use of Zephaniah 3 in John 12*, 99.

All these features disclose that 3:8–20 is an integrated unit of prophecy about *the future*, to be read as a whole. This is so, despite understanding the imperatives (inherently future) in 3:14 as being grounded in the *qatal* verbs (accomplished deliverance) of 3:15.[13]

The Argument and Function of 3:11–20

Now, with respect to the internal structure of the three subunits in 3:11–20b, the following features are clear. First, 3:11–13 includes two basic parts: The asyndetic temporal phrase "in that day" introduces the details of the promise in 3:11a. Then 3:11c–13 supplies two bases for the promise, the first marked by כִּי־אָז ("for then") and each containing a first-person statement of what God will accomplish (3:11b with *yiqtol*, 12a with *weqatal*) followed by a non-first-person statement of result (3:11c, 12b). The latter is then explicated through three coordinated negative clauses (. . . לֹא וְלֹא . . . וְלֹא) (3:13a–c), the last of which is followed by a threefold rationale initiated by כִּי ("because") (3:13d–f).

Second, 3:14–15 supplies an intrusive call to joy as part of the motivation to "wait for me!" in 3:8. Zephaniah gives four semantically similar imperatives in three groupings of asyndetic charges to rejoice, the last two imperatives being conjoined. Following this charge are two asyndetic reasons to rejoice that each includes a statement and explication (15a–b, c–d).

Scholars rightly emphasize the imperatives in 3:14. Though the commands do not directly build upon the primary exhortations in 2:1, 3 and 3:8, they especially motivate God's charge "wait for me!" (3:8) by supplying the book's rhetorical high point. Thus, Tachick has noted that 3:14–15 contain Longacre's six proposed markers for surface structure peak:[14]

1. *Rhetorical underlining:* Like a heightened drumbeat at a song's end, Zephaniah uses four pounding imperatives in 3:14, which is more than in any other verse in the book. The sharp, broken nature of the outbursts suggests that the prophet cannot contain his joy.
2. *Concentration of participants:* In 3:14, the prophet climactically "crowds the stage" by addressing several chief personalities or figures related to those members who appear elsewhere in the book: "daughter" (3:10), "Zion" (3:16), "Israel" (2:9; 3:13, 15), and "Jerusalem" (1:4, 12; 3:16; cf. 3:1, 11). When speaking of 3:14–20 together, Berlin rightly notes, "All of the main 'characters'—

---

13. Similarly, Ben Zvi, *Book of Zephaniah*, 246.

14. Tachick, *Use of Zephaniah 3 in John 12*, 101–7; see Longacre, *The Grammar of Discourse*, 38–48.

God, Israel, and the nations—who earlier were bringing judgment or suffering destruction are here joined together."[15]

3. *Heightened vividness:* Unlike his earlier pattern of repeating verbal roots in 2:1 (קשש, "to bundle") and 2:3 (בקש, "to seek"), Zephaniah adds color and dimension to his call to rejoice by using four imperatives from different roots in 3:14 (רנן, "to sing aloud"; רוע, "to shout"; שמח, "to be merry"; עלז, "to exult"). He also vividly changes from masculine plural to feminine singular in three of the four imperatives, thus noting the unity that has come to the transformed, multiethnic "Israel."

4. *Change of pace:* In 2:1, 3 and 3:8, various adverbial particles supplied marked reasons to heed Zephaniah's imperatives (בְּטֶרֶם, "before," 3x in 2:2a, c, d; כִּי, "for" in 2:4a; כִּי, "for" 2x in 3:8b, 9a), but in 3:14 the prophet simply expresses his charges in staccato fashion and then adds two unmarked reasons to rejoice in 3:15.

5. *Change of vantage point and/or orientation:* Whereas the initial two-thirds of the book motivates the audience by visions of dread (save for the brief statements of hope in 2:7, 9c–d, 11c), 3:9–20b inspires patient trust among the remnant by portraying amazing vistas of joyous and global salvation.[16] This shift is perhaps nowhere more pronounced than in the threefold call of 3:14 to celebrate proleptically because of God's certain deliverance in 3:15. Altering the time perspective from *judgment is coming* in 2:1–4 and 3:8 (e.g., "before the day . . . comes" in 2:2; "perhaps you may be hidden" in 2:4; "the earth will be consumed" in 3:8) to *judgment is past* in 3:15 (using *qatal* verbs) highlights the prophetic outburst in 3:14 calling for joy amid the waiting.

6. *Incidence of particles and onomatopoeia:* The presence of prose particles 7. (אֶת/אֲשֶׁר/הַ⊙) helps to formally distinguish prose from poetry.[17] The subunit 3:11–13 has three such particles (3:11a, including בַּיּוֹם), and 3:16–20b has eighteen;[18] 3:14–15 has none. This indicates that these verses are more of a didactic intrusion encouraging celebration.

The way 3:14–15 stand out in the book's overall macrostructure further highlights the distinct and elevated rhetorical role these two verses play in Zephaniah's

---

15. Berlin, *Zephaniah,* 148.

16. Achtemeier writes, "The Book of Zephaniah ends in almost unimaginable joy" (Achtemeier, *Nahum–Malachi,* 86). Similarly, Robertson observes that Zephaniah includes at its front "one of the most awesome descriptions of the wrath of God in judgment found anywhere in Scripture" and then at its end "one of the most moving descriptions of the love of God for his people found anywhere in Scripture" (Robertson, *Books of*

Nahum, Habakkuk, and Zephaniah, 334). Jesus's blood and righteousness alone ultimately clarify how Yahweh can justly deliver any from his encroaching wrath (Exod 34:6–7; Rom 3:23–26).

17. See Andersen and Forbes, "'Prose Particle' Counts of the Hebrew Bible," 165–83.

18. The article occurs eleven times (Zeph 3:16a [2x], 19a [2x], 19b, c, d, 20a [3x], 20b) and אֶת־ occurs seven times (19a, 19b, 20a [2x], 20b [3x]).

argument. As highlighted in the Structure and Literary Form discussion at 3:8–10, the overall flow of 2:1–3:20b contains a remarkable parallel symmetry between stages 1 and 2 of Zephaniah's exhortation, and the balance is broken only at 3:14–15. Here the discursive directive speech (3:14–15) intrudes between the two motivating promise sections (3:11–13, 16–20b), while in stage 1 the two unmarked reasons stand directly adjacent (2:5–15; 3:1–7).

Figure 8.4: Zeph 3:14–15 as Motivational Peak in the Balanced Structure of Zephaniah's Stage 1 and 2 Exhortations	
Stage 1: The Appeal to Seek YHWH Together to Avoid Punishment (2:1–3:7)	
A. The Charge to Unite in Submission to YHWH (2:1–2)	
B. The Charge to Seek YHWH in Righteousness and Humility (2:3–4)	
1. The Charge to Seek YHWH (2:3)	Commands (2mp imperatives)
2. An Initial Reason to Seek YHWH: The Devastation of Philistia (2:4)	Initial basis fronted with "for" (כִּי)
C. Further Reasons to Seek YHWH Together (2:5–3:7)	Two unmarked reasons, both beginning with "Woe!" (הוֹי)
1. The Lamentable State and Fate of the Rebels from the Foreign Nations (2:5–15)	
2. The Lamentable State and Fate of the Rebels from Jerusalem (3:1–7)	
Stage 2: The Appeal to Wait for YHWH to Enjoy Salvation (3:8–20b)	
A. The Charge to Wait for YHWH to Act (3:8–10)	
1. The Charge to Wait for YHWH (3:8a)	Command (2mp imperative)
2. Two Reasons to Wait for YHWH (3:8b–10)	Two initial bases, both fronted with "for" (כִּי)
B. Promises to Motivate Waiting for YHWH: The Remnant's Satisfying Salvation (3:11–20b)	
1. The Promise that YHWH Will Not Shame Jerusalem (3:11–13)	Two unmarked promises, both introduced by "in that day" (בַּיּוֹם הַהוּא) but separated by the discursive charge.
2. A Discursive Charge to Rejoice as if the Great Salvation Has Already Occurred (3:14–15)	
3. The Promise That YHWH Will Save Completely (3:16–20b)	

Third, grasping the flow of thought in 3:16–20b is challenged by the difficult Hebrew in 3:18. The subunit likely has two parts (3:16–18, 19–20b), each detailing from a different angle promises that YHWH will completely save his remnant.

The first section opens with the promise that "in that day" of YHWH's rising, someone will declare to personified Jerusalem that they need not fear. The speech frame occurs in 3:16a, and then 3:16b–18 details the speech itself. The prohibition not to fear comes in 3:16b–c both as charge and explication, and then two unmarked reasons to avoid fear follow (3:17, 18). Some interpreters end the quotation at 3:17 (e.g., CSB). However, the verb אסף ("to gather") being in the *qatal* in 3:18 suggests that the future speech treats the ingathering as a past reality. And because God's assembling the world's peoples both for punishment (1:2–3; 3:8, using both אסף, "to gather," and קבץ, "to assemble") and deliverance (3:19–20b, using קבץ; cf. 3:10) is still *future* in relation to Zephaniah's present time, the treatment of the ingathering as past in 3:18 indicates that the verse is still part of the citation of what *will be* declared on the day of YHWH.

The second section opens with the arresting הִנְנִי ("Look, I!"), an asyndetic marker of immediate significance that returns the prophet's argument to his present time (3:19a). What follows treats the deliverance at the day of YHWH as *future*. God first pledges to fully save those he once banished (3:19) and then expounds on this promise in more personal terms (3:20a–b). The book then ends in much the same way it began (1:1), declaring "YHWH has spoken" all that precedes (3:20c).

Zephaniah 3:11–20b provides the book's highest-level motivations for jointly seeking and waiting, looking and longing (2:1, 3; 3:8). Each of the three units (3:11–13, 14–15, 16–20b) are dominated by feminine singular forms that refer to the newly transformed city Jerusalem—a city that is no longer "rebellious and defiled" or "oppressive" (contrast 3:1–7) but is now filled with an international "afflicted and needy people" who "will take refuge in the name YHWH" (3:12a–b). Zephaniah closely ties the city in 3:11–20b with the remnant of Israel (3:13, 15). But the feminine persona of this transformed Jerusalem also connects with the "daughter of my scattered ones" (3:10), the international peoples who are offering their worship before God, whose presence the book solely associates with Jerusalem (1:12; 3:5, 15, 16–17). Thus, like other prophets (e.g., Isa 54:2–3; Jer 3:17), Zephaniah links Jerusalem with some "from every tribe and language and people and nation" (Rev 5:10) and equates this transformed city with the new Israel. Other texts relate this church with "the Israel of God" (Gal 6:16) and with the heavenly new Jerusalem (Gal 5:25–26; Heb 12:22) that is "prepared as a bride adorned for her husband" (Rev 22:2).

In the way that the unit directly supports the command to "wait" in Zeph 3:8, the whole is part of the prophetic exhortation. Nevertheless, because 3:11–20b is principally focused on future hope of deliverance and accompanied by prohibitions not to fear, the unit itself is a "prophetic announcement of salvation."[19]

Explanation of the Text

1. The Promise That YHWH Will Not Shame Jerusalem (3:11–13)

In 3:8b–10, Zephaniah clarified that "waiting" for YHWH is necessary because of God's inevitable coming global punishment and resulting global restoration. The lack of conjunction at the head of 3:11 and the following cohesive content suggest that 3:11–20b clarifies the implications of this new creation work for the multiethnic remnant whom

---

19. Sweeney, *Isaiah 1–39*, 531.

Zephaniah associates with YHWH's presence and, therefore, identifies with the redeemed city Jerusalem (Zeph 3:9–10). That is, these verses supply the most personal, ultimate motivation for the faithful in Judah and other lands to continue trusting YHWH together. For those who add enduring hope (3:8) to their unified seeking of YHWH (2:1, 3), the restoration through the fires of punishment will include God removing shame and preserving the broken (3:11–13), bringing their joy to completion in view of his irreversible victory (3:14–15), and culminating worldwide deliverance for the glory of his name (3:16–20b). Thus, the calls of the book's body for God's people to seek him together and wait for him (2:1, 3; 3:8) amount to the Savior's invitation to satisfaction that will result in the consummation of the remnant's joy in God and God's joy in his redeemed.

a. The Details of the Promise (3:11a)

YHWH further motivates his faithful remnant to "wait" for him (Zeph 3:8a) by promising that, "in that day" (בַּיּוֹם הַהוּא) of judicial action (3:8a), the prior rebellious city of Jerusalem will *not* remain in a shameful state before God. In 3:8–10, YHWH addressed the remnant community's individual members from Judah and other lands with a masculine plural imperative. In 3:11a, feminine singular verbs and pronouns indicate his focus is now on the new Jerusalem. This collective city represents the international assembly of worshipers—"the daughter of my scattered ones"—who has gathered to God's presence (3:9–10).

Before his day of wrath, he used all feminine singular language to characterize Jerusalem as a "rebellious and defiled one—the oppressive city" (3:1). Indeed, whereas he hoped that she would fear him and receive instruction, her inhabitants "corrupted all *their deeds* [עֲלִילוֹתָם]" (3:7) by syncretistic worship (1:4–6) and complacency (1:12), apathy for God (2:1), and resisting and ignoring his instruction (3:2). Their leaders were violent and deceptive (1:9) and practiced iniquity (3:3–4), yet they felt no "shame" (בֹּשֶׁת) for their disgraceful acts (3:5). Jerusalem had become like her pagan neighbors, joining them in sinning "against YHWH" (לַיהוָה, 1:17) and, by this, breaking both the Mosaic covenant (cf. Jer 11:10; 31:31–32; Dan 9:11) and the enduring covenant with creation (Isa 24:5; Zech 11:10). The just result could only be Jerusalem's desolation (Zeph 3:7; cf. Lev 26:14–39; Deut 28:15–68).

Nevertheless, in Zeph 3:11a, YHWH's "purposed" "decree" to curse Jerusalem's rebels (Zeph 2:2; 3:7) will not result in complete and permanent destruction. With compassion (cf. Deut 4:31), he will protect his faithful remnant (cf. Zeph 2:3, 2:7, 9), now completely comprising the new Jerusalem. While he will punish the unrepentant, the result will be that the city will not "be ashamed" (בּוֹשׁ; cf. Isa 61:7; Joel 2:26–27).[20] Its members will loathe their past iniquity (Ezek 20:43; 36:31), but they will not be guilty or have guilty consciences.[21] Truly, "Whoever justifies a wicked man and condemns a righteous man is an abomination to YHWH" (Prov 17:15; cf. Rom 4:5). Thus, Jerusalem's shameless

---

20. Cf. Isa 29:22–23; 45:17; Rom 10:11. The text likely means that the city will not "be ashamed" (so NET; cf. NKJV; Motyer, "Zephaniah," 953) rather than be "put to shame" (so NRSVue, ESV, NIV, CSB; J. M. P. Smith, "Book of Zephaniah," 250–51; Berlin, *Zephaniah*, 135; Patterson, *Nahum, Habakkuk, Zephaniah*, 333) since the text uses the *qal* stative of בּוֹשׁ and

not the *hiphil*. Furthermore, the focus is less on the members' mere feeling of guilt (so NASB20) and more on their shame-free state before YHWH. Cf. Pss 22:6[5]; 25:3; 31:18[17]; 109:28; Isa 49:23; 54:4; Rom 9:33.

21. Shepherd, *Commentary on the Book of the Twelve*, 373.

state requires that God must have satisfied his justice and transformed the collective city so that it will never reject him again (cf. Jer 32:40).[22]

By recalling Zeph 3:7 (cf. 1:17), YHWH declares that he will redeem Jerusalem despite "all *your deeds* by which you revolted against me" (מִכֹּל עֲלִילֹתַיִךְ אֲשֶׁר פָּשַׁעַתְּ בִּי). The verb פשע ("to break") and noun פֶּשַׁע ("breach") commonly refer to specific, willful legal transgressions of an inferior toward a superior (e.g., Gen 50:17; 2 Kgs 8:20, 22; Prov 28:24).[23] The construction פשע plus preposition בְּ ("with") plus God as the object is common within the Latter Prophets; to "break with God" means to create a fissure in the covenant relationship and thus "to revolt" against him.[24] Solomon previously used this phrase at the temple's dedicatory prayer, pleading that YHWH would "forgive your people who have sinned against you *and all their breaches that they broke with you* [i.e., crimes by which they have revolted against you]" (וּלְכָל־פִּשְׁעֵיהֶם אֲשֶׁר פָּשְׁעוּ־בָךְ, 1 Kgs 8:50). Zephaniah's wording reveals that YHWH will answer this prayer.

b. The Bases of the Promise (3:11b–13)

Marked by the particles כִּי־אָז ("for then") (3:11b), YHWH now makes two promises for why Jerusalem will not experience shame. He will perform two contrasting actions related to those in Jerusalem (3:11b, 12a), each with shame-averting results for the city (3:11c, 12b–13).

(1) Basis 1: YHWH's Removal of the Proud (3:11b–c)

(a) The Divine Promise (3:11b)

YHWH continues second feminine singular address and pledges that Jerusalem will not be humiliated because he will "remove from your midst the exultant ones of your boast" (אָסִיר מִקִּרְבֵּךְ עַלִּיזֵי גַּאֲוָתֵךְ, Zeph 3:11b) when ("in that day") he rises as covenant witness (כִּי־אָז, "for then"). Earlier we learned that both "YHWH" and the oppressive "officials" were *in the midst* (בְּקֶרֶב) of Zephaniah's Jerusalem (3:3a, 5a). Now YHWH promises that his future eschatological judgment will fully eradicate from his temple-presence all who arrogantly oppose him.

Following Isaiah's use of the singular adjective עַלִּיז ("exultant") to characterize both Jerusalem (Isa 22:2; 32:13; cf. 5:14) and Tyre (23:7) as prideful, Zephaniah earlier employed the term to describe the arrogant city Nineveh that God also promised to wipe out (Zeph 2:15). Similarly, the term גַּאֲוָה commonly refers to one's "boast" in the form of arrogance or conceit, which YHWH commits to punish (Ps 31:23[24]; Isa 13:11) in both Israel (Ps 73:6; Isa 9:8) and places like Moab (Isa 16:6;

---

22. The tower of Babel was a counterfeit Eden, but Zephaniah has stressed its reversal and the people's return to the true "Eden" by following the rivers of life (Zeph 3:9–10; cf. Gen 2:10–14). The lack of "shame" he now highlights amid the new Jerusalem likely recalls the lack of shame (hithpolel בוש) the first man and woman originally enjoyed in the garden of Eden (Gen 2:25). Even if God clothing them signified their maturity (so William N. Wilder, "Illumination and Investiture: The Royal Significance of the Tree of Wisdom in Genesis 3," *WTJ* 68 [2006]: 51–69), the shameless nakedness of marital intimacy (e.g., Prov 5:15–20) still anticipates the shameless life Christ's "bride," the church, enjoys before her heavenly "husband" (e.g., Eph 5:25–27; Rev 14:4).

23. See Alex Luc, "פָּשַׁע (pāšaʿ)," *NIDOTTE* 3:703; Rolf

Knierim, "פֶּשַׁע pešaʿ Crime," *TLOT* 2:1033–37. Knierim stresses that, "Although [the term] always implies a conscious behavior, the term *per se* does not describe the attitude but the criminal act that consists in removal of property or breach of relationship" (Knierim, "פֶּשַׁע pešaʿ Crime," *TLOT* 2:1036). He, thus, says that the term "does not mean sin." In contrast, both attitudes and acts are moral lapses against the divine standard and, therefore, qualify as sin. As such, Luc seems more correct to compare the term to less restrictive terms like חטא ("miss the mark, sin") and עון ("to bend, commit iniquity"), which Scripture can associate with various offenses, regardless of social status (e.g., חָטָא in 1 Sam 19:4; 26:21; עָוֹן in 2 Sam 3:8).

24. See Isa 1:2; 43:27; 66:24; Jer 2:8, 29; 3:13; 33:8; Ezek 2:3; 18:31; 20:38; Hos 7:13.

25:11; Jer 48:29; cf. Zeph 2:8–10). Nevertheless, the term can also refer to YHWH or Israel's "boast" with respect to God's eminence or majesty (Deut 33:26; Ps 68:34[35]) or Israel's source of strength (Deut 33:29). In Zeph 3:11b, the second singular pronominal suffix indicates that the term deals in some way with Jerusalem's "boast."

Specifically, YHWH promises to remove "the exultant ones of your [i.e., Jerusalem's] boast" (עַלִּיזֵי גַּאֲוָתֵךְ) (Zeph 3:11b), which will result in a context where the city "will no more increase arrogance [וְלֹא־תוֹסִפִי לְגָבְהָה] at the mountain of my holiness" (3:11c). Both eliminating "the exultant ones" and reducing those who "are high" or "arrogant" (גבה; cf. Isa 3:16–17; Jer 13:15–16; Ezek 16:50) show that the "exultant" here are the proud, whom YHWH will remove from his presence on his day of fury. But what does "the exultant ones of Jerusalem's boast" mean? Gesenius treats the genitive relationship in the construct phrase עַלִּיזֵי גַּאֲוָתֵךְ as one of attribute or quality with the pronominal suffix referring to the compound idea (i.e., Jerusalem's proudly exultant ones).[25] Most contemporary English translations follow this reading (see NRSVue, NASB20, NET, ESV, NIV, CSB), and it fits the context well. This interpretation may restrict those whom YHWH eradicates to *Judean* rebels who inhabited Jerusalem (cf. Zeph 1:4–6, 8–13; 3:1–7). However, throughout the book YHWH's presence is within Jerusalem (e.g., 3:5, 11), and his gathering some from all nations to himself to both punish (3:8) and redeem (3:9–10) may suggest that the haughty associated here with the city include a larger group.

Indeed, two factors suggest a broader referent and that the genitive relationship in עַלִּיזֵי גַּאֲוָתֵךְ may, against Gesenius, be objective-adversative (i.e., the presumptuous ones who exult over Jerusalem's boast, which is YHWH):[26] (1) YHWH's promise to "remove" (*hiphil* of סור) the arrogant in 3:11c anticipates the declaration in 3:15a–b that he "has removed" (*hiphil* of סור) Jerusalem's judgments, which are then clarified as her collective enemy (both within and without) that operated as God's agent of covenant curse. The proud ones in 3:11b–c, therefore, are likely more than just the arrogant Judeans. (2) In 3:11b, YHWH is likely intentionally alluding to Isa 13:3 and applying it typologically, and the meaning of Isa 13:3 points to an adversative construct relationship that includes a referent broader than Judeans.[27]

In Isa 13:3, Babylon is YHWH's hostile agent that will bring Jerusalem to ruin: "I myself have commanded *my consecrated ones* [מְקֻדָּשָׁי]; also *I have called* [קָרָאתִי] my mighty ones for my anger—*the exultant ones of my boast* [עַלִּיזֵי גַּאֲוָתִי]." In Zeph 3:11b YHWH likely intentionally recalls Isaiah's prophecy about Babylon since עַלִּיז ("exultant") occurs only in Isaiah and Zephaniah and only these two passages employ the plural of עַלִּיז in construct with גַּאֲוָה plus suffix.[28] Increasing this allusion's likelihood is that Zephaniah probably already alluded to Isa 13:3 in Zeph 1:7 by saying that YHWH "has consecrated his invited ones" (הִקְדִּישׁ קְרֻאָיו) as agents of Jerusalem's slaughter.

This genitive relationship within the construct chain of Isa 13:3 could be (1) objective in the sense of an action done to/for another (i.e.,

---

25. GKC §135n; cf. Joüon §129f.

26. See Joüon §129e.

27. For a defense that Zephaniah uses Isaiah 13, see H. L. Ginsberg, "Gleanings from First Isaiah," in *Mordecai Kaplan Jubilee Volume on the Occasion of His Seventieth Birthday* (New York: Jewish Theological Seminary of America, 1953), 245–59.

28. Against Berlin, who says the phrase in Isa 13:3 "has a rather different nuance" (Berlin, *Zephaniah*, 136), Delitzsch rightly affirms, "We could hardly expect to find it employed by two authors who stood in no relation whatever to one another" (Delitzsch, "Isaiah," 10:193 (1:295).

the Babylonians rejoice in YHWH's majesty),[29] (2) objective in the sense of an action done against another (i.e., the Babylonians presumptuously exult over YHWH's eminence),[30] (3) one of agency or purpose (i.e., the Babylonians exulting [over Jerusalem] is the means for YHWH's boast),[31] or (4) one of attribute or quality (i.e., the Babylonians are YHWH's proudly exulting ones).[32] Option 1 is unlikely since later in the chapter God promises to judge Babylon for *not* celebrating (Isa 13:11; cf. Hab 1:11). YHWH stressing in Isa 13:3 that he has consecrated the Babylonians as vehicles of his wrath supports option 3; however, the bulk of the chapter focuses on their role not as warriors to see YHWH exalted but as divine enemies whom he will overcome (Isa 13:19). Option 4 fails in a comparable way since the greater context stresses not how the Babylonians are linked with YHWH (*my* proudly exultant ones) but rather that they are distinct from him as objects of his just rage. As such, option 2 is most likely: YHWH would put down Babylon for failing to acknowledge his supremacy while serving as instruments of his justice (cf. 10:15).

So, what implications arise if indeed Zeph 3:11b intentionally alludes to Isa 13:3? The following reflections account for understanding Zeph 3:8–10 as indicating that the prophet focuses not on Jerusalem's 586 BC destruction but on the global and future day of punishment and new creation that Jesus Christ's first and second appearances fulfill.[33]

First, in Isa 11:3 גַּאֲוָה refers to YHWH's majesty rather than human pride. In Zeph 3:11b, it apparently refers to the same thing. God is Jerusalem's "boast" like Deut 33:29 characterizes him as the essence of Israel's triumph: "Happy are you, O Israel!

Who is like you—a people saved by YHWH, the shield of your help and the one who is *the sword of your boast* [חֶרֶב גַּאֲוָתֶךָ]?" YHWH gets all the glory for his people's victories and exaltation, and when he establishes "the mountain of the house of YHWH . . . as the highest of the mountains" (Isa 2:2) and when he brings low the haughtiness of man, then he "*alone* will be exalted on that day" (2:11, 17).

Second, in Isa 13:3 the pompously exultant Babylonians are Jerusalem's enemies carrying YHWH's judgments of destruction (see Zeph 3:15a–b). As such, when God promises to remove the arrogant from his central sanctuary in the eschatological era, he is reading the earlier statements about Babylon typologically as words about anyone standing against God, his ways, and his faithful people.[34] As YHWH later affirms, he will deal "with all who afflict you" (Zeph 3:19a). Significantly, already in Isa 13, YHWH treats the Babylonians as mere signposts for anyone deserving his wrath: "And I will visit evil on the world and on wicked ones their iniquity" (Isa 13:11). Thus, Zephaniah is reading the text as Isaiah himself already intended.

Third, this means that the arrogant "exultant ones" whom God promises to uproot from Jerusalem would include all who arrogantly resist YHWH's sovereign control—those associated with "the remnant of the Baal" among the Judeans (Zeph 1:4–6) and those from the broader world who "against YHWH . . . have sinned" (1:17c). He would treat them like the prideful Nineveh (2:15; cf. Ezek 20:38; Mal 4:1[3:19]), and man-centered pride would no longer characterize the city in which YHWH's presence resided.

---

29. So "גַּאֲוָה," *HALOT* 168; see GKC, §128.h; Joüon, §129e.

30. So "עָלָיו," *HALOT* 833; see Joüon, §129e.

31. Cf. GKC, §128q; Joüon, §129f.

32. So GKC, §135n; Joüon, §129f; Patterson, *Nahum, Habakkuk, Zephaniah*, 333.

33. This contrasts with Sweeney, who attempts to read this entire unit against the backdrop of the Josianic reforms (see Sweeney, *Zephaniah*, 188–90).

34. Cf. 1 Pet 5:13; Rev 16:17–18:24.

(b) The Result (3:11c)

YHWH affirms that the result of cleansing Jerusalem is that the city will "no more increase arrogance at the mountain of my holiness." Like the Amorites of old whom God only destroyed after their wickedness had reached its providential limit (Gen 15:16; cf. Dan 8:23),[35] Jerusalem's self-reliance and rebellion could only grow so far. The reality of God's holy presence would finally demand that he cleanse his sacred space and people.

Translators commonly render the phrase "the mountain of my holiness" (הַר קָדְשִׁי) as "my holy mountain,"[36] viewing (1) the singular suffix to belong to the compound idea and (2) the absolute noun קֹדֶשׁ ("holiness, something holy") to attribute the quality of holiness to the "mountain" (הַר).[37] Other texts make plain that "the mountain" is the future "Jerusalem" or "Zion,"[38] and some parallel texts indicate that the phrase highlights *YHWH's* holiness, which alone makes the mountain holy. For example, by alluding to his garden sanctuary in Eden, YHWH speaks of "the mountain of the holiness of God" (הַר קֹדֶשׁ אֱלֹהִים; Ezek 28:14; cf. Gen 2:10; Exod 15:17); the threefold construct chain emphasizes that the holiness is *God's*, not something inherent to the mountain. Later, YHWH promises that "Jerusalem will be called the faithful city and the mountain of YHWH of armies, the mountain of the holiness" (Zech 8:3). Only because YHWH "dwells in Zion, the mountain of my holiness," will

"Jerusalem . . . be holy" (Joel 3:17[4:17]; cf. Obad 16–17). The holy God dwelling there requires that he cleanse the site of all polluted and contagious sinners. He has entered an even greater conquest than in Joshua's days (Josh 5:15). He will now do away with everything opposing his character.

YHWH uses mountain imagery for Jerusalem to highlight that, in the end, he alone will be exalted (see Isa 2:2, 11; Mic 4:1) as he reigns preeminent from his transformed city, ever satisfying his purified world (Zeph 3:14; cf. Exod 15:17–18; Jer 31:10–14). God's mountain is the emanating center of his eternal reign. Here he secures refuge and deliverance and proves human conceit to be folly (e.g., Pss 15:1; 43:3; Isa 57:13). This is the place at which the faithful remnant from all nations will gather to YHWH (Zeph 3:9–10)[39] and the messianic king will rule them (Ps 2:6; Isa 11:1–5, 9).[40]

(2) Basis 2: YHWH's Leaving the Humble (3:12–13)
(a) The Divine Promise (3:12a)

YHWH continues his second-person address to Jerusalem and now gives a second reason the purged city will exist without shame. When he cleanses her midst (מִקִּרְבֵּךְ) from all arrogance (3:11b), he promises to preserve a remnant, using the *hiphil* (causative) form of the verb שאר, the same root found in the masculine noun שְׁאָר ("remnant") in 1:4 and the feminine noun שְׁאֵרִית ("remnant") in 2:7, 9 and 3:13. Specifically, he will

---

35. Cf. Matt 23:32; 1 Thess 2:16.

36. Compare the versions (e.g., NIV, ESV, NRSVue, NASB, NET, NLT) in the following passages: Pss 2:6; 3:5[4]; 15:1; 43:3; 48:2[1]; 99:9; Isa 11:9; 56:7; 57:13; 65:11, 25; 66:20; Ezek 20:40; Dan 9:16; Joel 2:1; 4:17[3:17]; Obad 16.

37. See GKC §128p, §135n.

38. See Ps 2:6; Isa 66:20; Joel 4:17[3:17]; Obad 16–17; Zech 8:3.

39. Cf. Isa 2:2; 25:6–8; 56:7; 66:20; Jer 3:15; Mic 4:2; Zech 8:20–23; 14:16.

40. The OT authors often characterized the garden sanctu-

ary in Eden, then Mount Sinai/Horeb, and finally Mount Zion as the hub of God's earthly reign (e.g., Exod 3:1; 15:17–18; Ps 48; Ezek 28:13–16). Recalling the original divine mountain paradise in Eden likely prompted the ancients in Mesopotamia and the Levant to believe humans encountered the "gods" at cosmic mountains (see Clifford, *The Cosmic Mountain in Canaan and the Old Testament*). For Matthew's use of this OT background to elevate Messiah Jesus, see T. L. Donaldson, *Jesus on the Mountain: A Study in Matthean Theology*, JSNTSup 8 (Sheffield: Sheffield Academic, 1990).

"cause to remain" (הִשְׁאַרְתִּי) in Jerusalem's midst (בְּקִרְבֵּךְ) "an afflicted and needy people" (עַם עָנִי וָדָל) (3:12a). Dumbrell relates the adjective עָנִי ("afflicted") to a condition and the adjective עָנָו ("bent over, humble") to a posture.[41] In 2:3a, Zephaniah called "all the humble of the land" (כָּל־עַנְוֵי הָאָרֶץ) to seek YHWH (2:3a), thus focusing on their dependent countenance. Here, however, he speaks of the "afflicted" remnant to highlight both their broken but delivered state and their endurance through trial (cf. Jer 31:34; 50:20).

In Zeph 3:12 God aligns the "afflicted" (עָנִי) with the "needy, poor" (דָל). Sabottka and Lohfink restrict the prophet's focus to the economically "poor,"[42] a class to which דָל can certainly refer (e.g., Prov 10:15; Jer 39:10). Nevertheless, דָל can also point to the "weak" (Gen 41:19; Judg 6:15), the "insignificant" (Jer 5:4), and, most commonly, the "needy, vulnerable, or defenseless" (e.g., Exod 23:3; Lev 19:15; Isa 11:4).[43] This latter meaning is natural when the term parallels עָנִי, as happens here (cf. Ps 82:3; Prov 22:22).[44] Furthermore, in Zeph 3:11–12 God particularly contrasts the afflicted "poor" and the arrogant rather than socioeconomic classes.

That is, YHWH is "describing a moral attribute rather than a social status."[45] Those YHWH will save exhibit a meek and dependent disposition and not necessarily material lack.[46]

Who are the "afflicted and needy"? They are the "lame" and the "banished" at the book's end whom YHWH characterizes as having been ill-treated but whom he promises to both "save" and "assemble" (3:19). But not every ill-treated person is part of this group. Though YHWH works justice for the weak (Deut 10:18; Ps 68:5[6]) and calls his people to do the same (Exod 22:22; Deut 27:19),[47] he will not show compassion on the unrepentant, regardless of their apparent need (Lev 19:15; Isa 9:17; Ps 146:9).[48] He will remove the arrogant (Zeph 3:11) but leave those who will "call on" and "take refuge in the name YHWH" (3:9a, 12b). Only those "seeking" and "waiting" for YHWH will avoid his day of wrath and enjoy his holy presence in the new Jerusalem (Zeph 2:3; 3:8).[49]

God names those ingathered and preserved in the new Jerusalem a singular "people" (עַם). Within the book, the noun עַם occurs four other times in the singular and twice in the plural:

---

41. Dumbrell writes: "עָנִי means to have been humbled, afflicted by necessity or circumstances, stressing difficulty of the condition and implying . . . some kind of disability present. . . . עָנָו means, basically, bent over (under the pressure of circumstances) and consequently, as affliction does its proper work, humble" (Dumbrell, "עָנָו, עָנִי [ʿānāw; ʿānî]," NIDOTTE 3:451–52).

42. Sabottka, Zephanja, 65–66; Lohfink, "Zephaniah and the Church of the Poor," 113–18.

43. For the latter category, see also, e.g., Job 5:16; Pss 41:2[1]; 72:13; Isa 14:30; 25:4.

44. See also Job 34:28; Isa 10:2; 26:6. So, too, Ben Zvi, Book of Zephaniah, 233.

45. Robertson, Books of Nahum, Habakkuk, and Zephaniah, 331; cf. A. Vanlier Hunter, "Seek the Lord!: A Study of the Meaning and Function of the Exhortations in Amos, Hosea, Isaiah, Micah, and Zephaniah" (ThD diss., St. Mary's Seminary and University, 1982), 268; Vlaardingerbroek, Zephaniah, 203; Patterson, Nahum, Habakkuk, Zephaniah, 334.

46. Though Renz elsewhere portrays the prophet as confronting the urban rich and elevating the rural poor (Renz, Books of Nahum, Habakkuk, and Zephaniah, 525–26, 557, 561, 614, 618–19), he now rightly recognizes that what Zephaniah commends here and elsewhere "is not a low socioeconomic status as such but a certain attitude and lifestyle" (p. 620).

47. Cf. Jas 1:17.

48. Similarly, Calvin wrote, "But the Prophet speaks of the elect alone; for we see that many are severely afflicted, and are not softened, nor do they put off their former hardihood" (Calvin, "Habakkuk, Zephaniah, Haggai," 295–96; cf. Vlaardingerbroek, Zephaniah, 203).

49. These "afflicted and needy" must humbly follow the Messiah even through death (see Isa 42:2–3; 53:7; Zech 9:9; Matt 11:29; 12:19–20; Phil 2:7–8; 1 Pet 2:23) unto receiving the crown of life (Jas 1:12; Rev 2:10).

1. "All the people of Canaan" (Zeph 1:11)
2. "My people" and "the people of YHWH of armies" with respect to Israel as God's chosen, which in Zephaniah's day was the old covenant community consisting of both believing remnant and unbelieving rebel (2:8, 10)
3. "The remnant of my people" referring to the faithful Judeans/Israelites who live through the day of YHWH and help shape new covenant Israel (2:9)
4. The multiethnic "peoples" of the world whom YHWH will transform and who will gather to worship him through prayer and offering at the great day of judgment (3:9–10)
5. The "afflicted and needy people" here in 3:12 who are finding refuge in his presence at the mountain of his holiness
6. The pagan "peoples of the earth" (3:20b) among whom the "people" from 3:12 will coexist for a time while bearing witness to YHWH's greatness.

This commentary has already recounted how various OT authors before or contemporary with Zephaniah expected God would incorporate some of Israel's enemy peoples into his eschatological community.[50] Zephaniah has already noted how peoples descending from those once dispersed at Babel will pray to and serve YHWH in his presence at the transformed Jerusalem (Zeph 3:9–10; cf. 2:9, 11). Therefore, the "afflicted and needy people" in

Zeph 3:12 likely includes both "the remnant of my people" in 2:9 and many from other nations who have joined the faithful Judeans in seeking and waiting upon YHWH the King at the mountain of his holiness. That is, the ethnically diverse worshiping community of Judean and non-Judean *peoples* in 3:9–10 has together become the "afflicted and needy *people*" of 3:12a. And the positive result of their being in God's presence is that "they will take refuge in the name YHWH—the remnant of Israel" (3:13).

(b) The Result (3:12b–13f)

The result of YHWH's preserving care is that those in Jerusalem hidden from his wrath "will take refuge in the name YHWH" (וְחָסוּ בְּשֵׁם יְהוָה, 3:12b). Pairing the verb חסה ("to take refuge") plus divine object "you will never be ashamed" (לֹא תֵבוֹשִׁי, 3:11a) recalls similar declarations in Pss 25:20; 31:1[2]; and 71:1.[51] Moreover, Isaiah had declared, "YHWH has founded Zion, and in her *the afflicted ones of his people find refuge*" (יֶחֱסוּ עֲנִיֵּי עַמּוֹ, Isa 14:32).[52] As noted at Zeph 3:9, YHWH's name constitutes his total identity in all its pleasantness, perfection, and power.[53] While the OT commonly says people should take refuge in YHWH (e.g., 2 Sam 22:31; Ps 118:9–9; Prov 30:5), only here do we read of taking refuge in his *name*.[54] Elsewhere, to take refuge in YHWH means treasuring and trusting in his character, strength, promises, and presence (Isa 14:32; 57:13; Nah 1:7). This entails

---

50. See God Incorporating Enemy Peoples in Its Biblical Context within Canonical Significance of Zeph 2:5–15.

51. Ben Zvi, *Book of Zephaniah*, 231. Zephaniah mainly differs by stressing the durative (with לֹא) rather than punctiliar (with אַל) state of shamelessness. For this temporal distinction between negations, see *BHRG*, §19.5.2.1, §41.3(1).

52. Cf. Matt 5:3.

53. Stuart, "Names, Proper," *ISBE* 3:483–88; Ross, "שֵׁם," *NIDOTTE* 4:147–51.

54. Conceptually, Prov 18:10 states the same idea: "A strong

tower is the name YHWH; in it runs a righteous man, and he becomes inaccessible [to his enemies]." Ben Zvi thinks the unique phrasing of Zeph 3:12 has something to do with the mention of calling on YHWH's name in 3:9 (Ben Zvi, *Book of Zephaniah*, 231). Sweeney goes further by proposing that Zephaniah's use of "name" recalls Deuteronomy (see Deut 12:5, 11; 14:23; 16:2, 6, 11; 26:2) and shows that the prophet depended "on literature employed to support Josiah's reform" (see 2 Kgs 22:8, 11; cf. Deut 29:21; 30:10; 31:26) (Sweeney, *Zephaniah*, 190).

enjoying his blessing (Pss 2:12; 34:8) and protection (18:2, 30; 144:2; Prov 30:5), resting in his goodness (Ps 31:19) and rescue (34:22), and embracing his help (37:40) and care (Nah 1:7). "The remnant of Israel" will do such things (Zeph 3:13), as they delight in YHWH's presence, shelter, and preserving care (2:3; 3:5, 7) by seeking and inquiring of him (1:6; 2:3), heeding and trusting in him (3:2), and calling on his name through praise and prayer (3:9). On this verse, Calvin noted, "We hence see for what purpose God deprives us of all earthly trust, and takes away from us every ground of glorying; it is, that we may rely only on his favour."[55]

Zephaniah ironically uses the masculine form for Judah's "remnant of the Baal" (שְׁאָר הַבַּעַל) in 1:4. He then refers more positively to YHWH's faithful ones (whom he will preserve through his global fury) by using the feminine "remnant" (שְׁאֵרִית) three times and the alternative "remainder" (יֶתֶר) one time:[56]

1. "The remnant of the house of Judah" (שְׁאֵרִית בֵּית יְהוּדָה) who will possess and inhabit the area of Philistia once God destroys these enemies (2:7)[57]
2. "The remnant of my people . . . and the remainder of my nation" (שְׁאֵרִית עַמִּי . . . וְיֶתֶר גּוֹיִי) who will plunder and inherit Moab and Bene-Ammon amid the new creation (2:9)[58]
3. "The remnant of Israel" (שְׁאֵרִית יִשְׂרָאֵל) who

will take refuge in YHWH's name at the mountain of his holiness in the day of his wrath (3:13)[59]

These groups are probably a single remnant, which the book progressively discloses.[60] Two reasons suggest we must interpret "the remnant of Israel" in 3:13 in relation to the globally-inclusive, omni-ethnic community of worshipers defined in 3:9–10, all of whom are associated with the new Jerusalem at the mountain of YHWH's holiness: (1) The grammatical antecedent subject of the third person plural verb וְחָסוּ ("and they will take refuge") in 3:12b is the collective "afflicted and needy people" of 3:12a. (2) The phrase "the remnant of Israel" is a dislocated collective appositive referring to this same group and not merely a subset of it. Thus, YHWH here calls his single eschatological people "the remnant of Israel," which will consist of some from Judah and other nations who have sought YHWH together and waited for him (2:1, 3; 3:8). In 2:9, YHWH already hinted at including the nations by saying "the remainder of my nation will inherit them"—namely, Moab and Bene-Ammon, claiming not only their territory but also some from the peoples themselves!

The genitive relationship in the phrase "the remnant of Israel" could be appositional with the proper name clarifying the group's makeup (= "the remnant [that is] Israel").[61] However, since

---

55. Calvin, "Habakkuk, Zephaniah, Haggai," 295.

56. For more on "remnant," see the discussion at Zeph 2:7.

57. Zephaniah 2:7 alone combines שְׁאֵרִית יְהוּדָה ("the remnant of Judah") with בֵּית ("house"). The phrase שְׁאֵרִית יְהוּדָה ("the remnant of Judah") occurs without בֵּית ("house") in Jer 40:5; 42:15, 19; 43:5; 44:12, 14, 28, but none of these texts refer to an eschatological remnant.

58. Zechariah 8:6, 11–12 speak of the שְׁאֵרִית הָעָם ("the remnant of the people") in a comparable future prediction, whereas other occurrences refer to an immediate group (cf. Neh 7:71; Jer 41:10, 16; Hag 1:12, 14; 2:2).

59. For the phrase שְׁאֵרִית יִשְׂרָאֵל ("the remnant of Israel"),

see also 1 Chr 12:39 [שְׁרִית]; 2 Chr 34:9; Jer 6:9; 31:7; Ezek 9:8; 11:13; Mic 2:12; cf. Isa 46:3. All those passages from the writing prophets refer to a future remnant whom God will preserve through punishment. For שְׁאָר יִשְׂרָאֵל, see Neh 11:20 and Isa 10:20, the latter of which is comparable to Zeph 3:12.

60. So also Ben Zvi who says that the "house of Judah" in Zeph 2:7 and "Israel" in 3:12–14 are "one single referent" (Ben Zvi, Book of Zephaniah, 308), the former geopolitical and the latter "religious, ideological" (Ben Zvi, Book of Zephaniah, 234; cf. Berlin, Zephaniah, 136).

61. See GKC §128k and Jouön §129f, which refer to this as "the genitive of proper noun." Cf. "the river Euphrates"

this is a "remnant" of a greater group and the book's comparable construct chains most naturally express origin or possession,[62] God probably intends the same here.[63] "Israel" is the general title for YHWH's special covenant partner that he earlier identifies as "Judah" (1:4)[64] and "the nation not longing" (2:1) though it contained some the prophet called "the humble of the land" (2:3). The use of "Israel" also points to a reunified nation, which Josiah's reforms sought (2 Kgs 23:15–20; cf. 2 Chr 34:33; 35:18) and prophets predicted would eventually occur (e.g., Ezek 37:16–22).[65] The "remnant" originating in this group is specifically these humble Israelites along with countless others from the nations who have now been "built into the midst of my people" (Jer 12:16). With new identities, they are not counted among the "nations" whom YHWH will destroy but instead are "foreigners" united with God's servant Jacob/Israel (30:8–11). Within the single covenant family, these former outsiders are adopted "daughters" (Ezek 16:61), all of which are considered the offspring of Jerusalem (Ps 87; Isa 53:10–54:3). Though terse, the argument's flow suggests this interpretation.

God now clarifies what it will mean for "the remnant of Israel" to "take refuge in the name YHWH." God uses three conjoined לֹא plus long (i.e., indicative; the actual forms are not visibly "long") *yiqtol* prohibitions (Zeph 3:13a–c), each

carrying durative or timeless force.[66] The first is asyndetic, suggesting that the embedded unit clarifies what precedes, and the conjunction *waw* links the next two. These three clauses are then followed by three more conjoined ground clauses, the first fronted by כִּי ("because"); together they clarify why the three negative affirmations are true.

Explicating 3:12b, Zephaniah notes the remnant "will never do wrong" (לֹא־יַעֲשׂוּ עַוְלָה) (3:13a). The feminine noun עַוְלָה ("wrong") occurs minimally in the writing prophets and always in relation to evil acts like testifying falsely (Isa 59:3), violating others (Ezek 28:15), murdering (Hos 10:13), and leading in harmful ways (Mic 3:10; Hab 2:12). Zephaniah said earlier that YHWH "never does wrong" (לֹא יַעֲשֶׂה עַוְלָה, Zeph 3:5),[67] and those in the new Jerusalem will imitate him. They will now reflect, resemble, and represent YHWH more purely, aligning with their original design as those made in the image of the living God (Gen 1:26–28).[68]

The next two negative predictions each address the absence of falsehood in the new Jerusalem. "The remnant of Israel" will never "speak a lie, and in their mouth will never be found a tongue of deceit" (וְלֹא־יְדַבְּרוּ כָזָב וְלֹא־יִמָּצֵא בְּפִיהֶם לְשׁוֹן תַּרְמִית, 3:13b–c).[69] Earlier the prophet said Jerusalem's religious leaders corruptly enacted מִרְמָה ("deception, fraud," Zeph 1:9), a noun related to תַּרְמִית ("deceit") used here in Zeph 3:13. Previously, Jerusalem was "the

---

(נְהַר פְּרָת, e.g., Gen 15:18), "the land *of* Canaan" (אֶרֶץ כְּנַעַן, e.g., 13:12), and "the maiden Israel" (בְּתוּלַת יִשְׂרָאֵל, Jer 18:13; Amos 5:2).

62. See, e.g., "the remnant of the house of Judah" (Zeph 2:7); "the remainder from my nation" (2:9); "the daughter of my scattered ones" (3:10).

63. See GKC §128g; Joüon §129d, f.

64. As noted at Zeph 2:7, Josiah's "Judah" included many from the northern tribes who, after Samaria's downfall (723 BC) reasserted YHWH worship in Jerusalem (2 Chr 34:6–9; cf. 2 Kgs 23:16, 19; 2 Chr 11:13–17; 15:9; 30:1, 5, 10–11, 25). "The remnant of Judah," therefore, represents a purified and reunited "Israel."

65. Sweeney limits the group to the former (Sweeney, *Zephaniah*, 191–92) but fails to account enough for the universal, longer-range aspects of the context overviewed in Zeph 3:8–10 and continued in 3:11–13 in view of the phrase "at that time" (3:11a; cf. 3:16a).

66. *BHRG*, §19.5.2.1, §41.9[1b].

67. Cf. 2 Chr 19:7; Ps 92:16[15].

68. Cf. Achtemeier, *Nahum–Malachi*, 84.

69. The verb דבר ("to speak") occurs with singular כָּזָב ("lie") in Pss 5:7; 58:4; Dan 11:27 and with plural כְּזָבִים ("lies") in Judg 16:10, 13 and Hos 7:13.

oppressive city" (3:1) through its leaders' deceptive words (1:9; 3:3–4).[70] But now, with a "purified lip" (3:9), the worshipers in the new Jerusalem will speak prayer and praise rather than treachery, following in the messianic servant's path (Isa 53:9; 1 Pet 2:22).[71]

Wrongdoing and lies will be absent among the new creational community *because* (כִּי) "they will graze and lie down, and there will be none who cause trembling" (Zeph 3:13d–f). As in 2:6–7, YHWH applies shepherding imagery to his people. In the great Shepherd's presence (Gen 48:15; Ps 23:1; Eccl 12:11)[72] and with all potential harm removed, those on the mountain of YHWH's holiness now freely live and rest without sin. The explicit use of the pronoun "they" (הֵמָּה) is emphatic, stressing that the multiethnic "remnant of Israel" and "afflicted and needy people" will enjoy such tranquility.[73] Sweeney rightly observes how the imagery "appears to replicate the tranquility and peace of the garden of Eden,"[74] which is exactly how other texts describe the new Jerusalem (e.g., Isa 51:3; Ezek 36:35).[75]

The phrase "and there will be none who cause trembling" (וְאֵין מַחֲרִיד) recalls Moses's restoration blessing (Lev 26:5–6) and parallels the same phrase the prophets use to describe God's people's future state in the new creation (e.g., Jer 30:10; Ezek 34:28; Mic 4:4). God will now reverse the covenant curse of being another's prey (Deut 28:26; Jer 7:33) and provide for and protect his children, who will know and live for YHWH (Ezek 34:25–31; 36:26–28).

Fearing nothing in the heavens and the earth implies that "the remnant of Israel" will indeed fear God and receive his instruction (Zeph 3:7). And fearing YHWH alone naturally leads to both human faithfulness and divine pleasure (cf. Ps 147:10–11). At Sinai, Moses declared the natural pattern: "God has come to test you and that his fear may be on your face so that you will not sin" (Exod 20:20). Truly encountering God leads to fearing him, which in turn generates holiness (cf. Deut 17:18–20; 31:11–12). In contrast, giving into sin is always a failure to fear God enough and often signals the presence of misguided fears of people or things.

2. A Discursive Charge to Rejoice as if the Great Salvation Has Already Occurred (3:14–15)

The hope YHWH unveils in 3:11–13 now unexpectedly leads Zephaniah to command his listeners to celebrate in the present (3:14). Two unmarked reasons that treat God's victorious, saving work as if it has already happened then ground his charges (3:15). While the book's two-stage exhortation (2:1, 3; 3:8) climaxes with the charge to "wait" on YHWH in 3:8, 3:14–15 supply the sermon's rhetorical peak (see Structure and Literary Form above) by uniquely arousing attention and showing why the appeal to submit to God that shapes the book's body (2:1, 3; 3:8) is ultimately an invitation to satisfaction.

a. Three Calls to Rejoice (3:14)

Zephaniah stacks four imperatives in three asyndetic groupings, each with different roots:

---

70. Earlier prophets noted how Israel multiplied deceitful statements and found protection in a "lie" (כָּזָב) (Isa 28:15, 17; Hos 12:2) rather than in YHWH (e.g., Isa 25:4; Jer 17:17; Joel 4:16[3:16]).

71. Cf. Isa 59:21; John 1:47; Rev 14:5.

72. Cf. Ps 80:2; Ezek 34:15, 23; 37:24; Mic 5:3[4]; Zech 11:7; 13:7; John 10:11, 14, 16; Heb 13:20; 1 Pet 2:25; 5:4; Rev 7:17.

73. Motyer, "Zephaniah," 954. Motyer properly identifies the nations of 3:9–10 in this group, but he wrongly distinguishes them from "the remnant of Israel."

74. Sweeney, *Zephaniah*, 192.

75. Cf. Gen 2:8–14 with Isa 11:6–9; 65:17–25; Rev 21:1–4; 22:1–5.

"Sing aloud, O daughter of Zion! Shout, O Israel! Be merry, and exult with all heart, O daughter of Jerusalem!" (רָנִּי. . . . הָרִיעוּ. . . . שִׂמְחִי וְעָלְזִי).[76] Each verb expresses loud rejoicing, and together they express multiorbed, multisensory praise to God. Whereas in 3:8b–13 YHWH used a longing for deliverance to motivate present trust ("wait," 3:8a), here that future desire creates present delight and current jubilation.

Isaiah commonly clarifies the tone worship will take in the new creation with the verb רנן ("sing aloud").[77] Indeed, the once waste places of Jerusalem and the whole creation will carol [רנן] in witness to YHWH's saving work.[78] Though the *hiphil* of רוע ("shout") often denotes sounds of alarm in the presence of terror, Zechariah later appears to allude to Zeph 3:14–15 when he uses it to announce the arrival of the righteous king who brings salvation: "Rejoice greatly, O daughter of Zion! *Shout* [הָרִיעִי], O daughter of Jerusalem! Look—your king comes to you, righteous and victorious is he!" (Zech 9:9; cf. Isa 44:23). Thus, by connecting Zeph 3:14–15 to other texts in the prophets, Zechariah himself knew God would accomplish through the Messiah the victory Zephaniah foretells. Isaiah notes that when YHWH saves his waiting throng, the redeemed will declare, "This is YHWH! We have waited for him; let us be glad *and be merry* [וְנִשְׂמְחָה] in his salvation" (Isa 25:9; cf. 56:7). Indeed, all of YHWH's delivered servants "will be merry" (יִשְׂמְחוּ) (65:13) and do so with the flourishing new

Jerusalem (66:10).[79] Thus, as in Zeph 3:14, YHWH urges through Zechariah, "*Sing aloud and be merry, O daughter of Zion* [רָנִּי וְשִׂמְחִי בַּת־צִיּוֹן], for look—I am coming and will dwell in your midst" (Zech 2:10[14]). As for the infrequent verb עלז ("exult"), the psalmist uses it twice to celebrate God's saving acts (Pss 28:7; 68:4[5]), but among the Prophets only Hab 3:18 includes a comparable context, as Habakkuk declares that he will "exult" in YHWH as he faces the prospect of YHWH's judgment day and deliverance of his anointed (cf. Hab 3:1–16).

Of the three imperatival groupings, the first and third are uniquely feminine singular and addressed to the "daughter of Zion" (בַּת־צִיּוֹן) and the "daughter of Jerusalem" (בַּת יְרוּשָׁלָם), respectively. In contrast, the second imperative is masculine plural like those in 2:1, 3 and 3:8 and linked with "Israel" (יִשְׂרָאֵל). Some interpreters view the construct phrases the "daughter of Zion" and the "daughter of Jerusalem" as appositional genitives dealing with a proper noun, such that they only express endearment (= "daughter Zion/Jerusalem"—i.e., the daughter *who is* Zion/Jerusalem") (e.g., NRSVue, NET, NIV, CSB).[80] While possible, the "daughter" (בַּת) language suggests a genitive of origin,[81] a common genitival relationship within Zephaniah.[82] Thus, the once "oppressive city" has birthed a new more faithful one that God has lovingly ransomed from its inherited empty ways (cf. Isa 62:11; 1 Pet 1:18).[83]

The second singular form of the first, third, and fourth imperatives clarifies that the city is still being

---

76. Cf. *hithpolel* and *qal* of קשש, "gather" 2x in 2:1; *piel* of בקש, "seek" 3x in 2:3; *piel* of חכה, "wait" 1x in 3:8.

77. Cf. Isa 24:14; 26:19; 35:6, 10; 51:11; 52:8–9; 54:1; 65:14.

78. See Isa 35:1–2; 44:23; 49:13; 55:12.

79. Zephaniah's note that those who "serve" (עבד) YHWH should "be merry" (שמח) (Zeph 3:9, 14) echoes YHWH's declaration through Isaiah: "My servants will be merry" (עֲבָדַי יִשְׂמָחוּ, Isa 65:13).

80. See Song 7:1. So Joüon §129f; cf. GKC §128k. See also W. F. Stinespring, "No Daughter of Zion: A Study of the Appo-

sitional Genitive in Hebrew Grammar," *Enc* 26 (1965): 133–41; Ball, *Rhetorical Study of Zephaniah*, 265; Roberts, *Nahum, Habakkuk, and Zephaniah*, 219; cf. Berlin, *Zephaniah*, 141.

81. See GKC §128g; Joüon §129d, f.

82. See "the remnant of the house of Judah" (Zeph 2:7), "the remnant of my people" (2:9c), "the remainder of my nation" (2:9d), "the daughter of [= *from*] my scattered ones" (בַּת־פּוּצַי) (2:10), and "the remnant of Israel" (3:13).

83. So too Floyd, *Minor Prophets, Part 2*, 238.

addressed, but the reference now being the "daughter of Zion/Jerusalem" highlights that the prophet speaks *not* to the Jerusalem of his day but to the remnant who will become the future, transformed, new city (cf. Isa 1:26).[84] Furthermore, the shift here from "the remnant of Israel" (שְׁאֵרִית יִשְׂרָאֵל) in 3:13 to only "Israel" in 3:14b suggests that the multiethnic "remnant of Israel" has now become God's new "Israel," a freshly established singular people.[85] And Zephaniah framing the plural address to the transformed members of "Israel" with a singular address to the transformed city reveals the strong theological tie between the place and the people, even those residing in former enemy territories (Zeph 3:7, 9; cf. Ps 87). Zephaniah likely envisions the city boundaries expanding so that they are coterminous with every Israelite's location, for God's glory that is centered at the mountain of his holiness and the new Jerusalem will encompass the earth.[86]

For Zephaniah, these are all *future* realities. Nevertheless, his present-time imperatives suggest that he is so convinced of the future salvation that it should spark present joy in the remnant from Judah and other lands. He is calling those who will ultimately become the one, transformed people of God, the church, to let their joyful hope become present praise.[87]

b. Two Reasons to Rejoice (3:15)

Zephaniah now supplies two grammatically unmarked reasons the preserved future remnant should rejoice.[88] The reasons relate to (1) what YHWH has (i.e., will have) done in removing Jerusalem's curses (3:15a–b), (2) where he is (3:15c), and (3) what this necessitates (3:15d). The lack of conjunction on the two clauses bearing an explicit subject (3:15a, c) supports this reading since it most naturally signals some form of explication, which context suggests is causal.

(1) YHWH's Removal of the Curses (3:15a–b)

The first reason the future transformed city should sing is because "YHWH has removed your judgments; he has turned away your enemy." The initial statement declares what God has accomplished, and the second, now without an explicit subject and signaled by asyndeton, clarifies the nature of his act. Specifically, YHWH has taken away Jerusalem's "judgments" (מִשְׁפָּטַיִךְ), namely, her "enemy" (אֹיְבֵךְ). Having addressed the charges, carried out his sentence, and appeased his wrath,

---

84. Characterizing Jerusalem's offspring as feminine points to a transformed city and not to the female population (against Renz, *Books of Nahum, Habakkuk, and Zephaniah*, 627–28).

85. Cf. Gal 6:15–16; Eph 2:13–22. See G. K. Beale, "Peace and Mercy upon the Israel of God: The Old Testament Background of Gal. 6,16b," *Bib* 80 (1999): 204–23; cf. G. K. Beale, *A New Testament Biblical Theology: The Unfolding of the Old Testament in the New* (Grand Rapids: Baker Academic, 2011), 722–24.

86. Cf. Isa 4:2–6; 11:9; 54:1–3; 65:17–18, 25; Jer 3:16–18; Dan 2:34–35, 44–5; Rev 21:1–3, 9–11, 23–22:5. For more on this teaching, see the comments above on Zeph 2:9, 11 and G. K. Beale, *The Temple and the Church's Mission: A Biblical Theology of the Dwelling Place of God*, NSBT 17 (Downers Grove, IL: InterVarsity Press, 2004), 365–76; Beale, *New Testament Biblical Theology*, 639–44.

87. Similarly, Calvin asserted: "The Prophet . . . encourages the faithful to rejoice, as though he saw with his eyes what he had previously promised . . . [and] as though they were already . . . in possession of what they had prayed for . . . [and] as though they were already enjoying that happiness, which was yet far distant" (Calvin, "Habakkuk, Zephaniah, Haggai," 299). In Floyd's words, Zeph 3:14–15 engenders "anticipatory joy" (Floyd, *Minor Prophets, Part 2*, 245; cf. Calvin, "Habakkuk, Zephaniah, Haggai," 299; Robertson, *Books of Nahum, Habakkuk, and Zephaniah*, 336; Roberts, *Nahum, Habakkuk, and Zephaniah*, 222.). The future impacts the way we should live in the present (cf. Isa 2:5 with 2:2–4 and Mic 4:5 with 4:1–4).

88. So, too, J. M. P. Smith, "Book of Zephaniah," 256; Ben Zvi, *Book of Zephaniah*, 238; Vlaardingerbroek, *Zephaniah*, 209; Sweeney, *Zephaniah*, 198.

God now promises to overcome the curse with a blessing.

The God who displays his "judgment" (מִשְׁפָּט) morning by morning (3:5) and whose "judgment" (מִשְׁפָּט) is to punish the world's evildoers (3:8; cf. 2:3) will remove the new Jerusalem's "judgments" (מִשְׁפָּטַיִךְ). This likely refers to his halting the covenant curses of enemy oppression, which shaped the "decree" (2:2) that he "purposed to visit" against the city (3:7; cf. e.g., Lev 26:16–17; Deut 28:43–44). To end the curses means that he has "turned away" Jerusalem's "enemy." The switch from plural "judgments" to singular "enemy" is unexpected, leading many translations to render both forms as plural (e.g., LXX, Vulg., Syr., Tg. Neb., NRSVue, ESV, NASB20). However, the singular has solid textual support (so NKJV, NET, NIV, CSB). The "enemy" could refer to the devil. Prophets like Isaiah attach the work of global evil to a demonic figure (e.g., Isa 14:12; 27:1), and the NT at times applies the singular "enemy" to the devil (Matt 13:39; Luke 10:19; cf. T. Dan 6:3). Nevertheless, Zephaniah elevates YHWH as the one Jerusalem should fear more than any other person. As such, the "enemy" in Zeph 3:15 could be God himself, as in other parallel texts (see Isa 63:10; Jer 30:14; Lam 2:4–5).[89] However, because YHWH promises to remove the arrogant abusers from Jerusalem's midst (3:11) with the same *hiphil* verb סור, the singular "enemy" (אֹיֵב) in

3:15 likely refers to a class[90] of all those who caused and carried out the divine judgments—both those *within* the city (cf. 1:9; 3:1–4, 11, 18–19) and those *outside* it (2:4–15; 3:18–19).[91] Such a group is at least the most direct referent.

Earlier, the *future* reality of YHWH pouring his wrath upon all the earth's unrepentant sinners and self-exalting oppressors motivated the faithful to "wait" for him (3:8). However, now through his use of Hebrew *qatal* verbs (הֵסִיר "has removed"; פִּנָּה "has turned away"), he treats the punishments he intended for Jerusalem as already complete (much like in 2:11 and 15 with respect to the earth's gods and Assyria's capital Nineveh).[92] Apart from Zephaniah's referring to Judah's Baal followers as a "remnant" (1:4) and to Cush's accomplished demise (2:12), the book makes no hint that God *already* completed or even initiated judgment and its resulting salvation. Some scholars posit that the prophet refers to the Assyrians, whom YHWH had already begun to remove in Zephaniah's day.[93] However, both the specific statements against Assyria in 2:13–15 and the more general statements regarding global destruction (e.g., 1:2–3, 14–18; 3:8) all treat God's punishment as *future*. Others posit that the prophet's message has developed, moving from pre-reform in 1:2–3:13 to post-reform in 3:14–20, a shift that thus "warrants the eventual fulfillment of all that has been prophesied."[94] However, the

---

89. See Renz, *Books of Nahum, Habakkuk, and Zephaniah*, 628.

90. So too Ball, *Rhetorical Study of Zephaniah*, 181; Ben Zvi, *Book of Zephaniah*, 241; Vlaardingerbroek, *Zephaniah*, 207; cf. *IBHS*, 114–15 (§7.2.2).

91. Berlin, *Zephaniah*, 143.

92. Though finding it possible, Renz does not "find it plausible that Zephaniah offered such an 'idyllic portrayal of Jerusalem's secure and peaceful future' as an imminent prospect in the 620s" (Renz, *Books of Nahum, Habakkuk, and Zephaniah*, 623–24). Renz's approach fails to recognize that Zephaniah's God controls history and foretold such an eschatological future through prophets as early as Moses (e.g., Deut 30:1–14; Isa

11:1–12:6; 35; Hos 2:14–23; Amos 9:11–15; Mic 5:1–4a[2–5a]). For more on what grammarians term the "perfect of certitude" among other things, see GKC, §106l–n; *IBHS*, §30.5.1e; Joüon, §112h; Williams and Beckman, *Williams' Hebrew Syntax*, §165; *BHRG*, §19.2.5.1, 539. Though Ben Zvi recognizes the absence of an explicit causal כִּי ("because"), he compares Zeph 3:14–15 to "a call to praise," which consistently employs verbs other than *yiqtol* to establish the reason for praise (e.g., Exod 15:21; Pss 9:12–13[11–12]; 106:1; 107:1; 117:1–2; 118:1; 136:1; Jer 20:13) (Ben Zvi, *Book of Zephaniah*, 238).

93. E.g., Sweeney, *Zephaniah*, 198, 200.

94. Floyd, *Minor Prophets, Part 2*, 176.

whole book presents itself as a single oracle that Zephaniah likely gave during the Feast of Ingathering in 622 BC, and this calls us to consider another option.[95]

Zephaniah views the day of YHWH as *near* (1:7, 14)—as both certain and *future* (1:4, 8–9, 12–13; 3:7–8),[96] and he urges his listeners to set out and patiently pursue YHWH together (2:1, 3; 3:8) *before* his decree is born (2:2). Nevertheless, as part of the book's intensifying literary turbulence,[97] the prophet makes the certainty of *future* joy after the day of YHWH the catalyst for the present joy amid pain.[98] In Smith's words, "The prophet transports himself in imagination to the future for which he so ardently longs and proceeds to describe it as though it were actually realized."[99]

God's trustworthiness guarantees he will fulfill his promise, which enables experiencing tomorrow's joy today. Thus, Zephaniah's call to *present* joy, a delight growing out of hope, accompanies his call to *presently* "seek" YHWH together and to "wait" for him (cf. Hab 3:17–19).[100] Other prophets make similar appeals to celebrate YHWH's eschatological salvation (e.g., Isa 12:5–6; Joel 2:21–23; Zech 2:10), which ultimately comes through his messianic king (Zech 9:9). Zephaniah's readers must rise above their earthly trials by tireless trust,

as the hope of future joy sustains their present pursuit of God, just as it would Christ (Isa 53:11; cf. Heb 12:3).

YHWH's commitment to remove Jerusalem's judgments means that he will eliminate every internal and external obstacle to his people's Godwardness, deal with their sin, and fully appease his wrath. Such is indeed a cause to celebrate. On this, Motyer writes, "It is one thing to deal with sin within the sinner so that conscience no longer accuses (Zeph 3:11): this is the guiltiness of sin. It is a different thing to deal with sin as it outrages the holy character of God: this is the offense of sin, and it constitutes a deeper and more necessary work, for there can be no salvation until God is satisfied."[101] YHWH removing his judgments highlights complete freedom from the curse.[102]

(2) YHWH's Nearness (3:15c–d)

Zephaniah now raises YHWH's promised nearness as a second reason that the future transformed Jerusalem ought to shout for joy: "Israel's King, YHWH, is in your midst" (מֶלֶךְ יִשְׂרָאֵל יְהוָה בְּקִרְבֵּךְ). Then, using the first of the book's two prohibitions (cf. 3:16b), the prophet infers that, because YHWH will be close, the remnant should "never fear evil again!" (לֹא־תִירְאִי רָע עוֹד).

---

95. For more on this link, see the comments at Zeph 1:2–3. The important matter here is that the book's present shape treats the whole as an intentionally crafted composite. For the movement from prophetic speech to prophetic book, see Block, *Book of Ezekiel: Chapters 1–24*, 17–23.

96. Cf. Zeph 3:8b–10, 11–13, 16–17, 19–20.

97. For Zeph 3:14–15 as Zephaniah's rhetorical peak, see Structure and Literary Form above, along with Tachick, *Use of Zephaniah 3 in John 12*, 101–7.

98. As already noted, the numerous parallels that 3:14–15 has with 3:8–13 and 3:16–20 further support that (1) Zeph 3:14–15 is intrusive, (2) the imperatives in 3:14 are *not* operating like the imperatives in 2:1, 3 and 3:8, and (3) the *qatal* verbs in 3:15 are indeed "perfects of certitude" (see Structure and Literary Form above).

99. J. M. P. Smith, "Book of Zephaniah," 256.

100. See also Rom 5:2; 12:12.

101. Motyer, "Zephaniah," 956–57.

102. Ben Zvi asserts that Zeph 3:15 does not refer in any way to "YHWH as a divine warrior who vanquishes his enemies and becomes king" (Ben Zvi, *Book of Zephaniah*, 243). However, while YHWH is already Israel's King, the context of YHWH's day presents him as a Warrior (Zeph 1:14–18) and as "a Mighty One" who will "save" (3:17) by removing his judgments. Furthermore, when his judgments can refer to individuals as both *agents* (see Isa 54:16; of Assyria: Isa 7:20; 10:5; Mic 6:9; of Israel: Isa 41:15; of Persia: Isa 45:1; of Babylon: Isa 13:3, 5, 13; Jer 50:21; Ezek 30:24–25) and *objects* of his wrath (of Assyria: Isa 10:12, 18; 14:25; 30:31; 31:8; 37:7; of Babylon: Jer 50:23).

Zephaniah calls Jerusalem's great deliverer "Israel's King" (מֶלֶךְ יִשְׂרָאֵל, Zeph 3:15c), the full title of which Scripture applies to YHWH only here and in Isa 44:6 (cf. Isa 41:21; Jer 10:7).[103] Elsewhere, the phrase refers to human kings of the united kingdom or the divided Northern or Southern Kingdoms.[104] Earlier, Zephaniah called him "Sovereign YHWH" (1:7a) to highlight his absolute ability to bring his day of fury. Later, God labeled himself "YHWH of armies, the God of Israel" (2:9a), to stress not only that he was for his people but that no enemy force could rival his warriors. Now, Zephaniah uses the title "Israel's King" plus the appositive "YHWH" to present the causer of all things not only as (1) the new Israel's supreme Monarch (cf. Num 23:21; Deut 33:5; Ezek 20:33) but also as (2) the preeminent, true Savior and Ruler of the universe since he will eradicate global hostility and deliver (cf. Isa 43:11; 44:6; 45:21).[105]

Later, the Canonical and Theological Significance section will note how the NT relates the phrase "Israel's King" to Jesus. Presently, at least three factors make Zephaniah calling YHWH "Israel's King" significant. First, while "Josiah the son of Amon" was "Judah's king" in the prophet's day (Zeph 1:1), he was not Judah's ultimate Lord. All of Israel's leaders in both the united and divided kingdoms were supposed to represent and never replace YHWH's governance (Deut 17:18–20). Instead, they rejected YHWH as king and covenant Lord (cf. 1 Sam 8:7; 2 Kgs 17:14–18; Jer 3:6–11), and eventually Manasseh's rebellious reign made Judah's

downfall inevitable (2 Kgs 21:11–12; 23:26–27). During Zephaniah's adult life King Josiah "turned to YHWH with all his heart" (23:25). Thus, Zephaniah and Josiah both elevated YHWH's kingship above all else, and the future, after experiencing the curse, would prove God's supremacy.

Second, use of "King" (מֶלֶךְ) in Zeph 3:15c repeats the same title the remnant of Baalists in Judah sinfully ascribed to their chief divine authority (מַלְכָּם "their king," 1:5). This wordplay makes clear that YHWH of Israel is the supreme Ruler of all things visible and invisible. He alone "has made lean all the gods of the earth, so that all the coastlands of the nations will bow down to him, each from his place" (Zeph 2:11b–c; cf. Zech 14:9; Rev 22:3–4).

Third, Zephaniah associates God's kingship with "Israel." This association not only establishes YHWH's continuity with his past (old) covenant (see Zeph 2:9; cf. 3:13) but it also firmly links him to the newly transformed, multiethnic, single people of God, the new "Israel" of 3:14 (cf. 3:9–10). This new "Israel" is the transformed covenant community that Zephaniah associates with YHWH's cleansed city and the mountain of his holiness (3:11–13).

Having proved his majesty and supremacy by famishing "all the gods of the earth" (2:11; cf. 3:8) and by eradicating Jerusalem's enemy (3:15a–b), YHWH's royal presence would rest in the city's midst and shelter the redeemed people. This indeed is cause to rejoice (3:14) and removes the remnant's need to fear evil (3:15d). The clause

---

103. Scripture frequently depicts YHWH as "King" (מֶלֶךְ)—e.g., Num 23:21; 1 Sam 12:12; Ps 149:2; Isa 33:22; Jer 10:10; Ezek 20:33; Mic 2:13; Mal 1:14; Zech 14:9. For a thorough discussion of YHWH's kingship and reign in Scripture, see J. A. Soggin, "מָלַךְ *melek* (king)," *TLOT* 2:672–80.

104. United kingdom (e.g., 1 Sam 26:20; 2 Sam 6:20; 2 Kgs 23:13), Northern Kingdom (e.g., 1 Kgs 15:17; 22:3–4; 2 Kgs 3:9), Southern Kingdom (e.g., 2 Chr 21:2; cf. 21:4). The OT never uses this phrase to refer to the coming messianic de-

liverer, though it certainly implies such in the way it envisions him as a new David and better Solomon.

105. See also Deut 4:35, 39; 32:39; Ps 83:19[18]; Hos 13:4. Gray notes four features common to most passages addressing YHWH's kingship: YHWH's (1) conflict with disorder or the powers of evil, (2) victory, (3) manifestation as king, and (4) assigning the proper place to the cosmos and chaos (John Gray, "The Kingship of God in the Prophets and Psalms," *VT* 11.1 [1961]: 1–2).

לֹא־תִירְאִי רָע עוֹד could either be (1) resultative and predictive (= "you will never fear evil again") or (2) prohibitive and directive, aligning with the earlier four imperatives (= "Never fear evil again!"). As in the Ten Words (e.g., Deut 5:17–21), the fronted nature of the negative לֹא plus *yiqtol* suggests it is a non-indicative, durative prohibition that recalls the imagery of 3:12–13 (option 2).[106] The "afflicted and needy people" dwelling in the new Jerusalem's "midst" (בְּקִרְבֵּךְ, 3:12a) will find refuge in the name YHWH (3:12b) as he resides in the city's "midst" (בְּקִרְבֵּךְ, 3:15c). There, the peoples will enjoy motivation for holiness (3:13a–c) and should "never fear evil again!" as "they will graze and lie down, and there will be none who cause trembling" (3:13d–f). As the psalmist declared, "I will not fear evil, for you are with me" (לֹא־אִירָא רָע כִּי־אַתָּה עִמָּדִי, Ps 23:4; cf. 3:6; 27:1), so Jerusalem would rest in perfect peace within YHWH's presence.[107]

In Scripture, the verb "to fear" (I-ירא) expresses a spectrum of negative or positive emotions, depending on the verb's context and object. Zephaniah has already characterized YHWH as "fearsome" (נוֹרָא, 2:11a), and YHWH's wrath was coming against Jerusalem because she failed to "fear me" (תִירְאִי אוֹתִי, 3:7b). Zephaniah pits proper reverence of YHWH (3:7b) against dread of evil (3:15d) since the faithful and free need not fear "evil" (רָע) again (3:15d). The former will continue; the latter will be no more (cf. Jer 32:30; Matt 10:28). Thus, while YHWH creates both good and harm (Eccl 7:13–14; Isa 47:5) and orchestrates blessing and curse (Deut 11:26; 32:39; Judg 2:15), he "is righteous" and "never does

wrong" (Zeph 3:5a–b), dwells in holiness (3:11c), and will forever eliminate evil from his people's presence (3:15d).[108]

This "evil" includes the internal and external "enemy" of Zeph 3:15a–b[109]—those who practice violence and deception (1:9; cf. 3:3–4), who taunt, reproach, and are haughty (2:8b–c, 10b–c, 15b–c; 3:11b–c), and who abuse and cause trembling (3:1, 13f, 19a).[110] It would also include those making idols (1:3b), the remnant of the Baal who were practicing false worship (1:4b), the pagan and worldly merchants (1:11), the complacent (1:12), those not longing for or seeking YHWH (2:1b, 3a–c), those resisting God and remaining unresponsive (3:2), those doing wrong but lacking shame (3:5e), those not fearing God or receiving instruction (3:7b–c), those corrupting their deeds (3:7f), and all those throughout the world engaged in any form of sin against YHWH (1:17c). Therefore, the "evil" that the remnant need not fear would include both persecution and all obstacles to sanctification—anything that could be done against them from outside *and* any wrong that could have previously welled up from inside. Their relationship with YHWH's presence will be completely safe with no potential of apostasy (see Jer 32:40; Zeph 1:6).

3. The Promise That YHWH Will Save Completely (3:16–20b)

The temporal marker "in that day" (בַּיּוֹם הַהוּא) introduces the unit of 3:16–20b, parallels the same phrase beginning 3:11–13, and refers to "the day of

---

106. On the distinction between לֹא plus (long) *yiqtol* marking a durative prohibition and אַל plus (short) *yiqtol* signaling an immediate, time-bound prohibition, see *BHRG*, §19.3.5.1.

107. Sweeney notes that salvation oracles commonly include "the reassurance formula" אַל תִּירָא ("do not fear"), which stresses the reality of future security (Sweeney, *Zephaniah*, 200; cf. Sweeney, *Isaiah 1–39*, 547).

108. Cf. Rev 21:4, 27–22:5.

109. Compare the feminine רָעָה for covenant curse in Judg 2:15 and the masculine רָע as the opposite of well-being in Isa 45:7.

110. These are "those who kill the body but cannot kill the soul" (Matt 10:28; cf. Luke 12:4).

[YHWH's] rising as a witness" in 3:8a (cf. 1:7–10, 14–16, 18; 2:2–3). In 3:15, Zephaniah anticipated this time (as if already accomplished) when the universe's true King would deliver his believing remnant and reveal his presence among them. Zephaniah 3:16–20b expands on 3:11–13 and further clarifies the implications of YHWH's cleansing and new creational work highlighted in 3:8b–10 by supplying another foundational promise to motivate waiting for YHWH (3:8a). Furthermore, 3:16–20b continues the feminine singular address found in 3:11–13 by which YHWH addresses the restored city Jerusalem.

3:16–20b also develops the context of salvation that 3:14–15 celebrates by stressing in promissory fashion the consummate salvation's content. This includes (1) the remnant's not fearing evil (3:15, 16), (2) YHWH addressing the transformed city as the only Zion/Jerusalem (3:14, 16a–b), (3) God dwelling amid the new city (3:15, 17), (4) God relieving the redeemed of all abusers (3:15, 18–19), and (5) the threefold joy that now focuses on YHWH's delight in his redeemed (3:14, 17).

Just as YHWH's first-person voice foregrounded 3:11–13, so too he is apparently the main speaker in 3:16–20b (see esp. 3:18, 19–20b). Nevertheless, his own voice gets mingled with that of the future prophetic mouthpiece when he reports a future speech, the longest in the book (3:16b–18; cf. 1:12d–e; 2:15b–c; 3:7b–c).

a. The Prediction of a Future Speech Prohibiting Fear (3:16–18)

The unit opens with YHWH predicting a future unnamed messenger's speech to Jerusalem on the day of judgment (3:16a). The speech's contents then follow (3:16b–18).

(1) The Prediction of the Future Speech (3:16a)

"In that day" (בַּיּוֹם הַהוּא) of punishment (3:8a) when King YHWH cleanses his sacred mountain (3:11–13) and delivers the new and rejoicing Israel (3:14–15), he promises that the transformed city Jerusalem will receive a speech. This speech's contents should further motivate the remnant of Zephaniah's day to "wait" for YHWH (3:8a). YHWH's passive "it will be said" (niphal yiqtol יֵאָמֵר) leaves the specific speaker's identity unclear and accentuates the speech's content. Nevertheless, the speaker's role as a prophetic messenger is certain since, as is common throughout the book, his words (3:16–17) blend with YHWH's (3:18) without signaling a new speech act. That the speech addresses "Jerusalem" and not the remnant "daughter" of the old city (3:14a, d) implies the "daughter of Zion/Jerusalem" (3:14a, d) has now become the whole city. The close context from 3:9–10 further suggests this new city's makeup is the multiethnic redeemed remnant.

(2) The Contents of the Future Speech (3:16b–18)

The quotation runs from 3:16b–18 and includes both a charge not to fear (3:16b–c) and two reasons for this prohibition (3:17–18). The prophetic voice foregrounds 3:16b–17, treating YHWH in third person, but then YHWH's voice leads with first-person speech in 3:18. Since Zephaniah has many similar participant shifts without any marker, the change should not influence our reading 3:16b–18 as a single embedded prophetic quotation. The temporal phrases "at that time" (בָּעֵת הַהִיא) in 3:19a and 20a signal that the citation ends after 3:18. These phrases both echo the "in that day" (בַּיּוֹם הַהוּא) of 3:11a and 16a and reestablish the context as Zephaniah's present by treating the day of YHWH as future.[111]

---

111. By missing the return to Zephaniah's present in 3:19–20b, Wendland and Clark maintain that 3:18–20b is one first-person speech (Wendland and Clark, "Zephaniah," 33–34).

(a) The Prohibition Not to Fear (3:16b–c)

Two asyndetic negative commands open the unknown speaker's address with the second developing the first: "Do not fear! O Zion, may your hands not grow slack" (אַל־תִּירְאִי צִיּוֹן אַל־יִרְפּוּ יָדָיִךְ). While some translations include the vocative "O Zion" with 3:16b (e.g., NRSVue, NASB20, NET, ESV, NIV), the Masoretic cantillation treats it as introducing 3:16c by placing צִיּוֹן ("Zion") *after* the *athnakh* (see above; cf. NKJV, CSB). The construction אַל plus short *yiqtol* commonly marks urgent, one-time prohibitions.[112] This contrasts with the timeless prohibition structure לֹא plus long (i.e., indicative; the actual form is not visibly "long") *yiqtol* in 3:15d: "Never fear evil again!" The verb "to fear" (ירא-I) is the same in both instances, but the quotation in 3:16b addresses that future day's realities, which will include in it a potential reason to dread.[113] Stated differently, the immediate charge not to fear indicates an already-but-not-yet quality to the day of YHWH, for while God will ultimately eradicate evil completely, the "day" will include a season wherein the presence of sustained potential harm will tempt the remnant to fear.[114]

Unlike 3:15d, 3:16b does not explicitly state what the remnant could but should not fear. However, because 3:17b portrays YHWH as a "Mighty One" who "will save," the messenger likely focuses on hostile external (and perhaps internal) forces standing against God, his ways, and his people (cf. 3:11b, 13f, 15a–b, 19a). Yet even in their presence, the remnant need not fear.[115]

Scripture commonly pairs the verb רפה ("to grow slack, sink) or the adjective רָפָא ("slack, feeble") with the plural noun יָדִים ("hands") to figuratively express lack of courage in reaction to a message or event—a paralysis of the will and body often caused by shock in the wake of terror (e.g., 2 Chr 15:7; Isa 13:7; Jer 6:24).[116] Beside not feeling fear, the city should not act fearfully. The believing remnant must awaken from their stupor, confident in YHWH's presence, favor, and sovereignty. Zephaniah may be alluding to Isaiah's earlier declaration, which also predicts God's eschatological renewal and promised salvation: "Strengthen weak hands [יָדַיִם רָפוֹת], and staggering knees make strong! Say to those with a panicked heart, 'Be strong! Do not fear [אַל־תִּירָאוּ]! Look, your God . . . will come and save you [וְיֹשַׁעֲכֶם]'" (Isa 35:3–4).[117]

(b) Two Reasons Not to Fear (3:17–18)

YHWH's messenger now gives two reasons to take courage. The saving Warrior is near (Zeph 3:17), and YHWH has already gathered his remnant whom he will save (3:18).

- Reason 1: The Saving Warrior's Nearness (3:17)

The first reason the city should rest is "YHWH your God is in your midst" (בְּקִרְבֵּךְ), not as a vengeful covenant Lord but as the delivering King (3:17a). This statement of YHWH's presence with Zion recalls the basis for joy in 3:15c. But here the extended "YHWH *your* God," with the additional feminine singular pronominal suffix (יְהוָה אֱלֹהַיִךְ),

---

112. *BHRG*, §19.5.2.1, §41.3(1).

113. For אַל תִּירְאִי ("Do not fear!") in the Latter Prophets, see also Isa 7:4; 35:4; 40:9; 41:10, 13–14; 43:1, 5; 44:2; 54:4; Jer 30:10; 46:27–28; Joel 2:21–22; Hag 2:5; Zech 8:13–15.

114. So also Vlaardingerbroek, who sees Zephaniah predicting "a state of salvation, but not in the sense of an indestructible and unthreatened state of well-being" (Vlaardingerbroek, *Zephaniah*, 213).

115. Christians' present experience in the church age now fulfills Zephaniah's prediction of certain security amid objects of dread for the believing remnant.

116. See Motyer, "Zephaniah," 957; cf. Vlaardingerbroek, *Zephaniah*, 213.

117. Cf. Heb 12:12; 13:6; Rev 2:10.

emphasizes the supreme deity's personal identification with his eschatological city, which now is transformed from its once "oppressive" and "corrupt" ways (3:1, 7; cf. 3:11–13, 19).

Next comes a key implication of his nearness: "As a Mighty One, he will save!" (3:17b). The asyndetic clause likely indicates that God's presence ensures complete deliverance. The fronted substantival adjective "Mighty One" (גִּבּוֹר) recalls 1:14c. There, YHWH was a Warrior punishing rebels; now he is the Savior.[118] The adjective's first position signals the indicative, predictive nature of the following *yiqtol*. With the *hiphil* of the verb יָשַׁע ("to save"), YHWH delivers his people from human enemies (e.g., Exod 14:30; Judg 2:18; Isa 49:25), other evil, affliction, or distress (e.g., 1 Sam 10:19; Ps 34:6[7]; Isa 46:7), and even from sin (Ezek 36:29; 37:23; cf. Jer 4:14). Here, God promises to deliver from all causes of fear hindering one's ability to persevere.

The speech itself highlights how the day of YHWH itself will include an overlap in time, wherein YHWH will have already appeared but not yet fully saved. But the reality of his presence ensures that he will! As the supreme and royal "Mighty One" (cf. Deut 10:17; Ps 24:8; Isa 42:13) who escalates his original exodus redemption (Exod 15:1–3; Num 24:7–8),[119] YHWH will fully deliver his people. He will rescue the collective remnant now associated with Jerusalem from their sins (Zeph 1:17–18; 3:9, 11) and from his judicial curses (3:15; cf. Isa 25:4, 8–9; 63:1),

including the removal of all proud abusers (Zeph 3:11, 15, 19).[120]

Not only this, God himself will revel in his redeemed in a threefold way that matches the threefold charge in 3:14 for the remnant city to rejoice. The three statements are not conjoined but independent and contain fronted *yiqtols* (in gray) followed by prepositional phrases:

Figure 8.5: Zeph 3:17c–e in the NET Bible	
MT	**NET**
יָשִׂישׂ עָלַיִךְ בְּשִׂמְחָה	He takes great delight in you;
יְחַדֵּשׁ[121] בְּאַהֲבָת	he renews you by his love;
יָגִיל עָלַיִךְ בְּרִנָּה	he shouts for joy over you

Following the predictive indicative *yiqtol* יוֹשִׁיעַ ("he will save") in 3:17b, most modern translations treat the three first-position *yiqtols* as emphatic, predictive indicatives, as in the ESV: "*He* will *rejoice* over you with gladness; *he will quiet* you by his love; *he will exult* over you with loud singing" (3:17c–e; cf. NKJV, NRSVue, NASB20, NIV, CSB). Others, like the NET, treat them as emphatic, present continuous indicatives, which is one way fientive (i.e., those dealing with activities rather than states) *yiqtols* function in certain contexts: "*He takes* great *delight* in you; *he renews* you by his love; *he shouts* for joy over you" (cf. YLT, italics added).[122] While both renderings fit the context, only the former aligns with the promissory orientation of 3:17b. However, *yiqtol* verbs in the first

---

118. Ben Zvi identifies this movement from punishment (Zeph 1:14) to salvation (3:17), but he minimizes too much the conquest-warrior motif that is present in both texts (Ben Zvi, *Book of Zephaniah*, 249, 287).

119. Cf. Isa 11:11–12:6; Jer 16:14–15; Ezek 20:36–38, 41–42; Luke 9:30–31.

120. Isaiah applies the title "Mighty One" (גִּבּוֹר) to YHWH (Isa 10:21; 42:13) and to his messianic King (9:5[6]).

121. I here follow the LXX, which reads the Hebrew as יְחַדֵּשׁ rather than the MT's יַחֲרִישׁ. On this change, see below.

122. For more on fientive *yiqtols* expressing present tense, see Brian L. Webster, *The Cambridge Introduction to Biblical Hebrew* (Cambridge: Cambridge University Press, 2009), 295–305; Brian L. Webster, "The Perfect Verb and the Perfect Woman in Proverbs," in *Windows to the Ancient World of the Hebrew Bible: Essays in Honor of Samuel Greengus*, ed. Bill T. Arnold, Nancy L. Erickson, and John H. Walton (Winona Lake, IN: Eisenbrauns, 2014), 261–71; DeRouchie, *How to Understand and Apply*, 193–99.

position usually express non-indicative volitional modality,[123] which in this setting would mean the certainty of coming salvation moves the speaker to bless the city with hope in direct alignment with previous promises. Thus, the syntax probably yields this interpretation: "*May he rejoice* [יָשִׂישׂ] over you with merriment; *may he renew* [יְחַדֵּשׁ] with his love; *may he celebrate* [יָגִיל] over you with song!" Robertson rightly asserts, "That the Holy One should experience ecstasy over the sinner is incomprehensible" apart from blood-bought grace (cf. Luke 15:7, 10).[124] We will consider each clause in turn.

First, the prophetic mouthpiece expects YHWH to "rejoice" (שׂושׂ) over the city with "merriment" (שִׂמְחָה, 3:17c). Nearly a millennium before Zephaniah, Moses promised Israel that sometime after cursing the sinful nation (Deut 28:63) God would "return to rejoice [לָשׂושׂ] over you for good, just as he rejoiced [שָׂשׂ] over your fathers" (30:9). Jeremiah recalled this promise in Zephaniah's day (Jer 32:41), and the spokesperson is likely alluding to the same promise here, believing that YHWH will fulfill it.[125] Isaiah, too, declared of the transformed city Jerusalem, "Like a bridegroom's joy over a bride, your God will rejoice [יָשִׂישׂ] over you"

(Isa 62:5; cf. 65:19). The "merriment" (שִׂמְחָה) recalls the related verb used earlier in 3:14c to charge "the daughter of Jerusalem" to "be merry!" (שִׂמְחִי) in the wake of King YHWH's delivering act.

Second, at the day YHWH's presence returns to the city, the messenger will petition that Yahweh "renew by his love" (יְחַדֵּשׁ בְּאַהֲבָתוֹ) (3:17d). God's "love" (אַהֲבָה) moved him to rescue Israel from Egypt (Deut 7:8), to give them kings like Solomon (1 Kgs 10:9; 2 Chr 2:11[10]; 9:8), and to sustain them even when rebellious (Isa 63:9; Jer 31:3; Hos 3:1). And he promises to pour forth this same "love" in the days of restoration (Isa 43:4; Hos 14:4). The MT has the verb יַחֲרִישׁ, which is the *hiphil* of II חרשׁ and which many English translations render "to [make] quiet" (so NKJV, NASB20, ESV). With this form, God's "quieting" could mean either that he will calm the fears of this once-oppressed city (cf. Jer 4:19) or that he will cause her to "be silent," making the remnant's cries for help or clarity unnecessary (cf. Exod 14:14; Isa 41:1; Job 6:24).[126] However, neither of these options is likely, for, as both the NET notes and Webster rightly indicate, the *hiphil* stative verb חרשׁ always means "to *keep, be,* or *become* silent" rather than "to *make* silent" (e.g., Ps 50:21; Isa 42:14; Hab 1:3).[127] Thus, the

---

123. Robert D. Holmstedt, "The Typological Classification of the Hebrew of Genesis: Subject-Verb or Verb-Subject?," *JHebS* 11 (2011): 2–39; Robert D. Holmstedt, "Investigating the Possible Verb-Subject to Subject-Verb Shift in Ancient Hebrew: Methodological First Steps," *KUSATU* 15 (2013): 3–31; cf. Garrett and DeRouchie, *A Modern Grammar for Biblical Hebrew,* 39–40; DeRouchie, *How to Understand and Apply,* 199–201.

124. Robertson, *Books of Nahum, Habakkuk, and Zephaniah,* 340.

125. Cf. Robertson, *Books of Nahum, Habakkuk, and Zephaniah,* 342–43.

126. The context of "fear" that Zeph 3:16b–c establishes and the similar *hiphil* uses of the verb חרשׁ elsewhere make the meaning "to quiet, silence" more likely for the reading חרשׁ in 3:17d than the homonym I חרשׁ ("to plough") (but see below for another possibility). However, sometimes the *niphal* of חרשׁ refers metaphorically to YHWH's "tilling" Jerusalem's

unproductive ground (i.e., the wicked majority) in order to plant a new garden for himself (i.e., transforming the city into a new creation for his and his redeemed ones' joy) (cf. Jer 26:18; Mic 3:12).

127. See NET under Zeph 3:17; Brian L. Webster, "A Reversal of Fortunes: What Comfort! Zephaniah 3:17," in *Devotions on the Hebrew Bible: 54 Reflections to Inspire and Instruct,* ed. Milton Eng and Lee M. Fields (Grand Rapids: Zondervan, 2015), 105–7. Both *HALOT* and *DCH* identify the meaning of "reduce to silence" or "make silent" in Job 11:3 בַּדֶּיךָ מְתִים יַחֲרִישׁוּ = "Should your babble silence men?" ESV; cf. NKJV, NRSVue, NASB20, NIV, CSB) ("חרשׁ II," *HALOT* 358; "חרשׁ II," *DCH* 3:323–34). However, because the verb יַחֲרִישׁוּ ("they will/should be silent") is plural and בַּד ("loose talk, babble") is the object of the plural subject מְתִים ("people"), the NET's translation is better: "Should people remain silent at your idle talk?"

NASB20 translates the clause, "He will be quiet in his love," and the NIV reads, "In his love he will no longer rebuke you" (Zeph 3:17d).[128] The NIV's rendering of YHWH's anger being quieted in his love appears contextually driven, for God's silence in speech does not easily align with the verbs of "rejoicing" (שׂישׂ) and "celebration" (גיל) and the nouns of "merriment" (שִׂמְחָה) and "song" (I רִנָּה). Nevertheless, Motyer sees God progressing "from the feeling of joy (3:17c) to the silence of adoration (3:17d) to vocal exultation (3:17e)."[129] This is a more likely reading, for elsewhere the state of "silence" that the verb חרשׁ expresses always lacks speech or sound rather than quieted anger. Nevertheless, rejoicing with merriment in 3:17c seems to express more than feeling, suggesting that the speaker did not envision a progression of divine affection.

Significantly, the LXX translated the clause in 3:17d, "And he will renew you in his love" (καὶ καινιεῖ σε ἐν τῇ ἀγαπήσει). The Greek translator apparently read the *piel* יְחַדֵּשׁ ("he will renew")[130] from the verb חדשׁ ("to make new, restore") with *daleth* (ד), rather than the *hiphil* יַחֲרִישׁ ("may he quiet") with *resh* (ר), as in the MT. The NRSVue, the NET, and the NASB20 margin all have "renew," which is the best lexical reading.[131] Perhaps the

Hebrew text does not specify the object of the renewal since YHWH's eschatological work will exceed a single place or people and include the entire universe—a new heavens and a new earth (cf. Isa 43:19–21; 65:17; 66:22).[132]

The relatively infrequent verb חדשׁ occurs in some comparable contexts. For example, when envisioning how, in the days of restoration following the exile, the anointed, Spirit-empowered herald of the good news will heal and free many so that they may become oaks of righteousness and that YHWH may be glorified, Isaiah also highlights that, in turn, *they will renew* [וְחִדְּשׁוּ] the wasted cities, what was desolated for many generations" (Isa 61:4).[133] Similarly, following Jerusalem's destruction in 586 BC, the lamenting prophet prays, "Cause us to return, O YHWH, to yourself, so that we may return; *renew* [חַדֵּשׁ] our days as of old" (Lam 5:21). The future prophetic messenger believes that YHWH will indeed fulfill this prayer.

Third, the hope is that YHWH will "celebrate over you [Zion] with song" (יָגִיל עָלַיִךְ בְּרִנָּה, Zeph 3:17e). Like a father who "celebrates" (גיל) or "makes merry" (שׂמח) over a righteous child (Prov 23:24–25), so God delights in his people (cf. Pss 147:11; 149:4; cf. 35:27).[134] God's melody (רִנָּה) will provide an antiphonal chorus to the "loud singing"

---

128. Achtemeier renders the clause, "He will hold his peace in his love," meaning that "the war cry of 1:14 is stilled" (Achtemeier, *Nahum–Malachi*, 85; cf. Ben Zvi, *Book of Zephaniah*, 251–52).

129. Motyer, "Zephaniah," 958.

130. Or יְחַדְּשֵׁךְ ("he will renew *you*") with object suffix. Perhaps the translator understood the pronominal object as "you" by ellipsis, or perhaps an original object suffix ךְ was lost through haplography, the final כ being dropped before the similar looking ב at the beginning of the next word (so, too, Harris and Burer, *The NET Bible*, under Zeph 3:17).

131. The switch from the more original יחדשׁ (from חדשׁ) to יחרישׁ (from חרשׁ) likely arose by confusing *daleth* and *resh* and since in later Aramaic the verb חרשׁ, which remained stative and intransitive in the Peal (= "to be choked, obstructed")

could become transitive and factitive in the *pael* (= "to choke, entangle"). See, e.g., the *pael* participle מְחַרְשָׁן 2x in Tg. Neb. Ezek 13:20 as "choking/entangling [souls to destroy them]." See Jastrow, "חֲרַשׁ," *Dictionary*, 507. It may also be that the Zephaniah's new exodus motif moved a later scribe to read יחרישׁ (cf. Exod 14:14) over יחדשׁ. Among those following this emendation include John Owen in Calvin, "Habakkuk, Zephaniah, Haggai," 304n1; J. M. P. Smith, "Book of Zephaniah," 257, 262; G. Smith, *Book of the Twelve Prophets*, 2:73; House, *Zephaniah*, 133; Patterson, *Nahum, Habakkuk, Zephaniah*, 341.

132. See also Rom 8:20–21; 2 Pet 3:13; Rev 21:1.

133. Cf. Isa 44:26; 58:12; 65:21; Ezek 36:33; Amos 9:14; Zech 1:16–17.

134. This is similar to the pleasure he has in his Son (Matt 3:17; 12:18; 17:5; 2 Pet 1:17).

(רָנַן) of the original Zion's transformed daughter (Zeph 3:14a; cf. Isa 35:6; 51:11), which will itself match that of the whole creation (e.g., 35:2; 44:23). Within Scripture, YHWH sings only in Zeph 3:17e.[135] Nevertheless, as God will "rejoice" (שִׂישׂ) over the new Zion in both Isa 62:5 and Zeph 3:17c, YHWH "celebrates" (גִּיל) over the transformed city in both Isa 65:17–19 and Zeph 3:17e, where such delight captures his joy over the entire renewed creation:

> For look, I am about to create new heavens and a new earth, and the former things will neither be remembered, nor will they rise on a mind. But *rejoice* [שִׂישׂוּ] *and celebrate* [וְגִילוּ] unto eternity with respect to that which I am creating. For look, I am creating Jerusalem as a *celebration* [גִּילָה] and her people as a *joy* [מָשׂוֹשׂ]. And I will celebrate [וְגַלְתִּי] in Jerusalem, and I will rejoice [וְשַׂשְׂתִּי] in my people. (Isa 65:17–19)

• Reason 2: YHWH's Gathering of His Remnant (3:18)

YHWH having already fulfilled his second exodus ingathering in this future day is a second explicit reason why Zion should be courageous. This ingathering implies that he will complete his saving act and bring his people into full rest. However, others contest this reading.

Scholars generally view this verse's Hebrew as the book's most difficult: נוּגֵי מִמּוֹעֵד אָסַפְתִּי מִמֵּךְ הָיוּ מַשְׂאֵת עָלֶיהָ חֶרְפָּה.[136] The following features divide interpreters:

1. The *yiqtol* of 3:17b set a future-oriented context for the previous unit, which leads most English translators to treat one (NASB20, NIV) or both (NRSVue, ESV, CSB) of the verbs in 3:18 as future, even though the verbs are *qatal*.[137]

2. The *athnakh* that divides the verse leaves two finite verbs in the initial half and none in the second, which leads some to disregard the Masoretic cantillation at this point (e.g., NRSVue, ESV, NIV, CSB against NASB20, NET).

3. Following the Septuagint, some link the initial two words with the end of the previous clause (e.g., NRSVue).

4. While translations commonly render מוֹעֵד as "feast(s)/festival(s)," the noun מוֹעֵד means only "something appointed," which leads commentators to differ on whether YHWH is highlighting an appointed *time* (e.g., a sacred festival; Hos 9:5; 12:10), *place* (e.g., a location for meeting; Lam 2:6), or *thing* (e.g., an assembly; Isa 14:13).

5. The switch from second feminine singular (מִמֵּךְ "from you") to third feminine singular (עָלֶיהָ "on her") is difficult, leaving the actual referents unclear and leading some to emend the text.

6. The meaning of מַשְׂאֵת ("burden; present, tribute") is not clear within the context.

Consider the variation in the following translations:

---

135. Unless in Isa 5:1 YHWH is the one singing (שִׁיר) over his and his "beloved" Son's vineyard (cf. Mark 12:1, 6).

136. Hadjiev attributes Zeph 3:18's apparent disjointedness to a later editor who unsuccessfully attempted to connect the book's conclusion (3:18–20) to the preceding passage (Tchavdar S. Hadjiev, "The Translation Problems of Zephaniah 3,18: A Diachronic Solution," *ZAW* 124.3 [2012]: 416–20). In contrast, Motyer suggests that difficult Hebrew may deliberately reflect Zephaniah's excitement for God's day of complete

deliverance (Motyer, "Zephaniah," 960). For other potential intentional grammatical solecisms in prophetic materials, see, e.g., Daniel I. Block, "Text and Emotion: A Study in the 'Corruptions' in Ezekiel's Inaugural Vision (Ezekiel 1:4–28)," *CBQ* 50 (1988): 418–42; G. K. Beale, *John's Use of the Old Testament in Revelation*, JSNTSup 166 (Sheffield: Sheffield Academic, 1998), 318–55.

137. An exception is the NET, which renders both verbs with past tense.

Figure 8.6: Different Translations of Zephaniah 3:18

MT

נוּגֵי מִמּוֹעֵד אָסַפְתִּי מִמֵּךְ הָיוּ מַשְׂאֵת עָלֶיהָ חֶרְפָּה:

LXX and NETS

... ὡς ἐν ἡμέρᾳ ἑορτῆς. καὶ συνάξω τοὺς συντετριμμένους· οὐαί, τίς ἔλαβεν ἐπ᾽ αὐτὴν ὀνειδισμόν;	... as on a day of a feast. And I will gather those who are shattered. Alas, who took up a reproach against her?

NRSVue and NASB20

NRSVue	NASB20
... as on a day of festival. I will remove disaster from you, so that you will not bear reproach for it.	"I will gather those who are worried about the appointed feasts—They came from you, *Zion; The* reproach *of exile* is a burden on them."

NET and ESV

NET	ESV
"As for those who grieve because they cannot attend the festivals— I took them away from you; they became tribute and were a source of shame to you."	I will gather those of you who mourn for the festival, so that you will no longer suffer reproach.

NIV and CSB

NIV	CSB
I will remove from you all who mourn over the loss of your appointed festivals, which is a burden and reproach for you.	I will gather those who have been driven from the appointed festivals; they will be a tribute from you and a reproach on her.

My approach to this verse allows the Hebrew text to stand in its present Masoretic form and treats the shift from *yiqtol* in 3:17 (4x) to *qatal* in 3:18 (2x) as significant. Elsewhere in the book, intrusive *qatal* verbs treat future events as having already occurred (2:11, 15; 3:15). Here, however, the speech act is something declared in the future, and the switch to *qatal* suggests divine activity that is indeed past to awaken hope for the further future. From the perspective of this end-times prophetic mouthpiece, Zion should not fear now that the day of YHWH has come because God has already begun and will complete his eternal saving work: "Those tormented from an appointed time I have gathered. They were away from you; a burden was on her, a reproach" (3:18).

The phrase rendered "those tormented" is a *niphal* masculine plural participle, likely from I יגה. This verb always expresses grief or affliction caused by another, usually YHWH in relation to Judah's exilic suffering (e.g., Isa 51:23; Lam 3:32–33).[138] The preposition מִן on the indefinite מוֹעֵד ("an appointed time, place, thing") could be (1) *causal* (= "those tormented *because of* [their inability to enjoy] an appointed event—e.g., a feast), (2) *separative* (= "those tormented *from* an appointed group or place—e.g., an assembly or the temple), or (3) *temporal* (= "those tormented *since* an appointed time—e.g., a day of punishment"). Most English translations follow the first option, and Lam 1:4–5 supports it as a nearly contemporary text that describes Jerusalem after Babylon destroyed it with

---

138. The verb could possibly mean "those separated" and be from יגה II ("to remove"), which occurs elsewhere only in 2 Sam 20:13 as a *hiphil*. יגה II is an alternative form of הגה II (see

"יגה II," *HALOT* 385). In the *qal* it means "to expel, drive away," and it once describes Judah's exile (Isa 27:8; cf. Prov 25:4–5).

the proper nouns צִיּוֹן ("Zion"), the verb I יגה ("to torment"), and the noun מוֹעֵד referring to some sacred gathering like a "feast": "The roads unto Zion are mourning without those coming for *a feast* [מוֹעֵד]. . . . Her women of marriageable age are *tormented* [נּוּגוֹת]. . . . Her enemies are at ease, because YHWH *has tormented* [הוֹגָה] her on account of the multitude of her offenses" (Lam 1:4–5c).

Israel was to gather to the central sanctuary for three annual festivals (Deut 16:16), and Zephaniah has likely already used the verb אסף ("to gather") to recall the Feast of Ingathering (אָסִיף; Deut 16:13), also known as the Feast of Sukkot/Booths (see Zeph 1:2–3, 5, 7). However, mentioning a "feast" (singular) here seems intrusive, and one should consider options closer to Zephaniah's argument since מוֹעֵד could refer to any "appointed time, place, or thing."

Commentators disagree whether those tormented in 3:18 are the faithful remnant whom God has recovered or the condemned rebels whom he has weeded out. Those affirming they are rebels see the verb אסף ("to gather") in 3:18a directly recalling the comparable uses of אסף in the punishment contexts of 1:2–3 and 3:8.[139]

For example, Floyd believes in 3:18 that YHWH will keep his promises in 1:8–9, 12–13 and 3:11 to remove from the community "those with feelings opposed to the rejoicing" urged on the daughter of Zion in 3:14–17.[140] He reads מִמּוֹעֵד as "from the

assembly" and renders the verse, "Those from the assembly who were sorrowful I have removed from you; they were a burden on her, a reproach."[141] He also believes the shift from second feminine singular ("you") to third feminine singular ("her") distinguishes the new purified "Zion" ("you") from her rebellious mother ("her"), as 3:14 called the remnant "the daughter of Zion/Jerusalem" (3:14a, d).[142]

Sweeney notes that מוֹעֵד can denote a fixed time of divine punishment or intrusion like the day of YHWH (e.g., Hab 2:3; Dan 8:19) and not just a sacred event like a festival (e.g., Isa 33:20; Lam 2:7) or a specific group like an assembly (e.g., Num 6:2; Lam 1:15).[143] Given the book's whole message, he translates 3:18 with this meaning for מוֹעֵד: "Those who have suffered from the appointed time when I punished you were a burden upon her, a reproach."[144] He decides that (1) the grieved ones were those suffering "punishment or exile at YHWH's appointed time of judgment"[145] and (2) the prepositional phrase with a third feminine singular object (עָלֶיהָ "on her") specifies the enigmatic מַשְׂאֵת ("burden") to mean a sacred offering that God rendered by punishing and purging the city (cf. the language and imagery of sacrifice in 1:7, 17–18; 3:8).[146]

While these more negative readings are possible, "those tormented" more likely refers to the faithful

---

139. E.g., Floyd, *Minor Prophets, Part 2*, 237–38; Sweeney, *Zephaniah*, 204; Renz, *Books of Nahum, Habakkuk, and Zephaniah*, 635n.e, 638–41.

140. Floyd, *Minor Prophets, Part 2*, 237.

141. Floyd, *Minor Prophets, Part 2*, 237. While מִמּוֹעֵד has no definite article (= מִן-הַמּוֹעֵד), the speech in 3:16b–18 is poetic, so it may not include this prose particle that does appear in the surrounding context (1x in 3:16 and 6x in 3:19–20b). Floyd's translation disregards both the *munakh* (♀) and *athnakh* (♀) by linking מִמֵּךְ with what precedes and הָיוּ with what follows.

142. Floyd, *Minor Prophets, Part 2*, 238.

143. Sweeney, *Zephaniah*, 204.

144. Sweeney, *Zephaniah*, 193. Sweeney's attempt to have

נּוּגֵי מִמּוֹעֵד and הָיוּ within the same clause unnaturally makes אָסַפְתִּי מִמֵּךְ into an unmarked relative clause and disregards the *munakh* (♀) that links מִמֵּךְ to the verb הָיוּ. Instead, נּוּגֵי מִמּוֹעֵד is the direct object of the verb אָסַפְתִּי, and מִמֵּךְ is a focus modifier that fronts הָיוּ. See the commentary at Zeph 1:2–3 for why אסף in Zephaniah means "to gather" and does not by itself express the act of punishing.

145. Sweeney, *Zephaniah*, 204–5.

146. Sweeney, *Zephaniah*, 205. מַשְׂאֵת can refer to a "present" from one of greater social status to a lesser (e.g., Gen 43:34; 2 Sam 11:8; Esth 2:18) or "tribute, tax" from lesser to greater (Amos 5:11), which includes religious contributions (2 Chr 24:6–9; Ezek 20:40).

remnant from all nations whom YHWH has gathered and whom he will completely save. At least two elements from the immediate context support this conclusion.

First, while the book uses the verbs אסף ("to gather") and קבץ ("to assemble") for YHWH's eschatological ingathering of his global *enemies* (1:2–3; 3:8),[147] in this unit God twice "assembles" (קבץ) his *redeemed* on that future day (3:19–20b).[148] The single eschatological ingathering that Zephaniah envisions will include both prisoners of war and those whom God has freed (cf. 2:11).[149] The positive use of קבץ within the same unit of Zeph 3:16–20b strongly suggests that the verb אסף ("to gather") in 3:18a depicts the new exodus of some ethnic Israelites and some once foreigners as fulfilled and ensuring their lasting place of rest.[150]

Second, YHWH already spoke of such an influx by noting that international worshipers, the daughter of those he scattered at the tower of Babel, would bring tribute to YHWH at his sacred abode on his day of worldwide ingathering (3:9–10). Since YHWH is presently addressing the new Zion, it is logical for him to comment on her already assembled inhabitants.

"Those tormented" (נוּגֵי מִמּוֹעֵד) are those who have heeded YHWH's just decree by humbling themselves (2:3a). They are the "afflicted and needy" who will "take refuge in the name YHWH" (3:12), and they are "the lame one and the banished one" whom God has drawn near and will heal

(3:9–10, 19b–c). Sweeney rightly reads מִמּוֹעֵד as temporal, but it is indefinite ("from *an* appointed time") and likely refers to whatever appointed time of suffering the grieved ones endured (cf. e.g., 2:2a; 3:7d). It is these that YHWH has "gathered" (אָסַפְתִּי; cf. 3:10). This gathering ensures that he will complete the transformation he has begun and is one reason why the new Zion can be courageous during sustained trials (3:16).

The clause "they were away from you" (מִמֵּךְ הָיוּ) addresses the future Jerusalem's inhabitants' spatial or temporal separation from their future home, and the focus-fronting of the prepositional phrase may highlight a sense of divine anguish over the distance. In a real sense, those seeking YHWH together and waiting for him (2:1, 3; 3:8) were exiles awaiting lasting rest.[151]

The last clause details the specific significance of the remnant's separation from the new Jerusalem. This meant that the old city sat under a weight of chastisement. "A burden was on her, a reproach" (מַשְׂאֵת עָלֶיהָ חֶרְפָּה), which simply extended the "reproach" (חֶרְפָּה) Moab and Bene-Ammon had brought upon her in Zephaniah's day (2:8a; cf. 2:8b, 10b). Yet, because YHWH had already "gathered" his humble remnant, "the earth, their [place of] shame" once associated with Zion was now becoming a place of joy and praise (3:14, 19d). Therefore, she need not fear or let her hands grow slack (3:16b–c).[152] In sum, Zeph 3:18 gives a second reason his faithful remnant should be courageous

---

147. Cf. Isa 24:21–22; Jer 8:13; Hos 4:3–6; Zech 14:2.

148. Cf. Isa 11:12; Ezek 11:17; Mic 2:12; 4:6; John 11:50–52.

149. Cf. Matt 3:12; 13:30, 40–42; 25:32. For more on this single eschatological ingathering, see DeRouchie, "YHWH's Future Ingathering in Zephaniah 1:2," 173–91. Renz's proposal that YHWH has "gathered" (אסף) his enemy in 3:18 but has yet to "assemble" (קבץ) his remnant in 3:19–20 is unlikely since in 3:8b אסף ("to gather") and קבץ ("to assemble") synonymously describe God ingathering the wicked (3:8c) and remnant (3:9–10) (Renz, *Books of Nahum, Habakkuk, and Zephaniah*, 637).

150. See, e.g., Isa 11:10–12:6; 49:5–6; Jer 23:3–8; Mic 7:14–20; Zech 8:20–23. Ben Zvi notes that the "ingathering" found in Zeph 1:2–3 and 3:18–19 "represents one of the main transformations in the book, i.e., from 'divine gathering' in order to punish to 'divine gathering' to save, to bring to the ideal status" (Ben Zvi, *Book of Zephaniah*, 324).

151. Cf. Phil 3:20–21; Heb 11:13; 1 Pet 1:1, 17; 2 Pet 2:11.

152. For other positive treatments of Zeph 3:18, see, e.g., Ben Zvi, *Book of Zephaniah*, 252–54.

Part III.2: Stage 2: The Appeal to Wait for YHWH to Enjoy Salvation

when YHWH's day arrives: Since God will have fulfilled his promised second exodus ingathering, the people can be certain he will also bring full salvation and rest.

b. The Promissory Implications of the Future Speech (3:19–20b)

The arresting "Look, I . . ." (הִנְנִי) that opens 3:19 marks what follows in 3:19–20b as significant. These verses' content both confirms key points of salvation already known and mark the end of Zephaniah's message.[153] The two occurrences of "at that time" (בָּעֵת הַהִיא) in 3:19a and 20a likely refer to the time of the preceding speech act in 3:16b–18, which itself will be proclaimed "in that day" (בַּיּוֹם הַהוּא, 3:16a)—namely, the eschatological period when YHWH will rise to judge the world (3:8; cf. 1:7–10, 14–16, 18; 2:2–3).

(1) Jerusalem's Complete Salvation (3:19)

YHWH now continues his first-person address to the new city Jerusalem (= feminine singular "you") that has dominated both subsections fronted with "in that day" (בַּיּוֹם הַהוּא, 3:11–13, 16–20b): "Look, I will be dealing with all who afflict you at that time" (הִנְנִי עֹשֶׂה אֶת־כָּל־מְעַנַּיִךְ בָּעֵת הַהִיא). The participle of עשׂה ("to do") plus אֶת־ meaning "deal with" occurs elsewhere (e.g., Ps 109:21; Jer 18:23; Ezek 22:14), and here the time marker "at that time" (בָּעֵת הַהִיא) orients the whole participial clause as being future.

YHWH signals that the timestamp functions differently here than in 3:11a and 3:16a by employing the phrase "at that time" rather than "in that day" (cf. 3:11a, 16a) and placing the temporal

marker at the end of the clause. Instead of beginning its own subsection, 3:19 intimately relates to the preceding foretold speech act (3:16–18). The temporal marker's final placement signals that the phrase itself modifies the near object phrase "all those afflicting you" (אֶת־כָּל־מְעַנַּיִךְ), and the most direct referent for this activity is the preceding speech's future time frame. Thus, the ones "afflicting" the city (3:19a) are the implied objects of potential fear in 3:16b and the adversaries from whom the "Mighty One . . . will save" his remnant people (3:17b). Roberts believes these "probably include both the arrogant Judean officials who formerly dominated and oppressed the city (vv. 1–5, 11) and the foreign nations whom Yahweh used to purge the city of these officials (v. 8)."[154] The substantival *piel* participle of II ענה ("to afflict") recalls both the related substantival adjective "humble ones" (עֲנָוִים), whom the prophet called to "seek *humility* [עֲנָוָה]" (2:3a, c), and the "afflicted" (עָנִי) people whom YHWH promised to preserve and to separate from their once haughty oppressors (3:11–12a). Thus, "those afflicting" the new city in 3:19a are those who carry on the self-exulting arrogance of the enemies within (e.g., 1:9; 3:1–4) and without (e.g., 1:17–18; 2:8, 10, 15) Zephaniah's present Jerusalem that YHWH has already promised to destroy (3:11, 15; cf. 2 Sam 7:10; Isa 60:14).

Participle clauses like the one in Zeph 3:19a most commonly express "continuous action that takes place simultaneously with the reference time of an event," and usually an associated finite verb signals them.[155] In this context, the two future-oriented *weqatal* verbs of 3:19b–c express that main event. YHWH declares that when he confronts the

---

153. Cf. Garrett and DeRouchie, *A Modern Grammar for Biblical Hebrew*, 321–23; DeRouchie, *How to Understand and Apply*, 205–6.

154. Roberts, *Nahum, Habakkuk, and Zephaniah*, 223.

155. *BHRG*, §20.3.3(1); cf. Peter Theodore Nash, "The Hebrew Qal Active Participle: A Non-Aspectual Narrative Background Element" (PhD diss., University of Chicago, 1992), 132.

abusers (Zeph 3:19a), "I will save the lame one, and the banished one I will assemble" (וְהוֹשַׁעְתִּי אֶת־הַצֹּלֵעָה וְהַנִּדָּחָה אֲקַבֵּץ, 3:19b–c). Here God portrays Jerusalem as a crippled, homeless bride that he will now restore.[156] These two clauses' verb-object / object-verb structure often signals contrastive matching, which would mean that God's "saving" and "assembling" concern a common event yet are distinct acts in YHWH's mind.[157] This grammar reinforces from 3:17–18 that YHWH's single day will include a period in which YHWH will have already "gathered" and yet not have completely "saved."[158]

YHWH recalls the promise in 3:17b by using the same *hiphil* verb ישע ("to save") and now declares that he will "save the lame"—or perhaps better, "her who is lame" (וְהוֹשַׁעְתִּי אֶת־הַצֹּלֵעָה). The feminine singular substantival participle הַצֹּלֵעָה ("the lame one") portrays Jerusalem as a limping female, who was left wounded and unhealthy in her former "rebellious and defiled," even "oppressive," state (3:1). Yet YHWH commits to rescue her since she is the one who heeded Zephaniah's call to seek YHWH together (2:1, 3). The prophets often portray God

saving the redeemed at the age's end as delivering the maimed and the weak.[159] Certainly, this includes "the afflicted and needy" state of those who bear physical disabilities, some due to the abuses of others (see 3:12a, 19a).[160] But the imagery goes further, pointing to the figurative brokenness of the redeemed in their sinful state.[161] Thus, Motyer asserts, "The 'lame' is the one whose internal weakness makes him helpless."[162]

Along with healing the limping city, YHWH promises to "assemble" (קבץ) "the banished" (הַנִּדָּחָה) city, most clearly by reconciling her to himself. Scripture usually employs the verb I נדח ("to banish") to describe either Israel's state amid exile (*niphal*)[163] or God's actions that caused Israel's exile (*hiphil*).[164] Building on Moses's original promise (Deut 30:4), many of these texts also include the verb קבץ and predict the great eschatological ingathering of those once separated from God.[165] What is distinctive about Zeph 3:19, however, is that the feminine singular *niphal* substantival participle הַנִּדָּחָה ("the banished one") shows that YHWH is describing not the people in general but the city Zion herself as an unfaithful bride whom he

---

156. Cf. J. M. P. Smith, "Book of Zephaniah," 259.

157. DeRouchie, *How to Understand and Apply*, 223–24; cf. Dempster, "Linguistic Features of Hebrew Narrative," 84–87.

158. While unhelpfully focusing on Judah as a whole and not the faithful transnational remnant, Timmer notes, "Once Judah has been restored, an unidentified . . . [group] still exists in the capacity of renewed Judah's 'enemies' (אֹיְבֵךְ, 3:15) and 'oppressors' (כָּל מְעַנַּיִךְ, 3:19)" (Timmer, *Non-Israelite Nations*, 153).

159. E.g., Isa 35:5–6; 42:16; Jer 30:17; 31:8; Ezek 34:16; Mic 4:6–7.

160. Cf. Isa 53:4 with Matt 8:16–17.

161. Similarly, Isaiah depicted the Israelite community's wickedness as sickness (Isa 1:5–6). Nevertheless, using feminine singular address, God promises to redeem the crippled Jerusalem resulting in fully restoring those who repent (1:24–28). YHWH will "bind the brokenness of his people [חָבַשׁ . . . אֶת־שֶׁבֶר עַמּוֹ]" and "heal the blow of his injury" (30:26) through his Spirit-empowered servant-person, who will "bind up [לַחֲבֹשׁ] those broken of heart" (61:1).

162. Motyer, "Zephaniah," 961.

163. E.g., Ps 147:2; Isa 27:13; Jer 30:17; 40;12; 43:5; 49:5.

164. E.g., Jer 16:15; 23:8; 24:9; 27:10, 15; 46:28; 50:17; Ezek 4:13; Dan 9:7.

165. קבץ occurs in the *niphal* in, e.g., Neh 1:9; Isa 11:12; 56:8; Mic 4:6; and in *hiphil* in, e.g., Jer 23:2–3; 29:14, 18; 32:37. Some scholars believe that in Zeph 3:19–20, the mention of return from exile and overall eschatological flavor reveals these verses to be secondary and to demand a post-monarchic date (e.g., Gerleman, *Zephanja*, 66; Rudolph, *Micha, Nahum, Habakuk, Zephanja*, 299–300; Ball, *Rhetorical Study of Zephaniah*, 198; Ben Zvi, *Book of Zephaniah*, 257). While such views questionably deny the possibility of divine prediction, Motyer correctly notes that we should expect both messages of punishment and hope side by side in the preexilic era since YHWH's very name, upon which the prophetic ministry rested, "forbids him to be only judge or redeemer; he must be both" (cf. Exod 3:15; 34:6–7; Motyer, "Zephaniah," 957).

rejected but whom he will draw back to himself.[166] Three other prophetic texts use feminine singular forms to speak comparably of Jerusalem's disabled or sick state from which God intends to heal (Jer 30:16–17; Ezek 34:16; Mic 4:6–7). While all these texts are significant, Mic 4:6–7 receives added comment because it includes the identical feminine singular participle הַצֹּלֵעָה ("the lame one"), which occurs in the OT only in Mic 4:6–7 and Zeph 3:19.

In that day—the utterance of YHWH—I will gather *the lame one* [fs, הַצֹּלֵעָה], *and the banished one* [fs] *I will assemble* [וְהַנִּדָּחָה אֲקַבֵּצָה]—even the one against whom I worked evil. *And I will place the lame one* [וְשַׂמְתִּי אֶת־הַצֹּלֵעָה] for a remnant *and the banished one* [וְהַנַּהֲלָאָה] for a strong nation. And YHWH will reign over them at Mount Zion from now and unto forever. (Mic 4:6–7)

Micah's words follow his predictions that Jerusalem would become a heap of ruins under God's fury (Mic 3:12) and that, in the latter days, the nations will gather to a restored and elevated Zion where they will hear YHWH's Torah and find both justice and peace (4:1–4). The stress on YHWH's reign over his transformed people also anticipates the promise that a ruler in Israel would rise from Judah to shepherd a worldwide flock in the strength and majesty of God, resulting in peace on earth (5:2–5). Hence, as YHWH has already stressed in Zeph 3:9–10, his commitment to heal and reassemble Jerusalem includes his incorporating those nonnative Israelites who hear God's words of judgment, seek YHWH together with Ju-

dah's remnant, wait for God in hope, and gather as worshipers to his presence (Zeph 2:1, 3; 3:8, 9–10). Furthermore, if Zephaniah is intentionally identifying his predictions with Micah's, then Zephaniah too saw the Messiah as being instrumental in this coming global healing.

Isaiah foresaw something similar. He first highlighted how foreigners who join YHWH will serve priestly roles on the mountain of his holiness and how YHWH's temple will be a house of prayer for all peoples (Isa 56:6–7). Then he adds, "The utterance of YHWH *who assembles the banished of Israel* [מְקַבֵּץ הִדְחֵי יִשְׂרָאֵל]: More *I will assemble* [אֲקַבֵּץ] unto it *for those assembled to it* [לְנִקְבָּצָיו]" (56:8).[167] And again, "And I . . . am coming *to assemble* [לְקַבֵּץ] all the nations and the tongues, and they will come and will see my glory" (66:18).[168]

Having affirmed that he will both heal and reconstitute Jerusalem, YHWH now pledges, "And I will place them for praise and for a name in all the earth, their [place of] shame" (וְשַׂמְתִּים לִתְהִלָּה וּלְשֵׁם בְּכָל־הָאָרֶץ בָּשְׁתָּם) (Zeph 3:19d). Some interpreters read the masculine plural object suffix on the *weqatal* verb שִׂים ("to place") as a mere enclitic *mem*,[169] which allows them to treat בָּשְׁתָּם ("their shame") as the direct object.[170] Hence, the ESV reads, "I will change their shame into praise and renown in all the earth" (cf. NRSVue, NASB20, NET). This questionable construal creates an irregular syntactic structure by (1) reading what is naturally an object suffix as an enclitic, (2) requiring an alternative word-order of Verb-Modifier-Object rather than the more common Verb-Object-Modifier, and (3) disregarding the Masoretes by locating the verb

---

166. See further the comments at Zeph 2:4.

167. Isa 56:8b reads, עוֹד אֲקַבֵּץ עָלָיו לְנִקְבָּצָיו. עוֹד is here rendered with the sense of "still more" (cf. e.g., Gen 8:21; 2 Sam 21:15; 1 Kgs 22:7), and the preposition on לְנִקְבָּצָיו is a לְ of advantage: "for the benefit of those assembled to it."

168. Cf. John 10:16; 11:51–52.

169. "The enclitic *mêm* is an archaic suffix occasionally

affixed to the end of a word . . . [whose] meaning and function . . . are . . . unknown" (*BHRG*, §28.2). For cross-linguistic usage, see David Crystal, *A Dictionary of Linguistics and Phonetics*, 5th ed., Language Library (Malden, MA: Blackwell, 2003), 76, under "clitic."

170. See Sabottka, *Zephanja*, 139; Rudolph, *Micha, Nahum, Habakuk, Zephanja*, 294; Kapelrud, *Message of the Prophet*

and its object in different cantillation units (following the disjunctive *zaqeph qaton* [◌֔] on וּלְשֵׁם).

Alternatively, Ball renders the whole grouping of words into two clauses with the second verb being elliptical: "I will transform them into a praise, and their shame into a name in all the earth."[171] Though this reading has more natural syntax than the one above, Zephaniah minimally uses ellipsis (cf. 1:13b; 2:4b, 9b). This reading also disregards both the conjunctive *munakh* (◌ֽ) under לִתְהִלָּה ("for praise") that links this phrase to וּלְשֵׁם ("and for a name") and the disjunctive *zaqeph qaton* (◌֔) on וּלְשֵׁם that gives a brief pause after the compound prepositional phrase unit.

Still, others read the text as if there were no definite article on הָאָרֶץ ("the land"), which then allows בָּשְׁתָּם ("their shame") to stand as the absolute noun in a compound construct chain *בְּכָל־אֶרֶץ בָּשְׁתָּם ("in all the land of their shame"). Tg. Neb., the Vulgate, and Roberts adopt this approach. Roberts translates the whole, "I will make them renowned and famous in every land of their shame."[172] Both the NKJV and NIV follow a similar pattern.

The best reading results in a comparable sense but does not require the questionable emendation. Two options, both with the same basic meaning, are possible, but the first requires the intrusion of a present-time unlexicalized verb, which would

be foreign to the future-oriented context.[173] First, בָּשְׁתָּם may be an unmarked relative clause, resulting in a translation like, "And I will place them for praise and for a name in all the earth, which is their shame."[174] Second, בָּשְׁתָּם ("their shame") may be a noun in descriptive apposition to הָאָרֶץ ("the earth"), resulting in the translation, "And I will place them for praise and for a name in all the earth, their [place of] shame."[175]

Because the initial part of 3:19 only addresses the city, using feminine singular forms, the third masculine plural object ("them") and possessive ("their") suffixes are unexpected in 3:19d. The return to masculine plural, however, recalls the book's main imperatives (2:1, 3; 3:8), which refer to the faithful remnant from Judah and other lands. It also points back to the masculine plural group "Israel" that Zephaniah urged to "shout" (3:14b) in view of the certainty of their coming salvation (3:15). This newly redefined "Israel" is nothing less than the reconstituted people of God from all the nations (3:9–10) who together make up the "daughter" city of Zephaniah's "Zion/Jerusalem" and who now sing and rejoice (3:14a, c, d).[176] As such, the "lame" and "banished" city that YHWH has saved and assembled (3:19b–c) is indeed filled with members whom he will now purposefully position.

Some interpret 3:19 to say that the onlooking

Zephaniah, 109; Berlin, *Zephaniah*, 147; O'Connor, *Hebrew Verse Structure*, 262; Sweeney, *Zephaniah*, 207; Patterson, *Nahum, Habakkuk, Zephaniah*, 343–44.

171. Ball, *Rhetorical Study of Zephaniah*, 196, 295; cf. Gerleman, *Zephanja*, 66.

172. Roberts, *Nahum, Habakkuk, and Zephaniah*, 219; cf. Calvin, "Habakkuk, Zephaniah, Haggai," 309, 311; House, *Zephaniah*, 126. Similarly, Ben Zvi (*The Book of Zephaniah*, 258–59) aligns Zeph 3:19d with Josh 8:11; 1 Kgs 14:24; Jer 25:26; 31:40; and Ezek 45:16a—all texts in which GKC views the presence of an article as "doubtful" because it is "found before a noun already determined in some other way" yet, "being usual after כָּל־, has been mechanically added" (GKC, §127f, g).

173. A third option reads the final words after the *zaqeph*

qaton as their own clause and leaves the relationship of the two parts undefined: "And I will place them for praise and for a name; in all the earth was/is their shame." Its weaknesses are the that it introduces a strong sense of disjunction and unnaturally requires this future-dominated context to have past or present time in the second clause.

174. Cf. Motyer, "Zephaniah," 961.

175. So also Keil, "Twelve Minor Prophets," 10:463 (2:163).

176. Against Renz, who believes the end of Zeph 3:19 is "more narrowly focused than v. 9 in that it is only concerned with the reputation of the Judahite remnant" (Renz, *Books of Nahum, Habakkuk, and Zephaniah*, 642), after 3:8 the text equates the remnant of Israel with those from the nations, now in Jerusalem, whom YHWH has transformed.

world will admire and acclaim those God redeemed. For example, the NIV translates 3:19d: "I will give them praise and honor in every land where they have suffered shame" (cf. NET, CSB). Truly, in many closely associated texts, God promises to exalt his own before the eyes of rebel nations (e.g., Isa 56:5; 62:2–4).[177] Yet the glory of Jerusalem will be the glory YHWH displays through her: "But on you YHWH will rise, and his glory will be seen on you. And nations will walk to your light, and kings to the brightness of your rising" (60:2–3).

While the preposition לְ ("to, for") can mark the direct object of the verb (e.g., Lev 19:18; Deut 9:27; Jer 31:34),[178] in Zeph 3:19d the preposition לְ plus noun construction more likely expresses purpose, such that YHWH "will place them *for* praise and *for* a name" (וְשַׂמְתִּים לִתְהִלָּה וּלְשֵׁם).[179] Indeed, praise and a name will in some way relate to the remnant, but the acclaim is not necessarily limited to them. Several parallel texts support this reading.

Jeremiah elaborates on Moses's earlier promise (Deut 26:19; cf. 28:10) and offers the two closest parallel texts to Zeph 3:19d. Both suggest that the honor God's people enjoy results in onlookers exalting *him* above all. Early in Jeremiah's ministry, YHWH announced that he set his affections on Israel and Judah "that they might be *to me* for a people and for a name and for praise and for glory" (לִהְיוֹת לִי לְעָם וּלְשֵׁם וְלִתְהִלָּה וּלְתִפְאָרֶת); nevertheless, "They would not listen" (Jer 13:11). Similarly,

in a text similar to Zeph 3:19d, YHWH asserts through Jeremiah that the eschatological Jerusalem "will be *to me* for a name of joy, for praise, and for glory before all the nations of the earth" (וְהָיְתָה לִי לְשֵׁם שָׂשׂוֹן לִתְהִלָּה וּלְתִפְאֶרֶת לְכֹל גּוֹיֵי הָאָרֶץ, 33:9).

Isaiah had foreseen that God's new creational work will "be to YHWH for a name" (וְהָיָה לַיהוָה לְשֵׁם, Isa 55:13). And YHWH would pledge through Ezekiel's new covenant promise, "And I will display as holy my great name—the one profaned by the nations" (וְקִדַּשְׁתִּי אֶת־שְׁמִי הַגָּדוֹל הַמְחֻלָּל בַּגּוֹיִם, Ezek 36:23; cf. 39:25). Zechariah, too, would foresee that on the future day in which YHWH would save his people, the remnant flock of God will be "like the jewels of a crown" that will radiate "*his* goodness" (טוּבוֹ) and "*his* beauty" (יָפְיוֹ) (Zech 9:16–17)![180]

Sweeney rightly concludes that God exalting his people "will provide a basis by which YHWH will be praised and recognized throughout the entire world."[181] In Shepherd's words, "The LORD will give his people a 'name' (i.e., renown) among the nations, precisely because they will truly bear his name. . . . He is acting for the sake of his name, which the people bear."[182]

The sphere in which the redeemed remnant will magnify YHWH is "in all the earth, their [place of] shame" (בְּכָל־הָאָרֶץ בָּשְׁתָּם, Zeph 3:19d). In the book, אֶרֶץ refers both to the "earth" broadly (1:18; 2:11; 3:8, 20b) and to specific national "land" more restric-

---

177. Cf. Isa 60:18; 62:6–7; 65:15; 66:22; Rom 2:29; 1 Cor 4:5; 1 Pet 1:7; 5:4.

178. According to Joüon and Muraoka, this function occurs most often in later biblical Hebrew, likely under the influence of Aramaic (Joüon, §125k). They see it, for example, in 1 Chr 16:37; 22:19; 25:1; 29:22; 2 Chr 6:42; 17:3–4; 20:3; 31:21; 34:3; Ezra 8:16. Cf. Williams and Beckman, *Williams' Hebrew Syntax*, §273b; *BHRG*, §39.11(2).

179. Cf. Gen 22:7; 31:52. For לְ expressing purpose with a noun, see Williams and Beckman, *Williams' Hebrew Syntax*, §277; *BHRG*, §39.11(6.d).

180. See also Matt 5:16; 9:8; John 15:8; 2 Cor 9:13; Phil 1:11; 2 Thess 1:10. For a less developed form of this reading of Zeph 3:19–20b, see Jason S. DeRouchie, "Made for Praise: Zephaniah 3:20," in *Devotions on the Hebrew Bible: 54 Reflections to Inspire and Instruct*, ed. Milton Eng and Lee M. Fields (Grand Rapids: Zondervan, 2015), 108–10.

181. Sweeney, *The Twelve Prophets*, 524.

182. Shepherd, *Commentary on the Book of the Twelve*, 372, 375.

tively (2:3, 5). The full phrase כָּל־הָאָרֶץ specifically recalls the global punishment that both 1:18 and 3:8 highlighted and clarifies that the scope of the reversal in 3:19d is indeed worldwide (= "all the earth").

The whole earth was the sphere of the Jerusalem remnant's "shame" (בֹּשֶׁת), which appears to have derived in a twofold way. First, it related to the "oppressive" makeup of Zephaniah's Jerusalem, which was filled with leaders who did wrong yet never knew "shame" (בֹּשֶׁת) (3:1, 5). In the exile, Jerusalem's population was dispersed throughout the inhabited world, bringing the city under a "burden" and causing her to suffer "reproach" (3:18c). Even before this, though, God's people suffered "disgrace" and "abuses" from the nations at large (2:8, 10), such that YHWH's counter would be to humiliate "all the gods of the earth" (2:11). Thus, he promised the new Jerusalem that in the day of his rising, "*You will never be put to shame* [לֹא תֵבוֹשִׁי] on account of all your deeds by which you have revolted against me" (3:11a).

Second, the remnant's global shame stemmed from the tower of Babel's universal impact (Gen 11:1–9), the reversal of which the prophet alluded to in Zeph 3:9–10 (cf. 2:5–15). Humanity had sinned against YHWH (1:17), and so he would bring "a complete, even terrifying, end" to "all the inhabitants of the earth" (1:18). Yet God would hide his remnant from this wrath (2:3). This remnant consists of some native Israelites and some from other nations seeking YHWH (2:3; 3:9–10). YHWH would "change for [this remnant] a purified lip so that all of them may call on the name YHWH, to serve him with one shoulder" (3:9). These multiethnic, prayerful, afflicted, and needy worshipers would gather to and find refuge in YHWH's presence at the mountain of his holiness (3:10, 11–13) and together be God's new Israel

(3:14b). The global rebellion and shame would, therefore, be reversed as God would place this newly transformed people "for praise and for a name in all the earth" (3:19).[183]

(2) The Remnant's Complete Participation (3:20a–b)

YHWH stressed Jerusalem's complete salvation in 3:19. Now in 3:20, he says that the remnant will completely participate in this reality. Zephaniah 3:19 addressed the new Jerusalem with feminine singular language ("all who afflict *you*") and then developed the redemption of the lame and banished city in an impersonal way, speaking of placing "*them*" for fame and "*their* (place of) shame." By contrast, in 3:20a–b, YHWH returns to second masculine plural address ("you/your") and by this concludes with personal words of assurance to the faithful remnant using the same speech patterns with which the rest of the book issues its primary appeal to patiently pursue YHWH together (see the masculine plural imperatives in 2:1, 3; 3:8; cf. 3:14b).

The prepositional phrase בָּעֵת הַהִיא ("At that time") references 3:19 when YHWH "will save . . . and assemble" his broken and banished city. The second prepositional phrase (וּבָעֵת קַבְּצִי אֶתְכֶם, "even at the time of my assembling you") reinforces this temporal reference. The phrase itself is grammatically dislocated to the clause's end due to its length, and the infinitive construct of קבץ ("to assemble") recalls God's promised actions in 3:19. The non-fronted position of the *hiphil yiqtol* אָבִיא ("I will bring") marks the action as indicative and promissory.

The language again recalls the promise of Deut 30:4–5, where YHWH asserts of those who will be part of his new covenant work, "If *your banished*

---

183. Cf. Isa 29:22–23; 45:17; 61:7; Joel 2:26–27.

one [נִדַּחֲךָ] is at the end of the heavens, from there YHWH your God *will assemble you* [יְקַבֶּצְךָ], and from there he will take you. *And YHWH your God will bring you* [וֶהֱבִיאֲךָ] into the land that your fathers possessed, with the result that you will possess it." Like Zephaniah, other OT prophets draw on this promise, using both the *qal* of קבץ ("to assemble") and the *hiphil* of בוא ("to bring"), and they envisioned a final ingathering that includes repentant Israelites and individuals from other nations.[184]

Some scholars see Zephaniah's promise finding "immediate fulfillment in the return from the seventy years of exile."[185] However, while such a return typologically foreshadowed the greater return that would follow, it does not directly fulfill it. Such is clear because it was not accompanied by an international ingathering for punishment and renewal as signaled in Zeph 3:8–10 and pointed to in the temporal markers like "in that day" (3:16a) and "at that time" (3:19a, 20a).[186]

YHWH now uses a logical clause to restate from Zeph 3:19d the culminating thrust of his restorative, ingathering work. The reason why he will "bring" his people to himself is *because* (כִּי, "for") "I will give you for a name and for praise among all the peoples of the earth" (אֶתֵּן אֶתְכֶם לְשֵׁם וְלִתְהִלָּה

בְּכֹל עַמֵּי הָאָרֶץ). Beyond what was already affirmed in 3:19d, these words both personalize the pledge through second masculine plural address and emphasize God elevating his people for renown "among all the peoples of the earth" (בְּכֹל עַמֵּי הָאָרֶץ) (3:20b).

God will vindicate the very divine jealousy that drives the day of YHWH (1:18; 3:8) by majestically saving his saints before an onlooking enemy world (see the discussion at 3:19). Again, Zephaniah develops his new exodus motif by echoing the original event (cf. Exod 15:14–16). Moses had anticipated that Israel's perfect obedience to the Torah would have resulted in those outside standing in awe: "And all the peoples of the earth will see that the name YHWH has been called on you, and they will be afraid of you" (Deut 28:10). This will happen in YHWH's day, likely because God has now transformed his people through the perfect obedience of Christ. Timmer notes that in 3:20 the treatment of the outside onlookers as a group (using כל ["all"]) implies "that this final form of the 'peoples' no longer includes those who were to be transformed per 3:9."[187] The result is that "Zion's former enemies are either transformed (3:9) or, as in 3:13, 15, 19, 20, rendered incapable of further opposition and made the audience of Zion's final exaltation."[188]

---

184. The prophets tag the community members Israel's "offspring" (Isa 43:5), "the survivors of the nations" (45:20; cf. 49:18; 60:4; 66:18), Israel's "remnant," "house," and "people" (Jer 31:8; Ezek 36:24; 37:21; cf. 38:8; Zech 10:10), and God's scattered "sheep" (Ezek 34:13; cf. Isa 56:8; John 10:16; 11:52). See the commentary at Zeph 3:9–10 and God Incorporating Enemy Peoples in Its Biblical Context within Canonical Significance of Zeph 2:5–15.

185. Bailey, "Zephaniah," 499. Renz sees "initial fulfillment" of these promises in the initial return to the land and believes the author (who for Renz was Zephaniah's later disciple) would not have expected eschatological interpretations or application; nevertheless, he admits that the wording of Zeph 3:19–20 likely generated later readers' hope "for a future 'messianic age' whose contours could be filled out with the help of other texts" (Renz, *Books of Nahum, Habakkuk, and Zephaniah*, 645).

186. The Canonical and Theological Significance section will associate the initial fulfillment of this part of Zephaniah's oracle with God punishing Christ for the sins of the many and with God's new covenant ingathering of the church that Jesus's death ignites.

187. Timmer, *Non-Israelite Nations*, 165 and n51.

188. Timmer, *Non-Israelite Nations*, 165. Zephaniah envisions only two groups in 3:16–20: (1) the multiethnic Zion and (2) God's enemies who will recognize the new Zion's glory, not be able to harm God's saints permanently (cf. John 11:25–26), and bow down before YHWH as prisoners of war (Zeph 2:11; cf. Isa 45:23). Timmer incorrectly posits a third group who are neither YHWH's worshipers nor his enemies (p. 224).

Since the unit began in 3:16, Zephaniah has envisioned the day of YHWH having an inaugurated but not yet consummated state, with God redeeming his people in stages.[189] In that "day," those already "gathered" who are tempted to "fear" find hope in God's promise to fully "save" (Zeph 3:16–18). Zephaniah 3:19–20b now adds that, when YHWH assembles the faithful, he will give them positions of honor while a broader population of rebel observers continues to exist.

The book's beginning indicated that "everything from on the face of the ground" that YHWH will "gather" for eschatological judicial assessment and ultimately cut off includes the broader group (Zeph 1:2–3; cf. 1:17–18; 3:8). But here at the book's end, YHWH pledges that at the same time he will also "gather" (3:18), "assemble" (3:19c, 20a), and "bring" (3:20a) a righteous remnant for his name's sake. This remnant will temporarily reside amid hostile peoples whom he will ultimately overcome. God declares that this will happen "in my restoring your circumstances before your eyes" (בְּשׁוּבִי אֶת־שְׁבוּתֵיכֶם לְעֵינֵיכֶם). The prophet uses a similar phrase but with a singular noun in 2:7 when noting how YHWH would visit the house of Judah's remnant "and restore their circumstance" (וְשָׁב שְׁבוּתָם)—that is, return them to a state of covenant reconciliation and blessing.[190] The type-2 (with *yod*) plural noun suffix on שְׁבוּת (i.e., יכֶם)

occurs only in 3:20b and Ezek 16:53. This irregularity moves some grammarians to treat the form as a mere scribal error.[191] Regardless, there is no substantive difference in meaning between the singular and plural usage. Both Zeph 3:20b and Ezek 16:53 are restoration prophecies, and the latter explicitly highlights the eschatological people's global diversity.

YHWH promises the restoration will happen "before your eyes" (לְעֵינֵיכֶם) to emphasize the experience's personal and direct nature.[192] It may also reinforce what God means by setting his people "for a name and for praise" since their salvation will result in their witnessing "all the coastlands of the nations" recognize that YHWH is indeed God (Zeph 2:11; cf. Zech 14:9).[193] Nevertheless, if YHWH's salvation is still a distant future from Zephaniah's perspective, how can God assert that the faithful remnant among the prophet's contemporaries will personally witness this work? While Zephaniah could be thinking of the faithful remnant only collectively and representatively, Robertson proposes that Zephaniah may be foreshadowing the resurrection just as YHWH did through other prophets.[194] In such an instance, Zephaniah may have in mind something akin to the souls of faithful saints who were martyred or who died of natural causes but who "came alive and reigned with Christ a thousand years" (Rev 20:4).

---

189. The NT testifies to the kingdom's inaugurated but not yet final status (e.g., Rom 8:18–24; Eph 1:3–14; Heb 9:28). For a defense that what Zephaniah envisions begins with Christ's first coming, see the discussion of The Inaugurated Kingdom in the Canonical and Theological Significance section below.

190. See the discussion at Zeph 2:7 for why I render שְׁבוּת as "circumstance" and see it as a restoration of former well-being (e.g., NRSVue, NASB20, NET, ESV, NIV, CSB) rather than as a reversal of "captivity" (e.g., LXX, Vulgate, Tg. Neb., Peshitta, KJV). See also Bracke, "*šûb šebût*," 233–44.

191. So GKC, §91.l; cf. Hans Bauer, Pontus Leander, and Paul Kahle, *Historische Grammatik der Hebräischen Sprache des Alten Testamentes* (Halle: Niemeyer, 1922), §29.b'.

192. Motyer, "Zephaniah," 962. Both Smith and Vlaardingerbroek propose the phrase "before your eyes" means "in your own lifetime" (J. M. P. Smith, "Book of Zephaniah," 260; Vlaardingerbroek, *Zephaniah*, 217). However, the context suggests that YHWH is envisioning a personal experience *after* this present lifetime.

193. See also Rom 14:11; Phil 2:10–11.

194. Robertson, *Books of Nahum, Habakkuk, and Zephaniah*, 346–47. See Deut 32:39; Job 19:25–26; Isa 26:19; Dan 12:2; Hos 6:1–3; cf. Matt 22:32.

Canonical and Theological Significance

Jesus, the World's Savior-King

The discussion on Zeph 3:8–10 noted how Jesus's death and resurrection and the church's birth at Pentecost initially fulfill Zephaniah's vision of the day of YHWH as both punishment and renewal. John 12:13, 15 alluding to Zeph 3:14–15 also supports this conclusion.

Long ago, Jerome claimed that at least some of Zephaniah's prophecies had already been accomplished since the NT associates Zech 9:9 with Jesus's triumphal entry, and the call to rejoice in Zeph 3:14 resembles the call in Zech 9:9.[195] Scholars often see John's account of Jesus's triumphal entry as citing Ps 118:25–26 [LXX 117:25–26] and Zech 9:9: "They took branches of palm trees, and they went out to meet him and shouted, 'Hosanna! Blessed is he who comes in the name of the Lord, even *Israel's King*!' And after Jesus found a young donkey, he sat on it, just as it is written, '*Do not be afraid, daughter of Zion*; look, your king is coming, sitting on a donkey's colt" (John 12:13–15). However, some interpreters miss that Ps 118 does not include the phrase "Israel's King" and that the opening charge in Zech 9:9 is actually "rejoice" rather than "fear not." These differences indicate that John is also alluding to Zeph 3:14–15,[196] the only place in the OT that groups "Israel's King," "never fear," and "daughter of Zion."[197]

Tachick rightly sees at least three hermeneutical applications of Zeph 3:14–15 in John's narrative. First, the apostle marked Jesus's coming triumph as directly fulfilling Zephaniah's prediction of YHWH's end-times reign.[198] Second, the ordering in Zeph 3:8–20 may have informed John's account: (1) Jerusalem joyfully shouting (John 12:13; cf. Zeph 3:14) (2) because of Jesus's kingship (John 12:13; cf. Zeph 3:15c); (3) exhorting the daughter of Zion to not fear (John 12:15; cf. Zeph 3:15d with 3:14a); (4) the world going after Jesus (John 12:19; cf. Zeph 3:9–10, 19–20).[199] Third, despite

---

195. Jerome, *Commentaries on the Twelve Prophets*, ed. Thomas P. Scheck, 2 vols., *Ancient Christian Texts* (Downers Grove, IL: InterVarsity Press, 2016), 613.

196. See esp. Tachick, *Use of Zephaniah 3 in John 12*; cf. Raymond E. Brown, *The Gospel According to John (I–XII): Introduction, Translation, and Notes*, AB (New Haven: Yale University Press, 1966), 458–63; Robertson, *Books of Nahum, Habakkuk, and Zephaniah*, 388; A. C. Brunson, *Psalm 118 in the Gospel of John: An Intertextual Study on the New Exodus Pattern in the Theology of John*, WUNT 2.158 (Tübingen: Mohr Siebeck, 2003), 225–36, 258, 277; Ruth Sheridan, *Retelling Scripture: 'The Jews' and the Scriptural Citations in John 1:19–12:15*, BibInt 110 (Leiden: Brill, 2012), 222, 226–28; Adam Kubiś, *The Book of Zechariah in the Gospel of John*, EBib 64 (Pendé: Gabalda, 2012), 82–92.

197. The parallel exists only in the Hebrew text of Zeph 3:15d. The LXX read אַל־תִּירְאִי ("you will not *fear*") as אַל־תִּרְאִי ("you will not *see*"), from the root ראה ("to see") instead of ירא ("to be afraid, fear"), resulting in the translation οὐκ ὄψῃ κακὰ οὐκέτι ("You will not see evil any longer"). For the connections between Zeph 3:14–15 and Zech 9:9–10, see Shepherd, *Commentary on the Book of the Twelve*, 373–74.

198. Tachick, *Use of Zephaniah 3 in John 12*, 176–77; cf. 202–7.

199. Tachick, *Use of Zephaniah 3 in John 12*, 178–81. Besides Zeph 3:8–20, Tachick affirms Brendsel's assertion that the apostle also used Isa 52:7–12 as a blueprint for Jesus's entry. See Daniel J. Brendsel, *"Isaiah Saw His Glory": The Use of Isaiah 52–53 in John 12*, BZNW 208 (Berlin: de Gruyter, 2014), 181.

Jerusalem's worshipers' probable nationalistic intentions, John's portrayal ironically exalts Jesus as the world's saving King and Satisfier.[200]

Theologically, John's use of Zeph 3:14–15 closely associates King Jesus with YHWH. With Jesus's entering Jerusalem, God began to fulfill Zephaniah's prediction of YHWH's arrival,[201] the end of exile, and the dawn of the new creation.[202] Jesus's correspondence to God in this text is but one more in a Gospel that proclaims Jesus's divinity (see esp. John 1:1, 18; 20:28–29).[203] As in Ps 118, Zephaniah (esp. 3:15, 17), and Zech 9, John maintains the Warrior-King motif by treating Jesus as both the agent of salvation (ὡσαννά, "Hosanna!" = הוֹשִׁיעָה נָּא, "Please save!") coming "in the name of the Lord" (John 12:13; cf. 12:47) and the agent of "judgment" defeating the chief "enemy," "the ruler of this world" (12:31).[204]

Furthermore, through his narrative, John incorporates Zephaniah's motif of a multiethnic ingathering.[205] Unlike Matt 21:5, John omits from his quotation of Zech 9:9 the detail that the king was coming "to you" (לָךְ/σοι) (John 12:15), which "avoids an ethnic limitation on Jesus's kingship."[206] With this, after the celebration at Jesus's entry into Jerusalem, the Pharisees declare that "the world [ὁ κόσμος] has gone away after him" (12:19), using a term that in John's writings usually means "people everywhere without racial distinction but who are lost and in rebellion against God" (e.g., 3:16–17; 12:46–47).[207] We also learn that "certain Greeks" wished "to see Jesus" (12:20–21), which validates John's global ingathering theme (cf. 10:15–16; 11:50–52; 12:11, 19).[208] Jesus's affirmation, "And I, after I have been lifted up from the earth,

---

200. Tachick, *Use of Zephaniah 3 in John 12*, 173–76.

201. Thus, in Christ YHWH is in our midst and thereby begins to fulfill Zephaniah's expectation that "Israel's King, YHWH, is in your midst" (Zeph 3:15). Furthermore, Jesus is the temple (John 2:21), who at Pentecost (see comments above on Zeph 3:9–10) comes to indwell the church through his Spirit (Matt 28:28; John 14:16–20; Rom 8:9–10; cf. Rev 21:3), thus fulfilling God's eschatological promise of divine presence (Ezek 37:23–24 with 2 Cor 6:16; cf. Ps 46:5; Isa 54:4–8; 57:14–19; 62:10–12; Joel 4:17, 21[3:17, 21]).

202. Tachick, *Use of Zephaniah 3 in John 12*, 181. No OT texts, whether Hebrew or Greek, apply the full phrase "Israel's king" (מֶלֶךְ יִשְׂרָאֵל / ὁ βασιλεὺς τοῦ Ἰσραήλ) to the coming Messiah (though they imply the reality). It does appear in some intertestamental texts (e.g., Pss. Sol. 17:21, 32, 42; cf. Sib. Or. 5:108) and NT texts (Matt 27:42//Mark 15:32; John 1:49; 12:13). Bauckham claims Jesus being "king" in John 12:13 is a Davidic messianic title, but he does not mention Zeph 3:14–15 (Richard Bauckham, "Messianism According to the Gospel of John," in *Challenging Perspectives on the Gospel of John*, ed. John Lierman, WUNT 2.219 [Tübingen: Mohr Siebeck, 2006], 59).

203. See Andreas J. Köstenberger, *A Theology of John's Gospel and Letters: The Word, the Christ, the Son of God*, Biblical The-

ology of the New Testament (Grand Rapids: Zondervan, 2009), 356–61; cf. Tachick, *Use of Zephaniah 3 in John 12*, 181–88.

204. Tachick, *Use of Zephaniah 3 in John 12*, 196–202. While the singular אֹיֵב ("enemy") in Zeph 3:15 likely refers collectively to all those who instigated and brought about Jerusalem's divine punishment, John may have drawn from it to identify the evil one as the ultimate transcendent "enemy" whom God promised to overcome.

205. Tachick, *Use of Zephaniah 3 in John 12*, 189–95.

206. Tachick, *Use of Zephaniah 3 in John 12*, 189.

207. D. A. Carson, *The Gospel according to John*, PNTC (Grand Rapids: Eerdmans, 1991), 435; cf. Lars Kierspel, *The Jews and the World in the Fourth Gospel: Parallelism, Function, and Context*, WUNT 2.220 (Tübingen: Mohr Siebeck, 2006), 157–60, 177.

208. Tachick, *Use of Zephaniah 3 in John 12*, 191. For a defense that these "Greeks" are Gentiles (cf. Acts 16:1; 21:28; Rom 1:16) and not Jews of the diaspora, see W. E. Moore, "Sir, We Wish to See Jesus—Was This an Occasion of Temptation?," *SJT* 20 (1967): 78; Johannes Beutler, "Greeks Come to See Jesus (John 12:20f)," *Bib* 71 (1990): 342–43; Carson, *The Gospel according to John*, 435; Andreas J. Köstenberger, *John*, BECNT (Grand Rapids: Baker Academic, 2004), 377.

will draw *all* to me" (12:32)—that is, all kinds of people without distinction, whether Jews or Gentiles—follows this statement. Thus, the evangelist links Jesus's life and ministry to Zephaniah's vision of the tower of Babel's reversal and the ingathering and transformation of a global community of worshipers celebrating before God in the new Jerusalem (Zeph 3:8–20). As the high priest Caiaphas had earlier prophesied, "Jesus would die for the [Jewish] nation, and not for the nation only, but also to gather into one the children of God who are scattered abroad" (John 11:51–52; cf. Isa 49:6).

Finally, John's allusion to Zeph 3:14–15 indicates that Jesus's entry into Jerusalem inaugurates Zephaniah's eschatological day of YHWH. The literary context supports this conceptual link.[209] Specifically, John notes that Jesus's entry as Warrior-King and worldwide Savior triggers the "hour" (ὥρα) of his glorification (John 12:27–28) and the "now" of both the world and its ruler's judgment (12:31). The apostle directly relates the "hour" and the "now" to what Jesus's death would accomplish (12:32–33; cf. 3:14–15; 8:28).[210] John often uses the term "hour" (ὥρα) to recall LXX Daniel's latter-day prophecies, which commonly use the singular or plural form of "hour" for the end time.[211] Only at the time of Jesus's death did this "hour" come (12:23, 27, 31).[212] Within John, this is the time for his glorification (12:23, 27; 17:1), departure from this world to return to the Father (13:1), and scattering of his disciples (16:32).[213]

Conceptually, all these realities align with Zephaniah's stress in 3:8–20 that on his day YHWH would both punish and renew by destroying his enemies and restoring his redeemed. Zephaniah associated these realities with "the day of YHWH" (יוֹם־יְהוָה/ἡ ἡμέρα κυρίου),[214] which he also referred to with phrases like "at that time" (בָּעֵת הַהִיא/ἐν ἐκείνῃ τῇ ἡμέρᾳ, cf. Zeph 1:12; 3:19–20). John prefers the language of "hour." Yet, he does mark Jesus's movement toward Jerusalem with a mention of "the day" (τὴν ἡμέραν) of his coming burial (John 12:7), which apparently foreshadows other mentions of "the last day" (τῇ ἐσχάτῃ ἡμέρᾳ) (e.g., 6:39–40; 7:37; 12:48).

---

209. Tachick, *Use of Zephaniah 3 in John 12*, 202–7.

210. Carson, *The Gospel according to John*, 439.

211. See Dan 8:17 (עֶת־קֵץ, "end time"/ὥραν καιροῦ, "an appropriate hour"); 8:19 (מוֹעֵד קֵץ, "appointed end"/ὥρας καιροῦ, "appropriate hours"); 11:6 (עִתִּים, "times"/ὥρας, "hours"); 11:35 (מוֹעֵד, "appointed [time]"/ὥρας, "hours"); 11:40 (עֵת קֵץ, "end time"/ὥραν συντελείας, "hours of consummation"); 11:45 (עַד־קִצּוֹ, "unto its end"/ὥρα τῆς συντελείας αὐτοῦ, "hour of its consummation"); 12:1 (בָּעֵת הַהִיא, "at that time"/ κατὰ τὴν ὥραν ἐκείνη, "according to that hour"); 12:45 (לְקֵץ, "to the end"/γάρ εἰσιν ἡμέραι καὶ ὧραι εἰς ἀναπλήρωσιν συντελείας, "for there are days and hours until the fulfillment of the end"). See Stefanos Mihalios, *The Danielic Eschatological Hour in the Johannine Literature*, LNTS 436 (London: T&T Clark, 2011), especially noting pp. 124–39 for his argument that Dan 12:1 stands behind the use of "hour" in John 12:23, 27; cf. G. K. Beale, "The Old Testament Background of the 'Last Hour' in 1 John 2,18," *Bib* 92.2 (2011): 231–54. For the translation "until *its* end" in Dan 11:45, see Jason Thomas Parry, "Desolation of the Temple and Messianic Enthronement in Daniel 11:36–12:3," *JETS* 54.3 (2011): 516–17.

212. Jesus's "hour" was yet to come prior to his death (John 2:4; 7:30; 8:20), but it was predicted (4:21, 23; 5:25, 28; cf. 16:25, 32).

213. Elsewhere we also learn that Jesus's eschatological "hour" was the time when the antichrist and numerous antichrists would rise (1 John 2:18), when he would return to the earth like a thief (Rev 3:3), when he would preserve his own through great tribulation (3:10), and when God will judge and harvest the earth (14:7, 15).

214. See Zeph 1:7, 14; cf. 1:8–10, 15–16, 18; 2:2–3; 3:8, 11, 16.

The Inaugurated Kingdom

An apparent feature of Zeph 3:16–20 was the prophet's portrayal of the day of YHWH as occurring in stages, such that the global ingathering and final salvation will not be simultaneous. Even after YHWH has "gathered" his remnant (3:18a), those "afflicting" Jerusalem (3:19a) will still be present to cause "fear" (3:16b). Nevertheless, "as a Mighty One," YHWH "will save" (3:17b) and do so by placing his redeemed "for praise and for a name" (3:19d) in the context of "all the peoples of the earth" (3:20b). All this will happen "in that day" (3:16a) when YHWH rises "as a witness" (3:8a) and sets out both to punish the rebels of the nations (3:8b–c) and to deliver a remnant offspring from the same (3:9–10).

This vision of an inaugurated but not final day of YHWH finds fulfillment as the NT depicts the period of the church in the new creation—a reality that in this transition of the ages is both already (2 Cor 5:17; Gal 6:15; cf. Rom 6:4) and not yet (2 Pet 3:13; Rev 21:1–2; cf. Rom 8:20–22). In this day, various shades and levels of dread and desire develop in stages, and salvation bears past (Eph 2:8), present (1 Cor 1:18), and future (Rom 5:9) elements. In Christ's first coming, the future has entered the middle of history, overcoming the old age, old covenant, and old creation with the new age, new covenant, and new creation. Jesus brings a seismic shift in redemptive history, as promise moves to fulfillment and what the OT anticipated is now realized (cf. Luke 16:16; Gal 3:24–25; 4:4).

Jesus's arrival brought the dawning light of the new creation (Matt 4:16–17; John 8:12), and those in Christ have already tasted "the powers of the age to come" (Heb 6:5). Indeed, "He appeared once for all at the end of the ages for the nullification of sin through the sacrifice of himself. . . . The Christ, having been offered once to bear sins for the many, will appear a second time without reference to sin to those eagerly awaiting him for salvation" (9:26, 28). When compared to the old covenant, Christ "has obtained a superior ministry, just as the covenant he mediates is better" and "is enacted on the basis of better promises" (8:6). Furthermore, "by a single offering he has perfected forever those who are being sanctified" (10:14).

Jesus has already delivered us from "the present evil age" (Gal 1:4; cf. Col 2:15), yet in such a way that there is still more to be revealed. "The sufferings of the present time are not worth comparing to the glory that is about to be revealed to us" (Rom 8:18) when this cursed creation "will be set free from its slavery unto corruption into the freedom of the glory of the children of God" (8:21). For believers, God has already "blessed us with all spiritual blessing in the heavenly places in Christ" (Eph 1:3), but the full enjoyment of this "inheritance" awaits "the redemption of the possession," when God will claim his own (1:14).

A vision of future salvation generates present joy, even amid various trials. Therefore, as Christian's await their future "inheritance that is imperishable and undefiled and unfading, kept in heaven," they are to "rejoice with joy unspeakable and filled with glory, obtaining the outcome of [their] faith—salvation of souls" (1 Pet 1:4, 9). And Christians "rejoice in hope" (Rom 12:12) and "exult on the basis of the hope of the glory of God" (5:2). What we dread or long for tomorrow, changes who we are today (2 Pet 1:4), such that future-oriented desire becomes present delight. This resembles Zephaniah's logic in 3:14–15 where he charges the faithful remnant to "sing aloud," "shout," "be merry and exult" with deep assurance as if the Warrior-King's victory, salvation, and joyous song were already fully realized. This hope sustains and brings joy, even under trial (cf. Phil 4:4–7; Jas 1:2–4).

A Proper Response

Stand Fearless Before Others and Persevere in Hope

Because "Israel's King," YHWH our God, is *already* with us through Jesus (Zeph 3:15, 17; Matt 1:23; 28:20), we *already* should not fear evil or give up (Zeph 3:13, 15–16; Matt 10:28; John 12:15). In the death of Christ, God reconciled his enemies, making them his friends (John 15:5; Rom. 5:10). And if the living God, to whom every knee will bow (Zeph 2:11; Isa 45:23), "is for us, who is against us? Indeed, he who did not spare his own Son but gave him up for us all, how will he not also with him graciously give us all things?" (Rom 8:31–32).

We still await the day when YHWH will finish dealing with all who afflict us (Zeph 3:19). However, through the cursing of Christ (Rom 8:3; Gal 3:13), God has *already* disarmed the enemies that once stood against us (Zeph 3:15; Col 2:15), thus making even our physical death gain (Phil 1:28; cf. Mark 10:29–30; John 11:25). "Since, therefore, the children share in blood and flesh, he even likewise partook of the same, so that through death he might destroy the one having power of death, that is, the devil, and might set free those, as many as were by fear of death through all of life, held in slavery" (Heb 2:14–15). Knowing that God is so much with us and for us, our souls can find rest and push ahead in fearless hope.

On the promise in Zeph 3:13 that "there will be none who cause trembling," Luther noted, "It is the glory of the kingdom of Christ that we are joyful and at peace through Christ, who has reconciled us to God; not that the cross will no longer be there in the future, not that the world and Satan are not going to set their traps for us; but that against all these the conscience is strengthened and secure, so that all these trouble it not at all."[215] May these realities embolden God's people to willingly proclaim the good news in the hardest places among the most difficult peoples on the planet, hoping in YHWH and not fearing others. And may we increasingly flourish in holiness, confident that God is already completely committed to us (Zeph 3:13, 15).

---

215. Luther, "Lectures on Zephaniah," 358.

Celebrate Jesus as Israel's Hoped-for Savior-King, Whose Arrival Initiates Zephaniah's Day of YHWH

Zephaniah commands that we "sing aloud, shout, be merry and exult!" (Zeph 3:14). He commands such rejoicing because YHWH is "Israel's King" who would heal the disabled, gather the banished, and deliver his multiethnic remnant from evil and oppression on the day of YHWH (3:9–10, 15, 17, 19). Within the Book of the Twelve, many of the prophets assert that God's future victory and peace-producing reign would happen through a human Davidic royal representative, who himself would be called "King" (e.g., Hos 3:5; Mic 5:2–5; Zech 9:9).

Also, as noted above, John identifies "Israel's King" to be Jesus (John 12:13, 15). His life-saving, disability-overcoming, and outcast-gathering ministry (5:3–9; 11:50–51; Matt 8:16–17) attracts the whole world (John 12:19–21). At Jesus's triumphal entry, the crowd's cry of "Hosanna" ("Please save!") (12:13) and his command "fear not" (12:15) together mark him as the one through whom God's wrath would be averted and the evil one overcome. These remarks also clarify Jesus's stress later in the narrative: "Now is the judgment of this world; now will the ruler of this world be cast out. And I, when I am lifted from the earth, will draw all people to myself" (12:31–32). Jesus's death and resurrection initially remove Zephaniah's "judgments" and overcome the "enemy" (Zeph 3:15). The statement regarding Jesus's being lifted from the earth recalls John 3 where Jesus declared his coming crucifixion to be the only means for moving one from death to life and for saving one from God's wrath (John 3:14–17, 36).

Embrace the Truth That YHWH Seeks His Own Glory by Liberating the Lame

At Zephaniah's close, God declares the ultimate end for which he delivers and transforms his faithful remnant: *his* glory. He will take and transform the "lame" and "banished" (3:19b–c)—those sick and separated—and place them "for praise and for a name" resulting in his veneration (Zeph 3:19d). Indeed, the very reason Yahweh will "assemble" and save through the great second exodus is *because* (כִּי) he is committed to shaping a God-treasuring community that will radiate *his* worth "among all the peoples of the earth" (3:20). He redeems an international community of supplicants whose transformed speech he enables to "call" upon *his* name to "serve" *him* together, bringing *him* the "offering" of which *he* is worthy (3:9–10). Assembled on "the mountain of [*his*] holiness," the "afflicted and needy" "take refuge" in *his* name and turn from sin (3:11–13), singing aloud and shouting and rejoicing because YHWH has acted (3:14–15).

Too often Christians affirm their desire to be God-centered but then live as if YHWH is man-centered. However, for him to remain God, he must exalt his glory above all else. "I am YHWH; that is my name, and my glory to another I will not give, nor my praise to graven images" (Isa 42:8; cf. 48:9, 11). "Stop regarding man in whose nostrils is breath, for of what account is he?" (2:22; cf. 40:15, 17). YHWH is truly preeminent over all—the Source, Sustainer, and ultimate End of all things. "For from him and through him and to him are all things. To him be glory forever" (Rom 11:36; cf. Heb 11:3). And in this context, because he is indeed the only Savior (Ps 146:3; Isa 43:11) and the highest Pleasure (Ps 16:11; Matt 13:44), he engages in the greatest act of love by calling us to live for his glory.

When YHWH rescues us who once were lacking his glory (Rom 3:23), our response must be to live in a way that makes much of God. YHWH's greatest passion (i.e., his glory) must become our greatest passion. Only then are we truly imaging him (Gen 1:26–27; Rom 8:29). Like the "mass of witnesses" of the past whose lives testified to the trustworthiness and worth of the living God (Heb 12:1; cf. ch. 11), God now calls us to be "those of whom the world was not worthy" (11:38; cf. 12:1–3), for "through Jesus Christ, to whom be glory unto forever," God works in us "what is pleasing in his sight" (13:21). "So, whether you eat or drink, or whatever you do, do all to the glory of God" (1 Cor 10:31; cf. Col 3:17, 23), and may we all ever bear witness to him, whether by life or by death (Acts 1:8; cf. Phil 1:20–21).

Peter prayed that the genuine faith of the elect exiles may result "unto praise and glory and honor at the revelation of Jesus Christ" (1 Pet 1:7), and he promises that "after the Great Shepherd appears, you will receive the crown unfading of glory" (5:4). Nevertheless, he also clarifies that the acclaim will be given not to Jerusalem's new community but *to the Lord*, as the onlookers observe the remnant's good works and "glorify God at the day of visitation" (2:12; cf. Matt 5:16). We glorify God when we display him as Sovereign, Savior, and Satisfier, trust him as Deliverer and Provider, surrender to him as Lord, follow him as the all-wise Guide, treasure and honor him as infinitely valuable, live for his fame, and depend on him for help. God loves his glory, and so should we, above all else.

Delight in YHWH Who Saves His People from His Wrath and from All Evil

God's bride rejoices in his goodness (Zeph 3:14–15; cf. Isa 65:18; Jer 31:10–14) and matches his promised mirth-filled melody (Zeph 3:17; cf. Ps 147:11) line for line. The more impressive the pardon, the more splendid the praise! As a "Mighty One" (Zeph 3:17), he is praiseworthy. Even more than in Zephaniah's day, we should celebrate our great Savior and the salvation he has *already* secured (3:14–15), knowing that doing so magnifies his worth and greatness (3:19–20). Our joy today is not based on present appearances but on what God has already done and promises to do (Hab 3:18–19; Rom 5:2–5; 1 Pet 5:10). Indeed, *already* God "has subjected all things under his feet" (Eph 1:22; cf. Heb 2:8). "Having disarmed the rulers and authorities," God has *already* "disgraced them in public, having triumphed over them" by the cross (Col 2:15; cf. Zeph 3:11, 19). *Already* "God's love has been poured into our hearts through the Holy Spirit who has been given to us" (Rom 5:5), such that God is truly in our midst (cf. Zeph 3:15, 17). God has *already* begun to gather his remnant (John 10:16; 11:51–52; cf. Zeph 3:18–20), has *already* inaugurated the new creation (2 Cor 5:17; Gal 6:15; cf. Zeph 3:9–10), and has *already* secured the complete and future victory for which Zephaniah rejoiced (3:14–15).

Jesus promised his disciples that some would be martyred but that "not a hair of your head will perish" (Luke 21:16, 18; cf. John 11:25). He urged them to deny themselves and suffer with him, yet he assured them that "whoever loses his life for my sake and the gospel will save it" (Mark 8:34–35). And he compelled them to a life of radical loss "for my sake and for the sake of the gospel," promising that they would "receive a hundredfold now . . . with persecutions, and in the age to come eternal life" (10:29–30). What we hope for tomorrow changes who we are today, and God's promising pleasure for all who dependently endure through pain provides an amazing motivation for holiness (2 Pet 1:4).

As was true for Jesus (Isa 53:11; Heb 12:2), the future joy for which we aim becomes our present joy that sustains (cf. Heb 10:34; 11:6, 26; 12:3). "Israel's King" and "Mighty One" who will destroy death as the last enemy (1 Cor 15:26), and who will completely save and sing over his redeemed desires to satisfy us with his goodness (Zeph 3:14–15, 17). Our gladness redounds to his glory (3:19–20), so may we today patiently pursue YHWH together in joy, embracing the Savior's invitation to satisfaction.

PART IV

Zephaniah 3:20c

The Subscription of the Savior's Invitation to Satisfaction

Main Idea of Zephaniah 3:20c

The subscription to the book declares that all the precedes was fully from YHWH.

I. The Superscription of the Savior's Invitation to Satisfaction (1:1)

II. The Setting of the Savior's Invitation to Satisfaction: A Call to Revere YHWH in View of His Coming Day (1:2–18)

III. The Substance of the Savior's Invitation to Satisfaction: Charges to Seek YHWH Together and ·to Wait (2:1–3:20b)

   III.1 Stage 1: The Appeal to Seek YHWH Together to Avoid Punishment (2:1–3:7)

   III.2 Stage 2: The Appeal to Wait for YHWH to Enjoy Salvation (3:8–20b)

➡ **IV. The Subscription of the Savior's Invitation to Satisfaction (3:20c)**

Literary Context of Zephaniah 3:20c

Echoing the superscription's characterization of the oracle as "YHWH's word" (1:1), the book now concludes with the brief declaration, "YHWH has spoken" (3:20c). This subscription follows the book body, which includes both the setting (1:2–18) and the substance (2:1–3:20b) of the Savior's invitation to satisfaction.

9
CHAPTER

Zephaniah 3:20c

A. YHWH Has Spoken

Main Idea of the Passage

Zephaniah's book concludes with the prophet indicating that what precedes was fully from God: "YHWH has spoken" (אָמַר יְהוָה).

> IV. **The Subscription of the Savior's Invitation to Satisfaction (3:20c)**
>
> →   A. **YHWH Has Spoken (3:20c)**

Literary Context

Because the whole book stands as a single oracle, the formula relates to all that precedes.

Translation and Exegetical Outline

(See page 310.)

Zephaniah 3:20c

20c [Y]	אָמַ֖ר יְהוָֽה׃	YHWH has spoken.

IV. The Subscription of the Savior's Invitation to Satisfaction (3:20c)

A. YHWH Has Spoken (3:20c)

Explanation of the Text

Zephaniah ends his book in a way similar to how he began. The superscription declared all that followed to be "YHWH's word" (1:1), and now we are told, "YHWH has spoken" (אָמַר יְהוָה). Prophetic oracles commonly end this way.[1] Connecting the whole book to God with the envelopment of 1:1 and 3:20c emphasizes the seriousness of the book's commands, the certainty of its predictions, and the trustworthiness of its promises.

The *qatal* form אָמַר ("he said") suggests that the preceding oracle was received prior to its inscription. The book only proposes Zephaniah himself as the one who both received and wrote down YHWH's revelation.[2]

Canonical and Theological Significance

That Zephaniah's book is from YHWH stresses that all it contains is both true and authoritative. To avoid punishment and enjoy salvation—even amidst suffering—, readers must "seek" YHWH together (2:1, 3) and "wait" for him (3:8), relishing already the joy set before them (3:14, 17). Patiently pursuing King YHWH together will most certainly result in prolonged pleasures in his presence, all for his glory and great joy. This is the essence of the Savior's invitation to satisfaction.

---

1. E.g., Amos 1:5, 15; 2:3; 5:16; 9:15; cf. Obad 18; Hag 2:23.
2. This statement does not rule out the use of a scribal amanuensis like Baruch (Jer 36:4, 32) who could have transcribed Zephaniah's words. However, because Zephaniah was himself part of the royal line and intimately aware of the political scene, Zephaniah himself could have written the oracle.

Scripture Index

Old Testament

Genesis

1:1 . . . . .91, 92
1:2 124
1:2–3 131
1:3 220
1:14 86
1:20–28 .81, 242
1:26–27 304
1:26, 28 81
1:26–28 273
1:28 . . . . .183, 187
2 199
2:5 80
2:7 127
2:10 269
2:10–14 . . . . .199, 242
2:13 . . . . .34, 242
2:15 . . . . .183, 187
3:8 38
3:14–24 93
3:15 . . . . 35, 36, 41, 47, 93
3:17–18 195
3:17–19 .32, 80
3:18 186
3:19 82
3:23 80
3:24 193
4:26 . . . . .36, 86, 243
5:1–3 94
6 199
6:7 80
6:11, 13 114

6:11–12 220
6:11–13 .38, 93
6:12–13 128
7:3–4, 23 80
8:8 80
8:20–22 . . . . .215, 222
8:21 . . . . .32, 81
8:22 215
9:6 166
9:9–10 216
9:11 32
10 . . . . .34, 36, 242
10:1–32 36
10:1–11:9 200
10:5 247
10:6 192
10:6, 10 241
10:6–20 36
10:10 251
10:10–11 200
10:32 241
10:32–11:9 . . . . .62, 200
11:1, 6–7 243
11:1–9 . . . . . 34, 45, 239, 243, 245, 295
11:4 .36, 86, 247
11:4, 6 243
11:4, 8 175
11:4, 8–9 243
11:17 247
11:7–9 .67, 199
11:7, 9 34
11:8–9 . . . . 34, 36, 241, 251
11:9 21
12:1–2d 94

12:2–3 96
12:3 . . . . . 45, 67, 68, 93, 184, 199, 250
13:12–17 187
14:22 189
15:1 90
15:5 86
15:6 163
15:16 269
15:18 35
15:18–19 249
17:4–6 35
17:7–8 94
17:8 249
18:19 160
19:24–26 32
19:25 186
19:26 186
19:36–38 184
22:16 185
22:17–18 45
22:17b–18 . . . . .96, 201
22:18 . . . . .67, 250
25:21 240
26:3–4 . . . . .35, 249
26:4 93
29:8 196
34:29 120
41:19 270
47:22 85
48:15 274
49:9–10 . . . . .131, 209
49:27 . . . . .210, 235
50:4 151
50:17 294

Exodus

2:4	35
2:16	85
3:14–15	63
3:14–16	47
3:20	83
4:22–23	94
5:7, 12	148
6:6–8	47, 63
7:5	83
8:21	159
9:15	83
9:29	168
10:22–23	124, 220
12:12	189
12:12–14	40
12:24	151
14:14	284
14:19–20, 24, 27	220
14:30	283
15:1–3	283
15:3	39
15:6, 12	83
15:7	148
15:11	188, 189
15:14–16	296
15:17	269
15:17–18	269
16:32	118
18:11	189
18:21	210
19:5	168
19:6	94
19:16	38
19:16–20	124
20:3	189
20:7	238
20:11	63, 189
20:18	124
20:20	106, 274
22:20	166, 205
22:22	270
23:3	270

23:16	70, 79, 94
25:9	249
27:20–21	118
28:38	109
29:38–46	214
29:44	110
32:12	32, 80
34:6	68
34:6–7	47, 63, 120, 161, 238
34:10	188
34:14	49
34:22	70, 79, 94

Leviticus

1:9, 15	127
5:4	238
9:1–10:3	39
9:24–10:3	208
10:10–11	84, 114, 211
11:18	196
14:41	127
15:31	83
16:15–22, 33–34	40
17:11	39, 109
18:21	88
18:26–30	83
19:12	89
19:15	270
19:18	294
19:33	205
20:22–24	83
21:7	162
23:23–25	79
23:26–32	79
23:33–43	94
24:3	118
26:5–6	274
26:14–33	219
26:14–39	151
26:16–17	277
26:18, 27–28	207
26:14–16,18, 21, 23–24, 27–28	223
26:14–39	265

Numbers

6:2	288
6:23–27	238
10:9	39, 124, 131
12:6, 8	62
13:28	33, 125, 130
13:29	117, 179
13:30	106
14:21	185, 251
14:22	206
15:32–33	148
15:38–40	112
23:21	279
23:23	159
23:24	209
24:7–8	283
24:9	131, 209
28–29	109
28:1–8	214
29:1–6	79
29:7–11	79
29:12–38	94
29:12–40	109
30:10	162
31:48	111
32:23	118
35:3	196
35:33	39

Deuteronomy

1:7	117, 210
1:16–17	214
1:28	125
2:9, 19	187
2:23	179
3:5	130
4:5–8	94
4:11	38, 124
4:12	123

Numbers (right column header)

26:18, 21, 23–24, 27–28	166, 218
26:22	217
26:25	149
26:33	120

Scripture Index

4:16–18 82
4:19 86
4:23–24 128
4:25–28 94
4:27 240
4:28 206
4:29 90
4:29–31 157
4:30–31 96
4:31 265
4:35, 39 93
5:7 84
5:7–9 90
5:9 86
5:11 238
5:17–21 280
5:22 124
6:4–5 206
6:7, 20–25 68
6:10 35
6:10–11 . . . . 33, 39, 120, 125, 129,
130 183
6:13 89
6:25 160
7:1–2 33
7:8 284
7:20 160
7:21 188
8:3 67
8:5 207
8:14 166
8:17 120
8:19–20 . . . . 33, 35, 130
8:20 123
9:1 . . . . 33, 125
9:4–5 . . . . 33, 169
9:27 294
10:14 . . . . 63, 168
10:17 . . . . 122, 127, 188, 189, 283
10:17–18 . . . . 67, 205, 214
10:17–19 166
10:18 270
10:20 89
11:26 280

12:2–14 92
12:5 83
13:10–11 166
14:17 196
16:2–8 9
16:13 . . . . 79, 87, 95, 288
16:13–15 94
16:16 . . . . 92, 288
16:18–19 210
16:20 . . . . 160, 163
17:3 86
17:12–13 166
17:14–20 124
17:18–20 . . . . 274, 279
18:15, 18 66
18:16 123
18:20–22 . . . . 63, 206
18:21–22 . . . . 11, 66
18:22 63
19:19–20 166
20:9 111
20:16–17 33
20:16–18 180
20:18 . . . . 33, 129
21:21 . . . . 166, 207
22:1–4 92
22:11–12 112
23:3 201
23:3–4 184
23:16–17 205
24:14 198
26:10 86
26:15 219
26:19 294
27:9 106
27:19 270
28:10 . . . . 294, 296
28:15–68 . . . . 151, 216, 219, 265
28:26 . . . . 109, 274
28:28–29 126
28:30, 39 . . . . 33, 39, 120, 121, 130
28:43–44 277
28:45, 62 206

28:49–52 . . . . 109, 110
28:52 125
28:53, 55, 57 123
28:63 284
28:65 126
29:21 8
29:23 186
30:1–14 96
30:3 240
30:4 291
30:4–5 295
30:7 . . . . 82, 123, 125
31:9 9
31:16–18 . . . . 94, 220
32:2–4 238
32:4 . . . . 166, 212
32:5 220
32:17 . . . . 91, 189
32:18 150
32:21 89
32:26–27 218
32:35–36 184
32:39 . . . . 92, 93, 280
32:47 67
33:5 279
33:10 211
33:26 267
33:27 219
33:29 . . . . 193, 267, 268

Joshua

5:13 193
5:15 269
6:5, 20 . . . . 33, 125, 130
6:15 220
6:21 180
7:11 126
11:22 183
13:2–3 . . . . 179, 183
13:3 161
15:12 . . . . 179, 183, 249
21:43 35
23:7 89
24:25 151

Judges

1:18	183
2:3	129
2:10	68
2:11, 13	92
2:12	90
2:15	280
2:18	283
3:1–3	179, 183
3:7	84
3:12	184
3:19	106
6:15	270
10:7	184
19:26	213

1 Samuel

2:29	219
2:30	185
5:3–5	113
5:5	85
6:2	85
8:7	89, 279
9:13	110
10:19	89, 283
12:12	89
12:20–21	127
15:22	208
17:45	86
27:1–7	161
28:6	62
28:10	89
30:25	151

2 Samuel

1:20	217
5:20	83
7:10	290
7:12–16	64
7:16	68, 96
7:23	188
8:2	243
8:2, 6	239

8:2, 11–12	185
12:26–31	185
12:30	88
18:21	65
22:12	38, 131
22:31	271
22:27	238

1 Kings

1:29–30	89
1:41	110
4:21	35, 239, 243
6:20–22	197
8:27	249
8:29	83
9:3	110
9:7	82
10:5	112
10:9	284
10:26	95
11:5, 7	88
11:5, 33	88
11:13, 36	83
12:31–32	84, 85
13:33–34	84, 85
13:34	80
14:23	92
17–18	84
17:3	239, 243
17:10, 12	148
17:24	67
18:21	83
18:28	93
19:18	93, 160
20:34	217
22:5	90
22:19	86, 189

2 Kings

3	185
7:9	230
8:7–15	169
8:20, 22	266
10:13	111

10:22	112
10:22–23	112
10:28	84
11:15	111
11:18	85
13:20	184, 185
17	195
17:5	216
17:6	217
17:7	218
17:7–8	90
17:10	92
17:13	63, 96, 210
17:13–15	94
17:14–18	279
17:16	87, 92
17:16–18	84
17:13	206
17:33	92
17:35–36	218
18–20	64
18:1	64
18:5	208
18:14	126
19:9	65, 192
19:20	208
19:23	197
20:21–21:18	6, 7
21	66
21:1–26	68
21:2	112
21:2–9	211
21:3, 5–6, 21	87
21:4–7	114
21:5	87, 97
21:6	9
21:11–12	279
21:11–15	213
21:13	249
21:19	64
21:19–26	7, 63
21:20	112

21–23 7
22–23 111
22:1 . . . . .8, 64
22:1–23:30 66
22:8 8
22:14 . . . . .112, 115
23:2–3 15
23:3, 21 8
22:4 113
22:13 159
22:19–20 137
23:4–25 .8, 9
23:4–5, 10, 24 66
23:5 . . . . .9, 84
23:5, 8–9, 20 86
23:5–6, 12–13 8
23:6, 10, 12–15, 24 89
23:26–27 279
23:10 88
23:12 87
23:13 88
23:15–16, 20 85
23:15–20 273
23:16, 19 182
23:21–23 9
23:25 . . . . .8, 66, 88
23:26–27 231
24:2 184
25:18 113

1 Chronicles
4:39–41 . . . . .65, 192
7:40 238
9:22 . . . . .113, 238
16:18 180
16:25 188
16:41 238
20:2 88
21:12 193
21:30 193
23:13 114

2 Chronicles
2:11, 10 284

7:14 157
9:8 284
19:18–19 131
12:3 .65, 192
13:11 118
13:14 131
14:9–15 . . . . .65, 192
15:4 157
15:7 282
19:7 212
20:1 184
20:4 149
21:16 . . . . .65, 192
23:4 113
26:15 217
28:23 81
29:7–8 118
30:17 109
30:27 219
32:15 219
33:12–16 7
33:14 115
34:6–9 182
34–35 111
34:3 8
34:3–7 8
34:3–35:19 66
34:14–15 8
34:22 112
34:29–35:19 8
34:33 273
35:18 273

Ezra
5:11 189

Nehemiah
3:38–39 115
4:20 39
5:18 238
8:3 213
8:11 106
9:6 . . . . .63, 86
9:25 . . . . .125, 130

9:30 62

Esther
1:1 . . . . .65, 192, 242

Job
1:6 189
2:10 238
3:24 230
5:10 217
5:14 126
6:24 284
8:21 238
12:7–8 81
12:25 126
15:6 238
15:22 . . . . .38, 131
15:24 124
20:7 127
21:5 217
21:12–13 120
21:27 211
24:4 157
24:14 210
27:16 112
28:26 151
33:3 238
34:10 212
34:32 159
36:6 213
36:23 159
37:12 159
38:27 124
39:24 39
40:30 117
41:26, 34 88
42:10 183

Psalms
1:6 97
2:6 269
2:7 151
2:8 201
2:9 46

2:12 272	34:8 272	78:56–57 90
3:6 280	34:14 238	79:5 128
8:4–5 86	34:22 272	82:1 189
8:6–8 81	35:26 185	82:3 270
9:9 213	35:27 285	83:4 6
9:18–19 157	37:1 212	86:9 190
10:4 120	37:10–11 157	87 . . . . 29, 238, 273, 276
10:12 157	37:11 157	87:4 . . . . 34, 180, 201, 241
10:12–13 157	37:40 272	87:4, 6 238
10:11, 13 119	40:10 238	89:7, 9 189
11:3 159	43:3 269	89:14 160
11:4 249	44:17 184	91:9 219
14:1 . . . . 120, 220	44:19 90	92:16 212
15:1 269	49:5–6 91	95:3 . . . . 88, 189
15:2 . . . . 159, 160	50:12–13 189	95:7–8 160
15:14 218	50:21 284	96:4 188
16:11 304	51:18–19 208	96:4–5 189
17:13 193	52:5 160	99:3 188
18:2, 30 272	53:2 . . . . 120, 220	101:8 . . . . 210, 212, 214
18:8–16 44	58:3 159	102:7 196
18:27 238	59 210	103:11 218
18:30 212	59:7–8, 15–17 210	103:20–21 189
18:43 127	60:10 180	104:11 196
22:28–30 190	62:9 207	105:3–4 90
23:1 274	63:4 238	105:4 157
23:4 280	63:12 89	105:11 180
24:8 . . . . 39, 283	68:4 275	106:37 189
25:20 271	68:5 270	108:10 180
27:1 280	68:32 241	109:21 290
27:5 . . . . 6, 160	68:33 122	115:4–8 206
27:8 157	68:34 267	115:9–11 207
28:7 275	69:35 81	115:15 189
29:2 189	71:1 271	116:4, 13, 17 239
29:4 122	71:3 219	118 . . . . 298, 299
29:25 236	71:23 238	118:8–9 198
31:1 271	72:17 96	118:9 91
31:19 272	72:19 251	118:9–9 271
31:20 160	73:6 266	118:25–26 298
31:21 6	73:10–11 120	119:3 159
31:23 266	73:28 208	119:13 238
33:4 67	76:3 219	119:75 160
33:20 . . . . 230, 234	76:9–10 157	119:89 67
34:6 283	78:4–8 68	119:105 67

Scripture Index

119:160 67
119:171 238
121:4 86
139:11–12 118
139:12 210
144:2 272
144:13 217
146:3 . . . . .91, 198, 304
146:7 213
146:9 270
147:10–11 274
147:11 . . . . .285, 304
147:18 67
148:2–5 189
148:6 151
148:8 67
149:4 285
149:5–9 110

Proverbs

3:7 218
3:12 207
3:14 127
5:2 238
8:13 218
10:15 270
10:27 218
11:4 127
15:8 208
15:9 97
15:33 160
16:17 218
16:18 . . . . .184, 188
17:15 265
18:5 198
18:10 238
22:16 198
22:22 270
23:24–25 285
24:28 238
27:2 238
28:14 160
28:22 129

28:24 266
30:5 .271, 272
30:20 159
31:24 117

Ecclesiastes

3:2 162
3:14 218
3:18 238
7:13–14 . . . . .93, 280
8:3 129
12:11 274

Song of Solomon

3:3 87
5:7 87

Isaiah

1:1 . . . . .62, 63
1:2 32
1:4 220
1:11 208
1:21–23 160
1:26 276
2:1, 6 179
2:2 . . . . .268, 269
2:2–3 .34, 250
2:2–4 .29, 249
2:3 . . . . .49, 191
2:6 . . . . 113, 166, 175
2:6–8 .33, 118
2:11, 17 268
2:12 125
2:17 191
2:22 198
3:6 81
3:13–15 205
3:14–15 209
3:16–17 267
4:2–4 95
4:2–6 108
4:5–6 249
5:8–22 178
5:11–13 119

5:14 266
5:16 213
5:17 202
5:24 148
5:25 83
5:26–30 122
5:30 38
6:5 106
7:23–25 186
8:13 218
8:17 .230, 234
8:20 211
9:1 215
9:7 96
9:8 266
9:12 207
9:17 270
10:3 . . . . 111, 124, 183
10:5 . . . . .39, 195, 216
10:5–12 194
10:6 217
10:21 32
10:23 128
11:1–5, 9 269
11:1–10 . . . . .41, 108
11:2 249
11:3 268
11:4 .157, 270
11:6 205
11:9 249
11:11 . . . . 124, 181, 189, 190, 241, 283
11:12 . . . . .32, 32
11:14 201
12:5–6 .32, 278
13 268
13–23 168
13:1–22 108
13:3 . . . . 32, 39, 109, 110, 267, 268
13:3–5 . . . . .109, 110
13:4 . . . . .32, 86
13:5 . . . . .39, 216
13:6 . . . . .40, 122
13:7 . . . . .32, 282

13:8 129	24:4–6 93	36–39 64
13:9, 11 126	24:5 . . . . .162, 265	40:8 67
13:9, 13 123	24:5–6 . . . . .82, 126, 216	40:25–26 87
13:10 . . . . .38, 131	24:17–18 118	41:1 284
13:11 . . . . 188, 266, 268	24:21–22 32	41:21 279
13:13, 19 . . . . .40, 108	24:22 . . . . .79, 111, 241	41:23 119
13:17 127	25:4 32	42:1 249
13:19 268	25:4, 8–9 283	42:4 249
13:19–20 186	25:9 . . . . .32, 275	42:8 303
14:2 201	25:11 267	42:13 . . . . 32, 122, 283, 283
14:4–23 251	26:3–4 208	42:14 284
14:12 277	26:12 159	42:14–16 151
14:13 286	27:1 277	42:22 120
14:22 82	28:22 128	42:24 217
14:26–27 82	28:24 80	42:25 . . . . 167, 207, 215
14:31 195	29:5 151	43:4 . . . . .32, 284
14:32 . . . . .32, 271	29:5–6 151	43:8 206
16:6 . . . . 184, 188, 266	29:6 . . . . .38, 111	43:9–13 11
17:6 185	29:9–12 206	43:10–11 190
17:13–14 151	29:13 238	43:11 . . . . .279, 303
18:1–2 . . . . .65, 241, 242	29:22–23 32	43:19–21 285
18:1–6 192	30:8 9	43:20 196
18:1, 7 . . . . .32, 240	30:8–12 206	43:27 . . . . .32, 93, 216
18:7 . . . . 34, 240, 241, 244	30:15 208	44:6 .32, 88, 279
19:18 238	30:18 234	44:6–8 11
19:19–25 190	30:22 127	44:23 275
19:21 . . . . 240, 243, 244	30:26 32	45:7 . . . . .91, 92, 189
19:21–22 32	30:30 38	45:14 . . . . 34, 49, 198, 241
19:22 240	32:13 . . . . .198, 266	45:17 32
19:25 238	32:14 196	45:19 163
20:1–6 . . . . .217, 223	33:7 122	45:21 279
20:3–4 192	33:14–16 . . . . .40, 160, 214	45:21–22 92
20:3–6 193	33:20 288	45:22 198
20:4 217	33:23 235	45:23 . . . . 49, 185, 190, 302
20:5–6 . . . . 65, 192, 218, 241	34:1–2, 5–6 109	46:1 196
20:6 . . . . .169, 214	34:2, 6 40	46:7 . . . . .283, 283
22:2 . . . . .198, 266	34:10–11 196	46:9–10 24
22:5, 12–14 109	34:11 197	47:5 280
22:12–14 39	35:5–6 32	47:8–9 162
22:14 . . . . .40, 109, 133	35:6, 10 32	47:8, 10 198
23:7 266	35:3–4 . . . . .32, 282	47:14 148
23:8 117	35:6 . . . . .187, 286	48:9, 11 303
23:9 188	37:9 . . . . .65, 192	49:3, 6 24

Scripture Index

49:5–6. 45
49:6. . . . . .96, 241, 300
49:7. .190
49:25. 283
50:1. .162
50:8, 10. 164
50:10. 249
51:1. . . . . .157, 163
51:1–2. . . . . .150, 163
51:3. . . . . .249, 274
51:4. .221
51:7. .184
51:11. 286
51:17, 22. 236
51:23. . . . . .32, 287
52:7. 29
52:10. 198
52:11. 238
52:13–53:12. . . . . .96, 109
53:1. . . . . .126, 164
53:5. . . . . .45, 133
53:9. . . . . .32, 164, 274
53:10–11. 44
53:10–54:3. 273
53:11. . . . . 40, 41, 133, 278, 305
54:1. . . . . .32, 162
54:2–3. . . . . .202, 264
54:3. .217
54:6. .162
54:9–10. . . . . .81, 216
55:3. 96
55:9–10. 32
55:13. . . . . .32, 294
56:4–5. 86
56:4–8. 32
56:5. .294
56:6. . . . . .240, 243
56:6–7. 292
56:7. .275
56:11. 209
57:9. 88
57:13. . . . . .269, 271
58:12. 187

59:3. .273
59:9. . . . . .213, 215
59:10. 126
59:12–13. 90
59:16. 126
59:21. 249
60:4. .244
60:6. .244
60:14. 290
60:15. 162
61:2. .134
61:4. . . . . 130, 187, 285
61:5. .201
61:7. . . . . .32, 265
62:2–4. 294
62:4. . . . . .120, 162
62:5. . . . . .32, 284, 286
62:11. . . . . .32, 275
62:12. 250
63:1. .283
63:9. .284
63:10. 277
64:4. . . . . 162, 230, 234, 252
65:10. 202
65:17. 285
65:17–18. 250
65:17–19. . . . . .32, 249, 286
65:18. . . . . .32, 304
65:18–22. 34
65:19. . . . . .41, 284
65:21–22. 130
66:1. .249
66:6. .119
66:12. 244
66:15. .32
66:15–16. . . . . .128, 134
66:16. 193
66:20. 244
66:20–21. . . . . 201, 240, 243
66:22. 285
66:24. .32

Jeremiah

1:1. . . . . .62, 63
1:2. 63
1:5. .110
2:15. 218
2:30. . . . . 166, 206, 207
3:3. .166
3:6–11. 279
3:7, 10. 210
3:8. . . . . .36, 162
3:8, 10. 207
3:11. .83
3:15. 203
3:16–17. 191
3:16–19. 249
3:17. . . . . .34, 264
3:25. 126
4:5. .149
4:7. . . . . .180, 218
4:9. .217
4:14. 283
4:19. 284
5:3. .207
5:4. .270
5:6. .209
5:7. 89
5:12–13. 119
5:21. 206
5:27. 114
5:28, 31. 114
6:1. . . . . .39, 124
6:7. .114
6:8. .120
6:11. 236
6:15. 111
6:20. 208
6:22–23. 108
6:24. 282
7:8. .208
7:22. 216
7:28. 206
7:31. . . . . .9, 68
7:33. 274

8:2 . . . . .87, 92	23:1–8 203	31:33 . . . . .164, 249
8:13 241	23:2 87	31:34 . . . . 41, 239, 270, 294
8:14 126	23:5 41	32:17 82
9:10 . . . . .218, 219	23:11 211	32:29 86
9:15 240	23:16 211	32:30 280
9:23–24 91	23:16–22, 32 211	32:35 88
9:24 166	23:18 189	32:40 . . . . 223, 266, 280
10:5 119	23:22 210	32:41 284
10:7 279	23:22, 28 .63	33:9 49
10:15 111	23:24 249	33:20 215
10:18 125	25:4 206	33:22 86
10:22 219	25:9 195	34:21–22 110
10:25 . . . . .109, 236	25:15 236	34:22 180
11:10 265	25:20 161	36:12 209
11:13 84	25:30 .39, 219	36:12, 21 .111
12:3 . . . . .109, 110	25:30–33 .82	36:14 64
12:14–17 241	25:33 . . . . .127, 193	36:26 . . . . .111, 160
12:16 273	25:36 115	38:6 111
13:11 .49, 294	26:10 . . . . .111, 209	38:7 65
13:15–16 267	27:3 169	39:10 270
13:23 65	27:5 82	39:16 65
15:8 161	27:5–6 206	39:18 208
16:2–3, 9 .83	27:5–8 195	42:14 39
16:4 127	27:22 .83, 183	43:5 111
16:19 123	28:9 40	43:10–13 . . . . .193, 195
17:1 249	28:16 32	44:1 241
17:5–8 208	29:5–7 . . . . .33, 129	44:25–27 .86
17:6 186	29:13 . . . . .90, 157	46–51 168
17:25 83	30:2–3 9	46:10 . . . . .37, 40, 109
18:7–10 .219	30:7 .124, 178	46:28 128
18:18 63	30:9 249	47:4 179
18:23 290	30:10 274	48:3 115
19:8 199	31:3 284	48:7 85
19:13 .86, 87	31:10–14 269	48:11–12 . . . . .40, 119
21:12 . . . . .210, 214	30:11 . . . . .202, 240	48:27–30 184
22:1–3 205	30:14 277	48:29 . . . . .188, 267
22:3 . . . . .205, 211	30:16 120	48:47 202
22:4–15 .197	30:16–17 292	49:1, 3 88
22:7 . . . . .109, 110	31:10–14 304	49:3 85
22:11–12 .83	31:18 207	49:6 202
22:21 206	31:26 62	49:22 219
23:1 202	31:31–32 265	50:2 189
23:1–4 209	31:32 162	50:4 . . . . .157, 159

50:6 202
50:14 126
50:20 270
50:22 116
50:39–40 186
51:7–8 119
51:20 39
51:27 . . . . .39, 124, 131
51:32 129
51:43 196
51:44 189
51:52 189
51:54 116
51:61–64 169
52:24 113

Lamentations

1:4–5 287
1:4–5c 288
1:13 128
1:15 288
2:3–4 128
2:4 236
2:4–5 277
2:6 . . . . .211, 286
2:7 288
2:11–12, 19 132
2:21 . . . . .68, 108, 217
3:22–23 212
3:32–33 287
4:4–5, 9 132
4:11 . . . . .128, 236
4:13 211
5:21 285

Ezekiel

1:3 63
4:17 217
5:10–11 228
5:15 184
7:8 236
7:14 131
7:19 127
7:19–20 81

7:22 6
7:27 129
8–11 119
8:4 .219, 249
8:10–12 93
8:14 93
9:3 249
10:4, 18–19 219
11:22–23 249
11:23 219
12:2 206
13 211
13:5 37
13:9 211
14:3–4 81
14:13 83
14:19 236
16:3 117
16:13 112
16:37 235
16:49–50 188
16:50 267
16:53 297
16:61 273
18:5, 9 205
18:5–9 . . . . .160, 205
18:7, 12, 16 205
20:33 279
20:38 . . . . .238, 268
20:40 244
20:43 265
21:24 193
22:14 290
22:19–22 235
22:25 209
22:25, 28 211
22:26 . . . . .84, 211
22:27 210
22:29 205
22:31 236
23:23 110
23:24 213
23:25 128

25:3, 6 184
25–32 168
25:16 179
26:7 195
27:30 122
28:14 269
28:15 273
28:26 . . . . .34, 130
29:13 241
29:16 . . . . 214, 218, 241
29:19 193
30:3 . . . . 38, 40, 122, 131, 162
30:4–5 192
30:15 236
30:25 193
31:3 197
32:7–8 38
32:11 193
33:3 39
33:33 40
34:2, 8 202
34:7–16 209
34:10 210
34:10, 12, 15 202
34:16 292
34:25–31 274
34:28 274
35:12–13 185
35:13 185
36:17–18 127
36:19 240
36:20–21 218
36:23 . . . . .42, 294
36:26–28 274
36:29 283
36:31 265
36:35 . . . . .249, 274
37:16–22 273
37:23 283
37:24–28 .42
37:27 41
38:9 124
38:17 . . . . .40, 108

Scripture Index

38:19 123
39:6 190
39:8 . . . . .40, 107
39:17–20 . . . . .46, 109
39:17, 20–21 . . . . .40, 109
39:21 214
39:25 294
44:7 189
44:22 162
46:18 205
47:13 180

Daniel

2:21 . . . . .91, 206
2:44–45 249
6:3 277
8:19 288
8:23 269
9:11 265
9:24 111
12:3 164

Hosea

1:1 .57, 62, 63
1:10–11 28
2:1–2 28
2:6 228
2:12 91
2:18–19 83
2:19 238
3:1 284
3:5 . . . . 40, 157, 202, 249, 303
4:3 . . . . .79, 81
5:8 131
5:10 236
5:15 157
6:1 207
6:1–2 28
6:5 . . . . 213, 214, 221
6:7 216
6:9 230
7:1 159
7:10 157
9:3, 6 241

9:5 286
9:9 220
10:5 84
10:13 273
11:1 216
11:10 131
11:10–11 .209
12:8 . . . . .33, 118
12:10 . . . . .206, 286
13:4 190
13:5–6 166
13:14 28
13:16 216
14:4 284
14:10 160

Joel

1:1 . . . . .62, 63
1:5 . . . . .40, 131
1:13–14 116
1:14 149
1:14–15 149
2:1 . . . . .39, 124
2:2 . . . . .38, 131
2:5 148
2:9 . . . . .40, 45, 118
2:9–10 131
2:11 . . . . .38, 39, 121
2:11, 31 188
2:11–13 41
2:11–14 214
2:14 . . . . .40, 160
2:21–23 278
2:25–26 28
2:26–27 265
2:28–29 . . . . 28, 41, 239, 247
2:28–31 44
2:28–32 247
2:30–31 38
2:31 . . . . .44, 121, 247
2:32 . . . . 28, 29, 41, 247
3:1–2 . . . . 28, 41, 239, 247
3:1–4 44

3:1–5 247
3:2 235
3:3–4 38
3:4 . . . . .121, 247
3:5 . . . . .29, 247
3:9–16 37
3:16 . . . . .39, 131, 209
3:17 269
4:2 235
4:9–16 37
4:16 . . . . .39, 131, 209
4:17 269
5 41

Amos

1:1 63
1:2 . . . . .39, 131, 209
1:6–8 161
2:7–8 93
2:8 93
3:4, 8 209
3:6 . . . . 39, 124, 131, 217
3:7 63
4:6–12 . . . . .207, 223
5:6 157
5:11 . . . . 33, 120, 121, 130
5:15 . . . . .40, 160
5:16–17 116
5:18 . . . . 37, 38, 108, 131
5:18, 20 . . . . 124, 131, 215
5:18–20 118
5:26 . . . . .86, 87, 88
6:2 161
6:6–12 167
8:4 157
8:12 90
9:2–4 118
9:3 160
9:7 . . . . .66, 179
9:8 . . . . .32, 80
9:10 119
9:11–12 . . . . .29, 202
9:11–14 42

Scripture Index

9:12 29
9:13–15 29

Obadiah

12, 14 123
14 124
15 . . . . 37, 162
16–17 269
18 148
20–21 29

Jonah

1:14 29
3:8 29

Micah

1:1 . . . . 62, 63
1:7 . . . . 91, 93
1:8–16 116
2:12 79
3:1–3 209
3:10 273
3:11 . . . . 40, 119, 211
3:12 292
4:1 269
4:1–4 . . . . 29, 249
4:4 274
4:6–7 292
4:7 249
4:11–12 79
4:12–13 235
5:2–4 203
5:2–5 . . . . 29, 40, 303
6:4 216
6:6–8 208
6:9 39
6:15 . . . . 33, 120, 121, 130
7:8–9 221
7:8–10 . . . . 213, 215
7:16–17 190

Nahum

1:1 63
1:2–8 29

1:7 . . . . 26, 161, 271, 272
1:10 148
3:1 206
3:7 196
3:19 199

Habakkuk

1:1 63
1:2–3 114
1:3 284
1:4 . . . . 160, 211
1:6 110
1:8 210
1:11 268
2:1–4 235
2:3 . . . . 230, 288
2:4 . . . . 29, 163
2:5 119
2:9–19 178
2:12 273
2:12, 19 178
2:16–17 . . . . 21, 177
2:20 106
3:1–16 275
3:16 123
3:17–19 . . . . 26, 278
3:18 275
3:18–19 304

Zephaniah

1:1 . . . . . 6, 9, 11, 12, 24, 34, 36, 48, 60,
67, 68, 106, 111, 136 192,
241, 279
1:2 . . . . 46, 80, 87, 95
1:2–3, 14–18 . . . . 37, 94
1:2–3b 78, 79, 95
1:2–3 . . . . . 6, 10, 32, 33, 36, 38, 70, 80,
81, 82, 94, 106, 126, 128, 199,
234, 245, 247
1:2–3, 5, 7 288
1:2–4, 18 220
1:2–6 . . . . 77, 94, 99, 106
1:2–18 . . . . 71, 135, 139, 145
1:2–2:3 14
1:2–3:20b 69

1:3 . . . . 32, 80, 90, 95, 186
1:3c 82
1:4 . . . . 6, 7, 9, 84, 88, 92, 97, 112,
160, 194, 222
1:4a 80
14c 84, 85
1:4–5 . . . . 7, 66, 189, 206
1:4–6 . . . . 8, 94, 93, 150, 195, 213, 268
1:4–6, 12 202
1:4–13 9
1:5 . . . . .85, 87, 88, 92, 126, 127,
208, 238
1:5b 87
1:6 . . . . 208, 239, 240, 280
1:6, 12 . . . . 33, 90, 91
1:7 . . . . .26, 37, 38, 39, 43, 46, 94, 131,
133, 134, 148, 267
1:7a 99, 105
1:7b 105, 122
1:7d 109
1:7b–13 108
1:7b–18 99
1:7–8 . . . . 95, 214
1:7–8, 17–18 208
1:7–10 105
1:7–13 121
1:7, 14 . . . . 26, 27, 45, 131
1:7, 17 128
1:7–18 . . . . 99, 105
1:8 209
1:8a 105
1:8b 183
1:8–9 . . . . 6, 8, 114, 115, 202, 214
1:8, 13, 18 118
1:9–10 27
1:9 . . . . 112, 113, 160
1:9, 11, 18 157
1:10–13 . . . . 63, 94
1:11 . . . . 105, 113, 118, 127, 130, 150,
179, 184, 188, 271
1:11b 33, 120
1:11–12 150
1:11–18 105

Scripture Index

1:12......40, 97, 111, 119, 120, 131, 205, 300

1:12a.....................105

1:12c.....................89

1:12d–e.....................211

1:12, 18.....................160

1:13.........27, 33, 121, 130, 183

1:14.....................37, 40, 121

1:14a.....................105, 121

1:14c.....................123

1:14–18.........37, 107, 108, 121

1:15......26, 38, 118, 126, 127, 131

1:15–16.......33, 44, 105, 130, 133

1:16.........39, 124, 125, 131, 217

1:17.........35, 39, 91, 127, 149, 162

1:17c.....................169

1:17d.....................126

1:17–18..........6, 121, 125, 283

1:18......33, 43, 44, 82, 89, 95, 109, 118, 127, 131, 134

2 199

2:1.....................148, 165

2:1–2.............38, 70, 149, 222

2:1, 3......40, 42, 116, 135, 137, 143, 159, 239

2:1–4.............152, 168, 214

2:1–3:20 ....99, 135, 145

2:2.....................223, 265

2:2a.....................150

2:2, 15.....................188

2:2–3.....................165

2:3........90, 92, 149, 151, 158, 163, 164, 165, 166, 202, 235, 270

2:3a.....................156

2:3b.....................205

2:3–4.....................166, 179

2:3, 7, 9.....................177

2:4.............162, 163, 184

2:4, 9, 13, 15.....................120

2:4–15.....................6, 9, 136

2:5.............117, 178, 183

2:5a.....................179

2:5c.....................180

2:5, 12.....................169

2:5–15.........7, 36, 179, 200, 204

2:5–3:7 ....36, 37, 168, 199

2:6.....................196, 203

2:6–7.........180, 182, 186

2:7.........34, 48, 111, 130, 182

2:7d.....................183

2:7, 9.........21, 83, 110, 160, 161

2:7–11.....................10

2:8c.....................185

2:8, 15.....................125, 184

2:8–10.....................267

2:8, 10.....................198

2:9......12, 130, 182, 228, 234, 279

2:9a.....................188

2:9b.....................185

2:9c–d.....................201

2:9, 11.....................65

2:9–11.....................201

2:10.....................166

2:10c.....................185, 188

2:11......49, 89, 127, 187, 197, 218, 223, 297, 302

2:11a.....................188, 189

2:11c.....................190

2:11–12.....................34, 243

2:11, 15.....................116

2:12......6, 36, 65, 192, 193, 200, 207, 217, 242

2:13.....................83

2:13c.....................196

2:13c–14a.....................195

2:13–15.............7, 193, 194

2:14b–d 196

2:14d–e.....................197

2:14c.....................197

2:15.........197, 198, 199, 205, 266

2:15b–c.....................198

3 221

3:1.....................178

3:1, 3–4, 11 202

3:1, 3–4, 19 115

3:1–2.....................91

3:1–2, 5, 7.....................202

3:1, 3.....................157

3:1–4, 7.....................9

3:1–5.....................160

3:1–5, 7.....................230

3:1–7.....................179

3:1–20.....................14

3:2....33, 39, 207, 208, 213, 216, 240

3:2–5.....................221

3:2b.....................207

3:3.....................210

3:3a.....................209

3:3b–c.....................210

3:3–4.........6, 8, 84, 115, 217, 219

3:4.....................84, 97, 211

3:4a.....................210

3:5....38, 49, 97, 211, 212, 213, 214, 220, 221, 222, 223

3:5a.....................212

3:5–b.....................280

3:5c.....................210, 212

3:6.........120, 125, 207, 218

3:6b–d.....................217

3:6c.....................217

3:6–7.........161, 166, 169, 214, 223

3:7......6, 37, 40, 48, 151, 161, 188, 207, 265, 266, 274

3:7b.....................218

3:7e–f.....................219

3:7, 9.....................276

3:8......12, 18, 21, 34, 37, 46, 79, 82, 89, 92, 94, 95, 107, 109, 131, 135, 165, 190, 208, 228, 230, 236, 246, 247, 264, 270

3:8, 14.........17, 33, 43, 44, 116

3:8–10.....6, 27, 37, 41, 44, 245, 246, 248, 251, 254, 268, 296, 298

3:8–13.....................260

3:8–20.....10, 47, 130, 134, 145, 187, 298, 300

3:8, 18.....................70, 240

3:936, 44, 237, 238, 239, 241, 243, 271

3:9–10.....6, 44, 49, 65, 67, 175, 187, 190, 191, 200, 243, 247, 248, 249, 250, 251, 252, 265, 269, 292, 295, 305

3:9–10, 12 110

Scripture Index

3:9–10, 13 45
3:9–10, 15, 19 44
3:9, 11 283
3:9–13 199
3:9–20 27
3:10 . . . . . .41, 44, 45, 65, 68, 191, 243, 244, 250
3:10–12 45
3:10, 18 45
3:11 . . . . 205, 220, 270, 278
3:11b 110, 266, 267, 268
3:11–12 . . . . .160, 270
3:11–13 160
3:11, 16 27
3:11, 1 215
3:11, 15, 19 283
3:11–20 . . . . .41, 161
3:12 . . . . 160, 249, 270, 271
3:13 . . 27, 83, 115, 130, 164, 202, 272, 279
3:13a 182
3:13d–f 274
3:14 . . . . .269, 275
3:14–15 . . . . . . .37, 260, 263, 275, 298, 299, 300, 304
3:14–20 41
3:15 . . . . . . .41, 42, 44, 88, 89, 116, 162, 240, 277, 302, 303
3:15a–b 280
3:15c 279
3:15–16 188
3:15, 17 41
3:15, 18 188
3:15, 19 . . . . .44, 49
3:16–17 49
3:16–18 . . . . .45, 297
3:16–20b .289
3:16–20 301
3:17 . . . . 47, 48, 49, 282
3:17d 285
3:17e .285, 286
3:18 . . . . .42, 289
3:18, 19–20 79
3:19 .291, 292
3:19a 290

3:19d .292, 294
3:19–20 . . . . 42, 49, 86, 300
3:20 . . . . .12, 49
3:20b 241

Haggai

1:1 . . . . .57, 63
1:6 27
1:11 27
1:12, 14 27
2:2 27
2:6–7, 21–22 . . . . .27, 29
2:7, 9 .27, 249
2:7–9 43
2:14 208
2:17 207
2:23 27

Zechariah

1:1 .57, 62, 63
2:10 .275, 278
2:11 29
2:17 106
3:8–9 . . . . .29, 202, 203
3:9 . . . . .40, 41, 47
4:2, 10 118
6:12–13 . . . . .40, 202
6:12–13, 15 . . . . .29, 249
7:9 .210, 214
7:11–12 63
7:12 62
7:14 217
8:3 269
8:16 214
8:20–23 250
8:21–22 159
8:22–23 49
8:23 . . . . .29, 34
9 299
9:5–7 161
9:6–8 208
9:9 . . . .37, 44, 275, 278, 298, 299, 303
9:9–10 41
9:9–11 202

9:14 . . . . .39, 124, 131
9:16–17 294
10:2 202
11:10 265
13:1 41
13:17–19 .203
14:1 37
14:1–2, 16 95
14:1–21 108
14:2 . . . . .36, 79, 241
14:2–3 235
14:7–9, 20 42
14:9 . . . . 239, 243, 279, 297

Malachi

1:1 63
1:4–5 223
1:5 . . . . .218, 169
1:10 208
1:11, 14 190
2:3 . . . . .39, 127
2:5–7 211
2:6 238
2:7 211
2:7–9 84
3:1 30
3:1–2 .41, 43
3:1–3, 23–24 95
3:3 244
3:13–14 120
3:19 .128, 268
3:23 .121, 188
3:23–24 . . . . .30, 43
4:1 . . . . 128, 148, 268
4:5 .121, 188
4:5–6 . . . . .30, 43, 95

Deuterocanonical Books

1 Maccabees (1 Macc)

4:36–59 108

New Testament

Matthew

1:23 . . . . 43, 302
3:11 95
3:11–12 43
3:12 . . . . 36, 38, 46, 95, 222
4:3–4, 7, 10 67
4:4 67
4:15–17 47
4:16–17 301
5:6, 10, 20 164
5:16 304
5:17–18 67
5:45 . . . . .215, 222
6:1 164
6:24 . . . . .92, 150
6:33 164
6:34 165
7:13–14 . . . . 91, 97
7:23 46
8:16–17 303
10:28 . . . . 165, 280, 302
11:9–15 43
11:28–29 250
11:28–30 41
12:36 46
13:24–30 36
13:30 95
13:39 277
13:41–42 97
13:44 304
13:44–46 91
16:24–25 92
19:26 92
21:5 299
23:1–3 67
24:29–30 131
24:30 46
24:31 .46, 131
24:36, 42 46
24:43 45
25:31–32 46
25:32 . . . . .95, 96
25:32, 46 36
25:34 46

25:46 97
26:29 46
27:45, 51 44
28:18–20 45
28:20 302

Mark

1:15 24
2:1 71
4:11–12 25
7:13 67
8:34–35 305
10:29–30 302
12:24 67
12:36 67
13:7 45
13:32 46
13:33–37 46
14:25 46
15:33 .44, 131

Luke

2:32 24
9:31 45
10:2 251
10:19 277
13:4–5 166
14:26–28 92
15:7, 10 284
15:8 118
16:16 . . . . .24, 301
16:28–31 67
17:24 46
21:16, 18 305
23:44 44
24:25 67
24:25–27 49
24:27 49
24:44 67
24:47 250

John

1:1 49
1:1, 18 299

1:1–3 222
1:14 43
1:29 . . . . .43, 134
2:19–21 249
2:19–22 43
3 . . . . .221, 303
3:14–17, 36 303
3:18 92
3:18–19 221
3:30 165
3:36 . . . . .97, 134, 221
4:19, 44 222
4:21, 23 250
5:18 49
5:39 49
5:46–47 67
6:14 222
6:24 97
6:35 . . . . .67, 250
6:39–40, 44, 54 46
7:40 222
8:12 301
9:17 222
10:16 .250, 305
10:35 67
11:51–52 . . . . .250, 305
11:25 . . . . .67, 302, 305
11:51–52 . . . . .45, 241, 300
12:7 300
12:13 . . . . .44, 298, 299
12:13, 15 . . . . 37, 41, 44, 303
12:13–15 298
12:15 . . . . 298, 299, 302
12:19 298
12:19–20 250
12:19–21 303
12:27–28 300
12:31 44
12:31–32 44
12:47 299
12:48 46
13:34–35 166
14:6 97

Scripture Index

14:9 49
15:5 302
20:28–29 299

Acts

1:1 248
1:2–3, 22 . . . . 37, 245
1:3 246
1:4 246
1:8 . . . . . . 45, 246, 247, 250, 251, 304
1:9–11 46
1:22 246
2 . . . . 245, 247
2:1–47 37
2:3–4, 11, 26 247
2:4 247
2:4–6 44
2:5 248
2:9–11 248
2:16–21 44
2:17–21 247
2:20 . . . . 44, 131, 247
2:21 . . . . 29, 247
2:40 247
2:42–47 247
3:18 49
3:18, 24 . . . . 15, 25, 42, 49, 67
3:25–26 45
4:27–28 11
4:33 246
5:29 165
7:42 25
7:42–43 86
8:26–39 44
8:26–40 . . . . 37, 245, 248
10:34–35 67
10:43 15
13:32–33 67
13:40 25
14:27 222
15:15 25
15:16–18 . . . . 29, 202
15:20 93

15:20–21 93
17:24 249
17:24–28 . . . . 91, 92
21:25 93
26:22–23 49
26:23 24

Romans

2:4 . . . . 97, 223
2:6, 13 164
2:8 134
2:13 164
3:23 304
3:27 91
4:4 91
4:5 265
5:1 164
5:1–5 47
5:1, 9–11 45
5:1, 18–19 133
5:2–5 304
5:5 304
5:9 . . . . 45, 301
5:9–10 47
5:10 . . . . 251, 302
5:18–19 . . . . 24, 44
6:4 301
8:1 134
8:3 302
8:7 92
8:13 92
8:18 . . . . 47, 301
8:20–21 . . . . 93, 252
8:20–22 301
8:29 304
8:31–32 302
9:26 28
10:13 29
10:13–15, 17 251
11:17–24 250
11:36 . . . . 11, 48, 304
12:1 . . . . 45, 250
12:12 302

9:23–24 91
12:18–21 224
13:10 164
13:11, 14 223
13:11–14 131
13:14 93
14:11 49
15:4 . . . . 24, 67
15:16 45
16:25–26 . . . . 24, 25

1 Corinthians

1:18 301
1:30–31 165
2:13–14 25
2:14 92
3:13 46
4:7 91
6:9–10 . . . . 91, 93
6:11 93
8:4, 6 92
8:4–13 93
10:7 91
10:11 . . . . 24, 25, 44
10:31 304
15:10 165
15:26 305

2 Corinthians

3:9 94
3:14 25
3:14–16 24
5:10 46
5:17 . . . . 44, 301, 305
5:21 44
10:17–18 165
12:10 92

Galatians

1:4 301
2:20 164
3:8, 29 45
3:13 . . . . 44, 133, 302
3:24–25 301

4:4 . . . . .24, 301
4:26 45
4:26–27 201
5:6 164
5:25–26 250
6:15 . . . . .44, 301, 305
6:16 264

Ephesians

1:3 301
1:11 . . . . .11, 24, 206
1:22 304
2:3 . . . . .93, 134
2:5 251
2:8 301
2:11–22 250
2:13–22 44
2:14–16 45
4:11 203
5:5 . . . . .91, 93
5:6 134
5:14 131

Philippians

1:20–21 304
1:28 302
2:6 49
2:10–11 222
2:12–13 92
4:4–7 302
4:5 45
4:6–7 . . . . .165, 252

Colossians

1:15 49
1:16 48
2:15 . . . . 223, 301, 302, 304
3:5 . . . . .91, 93
3:17, 23 304

1 Thessalonians

4:16 . . . . .46, 131
4:17 131
5:2 . . . . .45, 46
5:4 46

5:5, 8–9 . . . . .46, 132
5:9 134

2 Thessalonians

1:7–8 131
1:7–10 46
1:8–9 . . . . .132, 134
1:8–10 46
1:9–10 37
2:1–3 45

1 Timothy

4:4–5 93
6:17 91

2 Timothy

1:10 134
2:22 .164, 166
3:15–17 49
3:16 11
3:15–17 24
3:16–17 11
4:2 49
4:8 134

Titus

2:13 132

Hebrews

1:3 . . . . 48, 49, 67, 91, 92
2:8 304
2:14–15 302
2:15 165
3:13 165
4:9, 11 . . . . .41, 47
4:16 208
6:5 301
8:13 44
9:22 .39, 109
9:28 .47, 252
10:23–25 . . . . .47, 132, 252
10:27 134
10:34 305
11 304
11:3 304

11:6, 26 305
11:26 68
12:1 304
12:2 305
12:3 . . . . 252, 278, 305
12:11 167
12:14 165
12:22 . . . . .45, 250, 264
12:22–29 44
12:26–29 27
13:15–16 . . . . .45, 250

James

1:2–4 302
1:12 252
1:27 .166, 205
2:23 164
3:9 166
4:6 165

1 Peter

1:4, 9 302
1:7 304
1:10–11 . . . . .11, 25, 42, 62
1:10–12 . . . . .25, 49, 67
1:12 169
1:18 275
2:5 . . . . .45, 250
2:22 274
2:24 45
4:11 165
5:5 165
5:6–7 252
5:7 165
5:10 .252, 304
5:13 251

2 Peter

1:4 . . . . .42, 302, 305
1:20–21 11
1:21 .25, 62, 67
2:9 252
3:7–10 46
3:8–9 45

Scripture Index

3:9 120
3:10 . . . . 37, 46, 131, 132
3:13 301

1 John

2:15, 17 222
3:7 164
3:10 92
3:16 93
3:16–18 166
4:10–11 166
5:21 93

Revelation

1:3 45
3:2–3 46
3:3 46

3:19 223
4:11 91
5:5 131
5:8–14 222
5:9 222
5:9–10 . . . . .67, 250
5:10 264
6:12–13 131
7:9 222
7:9–10 . . . . .67, 239, 250
7:17 203
8:7 46
11:7 95
12:4 131
16:8–10 223
16:14 .46, 95

16:17–18:24 251
19:17–18 46
19:19 95
20:4 297
20:7–10 . . . . .40, 108
20:8 95
21:1–2 301
21:2 . . . . .45, 250
21:2, 10 250
21:8 93
21:22–22:5 250
21:23–25 .222
22:1–2 34
22:2 264
22:3–4 279
22:10 45

Extrabiblical Index

Ancient Near Eastern Literature

Annals of Tiglath-pileser III 161

The "Babel of Tongues" 242

The Babylonian Chronicle 7

The Bukān Inscription. 186

Code of Hammurabi. *See* Laws of Hammurabi

Enmerkar and the Lord of Aratta. . . . 242

The First Soldier's Oath 186

Hittite Treaty 18B Between Hattusili III of Hatti and Ulmi-Teshshup of Targhuntassa. 120

The Inscription of King Mesha. 185

The Inscriptions of Bar-gaʾyah and Matiʾel from Sefire. . . . 115, 120, 131

The Kirta Epic. 87

Lamentation over the Destruction of Sumer and Ur 124

The Laws of Hammurabi. 120

The Moabite Stone 161, 185

The Neo-Babylonian Empire and Its Successors 199

Petition for Reconstruction of Temple 85

Prayer to the Gods of the Night 86

Texts from Hammurabi to the Downfall of the Assyrian Empire 131, 186

The Treaty Between *KTK* and Arpad 115, 131

Ugaritic Rites for the Vintage 87

The Vassal Treaties of Esarhaddon . . 120

Texts from the Judaean Desert

Dead Sea Scrolls

1QHᵃ (Hodayot or Thanksgiving Hymns)

3:26 85

5:8 85

1QS (Rule of the Community)

III, 11 90

4Q76–82 XIIᵃ⁻ᵍ (Minor Prophets)

4Q76. 25

Naḥal Ḥever

ḤevXII gr (8Ḥev 1)

document. 25

XX, 25–26 95

Ancient Jewish Writers

Josephus

Jewish Antiquities (A.J.)

8.165–75. 65

10.180–85 186

Rabbinic Works

Babylonian Talmud (b.)

Baba Batra (B. Bat.)

13b, 14b 25

Megillah (Meg.)

15a 6, 63

Targums

Tg. Neb. (Targum of the Prophets) . . 88, 113, 116–17, 149, 179, 184, 196, 197, 205, 214, 218, 277, 285, 293

Greco-Roman Literature

Herodotus

Histories (Historiae)

2.159.2 162

Subject Index

Abrahamic covenant, 28–29, 30, 45, 94, 201, 250

abuse of power, 157–58. *See also* leaders

allusions
Old Testament, 31–35, 201, 244
scriptural, 36–38, 121

aristocracy. *See* leaders, political

arrogance. *See* pride

Assyria. *See also* Mesopotamia; Ninevah
demise of, 176–78, 194–95, 224
exile by, 83, 195
Ninevah, 195–99
northern kingdom and, 6, 83, 94, 207

astrology, worship of. *See* punishment, Baal worshipers; worshipers, star

atheism, 90, 91, 120, 149–50

atonement. *See* Christ, sacrifice

Babel, tower of,
promise concerning, 175, 194n, 240–44
punishment of, 200, 240, 295
reversal of, 21, 34, 36, 199–201, 242. *See also* worshipers, worldwide

Babylon, 6, 10–11, 251. *See also* Babylonians; Mesopotamia

Babylonian. *See also* Jerusalem; remnant
agents of punishment, 109–10, 186, 213, 267–68
exile, 11–12, 27–28, 123, 182, 184n68, 240n77, 295–96

Baal. *See also* Josiah
eradication of, 8, 77, 84
influence of, 78, 84
punishment of. *See* punishment, Baal worshippers
remnant of
defined, 7, 33, 78, 83–84

idolatrous, 84–86
prideful, 90
star-worshipers, 86–87
syncretistic, 87–89

Bene-Ammon
hope for, 177, 191, 201–2
judgment against, 34, 187–91
location of, 88n
plunder of, 187
punishment of
nature of, 185–86
reason for, 175–76, 184–85

blessings. *See also* curses
belief in, 126, 133n
from God. *See* covenant
restoration of, 33, 36, 67, 130, 244–48

Canaan. *See also* Josiah
allusion of, 33–34, 35
destruction of, 39, 101, 129–30, 169
influence of, 113
"people of," 117, 120, 179n37

Canaanite. *See* Baal; Canaan

changed, life. *See* curses; transformation

chastisement. *See* punishment

child sacrifice, 9, 114

Christ. *See also* messiah
day of YHWH and, 5, 30, 42–45, 131–32. *See also* day of YHWH
good shepherd, 202–3
Israel's hope, 303
kingdom of, 5, 248, 301–2. *See also* eschatology
resurrection, 38, 244–48, 297
return of, 45–47, 49, 97, 131–32. *See also* day of YHWH; eschatology
role within testaments, 24–25, 222
sacrifice, 39–40, 133–34

salvation through, 43–45, 96, 298–300, 303, 304–5

Zephaniah and, 164

church, New Testament, 244–48, 298–300. *See also* worshipers

"Coming Day of Punishment". *See also* day of YHWH; punishment
characteristics, 121–25
effects of, 125–29

complacency, 118–20. *See also* Jerusalem

covenant
Abrahamic, 28–29, 30, 45, 93–94, 129, 250
Mosaic, 30, 33–34, 47, 183, 216
new, 34, 44–45, 126n150, 208n221. *See also* Christ, kingdom of; church, New Testament

curses. *See also* blessings; covenant
belief in, 133n187
motivation of, 42, 67, 140, 207, 218. *See also* punishment
reversals of, 218, 276–78

Cush
destruction of, 34, 176–78, 192–94, 193n143, 209
identity of, 13, 64–65, 65n22–26, 190n111, 191–92, 192n131–32. *See also* Babel; foreigners; Nimrod
part of remnant, 21, 200, 238, 241–42
Zephaniah and. *See* Zephaniah, prophet

date of Zephaniah, disagreement of, 10. *See also* Zephaniah, authorship

day of
sacrifice, 105, 109
slaughter, 109–10
the Lord, 13n36, 46, 115n87, 161

wrath, 23, 30, 45–46, 71, 123, 133. *See also* day of YHWH; wrath

day of YHWH. *See also* punishment
  characteristics of
    divisive, 37–38
    imminent, 40–41, 104–5, 108–10, 121–22, 108n35
    terror filled, 38, 103, 123–25, 124n137
    torturous, 39–40, 122–23
  Christ's church, 42–46, 244–48. *See also* Christ
  common features, 19–20, 42, 107n28, 108n34, 130–31
  courage during
    full rest, 286–90
    salvation, 282–86
  defined, 107, 130, 131–32
  effects of, 95–96, 125–29
  fulfilled, 43–46, 244–45. *See also* Christ
  Jerusalem and, 109, 111–21. *See also* Jerusalem
  kingdom, 33–34. *See also* eschatology
  motivation, 42, 71, 107–10, 227–28. *See also* patience; reverence
  prior allusions to, 36–37
  prophecy of, 44, 298–300
  punishment during, 20–21, 37–41, 46–47. *See also* punishment
  renewal, 33–34, 41–42, 46–47, 199–201
  reverence of. *See* reverence
  textual boundaries, 100–105

deists, 119–20

destruction. *See also* day of YHWH
  complete, 41, 125, 128
  humanity's, 127–29
  Jerusalem, 108n35, 109
  global, 78–82, 94, 162, 242

discipleship, 134, 136, 166. *See also* missions

discipline
  for change, 160, 166–67, 207, 218–19, 223
  of leaders, 111. *See also* leaders
  of nations, 166–67, 176

distress, humanity's. *See also* day of YHWH; punishment
  promise of God, 125–26

reason for, 126–27

divine origin, 59, 63, 311. *See also* YHWH, word of; Zephaniah, book of

eschatology/-logical. *See also* judgment; remnant
  Christ's return, 45–46, 49, 220–21, 244–45, 268, 300n213
  definition, 9n18, 79–80
  global wrath, 79n20, 94, 105, 108n35, 128, 186, 235–38, 296
  ingathering, 36, 94–96, 200–202, 248, 286–90, 296
  new Jerusalem, 29–30, 33–34, 199–201, 237–40, 248–50
  present day context, 9, 13n36, 47, 164, 220–22

exile
  Assyrian, 83, 195
  Babylonian, 11–12, 27–28, 123, 182, 184n68, 240n77, 295–96
  reversal of, 241, 243, 304
  YHWH, by, 94, 157, 202, 221, 291

faithful
  remnant, 12–13, 36, 41, 49, 64, 130. *See also* ingathering
  return to being, 42, 143, 163–64. *See also* seeking

feasts and festivals. *See also* day of
  differing translations, 286–87
  of Baal, 87
  of God, 79n15
  of Ingathering, 9, 70, 87, 94–95, 108, 146, 148, 288

foreign(ers). *See also* Assyria; Babylon; Bene-Ammon; Canaan; Cush; Philistines; Moab
  curses on, 168–70
  fate of, 177–78
  influence of, 86n, 117, 130, 136, 156. *See also* idolatry
  nations, use of, 216–18
  punishment of, 216–20
    Assyria and Cushites, 191–99
    Moab and Bene-Ammon, 184–91. *See also* Assyria, Bene-Ammon, Cush, Moab
  reformation of, 201–2, 292. *See also* eschatology

"woe" to, 53–54, 124n137, 168–70, 175, 179, 184, 233, 263

foreshadowing. *See also* eschatology
  judgment, 38, 40, 99, 115n87, 217
  messianic, 29, 43, 202–3, 268, 297, 300. *See also* Christ
  new kingdom, 35, 99, 108, 199–200

genealogy, 62–63. *See also* Zephaniah, prophet

God. *See also* YHWH
  blessing of. *See* Christ; covenant; curses; remnant, restoration
  exaltation of, 22, 41, 47–49, 160, 303–4. *See also* humility
  joy of, 22, 49, 141, 261, 283–86, 304–5. *See also* seeking
  justice of, 223–24. *See also* judgment
  love of, 262n16, 284–85, 304–5
  presence, 278, 282–86
  promises of, 67–68, 96, 219n283, 254, 263–64, 280–81, 295–96. *See also* promises; worshipers, worldwide
  pursuit of, 5, 20–21, 60, 135, 154, 163–64, 233, 278. *See also* patience; seeking
  source of Zephaniah, 60, 62, 63
  sovereignty, 48, 107–10, 189, 279
  wrath of, 107–10, 127–29, 132–33, 246n104. *See also* day of YHWH; punishment

hermeneutic overview, 23
  messianic context, 28–30, 202–3
  minor prophet links, 26–27
  Old Testament allusions. *See* Old Testament allusions
  salvation in testaments, 24–25
  thematic plot, 27–28
  typology, 35, 94–95

Hezekiah, King, 64, 64n19–20, 66, 68, 159n27, 207–8

history
  background, 66. *See also* messenger; Zephaniah, book of
  preexilic, 11n27, 62–63, 114n79, 291n165
  prophecy, 11n27. *See also* prophecy
  redemptive, 24, 27, 82–83, 93–96. *See also* salvation

hope. *See also* patience; unity
for future, 278, 282–87, 301–2, 305
for humanity, 22, 132, 134, 150, 222–23, 302. *See also* worshipers, worldwide
for Judah. *See* eschatology; remnant
for remnant, 60, 130, 163, 191, 200, 231. *See also*
messianic, 6, 28–30, 96, 296n185
humanity. *See* day of YHWH; hope; punishment; salvation
humility. *See also* hope; seeking
Judah, 149–50, 158–60
obedient, 158–59
repentant, 96–98, 157–58, 218–20
saving
promise of, 269–71
refuge, 271–74
seeking, 153, 156, 160, 165–66

incarnation, 221. *See also* Christ; eschatology
idolatry
Baal. *See* Baal; Josiah, reforms
defined, 84, 90–91
Molech, 88, 88n80
pluralism, 97
polytheism, 89, 92
present day, 91–93
punishment for, 83–90, 280. *See* punishment
ingathering. *See also* eschatology
declaration of, 79–81
details, 81–82, 94–96
feasts of. *See* feasts
judgment, 36, 79–81, 124n140, 149, 287–89
worship during. *See* worshipers
Israel. *See also* Jerusalem
calling of, 93–94
disloyalty of, 6–7, 33–34, 83, 117, 218. *See also* foreigners; idolatry
destruction of, 6, 28n92, 63, 83, 94, 194–95, 216
hope for, 6, 24, 303
new, 5, 181–82, 263–64, 273n64, 295
leaders. *See* leaders; priests
punishment of, 40–41, 87, 96. *See also* punishment

Jeroboam I, 84–85
Jerusalem
characteristics of, 204–6, 215, 291
chosen, 294–95
destruction of, 94, 115–17, 150, 268, 292. *See also* punishment; wailing
elite of. *See* leaders
failures of
opposing YHWH, 141, 206–7, 216
repentant, 219–20
untrusting, 207–8. *See also* foreign, punishment of; leaders
healing of, 160–61, 290–95. *See also* seeking
judgment of, 107–10, 156
new, 13, 158–59, 281, 290–91, 293
Nineveh comparison, 204, 268
pride within, 97, 118–20, 215
priests. *See* leaders
punishment
implications for, 108, 111–20
waiting for, 228–30. *See also* punishment
salvation of, 290–95
Jesus. *See* Christ
John the Baptist, 43, 95
joy
God, of, 22, 49, 141, 261, 283–86, 304–5
new Jerusalem, of, 259–61, 278–80
remnant, 258, 264–65. *See also* remnant
Josiah, King
death, 162n49
reforms, 5–6, 7n7, 8n11, 11n27, 66, 85–89, 112, 178
reign, 6–9, 63–64, 66, 111n53, 114
righteous, 158n16, 178, 209, 279
Judah. *See also* day of YHWH
audience of Zephaniah, 13
chosen, 294–95
correction of, 12–13, 82, 130–31
elite of. *See* leaders
exile, 11n27. *See also* history
hope for, 143, 163, 182
wrath on. *See* punishment; seeking

judgment. *See also* punishment
"cutting off," 80, 82, 82n37, 83n45, 231n13
day of. *See* day of YHWH; wrath
deliverance from, 96–97, 120, 157–58, 160. *See also* humility; repentance
expressions of, 214–15
flood, 32–33, 80
global, 36, 46–48, 77–79, 79n20,108,
"hush" before, 26–27, 38, 73, 100, 134, 136, 159n25
ingathering, 36, 79–81, 94–96, 151, 200–202, 248, 286–90, 296
Judah, 14, 83, 115n87,
reversal of. *See* Babel, tower of
righteous, 212–14
salvation from, 96–98, 160–61, 214–15

king, usage of, 88–89. *See also* syncretism
King Josiah. *See* Josiah, King

lament. *See* wailing
lampstands, 118
leaders
ethics of, 111, 202, 208–9, 213
political
characteristics of, 209–10
punishment of, 111–13
punishment of, 118
religious
characteristics of, 7n7, 84, 210–11
punishment of, 113–15
set apart, 114
light
Christ as, 221,
judgment as, 220–22
LXX. *See* Septuagint

macro-segmentation. *See* macrostructure
macrostructure, alternative views. *See also* two-part argument
three-part structure, 14
prophetic drama, 13–15
dramatic prophecy, 15
thematic chiasm, 15–16, 138–139, 261–63

Subject Index

Masoretic Text, 25, 77–78, 87–88, 122, 157, 188, 197, 212–14, 216, 218–19, 230, 234, 283–85, 287

message, 6, 63

messenger
future, 281. *See also* prophecy
Zephaniah as, 63–66

messiah 96, 202–3
in Haggai-Malachi, 29–30
in Hosea-Habakkuk, 28–29
sacrificial lamb, 39–40

Mesopotamia, 84, 87, 192, 195n153, 199–200, 241n81, 269n40. *See also* Assyria; Babylon

Milcom, 85, 88, 88n80

minor prophets
arrangement of, 25–26
links to Zephaniah, 26–30

missions, 251. *See also* discipleship

Moab
hope for, 191
judgment against, 187–91
plunder of, 187
punishment of
nature of, 185–86
reason for, 184–85

Molech, 88, 88n80

motivation. *See also* day of YHWH; curses
patient, 42, 230–31
rhetorical, 20–22
saving, 20–22, 96–98, 99, 253–55
transformative, 71, 149

MT. *See* Masoretic Text

new Jerusalem
courage of, 282–83, 286
joy of, 278–80. *See also* God, joy of
people of, 270–71. *See also* worshipers, worldwide

Nimrod. *See* Babel, tower of

Nineveh. *See also* Babel, tower of
arrogance of, 176, 198–99
desolation of, 48, 196–97
end time characteristics, 224, 266, 268, 277
final destruction of, 7, 197–99, 199n187,
plea for, 195–96

oath taking, 89. *See also* syncretism

Old Testament allusions
"day of," 107–8, 245–48
global kingdom, 33–34
judgment, 32–33
reformation, 34
typology, 35

organization of Zephaniah. *See* Zephaniah, book of

outline of Zephaniah, 51–55

paganism. *See* idolatry

pantheism, 92, 189

patience. *See also* salvation, waiting for
for future, 136, 225–28, 234–37, 252, 261–63. *See also* eschatology
help with, 20–22, 165, 282–83
joy in, 264–65
motivation for, 42, 230–31
trust and, 136, 207, 231–32, 278, 302

Peshitta. *See* Syriac Peshitta

Philistia
as Canaan, 179
"woe" to, 171–75, 178–80, 204–5, 227

Philistines
devastation of, 161–63, 179–80
Judah's homeland and, 180–84
influence of, 118, 179

pluralism, 97

polytheism, 89, 92

practices, religious. *See also* syncretism
outer garb, 112–13
threshold, 113–14

pride
Assyria, 198
Babel's, 34
Bene-Ammon's, 48, 191, 194
destruction of, 60
human, 34, 112, 118–20, 125, 198, 223–24, 268
Jerusalem's, 97, 118–20, 198, 215, 266
Moab's, 48, 191, 194, 198
Ninevah's, 176, 198, 224, 268
Philistia's, 179
Tyre's, 266

priests. *See also* leaders, religious
illegitimate, 1, 7, 9, 11, 78, 84–87, 90

Israelite, 84
set apart, 114–15

promises, of God
protection, 265–66
purification, 35, 120, 254, 266–69
redemption, 263–64, 269–71
refuge, 271–74
salvation, 21–22, 290–95

prophecy. *See also* Old Testament allusions
allegiance to YHWH, 238–39
foreign nations, 168–70
Jesus' reign, 24–25. *See also* eschatology
messianic, 164, 264
prophetic discourse, 17
view by prophets, 26, 292

prophets
contemporary, 6
minor, 25–26

punishment. *See also* day of YHWH; Jerusalem; reverence, reason for
avoidance of, 19–20, 90, 218–20
Baal worshippers
atheism, 90, priests, 84–86
star-worshipers, 86n, 86–87
syncretism, 87–89
cataclysmic, 38
characteristics of
imminent, 121–22
terror filled, 123–25
torturous, 122–23
conquest, 38–39
"cutting off," 80, 82, 82n37, 83n45, 231n13
effects of
destruction, 127–29
distress, 125–27
features of, 131
global, 37–38, 72
international, 184–99. *See also* foreign(ers)
local, 82–90
near, 40–41, 49–50
priests, 7n7, 84, 113–15, 118, 210–11
sacrificial, 39–40, 107–10, 133–34
universal implications of, 186–87

rebels. *See* foreigners; Jerusalem

Subject Index

redemption, 27–28, 48, 93–96, 295–96, 301

redemptive reversal, 36

reformation. *See also* salvation
    foreign people, 201–2
    Josiah's, 5–6, 7n7, 8n11, 11n27, 66, 85–89, 112, 178

refuge. *See also* salvation
    in YHWH, 160–61

rejoice. *See* joy

remnant
    hope, 67–68, 289–90. *See also* joy
    "house of Judah," 13, 33–34, 182, 271–74
    land of the, 180–84, 199–201
    preservation of, 67–68
    punishment of Baal. *See* punishment, Baal worshippers

rejoicing
    call to, 274–76
    reason for, 276–80. *See also* God, joy of; new Jerusalem
    restoration of, 36, 130, 136, 231, 244–48, 283–84, 291n161
    seek YHWH, 135–36, 156–61. *See also* humility; seeking
    salvation of, 295–97. *See also* eschatology; patience

repentance. *See also* punishment; unrepentant
    humble in, 157–58, 161n37. *See also* humility
    reason for, 20, 38, 48, 149–50, 166–67, 177
    urgency of, 40–41, 97, 146, 151
    way for, 67–68, 120, 140n19, 169, 175–76, 218

restoration
    day of YHWH, 244–48
    remnant, 36, 130, 136, 231, 244–48, 283–84, 291n161

retribution. *See* punishment

reverence. *See also* YHWH
    call for, 19–17, 69–70, 106, 132–33
    "Hush/Silence," 72, 100, 106, 121. *See also* judgment; reverence
    need for, 105
    reason for
        effects of punishment, 125–29

imminence of punishment, 121–25, 230–31

impending punishment, 70–72, 107–10

implications of punishment, 111–20. *See also* God; punishment

rhetorical approach, 13, 20, 24–25. *See also* structure of Zephaniah

righteousness
    YHWH's, 211–12
    seeking, 160

sacrifice
    Christ's. *See* Christ
    restoration through,107–9

salvation. *See also* discipleship; judgment
    Christ and, 46–47, 304–5. *See also* Christ
    in testaments, 24–25, 246–48
    Judeans/Israel. *See* Babel, reversal
    motivation for, 20–22, 96–98, 99, 253–55. *See also* punishment
    multiethnic, 201–2, 233, 299–301. *See also* eschatology; worshipers, worldwide. *See also* worshipers
    remnant, 13, 282–86
    waiting for, 137, 229–30. *See also* patience; seeking
    victorious, 274–76, 287, 303, 304–5

"Savior's Invitation to Satisfaction"
    messenger of, 57–60. *See also* Zephaniah, prophet
    setting, 19–23, 69–70
    substance
        seek YHWH, 20–21, 154–56, 253, 311
        wait, 253–54. *See also* patience; seeking
    superscription of, 19, 57, 62–63
    theme, 50, 135

second coming, 131–32, 245–48. *See also* day of YHWH

seeking
    global, 159, 166
    how to, 156, 159–60
    humility, 153, 156, 160, 165–66
    reason for, 20–21, 143, 165–66, 230–32
    righteous, 163–64
    salvation, 253

unity in, 139n14, 165, 168. *See also* unity

self-reliance. *See* pride

Septuagint (LXX), 25, 62, 78, 81, 85, 87–89, 95, 106, 112, 114–17, 119, 123, 157, 181,184, 186, 188, 196–97, 205, 210, 213–14, 217–19, 230, 241, 246–47, 277, 283, 285–87, 297–98, 300

sermons, from Zephaniah, 49–50, 91–92, 97–98

"Silence!" *See* reverence; YHWH

sin. *See also* day of YHWH; idolatry; seeking; repentance
    global, 5, 27–28, 33, 37–38, 295
    local, 82–90

structure of Zephaniah
    disagreement concerning, 70–71
    macrostructure, 13–16. *See also* macrostructure, alternative views
    two-part argument, 16–23. *See also* two-part argument
    speaker
        YHWH, 71, 74, 139, 204, 258, 281
        Zephaniah, 258, 284, 285

syncretism, 8–9, 83, 87–89, 92, 97, 112n63, 113, 132n184, 157

Syriac Peshitta, 88–89, 116–17, 184, 196–97, 205, 214, 218–19, 235

Table of Nations, 34–36, 242

thematic plot, 27–28

togetherness. *See* unity

Torah
    discovery of, 7n7, 8–9, 66, 158
    future events, 29, 109, 249, 292, 296
    Josiah and, 8n11. *See also* Josiah, reforms
    teaching of, 84, 149, 164, 204, 211, 211n234. *See also* priests

Tower of Babel. *See* Babel, tower of; foreshadowing

transformation. *See also* repentance; reverence
    motivation for, 71, 149. *See also* patience; repentance; salvation
    of foreigners. *See* foreign(ers)
    of self, 132–33, 302, 305

338   *Subject Index*

trust. *See* patience

two-part argument
  argument diagrams, 17–19, 23
  "new form criticism," 16–17
  rhetorical motivation, 20–22
  Savior's invitation, 19–20, 22–23

typology, 35

unity. *See also* repentance; reverence
  avoid punishment, 20–21, 42, 135,
    137, 170–76
  Judah and, 143, 153
  need for, 146, 148–50
  repentance, 176–77
  strength in, 165
  time for, 150–51

unrepentant, 215, 222, 234, 236, 245–46.
  See also Jerusalem; leaders

voice
  prophet's, 60n5, 71, 74, 204, 208
  YHWH's, 15, 71, 74, 208–9, 254, 258,
    281, 307. *See also* God, word of

Vulgate, 88–89, 117, 179, 181, 184,
  196–97, 205, 213, 218, 230, 235,
  246, 293, 297

wailing. *See also* "woe"
  destruction of Jerusalem, 115–17
  loss of trade, 117–18

wait for God, 54–55, 141, 261–63. *See
  also* patience; seeking

warning, God's. *See also* day of YHWH;
  punishment
  coming judgment, 38, 42, 60, 97,
    223–24
  Israel and Judah, to, 12, 63,
    126–27,148–50, 166–67. *See also*
    Israel; Judah; unity

wealth
  idolism of, 97, 112n61, 116, 157. *See
    also* idolatry
  loss of, 118, 120, 127, 149. *See also*
    punishment

witness. *See* discipleship

"woe." *See also* reverence
  to foreign nations, 124n137, 168–70,
    175, 179, 184, 233, 263
  to Jerusalem, 141, 146, 190n111,
    204
  to Judah, 77, 227
  to Philistia, 171–75, 178–80, 204–5,
    227
  to remnant, 145

worship. *See also* idolatry
  Baal. *See* Baal
  idols. *See* idolatry, present day
  Milcom, 85, 88, 88n80
  Molech, 88, 88n80
  YHWH, 189–90. *See also* YHWH

worshipers. *See also* remnant
  multiethnic, 5, 21, 27–28, 30, 41–43,
    237–40, 271, 299–300
  present day, 45, 245, 250
  star, 86n
  worldwide, 30, 237–40, 244, 248–50

wrath. *See also* day of YHWH
  against foreign nations. *See*
    foreign(ers)
  coming. *See* day of YHWH
  global, 125, 177–78

YHWH. *See also* God
  actions of, 48, 139
  authority, 60, 168, 189, 238, 279
  call from, 21–22
  character of, 211–15, 303–4
  day of. *See* day of YHWH
  deliverance by, 246
  discipline by, 166–67, 218–20
  exaltation of, 47–49
  fear of, 21, 29, 37–39, 42 160, 280.
    See also reverence
  jealousy of, 169, 188–89
  King, 43. *See also* God, sovereignty
  renewal by, 41–46. *See also* Christ;
    eschatology

reverence toward, 19, 47–49, 69–70,
  72, 106. *See also* reverence;
  Jerusalem
surrender to, 145
waiting. *See* seeking
word of, 24–25, 63, 66–67, 309–11
wrath of, 2, 44–46, 103, 127–28,
  247. *See also* day of YHWH;
  punishment

Zephaniah, book of
  audience, 13, 136–37
  authorship, 6, 9–12
  comparison to prophets, 26–30
  exegetical outline, 23
  Hermeneutics, 23–30. *See also*
    Hermeneutic overview
  historic background, 6–9, 19, 63, 65.
    See also Josiah
  literary structure. *See*
    macrostructure, two-part
    argument
  macrostructure, 13–16. *See also*
    macrostructure, two-part
    argument
  Old Testament within, 30–32, 243
  outline of, 5, 51–55
  predictions within, 10–11. *See also*
    prophecy
  sermons from, 49–50
  superscription to, 57, 62
  theology, 9, 24–25, 35–37

Zephaniah, prophet. *See also* Zephaniah,
  book of
  influencers, 6–8, 26–30
  message, 8–9, 18, 43, 63–66. *See also*
    day of YHWH
  ministry of, 7–9
  personal background, 6, 36, 62–66,
    136
  proclamation, 50, 57, 59–60, 67.
    See also "Savior's Invitation to
    Satisfaction"
  redemption and, 93–96

Author Index

Achtemeier, Elizabeth, 107, 122, 126, 237, 262, 273, 285

Albright, W. F., 65, 192

Bailey, Waylon, 81–82, 111, 136, 150, 230, 254, 258, 296

Baker, David W., 64, 84, 109, 114, 116, 118–19, 123, 150, 158, 161, 169, 186, 188, 191, 199, 204, 211, 237, 242

Ball, Ivan Jay, Jr., 85, 87, 122–23, 138, 148, 151, 1563, 161, 187–89, 191–92, 205, 213, 215, 218, 220, 230, 234–35, 242, 275, 277, 291, 293

Beale, G. K., 9, 24, 37, 44, 90, 164, 206, 245

Bennett, Robert A., 65, 176, 276, 286, 300

Ben Zvi, Ehud, 7–8, 10, 13–14n, 25, 64, 81, 82, 83, 84–85, 89, 109, 114, 122, 123, 125–27, 148–49, 156–58, 160–63, 169, 178–79, 181–82, 185–87, 189–90, 192, 197, 199, 208–13, 215–16, 218–19, 231–32, 234–35, 240, 243–44, 259–61, 270–72, 276–78, 283, 285, 289, 291, 293

Berlin, Adele, 7, 10–11, 13, 33–34, 36, 62, 64–65, 81–82, 85, 88–89, 113, 117, 122–23, 125–28, 148, 151, 156, 158, 161–62, 168–69, 177–78, 180–81, 186, 189–90, 192–93, 195–97, 199, 206, 213, 215, 219, 235, 237, 241, 244, 261–62, 265, 267, 272, 275, 277, 293, 298

Berridge, John M., 6, 63

Block, Daniel I., xiv, xvi, 8, 60, 62, 80, 87–90, 128, 150, 169, 184, 196, 209, 218, 236, 278, 286

Brueggemann, Walter, 11

Butcher, Jerry Dale, 245, 247

Calvin, John, 85, 97–98, 109, 113, 118–20, 149, 158, 160–61, 183, 185, 198, 211, 213–14, 218, 224, 232, 235, 237, 240, 270, 272, 276, 285, 293

Clendenen, E. Ray, 26, 136, 163, 235, 258

Craigie, Peter C., 123

Dempster, Stephen, xvi, 25–26, 28, 138, 291

DeRouchie, Jason S., xvi, xxvii, 13, 17–18, 22, 24–25, 30, 33, 35, 37, 41, 47, 50, 72, 74, 77, 79, 81–82, 89–91, 94, 104, 120, 123, 133, 137–38, 140–41, 146, 154, 157–59, 163–64, 177, 183, 189, 206, 210, 215, 220, 232, 235–36, 369, 341, 351, 258, 283–84, 289–91, 294

Floyd, Michael H., 10–11, 14, 16–17, 34, 71–72, 74, 100, 104–106, 109, 116, 119, 136, 140, 150, 156, 158–59, 161, 169–70, 175–76, 183, 186–87, 190, 193–94, 196–97, 199–200, 216, 230, 232, 235, 242, 258–60, 275–77, 288

Gentry, Peter J., xvi, 10, 63, 82, 138, 240–41

Gowan, Donald E., 10, 63

House, Paul R., 13–15, 26, 28, 49, 213, 215, 218–19, 235, 237, 285, 293

Irsigler, Hubert., 10, 149, 156, 214–15, 228, 230, 232

Jerome, 246, 298

Kapelrud, Arvid S., 11, 13, 15, 148–49, 156–57, 161, 169, 213, 216, 292–93

Keil, Carl F., 8, 84, 88, 109, 111–13, 117, 126, 158, 161–62, 175, 185–87, 189, 191, 194, 196, 213–14, 230, 234, 237, 244, 293

Luther, Martin, 5, 109, 113, 117, 119, 126, 179, 195, 205–206, 213, 247–47, 302

Motyer, J. Alec., 11–13 62, 64, 70, 83, 86, 97, 104, 107, 109, 114, 116–17, 120, 122–23, 126–27, 132, 138, 141, 149, 151, 156, 158, 161, 163, 165, 177, 179–80, 185, 188, 190, 194–96, 198–99, 205–206, 208, 211–13, 215–16, 230–31, 234–35, 239, 242, 265, 274, 278, 282, 285–86, 291, 293

Patterson, Richard D., 17, 81, 86, 88, 106–107, 109, 113–14, 117, 123, 149, 153, 160, 170, 175, 178, 185, 191, 199, 214–15, 230, 232, 244, 254, 258, 265, 268, 270, 285, 293

Renz, Thomas., 8, 10–11, 64, 79, 94, 105–106, 109, 112–13, 116, 122–23, 126–28, 137–38, 148–49, 156–58, 161, 170, 175, 189–90, 193–94, 197, 204, 234, 236–37, 244, 270, 276–77, 288–89, 293, 296

Rice, Gene, 64–65, 192

Roberts, J. J. M., 8–10, 13, 64, 70, 79, 81, 83, 85–87, 108–109, 11–16, 125–26, 138–39, 148–49, 156, 161, 169, 178–81, 185, 187, 189, 191, 195–96, 198, 205, 210, 213–16, 219, 230–31, 237, 275–76, 290, 293

Robertson, O. Palmer, 9–11, 64, 96, 109, 112, 114, 124, 133, 149, 158, 175, 177–78, 183, 185, 187, 189, 191, 194, 196, 199, 206, 213, 230, 235, 237, 242, 262, 270, 276, 284, 297–98

Rudolph, Wilhelm, 8, 13, 148, 151, 160–61, 186–87, 189, 196, 205, 209, 215, 219, 228, 235, 291–92

Ryou, Daniel Hojoon, 138, 140–41, 148, 151, 156, 161, 170, 175, 186–87, 197, 216, 230, 235

Sabottka, Liudger, 112, 122, 127, 148–49, 157, 186, 188–89, 197, 205, 213–14, 270, 292

Seybold, Klaus, 6, 13, 108–109, 111, 113–14, 128, 156, 187, 196, 214, 220, 235

Sheehan, Clint, 9, 14, 16

Shepherd, Michael B., 25–27, 29, 64, 106–107, 115, 128, 130, 160–61, 163, 185, 202, 235, 244, 265, 294, 298

Smith, Craig A., 16

Smith, John Merlin Powis, 8, 10, 15, 64, 86, 111–13, 116, 119–20, 126, 132, 148, 150, 156, 158, 161, 178–80, 183, 187–88, 191–92, 196, 199, 205, 213–16, 218–19, 230–31, 235, 265, 276, 278, 285, 291, 297

Smith, George Adam, 231, 285

Smith, Ralph L., 64–65, 127, 169, 185, 205, 213–14, 216, 219–20, 235, 242

Smith, Robert Houston, 65

Sweeney, Marvin A., 6, 8–12, 14, 16–17, 60, 62, 64, 69, 71, 74, 77, 79, 81, 83, 85, 87, 95, 100, 104, 108–109, 111–16, 118–19, 125–26, 128, 138–40, 146, 148–51, 156–58, 161–63, 168–70, 175–78, 180, 185–87, 190–93, 196–97, 204, 206, 208–10, 212–16, 218, 220, 228, 230–32, 234, 237, 242, 244, 258, 264, 268, 271, 273–74, 276–77, 280, 288–89, 293, 294

Tachick, Christopher S., 15, 44, 116, 230, 258–61, 278, 298–300

Thomson, Ian H., 16

Timmer, Daniel C., 127, 169, 190, 194, 236–37, 291, 296

Vlaardingerbroek, Johannes, 7, 10, 13, 60, 70, 79–80, 82, 84, 86–87, 89–90, 94, 96, 106, 108, 111–13, 115–23, 125, 128, 138, 156, 158, 160–61, 168–69, 179–80, 183, 185, 188, 190–91, 196–97, 204, 209–10, 213, 216, 218, 220, 228, 231–32, 235, 237, 247, 270, 276–77, 282, 297

Walker, Larry L., 230

Watts, John D. W., 11, 26, 81, 150, 188, 193, 216

Wendland, Ernst R., 12–15, 71, 74, 118, 138–39, 141, 150, 156, 232–33, 258–60, 281

Westermann, Claus, 14, 146